Lecture Notes in Computer Science   4713

Commenced Publication in 1973
Founding and Former Series Editors:
Gerhard Goos, Juris Hartmanis, and Jan van Leeuwen

T0223196

Fred A. Hamprecht   Christoph Schnörr
Bernd Jähne (Eds.)

Pattern Recognition

29th DAGM Symposium
Heidelberg, Germany, September 12-14, 2007
Proceedings

 Springer

Volume Editors

Fred A. Hamprecht
Christoph Schnörr
Bernd Jähne
University of Heidelberg
Interdisciplinary Center for Scientific Computing, IWR/HCI
69120 Heidelberg, Germany
E-mail: ipsec@iwr.uni-heidelberg.de

Library of Congress Control Number: 2007934521

CR Subject Classification (1998): I.5, I.4, I.3.5, I.2.10, I.2.6, F.2.2

LNCS Sublibrary: SL 6 – Image Processing, Computer Vision, Pattern Recognition, and Graphics

ISSN	0302-9743
ISBN-10	3-540-74933-0 Springer Berlin Heidelberg New York
ISBN-13	978-3-540-74933-2 Springer Berlin Heidelberg New York

Springer is a part of Springer Science+Business Media

springer.com

© Springer-Verlag Berlin Heidelberg 2007
Printed in Germany

Typesetting: Camera-ready by author, data conversion by Scientific Publishing Services, Chennai, India
Printed on acid-free paper   SPIN: 12122677   06/3180   5 4 3 2 1 0

Preface

In 1996, the 18th Annual Symposium of the Deutsche Arbeitsgemeinschaft für Mustererkennung (DAGM) was hosted by the recently established research group on image processing of the University of Heidelberg, headed at that time by a single associate professor (Jähne) at the Interdisciplinary Center for Scientific Computing (IWR).

This year, it was a pleasure to host again the 29th Annual Symposium of the DAGM in Heidelberg. Meanwhile, image processing at the IWR consists of three Chairs (Hamprecht, Schnörr, Jähne). It will be complemented in 2008 by the Heidelberg Center for Image Processing (HCI) and involve eight industrial partners as founding members.

This development reflects the fact that image processing and pattern recognition are research and business areas which keep growing in both volume and importance. The Fraunhofer Institute for Technological Trend Analysis (INT, Euskirchen) has recently identified image processing and pattern recognition among the "scientific-technical areas of the future"[1], and the National IT Summit has called for a strategic research effort to foster the real-world awareness of IT systems in its 2006 white paper on "HighTech Strategies for the Information Society." Such systems should be able to "understand" and to orient themselves in their environment, and the development of sophisticated techniques for image processing and pattern recognition is a prerequisite to meet these challenges.

DAGM made English its sole conference language in 2001. Since then, it has continuously strenghtened its position as the most important conference on pattern recognition and related fields (image processing, computer vision, machine learning) for the German-speaking community. It is increasingly attracting scientists from all over Europe and beyond.

The selection of contributions as oral or poster presentation does not signify a quality grading. Consequently, posters and oral presentations were given the same number of pages in these proceedings. The accepted papers have roughly been sorted by subject area, and within each section alphabetically by first author. During the symposium, much space was devoted to discussions by extending both the poster sessions and the discussions following the presentations.

We were honored to have the following three invited speakers at the symposium:

- *Sabine Huffel (KU Leuven, Belgium)*, Quantification and Classification of Magnetic Resonance Spectroscopic Images with Applications in Cancer Diagnosis
- *Robert Massen (University of Applied Sciences, Constance and Baumer Inspection GmbH, Germany)*, History of the German Machine Vision Industry and Its Influence on Academic Research

---

[1] www.zukunftsstiftung.at/innovationstag/pdf/Technologie-%20und%20Innovationstrends_Kretschmer.pdf

- *Shimon Ullman (Weizmann Institute of Science, Israel)*, Image Interpretation by Feature Hierarchies

We would like to extend our sincere thanks to:

- All authors and attendees who helped make this symposium a success
- All reviewers from the Program Committee whose dedication and timely reporting helped ensure the punctuality of the selection process
- UniTT, Barbara Werner and Karin Kubessa-Nasri for their commitment to ensuring a smooth organization
- Our own labs who helped in the elimination of many of the typos that remained in the final submissions
- Björn Andres and Thorsten Dahmen for their help with the compilation of the proceedings

Last but not least, we would like to thank:

- Robert Bosch GmbH (Gold Corporate Contributor),
- MVTec Software GmbH (Silver Corporate Contributor),
- Basler, PCO imaging, Philips, Silicon Software, Stemmer, and Volume Graphics (Bronze Corporate Contributors)

for their donations that allowed, in particular, low registration fees for students.

We were happy to host the 29th Annual Symposium in Heidelberg and look forward to DAGM 2008 in Munich!

September 2007

Fred Hamprecht
Christoph Schnörr
Bernd Jähne

Organization

Program Committee 2007

T. Aach	RWTH Aachen
H. Bischof	University of Graz
J. Buhmann	ETH Zürich
H. Burkhardt	University of Freiburg
D. Cremers	University of Bonn
J. Denzler	University of Jena
B. Flach	TU Dresden
W. Förstner	University of Bonn
D. Gavrila	Daimler Chrysler
F. A. Hamprecht	University of Heidelberg
J. Hornegger	University of Erlangen
B. Jähne	University of Heidelberg
X. Jiang	University of Münster
R. Koch	University of Kiel
U. Köthe	University of Heidelberg
W.-G. Kropatsch	TU Wien
H. Mayer	BW-Universität München
R. Mester	University of Frankfurt
K.-R. Müller	University of Potsdam
H. Ney	RWTH Aachen
K. Obermayer	TU Berlin
K. Rohr	University of Heidelberg
B. Schiele	University of Darmstadt
C. Schnörr	University of Heidelberg
B. Schölkopf	MPI Tübingen
G. Sommer	University of Kiel
C. Stiller	University of Karlsruhe
T. Vetter	University of Basel
F. M. Wahl	University of Braunschweig
J. Weickert	Saarland University

Prizes 2006

Olympus Prize

The Olympus Prize 2006 was awarded to

Daniel Keysers and *Andrés Bruhn*

for their outstanding contributions to the area of pattern recognition and image understanding.

DAGM Prizes

The main prize for 2006 was awarded to:

Paul Ruhnau, Annette Stahl, Christoph Schnörr: On-line Variational Estimation of Dynamical Fluid Flows with Physics-Based Spatio-temporal Regularization

Simon Winkelbach, Sven Molkenstruck, Friedrich M. Wahl: Low-Cost Laser Range Scanner and Fast Surface Registration Approach

Further DAGM prizes for 2006 were awarded to:

Janina Schulz, Thorsten Schmidt, Olaf Ronneberger, Hans Burkhardt, Taras Pasternak, Alexander Dovzhenko, Klaus Palmet: Fast Scalar and Vectorial Grayscale-Based Invariant Features for 3D Cell Nuclei Localization and Classification

Edgar Seemann, Bernt Schiele: Cross-Articulation Learning for Robust Detection of Pedestrians

Table of Contents

Calibration, Pose Estimation and Depth

Self-calibration with Partially Known Rotations.................... 1
  Ferid Bajramovic and Joachim Denzler

A Combined Approach for Estimating Patchlets from PMD Depth
Images and Stereo Intensity Images 11
  Christian Beder, Bogumil Bartczak, and Reinhard Koch

View-Based Robot Localization Using Spherical Harmonics: Concept
and First Experimental Results 21
  *Holger Friedrich, David Dederscheck, Kai Krajsek, and
  Rudolf Mester*

Clustered Stochastic Optimization for Object Recognition and Pose
Estimation 32
  Juergen Gall, Bodo Rosenhahn, and Hans-Peter Seidel

Unambiguous Dynamic Diffraction Patterns for 3D Depth Profile
Measurement 42
  Dominik Lubeley

Point Matching Constraints in Two and Three Views 52
  Klas Nordberg

A Multi-view Camera System for the Generation of Real-Time
Occlusion-Free Scene Video 62
  Alparslan Yildiz and Yusuf Sinan Akgul

Motion, Tracking and Optical Flow

Selection of Local Optical Flow Models by Means of Residual
Analysis 72
  Björn Andres, Fred A. Hamprecht, and Christoph S. Garbe

Calibration of a Multi-camera Rig from Non-overlapping Views 82
  Sandro Esquivel, Felix Woelk, and Reinhard Koch

Fluid Flow Estimation Through Integration of Physical Flow
Configurations.. 92
  Christoph S. Garbe

Rigid Motion Constraints for Tracking Planar Objects 102
  Olaf Kähler and Joachim Denzler

Detectability of Moving Objects Using Correspondences over Two and
Three Frames 112
  Jens Klappstein, Fridtjof Stein, and Uwe Franke

An Analysis-by-Synthesis Camera Tracking Approach Based on
Free-Form Surfaces... 122
  Kevin Koeser, Bogumil Bartczak, and Reinhard Koch

An Adaptive Confidence Measure for Optical Flows Based on Linear
Subspace Projections 132
  Claudia Kondermann, Daniel Kondermann, Bernd Jähne, and
  Christoph Garbe

Bayesian Model Selection for Optical Flow Estimation 142
  Kai Krajsek and Rudolf Mester

Illumination-Robust Variational Optical Flow with Photometric
Invariants 152
  Yana Mileva, Andrés Bruhn, and Joachim Weickert

Online Smoothing for Markerless Motion Capture 163
  Bodo Rosenhahn, Thomas Brox, Daniel Cremers, and
  Hans-Peter Seidel

Occlusion Modeling by Tracking Multiple Objects 173
  Christian Schmaltz, Bodo Rosenhahn, Thomas Brox,
  Joachim Weickert, Daniel Cremers, Lennart Wietzke, and
  Gerald Sommer

Simultaneous Estimation of Surface Motion, Depth and Slopes Under
Changing Illumination 184
  Tobias Schuchert and Hanno Scharr

Recursive Estimation with Implicit Constraints 194
  Richard Steffen and Christian Beder

Optimal Dominant Motion Estimation Using Adaptive Search of
Transformation Space 204
  Adrian Ulges, Christoph H. Lampert, Daniel Keysers, and
  Thomas M. Breuel

A Duality Based Approach for Realtime TV-L^1 Optical Flow 214
  C. Zach, T. Pock, and H. Bischof

Segmentation

Semi-supervised Tumor Detection in Magnetic Resonance Spectroscopic
Images Using Discriminative Random Fields.......................... 224
  L. Görlitz, B.H. Menze, M.-A. Weber, B.M. Kelm, and
  F.A. Hamprecht

Regularized Data Fusion Improves Image Segmentation 234
    Tilman Lange and Joachim Buhmann

Perception-Based Image Segmentation Using the Bounded Irregular
Pyramid 244
    Rebeca Marfil, Antonio Bandera, and Francisco Sandoval

Efficient Image Segmentation Using Pairwise Pixel Similarities 254
    Christopher Rohkohl and Karin Engel

WarpCut – Fast Obstacle Segmentation in Monocular Video 264
    *Andreas Wedel, Thomas Schoenemann, Thomas Brox, and
    Daniel Cremers*

Filters and Image Improvement

Comparison of Adaptive Spatial Filters with Heuristic and Optimized
Region of Interest for EEG Based Brain-Computer-Interfaces 274
    *Christian Liefhold, Moritz Grosse-Wentrup, Klaus Gramann, and
    Martin Buss*

High Accuracy Feature Detection for Camera Calibration: A
Multi-steerable Approach 284
    Matthias Mühlich and Til Aach

A Subiteration-Based Surface-Thinning Algorithm with a Period of
Three 294
    Kálmán Palágyi

Holomorphic Filters for Object Detection 304
    Marco Reisert, Olaf Ronneberger, and Hans Burkhardt

Peer Group Vector Median Filter 314
    Bogdan Smolka

Image Statistics and Local Spatial Conditions for Nonstationary
Blurred Image Reconstruction 324
    Hongwei Zheng and Olaf Hellwich

Object and Pattern Recognition

The Minimum Volume Ellipsoid Metric 335
    Karim T. Abou-Moustafa and Frank P. Ferrie

An Attentional Approach for Perceptual Grouping of Spatially
Distributed Patterns 345
    Muhammad Zaheer Aziz and Bärbel Mertsching

Classifying Glaucoma with Image-Based Features from Fundus
Photographs 355
    Rüdiger Bock, Jörg Meier, Georg Michelson, László G. Nyúl, and
    Joachim Hornegger

Learning to Recognize Faces Incrementally 365
    O. Deniz, J. Lorenzo, M. Castrillon, J. Mendez, and A. Falcon

Short-Term Tide Prediction 375
    Nils Hasler and Klaus-Peter Hasler

Extraction of 3D Unfoliaged Trees from Image Sequences Via a
Generative Statistical Approach 385
    Hai Huang and Helmut Mayer

Greedy-Based Design of Sparse Two-Stage SVMs for Fast
Classification 395
    Rezaul Karim, Martin Bergtholdt, Jörg Kappes, and
    Christoph Schnörr

How to Find Interesting Locations in Video: A Spatiotemporal Interest
Point Detector Learned from Human Eye Movements 405
    Wolf Kienzle, Bernhard Schölkopf, Felix A. Wichmann, and
    Matthias O. Franz

A Fast and Reliable Coin Recognition System 415
    Marco Reisert, Olaf Ronneberger, and Hans Burkhardt

3D Invariants with High Robustness to Local Deformations for
Automated Pollen Recognition..................................... 425
    Olaf Ronneberger, Qing Wang, and Hans Burkhardt

The kernelHMM: Learning Kernel Combinations in Structured Output
Domains 436
    Volker Roth and Bernd Fischer

Intrinsic Mean for Semi-metrical Shape Retrieval Via Graph Cuts 446
    Frank R. Schmidt, Eno Töppe, Daniel Cremers, and Yuri Boykov

Pedestrian Recognition from a Moving Catadioptric Camera........... 456
    Wolfgang Schulz, Markus Enzweiler, and Tobias Ehlgen

Efficient Learning of Neural Networks with Evolutionary Algorithms ... 466
    Nils T. Siebel, Jochen Krause, and Gerald Sommer

Robust High-Speed Melt Pool Measurements for Laser Welding with
Sputter Detection Capability 476
    Nicolaj C. Stache, Henrik Zimmer, Jens Gedicke,
    Alexander Olowinsky, and Til Aach

Learning Robust Objective Functions with Application to Face Model
Fitting 486
  Matthias Wimmer, Sylvia Pietzsch, Freek Stulp, and Bernd Radig

Analyzing the Variability of the 3D Structure of Chromatin Fiber
Using Statistical Shape Theory 497
  *Siwei Yang, Sandra Götze, Julio Mateos-Langerak, Roel van Driel,
  Roland Eils, and Karl Rohr*

Registration

Image-Matching for Revision Detection in Printed Historical
Documents 507
  Joost van Beusekom, Faisal Shafait, and Thomas M. Breuel

Stochastic Optimization of Multiple Texture Registration Using Mutual
Information 517
  Ioan Cleju and Dietmar Saupe

Curvature Guided Level Set Registration Using Adaptive Finite
Elements 527
  Andreas Dedner, Marcel Lüthi, Thomas Albrecht, and Thomas Vetter

Spline-Based Elastic Image Registration with Matrix-Valued Basis
Functions Using Landmark and Intensity Information................. 537
  Stefan Wörz and Karl Rohr

Unifying Energy Minimization and Mutual Information Maximization
for Robust 2D/3D Registration of X-Ray and CT Images 547
  Guoyan Zheng

Author Index 559

Self-calibration with Partially Known Rotations

Ferid Bajramovic and Joachim Denzler

Chair for Computer Vision, Friedrich-Schiller-University Jena
{bajramov,denzler}@informatik.uni-jena.de
http://www4.informatik.uni-jena.de

Abstract. Self-calibration methods allow estimating the intrinsic camera parameters without using a known calibration object. However, such methods are very sensitive to noise, even in the simple special case of a purely rotating camera. Suitable pan-tilt-units can be used to perform pure camera rotations. In this case, we can get partial knowledge of the rotations, e.g. by rotating twice about the same axis. We present extended self-calibration algorithms which use such knowledge. In systematic simulations, we show that our new algorithms are less sensitive to noise. Experiments on real data result in a systematic error caused by non-ideal hardware. However, our algorithms can reduce the systematic error. In the case of complete rotation knowledge, it can even be greatly reduced.

1 Introduction

For many computer vision tasks, the intrinsic camera parameters have to be known. Classic calibration uses a calibration pattern with known geometry and easily detectable features to establish correspondences between known 3D points and 2D image points. However, having to use such a pattern is not very convenient and sometimes impossible. Luckily, there are self-calibration methods, which estimate the intrinsic camera parameters from images taken by a moving camera *without* knowledge about the scene. For an overview, the reader is referred to the literature [1]. An important special case is self-calibration from a purely rotating camera as introduced by Hartley [2,1].

However, most self-calibration methods are very sensitive to noise [3,1]. They work well at low noise levels, but most often have serious problems at higher noise levels. On the other hand, in many practical situations, additional knowledge is available, which can be used to increase the robustness of self-calibration. De Agapito, Hayman and Reid [6] exploit a priori knowledge on the intrinsic parameters by using a MAP estimator. In this paper, we focus on rotation knowledge. Hartley [2] mentions the possibility to incorporate known rotation matrices into the nonlinear refinement step and reported greatly improved self-calibration results. Frahm and Koch [4,5] have presented a linear approach that uses known relative orientation provided by an external rotation sensor.

In practice, however, there are cases in between no and full rotation knowledge. For example, a pan-tilt-unit is often used to perform rotations about one of two physical rotation axes at a time. To the best of our knowledge, using such a priori information to improve self-calibration has not been systematically studied. In this paper, we give an overview of different kinds of partial rotation information with real pan-tilt-units in mind, and show how this knowledge can be incorporated into a nonlinear

F.A. Hamprecht, C. Schnörr, and B. Jähne (Eds.): DAGM 2007, LNCS 4713, pp. 1–10, 2007.

self-calibration procedure. We demonstrate the improvements gained by our new algorithms in systematic simulations and also in experiments with real hardware.

The paper is organized as follows: In Section 2 we give a repetition of self-calibration for a rotating camera. Section 3 describes how partial rotation information can be incorporated into the self-calibration procedure in various situations. Our new algorithms are evaluated in Section 4. Finally, we give conclusions in section 5.

2   Self-calibration of a Rotating Camera

2.1   Camera Model

First of all, we introduce the camera model and some notation. The pinhole camera model [1,7] is expressed by the equation $\lambda p = K p_C$, where p_C is a 3D point in the camera coordinate system, $p = (p_x, p_y, 1)^T$ is the imaged point in homogeneous 2D pixel coordinates, $\lambda \neq 0$ is a projective scale factor and $K \stackrel{\text{def}}{=} ((f_x, s, o_x), (0, f_y, o_y), (0, 0, 1))^T$ is the camera calibration matrix, where f_x and f_y are the effective focal lengths, s is the skew parameter and (o_x, o_y) is the principal point. The relation between a 3D point in camera coordinates p_C and the same point expressed in world coordinates p_W is $p_C = R_o p_W + t$, where R_o is the orientation of the camera and t is the position of its optical center. Thus, p_W is mapped to the image point p by the equation $\lambda p = K(R_o p_W + t)$.

2.2   Linear Self-calibration

We will give a very brief repetition of Hartley's linear self-calibration algorithm [2,1] for a purely rotating camera. In this situation, without loss of generality, we can assume $t = 0$. Taking a second image $p' = (p'_x, p'_y, 1)^T$ of the point p_W with camera orientation R'_o then results in $\lambda' p' = K R'_o p_W$, where $\lambda' \neq 0$ is another scale factor. The points p and p' correspond. By eliminating p_W, we get (cf. [1]):

$$\lambda'' p' = KRK^{-1} p \quad \text{with} \quad R \stackrel{\text{def}}{=} R'_o R_o^T \quad \text{and} \quad \lambda'' \stackrel{\text{def}}{=} \lambda'/\lambda \ . \tag{1}$$

In this formulation, R is the relative camera rotation. The transformation $\lambda'' p' = Hp$ maps p to p', where $H \stackrel{\text{def}}{=} KRK^{-1}$ is the *infinite homography*. It is related to the *dual image of the absolute conic* $\omega^* \stackrel{\text{def}}{=} KK^T$ by the equation $\omega^* = H\omega^* H^T$. Now, given $n \geq 2$ rotations of the camera (not all about the same axis), the self-calibration problem can be solved linearly by the following algorithm:

Input: A set of point correspondences $\{(p_{i,j}, p'_{i,j}) \mid 1 \leq i \leq n, 1 \leq j \leq m_i\}$, where $n \geq 2$ is the number of image pairs and m_i is the number of point correspondences for pair i. For numerical reasons [1,8], we normalize pixel coordinates throughout the paper to the range $[-1, 1]$ by applying a translation and an isotropic scaling.
1. For each image pair i, estimate the inter-image homography H'_i from the point correspondences of image pair i and enforce $\det(H_i) = 1$ by setting $H_i = \det(H'_i)^{-\frac{1}{3}} H'_i$.
2. Solve the set of equations $\{\omega^* = H_i \omega^* H_i^T \mid 1 \leq i \leq n\}$ for ω^* (linear least squares).
3. Compute K from $\omega^* = KK^T$, e.g. by Cholesky decomposition of $(\omega^*)^{-1}$.

Note that Hartley and Zisserman [1] require the homographies H_i to be expressed with respect to a common reference image. It is obvious that this requirement is *not* necessary, as only the *relative* orientations R_i of pairs of views are required.

2.3   Nonlinear Refinement

With equation (1) in mind, the self-calibration problem for a rotating camera with constant intrinsic parameters K can be defined as the solution of the following optimization problem (similar to Hartley's and Zisserman's nonlinear refinement [1]):

$$K = \operatorname*{argmin}_{K} \min_{(R_i \in SO(3))_{1 \leq i \leq n}} \sum_{i=1}^{n} \sum_{j=1}^{m_i} d\left(KR_iK^{-1}p_{i,j}, \lambda''_{i,j}p'_{i,j} \right)^2 , \qquad (2)$$

where $SO(3) = \{ R \in \mathbb{R}^{3 \times 3} \mid RR^T = I \wedge \det(R) = 1 \}$ denotes the rotation group and $d(\cdot, \cdot)$ is the Euclidean distance of 2D points in homogeneous coordinates. There are two advantages of the nonlinear formulation of the problem. First, the distance $d(\cdot, \cdot)$ is a geometrically meaningful measure on the point correspondences. Second, the constraint, that K is constant, will be enforced directly, which is impossible for the homography estimation part of the linear algorithm. The nonlinear optimization problem in equation (2) can be solved by finding a good initial approximation to the solution and refining that using a local nonlinear optimization algorithm. We use a modern second order Trust Region algorithm [9]. The initial solution for K is provided by the linear self-calibration method described above. The rotation matrices can be initialized as follows: compute $R_i = K^{-1}H_iK$ and enforce the constraint $R_i \in SO(3)$ by setting all singular values of R_i to one. The gradient and the Hessian of the objective function in equation (2) (and all variants that will follow in the rest of the paper) can be gained symbolically in "closed form". We will leave out the details, as automatic differentiation methods can be applied.

2.4   Zero Skew

For modern cameras, we can often assume zero skew $s = 0$ [1]. This assumption can be easily incorporated into the optimization problem by initially setting $s = 0$ and removing s from the set of optimization parameters. In the linear algorithm, the assumption can also be applied [1].

3   Improved Self-calibration with Partially Known Rotations

Rotation information can be available to several different extents. The various cases of partially known rotations are summarized in Figure 1. We will subsequently explain these cases, and show how each kind of a priori knowledge can be incorporated into the nonlinear self-calibration procedure by presenting appropriate variants of equation (2) with modified parameterizations of the rotations R_i. Even though the new formulations may look more complicated, decreasing the dimension of the parameter space will (hopefully) reduce the over-adaptation to noise. Despite that, in the cases with known values of some parameters, the algorithms simply cannot introduce errors by misestimating them.

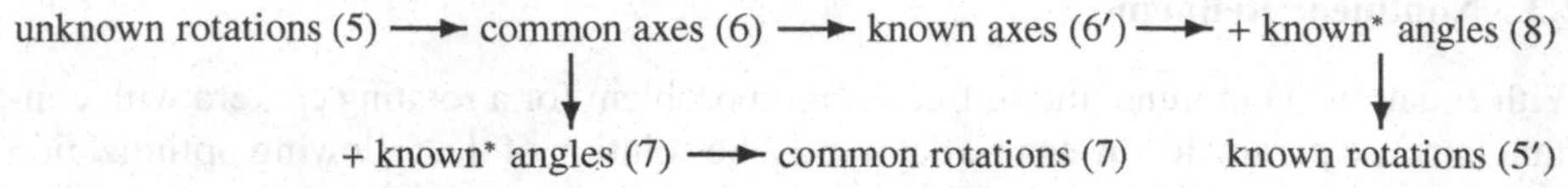

unknown rotations (5) ⟶ common axes (6) ⟶ known axes (6′) ⟶ + known* angles (8)

+ known* angles (7) ⟶ common rotations (7)   known rotations (5′)

Fig. 1. Cases of partially known rotations. The arrows indicate additional rotation knowledge, and "+ known* angles" means that, additionally, rotation angles are known up to a common scale factor. Numbers refer to equations, where (5′) and (6′) mean that a variation of the equation with fewer optimization parameters is used. Further explanations can be found in the text.

3.1 Unknown Rotations

Our starting point for using partial rotation information is the optimization problem in equation (2). First, we have a closer look at the rotation matrices. Enforcing the constraint $R_i \in SO(3)$ during the optimization can implicitly be achieved by using a minimal parameterization such as *exponential parameters* as suggested by Ma, Soatto, Kosecka and Sastry [10]. A rotation matrix R can be represented by a vector $w = (w_1, w_2, w_3)^T$ using Rodrigues' formula [10]:

$$R = \mathrm{Rod}(w) \stackrel{\text{def}}{=} I + \frac{S(w)}{\|w\|}\sin(\|w\|) + \frac{S(w)^2}{\|w\|^2}(1 - \cos(\|w\|)) \ , \tag{3}$$

using the skew symmetric matrix $S(w) \stackrel{\text{def}}{=} ((0, -w_3, w_2), (w_3, 0, -w_1), (-w_2, w_1, 0))^T$. The related *axis-angle* parameterization separates the rotation axis v and angle α explicitly at the cost of one additional parameter and the constraint $\|v\| = 1$:

$$R = \mathrm{Rod}(v, \alpha) \stackrel{\text{def}}{=} I + S(v)\sin(\alpha) + S(v)^2(1 - \cos(\alpha)) = \mathrm{Rod}(\alpha v) \ . \tag{4}$$

We prefer the axis-angle parameterization over exponential parameters only in cases of appropriate a priori knowledge, e.g. if v is known. For the following reasons, we do not use unit quaternions, even though they are very popular:

- They do not provide a minimal parameterization, as they have four parameters, and the unit quaternion constraint is required (similar to axis-angle).
- The close relationship between exponential parameters and the axis-angle representation helps pinpoint the precise differences between the various cases of partial rotation knowledge, as will become evident in the rest of the paper.
- There is no clear agreement as to which parameterization is best [11].

Applying exponential parameters to equation (2), we get the following nonlinear optimization problem, which has a total of $3n + 5$ parameters:

$$K = \underset{K}{\arg\min} \ \underset{(w_i)_{1 \le i \le n}}{\min} \sum_{i=1}^{n} \sum_{j=1}^{m_i} d\left(K\mathrm{Rod}(w_i)K^{-1}p_{i,j}, \lambda''_{i,j}p'_{i,j}\right)^2 \ . \tag{5}$$

For the initialization of the nonlinear optimization problem, we need to compute the rotation parameters w_i from the rotation matrices R_i [10].

3.2   Rotation About Two Axes Only

If the pan-tilt-unit is actively controlled for the purpose of self-calibration, it is possible to restrict rotations to be about one of the two physical rotation axes of the pan-tilt-unit *at a time*, such that there are only two mathematical rotation axes in total (Figure 1: "common axes"). In this case, rotations only have one parameter each (the rotation angle) and there are two degrees of freedom for each rotation axis. From a theoretical point of view, we can generalize this and allow $r \leq n$ rotation axes instead of only two. This results in $n + 2r + 5$ parameters. To obtain a suitable version of the optimization problem in equation (5), we replace exponential parameters by axis-angle and use only r instead of n rotation axes. Finally, we add constant indices k_i as a priori knowledge, which assign the correct rotation axis v_{k_i} to the rotation with index i, and get:

$$K = \underset{K}{\arg\min} \quad \underset{\substack{(\alpha_i)_{1 \leq i \leq n}, (v_k)_{1 \leq k \leq r} \\ \|v_k\| = 1 \text{ for all } k}}{\min} \sum_{i=1}^{n} \sum_{j=1}^{m_i} d\left(K\mathrm{Rod}(\alpha_i, v_{k_i})K^{-1}p_{i,j}, \lambda''_{i,j}p'_{i,j}\right)^2 \quad . \qquad (6)$$

Note that this formulation uses one parameter too much for each axis v_k. In this one case we trade minimality for simplicity and ignore the constraints $\|v_k\| = 1$ during the optimization. To initialize the common rotation axes, we take the average over all independent estimates which belong to the same axis. Throughout the paper, an according strategy is applied whenever two or more rotations have common parameters. If the rotation axes are known (Figure 1: "known axes"), the parameters v_k are constant and need not to be optimized, and we have a minimal parameterization with $5 + n$ parameters.

3.3   Rotation Angles Known Up to Scale

Things simplify even more if we have knowledge about the rotation angle. Using a pan-tilt-unit, relative rotation angles are often known in some device specific unit. If the pan-tilt-unit is calibrated and provides a mapping from machine units to radians, we get the actual angles. Otherwise, we assume a linear mapping from angles β_i in machine units to radians α_i: $\alpha_i = \theta_{k_i}\beta_i$, where θ_{k_i} is the unknown scale factor, which may be specific to each of the r rotation axes. This results in a total of $5 + 3r$ parameters for r unknown but fixed rotation axes (Figure 1: "common axes + known* angles"). To formulate an appropriate optimization problem, we begin with equation (5). We encode each axis *and* scale factor by *one* vector u_k. For each actual rotation, the appropriate vector u_{k_i} is multiplied by the known angle in machine units β_i to produce the exponential parameters (w_i in equation (5)). We now minimize over the vectors u_k:

$$K = \underset{K}{\arg\min} \quad \underset{(u_k)_{1 \leq k \leq r}}{\min} \sum_{i=1}^{n} \sum_{j=1}^{m_i} d\left(K\mathrm{Rod}(\beta_i u_{k_i})K^{-1}p_{i,j}, \lambda''_{i,j}p'_{i,j}\right)^2 \quad . \qquad (7)$$

If the rotation axes are known (Figure 1: "known axes + known* angles"), we start with the formulation in equation (6). The angles α_i are replaced by $\theta_{k_i}\beta_i$, and the values θ_k are the new optimization parameters ($5 + r$ parameters in total):

$$K = \underset{K}{\arg\min} \quad \underset{(\theta_k)_{1 \leq k \leq r}}{\min} \sum_{i=1}^{n} \sum_{j=1}^{m_i} d\left(K\mathrm{Rod}(\theta_{k_i}\beta_i, v_{k_i})K^{-1}p_{i,j}, \lambda''_{i,j}p'_{i,j}\right)^2 \quad . \qquad (8)$$

3.4   Common Rotations

It may be possible to control the pan-tilt-unit such that all rotations about each physical axis share the same angle (which we do not need to know). In other words, there are only two (or more generally: r) unknown rotation matrices (Figure 1: "common rotations"). Mathematically, this situation is a special case of equation (7) if we set $\beta_i = 1$ for all i. Thus, there is again a total of $5 + 3r$ parameters. This case is also a direct special case of equation (5) with fewer rotation parameters.

3.5   Known Rotations

Finally, rotations can be known completely ("known rotations"). In practice, such data can be provided by a dedicated rotation sensor (Figure 1: "known rotations"). Calibrated pan-tilt-units, as described above, are a further possibility ("known axes + known* angles" plus known scale factors θ_k). To get an appropriate optimization problem, we observe that this is a special case of *each* case presented above. We choose equation (5). The rotation parameters w_i are now constant and need not to be optimized.

This situation with only five parameters has already been briefly mentioned by Hartley [2], who used a similar nonlinear formulation. Frahm and Koch [4,5] investigated this case in more detail and presented a linear algorithm. Note, however, that these approaches cannot benefit from only *partially* known rotations.

3.6   A Note on Real Pan-Tilt-Units

All rotation knowledge in equation (2) and the above mentioned reformulations is expressed in the camera coordinate system. In the cases "common axes" and "common rotations", this seems uncritical at first sight, but really *is* an issue, as will be explained in this section. In the cases "known axes" and "known rotations" the problem is quite obvious: the alignment of the rotation axes with the camera coordinate system needs to be known. The additionally complicating issue, which is relevant to *all* cases of partial rotation knowledge, is that the alignment of the rotation axes with the camera coordinate system is typically *not* constant even though the camera is rigidly mounted onto (or into) the pan-tilt-unit. In most (if not all) pan-tilt-units, one of the rotation axes is placed "on top" of the other one. This means that the camera coordinate system is rigidly mounted relative to one of the rotation axes only. In case of the Directed Perception PTU-46-17.5, the pan mechanism rigidly rotates the tilt axis *and* the camera. However, the tilt mechanism only rotates the camera and does *not* affect the pan mechanism. Thus, tilting changes the alignment of the *pan* axis relative to the camera coordinate system. We can avoid this problem by keeping the tilt setting constant for *all* pan rotations, e.g. by first performing pan rotations and then tilt rotations.

4   Experiments

In the experiments, we investigate all cases of partially known rotations shown in Figure 1. We also include the linear standard algorithm. By simulation, we demonstrate how the influence of noise reduces when using partial rotation knowledge. We also present results for real hardware.

4.1 Simulation

For the simulation, we use a virtual pinhole camera with parameters $f_x^{(GT)} = f_y^{(GT)} = 100$, $s^{(GT)} = 0$, $o_x^{(GT)} = 150$, $o_y^{(GT)} = 100$. In normalized pixel coordinates, the values are: $f_x^{(GT,N)} = f_y^{(GT,N)} = 2/3$, $s^{(GT,N)} = o_x^{(GT,N)} = o_y^{(GT,N)} = 0$. These parameters are of course unknown to the self-calibration algorithms. Point correspondences are generated by projecting 100 3D points into the camera twice – before and after rotating the camera about its X or Y axis. Each resulting 2D point is modified by uniformly distributed, additive noise in the range $[-\phi/2, \phi/2] \times [-\phi/2, \phi/2]$. We systematically perform experiments for different values of the noise parameter ϕ. If one of the resulting 2D points of a corresponding pair lies outside of the image area $[0, 300] \times [0, 200]$, the pair is discarded. The 3D points are randomly generated by a uniform distribution on the cuboid $[-15000, 15000] \times [-10000, 10000] \times [-10000, 10000]$ (in pixel units). As an alternative, more difficult situation, we change the values of some parameters as follows: $f_x^{(GT)} = f_y^{(GT)} = 400$ (normalized: $f_x^{(GT)} = f_y^{(GT)} = 8/3$), 2000 3D points.

We perform a series of ten (relative) rotations about the Y axis followed by another ten rotations about the X axis. The rotation angle is $10°$ for each rotation. The initial configuration for the first sequence of rotations is $\boldsymbol{R_o} = \mathrm{Rod}((0, -25°, 0)^T)$, and $\boldsymbol{R_o} = \mathrm{Rod}((0, 0, -25°)^T)$ for the second one. We measure the error of the self-calibration result $\boldsymbol{K}^{(N)}$ by computing the Frobenius norm of the difference between $\boldsymbol{K}^{(N)}$ and the ground truth data $\boldsymbol{K}^{(GT,N)}$, both expressed in normalized pixel units: $e_F = \left\| \boldsymbol{K}^{(N)}, \boldsymbol{K}^{(GT,N)} \right\|_2$. If the self-calibration fails, e.g. because ω^* is not positive definite, we set $e_F = \infty$. Each experimental setup is simulated 100 times with identical parameters. For the final evaluation, we compute the median of e_F over all 100 runs.

Results: Figure 2 (left) shows the results of the simulation in the simple situation. You can clearly see the improvements gained by using partial rotation knowledge. As expected, a greater amount of rotation knowledge leads to better results. The linear algorithm is outperformed by the nonlinear ones, and additional rotation knowledge further improves the results. However, there is a clustering in the plots: "common axes", "common axes + machine angles" and "common rotations" perform almost equally well. The same is the case for "known axes" and "known axes + machine angles". Obviously, in this experiment, knowing rotation angles up to scale does *not* further improve self-calibration. However, there is a pronounced difference between "common axes", "known axes" and completely "known rotations". Knowing only "common axes" is already better than "unknown rotations", although this is clearly visible only for high noise levels. Note how these results agree with the hierarchy in Figure 1.

The results for the difficult situation are shown in Figure 2 (right). Note that the scale of the error axis is more than ten times larger in the right plot revealing that this situation *is* actually a lot more difficult. As far as the ranking of the algorithms is concerned, the main impression is the same. However, there are a few interesting differences to the simple situation. The most striking one is the large improvement gained by completely "known rotations". Beginning with noise level $\phi = 6$, there *is* now also an improvement gained by knowing angles up to scale in the case of "common axes". However, in the case "known axes + known* angles" there is a serious problem. The reason for this might be some bad local minimum, which cannot be overcome

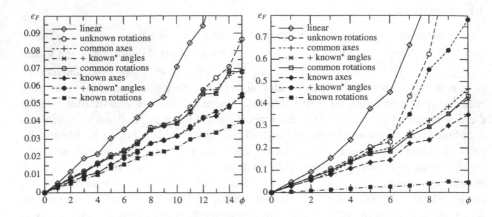

Fig. 2. Median of Frobenius error e_F for various noise levels ϕ. Left: simple situation ($f_x^{(GT)} = f_y^{(GT)} = 100$). Right: difficult situation ($f_x^{(GT)} = f_y^{(GT)} = 400$). Note the different scalings of the Y axes.

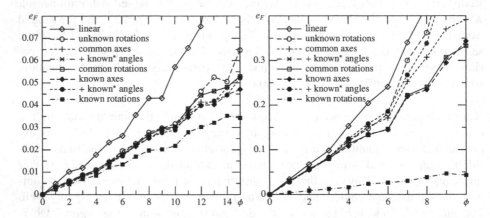

Fig. 3. Median of Frobenius error e_F for various noise levels ϕ with the assumption of zero skew. Left: simple situation ($f_x^{(GT)} = f_y^{(GT)} = 100$). Right: difficult situation ($f_x^{(GT)} = f_y^{(GT)} = 400$). Note the different scalings of the Y axes.

in the restricted seven dimensional space given a bad initialization for the angle scale parameters. A further possible explanation would be problems during the optimization caused by ill-conditioned Hessians, as might occur if the initialization is too bad.

The results for the zero skew variants of the algorithms are shown in Figure 3. The first important observation is that the error is reduced further. However, the improvement gained by (correctly) assuming zero skew is different for the various algorithms. As the good algorithms seem to gain less, the difference between the results for the various types of partial rotation knowledge is much smaller, but still visible. The case of completely "known rotations" distinguishes surprisingly well from the rest.

Table 1. Median Frobenius errors e_F and median relative errors in percent on the normalized focal length $e_r = 100|f_x^{(N)} - f_x^{(GT,N)}|/f_x^{(GT,N)}$ for the experiments on real data ($f_x^{(GT,N)} = 2.4098$)

| | base algorithm | | | | zero skew variant | | | |
| | t10 | t5 | o10 | o5 | t10 | t5 | o10 | o5 |
algorithm	e_F e_r	e_F e_r	e_F e_r	e_F e_r	e_F e_r	e_F e_r	e_F e_r	e_F e_r
linear	1.11 35	1.13 35	1.29 38	1.24 38	1.11 35	1.13 34	1.26 37	1.23 38
unknown rotation	1.04 36	1.06 35	1.24 44	1.20 40	1.04 35	1.06 35	1.21 44	1.18 40
common axes	1.00 35	1.04 34	1.13 41	1.13 38	0.99 34	1.04 34	1.13 41	1.12 38
+ known* angles	0.99 34	1.01 34	1.13 37	1.15 36	0.98 33	1.00 33	1.13 37	1.14 36
common rotations	0.99 34	1.01 34	1.13 37	1.15 36	0.98 33	1.00 33	1.13 37	1.14 36
known axes	1.17 37	1.15 35	1.34 44	1.22 40	0.97 33	1.03 33	1.05 38	1.08 37
+ known* angles	1.12 35	1.13 35	1.30 38	1.24 38	1.11 35	1.13 34	1.26 37	1.23 38
known rotations	0.12 2	0.12 2	0.17 2	0.15 2	0.12 2	0.12 2	0.17 2	0.15 2

4.2 Real Camera

For the experiments with real hardware, we use a Sony DFW-VL500 progressive scan firewire camera mounted onto a Directed Perception PTU-46-17.5 pan-tilt-unit such that the tilt axis is parallel to the X axis of the camera coordinate system, and the pan axis for tilt setting 0 is parallel to the Y axis. Note that this setup violates the pure rotation assumption, i.e. the translation vector t is *not* zero. Lacking ideal hardware, we nonetheless assume rotation about the X and Y axis of the camera coordinate system. Note that this problem is *not* specific to our approach, but common to the vast majority of the rotational self-calibration literature. We also adopt the further common simplification of ignoring camera distortions.

The pan-tilt-unit performs two rotation subsequences similar to the setup in the simulation. We use two different scenes for the experiments: a wall with artificial texture (t), which is well suited for point tracking, and a typical office environment (o). For each scene, we record one sequence with 10° rotations and another one with 5° rotations. Each of the four sequences (t10, t5, o10, o5) is repeated ten times with a randomly modified initial pan-tilt configuration. The videos are available online at http://www4.informatik.uni-jena.de/selfcalib. To get point correspondences, we track up to 200 points using KLT tracking [12]. All points which could be tracked from the beginning to the end of each 5° or 10° subsequence, respectively, are used as point correspondences.

A ground truth estimation of the camera parameters is performed using Zhang's [13] method. As in the simulation, we compute the median (over ten sequences) of the Frobenius error of the self-calibration results in normalized pixel units. The results are listed in Table 1. For all algorithms, except for "known rotations", the error is very large. Actually, the focal lengths f_x and f_y are severely overestimated throughout the experiments. The reason for this is very probably a violation of model assumptions: pure rotation about the optical center and a distortion-free camera. Given the good optics of the test camera, we expect the non-ideal pan-tilt-unit to cause most of the systematic error. Note, however, that our algorithms with partial rotation knowledge are able to reduce the systematic error in most cases. The algorithm with completely "known rotations" can even greatly reduce it and produce reasonable results.

5 Conclusions

We have presented improvements for rotational self-calibration with partially known rotations, which are available, e.g., when using a pan-tilt-unit to rotate the camera. The knowledge is exploited by restricting the rotation parameterization in a nonlinear self-calibration algorithm. In systematic simulations, we showed that our new algorithms can reduce the sensitivity to noise. The experiments on real data revealed a systematic error, probably caused by non-zero translation. Our algorithms with partial rotation knowledge were able to reduce this error. In case of full rotation knowledge, the remaining error was very small in comparison.

As future research, given the problems with the non-ideal pan-tilt-unit, we plan to extend our approach to be able to deal with the case of constant non-zero translation. We also plan to extend our formulation of partial rotation knowledge such that we do not have to express the rotation axes in the camera coordinate system.

References

1. Hartley, R., Zisserman, A.: Multiple View Geometry in Computer Vision, 2nd edn. Cambridge University Press, Cambridge (2003)
2. Hartley, R.I.: Self-Calibration of Stationary Cameras. International Journal of Computer Vision 22(1), 5–23 (1997)
3. Quan, L., Triggs, B.: A Unification of Autocalibration Methods. In: Proceedings of the Fourth Asian Conference on Computer Vision, pp. 917–922 (2000)
4. Frahm, J.M.: Camera Self-Calibration with Known Camera Orientation. PhD thesis, Institut für Informatik, Universität Kiel (2005)
5. Frahm, J.M., Koch, R.: Camera Calibration with Known Rotation. In: Proceedings of the IEEE International Conference on Computer Vision, vol. 2, pp. 1418–1425 (2003)
6. de Agapito, L., Hayman, E., Reid, I.D.: Self-Calibration of Rotating and Zooming Cameras. International Journal of Computer Vision 45(2), 107–127 (2001)
7. Trucco, E., Verri, A.: Introductory Techniques for 3D Computer Vision. Prentice-Hall, Englewood Cliffs (1998)
8. Hartley, R.I.: In defense of the eight-point algorithm. IEEE Transactions on Pattern Analysis and Machine Intelligence 19(6), 580–593 (1997)
9. Conn, A.R., Gould, N.I.M., Toint, P.L.: Trust-Region Methods. SIAM Society for Industrial and Applied Mathematics, Philadelphia (2000)
10. Ma, Y., Soatto, S., Košecká, J., Sastry, S.: An Invitation to 3D Vision, Springer, Heidelberg (2004)
11. Schmidt, J., Niemann, H.: Using Quaternions for Parametrizing 3-D Rotations in Unconstrained Nonlinear Optimization. In: Proceedings of the Vision Modeling and Visualization Conference, pp. 399–406 (2001)
12. Shi, J., Tomasi, C.: Good Features to Track. In: Proceedings of the IEEE Conference on Computer Vision and Pattern Recognition, pp. 593–600. IEEE Computer Society Press, Los Alamitos (1994)
13. Zhang, Z.: Flexible Camera Calibration by Viewing a Plane from Unknown Orientations. In: Proceedings of the IEEE International Conference on Computer Vision, pp. 666–673. IEEE Computer Society Press, Los Alamitos (1999)

A Combined Approach for Estimating Patchlets from PMD Depth Images and Stereo Intensity Images

Christian Beder, Bogumil Bartczak, and Reinhard Koch

Computer Science Department
Universiy of Kiel, Germany
{beder,bartczak,rk}@mip.informatik.uni-kiel.de

Abstract. Real-time active 3D range cameras based on time-of-flight technology using the Photonic Mixer Device (PMD) can be considered as a complementary technique for stereo-vision based depth estimation. Since those systems directly yield 3D measurements, they can also be used for initializing vision based approaches, especially in highly dynamic environments. Fusion of PMD depth images with passive intensity-based stereo is a promising approach for obtaining reliable surface reconstructions even in weakly textured surface regions.

In this work a PMD-stereo fusion algorithm for the estimation of patchlets from a combined PMD-stereo camera rig will be presented. As patchlet we define an oriented small planar 3d patch with associated surface normal. Least-squares estimation schemes for estimating patchlets from PMD range images as well as from a pair of stereo images are derived. It is shown, how those two approaches can be fused into one single estimation, that yields results even if either of the two single approaches fails.

1 Introduction

Vision-based passive stereo systems [1] and active systems such as structured light or laser scanners [2] are complementary methods to measure 3D depth of a scene. However, the application domain of all this systems is restricted. For instance the algorithmic complexity of stereo systems is quite high and they are not applicable in case of weakly textured surfaces. Laser scanners and structured light approaches on the other hand cannot cope with moving objects, because capturing is not instantaneous for this systems.

A new promising development for the area of surface reconstruction, that is able to cope with those caveats of the existing techniques, is the Photonic Mixer Device (PMD), which measures distances directly for a two dimensional field of pixels based on the time of flight of incoherent, modulated infrared light. Recently PMD cameras have been developed that are capable of capturing reliable depth images directly in real-time. Those cameras are compact and affordable, which makes them attractive for versatile applications including surveillance and computer vision [3]. The successful application of this technology in Structure

F.A. Hamprecht, C. Schnörr, and B. Jähne (Eds.): DAGM 2007, LNCS 4713, pp. 11–20, 2007.

from Motion [4], motion capturing [5] and face tracking[6] have been demonstrated.

In [7] the complementary nature of stereo vision based systems and PMD cameras is discussed qualitatively and a simple method for fusing the information gathered from those two system is proposed. Yet neither a quantitative comparison of both systems nor a statistically optimal fusion is done. Recently, a systematic and quantitative comparison of both approaches was investigated in [8]. The evaluation showed that a combination of both approaches, either by initialisation of stereo with PMD, or by fusion of both methods, could prove beneficial. However, no systematic analysis of a statistically optimal fusion of both modalities exists.

The main contribution of this work is therefore the development of a statistically optimal fusion of both systems based on the estimation of patchlets [9], i.e. small planar surface patches with an associated surface normal, being a very useful surface representation for tasks such as segmentation [10] and visualization [11].

First a short introduction to the technology underlying the PMD image formation will be given in section 2 in order to provide some background information.

Then in section 3 two least-squares estimation schemes for the PMD images as well as for the stereo images will be presented and it will be shown, how optimal estimates for the patchlets together with their covariance matrices can be obtained. While the PMD camera provides direct geometric measurements, which are used in the estimation of the patchlet, the stereo matching is based on estimating a local homography between the images [12,13,14], which optimally aligns the image intensities between the stereo image pair [15,16,17]. Because both estimation schemes have the same structure, a fused estimation using input data from both sources is possible.

In section 4 a brief quantitative analysis of the three approaches on synthetic images for different noise levels will be presented and some surface reconstructions from real images will be shown.

2   The PMD-Camera

We will first give some background information on the Photonic Mixer Device (PMD), which is a semiconductor structure based on CCD- or CMOS-technology [18]. Integrated in an image sensor array it is capable of modulating the current that is generated by received light intensities in every single pixel. This can be utilized to build affordable cameras that are able to measure depth with high precision. One such camera is shown in figure 3. It mainly consists of a camera with the PMD sensor and light emitter arrays that are used to send out modulated light. The light is reflected by 3D scene points and received by the PMD image sensor.

The depth measurement performed with a detector using the Photonic Mixer Device is based on the time of flight principle. Different approaches for measuring the time-of-flight with light exist [19]. One method suitable for the use with the

PMD is to modulate the emitted light intensity with a periodic pattern. Depending on the "time of flight" a phase shift of the periodic pattern is observable. The PMD-Camera is able to extract this phase shift in every pixel.

Though different intensity modulations using square waves or pseudo noise coding are possible, the use of a sinusoidal signal is technically well realizable [20]. Generally an intensity wave $I(x, t) = I_0 + I_A \cos(2\pi\nu_m(t + \frac{x}{c}) + \varphi_0)$ with modulation frequency ν_m, propagation speed c and initial phase φ_0 is sent out. At two points x_0 and x_1 of the wave the phase shift

$$\Delta\varphi = 2\pi\nu_m(x_1 - x_0)/c \qquad (1)$$

is observable. Extracting this shift from the wave therefore delivers the distance between x_0 and x_1. Due to the repetitive nature of the wave the non-ambiguous wavelength of the measurement is $\lambda_{max} = c/\nu_m$. The effective measurement range is $\frac{\lambda_{max}}{2}$ because light wave has to return to its source to be detected. Typically a modulation frequency of $\nu_m = 20\text{MHz}$ is used which gives the camera 7.5 meters of unambiguous depth range. Reflections from distances beyond this range might cause measurement errors due to phase wrapping, however usually the reflected light intensity is too small to cause such errors. For very small distances below 2m, the reflected strong light intensity might cause nonlinear saturation effects which might limit the accuracy and cause bias [3]. Therefore, the usable range was chosen between $2 - 7.5$ meters.

The phase difference is measured by cross correlation between the sent and received modulated signal by the PMD chip. Since the resolution of the phase difference measurement is independent from distance, the achievable depth resolution is independent from scene depth. This is in contrast to stereo triangulation where depth accuracy is proportional to inverse depth.

After taking depth calibration and lens distortions [21,3] into account, the model of a central perspective projection for the geometric description of the PMD-Camera measurements can be utilized.

3 Estimation of Patchlets

In the following two patchlet estimation schemes for PMD images as well as stereo images based on the Gauss-Markoff-Model [22] will be presented. Because the structure of both estimations is identical, both approaches can easily be fused, which will be shown in section 3.3.

3.1 Estimation of Patchlets from PMD Images

The PMD-camera determines for each ray direction corresponding to pixel $\mathbf{x}$ its distance λ to the optical center. If the camera geometry is given by a projection matrix [23, p.141f] as

$$P_3 = K_3(R_3|t_3) \qquad (2)$$

then the corresponding 3d point is obtained directly from the distance λ as

$$X = \frac{\lambda R_3^T K_3^{-1} x}{\sqrt{x^T K_3^{-T} K_3^{-1} x}} - R_3^T t_3 \tag{3}$$

This 3d point lies on the plane $(n^T, d)^T$, if

$$X^T n + d = 0 \tag{4}$$

or equivalently

$$\left(\sqrt{x^T K_3^{-T} K_3^{-1} x} t_3^T R_3 - \lambda x^T K_3^{-T} R_3 \right) n' = \sqrt{x^T K_3^{-T} K_3^{-1} x} \tag{5}$$

using the substitution $n' = \frac{n}{d}$ to parameterize the plane. This expression is linear in the plane parameters n' so that initial values are easily computed. Solving this expression for the unknown depth λ yields

$$\lambda = \sqrt{x^T K_3^{-T} K_3^{-1} x} \frac{t_3^T R_3 n' - 1}{x^T K_3^{-T} R_3 n'} \tag{6}$$

Now using the Jacobian

$$a^T(x, \lambda, n_0') = \frac{\partial \lambda}{\partial n'} \tag{7}$$

$$= \frac{\sqrt{x^T K_3^{-T} K_3^{-1} x}}{\left(x^T K_3^{-T} R_3 n' \right)^2} \left(x^T K_3^{-T} R_3 n' t_3^T R_3 - (t_3^T R_3 n' - 1) x^T K_3^{-T} R_3 \right) \tag{8}$$

the Taylor expansion of this expression then yields for every point on the plane

$$\underbrace{a^T(x, \lambda, n_0')}_{a_i^T} \underbrace{(n' - n_0')}_{\Delta n'} \approx \underbrace{\lambda - \sqrt{x^T K_3^{-T} K_3^{-1} x} \frac{t_3^T R_3 n_0' - 1}{x^T K_3^{-T} R_3 n_0'}}_{\Delta l_i} \tag{9}$$

In the following section a similar expression will be derived for the stereo system.

3.2   Estimation of Patchlets from Stereo Images

Given a calibrated stereo system with the first camera being

$$P_1 = K_1(I_3 | 0_3) \tag{10}$$

and the second camera being

$$P_2 = K_2(R_2 | t_2) \tag{11}$$

with the known rotation matrix R and translation vector t, the homography relating points on the plane $(n^T, d)^T$ from the first into the second camera is given by [23, p.314]

$$H = K_2 \left(R_2 - t_2 \frac{n^T}{d} \right) K_1^{-1} \tag{12}$$

which is linear in the vector $n' = \frac{n}{d}$. Hence, points on the plane are transformed according to

$$x_2 = H(n')x_1 = K_2 R_2 K_1^{-1} x_1 - ((x_1^T K_1^{-T}) \otimes (K_2 t_2)) n' \tag{13}$$

We now assume, that the grey value of corresponding points is equal in the two images. Using the Euclidean normalization function

$$h(x) = h \begin{pmatrix} u \\ v \\ w \end{pmatrix} = \frac{1}{w} \begin{pmatrix} u \\ v \end{pmatrix} \tag{14}$$

this is expressed in terms of the two images I_1 and I_2 as

$$I_1(h(x_1)) = I_2(h(x_2)) \tag{15}$$

or substituting equation (13)

$$I_1(h(x_1)) = I_2(h(K_2 R_2 K_1^{-1} x_1 - ((x_1^T K_1^{-T}) \otimes (K_2 t_2)) n')) \tag{16}$$

Applying chain rule, the partial derivatives of this expression are given by

$$b^T(x_1, n') = \frac{\partial}{\partial n'} I_2(h(K_2 R K_1^{-1} x_1 - ((x_1^T K_1^{-T}) \otimes (K_2 t)) n')) \tag{17}$$

$$= -(\nabla I_2)(h(H(n')x_1)) J(H(n')x_1) K_2 t_2 x_1^T K_1^{-T} \tag{18}$$

with the Jacobian of the normalization function being

$$J = \frac{\partial}{\partial x} h = \begin{pmatrix} \frac{1}{w} & 0 & -\frac{u}{w^2} \\ 0 & \frac{1}{w} & -\frac{v}{w^2} \end{pmatrix} \tag{19}$$

Hence, the Taylor expansion of equation (16) yields for every point on the plane

$$\underbrace{b^T(x_1, n_0')}_{b_j^T} \underbrace{(n' - n_0')}_{\Delta n'} \approx \underbrace{I_1(h(x_1)) - I_2(h(H(n_0')x_1))}_{\Delta m_j} \tag{20}$$

This equation is compatible with equation (9), so that a fused best linear unbiased estimation is possible as shown in the next section.

3.3 The Fused Estimation

Using a window containing N points from the PMD depth image and M points from the stereo intensity images on the patchlet, the plane parameter updates may be estimated iteratively as [22]

$$\widehat{\Delta n'} = \left(\sum_{i=1}^{N} \sigma_{l_i}^{-2} a_i a_i^T + \sum_{j=1}^{M} \sigma_{m_j}^{-2} b_j b_j^T \right)^{-1} \left(\sum_{i=1}^{N} \sigma_{l_i}^{-2} a_i \Delta l_i + \sum_{j=1}^{M} \sigma_{m_j}^{-2} b_j \Delta m_j \right) \tag{21}$$

having the expected covariance matrix

$$\Sigma_{\widehat{n'}\widehat{n'}} = \left(\sum_{i=1}^{N} \sigma_{l_i}^{-2} a_i a_i^T + \sum_{j=1}^{M} \sigma_{m_j}^{-2} b_j b_j^T \right)^{-1} \tag{22}$$

where $\sigma_{m_j}^2$ is twice the variance of the image noise for stereo pixels and $\sigma_{l_i}^2$ is the variance of the distance uncertainty of the PMD camera. Note, that those quantities need only be specified up to scale so that only the relative weighting between the stereo system and the PMD system is required.

To specify this relative weighting the variance factor can be estimated from the residuals as

$$\widehat{\sigma}_0^2 = \frac{1}{N + M - 3} \left(\sum_{i=1}^{N} \sigma_{l_i}^{-2} (\Delta l_i - a_i^T \Delta n')^2 + \sum_{j=1}^{M} \sigma_{m_j}^{-2} (\Delta m_j - b_j^T \Delta n')^2 \right) \tag{23}$$

By looking at the variance factors resulting from estimations with $N = 0$ and $M = 0$ respectively the relative weights can be determined.

Putting everything together we obtain three different patchlet estimation algorithms, namely using only the depth images, using the depth image for initialization (cf. equation (5)) and the stereo images for the estimation and finally a fused approach using all available data. In the following section those three alternatives will be compared.

4   Results

For evaluating the performance of the fused estimation scheme a stereo-rig was used, which is shown in figure 3. It consists of two Sony cameras which deliver images with a resolution of 1024×768 pixels and a field of view of $40° \times 32°$. The PMD camera in the middle is PMDTechs model 3K-s with a resolution of 64×48 pixels over a viewing angle of $22° \times 17°$. Hence, we used windows of 20×20 pixels in the intensity images and windows of 3×3 pixels in the depth images in order to cover approximately the same viewing angle with both systems. The rig was calibrated using a calibration pattern so that the internal parameters of each of the three camera as well as the relative poses of all cameras with respect to the

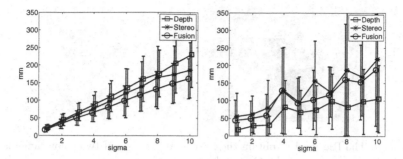

Fig. 1. *Left:* Expected standard deviation of estimated patchlet distance against image noise standard deviation. *Right:* Average distance of the estimated patchlets from ground truth against image noise standard deviation.

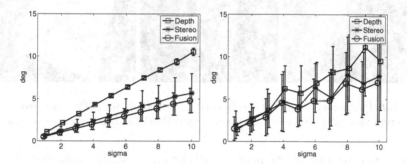

Fig. 2. *Left:* Expected standard deviation of estimated patchlet angle against image noise standard deviation. *Right:* Average angular distance of the estimated patchlets from ground truth against image noise standard deviation.

left stereo camera are known. The stereo system had a baseline of approximately 30 cm and the orientation was close to standard stereo geometry.

We started by generating synthetic data using the calibration parameters of the real rig to produce three images of a well-textured plane $3m$ in front of the camera. We then added white noise of different standard deviation to the three images and estimated 100 patchlets on the surface. The distance of the estimated patchlets from the ground truth as well as the expected standard deviation of the distance is plotted against the added image noise in figure 1. The expected accuracy plotted on the left hand side is worst for the approach depending solely on the PMD images due to the low resolution of the depth image. The accuracy is better for the estimation initialized with the depth image and optimized using the intensity images. Best results are expected for the completely fused approach. However, as the patchlets are estimated at equally distant sample-points rather than only at positions of high intensity gradient, the mean distance from the ground truth is worse for the texture-dependent intensity based estimation than for the other two approaches and the variation is high over the set of

Fig. 3. *Left:* The Rig used to obtain the results. It consists of two color cameras that frame the PMD-Camera. *Right:* One of the stereo images.

Fig. 4. *Left:* Patchlets from purely depth based estimation. *Middle:* Patchlets from stereo based estimation using depth initialization. *Right:* Patchlets from fused estimation.

patchlets. On the average the purely depth based approach performed best and the fused approach, being an average over both, lies somewhere in between. This is depicted on the right hand side of figure 1.

Figure 2 shows the same analysis for the normal angle. On the right hand side the angular difference to the ground truth is plotted against the image noise while on the left hand side the expected accuracies are plotted. Here the purely depth map based method is inferior to the intensity based estimation while the fused approach yields the best results.

Now we will present some results on real data. We used the rig depicted on the left hand side of figure 3 and took a picture of the scene shown on the right hand side. The resulting patchlets are depicted in figure 4. We removed patchlets, where the angular accuracy was below a common threshold of 10° in order to demonstrate the capabilities of the different methods. On the left hand side of figure 4 the remaining patchlets for the purely depth image based estimation are shown. It can be seen, that the angular accuracy of the patchlet estimation increases with distance for the depth image, because the surface covered increases and the distance measurement accuracy is equal over the whole image. Further observe, that the dark regions are measured slightly off the plane. The middle picture shows the remaining patchlets for the intensity based estimation with depth initialization. As expected only the textured regions of the image yield good patchlets. Finally the fused estimate yields the patchlets depicted on the right hand side of figure 4. As expected, the best accuracy is achievable using the statistically optimal fused method.

5   Conclusion

We have presented a fused estimation scheme for patchlet based surface reconstruction from stereo images as well as PMD range images. It has been shown, how the two systems can be integrated yielding more accurate surface reconstructions than either system alone.

The PMD camera yields an accurate direct distance measurement for each pixel and is therefore required for initializing each of the three proposed algorithms. However, the low resolution of current PMD cameras is the major factor limiting the stand-alone applicability of such a system.

Stereo intensity based systems on the other hand have a much higher resolution but their depth accuracy is depending on texture and object distance. Furthermore some initialization is required for those systems to work robustly.

Hence, both systems can be considered complementary in terms of resolution, depth accuracy and scene coverage. The proposed fusion of both approaches therefore constitutes a method for obtaining accurate and robust scene reconstructions including surface normals using a camera rig such as the one depicted in figure 3.

Acknowledgements

The PMD camera used in the experiments is courtesy of Alexander Prusak and Hubert Roth, University of Siegen, Germany.

This work was supported by the German Research Foundation (DFG), KO-2044/3-1.

References

1. Scharstein, D., Szeliski, R., Zabih, R.: A taxonomy and evaluation of dense two-frame stereo correspondence algorithms (2001)
2. Hoppe, H., DeRose, T., Duchamp, T., Halstead, M., Jin, H., McDonald, J., Schweitzer, J., Stuetzle, W.: Piecewise smooth surface reconstruction. Computer Graphics 28(Annual Conference Series), 295–302 (1994)
3. Lindner, M., Kolb, A.: Lateral and depth calibration of pmd-distance sensors. In: Bebis, G., Boyle, R., Parvin, B., Koracin, D., Remagnino, P., Nefian, A., Meenakshisundaram, G., Pascucci, V., Zara, J., Molineros, J., Theisel, H., Malzbender, T. (eds.) ISVC 2006. LNCS, vol. 4292, pp. 524–533. Springer, Heidelberg (2006)
4. Streckel, B., Bartczak, B., Koch, R., Kolb, A.: Supporting structure from motion with a 3d-range-camera. In: Ersbøll, B.K., Pedersen, K.S.(eds.) SCIA 2007. LNCS, vol. 4522. Springer, Heidelberg (2007)

5. Grest, D., Koch, R.: Single view motion tracking by depth and silhouette information. In: Scandinavian Conference on Image Analysis (SCIA07) (2007)
6. Gokturk, S., Tomasi, C.: 3d head tracking based on recognition and interpolation using a time-of-flight depth sensor. In: Proc. CVPR, pp. 211–217 (2004)
7. Kuhnert, K., Stommel, M.: Fusion of stereo-camera and pmd-camera data for realtime suited precise 3d environment reconstruction. In: IEEE/RSJ International Conference on Intelligent Robots and Systems (IROS) (October 2006)
8. Blank for review
9. Murray, D.R.: Patchlets: a method of interpreting correlation stereo 3D data. PhD thesis, The Univeristy of British Columbia, Vancouver, Canada (2004)
10. Murray, D., Little, J.J.: Segmenting correlation stereo range images using surface elements. In: 3DPVT '04: Proceedings of the 3D Data Processing, Visualization, and Transmission, 2nd International Symposium on (3DPVT'04), Washington, DC, USA, pp. 656–663. IEEE Computer Society Press, Los Alamitos (2004)
11. Szeliski, R., Tonnesen, D.: Surface modeling with oriented particle systems. Computer Graphics 26(2), 185–194 (1992)
12. Molton, N.D., Davison, A.J., Reid, I.D.: Locally planar patch features for realtime structure from motion. In: Proc. British Machine Vision Conference, BMVC (September 2004)
13. Pietzsch, T., Grossmann, A.: A method of estimating oriented surface elements from stereo images. In: Proc. British Machine Vision Conference (2005)
14. Pritchett, P., Zisserman, A.: Wide baseline stereo matching. In: Proceedings of the International Conference on Computer Vision, pp. 754–760 (1998)
15. Baker, S., Matthews, I.: Lucas-kanade 20 years on: A unifying framework: Part (2002)
16. Lucas, B., Kanade, T.: An iterative image registration technique with an application to stereo vision. In: IJCAI'81, pp. 674–679 (1981)
17. Triggs, B.: Detecting keypoints with stable position, orientation, and scale under illumination changes. In: Proceedings of European Conference on Computer Vision, pp. 100–113 (2004)
18. Xu, Z., Schwarte, R., Heinol, H., Buxbaum, B., Ringbeck, T.: Smart pixels - photonic mixer device (pmd). In: Mechatronics and Machine Vision in Practice, pp. 259–264 (1998)
19. Lange, R., Seitz, P., Biber, A., Schwarte, R.: Time-of-flight range imaging with a custom solid state image sensor. In: Tiziani, H.J., Rastogi, P.K. (eds.) Proc. SPIE. September 1999. Laser Metrology and Inspection, vol. 3823, pp. 180–191 (1999)
20. Zhang, Z.: Untersuchung und Charakterisierung von Photomischdetektor-Strukturen und ihren Grundschaltungen. PhD thesis, Department of Electrical Engineering And Computer Science at Univeristy of Siegen (December 2003)
21. Kahlmann, T., Remondino, F., Ingensand, H.: Calibration for increased accuracy of the range imaging camera swissrangertm. In: IEVM06 (2006)
22. Förstner, W., Wrobel, B.: Mathematical concepts in photogrammetry. In: McGlone, J.C., Mikhail, E.M., Bethel, J. (eds.) Manual of Photogrammetry. ASPRS, pp. 15–180 (2004)
23. Hartley, R.I., Zisserman, A.: Multiple View Geometry in Computer Vision. Cambridge University Press, Cambridge (2000)

View-Based Robot Localization
Using Spherical Harmonics:
Concept and First Experimental Results

Holger Friedrich, David Dederscheck, Kai Krajsek, and Rudolf Mester

Visual Sensorics and Information Processing Lab
J.W. Goethe University, Frankfurt, Germany
{holgerf,davidded,krajsek,mester}@vsi.cs.uni-frankfurt.de
http://www.vsi.cs.uni-frankfurt.de

Abstract. Robot self-localization using a hemispherical camera system can be done without correspondences. We present a view-based approach using view descriptors, which enables us to efficiently compare the image signal taken at different locations. A compact representation of the image signal can be computed using Spherical Harmonics as orthonormal basis functions defined on the sphere. This is particularly useful because rotations between two representations can be found easily. Compact view descriptors stored in a database enable us to compute a likelihood for the current view corresponding to a particular position and orientation in the map.

1 Introduction

Omnidirectional vision has become increasingly popular for the purpose of robot localization during the last years. Many approaches rely on compact image descriptors [21,1,5], [11,8] (using principal component analysis) [19,18] (using Fourier descriptors), [13] (using Haar integrals) to store and compare views efficiently. There are also approaches combining both compact descriptors and local features, e.g. [14].

We present a view-based method for robot localization in a known environment. A mobile robot equipped with an omnidirectional camera system provides a spherical image signal $s(\theta, \phi)$, i.e. an image signal defined on a sphere. In our experiments performed so far, the omnidirectional images were obtained from a simulated ultra-wide angle lens camera mounted face up on the robot, yielding rectangular images which can be mapped on the semi-sphere in a straightforward manner. These images were converted into *view descriptors*, i.e. *low dimensional vectors* (Fig. 1). The robot localization task is performed by comparing the current view descriptor to those stored in a database of views. Given a suitable distance metric, this yields a likelihood of the robot location. The image descriptors used here are not rotation invariant; due to their particular structure it is possible to estimate the orientation (rotation compared to a reference pose) of the current view. Our view representation is obtained by performing a linear

F.A. Hamprecht, C. Schnörr, and B. Jähne (Eds.): DAGM 2007, LNCS 4713, pp. 21–31, 2007.

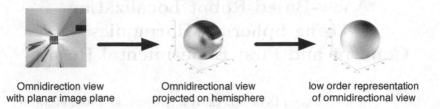

Omnidirection view | Omnidirectional view | low order representation
with planar image plane | projected on hemisphere | of omnidirectional view

Fig. 1. Computing an omnidirectional image signal from a planar wide angle image. The resulting hemispherical image signal is reflected at the equator to obtain an spherical image signal. The right image is a visualization of a low order Spherical Harmonic descriptor that approximates the omnidirectional image signal.

spectral transform, that is by expanding the spherical image signal $s(\theta, \phi)$ in orthonormal basis functions $b_i(\theta, \phi)$ according to

$$s(\theta, \phi) = \sum_i a_i \cdot b_i(\theta, \phi). \tag{1}$$

This is possible for any square integrable signal $s(\theta, \phi)$ defined on the sphere. Let $\bar{b}$ denote the complex conjugate of b. We obtain the coefficients a_i by

$$a_i = \int_0^{2\pi} \int_0^{\pi} s(\theta, \phi) \cdot \overline{b_i(\theta, \phi)} \cdot \sin\theta \, d\theta \, d\phi. \tag{2}$$

Our approach benefits from using *Spherical Harmonics* (Fig. 3) as basis functions b_i since they show the same nice properties concerning rotations which the Fourier basis system has with respect to translations. Rotations are mapped into a kind of *generalized phase changes*.

All views in the database are labeled with their corresponding location in the map (see Fig. 2); thus finding a match in the database – in principle – solves the localization task. We briefly discuss some obvious problems such as variations in illumination and impact of occlusions in Sec. 6. For each given view at an initially unknown robot position and orientation, a figure of (dis-)similarity to any other view in the database can be generated directly from the compact

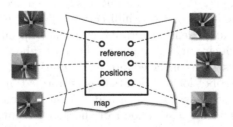

Fig. 2. A known environment is represented by a map containing view descriptors. These are obtained from images taken at reference positions.

vector representation of these views; this allows for more sophisticated temporal self-localization strategies [22], e. g. using particle filters.

In order to compare a given descriptor to those stored in a database, an operation has to be performed on the descriptor that corresponds to (virtually) *de*-rotating the corresponding view. Hence, for finding a measure of similarity between two views, de-rotation has to be performed as an integral part of the comparison. The estimation of 3D rotation between spherical signals has been investigated in different contexts in the last years [16,17,15,10]. For our application, a fast solution is of particular importance since we have to compare many pairs of descriptors. It is therefore useful to exploit group theoretical properties of Spherical Harmonics in order to eliminate those descriptors which cannot correspond to the same image signal (=pruning a search tree). This can be done by comparing the 'amplitude spectrum' while disregarding the 'phase'

The following sections deal with some essential mathematical characteristics of Spherical Harmonics, de-rotation and similarity measurement. The paper is concluded with a description of our experimental setup and the experimental results that we have obtained so far.

2   Spherical Harmonics

Here we emphasize some facts about Spherical Harmonics (Fig. 3) which are of particular interest for the matching and self localization task. For further group theoretical facts see [16] and [6]. Let

$$N_{\ell m} = \sqrt{\frac{2\ell+1}{2} \frac{(\ell-|m|)!}{(\ell+|m|)!}}, \; \ell \in \mathbb{N}_0, \, m \in \mathbb{Z} \tag{3}$$

and $P_{\ell m}(x)$ the Associated Legendre Polynomials [23].

The Spherical Harmonics $Y_{\ell m}(\theta, \phi)$ are defined as

$$Y_{\ell m}(\theta, \phi) = \frac{1}{\sqrt{2\pi}} \cdot N_{\ell m} \cdot P_{\ell m}(\cos \theta) \cdot e^{im\phi} \tag{4}$$

with $e^{im\phi}$ being a complex-valued phase term. ℓ ($\ell > 0$) is called *order* and m ($m = -\ell..+\ell$) is called *quantum number* for each ℓ. Note that slightly different notations of this definition exist. Some authors disregard the so called Condon-Shortley phase $(-1)^m$ in the definition of the associated Legendre polynomials. We do not omit this factor and conform to the notation of [23,12].

Spherical Harmonics have several properties that we would like to exploit in the following sections: Each set of Spherical Harmonics of order ℓ forms an orthonormal basis of dimension $2\ell+1$; Spherical Harmonics of orders $0 \ldots \ell$ form an orthonormal basis of dimension $(\ell + 1)^2$, i. e.

$$\int_0^{2\pi} \int_0^\pi \overline{Y_{\ell m}(\theta, \phi)} \cdot Y_{\ell'm'}(\theta, \phi) \cdot \sin \theta \, d\theta \, d\phi = \delta_{\ell\ell'} \cdot \delta_{mm'} \tag{5}$$

where $\delta_{\ell m}$ is the Kronecker delta function. The complex conjugate of a Spherical Harmonic function is simple to obtain:

$$Y_{\ell,-m}(\theta, \phi) = (-1)^m \cdot \overline{Y_{\ell m}(\theta, \phi)}. \tag{6}$$

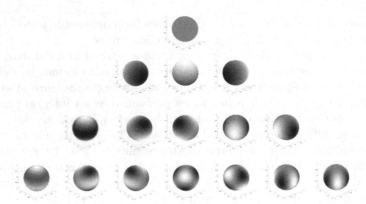

Fig. 3. A Spherical Harmonic function is a periodic function on the unit sphere which has ℓ maxima. The rows show Spherical Harmonics of *orders* $\ell = 0, 1, 2, 3$; columns show $m = 2\ell + 1$ functions for each order ℓ.

To approximate a signal $s(\theta, \phi)$, i.e.

$$s(\theta, \phi) = \sum_{\ell=0}^{\infty} \sum_{m=-\ell}^{\ell} a_{\ell m} \cdot Y_{\ell m}(\theta, \phi) \tag{7}$$

we need to compute the coefficients $a_{\ell m}$ using Eq. 2

$$a_{\ell m} = \int_0^{2\pi} \int_0^{\pi} s(\theta, \phi) \cdot \overline{Y_{\ell m}(\theta, \phi)} \cdot \sin \theta \, d\theta \, d\phi. \tag{8}$$

In practice, this is done using Spherical Harmonics of order $\ell = 0$ up to a small number, e. g. $\ell = 4$. It may also be useful to use real-valued Spherical Harmonics as defined in [12]. Eq. 6 implies that the number of coefficients stays the same for real-valued or complex-valued Spherical Harmonics. Hints on implementation can be found in [3,7].

3   Rotation Estimation

For general robot self-localization, we have to determine the 3D rotation between two Spherical Harmonic representations of image signals. This problem has already been investigated [2], and more recently in [15,16,10]. As an initial test case, we have chosen a mobile robot moving on a plane. For this particular application we only need to deal with 1D rotation estimation.

3.1   Rotations

The 3D case. Recall that Spherical Harmonics of order ℓ form a basis. Any 3D rotation can be expressed as a *linear transformation* (i. e. multiplication with an unitary matrix U_ℓ) and *does not mix coefficients of different order ℓ.* Hence rotations retain the distribution of spectral energy among different orders [16]. This is a unique characteristic of Spherical Harmonics which makes them so particularly useful, amongst others for the purpose of robot ego-localization pursued here. Applying a 3D rotation to a spherical function represented by coefficients a_{jk} yields new coefficients b_{jk} according to

$$
\begin{pmatrix} b_{00} \\ b_{10} \\ b_{11} \\ b_{1,-1} \\ \vdots \\ \vdots \\ b_{2,-2} \end{pmatrix} = \underbrace{\begin{pmatrix} \boxed{U_{\ell=0} } & & 0 \\ & U_{\ell=1} & \\ & & \\ 0 & & U_{\ell=2} \\ & & \end{pmatrix}}_{\Lambda_R} \begin{pmatrix} a_{00} \\ a_{10} \\ a_{11} \\ a_{1,-1} \\ \vdots \\ \vdots \\ a_{2,-2} \end{pmatrix} \tag{9}
$$

The 1D case: rotation about Z-axis. Since the robot moves on a plane in our current configuration, the problem of de-rotation is simplified somewhat. Recalling the definition of the complex-valued Spherical Harmonics, the implications of a rotation of φ about the Z-axis are as follows:

$$
Y_{\ell m}(\theta, \phi + \varphi) = \frac{1}{\sqrt{2\pi}} \cdot N_{\ell m} \cdot P_{\ell m}(\cos\theta) \cdot c^{i\, m\, (\phi + \varphi)} = e^{i\, m\, \varphi} \cdot Y_{\ell m}(\theta, \phi).
$$

The rotation matrix becomes much simpler because it changes into a diagonal matrix with elements $e^{-im\varphi}$:

$$
\begin{pmatrix} b_{00} \\ b_{10} \\ b_{11} \\ b_{1,-1} \\ \vdots \\ \vdots \\ b_{2,-2} \end{pmatrix} = \begin{pmatrix} \boxed{1} & & & & & 0 \\ & 1 & & & & \\ & & e^{-i\varphi} & & & \\ & & & e^{i\varphi} & & \\ & & & & 1 & \\ & & & & & e^{-i\varphi} \\ 0 & & & & & e^{i\varphi} \\ & & & & & e^{-2i\varphi} \\ & & & & & e^{2i\varphi} \end{pmatrix} \begin{pmatrix} a_{00} \\ a_{10} \\ a_{11} \\ a_{1,-1} \\ \vdots \\ \vdots \\ a_{2,-2} \end{pmatrix} \tag{10}
$$

3.2   De-rotation

Currently our implementation is based on direct non-linear estimation of φ similar to the method described in [17]. In this method, the 3D-rotation Λ_R for view descriptors a and b is determined such that $||b - \Lambda_R a||_2^2$ is minimized. This corresponds to the mean square signal difference between both signal approximations integrated over the sphere, as it will be discussed in more detail later in Sec. 4.1. The constraint of mere 1-axis rotation which has been maintained in our experiments so far, leaving full 3D, 6 DoF pose estimation to future investigations, leads to simplifications: we have to determine the angle φ that minimizes $\sum_\ell \sum_{m=-\ell}^{\ell} (b_{\ell m} - e^{-im\varphi} a_{\ell m})^2$. We emphasize that full 3D de-rotation is possible [17,16] for other robot configurations, that is, the spherical harmonic approach is even more interesting and attractive in that case.

4 Localization

4.1 Similarity Measure

Similarity between two image descriptors, a for signal $g(\theta, \phi)$ and b for signal $h(\theta, \phi)$, can be defined in a natural way. We define the *dissimilarity* Q as the squared difference of the two regarded image signals in the Spherical Harmonic domain up to order ℓ:

$$
\begin{aligned}
Q &= \int_0^{2\pi} \int_0^{\pi} (g(\theta, \phi) - h(\theta, \phi))^2 \cdot \sin\theta \, d\theta \, d\phi \\
&\stackrel{Eq. 7}{=} \int_0^{2\pi} \int_0^{\pi} \left(\sum_{\ell=0}^{\infty} \sum_{m=-\ell}^{\ell} (a_{\ell m} - b_{\ell m}) \cdot Y_{\ell m}(\theta, \phi) \right)^2 \cdot \sin\theta \, d\theta \, d\phi \\
&\stackrel{Eq. 5}{=} \sum_{\ell=0}^{\infty} \sum_{m=-\ell}^{\ell} \sum_{\ell'=0}^{\infty} \sum_{m'=-\ell'}^{\ell'} (a_{\ell m} - b_{\ell m}) \cdot (a_{\ell' m'} - b_{\ell' m'}) \cdot \delta_{\ell \ell'} \cdot \delta_{mm'} = \|a - b\|_2^2
\end{aligned}
$$

This result is of course not very astonishing, taking into account the fact that the regarded basis signals form an orthonormal basis. The measure Q is of course sensitive to any rotation between the signals. Hence, to find the minimum dissimilarity of two view descriptors we must de-rotate them first.

4.2 A Concept for a Rotation Invariant Similarity Measure

As we mentioned in Sec. 3.1, the norms of the subgroups of coefficients belonging to Spherical Harmonics of the same order are invariant to arbitrary 3D rotations of the signal. Thus L_2 norms, one for each order of Spherical Harmonics, can be considered as a kind of *energy spectrum* of the omnidirectional signal.

This energy spectrum is an efficient means for comparing pairs of spherical signals [9]. With a proper metric which should be derived from statistical models of the signal and the expected noise, spherical signals can be compared to each other even without performing the 'de-rotation'. If the energy spectrum is identical or similar, the particular spherical signals *can* be identical but they need not to be so. However, if their energy spectra are significantly different, both signals cannot be identical.

4.3 Robot Localization Algorithm

Robot localization can be done the following way:

For each reference location

1. use the fast rotation invariant similarity measure to drop unlikely views,
2. try to find the best matching rotation for the current image descriptor and de-rotate the current descriptor,
3. compute the similarity according to Sec. 4.1.

This yields a similarity map, which in all our experiments performed so far, has a distinct extremum at the true location of the robot. It can, however, also contain other extrema, i. e. different poses which have a similar likelihood. Considering the fact that man-made environments have certain regularities, which may result in similar views at several distinct positions, this is not too astonishing, forming a general problem of view-based navigation. At each instant, however, we have prior knowledge about the robots previous course and its previous pose(s), which is presumably always sufficient to disambiguate the current pose estimation process. Such strategies are well-known in robot navigation, and have been, amongst many others, described by Thrun et al. [22] ('Monte Carlo Localization'), or Menegatti et al. [19] (using other image descriptors).

5   Experimental Results

For our experiments, we currently use simulated image data rendered by ray tracing software. Using the 3D modeling software BLENDER [4], we have created an artificial environment resembling an office area, which provides an experimental area for a simulated robot (see Fig. 4). An upwards facing wide-angle perspective camera with a field of view of approx. $172.5°$ yields the simulated input images of the robot. The resulting images can be projected onto a hemisphere. This hemispherical signal is extended to a full spherical signal by suitable reflection at the equator. Subsequently, the spherical signal can be approximated by Spherical Harmonics. Of course, a direct expansion of the 2D wide-angle images into Spherical Harmonics is possible without the detour of projecting the perspective signal onto the sphere. We use Spherical Harmonics up to order $\ell = 4$. The reflection across the equator introduces an additional symmetry to the spherical image signal. Hence, additional constraints exist on the coefficients of the Spherical Harmonics.

Prior to performing a localization of the robot, we must create a set of reference frames and calculate its corresponding view descriptors. The view-attributed map needed for performing the robot localization must be computed beforehand; in a real application, the robot and a precision localization device will be driven through the envisaged environment while the views and the corresponding poses are recorded.

For our localization experiment, we have rendered a series of frames with the robot moving along a fixed path (Fig. 4(a)). To obtain realistic sequences of images, each taken at a definite position, a sequence of poses is recorded by a control script while the robot moves along a given path. The resulting list is then used to place the camera for the rendering process.

The images in Fig. 5 are maps of the simulation environment showing a measure corresponding to the likelihood of the robot location, calculated at discrete positions along the motion path. Note that these positions are in general *not* aligned with the grid and the heading direction of the robot is not aligned with the direction the grid was built with.

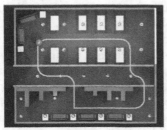

(a) Environment from bird's eye perspective. The path of the robot is marked.

(b) Simulated view of a normal camera facing forwards.

(c) Robot with camera facing upwards.

(d) Wide angle view facing upwards.

Fig. 4. Views of our simulated office environment

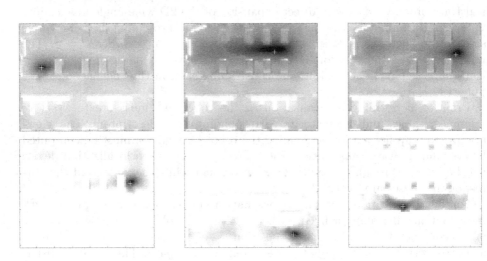

Fig. 5. These plots show the dissimilarity between current view descriptors obtained at six different positions of the path of the robot and the reference views from the database. The shown results have been obtained using a position grid with a spacing of 0.2 m and a total of 4636 view descriptors. Dark areas mark likely positions; white crosses mark the true position. The lower row additionally uses the rotation invariant measure to drop view descriptors beforehand if their energy spectra deviate excessively.

6 Next Steps Towards Realistic View Representations: An Outlook

So far, the view-based representation of the environment in which self-localization shall be performed has been described as a static one, where only one spherical view for each reference location has to be regarded. However, every realistic environment in which a robot will move is subject to various changes, particularly in illumination. Therefore, the content of the database has to consider this appropriately. We propose to represent the set of possible views (under varying illumination etc.) by a stochastic model of low order, as extracted from a larger training set of images. We denote such a model here as a *'dynamic spherical view model' (DSVM)*. In the case of 'normal' rectangular image areas, such models have already been successful for (non-spherical) background modeling [20]. Such a stochastic model inherently induces a suitable and statistically correct metric for the matching process, i. e. the Mahalanobis distance induced by the covariance matrix of the dynamic spherical view model.

In conventional 1D or n-D signal processing a second order description of the signal statistics in terms of covariance functions is sufficient to derive a canonical representation of the signal. This canonical representation is basically the result of a linear transform into a new coordinate system such that the covariance between any pair of different spectral coefficients is zero (*principal component analysis [PCA]* or *Karhunen-Loeve transform [KLT]*). The transfer of this approach to the spherical domain leads to a very practical statistical model for signal processes defined on the spherical domain. Using such a model, a PCA representation of spherical stochastic processes (here: spherical stochastic models for typical omnidirectional signals) can be developed.

The spherical PCA model for omnidirectional signals is a highly practical means for performing any kind of signal processing for *incomplete* spherical data. For example, it allows to compare a given spherical signal with other signals stored in a database even if the input signal contains areas where the signal value is not known or very largely destroyed (occlusions, . . .). The potential and usefulness of a statistically correct procedure for comparing *incomplete* data cannot be overestimated.

These statistical extensions of the self-localization approach using Spherical Harmonics still remain to be performed in investigations planned for the near future. We hope that by the paper presented here the feasibility of the baseline approach and the attractiveness of using Spherical Harmonics for omnidirectional vision and recognition could be conveyed.

References

1. Blaer, P., Allen, P.: Topological mobile robot localization using fast vision techniques. In: International Conference on Robotics and Automation, vol. 1, May 2002, pp. 1031–1036 (2002)
2. Burel, G., Henoco, H.: Determination of the orientation of 3D objects using Spherical Harmonics. Graph. Models Image Process. 57(5), 400–408 (1995)

3. Driscoll, J.R., Healy Jr., D.M.: Computing Fourier transforms and convolutions on the 2-sphere. Adv. Appl. Math. 15(2), 202–250 (1994)
4. The Blender Foundation. Blender (2007), http://www.blender.org
5. Gonzalez-Barbosa, J.-J., Lacroix, S.: Rover localization in natural environments by indexing panoramic images. In: Proceedings of the ICRA '02 IEEE International Conference on Robotics and Automation, pp. 1365–1370. IEEE, Los Alamitos (2002)
6. Groemer, H.: Geometric Applications of Fourier Series and Spherical Harmonics. In: Encyclopedia of Mathematics and Its Applications, Cambridge Univ. Press (1996)
7. Healy Jr., D.M., Rockmore, D.N., Kostelec, P.J., Moore, S.: FFTs for the 2-sphere – improvements and variations. Journal of Fourier Analysis and Applications 9(4), 341–385 (2003)
8. Jogan, M., Leonardis, A.: Robust localization using an omnidirectional appearance-based subspace model of environment. Robotics and Autonomous Systems 45, 57–72 (2003)
9. Kazhdan, M., Funkhouser, T., Rusinkiewicz, S.: Rotation invariant Spherical Harmonic representation of 3D shape descriptors. In: Kobbelt, L., Schröder, P., Hoppe, H. (eds.) Eurographics Symposium on Geometry Processing (June 2003)
10. Kovacs, J.A., Wriggers, W.: Fast rotational matching. Acta Crystallographica Section D 58(8), 1282–1286 (2002)
11. Kröse, B., Vlassis, N., Bunschoten, R., Motomura, Y.: A probabilistic model for appearance-based robot localization. Image and Vision Computing 19(6), 381–391 (2001)
12. Kudlicki, A., Rowicka, M., Gilski, M., Otwinowski, Z.: An efficient routine for computing symmetric real Spherical Harmonics for high orders of expansion. Journal of Applied Crystallography 39, 501–504 (2005)
13. Labbani-Igbida, O., Charron, C., Mouaddib, E.M.: Extraction of Haar integral features on omnidirectional images: Application to local and global localization. In: DAGM-Symposium, pp. 334–343 (2006)
14. Levin, A., Szeliski, R.: Visual odometry and map correlation. In: IEEE Conf. on Comp. Vision and Pattern Recognition, June 2004, vol. I, pp. 611–618. IEEE Computer Society Press, Los Alamitos (2004)
15. Makadia, A., Daniilidis, K.: Direct 3D-rotation estimation from spherical images via a generalized shift theorem. In: IEEE Comp. Society Conference on Computer Vision and Pattern Recognition (CVPR '03), vol. 2, pp. 217–224 (2003)
16. Makadia, A., Daniilidis, K.: Rotation recovery from spherical images without correspondences. IEEE Transactions on Pattern Analysis and Machine Intelligence 28(7), 1170–1175 (2006)
17. Makadia, A., Sorgi, L., Daniilidis, K.: Rotation estimation from spherical images. In: Proceedings ICPR'04, vol. 3 (2004)
18. Menegatti, E., Maeda, T., Ishiguro, H.: Image-based memory for robot navigation using properties of the omnidirectional images (2004)
19. Menegatti, E., Zoccarato, M., Pagello, E., Ishiguro, H.: Hierarchical image-based localisation for mobile robots with monte-carlo localisation. In: Proceedings ECMR'03, Warsaw, Poland, September 2003, pp. 13–20 (2003)
20. Oliver, N., Rosario, B., Pentland, A.: A bayesian computer vision system for modeling human interaction. In: Proceedings ICVS'99, pp. 255–272 (1999)

21. Pajdla, T., Hlavac, V.: Zero phase representation of panoramic images for image based localization. In: Comp. Analysis of Images and Patterns, pp. 550–557 (1999)
22. Thrun, S., Burgard, W., Fox, D.: Probabilistic Robotics. The MIT Press, Cambridge (2005)
23. Weisstein, E.W.: Legendre Polynomial. A Wolfram Web Resource (2007), http://mathworld.wolfram.com/LegendrePolynomial.html

Clustered Stochastic Optimization for Object Recognition and Pose Estimation*

Juergen Gall, Bodo Rosenhahn, and Hans-Peter Seidel

Max-Planck-Institute for Computer Science,
Stuhlsatzenhausweg 85, 66123 Saarbrücken, Germany
{jgall,rosenhahn,hpseidel}@mpi-inf.mpg.de

Abstract. We present an approach for estimating the 3D position and in case of articulated objects also the joint configuration from segmented 2D images. The pose estimation without initial information is a challenging optimization problem in a high dimensional space and is essential for texture acquisition and initialization of model-based tracking algorithms. Our method is able to recognize the correct object in the case of multiple objects and estimates its pose with a high accuracy. The key component is a particle-based global optimization method that converges to the global minimum similar to simulated annealing. After detecting potential bounded subsets of the search space, the particles are divided into clusters and migrate to the most attractive cluster as the time increases. The performance of our approach is verified by means of real scenes and a quantative error analysis for image distortions. Our experiments include rigid bodies and full human bodies.

1 Introduction

Finding the 3D position and rotation of a rigid object in a set of images from calibrated cameras without any initial information is a difficult optimization problem in a 6-dimensional space. The task becomes even more challenging for articulated objects where the dimensionality of the search space is much higher, e.g., a coarse model of a human skeleton has already 24 degrees of freedom (DoF) yielding a 30-dimensional space. Although the initial pose is essential for many state-of-the-art model-based tracking algorithm, e.g. [1,2,3], relatively little attention was paid to the initialization of rigid and articulated models. A manual initialization is usually required, which is time demanding and assumes some expertise on the model and on the world coordinate system.

Depending on the image features, there are several techniques for pose estimation in the literature. Edge-based approaches, e.g. [4,5,6], align curves or lines of the model to detected edges. They work best for homogeneous objects, however, textured objects and cluttered background typically involve many edges that are not related to the model. Texture-based approaches [7,8] use correspondences between the textured model and an image for pose estimation. Separate from the

---

* Our research is funded by the MPC for Visual Computing and Communication.

F.A. Hamprecht, C. Schnörr, and B. Jähne (Eds.): DAGM 2007, LNCS 4713, pp. 32–41, 2007.

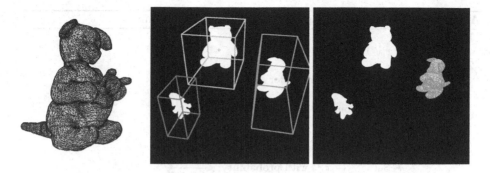

Fig. 1. From left to right: *a)* 3D model of object. *b)* Potential bounded subsets of the search space. *c)* Projection of the mesh. The pose is correctly estimated.

fact that they require textured surfaces for self-initialization, the texture needs to be registered to the model beforehand, i.e., a manual initialization is done for the texture acquisition during preprocessing.

Our approach for solving the initialization problem estimates the pose of rigid and articulated objects by minimizing an energy function based only on the silhouette information. Although we are not restricted to silhouettes, the object region has the advantage that it is an appearance independent feature that can be easily extracted from a single frame, e.g. by background subtraction. Since an initial guess is not available, local optimization algorithm like iterative closest point (ICP) [9,10] are not suitable for this task. For finding the exact pose, we use a novel particle-based global optimization, called *interacting simulated annealing* [11], that converges to the global optimum similar to simulated annealing [12]. In order to deal with multiple objects, we extend the work in [11] by clustering the particles with respect to previously detected bounded subsets of the search space.

After a brief introduction to interacting simulated annealing in Section 2, we give details of our method in Section 3. In Section 4, some extensions for human bodies are explained. The experimental results are discussed in Section 5 followed by a brief conclusion.

2   Interacting Simulated Annealing

Interacting particle systems are well-known as particle filter [13] and approximate a distribution of interest η_t by $\eta_t^n := \sum_{i=1}^{n} \pi^{(i)} \delta_{X^{(i)}}$, where δ is the Dirac measure and $X^{(i)}$ are n random variables, termed particles, weighted by $\pi^{(i)}$. In the case of *interacting simulated annealing (ISA)*, the distribution is proportional to a Boltzmann-Gibbs measure

$$g_t(dx) = \exp\left(-\beta_t V(x)\right) \lambda(dx), \tag{1}$$

where $V \geq 0$ is the energy function to minimize, β_t is an annealing parameter that increases with t, and λ is the Lebesgue measure.

Algorithm 1. Interacting Simulated Annealing Algorithm

---

1. Initialization
   - Sample $x_0^{(i)}$ from η_0 for all i
2. Selection
   - Set $\pi^{(i)} \leftarrow \exp(-\beta_t V(x_t^{(i)}))$ for all i
   - For i from 1 to n:
       Sample κ from $U[0,1]$
       If $\kappa \leq \epsilon_t \pi^{(i)}$ then
       ⋆ Set $\check{x}_t^{(i)} \leftarrow x_t^{(i)}$
       Else
       ⋆ Set $\check{x}_t^{(i)} \leftarrow x_t^{(j)}$ with probability $\frac{\pi^{(j)}}{\sum_{k=1}^n \pi^{(k)}}$
3. Mutation
   - Sample $x_{t+1}^{(i)}$ from $K_t(\check{x}_t^{(i)}, \cdot)$ for all i and go to step 2

In contrast to particle filter that estimate the posterior distribution for a sequence of images, we apply ISA for estimating the global optimum in still images where no initial information is available. For this purpose, the steps *Selection* and *Mutation* of Algorithm 1 are iterated until the global minimum of V is well approximated. During the selection, the particles are weighted according to a given energy function V where greater weight is given to particles with a lower energy. The weights associated to the particles refer to the probability that a particle is selected for the next step. We used the parameter $\epsilon_t = 1/\sum_{k=1}^n \pi^{(k)}$ for selection since it has slightly better convergence properties than $\epsilon_t = 0$, see for instance [14,11]. If a particle is not accepted with probability $\epsilon_t \pi^{(i)}$, a new particle is selected from all particles, e.g. by multinomial sampling. The selection process removes particles with a high energy while particles with a low energy are reproduced each time they are selected. An overview of various resampling schemes can be found in [15]. In the second step, the selected particles are distributed according to Markov kernels K_t specified by a modified dynamic variance scheme, which we propose in Section 3.4.

While the annealing scheme prevents the particles from getting stuck in local minima, the dynamic variance scheme focuses the search around selected

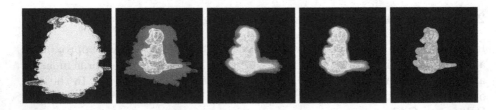

Fig. 2. Particles at $t = 0, 5, 10, 15$ and 19 for ISA. Particles with a higher weight are brighter, particles with a lower weight are darker. The particles converge to the pose with the lowest energy as t increases. **Most left:** Equally weighted particles after initialization. **Most right:** Estimate after 20 iterations.

particles. When t increases only particles with low energy are selected and the search is concentrated on a small region, see also Figure 2. Indeed, it has been shown that ISA approximates a distribution η_t that becomes concentrated in the region of global minima of V as t tends to infinity provided that the annealing scheme β_t increases slow enough and the search space is bounded [16]. In [11], the authors evaluated several annealing schemes and parameter settings. In our experiments, a polynomial scheme, i.e.

$$\beta_t = (t+1)^b \quad \text{for some } b \in (0,1), \tag{2}$$

performed well with $b = 0.7$.

3   Clustered Optimization

3.1   Initial Subsets

Having a binary image for each camera view, where pixels that belong to the foreground are set to 1 else to 0, the pixels are first clustered with respect to the 8-neighbor connectivity. In order to make the system more robust to noise, clusters covering only a very small area are discarded. In the next step, the 4 corners of the bounding box of each cluster are determined and the projection ray for each corner is calculated. The projection rays are represented as Plücker lines [17], i.e., the 3D line is determined by a normalized vector d and a moment m such that $x \times n = m$ for all x on the line. Provided that two projection rays from different views are not parallel, the midpoint p of the shortest line segment between the two rays l_1 and l_2 is unique and can be easily calculated. If the minimum distance between l_1 and l_2 is below a threshold, p is regarded as a corner of a convex polyhedron. After 8 corners of the polyhedron are detected for two clusters from two different views, the bounding cube is calculated as shown in Figure 1 b). In the case of more than two available camera views, each pair of images – starting with the views containing the most clusters – is checked until a polyhedron is found. The corners are similarly refined by calculating the midpoint of the shortest line segment between a ray from another view and a corner of a polyhedron. The resulting bounding cubes provide the initial bounded subsets of the search space. We remark that the algorithm is not very sensitive to the thresholds as long as the searched object is inside a bounding cube. This can be achieved by using very conservative thresholds.

3.2   Particles

Since we know the 3D model, the pose is determined by a vector in $\mathbb{R}^{6+m}$, i.e., each particle is a $6 + m$-dimensional random vector where m is the number of joints. The rigid body motion M is represented by the axis-angle representation given by the 6D vector $(\theta\omega, t)$ with $\omega = (\omega_1, \omega_2, \omega_3)$ and $\|\omega\|_2 = 1$. The mappings from $\theta\omega$ to a rotation matrix R and vice versa can be efficiently computed by the Rodriguez formula [18] and are denoted by $\exp(\theta\omega)$ and $\log(R)$, respectively.

Since ISA approximates a distribution by finite particles, we take the first moment of the distribution as estimate of the pose, i.e., the mean of a set of rotations $r^{(i)}$ weighted by $\pi^{(i)}$ is required.[1] This can be done by finding a geodesic on the Riemannian manifold determined by the set of 3D rotations. When the geodesic starting from the mean rotation in the manifold is mapped by the logarithm onto the tangent space at the mean, it is a straight line starting at the origin, see [19]. The tangent space is called exponential chart. Hence, the weighted mean rotation $\bar{r}$ satisfies

$$\sum_i \pi^{(i)} \left(\bar{r}^{-1} \star r^{(i)} \right) = 0,$$
(3)

where $r^{(j)} \star r^{(i)} := \log \left(\exp(r^{(j)}) \cdot \exp(r^{(i)}) \right)$ and $r^{-1} := \log \left(\exp(r)^T \right)$. The weighted mean can thus be estimated by

$$\hat{r}_{t+1} = \hat{r}_t \star \left(\frac{\sum_i \pi^{(i)} \left(\hat{r}_t^{-1} \star r^{(i)} \right)}{\sum_i \pi^{(i)}} \right).$$
(4)

3.3   Initialization

Due to multiple objects as shown in Figure 1, each particle belongs to a certain cluster C given by the bounding cubes and denoted by $x^{(i,C)}$. At the beginning, a small number of particles is generated with different orientations located in the center of the cube for each cluster. The complete set of particles is initialized by randomly assigning each particle the values of one of the generated particles. Afterwards, each particle is independently diffused by a normal distribution with mean $x^{(i,C)}$ and a diagonal covariance matrix with fixed entries except for the translation vector t where the standard deviations are given by the edge lengths of the cube divided by 6 such that over 99.5% of the particles are inside the cube.

3.4   Mutation

The dynamic variance scheme for the mutation step is implemented by cluster dependent Gaussian kernels $K_t^{(C)}$ with covariance matrices $\Sigma_t^{(C)}$ proportional to the sampling covariance matrix of each cluster:[2]

$$\Sigma_t^{(C)} := \frac{d}{|C| - 1} \sum_{\substack{i=1 \\ i \in C}}^{n} (x_t^{(i,C)} - \mu_t)_\rho (x_t^{(i,C)} - \mu_t)_\rho^T, \quad \mu_t := \frac{1}{|C|} \sum_{\substack{i=1 \\ i \in C}}^{n} x_t^{(i,C)},$$
(5)

where $|C|$ is the number of particles in cluster C and $((x)_\rho)_k = \max(x_k, \rho)$ for the kth dimension. The value $\rho > 0$ ensures that the variance does not become

---

[1] The density could also be estimated by kernel smoothing from the particles in order to take the peak of the density function as estimate. However, kernel smoothing is more expansive than calculating the first moment of a density and it also needs to be performed in the space of 3D rotations.

[2] Samples from a multivariate normal distribution $\mathcal{N}(\mu, \Sigma)$ can be drawn via a Cholesky decomposition $\Sigma = AA^T$: $x = \mu + Az$ where z is drawn from $\mathcal{N}(0, I)$.

zero for any dimension. In practice, we set $d = 0.4$ and compute only a sparse covariance matrix, see also Section 4.

3.5   Selection

Since each particle defines the pose of the model, the fitness of a particle $x \in \mathbb{R}^{6+m}$ can be evaluated by the difference between the original image and the template image that is the projected surface of the model. For this purpose, we apply a signed Euclidean distance transformation [20] on the silhouette image I_v and on the template $T_v(x)$ for each view v. The energy function is defined by $V(x) := \frac{\alpha}{r} \sum_{v=1}^{r} V_v(x)$ with

$$V_v(x) := \frac{1}{2|T_v^+(x)|} \sum_{p \in T_v^+(x)} |T_v(x,p) - I_v(p)| + \frac{1}{2|I_v^+|} \sum_{p \in I_v^+} |T_v(x,p) - I_v(p)|, \quad (6)$$

where I^+ denotes the set of strictly positive pixels of an image I. The normalization constant $\alpha = 0.1$ ensures that V is approximately in the range between 0 and 10, which is suitable for the selected annealing scheme.

The resampling step is cluster independent, i.e., the particles migrate to the most attractive cluster where the particles have more weight and give more offspring. At the end, there are no particles left where the silhouettes do not fit the model, see Figure 1 c).

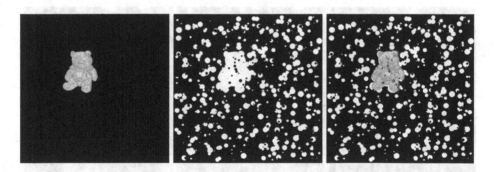

Fig. 3. From left to right: *a)* Estimated pose without noise. The error is less than $1mm$ (median). *b)* Silhouettes are randomly distorted by 500 white and 500 black circles. *c)* Median estimate with error less than $4cm$.

4   Human Bodies

While for rigid bodies the correlation between the parameters is neglected due to computational efficiency, correlation between connected joints in the human skeleton are incorporated. That is, the correlation of the joints that belong to the same skeleton branch, e.g. the left leg, are calculated in the dynamic variance scheme (5) while correlations with joints to other branches are set to zero.

In order to focus the search on poses with higher probabilities, prior knowledge is incorporated into the energy function as soft constraint. The probability of a pose p_{pose} is estimated by a Parzen-Rosenblatt estimator with Gaussian kernels [21,22] over a set of subsamples from different motions from the CMU motion database [23]. Since the dependency between the joints of the upper body and the joints of the lower body is low, the sample size can be reduced by splitting p_{pose} up into two independent probabilities p_{pose}^u and p_{pose}^l, respectively. Hence, the energy function is extended by

$$V(x) := \frac{\alpha}{r} \sum_{v=1}^{r} V_v(x) - \frac{\eta}{2} \ln \left(p_{pose}^u(x) p_{pose}^l(x) \right), \tag{7}$$

where $\eta = 2.0$ regulates the influence of the prior. Moreover, the mean and the variance of the joints in the training data is used to initialize the particles. To get rid of a biased error from the prior, the final pose is refined by ICP [9,10] that is initialized by the estimate of ISA.

5   Results

For the error analysis, synthetic images with silhouettes of the bear were generated by projecting the model for 3 different views. The error was measured by

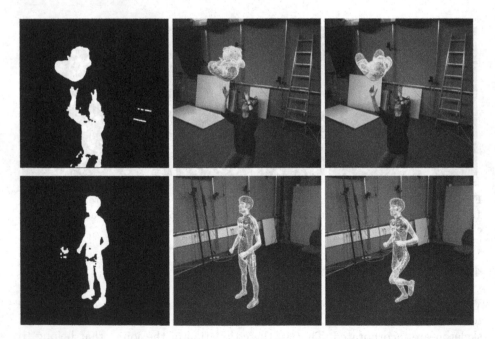

Fig. 4. Estimates for a real scene. 3 views were segmented for the bear and 4 views for the human (Only one is shown). **Most left:** Silhouettes from background subtraction.

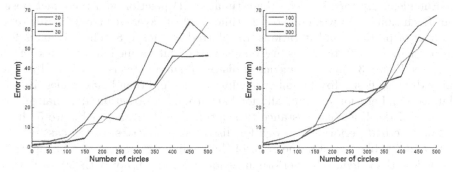

Fig. 5. Average error of the estimates for different numbers of iterations and 200 particles *(left)* and for different numbers of particles and 25 iterations *(right)*. 200 particles and 25 iterations are sufficient for rigid bodies.

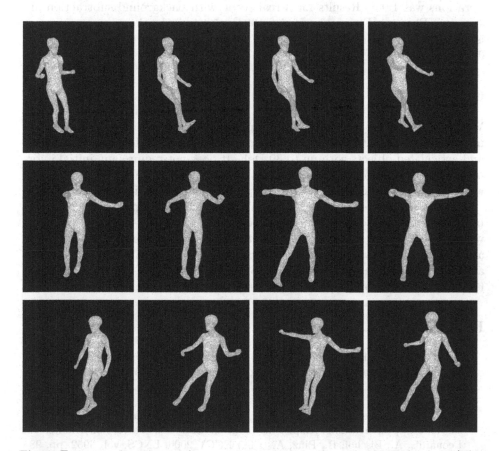

Fig. 6. Estimates for 12 poses from a motion sequence from the CMU database (The estimated poses of the human model are projected onto the silhouette images). Each row shows one of the three views.

the Euclidean distance between the estimated 3D position and the exact position. Each simulation was repeated 25 times and the average errors for different numbers of particles and iterations are plotted in Figure 5. The estimates for 200 particles and 30 iterations are very accurate with a median error less than $1mm$, see Figure 3 a). The influence of distorted silhouettes is simulated by randomly drawing first a fixed number of white circles and then black circles. Holes, dilatation and erosion are typically for background subtraction and change the outcome of the Euclidean distance transform. The diagrams in Figure 5 show that our method performs also well for distorted silhouettes. In the case of 500 white and 500 black circles, the error of the median estimate shown in Figure 3 is still less than $4cm$. The performance for a human body with 30 DoF was tested by generating synthetic images with silhouettes for 12 single poses from a sequence of the CMU database that was not used for the prior. The estimates are given in Figure 6. The average error of the joints for 400 particles and 40 iterations was $1.05°$. Results for a real scene with background subtraction are shown in Figure 4. For images of size 1004×1004 pixels, the computation cost is given by number of views × number of iterations × number of particles × 0.0346 seconds.

6   Discussion

We proposed an accurate and robust approach, which relies on a global optimization method with clustered particles, for estimating the 3D pose of rigid and articulated objects with up to 30 DoF. It does not require any initial information about position or orientation of the object and solves the initial problem as it occurs for tracking and texture acquisition. Our experiments demonstrate that the correct pose is estimated when multiple objects appear. It could also be extended to the case when the object is not visible by rejecting estimates with an high energy. In general, our method can be easily modified for certain applications, e.g., by including prior as we did for humans. Other possibilities are multi-cue integration and exploitation of an hierarchical structure, however, these features are object specific and not suitable for a general solution.

References

1. Bray, M., Kohli, P., Torr, P.: Posecut: Simultaneous segmentation and 3d pose estimation of humans using dynamic graph-cuts. In: Leonardis, A., Bischof, H., Pinz, A. (eds.) ECCV 2006. LNCS, vol. 3952, pp. 642–655. Springer, Heidelberg (2006)
2. Brox, T., Rosenhahn, B., Cremers, D., Seidel, H.P.: High accuracy optical flow serves 3-d pose tracking: Exploiting contour and flow based constraints. In: Leonardis, A., Bischof, H., Pinz, A. (eds.) ECCV 2006. LNCS, vol. 3952, pp. 98–111. Springer, Heidelberg (2006)
3. Rosenhahn, B., Brox, T., Weickert, J.: Three-dimensional shape knowledge for joint image segmentation and pose tracking. Int. J. of Computer Vision 73(3), 243–262 (2007)

4. Lowe, D.: Three-dimensional object recognition from single two-dimensional images. Artificial Intelligence 31(3), 355–395 (1987)
5. Lowe, D.: Fitting parameterized three-dimensional models to images. IEEE Trans. on Pattern Analysis and Machine Intelligence 13(5), 441–450 (1991)
6. Ansar, A., Daniilidis, K.: Linear pose estimation from points or lines. IEEE Trans. on Pattern Analysis and Machine Intelligence 25(5), 578–589 (2003)
7. Gall, J., Rosenhahn, B., Seidel, H.P.: Robust pose estimation with 3d textured models. In: Chang, L.-W., Lie, W.-N. (eds.) PSIVT 2006. LNCS, vol. 4319, pp. 84–95. Springer, Heidelberg (2006)
8. Lepetit, V., Pilet, J., Fua, P.: Point matching as a classification problem for fast and robust object pose estimation. IEEE Conf. on Computer Vision and Pattern Recognition 2, 244–250 (2004)
9. Besl, P., McKay, N.: A method for registration of 3-d shapes. IEEE Trans. on Pattern Analysis and Machine Intelligence 14(2), 239–256 (1992)
10. Zhang, Z.: Iterative point matching for registration of free-form curves and surfaces. Int. J. of Computer Vision 13(2), 119–152 (1994)
11. Gall, J., Potthoff, J., Schnörr, C., Rosenhahn, B., Seidel, H.P.: Interacting and annealing particle systems – mathematics and recipes. J. of Mathematical Imaging and Vision (to appear, 2007)
12. Kirkpatrick, S., Jr., C.G., Vecchi, M.: Optimization by simulated annealing. Science 220(4598), 671–680 (1983)
13. Doucet, A., de Freitas, N., Gordon, N. (eds.): Sequential Monte Carlo Methods in Practice. Springer, New York (2001)
14. Gall, J., Rosenhahn, B., Seidel, H.P.: An Introduction to Interacting Simulated Annealing. In: Human Motion - Understanding, Modeling, Capture and Animation, Springer, Heidelberg (to appear, 2007)
15. Douc, R., Cappe, O., Moulines, E.: Comparison of resampling schemes for particle filtering. In: Int. Symposium on Image and Signal Processing and Analysis, pp. 64–69 (2005)
16. Moral, P.D.: Feynman-Kac Formulae. In: Genealogical and Interacting Particle Systems with Applications, Springer, New York (2004)
17. Stolfi, J.: Oriented Projective Geometry: A Framework for Geometric Computation. Academic Press, Boston (1991)
18. Murray, R., Li, Z., Sastry, S.: A Mathematical Introduction to Robotic Manipulation. CRC Press, Boca Raton, FL (1994)
19. Pennec, X., Ayache, N.: Uniform distribution, distance and expectation problems for geometric features processing. J. of Mathematical Imaging and Vision 9(1), 49–67 (1998)
20. Felzenszwalb, P., Huttenlocher, D.: Distance transforms of sampled functions. Technical Report TR2004-1963, Cornell Computing and Information Science (2004)
21. Gall, J., Rosenhahn, B., Brox, T., Seidel, H.P.: Learning for multi-view 3d tracking in the context of particle filters. In: Bebis, G., Boyle, R., Parvin, B., Koracin, D., Remagnino, P., Nefian, A., Meenakshisundaram, G., Pascucci, V., Zara, J., Molineros, J., Theisel, H., Malzbender, T. (eds.) ISVC 2006. LNCS, vol. 4292, pp. 59–69. Springer, Heidelberg (2006)
22. Brox, T., Rosenhahn, B., Kersting, U., Cremers, D.: Nonparametric density estimation for human pose tracking. In: Franke, K., Müller, K.-R., Nickolay, B., Schäfer, R. (eds.) Pattern Recognition. LNCS, vol. 4174, pp. 546–555. Springer, Heidelberg (2006)
23. CMU: Graphics lab motion capture database, http://mocap.cs.cmu.edu/

Unambiguous Dynamic Diffraction Patterns for 3D Depth Profile Measurement

Dominik Lubeley

Communication Technology Institute
University of Dortmund
Germany

Abstract. The projection of fixed patterns in active 3d measurement systems is deteriorated by ambient lighting. Moreover classic projection patterns lead to ambiguities during pattern detection in the digital signal processing phase. Therefore a dynamic, diffraction based pattern projection system is introduced which can adapt to ambient lighting conditions. For error-free laser pattern detection a method for the design of unambiguous projection patterns is presented.

1 Introduction

Active optical 3d measurement systems use pattern projection for triangulating depth profiles of textureless objects or scenes. In situations with low ambient lighting, structured light approaches like gray code projections with additional phase shift can be used which illuminate the whole measurement space with incoherent light. The pattern contrast is reduced in situations with stronger ambient lighting. In order to improve the performance coherent laser projectors can be used which are capable of bundling their intensity by diffraction – if they are based on dynamic diffraction gratings. This paper describes the generation of arbitrary laser patterns based on a Liquid Crystal on Silicon (LCoS) microdisplay used as a dynamic phase grating. Having the opportunity to generate arbitrary laser patterns, an algorithm for the creation of unambiguous patterns is presented. In contrast to normal evenly spaced patterns, every point can be detected and assigned to its correct source without ambiguities, even when occlusion, wrong or missing detections occur.

2 Classic Triangulation

Laser patterns for 3d measurement can be realized with a laser projector either based on geometrical optics using mirrors for beam redirection or wave optics for beam diffraction. While redirection is based on temporally intensity modulation of the total pattern – like line by line scanning, complex phase modulated diffraction patterns are displayed simultaneously.

To use either projection method in conjunction with a camera for depth profile measurement the system has to be calibrated for example by using the algorithm

F.A. Hamprecht, C. Schnörr, and B. Jähne (Eds.): DAGM 2007, LNCS 4713, pp. 42–51, 2007.

presented by Zhang [1]. The extrinsic parameters position and orientation as well as the intrinsic parameters focal length and distortion have to be determined. While this is a typical procedure for camera calibration, the projector has first to be modelled as an inverse camera.

With known geometry the whole triangulation process uses vector algebra. Pattern points are modelled as straight lines

$$\mathbf{x}_{3d} = \mathbf{x}_{P,0} + r\mathbf{x}_{Ray} \tag{1}$$

originating from the optical centre $\mathbf{x}_{P,0}$ of the projector, whereas lines in the pattern are planes in the object space.

Centres of pattern points are detected using Gaussian fitting over several pixels in the camera image. The corresponding ray is assigned by selecting the 2d projection of the 3d straight line with the minimum distance to the detected centre.

2.1   Classic Patterns

Typical patterns for laser projections are lines or dot structures. Since lines consume much laser intensity and cannot be used for 2d depth profiles in one measuring process this paper concentrates on discrete dot structures which can be projected by the LCoS based spatial light modulator (SLM).

Typical diffraction gratings use a fixed phase distribution with structure sizes in the nanometre range on a glass substrate. With their fixed phase function they project a fixed diffraction pattern, for example 19×19 points with constant inter beam angle. The fixed grating cannot adapt to different lighting conditions and even worse: Most patterns do not allow an unambiguous detection as described in Sect. 4.

3   LCoS Microdisplays as Dynamic Phase Gratings

Switching from static phase gratings to a SLM, diffraction patterns can be projected dynamically. Since amplitude gratings have little diffraction efficiency, a phase grating based on a HD-LCoS microdisplay with high fill ratio was used for high efficiency. To project an intensity distribution of $I(u,v) = |G(u,v)|^2$ the corresponding phase distribution $\phi(x,y)$ with values between 0 and 2π can be calculated. Input laser plane $g(x,y)$ and diffraction pattern plane $G(u,v)$ are mathematically linked through the diffraction grating with phase shift $e^{j\phi(x,y)}$ by a Fourier transformation in the Fraunhofer region [4]:

$$G(u,v) = |G(u,v)|e^{j\phi(u,v)} = \mathcal{F}\{g(x,y)\} = \mathcal{F}\{|g(x,y)|e^{j\phi(x,y)}\} \ . \tag{2}$$

Therefore the phase distribution can be calculated using an iterative Fourier transform approach as described in [2,3].

As an example for a classical triangulation pattern an 18×18 dot matrix is depicted in Fig. 1 with the calculated phase distribution according to [2] and the measured intensity of the laser pattern.

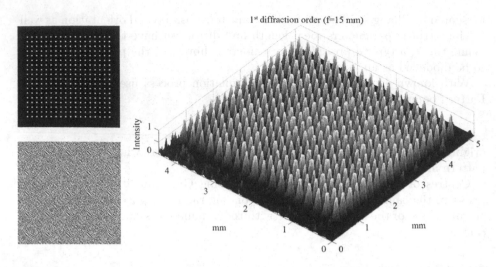

Fig. 1. Blueprint of 18 × 18 pattern (top left), phase distribution (bottom left), measured intensity of 1st diffraction order (right)

4   Unambiguous Patterns for Error Free Triangulation

To understand the ambiguity of triangulation patterns the projector and camera geometry in object space is shown in Fig. 2. An easy case with the projector centred above the camera with just a x-axis rotation is sketched without loss of generality. The projection pattern is a 3 × 3 dot matrix with constant inter beam angle. The intersections of each ray with the object space as well as their projections on the border of the image space are marked. Each 3d ray (1) can be projected to a 2d line

$$\mathbf{x}_{2D} = \mathbf{P}\mathbf{x}_{3D}z^{-1} \qquad (3)$$

in the 2d image space which passes through its projected border point, the entrance into the image space.

Remembering epipolar geometry of multiview systems [5] the projector can be regarded as a second, inverse camera. Every projected ray of the projector has an epipolar line in the camera image where its detected reflection can be found. In Fig. 2 the epipolar lines are parallel since their epipol is at infinity in a constellation with the baseline parallel to the image plane. Both camera and projector have the same z-value of zero in camera coordinates. Depending on the projector positioned before $(z > 0)$ or behind $(z < 0)$ the camera, the epipolar lines are either diverging or converging. Therefore the minimum distance between all epipolar lines is reached either at the border of the image considering divergent lines or at the imaged point of infinity of a ray if the rays are converging. The minimum distance between epipolar lines is named 2d conflict distance within this paper.

If this distance gets too small, detected pattern points cannot be assigned to their corresponding ray. If the distance gets close to zero as for the three spots

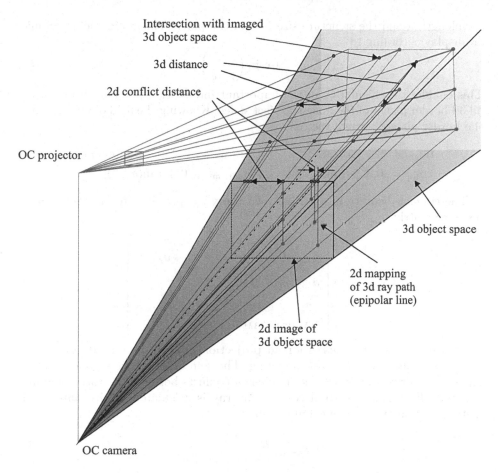

Fig. 2. Projection of 3d object space

in the centre column in this example, the situation gets ambiguous. The 3d ray path in object space has the same 2d projection for all three lines. Solving the correspondence problem for these three lines is impossible, if only one pattern point was not detected due to occlusion or contrast problems.

In bigger projection patterns this effect can escalate and corrupt lots of sample points, not only of the same column or row if the orientation between projector and camera changes to a slightly more complex setup.

Knowing the intrinsic matrix of a projector

$$\mathbf{K}_P = \begin{bmatrix} f_x & 0 & c_x \\ 0 & f_y & c_y \\ 0 & 0 & 1 \end{bmatrix} \tag{4}$$

the field of view in both directions can be calculated. In case of the laser projector the field of view can be calculated even easier knowing the illuminating wavelength λ and the structure size $p_{x,y}$ of the pixel elements in the LCoS microdisplay according to

$$\delta_{x,y} = \arcsin\left(\frac{\lambda}{p_{x,y}}\right) . \tag{5}$$

This enables the calculation of the important intersection points of Fig. 2 with all 3d border planes of the imaged object space. Knowing the field of view reveals the border planes' normal vectors

$$\begin{aligned}
\mathbf{n}_{\text{right}} &= [-1, 0, \tan(\delta_x/2)]^T & \mathbf{n}_{\text{left}} &= [-1, 0, -\tan(\delta_x/2)]^T \\
\mathbf{n}_{\text{top}} &= [0, 1, -\tan(\delta_y/2)]^T & \mathbf{n}_{\text{bottom}} &= [0, 1, \tan(\delta_y/2)]^T .
\end{aligned} \tag{6}$$

The conflict distance in pixel between every ray pair is noted in the conflict distance matrix

$$\mathbf{C}_{\text{Pattern}} = \begin{bmatrix}
0 & a_{21} & a_{31} & \cdots & & a_{N1} \\
a_{12} & 0 & a_{32} & \cdots & & a_{N2} \\
a_{13} & a_{23} & 0 & \ddots & & \vdots \\
\vdots & \vdots & \vdots & \ddots & & a_{N(M-1)} \\
a_{1M} & a_{2M} & a_{3M} & a_{(N-1)M} & & 0
\end{bmatrix} . \tag{7}$$

This matrix serves as basis for all projection pattern designs. It brands all elements smaller than $d_{\min}$ as conflicting. The sum of all conflicting elements in one column or row indicates the number of conflicts between the corresponding ray and all others. The total cost of one ray is calculated as the sum of all distances of one ray in one column or row

$$c(m) = \frac{1}{\sum_{n=1}^{N} \mathbf{C}_{\text{Pattern}}(n, m)} . \tag{8}$$

4.1   Modification of Desired Patterns

Instead of designing new unambiguous patterns a way of modifying desired patterns is introduced.

The total cost function (8) is not appropriate for optimizing the pattern. Rather the conflict distance matrix $\mathbf{C}_{\text{Positions}}$ for all possible ray positions has to be calculated. Having a spatial light modulator for beam diffraction or a step motor positioned mirror for beam redirection in mind, there exist N discrete horizontal and M discrete vertical positions forming a total of $N \cdot M$ possible ray positions. $\mathbf{C}_{\text{Positions}}$ thus consists of $2(N \cdot M)^2$ elements.

With $\mathbf{C}_{\text{Pattern}}$ having conflicting elements smaller than $d_{\min}$, the desired pattern has to be modified. The pattern itself is represented by a pattern matrix $\mathbf{P}$ with dimension $N \times M$ for all possible rays as illustrated in Fig. 1 (top left) and Fig. 4 (top left). As a trivial solution the most conflicting elements with the highest total cost (8) could be deleted. A more refined method is described here.

Within an iterative process, rays are translocated to less conflicting positions, until all conflicts are solved. Only one ray is moved within every iteration cycle.

To decide which ray has to be moved to which neighbouring position, a cost function is computed for each of the $N \cdot M$ possible positions at the start of each iteration. During evaluation the inverse minimum conflict distance

$$c(n, m) = \frac{1}{\min \left(\mathbf{C}_{\text{Positions}}(u, v) | [u, v] \in \text{Patternpoints} \right)} \tag{9}$$

with Patternpoints as the set of indices of active pattern points in $\mathbf{P}$ proved to be a good cost indicator.

Selected rays have to be moved to neighbouring positions with the aim to get a conflict-free, unambiguous projection pattern. Using (9) as the cost indicator, the most conflicting rays have to be moved first. Due to the two competing optimization goals

- pattern conflict avoidance and
- pattern affinity to the desired pattern,

a rating function for neighbouring positions $[n, m]$ compared to the actual position $[n_{\text{actual}}, m_{\text{actual}}]$ within a maximum distance $d_{\max}$ is needed

$$v(n, m) = \frac{c(n, m)/c(n_{\text{actual}}, m_{\text{actual}})}{d} - \mathbf{M}_{\text{Extra}}(n, m) \ . \tag{10}$$

To avoid deadlock situations of rays oscillating between two positions because the surrounding positions are even more expensive, an extra cost memory $\mathbf{M}_{\text{Extra}}$ is introduced. It raises the price of a previous position, when a ray is moved. After a few iterations the ray will leave the deadlock positions, since they get more and more expensive. To prevent wasted positions, the extra cost memory is halved every iteration, so that formerly used positions can be automatically reused after some time – maybe the whole neighbourhood of rays has changed in the meantime leading to a cheap settling position for other rays.

During the iteration the neighbouring position with the best improvement

$$\max(v(n, m) | d < d_{\max}) \tag{11}$$

for the most conflicting ray is selected as the new position and the cost function (9) has to be recalculated.

Always choosing the most conflicting ray can also end up in a deadlock situation, if the ray travels around neighbourhood positions which are all conflicting. They get more extra cost, but with the extra cost being halved every iteration they might be cheap enough for the ray to restart the circle.

First moving other rays away can lead to a better situation for the previously most conflicting ray. Therefore a ray memory $\mathbf{M}_{\text{Ray}}$ is used which adds extra cost to a formerly moved ray – not its position. This memory is also halved every iteration. The rays are sorted according to their cost $c(n, m)$ and indexed. The ray with the highest cost has index 1 at first. With $\mathbf{M}_{\text{Ray}}$ added, the resulting minimum is the index of the ray to be moved next:

$$\text{rayindex} = \min \left(\text{index}(\text{sort}(c(n, m))) + \mathbf{M}_{\text{Ray}} \right) \ . \tag{12}$$

Fig. 3. Projection pattern with conflicts

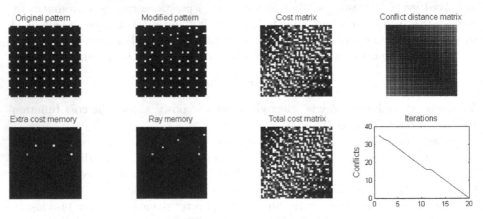

Fig. 4. Pattern modification

4.2   Simulation Results

To demonstrate the effects of ambiguous and unambiguous patterns, a triangulation setup with given depth map is simulated. The projector is positioned top right of the camera at $\mathbf{x}_{P,0} = [0.1\ \mathrm{m}, 0.1\ \mathrm{m}, 0\ \mathrm{m}]^T$ with an orientation of

Fig. 5. Modified projection pattern with specified 5 pixel minimum distance

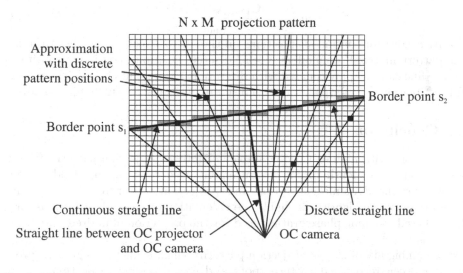

Fig. 6. Maximum number of conflict free, discrete rays in the projection pattern matrix

$[-5°, -10°]^T$. As an example a 9×9 dot pattern with a field of view of $30°$ is projected into the scene. All ray paths are simulated as well.

In Fig. 3 the ambiguities between ray 18, 41, 64 or 34, 57 and others can be seen. The ray paths are close and even overlapping.

The pattern modification according to Sect. 4.1 is shown in Fig. 4. The original desired pattern $\mathbf{P}$ is at the top left, $\mathbf{C}_{\text{Positions}}$ at the top right, the number of conflicts for every iteration step can be seen at the bottom right, the cost matrix (9) as well as the extra cost memory, total cost matrix and the ray memory after the last iteration step are also visualized.

After 20 iterations the modified pattern is conflict free. A minimum distance of $d_{\min} = 5$ pixel was the preset for this run of the modification algorithm.

As depicted in Fig. 5 the ray paths of the modified, unambiguous projection pattern always keep the preset minimum distance of 5 pixel. No matter where they hit the object plane, the detected dots can be assigned to the correct rays without ambiguities.

4.3   Estimation of Parallel Unambiguous Projection Rays

Often it is necessary to know the maximum number of unambiguous rays for a triangulation setup. Knowing extrinsic and intrinsic parameters of projector and camera, the vector $\mathbf{x}_{P,0} - \mathbf{x}_{C,0}$ between the optical centres can be calculated. The straight 2d line in the pattern matrix $\mathbf{P}$ in Fig. 6 which is orthogonal to this vector and passing the image centre, intersects the image border at the positions s_1 and s_2.

Getting the element $\mathbf{C}_{\text{Positions}}(s_1, s_2)$ reveals the conflict distance from these two rays – the distance between the two entrance points into the 2d image. The maximum number of unambiguous rays

$$n_{\max} = \frac{\mathbf{C}_{\text{Positions}}(s_1, s_2)}{d_{\min}} \tag{13}$$

is only correct for continuous positions on the line between s_1 and s_2. Although the pattern matrix $\mathbf{P}$ only offers $N \times M$ discrete positions, continuous positions on the line can be approximated with discrete pattern points beside it, verifying this estimation even for patterns with discrete positions. In Fig. 6, $n_{\max}$ is seven.

5   Conclusion

In situations with high or varying ambient lighting, projection patterns for triangulation based depth profile measurement need to be changed adaptively. A way for the dynamic generation and projection was introduced: iterative Fourier transform algorithms enable the calculation of phase distributions for a LCoS based dynamic phase grating used for the projection of desired diffraction patterns.

The ambiguity of classic projection patterns which leads to assignment problems between recognized pattern spots and corresponding projection rays in the signal processing phase is described. An algorithm for modifying desired projection patterns to eliminate ambiguities is introduced, which enables an assignment process without critical plausibility decisions – occlusions, wrong or missing detections have no influence.

The proposed projection patterns are not bound to diffraction based laser projections but can be applied to any kind of projection from conventional incoherent up to temporally triggered pattern projectors.

Acknowledgment

The author thanks the 'Deutsche Forschungsgemeinschaft' (DFG) which funded the presented researches as part of the DFG project 'Optische Tiefenprofilbestimmung auf der Basis adaptiv generierter Beugungsmuster' (KA 1697/4-1).

References

1. Zhang, Z.Y.: A Flexible New Technique For Camera Calibration. IEEE Transactions on Pattern Analysis and Machine Intelligence 22, 1330–1334 (2000)
2. Lubeley, D.: Laserprojektion auf Basis von Beugung – Bildwiedergabe und 3D-Erfassung. ITG-Fachbericht 199, Vorträge des 12. Dortmunder Fernsehseminars vom 20. bis 21. März 2007 in Dortmund, VDE-Verlag, pp. 197–200 (2007)
3. Fienup, J.R.: Phase Retrieval Algorithms – a Comparison. Applied Optics 21, 2758–2769 (1982)
4. Goodman, J.W.: Introduction to Fourier Optics, 3rd edn. Roberts & Co. Publishers, Englewood, Colo (2005)
5. Schreer, O., Kauff, P., Sikora, T.: 3D Videocommunication: Algorithms, Concepts and Real-Time Systems in Human Centred Communication. pp. 97–101, Chichester [u.a.]: Wiley (2005)

Point Matching Constraints in Two and Three Views

Klas Nordberg

Computer Vision Laboratory
Department of Electrical Engineering
Linköping University

Abstract. In the two-view case, point matching constraints are represented by the fundamental matrix. In the three-view case, the point matching constraints are indirectly represented by three trifocal tensors corresponding to the three camera matrices. A direct representation of the point matching constraints can be obtained by applying suitable transformations on the trifocal tensors. This paper discusses some issues related to point matching constraints. First, it presents a novel approach for deriving the constraints in terms of a generator space. Second, it shows that the resulting set of linearly independent constraints is 10-dimensional for the three-view case, a result which deviates from the literature on this subject. Third, in the case that the cameras have non-co-linear focal points, 9 of these 10 constraints can be obtained in a straight-forward way from the three fundamental matrices which we have in the three-view case. The last constraint can be obtained from the fundamental matrices but in a non-trivial way. The main result of the paper is a better understanding of the properties related to point matching constraints in three dimensions and how they are related to the corresponding two-view constraints.

1   Introduction

Matching constraints for points or lines in two or more images which correspond to the same point or line in 3D space is a well-explored area in computer vision. The basis is the standard representation of the mapping from a 3D point to a 2D point in terms of the *pin-hole camera model*:

$$\mathbf{y}_k \sim \mathbf{C}_k \, \mathbf{x}, \tag{1}$$

where $\mathbf{C}_k$ is the k-th camera matrix and $\mathbf{x}$ and $\mathbf{y}_k$ are homogeneous representations of a 3D point and its 2D image projection in the k-th camera. The symbol $\sim$ represents equality up to scaling.

The camera matrix $\mathbf{C}_k$ has a 1-dimensional null space N_k spanned by $\mathbf{n}_k$ which is the homogeneous representation of the camera focal point (or camera center). $\mathbf{C}_k^+$ is the pseudo-inverse of $\mathbf{C}_k$, satisfying $\mathbf{C}_k \mathbf{C}_k^+ = \mathbf{I}$ and $\mathbf{P}_k = \mathbf{C}_k^+ \mathbf{C}_k$ where $\mathbf{P}_k$ is the projection operator onto N_k. $\mathbf{C}_k^T$ and $\mathbf{C}_k^+$ have a 3-dimensional

F.A. Hamprecht, C. Schnörr, and B. Jähne (Eds.): DAGM 2007, LNCS 4713, pp. 52–61, 2007.

range which we can identify as $N_k^{\perp}$. An *epipole* $\mathbf{e}_{ij}$ is the mapping of focal point j with camera i: $\mathbf{e}_{ij} = \mathbf{C}_i \, \mathbf{n}_j$.

In the two-view case, $\mathbf{x}$ is projected onto two camera image points $\mathbf{y}_1, \mathbf{y}_2$ by means of two distinct cameras $\mathbf{C}_1, \mathbf{C}_2$. A constraint on the two image points can be described as

$$\mathbf{y}_1^T \mathbf{F}_{12} \, \mathbf{y}_2 = (\mathbf{y}_1 \otimes \mathbf{y}_2) \cdot \mathbf{F}_{12} = 0, \tag{2}$$

where $\mathbf{F}_{12}$ is the fundamental matrix corresponding to cameras 1 and 2, which can be computed directly from their matrices or estimated from a sufficiently large set of corresponding image points [2,1,3,4]. This constraint allows us to make a simple check whether or not two image points can correspond to the same 3D point. It should be noted that the constraint is necessary but not sufficient for $\mathbf{y}_1$ and $\mathbf{y}_2$ to correspond to the same $\mathbf{x}$. Consequently, if (2) is satisfied, the point pair $\mathbf{y}_1, \mathbf{y}_2$ can be said to be in hypothetical correspondence, which may be confirmed or rejected by further processing, e.g., comparing local image features in or around the two points. In the following presentation, $\mathbf{F}_{ij}$ denotes the fundamental matrix related to cameras i and j. It is assumed that the camera focal points (camera centers) of the two cameras are distinct, otherwise the concept of a fundamental matrix is not well-defined.

The standard approach for dealing with three-view matching constraints is described in terms of so-called trifocal tensors [5,6,7,4]. Let $\mathbf{C}_1, \mathbf{C}_2, \mathbf{C}_3$ be the three cameras which are assumed to have distinct focal points and let $\mathbf{x}$ and $\mathbf{L}$ be a 3D point and a 3D line which intersect. Let $\mathbf{y}_k$ be the homogeneous representation of the 2D point given by the mapping of $\mathbf{x}$ in camera k, and let $\mathbf{l}_k$ be the dual homogeneous representation of the 2D line given by the mapping of $\mathbf{L}$ in camera k. For this case, there exists a trifocal tensor $\mathbf{T}_1$, a third order tensor on $\mathbb{R}^3$, such that

$$(\mathbf{y}_1 \otimes \mathbf{l}_2 \otimes \mathbf{l}_3) \cdot \mathbf{T}_1 = 0. \tag{3}$$

If instead the projection of $\mathbf{x}$ is in views 2 or 3, there exist trifocal tensors $\mathbf{T}_2$ and $\mathbf{T}_3$ also for these cases. All three trifocal tensors can be derived from the camera matrices $\mathbf{C}_1, \mathbf{C}_2, \mathbf{C}_3$ only or estimated from a sufficiently large set of corresponding points and lines.

Clearly, the trifocal tensors provide matching constraints between corresponding point and lines in the three different views. By applying suitable transformations on a trifocal tensor, however, matching constraints for corresponding points in all three views can be obtained. For example, $\mathbf{T}_1$ can be transformed into nine tensors $\tilde{\mathbf{T}}_{1,k}, k = 1, \ldots, 9$ such that

$$(\mathbf{y}_1 \otimes \mathbf{y}_2 \otimes \mathbf{y}_3) \cdot \tilde{\mathbf{T}}_{1,k} = 0 \tag{4}$$

for image coordinates $\mathbf{y}_k$ corresponding to the same 3D point $\mathbf{x}$. The transformations which take place on the trifocal tensors are independent of the camera matrices and simply imply that the lines $\mathbf{l}_2$ and $\mathbf{l}_3$ are replaced by the symbols $\mathbf{y}_2 \times$ and $\mathbf{y}_3 \times$, where $\mathbf{y}_2$ and $\mathbf{y}_3$ are image points in views 2 and 3 which lie on lines $\mathbf{l}_2$ and $\mathbf{l}_3$, respectively. The same type of transformations can also be applied to $\mathbf{T}_2$ and $\mathbf{T}_3$ resulting in two more sets of 3×3 epipolar constraints.

In total the three trifocal tensors produce $3 \times 9 = 27$ constraints for corresponding points in three images. Already in [6] it was pointed out that the 9 point constraints which are produced from one trifocal tensor are linearly dependent. It is shown that 5 of the functional expressions which combine the elements of the tensor and the homogeneous image coordinates can be obtained from the other 4 by means of suitable linear combinations. The conclusion is that there are only 4 linearly independent constraints from each trifocal tensor, and since there are 3 such tensors, there must be in total 12 linearly independent point matching constraints for the three-view case, [4].

This analysis made on the number of linearly independent constraints is, however, not entirely correct. If we allow the coefficients of the linear combinations to take arbitrary forms, e.g., including the image coordinates, in fact any set of the constraints is linearly dependent of the others. For example, consider the two constraints

$$c_1(\mathbf{y}_1, \mathbf{y}_2, \mathbf{y}_3) = 0$$
$$c_2(\mathbf{y}_1, \mathbf{y}_2, \mathbf{y}_3) = 0. \tag{5}$$

Multiply the first equation by the left hand side of the second and the second by the left hand side of the first:

$$c_2(\mathbf{y}_1, \mathbf{y}_2, \mathbf{y}_3)\, c_1(\mathbf{y}_1, \mathbf{y}_2, \mathbf{y}_3) = 0$$
$$c_1(\mathbf{y}_1, \mathbf{y}_2, \mathbf{y}_3)\, c_2(\mathbf{y}_1, \mathbf{y}_2, \mathbf{y}_3) = 0, \tag{6}$$

and now we have two linearly dependent equations regardless of how c_1, c_2 are related. In view of this result, it appears more relevant to consider the number of linearly independent constraints which can be obtained by using coefficients which are *independent of the image coordinates* or, equivalently, how large is the smallest set of linearly independent tensors $\tilde{\mathbf{T}}_{i,k}$ for $i = 1, 2, 3$ and $k = 1, \ldots, 9$. As will be demonstrated in Section 4, this number is smaller than 12.

Another issue related to the point matching constraints derived from the trifocal tensors is how they may be related to the two-view constraints described by the corresponding fundamental matrices. The literature describes such relations, for example (1) a canonical set of three camera matrices can be computed from the three fundamental matrices, (2) from them the three trifocal tensors can be computed using the standard methods, and (3) by applying the above mentioned transformations the point matching constraints are obtained [4,8]. However, the concatenation of the three operations (1)–(3) results in a nontrivial mapping which does not reveal any explicit relations between the point matching constraints in two and three views.

1.1   This Paper

This paper presents a novel approach for deriving matching constraints, Section 2. This approach is then applied to point matching constraints in both two (Section 3) and three views (Section 4). As a result, we first obtain an explicit representation of the three-view point matching constraints in terms of a particular subspace of a particular vector space, and its dimensionality can easily be determined to be 10. In Section 5 the expressions which generate the two-view matching constraints, i.e. the fundamental matrices, are compared with the three view constraints and it can easily be seen that 9 of the latter can be obtained directly from the first. This result is valid for the case when the camera focal points are not co-linear. The 10-th dimension of the space of constraints can still be obtained from the fundamental matrices, but in a non-trivial way.

2 Matching Constraints

A common approach for the two cases of matching constraints discussed here is to start with a 3D point $\mathbf{x}$. In each camera view $\mathbf{x}$ is projected onto an image coordinate $\mathbf{y}_k$, (1). Then, a (multiplicative) joint image coordinate $\mathbf{Y}_{\text{joint}}$ is constructed as a tensor product of $\mathbf{y}_k$ from all views. This implies that $\mathbf{Y}_{\text{joint}} \sim \mathbf{C}_{\text{joint}} \mathbf{X}$, where $\mathbf{C}_{\text{joint}}$ is a *joint camera mapping* and $\mathbf{X}$ is either $\mathbf{x} \otimes \mathbf{x}$ or $\mathbf{x} \otimes \mathbf{x} \otimes \mathbf{x}$. Let X denote the linear span of all such $\mathbf{X}$, for all possible choices of $\mathbf{x}$, and let N denote the null space of $\mathbf{C}_{\text{joint}}$. The interesting space G is then defined as

$$G = \text{intersection of } N^{\perp} \text{ and } X^{\perp} \qquad \text{or, equivalently,}$$
$$G = \text{orthogonal complement of } \text{span}(N, X) \tag{7}$$

since it contains the *generating tensors* $\mathbf{G}$ of the matching constraints. For $\mathbf{G} \in G$ it follows that $(\mathbf{C}_{\text{joint}}^{+})^{T} \mathbf{G}$ is a matching constraint, denoted $\mathbf{F}$ for the two-view case and $\tilde{\mathbf{T}}$ for the three-view case. This follows directly from

$$\mathbf{Y}_{\text{joint}} \cdot ((\mathbf{C}_{\text{joint}}^{+})^{T} \mathbf{G}) \sim (\mathbf{C}_{\text{joint}} \mathbf{X})^{T} (\mathbf{C}_{\text{joint}}^{+})^{T} \mathbf{G} =$$
$$= \mathbf{X}^{T} \mathbf{C}_{\text{joint}}^{T} (\mathbf{C}_{\text{joint}}^{+})^{T} \mathbf{G} =$$
$$= \mathbf{X}^{T} (\mathbf{C}_{\text{joint}}^{+} \mathbf{C}_{\text{joint}})^{T} \mathbf{G} =$$
$$= \mathbf{X}^{T} \mathbf{P} \mathbf{G} = \mathbf{X}^{T} \mathbf{G} = 0, \tag{8}$$

where $\mathbf{P} = \mathbf{C}_{\text{joint}}^{+} \mathbf{C}_{\text{joint}}$ is the projection operator onto $N^{\perp}$. The second last equality follows from $\mathbf{G} \in N^{\perp}$ and the last equality follows from $\mathbf{G} \in X^{\perp}$ and $\mathbf{X} \in X$. Notice that since $G \subset N^{\perp}$ it follows that there are no null vectors of $\mathbf{C}_{\text{joint}}$ in G and, consequently, the dimensionality of G gives the number of linearly independent constraints.

In the following sections, this approach is applied to corresponding points in two and three views. This is done by describing in more detail the structure of the tensors $\mathbf{Y}_{\text{joint}}, \mathbf{C}_{\text{joint}}, \mathbf{X}, \mathbf{G}, \mathbf{P}$, and the vector spaces N, G, and X. In particular, the dimension of G is discussed in detail since it determines the number of linearly independent epipolar constraints.

The approach for constructing the matching constraints can be compared to the method presented in [9]. By means of the so-called Grassmannian tensor it is shown how matching constraints can be derived for the N-view case, resulting in explicit expression for the fundamental matrix or trifocal tensors in terms of the camera matrices. That approach, however, does not give a clear account for the dimensionality of the resulting constraints for the all-point case or how the two-view and three-view constraints are related. The approach proposed here, on the other hand, deals with both these issues and does so without a heavy mathematical formalism.

3 Point Matching Constraint in Two Views

Let $\mathbf{x}$ be a 3D point and consider its projection onto the two camera views:

$$\mathbf{y}_1 \sim \mathbf{C}_1 \, \mathbf{x}, \qquad \mathbf{y}_2 \sim \mathbf{C}_2 \, \mathbf{x}. \tag{9}$$

Form a *joint image coordinate* $\mathbf{Y}_{12}$ as

$$\mathbf{Y}_{12} = \mathbf{y}_1 \otimes \mathbf{y}_2 \sim (\mathbf{C}_1 \, \mathbf{x}) \otimes (\mathbf{C}_2 \, \mathbf{x}) = (\mathbf{C}_1 \otimes \mathbf{C}_2) \, (\mathbf{x} \otimes \mathbf{x}). \tag{10}$$

With this relation at hand, we also define a *joint camera mapping* $\mathbf{C}_{12} = \mathbf{C}_1 \otimes \mathbf{C}_2$ which allows us to write

$$\mathbf{Y}_{12} \sim \mathbf{C}_{12} \, (\mathbf{x} \otimes \mathbf{x}) = \mathbf{C}_{12} \, \mathbf{X}_{12} \tag{11}$$

for $\mathbf{X}_{12} = \mathbf{x} \otimes \mathbf{x}$. Let X_{12} denote the linear span of $\mathbf{X}_{12}$ for all $\mathbf{x}$. The null space of $\mathbf{C}_{12}$, denoted N_{12}, is 7-dimensional, and its orthogonal complement $N_{12}^{\perp} = N_1^{\perp} \otimes N_2^{\perp}$ is 9-dimensional $(7 + 9 = 16 = \dim(\mathbb{R}^4 \otimes \mathbb{R}^4))$. Define

$$\mathbf{C}_{12}^{+} = (\mathbf{C}_1^{+} \otimes \mathbf{C}_2^{+}) \tag{12}$$

which is a pseudo-inverse of $\mathbf{C}_{12}$ since

$$\mathbf{C}_{12}^{+} \mathbf{C}_{12} = (\mathbf{C}_1^{+} \otimes \mathbf{C}_2^{+}) \, (\mathbf{C}_1 \otimes \mathbf{C}_2) = (\mathbf{C}_1^{+} \mathbf{C}_1) \otimes (\mathbf{C}_2^{+} \mathbf{C}_2) = \mathbf{P}_1 \otimes \mathbf{P}_2 = \mathbf{P}_{12}, \tag{13}$$

where $\mathbf{P}_{12}$ is a projection operator onto $N_{12}^{\perp}$.

Next, we define

$$G_{12} = \text{intersection of } N_{12}^{\perp} \text{ and } X_{12}^{\perp} \tag{14}$$

or, equivalently,

$$G_{12} = \text{orthogonal complement of } \text{span}(N_{12}, X_{12}). \tag{15}$$

It was said above that $\dim(N_{12}) = 7$ and since X_{12} is the space of symmetric second order tensors on $\mathbb{R}^4$, we have $\dim(X_{12}) = 10$. However, $\mathbf{n}_k \otimes \mathbf{n}_k$ for $k = 1, 2$ lie in both of these two spaces, which otherwise are linearly independent. Consequently, $\dim(G_{12}) = 16 - (7 + 10 - 2) = 1$.

G_{12} contains *generating tensors* for a two-view epipolar constraint. Since G_{12} is 1-dimensional it is characterized by any non-zero element of this space. Let

$\mathbf{p}_1$ and $\mathbf{p}_2$ be the dual homogeneous representations of two distinct 3D planes which both includes the two focal points $\mathbf{n}_1$ and $\mathbf{n}_2$. This implies that

$$\mathbf{G}_{12} = \mathbf{p}_1 \otimes \mathbf{p}_2 - \mathbf{p}_2 \otimes \mathbf{p}_1 \tag{16}$$

is an element of $N_{\bar{12}}^{\perp}$. This $\mathbf{G}_{12}$ is a representation of the line which passes through both $\mathbf{n}_1$ and $\mathbf{n}_2$ in dual Plücker coordinates. Finally, it is also the case that $\mathbf{G}_{12} \in X_{\bar{12}}^{\perp}$ since $\mathbf{G}_{12}^{T}(\mathbf{x} \otimes \mathbf{x}) = 0$ for any $\mathbf{x}$. This implies that G_{12} is spanned by $\mathbf{G}_{12}$ in (16), and that a two-view epipolar constraint $\mathbf{F}$ is given by

$$\mathbf{F} = (\mathbf{C}_{12}^{+})^{T} (\mathbf{p}_1 \otimes \mathbf{p}_2 - \mathbf{p}_2 \otimes \mathbf{p}_1). \tag{17}$$

The fact that this $\mathbf{F}$ constitutes a matching constraints follows (8).

4   Point Matching Constraint in Three Views

Let $\mathbf{x}$ be a 3D point and consider its projection onto the three camera views which we assume have distinct focal points:

$$\mathbf{y}_1 \sim \mathbf{C}_1 \, \mathbf{x}, \qquad \mathbf{y}_2 \sim \mathbf{C}_2 \, \mathbf{x}, \qquad \mathbf{y}_3 \sim \mathbf{C}_3 \, \mathbf{x} \tag{18}$$

By means of the three-view joint camera matrix

$$\mathbf{C}_{123} = \mathbf{C}_1 \otimes \mathbf{C}_2 \otimes \mathbf{C}_2 \tag{19}$$

a three-view joint image coordinate $\mathbf{Y}_{123}$ can be defined as

$$\mathbf{Y}_{123} = \mathbf{y}_1 \otimes \mathbf{y}_2 \otimes \mathbf{y}_3 \sim (\mathbf{C}_1 \, \mathbf{x}) \otimes (\mathbf{C}_2 \, \mathbf{x}) \otimes (\mathbf{C}_3 \, \mathbf{x}) =$$
$$= (\mathbf{C}_1 \otimes \mathbf{C}_2 \otimes \mathbf{C}_3)(\mathbf{x} \otimes \mathbf{x} \otimes \mathbf{x}) = \mathbf{C}_{123}(\mathbf{x} \otimes \mathbf{x} \otimes \mathbf{x}) = \mathbf{C}_{123} \, \mathbf{X}_{123} \tag{20}$$

where $\mathbf{X}_{123} = \mathbf{x} \otimes \mathbf{x} \otimes \mathbf{x}$. Let X_{123} denote the linear span of $\mathbf{X}_{123}$ for all possible $\mathbf{x}$. $\mathbf{C}_{123}$ has a 37-dimensional null space N_{123} which, in turn, has a 27-dimensional orthogonal complement $N_{\bar{123}}^{\perp} = N_{\bar{1}}^{\perp} \otimes N_{\bar{2}}^{\perp} \otimes N_{\bar{3}}^{\perp}$ ($37 + 27 = 64 = \dim(\mathbb{R}^4 \otimes \mathbb{R}^4 \otimes \mathbb{R}^4)$). The joint camera mapping $\mathbf{C}_{123}$ has a pseudo-inverse:

$$\mathbf{C}_{123}^{+} = \mathbf{C}_1^{+} \otimes \mathbf{C}_2^{+} \otimes \mathbf{C}_3^{+} \tag{21}$$

which properties generalizes from (13) so that

$$\mathbf{P}_{123} = \mathbf{C}_{123}^{+} \mathbf{C}_{123} = \mathbf{P}_1 \otimes \mathbf{P}_2 \otimes \mathbf{P}_3 \tag{22}$$

is a projection operator onto $N_{\bar{123}}^{\perp}$.

We now define the space of generating tensors G_{123} as

$$G_{123} = \text{intersection of } N_{\bar{123}}^{\perp} \text{ and } X_{\bar{123}}^{\perp}, \qquad \text{or, equivalently,}$$
$$G_{123} = \text{orthogonal complement of } \text{span}(N_{123}, X_{123}). \tag{23}$$

We know that $\dim(N_{123}) = 37$ and since X_{123} is the space of completely symmetric third order tensors on $\mathbb{R}^4$, we have $\dim(X_{123}) = 20$. However, $\mathbf{n}_k \otimes \mathbf{n}_k \otimes \mathbf{n}_k$

for $k = 1, 2, 3$ lies in both of these two spaces, which otherwise are linearly independent, implying that $\dim(G_{123}) = 64 - (37 + 20 - 3) = 10$. Next, we describe a basis of G_{123}.

Apart from being distinct, here we consider the case that the focal points are also not co-linear. This implies that there is a unique 3D plane $\mathbf{p}_{00}$ which includes all focal points. Furthermore, we can also choose three arbitrary planes, $\mathbf{p}_{12}, \mathbf{p}_{23}, \mathbf{p}_{31}$, each of which is distinct from $\mathbf{p}_{00}$ and also includes two of the focal points:

$$\mathbf{p}_{ij} \text{ includes focal points } \mathbf{n}_i \text{ and } \mathbf{n}_j \text{ for } ij = 12 \text{ or } 23 \text{ or } 31. \qquad (24)$$

This amounts to four *distinct* 3D planes which are represented by four *linearly independent* vectors $\mathbf{p}_{00}, \mathbf{p}_{12}, \mathbf{p}_{23}$ and $\mathbf{p}_{31}$. Given these planes, the following relations are at hand

$$\mathbf{P}_1 \, \mathbf{p}_{00} = \mathbf{P}_2 \, \mathbf{p}_{00} = \mathbf{P}_3 \, \mathbf{p}_{00} = \mathbf{p}_{00}$$
$$\mathbf{P}_i \, \mathbf{p}_{ij} = \mathbf{P}_j \, \mathbf{p}_{ij} = \mathbf{p}_{ij} \qquad (25)$$

Define the 10 linearly independent tensors

$$\mathbf{G}_{123,1} = \mathbf{p}_{00} \otimes \mathbf{p}_{12} \otimes \mathbf{p}_{00} - \mathbf{p}_{12} \otimes \mathbf{p}_{00} \otimes \mathbf{p}_{00}$$
$$\mathbf{G}_{123,2} = \mathbf{p}_{00} \otimes \mathbf{p}_{12} \otimes \mathbf{p}_{23} - \mathbf{p}_{12} \otimes \mathbf{p}_{00} \otimes \mathbf{p}_{23}$$
$$\mathbf{G}_{123,3} = \mathbf{p}_{00} \otimes \mathbf{p}_{12} \otimes \mathbf{p}_{31} - \mathbf{p}_{12} \otimes \mathbf{p}_{00} \otimes \mathbf{p}_{31}$$
$$\mathbf{G}_{123,4} = \mathbf{p}_{00} \otimes \mathbf{p}_{00} \otimes \mathbf{p}_{23} - \mathbf{p}_{00} \otimes \mathbf{p}_{23} \otimes \mathbf{p}_{00}$$
$$\mathbf{G}_{123,5} = \mathbf{p}_{12} \otimes \mathbf{p}_{00} \otimes \mathbf{p}_{23} - \mathbf{p}_{12} \otimes \mathbf{p}_{23} \otimes \mathbf{p}_{00}$$
$$\mathbf{G}_{123,6} = \mathbf{p}_{31} \otimes \mathbf{p}_{00} \otimes \mathbf{p}_{23} - \mathbf{p}_{31} \otimes \mathbf{p}_{23} \otimes \mathbf{p}_{00}$$
$$\mathbf{G}_{123,7} = \mathbf{p}_{00} \otimes \mathbf{p}_{00} \otimes \mathbf{p}_{31} - \mathbf{p}_{31} \otimes \mathbf{p}_{00} \otimes \mathbf{p}_{00}$$
$$\mathbf{G}_{123,8} = \mathbf{p}_{00} \otimes \mathbf{p}_{12} \otimes \mathbf{p}_{31} - \mathbf{p}_{31} \otimes \mathbf{p}_{12} \otimes \mathbf{p}_{00}$$
$$\mathbf{G}_{123,9} = \mathbf{p}_{00} \otimes \mathbf{p}_{23} \otimes \mathbf{p}_{31} - \mathbf{p}_{31} \otimes \mathbf{p}_{23} \otimes \mathbf{p}_{00}$$
$$\mathbf{G}_{123,10} = \mathbf{p}_{12} \otimes \mathbf{p}_{23} \otimes \mathbf{p}_{31} - \mathbf{p}_{31} \otimes \mathbf{p}_{12} \otimes \mathbf{p}_{23} \qquad (26)$$

Given Equations (22) and (25), it follows directly that

$$\mathbf{P}_{123} \, \mathbf{G}_{123,k} = (\mathbf{P}_1 \otimes \mathbf{P}_2 \otimes \mathbf{P}_3) \, \mathbf{G}_{123,k} = \mathbf{G}_{123,k} \qquad (27)$$

which means that $\mathbf{G}_{123,k} \in N_{123}^{\perp}$ for $k = 1, \ldots, 10$. Also, each $\mathbf{G}_{123,k}$ is defined such that

$$(\mathbf{x} \otimes \mathbf{x} \otimes \mathbf{x}) \cdot \mathbf{G}_{123,k} = 0 \qquad (28)$$

for any $\mathbf{x} \in \mathbb{R}^4$, i.e., $\mathbf{G}_{123,k} \in X_{123}^{\perp}$ and, consequently, $\mathbf{G}_{123,k} \in G_{123}, k = 1, \ldots, 10$. All $\mathbf{G}_{123,k}$ are linearly independent which follows from the linear independence of $\mathbf{p}_{00}, \mathbf{p}_{12}, \mathbf{p}_{23}, \mathbf{p}_{31}$. Consequently, $\mathbf{G}_{123,k}, k = 1, \ldots, 10$ is a basis of G_{123} and

$$\tilde{\mathbf{T}}_k = (\mathbf{C}_{123}^{+})^{T} \, \mathbf{G}_{123,k}, \qquad k = 1, \ldots, 10 \qquad (29)$$

is a set of 10 linearly independent constraints, as proved by (8).

The case of co-linear focal points is not discussed here, but leads to the same conclusion; the space G is 10-dimensional and it is possible to construct a basis for G which, due to the co-linearity, is different from what is shown in (26).

5 How F and $\tilde{\mathbf{T}}_k$ Are Related

In this section we will investigate how the 10-dimensional space of point matching constraints for the three-view case is related to the three fundamental matrices which correspond to the three cameras.

The constraint generator $\mathbf{G}_{123,1}$ can be rewritten as

$$\mathbf{G}_{123,1} = \mathbf{p}_{00} \otimes \mathbf{p}_{12} \otimes \mathbf{p}_{00} - \mathbf{p}_{12} \otimes \mathbf{p}_{00} \otimes \mathbf{p}_{00} = (\mathbf{p}_{00} \otimes \mathbf{p}_{12} - \mathbf{p}_{12} \otimes \mathbf{p}_{00}) \otimes \mathbf{p}_{00}. \quad (30)$$

This means that the constraint $\tilde{\mathbf{T}}_1$ is given by

$$\tilde{\mathbf{T}}_1 = (\mathbf{C}_{123}^+)^T \mathbf{G}_{123,1} = (\mathbf{C}_{12}^+ \otimes \mathbf{C}_3^+)^T (\mathbf{p}_{00} \otimes \mathbf{p}_{12} - \mathbf{p}_{12} \otimes \mathbf{p}_{00}) \otimes \mathbf{p}_{00} = \quad (31)$$

$$= ((\mathbf{C}_{12}^+)^T (\mathbf{p}_{00} \otimes \mathbf{p}_{12} - \mathbf{p}_{12} \otimes \mathbf{p}_{00})) \otimes (\mathbf{C}_3^+ \otimes \mathbf{p}_{00}). \quad (32)$$

Since $\mathbf{p}_{00}$ and $\mathbf{p}_{12}$ are distinct and include the focal points $\mathbf{n}_1$ and $\mathbf{n}_2$ it follows from Section 3 that $\mathbf{p}_{00} \otimes \mathbf{p}_{12} - \mathbf{p}_{12} \otimes \mathbf{p}_{00}$ is a generator of $\mathbf{F}_{12}$, the fundamental matrix related to images 1 and 2:

$$\tilde{\mathbf{T}}_1 = \mathbf{F}_{12} \otimes (\mathbf{C}_3^+ \, \mathbf{p}_{00}) \quad (33)$$

This discussion can be applied to all generators $\mathbf{G}_{123,k}$ and corresponding constraints $\tilde{\mathbf{T}}_k$ for $k = 1, \ldots, 9$. The results is that all these 9 matching constraints in three views are directly related to matching constraints in two views. They are produced as the tensor product between a fundamental matrix and some vector in $\mathbb{R}^3$, e.g., the vectors of an ON-basis.

The remaining matching constraint, $\tilde{\mathbf{T}}_{10}$, which is generated by the generator $\mathbf{G}_{123,10}$, can also be derived from the fundamental matrices although not in the same straight-forward manner. To do this, however, we must assume that the camera focal points are not co-linear and that the fundamental matrices are *compatible*, i.e., that they satisfy

$$\mathbf{e}_{13}^T \mathbf{F}_{12} \mathbf{e}_{23} = \mathbf{e}_{21}^T \mathbf{F}_{23} \mathbf{e}_{31} = \mathbf{e}_{32}^T \mathbf{F}_{31} \mathbf{e}_{12} = 0 \quad (34)$$

relative to the epipoles $\mathbf{e}_{ij}$ [4]. These conditions are sufficient for assuring that the following transfer operations of points and lines are consistent over several transfers. In the ideal case they are always valid, but may not be so if the fundamental matrices have been estimated from noisy data.

The three planes $\mathbf{p}_{12}, \mathbf{p}_{23}, \mathbf{p}_{31}$ defined in (24) are epipolar planes. This means that

$$\mathbf{l}_{12} = (\mathbf{C}_1^+)^T \mathbf{p}_{12}, \quad \mathbf{l}_{23} = (\mathbf{C}_2^+)^T \mathbf{p}_{23}, \quad \mathbf{l}_{31} = (\mathbf{C}_3^+)^T \mathbf{p}_{31} \quad (35)$$

are epipolar lines relative to the epipoles $\mathbf{e}_{12}, \mathbf{e}_{23}, \mathbf{e}_{31}$, respectively. In the same way,

$$\mathbf{l}_{21} = (\mathbf{C}_2^+)^T \mathbf{p}_{12}, \quad \mathbf{l}_{32} = (\mathbf{C}_3^+)^T \mathbf{p}_{23}, \quad \mathbf{l}_{13} = (\mathbf{C}_1^+)^T \mathbf{p}_{31} \quad (36)$$

are epipolar lines relative to the epipoles $\mathbf{e}_{21}, \mathbf{e}_{32}, \mathbf{e}_{13}$, respectively. The last three epipolar lines can also be given by transferring of the first lines:

$$\mathbf{l}_{21} \sim \mathbf{F}_{12}^T [\mathbf{e}_{12}]_\times \mathbf{l}_{12}, \quad \mathbf{l}_{32} \sim \mathbf{F}_{23}^T [\mathbf{e}_{23}]_\times \mathbf{l}_{23}, \quad \mathbf{l}_{13} \sim \mathbf{F}_{31}^T [\mathbf{e}_{31}]_\times \mathbf{l}_{31}, \quad . \quad (37)$$

Now we can insert all these relations into the expressions for $\tilde{\mathbf{T}}_{10}$ given by Equations (26) and (29). This gives

$$\begin{aligned}
\tilde{\mathbf{T}}_{10} &= (\mathbf{C}_{123}^+)^T \, (\mathbf{p}_{12} \otimes \mathbf{p}_{23} \otimes \mathbf{p}_{31} - \mathbf{p}_{31} \otimes \mathbf{p}_{12} \otimes \mathbf{p}_{23}) = \\
&= (\mathbf{C}_1^+)^T \mathbf{p}_{12} \otimes (\mathbf{C}_2^+)^T \mathbf{p}_{23} \otimes (\mathbf{C}_3^+)^T \mathbf{p}_{31} - \\
&\qquad - (\mathbf{C}_1^+)^T \mathbf{p}_{31} \otimes (\mathbf{C}_2^+)^T \mathbf{p}_{12} \otimes (\mathbf{C}_3^+)^T \mathbf{p}_{23} = \\
&= \mathbf{l}_{12} \otimes \mathbf{l}_{23} \otimes \mathbf{l}_{31} - \mathbf{l}_{13} \otimes \mathbf{l}_{21} \otimes \mathbf{l}_{32} = \\
&= \mathbf{l}_{12} \otimes \mathbf{l}_{23} \otimes \mathbf{l}_{31} - \alpha \, \mathbf{F}_{31}^T [\mathbf{e}_{31}]_\times \mathbf{l}_{31} \otimes \mathbf{F}_{12}^T [\mathbf{e}_{12}]_\times \mathbf{l}_{12} \otimes \mathbf{F}_{23}^T [\mathbf{e}_{23}]_\times \mathbf{l}_{23}
\end{aligned} \qquad (38)$$

where α is a constant to be determined. This can, for example, be done by choosing two arbitrary matching points $\mathbf{y}_1$ and $\mathbf{y}_2$ in views 1 and 2, respectively, i.e., points which satisfy the epipolar constraint $\mathbf{y}_1^T \mathbf{F}_{12} \, \mathbf{y}_2 = 0$. These points uniquely determine a point $\mathbf{y}_3$ in the third view:

$$\mathbf{y}_3 = (\mathbf{F}_{12}^T \mathbf{y}_1) \times (\mathbf{F}_{23}^T \mathbf{y}_2). \qquad (39)$$

Now we have matching points in all three views and they must satisfy the epipolar constraint $(\mathbf{y}_1 \otimes \mathbf{y}_2 \otimes \mathbf{y}_3) \cdot \tilde{\mathbf{T}}_{10} = 0$. From this constraint, α can be found by solving a linear equation assuming that none of the points are lying on one of the epipolar lines.

In the case that all the above mentioned assumptions are valid, this α is uniquely determined regardless of how the matching points are found. By making different choices of the epipolar lines $\mathbf{l}_{12}, \mathbf{l}_{23}, \mathbf{l}_{31}$ the result is different instances of $\tilde{\mathbf{T}}_{10}$, parameterized by the 3D point $\mathbf{x}_0$ where the three epipolar planes cross. All these instances are linearly independent of $\tilde{\mathbf{T}}_1, \ldots, \tilde{\mathbf{T}}_9$ and together with these 9 constraints, they span the same 10-dimensional constraint space independent of $\mathbf{x}_0$.

In a practical situation, where the fundamental matrices are determined from noisy data, the matrices may not be compatible unless this condition is taken into account during their estimation. In the case of incompatible matrices, the estimation of $\tilde{\mathbf{T}}_{10}$ as well as the resulting space of constraints are more ambiguous. This implies that compatibility of the fundamental matrices is important if the three-view point matching constraints are determined from estimated fundamental matrices. Alternatively, in most practical situations it should be sufficient with the 9 point matching constraints which can be directly derived from the fundamental matrices and the final constraint dimension can be disregarded.

6 Summary

This paper has presented a novel approach to the derivation of matching constraints (Section 2) which only requires a basic understanding of tensor algebra; inner and outer products, and basic linear algebra; null spaces and intersection of vector spaces. When applied to point matching constraints in two and three views it shows that there are 10 linearly independent constraints in the three-view case, Section 4. In Section 5 it was shown that, in the case that the camera focal points are not co-linear, 9 of these 10 constraints can be obtained by a simple linear transformation from the three fundamental matrices. The 10-th constraint can also be produced from the fundamental matrices, but in a more complicated way and can in most cases be assumed to be redundant.

A practical side of this result is that, in the non-co-linear case for three views, if the corresponding fundamental matrices already are given (or estimated), 9 of the 10 three-view constraints can be obtained directly by means of simple linear transformations of the fundamental matrices. This operation has a much lower computational complexity than computing the canonical camera matrices from the fundamental matrices, computing the trifocal tensors from the camera matrices and transforming the trifocal tensors to point matching constraints.

Acknowledgment

This work has been made within the VISCOS project funded by the Swedish Foundation for Strategic Research (SSF).

References

1. Faugeras, O.: What can be seen in three dimensions with an uncalibrated stereo rig? In: Proceedings of European Conference on Computer Vision, pp. 563–578 (1992)
2. Faugeras, O., Luong, Q., Maybank, S.: Camera self-calibration: theory and experiments. In: Proceedings of European Conference on Computer Vision, pp. 321–334 (1992)
3. Hartley, R.: Estimation of relative camera positions for uncalibrated cameras. In: Proceedings of European Conference on Computer Vision, pp. 579–587 (1992)
4. Hartley, R., Zisserman, A.: Multiple View Geometry in Computer Vision, 2nd edn. Cambridge University Press, Cambridge (2003)
5. Shashua, A.: Trilinearity in visual recognition by alignment. In: Proceedings of European Conference on Computer Vision, pp. 479–484 (1994)
6. Shashua, A.: Algebraic functions for recognition. IEEE Trans. on Pattern Recognition and Machine Intelligence 17(8), 779–789 (1995)
7. Shashua, A., Werman, M.: On the trilinear tensor of three perspective views and its underlying geometry. In: Proceedings of International Conference on Computer Vision, pp. 920–925 (1995)
8. Shen, P.-Y., Wang, W., Wu, C., Quan, L., Mohr, R.: From fundamental matrix to trifocal tensor. Proc. SPIE, Vision Geometry VII 3454, 340–347 (1998)
9. Triggs, B.: Matching constraints and the joint image. In: Proceedings of International Conference on Computer Vision, Cambridge, MA, June 1995, pp. 338–343 (1995)

A Multi-view Camera System for the Generation of Real-Time Occlusion-Free Scene Video

Alparslan Yildiz and Yusuf Sinan Akgul

GIT Vision Lab
Department Of Computer Engineering
Gebze Institute Of Technology
Cayirova, Gebze, Kocaeli 41400
Turkey
{yildiz,akgul}@bilmuh.gyte.edu.tr

Abstract. This paper presents a novel multi-view camera system that produces real-time single view scene video which sees through the static objects to observe the dynamic objects. The system employs a training phase to recover the correspondences and occlusions between the views to determine the image positions where seeing through would be necessary. During the runtime phase, each dynamic object is detected and automatically registered between the views. The registered objects are learned using an appearance based method and they are later used to superimpose the occluded dynamic objects on the desired view. The occlusion detection is done using a very efficient and effective method. The system is very practical and can be used in real life applications including video surveillance, communication, activity analysis, and entertainment. We validated the system by running various tests in office and outdoor environments.

1 Introduction

The video produced by a camera with a 2D sensor array, i.e., the 2D video of a scene, is not sufficient to represent all the dynamic information about the 3D world. Yet, using 2D videos of real scenes to obtain dynamic real world information is very common in Computer Vision research and everyday life because of the wide availability and low cost of 2D cameras. One partial solution to the insufficiency of 2D videos is to use a multi-camera system to gather more than one 2D video of the scene from different angles. However, this solution introduces new problems such as occlusion analysis and it also makes the system more complex in terms of automatic or manual processing. To handle this complexity, it is desirable to produce a single "occlusion-free" 2D video of the scene using the images from a multi camera system. In order to establish a see through effect, the occluded dynamic objects of the scene would be clearly superimposed on the static scene objects that cause the occlusions. Such a system would be very useful both for automated and manual processing. For example, there are

F.A. Hamprecht, C. Schnörr, and B. Jähne (Eds.): DAGM 2007, LNCS 4713, pp. 62–71, 2007.

monocular object tracking systems for which occlusion is a serious problem. The blob based method of Haritaoglu *et al.* [3] uses a monocular method for the surveillance of people. Since it uses only 2D images from a single view, it relies on the detection of the blob merging for the occlusion detection. These types of tracking systems would benefit from our monocular "occlusion-free" scene images where the occluded humans are already marked clearly. Similar monocular object tracking methods include techniques that use object contours for occlusion detection, e.g. [5], and techniques that use depth ordering for the occlusion detection, e.g. [9]. An "occlusion-free" scene image would also be very useful for direct human interaction for entertainment, for communication, and also for manual video surveillance. For example, if we consider a security personnel of a department store, it might cause fatigue or some critical delays to switch between views of the store security cameras continuously. Using a single "occlusion-free" view to eliminate switching between views might be a better alternative for the manual activity tracking.

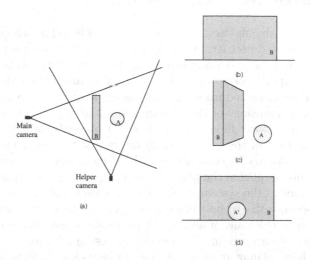

Fig. 1. (a) A scene containing a wall and a dynamic sphere. (b) View of the scene from main camera. (c) View of the scene from second camera. (d) "Occlusion-free" view of the scene for the main camera view.

In this paper, we present a novel system that uses a multi-camera setup to gather information about a scene and produce an "occlusion-free" view of the scene where the dynamic occluded objects are clearly marked (see Figure 1). The system is very efficient and it can work in real time on a general purpose home computer. The presented system includes an off-line training about the scene that will recover all the occluded regions. After the training, the system can work in real time to produce a 2D "occlusion-free" video of the scene from the point of view of one of the cameras.

There are systems in the literature addressing the occlusion problems with the multi-view camera setups. One category of such systems [8,4] uses the technique called synthetic aperture focusing, which requires about 100 cameras to simulate a very large physical aperture. Since large apertures receive light rays from many directions, it is possible to eliminate small occlusions and create new "see through" images. Our system is fundamentally different from these systems because we use only a few cameras instead of hundreds. Even though our system requires an off-line training about the scene, it is efficient enough to work in real time after the training. Finally, we do not place any restrictions on the occlusion size.

The rest of this paper is organized as follows: The detailed description of the proposed system is provided in Section 2. We provide the experimental results of the system in Section 3. Finally, we include a discussion about system usage possibilities, system limitations, and concluding remarks in Section 4.

2   "Occlusion-Free" Video Generation

Our approach in producing "occlusion-free" videos is based on using one or more helper cameras (i) to detect if a dynamic scene element is occluded on the main view, and (ii) to use the previously learned appearance of the occluded dynamic object image to superimpose on the main view. This means that the "occlusion-free" video will be produced from the viewing angle of the main camera. There are three basic assumptions of the system about the real world: (i) all the dynamic objects are always in contact with a 3D plane Π such as the ground, (ii) the static objects of the scene are stationary and the occlusions are always caused by the stationary objects, (iii) and the camera image planes have one of their axes roughly parallel to the plane Π. Although these assumptions might be seen as limitations of the system, they hold for a very wide range of real world applications because the scene elements that cause the occlusions are usually stationary, such as the walls of aisles in department stores, vertical columns in buildings, or heavy furniture in office environments. In addition, almost all work environments have planar grounds and the cameras can always be positioned with their X axes parallel to the ground.

The proposed system has two phases: training time and run time. The training is responsible for recovering the occluded image regions between the views. It also finds a perspective transform M_{ij} between the plane Π_i of helper camera i and the plane Π_j of the main camera j.

The direct way to perform the training of the scenes is to recover the 3D structure first using calibrated cameras. The recovered 3D structure would produce the occluded image regions and the perspective transforms. However, this approach is very difficult to implement in real life because establishing correspondences between two cameras with very different view points is not a trivial task. There are techniques in the literature that recover the occluded image regions directly such as the work of Zitnick and Kanade [10], but such techniques are not very helpful in our case because we need to find the image regions between views that correspond to occluded areas.

We developed a structured light solution for a more practical recovery of the occluded regions and their corresponding matches in the other views. Although, the structured light solution works very well indoors, for outdoor applications we need to switch to a laser scanner solution or the occlusion detection needs to be done manually.

2.1 Finding Occluded Areas Using Structured Light

Structured light has been used extensively to establish correspondences between camera pairs or between camera-projector pairs. One class of structured light methods, e.g. [2], uses color coding to project patterns on the scene, and the projected color patterns are used to find correspondences. These types of systems assume that the scene does not change the colors of the projected patterns. The other type of structured light systems project different patterns over time on the same scene under the assumption that the scene stays stationary. Gray codes [1] are one of the most popular among these methods and we employ an adaptation because our training stage is stationary and these methods are more robust against different types of objects in the scene. Our structured light method is similar to Scharstein and Szeliski [7]. The main difference of our work is that we use coded maps to resolve occlusion matches because our camera angles are very different compared to the stereo cameras used in [7]. Figure 2 (a-d) shows the result of this process for a scene with two occlusions (showing only low-order unique code bits).

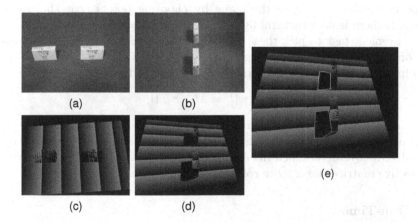

Fig. 2. (a) Main view of the scene with two occlusions. (b) Helper view of the scene. (c) low order u codes for the main view. (d) low order u codes for helper view. (e) Occluded areas found on the helper view.

Finding the occluded areas and their matches in the other images is the major task of the training phase. Although it is not required for a general solution, our occlusion detection method becomes very practical and robust if the structured light source is placed very close to the main view camera position with a roughly similar orientation. By using the unique codes, we find the occluded areas and the shadows which are the image regions where the unique codes cannot be found due to the occlusions. To find the occluded areas on the helper views, we find the *shadow area* O_i^m on unique code-map of each helper view i. We fit a convex hull for each O_i^m as shown in Figure 2-e to a scene with two occluded regions. We also use a minimum threshold value on the area of the regions so that we do not match shadows due to noise and other effects. If more than one projector is used, the structured light sources can be placed at other positions in the scene.

The last step of the training process is to find the perspective transformation between the views so that at runtime we can process the data that comes from the other views.

2.2   Perspective Transform Between Views

We need to define the mathematical relationship between views so that during the runtime if an occlusion of a dynamic object is detected, the information about that object can be taken from the other views. A perspective transform is sufficient to explain this relationship because our system assumes that all objects are in contact with the ground plane as explained in Section 2. Once the perspective transform between the images of the planes on two different views is estimated, the position of the dynamic occluded object on the main view can be estimated using the position of the object in the other views. We can estimate the perspective transform between the views using at least four corresponding points on the images of the plane. Note that it is trivial to automatically pick unique codes that belong to the plane by choosing points near the occluded regions. If there is no structural light available as in outdoor scenes, it is also a very convenient task to pick these points manually because this process will be done only once during the training time.

To find the perspective transform M_{ij} from view i to view j, we use

$$[wx\ wy\ w]_j^T = M_{ij}[x\ y\ 1]_i^T, \tag{1}$$

where $[x/w\ y/w]_j$ is a point from main view j and $[x\ y]_i$ is the corresponding point from helper view i. One can select more than four correspondences and solve the overdetermined linear system using least-squares to calculate the perspective matrices for a more robust solution.

2.3   Run-Time

During the run time, the system performs a two step algorithm for each frame from all helper views. The first step is to find blobs and decide whether blobs are inside any occluded area. The second step is to decide what to do with the blob.

First, the blob B_i^k that belongs to the dynamic object k is found on the helper view i, which can be done by subtracting the estimated background image from the current frame of the view i. Due to the system assumption of the planar environments, the dynamic object k has to intersect the ground plane Π_i at least in one 3D position. The projection of this position on the helper view i, which is called the *ground touching point(gtp)*, p_i^k, can be found easily: it is the pixel within the object blob B_i^k with the highest y value, assuming the coordinate center is on the upper left corner of the frame. It is guaranteed that $p_i^k \in \Pi_i$ and $p_i^k \in B_i^k$, so if the position of this pixel is transformed using the perspective transformation matrix between the helper view i and the main view, we can obtain the corresponding point on the main view. The corresponding main view point is calculated with the equation

$$p_j^k = M_{ij} p_i^k, \tag{2}$$

where p_i^k is *gtp* of the blob B_i^k on view i, and p_j^k is the corresponding point on view j, which is chosen to be the main view. Note that at this time, for a given pixel $r \in B_i^k$, the system knows if it is occluded by checking if $r \in O_i^m$ for all m as explained in Section 2.1.

As mentioned before, having all the occluded regions O_i^m at hand is not necessary. The perspective transformation will help to check if a blob is occluded or not. Once a blob B_i^k is found on the helper view i, its *gtp* p_i^k can be transformed to the main view to check if there is any blob standing where the transformed *gtp* points on the main view. If there is, then it is decided that the blob B_i^k is not occluded, otherwise it is occluded. This also makes it possible to adapt the system to changing occlusions and to changing backgrounds. To keep the things simple and to gain speed on computation, in our current experiments the occluded areas are found in the training phase.

The second step is to decide what to do with the blob B_i^k and will work differently for the occluded and non-occluded blobs. Let us first consider that object k is not standing on the occluded area, i.e. $p_i^k \notin O_i^m$ for any m. This means that the object k is visible from both the view i and the main view j. The system will now memorize both appearances B_i^k and B_j^k of the object k as a pair. Later this memory of appearances will be used to estimate the main view appearance of an occluded blob. To memorize, first, the system finds the corresponding object (if there is any) on the main view. It is sufficient to search the neighborhood of the point p_j^k (Equation 2) on the main view to find the corresponding blob B_j^k. If there is such a blob, then B_i^k and B_j^k are registered as a pair $\left(B_j^k, B_i^k \right)_t$ for the time frame t, resizing all blobs into a fixed bounding box. Note that, if we have more than one helper camera and if the same blob is visible from more than one helper view, then the above pair becomes an ordered set. Note also that this process is actually a simple appearance based object recognition learning technique.

Let us consider the other case where object k on the helper view i is on the occluded area, i.e. $\exists O_i^m$ and $p_i^k \in O_i^m$. It is obvious that there would be no matching blob on the main view at the corresponding position shown by the transformation (Equation 2). However, this position is very important because it marks the image region where the object k would have been shown if there were no occlusions. This means that if we had the appearance of the occluded dynamic object k from the main camera angle, we could have superimposed it at this location. Unfortunately, we do not have the occluded object image from the main camera view at this time instant because the object is only visible from the helper camera(s) and it is occluded for the main camera. However, it is very likely that the main camera has seen the dynamic object k many times while it was not occluded, which means that the system has a number of image pairs for this object in the memory. Therefore, making a search on the image pairs in the memory would retrieve this image. An optimization with the formula

$$min\ S(B_i^k, B_i(t, l)),\qquad(3)$$

performs this search to produce the image pair whose first component includes the image that we need to superimpose on the main view. $S(B_i, B_j)$ is a function that takes two blob images and returns a similarity value. $B_i(t, l)$ iterates over the second component of the blob pair $\left(B_j^l, B_i^l\right)_t$ for all blob pairs of view i, all frames t, and all blobs l. If the result from Formula 3 is lower than a threshold value, then the system does not have the image of the occluded object from the main camera view. In this case, the image to be painted on the main view can be chosen as the image of B_i^k. In other words, the blob detected on the helper view can directly be drawn on the main view at the position where the object would be standing. The direct application of the above method causes blinks in the generated video because the consecutively superimposed images might not be continuous. A considerable improvement for this approach is implemented in our system: it is known that moving objects like humans make periodical and continuous movements. Therefore, when the system does not have the image of the occluded object from the main camera view, the consequent main camera view appearances for the last match could be used for superimposing for most of the cases. In other words, given two image sequences starting with similar frames, we expect that these sequences will include similar images for the next few frames. In our experiments, 5 to 10 consequent frames are superimposed from the same sequence if we cannot find any matches. If the system still cannot find a suitable match, the helper view blob B_i^k itself is painted on the main view.

The activity detection and runtime module has to be very efficient because our system needs to process frames in real time. As a result, the blob storage and retrieval functions cannot be very complex. So, we used a basic Sum of Squared Differences (SSD) approach to implement the function S of Formula 3 due to its efficiency, as the registered pairs are at fixed size. Since the system has the blobs (masks) and appearances, only the pixels within the intersection of silhouettes of appearances are taken into SSD computation. Other alternatives for this effective appearance based approach would include employing a full scale object recognition module which would hurt the performance of the system in terms of running times.

3 Experiments

We tested our system both for experimental office environments and for more challenging outdoor environments. The office setup uses two CCD cameras and an ordinary projector to project patterns onto the scene. For the outdoor setup, however, we entered the plane Π correspondences and the occluded region O_i^m parameters manually because ordinary projectors are not very effective outdoors. Using a field laser scanner would achieve the same task if automatization is needed as in [6]. Figure 3 and Figure 4 shows some selected frames from the output of the experiments.

Main Camera   Helper Camera

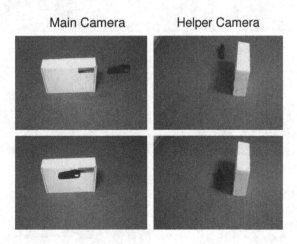

Fig. 3. Indoor experiment: A stapler object is pulled by a string behind an occlusion

Visual inspection of the results indicates that the system works very well for the more controlled office environments. All the occluded frames are handled very nicely and the occluded object positions are superimposed at the correct positions. The system also performs favorably for the outdoor experiments but there are some improvements that need to be made. Most of the problems with the outdoor experiments actually come from the blob detection phase which has to be very fast. If the blobs are detected correctly, then the rest of the system works very well. We observed that Formula 3 returns an acceptable appearance to be superimposed on the main camera view for most of the frames. We also observed that the system can process more than 15 frames per second for almost all the experiments on a regular computer.

Main Camera   Helper Camera

Fig. 4. Outdoor experiment: A person passing behind an occlusion

4 Discussion and Conclusions

We presented a multi-view camera system that produces real-time "occlusion-free" videos of scenes with stationary occlusions. The system is applicable in many practical tasks, such as in automated and manual video surveillance, entertainment, and human activity analysis. The system has several components each of which is optimized for speed because of the real time requirements.

We are working on several system improvements. The system currently uses a simple activity detection algorithm, which can be improved to include any gradual changes in the scene. It is also possible to handle changes in the static environments by double checking if a detected blob has a corresponding blob on the main view instead of an occlusion. Such an improvement is feasible and it can easily lead to the elimination of the training phase. It is also possible to improve the appearance based blob recognizer module of the system by utilizing a more sophisticated and efficient storage and retrieval system.

Overall, we are very encouraged with the current results and we think that this system will find many real world applications with great success.

References

1. Bitner, J.R., Erlich, G., Reingold, E.M.: Efficient Generation of the Binary Reflected Gray Code and its Applications. Communications of the ACM 19, 9 (1976)
2. Davies, C., Nixon, M.: Sensing Surface Discontinuities via Colored Spot. In: Proc. IEEE International Workshop on Image and Signal Processing, IEEE Computer Society Press, Los Alamitos (1996)
3. Haritaoglu, I., Harwood, D., Davis, L.S.: W4: Real-time surveillance of people and their activities. IEEE Trans. Pattern Anal. Mach. Intell. 22(8), 809–830 (2000)
4. Isaksen, A., McMillan, L., Gortler, S.J.: Dynamically reparameterized light fields. In: SIGGRAPH, pp. 297–306 (2000)
5. MacCormick, J., Blake, A.: A probabilistic exclusion principle for tracking multiple objects. International Journal of Computer Vision 39(1), 57–71 (2000)
6. Rioux, M.: Digital 3-d imaging: Theory and applications. In: Symposium on Photonic and Sensors and Controls for Commercial Applications, Boston, pp. 2–15 (1994)
7. Scharstein, D., Szeliski, R.: High-accuracy stereo depth maps using structured light. IEEE Computer Vision and Pattern Recognition (1), 195–202 (2003)
8. Vaish, V., Levoy, M., Szeliski, R., Zitnick, C.L., Kang, S.B.: Reconstructing occluded surfaces using synthetic apertures: Stereo, focus and robust measures. IEEE Computer Vision and Pattern Recognition (2), 2331–2338 (2006)
9. Wu, Y., Yu, T., Hua, G.: Tracking appearances with occlusions. IEEE Computer Vision and Pattern Recognition (1), 789–795 (2003)
10. Zitnick, C.L., Kanade, T.: A cooperative algorithm for stereo matching and occlusion detection. IEEE Trans. Pattern Anal. Mach. Intell. 22(7), 675–684 (2000)

Selection of Local Optical Flow Models by Means of Residual Analysis

Björn Andres, Fred A. Hamprecht, and Christoph S. Garbe

Interdisciplinary Center for Scientific Computing
University of Heidelberg, 69120 Heidelberg, Germany

Abstract. This contribution presents a novel approach to the challenging problem of model selection in motion estimation from sequences of images. New light is cast on parametric models of local optical flow. These models give rise to parameter estimation problems with highly correlated errors in variables (EIV). Regression is hence performed by equilibrated total least squares. The authors suggest to adaptively select motion models by testing local empirical regression residuals to be in accordance with the probability distribution that is theoretically predicted by the EIV model. Motion estimation with residual-based model selection is examined on artificial sequences designed to test specifically for the properties of the model selection process. These simulations indicate a good performance in the exclusion of inappropriate models and yield promising results in model complexity control.

1 Introduction and Related Work

In their well-known contribution [1], Black and Jepson propose to estimate optical flow independently for segmented spatiotemporal regions. Parameters of optical flow models are hence allowed to depend on non-trivial subsets of the spatiotemporal volume. The exploitation of the full potential of this approach involves the three challenging problems of motion segmentation, noise estimation and motion model selection. These problems are connected by the fact that violations of suitable models that exceed the scale of noise indicate segment borders. Gheissari et al. [2] comprehensively discuss this interrelation and demonstrate how local optical flow estimation, motion segmentation and motion model selection can be incorporated into an unsupervised motion segmentation framework. This paper focuses on the selection of suitable parametric optical flow models. While a simple model fails to approximate data of higher intrinsic complexity under low noise conditions, a complex model is prone to over-fitting in the presence of noise. Various information criteria have been proposed that penalize model complexity in order to avoid over-fitting. Among the most popular are Akaike's Information Criterion [3] as well as the Bayesian Information Criterion [4]. In the context of motion estimation, the model selection problem has been discussed by Wechsler et al. [5] as well as by Gheissari et al. [2]. However, "[...] *none of the existing model selection criteria is capable of reliably identifying the true underlying model* [...]. *The main reason is that the available*

F.A. Hamprecht, C. Schnörr, and B. Jähne (Eds.): DAGM 2007, LNCS 4713, pp. 72–81, 2007.
© Springer-Verlag Berlin Heidelberg 2007

information theoretic model selection criteria are based on the assumptions that noise is very small and the data size is large enough" [2]. Hence, Gheissari et al. suggest to consider the constraint surfaces of parametric models as thin plates and to penalize the strain energy of these plates according to a physical model. They show a successful application of this surface selection criterion (SSC) in a motion segmentation framework. As the SSC incorporates only second order derivatives of the model surfaces, it cannot be used to distinguish different linear models. Moreover, if information on the distribution of noise is available from camera calibration measurements or noise estimation, probabilistic model selection criteria that incorporate this information should be employed. This paper is intended to fill the gap between information theoretic penalization and heuristic surface modeling. Following the general idea of Cootes et al. [6], we suggest to assess parametric optical flow models by measuring the discrepancy between the empirical distribution of regression residuals and the probability density function (PDF) predicted from theory. This paper is organized as follows. In the next section, we formalize the concept of local optical flow to cast new light on the interrelation of optical flow estimation, motion segmentation and motion model selection. In terms of local optical flow, we then outline in section 3 the specifics of parameter estimation with respect to motion model selection. This includes equilibrated total least squares (ETLS) estimation under a suitably defined Errors-in-Variables (EIV) model. In section 4, the probability distribution of regression residuals is derived from the EIV model. Section 5 deals with simulations conducted to test the proposed model selector for its specific properties. We applied this method to artificial sequences featuring gray value structure on multiple scales. Real world video data as well as standard benchmark sequences such as the Yosemite sequence are not suitable to test for the specifics of model selection as the model selector has no intrinsic capability of overcoming the aperture problem.

2   Local Optical Flow

We formalize the concept of local optical flow in order to strengthen the interrelation of optical flow estimation, motion segmentation and motion model selection. If $n_x, n_y, n_t, n_c \in \mathbb{N}$, $P = \{1, \ldots, n_x\} \times \{1, \ldots, n_y\} \times \{1, \ldots, n_t\}$ and $C = \{0, \ldots, n_c\}$ then, the mapping $g : P \to C$ shall be referred to as an *irradiance signal*. Moreover, any mapping $g : \mathbb{R}^3 \to \mathbb{R}$ shall be termed an *ideal irradiance signal*. Herein, for $x \in P$, $g(x, y, t)$ may represent the mean irradiance onto the pixel indicated by (x, y) over the time interval indicated by t as measured with the finite intensity range and resolution given by C [7].

Definition 1 (Optical Flow). *Let $g : \mathbb{R}^3 \to \mathbb{R}$ be an ideal irradiance signal such that the first partial derivatives of g exist and let $(u, v)^T : \mathbb{R}^3 \to \mathbb{R}^2$. Then, $(u, v)^T$ shall be referred to as a field of optical flow precisely if*

$$\partial_t g + u \partial_x g + v \partial_y g = 0 \tag{1}$$

holds, which is is the well-known brightness change constraint equation *(BCCE).*

Definition 2 (Local Optical Flow). *Let* $g : \mathbb{R}^3 \rightarrow \mathbb{R}$ *be an ideal irradiance signal such that the first partial derivatives of g exist and let* $(u, v)^T : \mathbb{R}^3 \times \mathbb{R}^3 \rightarrow \mathbb{R}^2$. *Moreover, let* $\omega : \mathbb{R}^3 \times \mathbb{R}^3 \rightarrow \mathbb{R}_0^+$ *such that* $\forall \boldsymbol{x} \in \mathbb{R}^3 : \omega(\boldsymbol{x}, \boldsymbol{x}) > 0$. *Then,* $(u, v)^T$ *shall be referred to as a field of* local optical flow *with respect to* ω *precisely if*

$$\forall \boldsymbol{x}, \boldsymbol{x}' \in \mathbb{R}^3 : \omega(\boldsymbol{x}, \boldsymbol{x}')(\partial_t g(\boldsymbol{x}') + u(\boldsymbol{x}, \boldsymbol{x}')\partial_x g(\boldsymbol{x}') + v(\boldsymbol{x}, \boldsymbol{x}')\partial_y g(\boldsymbol{x}')) = 0 \ . \quad (2)$$

The mapping ω *shall then be referred to as an* aperture function *and, for all* $\boldsymbol{x} \in \mathbb{R}^3$, *the set* $U_\omega(\boldsymbol{x}) := \{\boldsymbol{x}' \in \mathbb{R}^3 | \omega(\boldsymbol{x}, \boldsymbol{x}') > 0\}$ *shall be termed the* motion neighborhood *of* $\boldsymbol{x}$. *In this paper, we refer to (2) as the* local brightness change constraint equation (LBCCE).

(Local) optical flow is often considered in conjunction with parametric models of u and v of which the parameters are estimated such that (1) and (2), respectively hold approximately. A way of looking at the definition of local optical flow is the following: Fix an $\boldsymbol{x} \in \mathbb{R}^3$. Now, the estimation of $(u, v)^T$ from the LBCCE for $\boldsymbol{x}$ is indeed the estimation of optical flow $(u', v')^T : \mathbb{R}^3 \rightarrow \mathbb{R}^2$ at this pixel on the data $U_\omega(\boldsymbol{x})$ namely, $\forall \boldsymbol{x}' \in \mathbb{R}^3 : u'(\boldsymbol{x}') = u(\boldsymbol{x}, \boldsymbol{x}') \wedge v'(\boldsymbol{x}') = v(\boldsymbol{x}, \boldsymbol{x}')$. Moreover, local optical flow $(u, v)^T : \mathbb{R}^3 \times \mathbb{R}^3 \rightarrow \mathbb{R}^2$ comprises optical flow $(u', v')^T : \mathbb{R}^3 \rightarrow \mathbb{R}^2$ as the special case in which it is assumed that $\forall \boldsymbol{x}, \boldsymbol{x}' \in \mathbb{R}^3 : u(\boldsymbol{x}, \boldsymbol{x}') = u'(\boldsymbol{x}') \wedge v(\boldsymbol{x}, \boldsymbol{x}') = v'(\boldsymbol{x}')$ i.e., for all $\boldsymbol{x}' \in \mathbb{R}^3$, $(u(\boldsymbol{x}, \boldsymbol{x}'), v(\boldsymbol{x}, \boldsymbol{x}'))$ is independent of $\boldsymbol{x}$. The generality of the LBCCE affords that $U_\omega(\boldsymbol{x})$ need not be, for instance, topologically connected and that, for $\boldsymbol{x}_1, \boldsymbol{x}_2 \in \mathbb{R}^3$ such that $\boldsymbol{x}_1 \neq \boldsymbol{x}_2$, $U_\omega(\boldsymbol{x}_1)$ and $U_\omega(\boldsymbol{x}_2)$ need neither be disjoint nor otherwise related. The aim in motion segmentation is to find a suitable aperture function ω that partitions the preimage of the irradiance signal i.e., $\forall \boldsymbol{x_1}, \boldsymbol{x_2} \in \mathbb{R}^3 : U_\omega(\boldsymbol{x_1}) = U_\omega(\boldsymbol{x_2}) \vee U_\omega(\boldsymbol{x_1}) \cap U_\omega(\boldsymbol{x_2}) = \emptyset$. In terms of local optical flow, the classical approach by Lucas and Kanade [8], to estimate optical flow for small identical spatiotemporal neighborhoods of each pixel, is to consider, for a given extension $d_s, d_t \in \mathbb{R}_0^+$ of these neighborhoods, the aperture function ω such that $\forall (x, y, t)^T, (x', y', t')^T \in \mathbb{R}^3 : \omega((x, y, t), (x', y', t')) = \Theta(d_s - |x' - x|)\Theta(d_s - |y' - y|)\Theta(d_t - |t' - t|)$ (with Θ denoting the Heaviside step function). Black and Jepson [1] investigate several parametric models of local optical flow, among these the local planarity assumption.

Definition 3 (Local Planarity (LPL)). *Let* $(u, v)^T : \mathbb{R}^3 \times \mathbb{R}^3 \rightarrow \mathbb{R}^2$ *and* $\omega : \mathbb{R}^3 \times \mathbb{R}^3 \rightarrow \mathbb{R}_0^+$. *Then,* $(u, v)^T$ *shall be called* locally planar *with respect to* ω *precisely if* $\exists p_1, \ldots, p_8 : \mathbb{R}^3 \rightarrow \mathbb{R} \ \forall (x, y, t)^T = \boldsymbol{x} \in \mathbb{R}^3 \ \forall (x', y', t')^T = \boldsymbol{x}' \in U_\omega(\boldsymbol{x})$:

$$\begin{pmatrix} u(\boldsymbol{x}, \boldsymbol{x}') \\ v(\boldsymbol{x}, \boldsymbol{x}') \end{pmatrix} = \begin{pmatrix} p_1(\boldsymbol{x}) \\ p_2(\boldsymbol{x}) \end{pmatrix} + \begin{pmatrix} p_3(\boldsymbol{x}) & p_4(\boldsymbol{x}) \\ p_5(\boldsymbol{x}) & p_6(\boldsymbol{x}) \end{pmatrix} \begin{pmatrix} x' - x \\ y' - y \end{pmatrix}$$
$$+ \begin{pmatrix} (x' - x)^2 & (x' - x)(y' - y) \\ (x' - x)(y' - y) & (y' - y)^2 \end{pmatrix} \begin{pmatrix} p_7(\boldsymbol{x}) \\ p_8(\boldsymbol{x}) \end{pmatrix} \ . \quad (3)$$

More restrictive models are obtained from LPL by imposing constraints on the parameter functions such as those to be found in Table 1. Given the LPL model,

Table 1. Parametric local optical flow models obtained from restrictions imposed on LPL. k indicates the number of parameter functions.

Code	k	Description	Restriction on LPL
LPL	8	Planar	none
LAF	6	Affine	$p_1 = p_2 = 0$
LDR	4	Divergence and Rotation	$p_1 = p_2 = 0, p_3 = p_6, p_4 = -p_5$
LSS	4	Stretch and Shear	$p_1 = p_2 = 0, p_3 = -p_6, p_4 = p_5$
LC	2	Constant	$p_1 = p_2 = p_3 = p_4 = p_5 = p_6 = 0$

define $a_g : \mathbb{R}^3 \times \mathbb{R}^3 \to \mathbb{R}^8$, $b_g : \mathbb{R}^3 \times \mathbb{R}^3 \to \mathbb{R}$ and $p : \mathbb{R}^3 \to \mathbb{R}^8$ such that $p := (p_1, \ldots, p_8)^T$ and $\forall (x, y, t)^T = x, (x', y', t')^T = x' \in \mathbb{R}^3$:

$$a_g(x, x') := \omega(x, x') \begin{pmatrix} \partial_x g(x') \\ \partial_y g(x') \\ (x' - x)\partial_x g(x') \\ (y' - y)\partial_x g(x') \\ (x' - x)\partial_y g(x') \\ (y' - y)\partial_y g(x') \\ (x' - x)^2 \partial_x g(x') + (x' - x)(y' - y)\partial_y g(x') \\ (x' - x)(y' - y)\partial_x g(x') + (y' - y)^2 \partial_y g(x') \end{pmatrix}, \quad (4)$$

$$b_g(x, x') := -\omega(x, x')\partial_t g(x') . \quad (5)$$

Then, the LBCCE shall be written as

$$\forall x, x' \in \mathbb{R}^3 : \quad a_g^T(x, x')p(x) = b_g(x, x') . \quad (6)$$

Analogous definitions of a_g, b_g and p exist for the parametric models LAF, LDR, LSS and LC. Optimized linear shift invariant (LSI) operators with finite impulse response (FIR) [9] are used to compute derivatives of (non-ideal) irradiance signals. The preimage of such a signal is finite and so is hence $U_\omega(x)$ for all $x \in P^1$. Finiteness allows to express (6) as a set of systems of equations.

Definition & Proposition 4 (LPL Data). *Let $g : P \to C$ be an irradiance signal, $\omega : P \times P \to \mathbb{R}_0^+$ such that $\forall x \in P : \omega(x, x) > 0$. Let $\forall x \in P : U_\omega(x) = \{x' \in P | \omega(x, x') > 0\}$, $m : P \to \mathbb{N}$ and $\forall x \in P : x'_1, \ldots, x'_{m(x)}$ such that $\{x'_1, \ldots, x'_{m(x)}\} = U_\omega(x)$. Moreover, consider a_g and b_g as defined in (4) and (5), respectively. Then,*

$$A_g(x) := \begin{bmatrix} a_g^T(x, x'_1) \\ \cdots \\ a_g^T(x, x'_{m(x)}) \end{bmatrix} \quad \text{and} \quad b_g(x) := \begin{bmatrix} b_g(x, x'_1) \\ \cdots \\ b_g(x, x'_{m(x)}) \end{bmatrix} . \quad (7)$$

---

[1] Only pixels $x \in P$ at suitable distance to the border of P such that the derivatives can be computed for all $x' \in U_\omega(x)$ are considered.

shall be termed the data matrix *and* data vector, *respectively of the LPL model.*
The LBCCE (6) is then equivalent to

$$\forall \boldsymbol{x} \in P : \quad A_g(\boldsymbol{x})\boldsymbol{p}(\boldsymbol{x}) = \boldsymbol{b}_g(\boldsymbol{x}) \ . \tag{8}$$

3   Parameter Estimation

We assume gray values to be corrupted by *additive* noise. The additive EIV model claims the existence of a true signal $\tau : P \to C$ and, for all $\boldsymbol{x} \in P$, a random variable $\epsilon(\boldsymbol{x})$ (noise) such that

$$\forall \boldsymbol{x} \in P : g(\boldsymbol{x}) = \tau(\boldsymbol{x}) + \epsilon(\boldsymbol{x}) \ . \tag{9}$$

Through the use of LSI operators, derivatives are approximated by linear combinations of gray values. The overlap of FIR masks in the computation of these derivatives at nearby pixels introduces correlation to the entries of A_g and $\boldsymbol{b}_g$. As these entries are linear in the derivatives, they can be decomposed with respect to (9) into

$$A_g(\boldsymbol{x}) = A_\tau(\boldsymbol{x}) + A_\epsilon(\boldsymbol{x}) \quad \text{and} \quad \boldsymbol{b}_g(\boldsymbol{x}) = \boldsymbol{b}_\tau(\boldsymbol{x}) + \boldsymbol{b}_\epsilon(\boldsymbol{x}) \ . \tag{10}$$

In the EIV model, it is assumed that $A_\tau(\boldsymbol{x})\boldsymbol{p}(\boldsymbol{x}) = \boldsymbol{b}_\tau(\boldsymbol{x})$ holds exactly as opposed to (8) which may be violated by the errors. As discussed comprehensively by Van Huffel [10], total least squares (TLS) would be the unique (with probability one) maximum likelihood estimator of the parameters $\boldsymbol{p}(\boldsymbol{x})$ if the entries of the matrix $[A_g(\boldsymbol{x}), \boldsymbol{b}_g(\boldsymbol{x})]$ stemmed from a multivariate normal distribution with zero mean and covariance matrix $\sigma^2 \mathbb{1}$. If these entries were known to be uncorrelated with zero mean and equal variance, TLS would still be a strongly consistent estimator. But in the present case, mutual correlation is introduced by the overlapping FIR masks of derivative operators. The idea in equilibration is to derive from the covariance matrices of the vectors $\text{vec}([A_g(\boldsymbol{x}), \boldsymbol{b}_g(\boldsymbol{x})])$ (column-wise vectorization of the matrix $[A_g(\boldsymbol{x}), \boldsymbol{b}_g(\boldsymbol{x})]$) square equilibration matrices $W_L(\boldsymbol{x})$ and $W_R(\boldsymbol{x})$ to estimate $\hat{\boldsymbol{p}}(\boldsymbol{x})$ by TLS on the data $W_L(\boldsymbol{x})[A_g(\boldsymbol{x}), \boldsymbol{b}_g(\boldsymbol{x})]W_R^T(\boldsymbol{x})$ instead of $[A_g(\boldsymbol{x}), \boldsymbol{b}_g(\boldsymbol{x})]$. $W_R^T(\boldsymbol{x})\hat{\boldsymbol{p}}(\boldsymbol{x})$ is then taken as an estimate of the initial problem. Mühlich [11] derives properties of equilibration matrices from the perturbation theory of eigenvectors and presents an algorithm to compute these iteratively from the covariance matrices of the vectors $\text{vec}([A_g(\boldsymbol{x}), \boldsymbol{b}_g(\boldsymbol{x})])$. If the aperture function $\omega : P \times P \to \mathbb{R}_0^+$ depends, for all $\boldsymbol{x}, \boldsymbol{x}' \in P$, only on the difference $\boldsymbol{x}' - \boldsymbol{x}$, there exist an $m \in \mathbb{N}$ such that $\forall \boldsymbol{x} \in P : |U_\omega(\boldsymbol{x})| = m$ as well as a common covariance matrix $C \in \mathbb{R}^{m \times (k+1)}$ (k being the number of model parameters) such that

$$\forall \boldsymbol{x} \in P : \quad \text{cov}(\text{vec}([A_g(\boldsymbol{x}), \boldsymbol{b}_g(\boldsymbol{x})])) = \text{cov}(\text{vec}([A_\epsilon(\boldsymbol{x}), \boldsymbol{b}_\epsilon(\boldsymbol{x})])) = C \ . \tag{11}$$

The equilibration matrices $W_L \in \mathbb{R}^{m \times m}$ and $W_R \in \mathbb{R}^{(k+1) \times (k+1)}$ are in this case independent of $\boldsymbol{x}$. Equilibration in the context of motion model selection is discussed in detail in [12]. The effect of equilibration is illustrated in Figure 1. It can be seen that the unequilibrated data is highly correlated as well as that some correlation remains after equilibration.

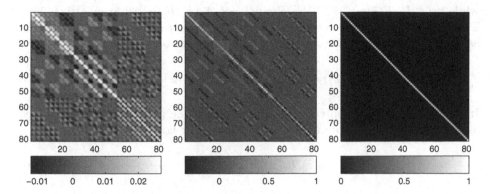

Fig. 1. LC ($k = 2$) local optical flow estimation from identical cuboidal $3 \times 3 \times 3$ motion neighborhoods ($m = 27$) is considered. Left: Identical covariance matrix $C \in \mathbb{R}^{81 \times 81}$ of the vectors $\text{vec}([A_g(\boldsymbol{x}), \boldsymbol{b}_g(\boldsymbol{x})])$, with structure owing to FIR masks. Middle: Covariance matrix of $\text{vec}(W_L[A_g(\boldsymbol{x}), \boldsymbol{b}_g(\boldsymbol{x})]W_R^T)$. Right: Unity matrix.

4 Residual Analysis

If the distribution of noise in the gray values is known, we propose to test regression residuals to be in accordance with the theoretically expected distribution. Given ETLS estimates $\hat{\boldsymbol{p}} : P \to \mathbb{R}^k$, the residuals are given by the mapping $\hat{\boldsymbol{r}} : P \to \mathbb{R}^m$ such that

$$\forall \boldsymbol{x} \in P: \quad \hat{\boldsymbol{r}}(\boldsymbol{x}) := W_L[A_g(\boldsymbol{x}), \boldsymbol{b}_g(\boldsymbol{x})]W_R^T \begin{pmatrix} \hat{\boldsymbol{p}}(\boldsymbol{x}) \\ -1 \end{pmatrix} . \tag{12}$$

In principle, the theoretical PDF of these residuals is determined by the joint PDF of the entries of $A_g(\boldsymbol{x})$ and $\boldsymbol{b}_g(\boldsymbol{x})$. The latter is obtained from the EIV model, the motion models, and the derivative operators. However, there is a direct influence to the residual PDF by the factor $[A_g(\boldsymbol{x}), \boldsymbol{b}_g(\boldsymbol{x})]$ as well as an indirect influence by the PDF of the estimates $\hat{\boldsymbol{p}}(\boldsymbol{x})$. In the following, we assume $\hat{\boldsymbol{p}}$ to be deterministic. Then, the residuals (12), expressed as

$$\forall \boldsymbol{x} \in P: \quad \hat{\boldsymbol{r}}(\boldsymbol{x}) = \underbrace{\left(\begin{pmatrix} \hat{\boldsymbol{p}}(\boldsymbol{x}) \\ -1 \end{pmatrix}^T W_R \otimes W_L \right)}_{=: \, R(\boldsymbol{x})} \text{vec}([A_g(\boldsymbol{x}), \boldsymbol{b}_g(\boldsymbol{x})]) , \tag{13}$$

are obtained from the deterministic linear mapping defined by the matrix $R(\boldsymbol{x})$, applied to the vector $\text{vec}([A_g(\boldsymbol{x}), \boldsymbol{b}_g(\boldsymbol{x})])$ of which the covariance matrix (11) is known. The covariance matrices of the residual vectors are therefore given by $C_r : P \to \mathbb{R}^{m \times m}$ such that $\forall \boldsymbol{x} \in P : C_r(\boldsymbol{x}) := \text{cov}(\hat{\boldsymbol{r}}(\boldsymbol{x})) = R(\boldsymbol{x})CR^T(\boldsymbol{x})$. From the Cholesky factorizations $L : P \to \mathbb{R}^{m \times m}$ such that $LL^T = C_r$ follows that $\hat{\boldsymbol{s}} := L^{-1}\hat{\boldsymbol{r}}$ is decorrelated i.e.,

$$\forall \boldsymbol{x} \in P: \quad \text{cov}(\hat{\boldsymbol{s}}(\boldsymbol{x})) = \mathbb{1}_m , \tag{14}$$

while $\forall x \in P : \mathbb{E}(\hat{s}(x)) = L^{-1}(x)R(x)\mathbb{E}(\text{vec}([A_g(x), b_g(x)]))$. From (10) follows $\mathbb{E}(\text{vec}([A_g(x), b_g(x)])) = \text{vec}([A_\tau(x), b_\tau(x)]) + \mathbb{E}(\text{vec}([A_\epsilon(x), b_\epsilon(x)]))$. Under the assumption that the entries of $[A_\epsilon(x), b_\epsilon(x)]$ have zero mean, it follows

$$\forall x \in P : \quad \mathbb{E}(\hat{s}(x)) = L^{-1}(x)W_L[A_\tau(x), b_\tau(x)]W_R^T \begin{pmatrix} \hat{p}(x) \\ -1 \end{pmatrix} \quad . \tag{15}$$

In practice, it depends on the appropriateness of the parametric model as well as on the empirical distribution of noise whether or not

$$[A_\tau(x), b_\tau(x)]W_R^T \begin{pmatrix} \hat{p}(x) \\ -1 \end{pmatrix} = 0 \tag{16}$$

holds, in which case it follows from (15) that

$$\mathbb{E}(\hat{s}(x)) = 0. \tag{17}$$

If, in addition, the noise in the gray values is i.i.d. according to a normal distribution with known variance then, it follows from (14) and (17) that the entries of the decorrelated residual vector $\hat{s}(x)$ from ETLS estimation form a set of independent standard normally distributed random variables. We therefore suggest to adaptively test this set of residuals, for each pixel $x \in P$, to be standard normally distributed. Deviations from the standard normal distribution are then taken as indications of inappropriateness of the motion model. We have therefor employed the Kolmogorov-Smirnov test, Pearson's χ^2 test, the Anderson-Darling test as well as the absolute difference of the vectors of the first 2,3,4 and 5 non-centered moments of the empirical and theoretical distribution.

5   Application and Results

In order to allow for motion estimation on real world video data or standard benchmark sequences such as the Yosemite sequence, the model selector has to be incorporated into a motion estimation framework that is capable of handling the aperture problem. If the model selector was examined separately on real data, the aperture problem as well as a possible incoherence of the true displacement and optical flow due to changes in illumination would distract from properties of the model selection process. Benchmark results from motion estimation frameworks on the other hand include effects from all components, be it confidence measures, motion segmentation or noise estimation techniques. Hence, in order to specifically test for properties of the model selector, we generated a variety of sequences from given two-dimensional displacement fields by warping of an initial frame. Gray value structure on multiple scales was introduced to this frame in order to avoid the aperture problem. Zero mean Gaussian noise was added to the sequences. In this special case, no framework is needed. A systematic study of the discrepancy between the true displacement field and optical flow estimates on this data can be trusted to indicate precisely the properties of the model selection process. Results from model selection are shown in Figure 2 for

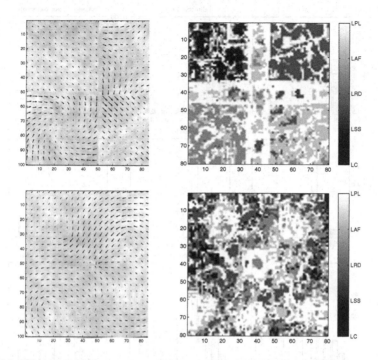

Fig. 2. Model selection from 11x11x3 motion neighborhoods of simulated sequences at 0.5% noise-to-signal amplitude ratio by comparison of 5 moments of the residual distribution. a) displacement field of the types sequence, b) according model selection, c) displacement field of the current sequence, d) according model selection.

a sequence featuring motion patterns of different parametric form (top) as well as for a simulated continuous current (bottom). From the different shading in Figure 2b, it can be seen that model selection is in accordance with the true displacement field. Motion patterns are identified correctly. The incidental choice of overly complex models is explained by the fact that a higher order model with the additional parameters correctly estimated as zero cannot be distinguished from the simpler model by means of residual analysis. The most complex model is correctly selected at motion discontinuities. Apart from the identification of motion patterns, an important application of model selection is to limit model complexity with respect to noise. While a complex model is appropriate at low noise levels model complexity has to be controlled with increasing noise in order to avoid over-fitting. Figure 3 shows the effect of model selection on the mean deviation of optical flow estimates from the true displacement field at 0.5%, 3% and 10% noise added to the continuous current sequence. The means were taken over the entire sequence. Amplitude and direction of the deviation were calculated together with the well-known angular error. Global choices of a single model (left part of each bar graph) are compared to adaptive model selection per pixel. In the latter case, errors from different (the selected) models are

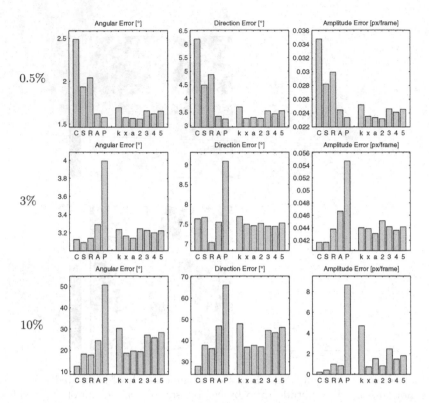

Fig. 3. Mean errors of optical flow estimation from 9x9x3 motion neighborhoods of a simulated continuous 2D current at different noise levels (top to bottom). Results for the models LC (C), LSS (S), LRD (R), LAF (A) and LPL (P), as well as for the adaptively selected models chosen by the KS test (k), the χ^2 test (x), the AD test (a) and the absolute difference of the vectors of the first 2,3,4 and 5 moments of the empirical and the theoretical distribution.

cumulated in the mean. Regardless which of the models LC (C), LSS (S), LRD (R), LAF (A) and LPL (P) is chosen globally, a situation exists in which the error is intolerably high compared to another model. This effect from global model assumptions causes a problem in applications with complex motion patterns and changing noise where a complex model, although needed to yield good estimates at low noise, performs weak at increasing noise levels. Considering model selection by Pearson's χ^2 test (x) or the Anderson-Darling test (a) which are the best performing model selectors, it can be seen from the top row of figure 3 that these adaptive estimators yield errors comparable to those obtained from the best global choices. The reason is that the residual-based model selector precisely excludes inappropriate models. At 3% and 10% noise, global model choices exist which are favorable to adaptive model selection. Nevertheless, the discrepancy is tolerable if the aim is to exclude the most complex models which perform poorly in this case. Results in model complexity control hence prove to be useful for applications where noise as well as the complexity of the displacement field vary. The slight limitation in model complexity control at high noise is due to the idealization of parameter estimates to be deterministic. However, this is not a principle drawback of residual analysis in motion model selection and effects are tolerable.

6 Conclusion and Perspectives

We have demonstrated that statistical testing of regression residuals is a viable approach to the model selection problem in motion estimation. The residual-based model selector is capable of precisely excluding inappropriate models. Its performance in model complexity control makes this model selector a particularly useful tool for applications where noise as well as the complexity of the displacement field vary. Slight limitations of the proposed method with tolerable effects are due to the idealization of equilibrated total least squares estimates to be deterministic. The incorporation of approximations to the distribution of TLS estimates is a promising starting point for future research.

References

1. Black, M.J., Jepson, A.: Estimating multiple independent motions in segmented images using parametric models with local deformations. In: IEEE Workshop on Motion of Non-Rigid and Articulated Objects, pp. 220–227. IEEE Computer Society Press, Los Alamitos (1994)
2. Gheissari, N., Bab-Hadiashar, A., Suter, D.: Parametric model-based motion segmentation using surface selection criterion. Computer Vision and Image Understanding 102, 214–226 (2006)
3. Akaike, H.: A new look at statistical model identification. IEEE Transactions on Automatic Control 19, 716–723 (1974)
4. Schwarz, G.: Estimating the dimension of a model. Annals of Statistics 6(461), 464 (1978)
5. Wechsler, H., Duric, Z., Li, F.Y., Cherkassky, V.: Motion estimation using statistical learning theory. PAMI 26(4), 466–478 (2004)
6. Cootes, T.F., Thacker, N., Taylor, C.J.: Automatic model selection by modelling the distribution of residuals. In: Heyden, A., Sparr, G., Nielsen, M., Johansen, P. (eds.) ECCV 2002. LNCS, vol. 2353, pp. 621–635. Springer, Heidelberg (2002)
7. Jähne, B.: Digital Image Processing. In: Concepts. Algorithms and Scientific Applications, vol. 6, Springer, Berlin (2005)
8. Lucas, B., Kanade, T.: An iterative image registration technique with an application to stereo vision. In: DARPA Image Understanding Workshop, pp. 121–130 (1981)
9. Scharr, H.: Optimale Operatoren in der Digitalen Bildverarbeitung. PhD thesis, University of Heidelberg, Heidelberg, Germany (2000)
10. Van Huffel, S., Vandewalle, J.: The Total Least Squares Problem: Computational Aspects and Analysis. SIAM, Philadelphia (1991)
11. Mühlich, M.: Estimation in Projective Spaces and Application in Computer Vision. PhD thesis, Johann Wolfgang Goethe Universität Frankfurt am Main (2005)
12. Andres, B.: Model selection in optical flow-based motion estimation by means of residual analysis. Diploma thesis, University of Heidelberg (2007)

Calibration of a Multi-camera Rig from Non-overlapping Views

Sandro Esquivel, Felix Woelk, and Reinhard Koch

Christian-Albrechts-University, 24118 Kiel, Germany

Abstract. A simple, stable and generic approach for estimation of relative positions and orientations of multiple rigidly coupled cameras is presented in this paper. The algorithm does not impose constraints on the field of view of the cameras and works even in the extreme case when the sequences from the different cameras are totally disjoint (i.e. when no part of the scene is captured by more than one camera). The influence of the rig motion on the existence of a unique solution is investigated and degenerate rig motions are identified. Each camera captures an individual sequence which is afterwards processed by a structure and motion (SAM) algorithm resulting in positions and orientations for each camera. The unknown relative transformations between the rigidly coupled cameras are estimated utilizing the rigidity constraint of the rig.

1 Introduction

Rigidly coupled cameras with non overlapping views appear in many scenarios: In the automotive industry f.e. rear view cameras and blind spot cameras gain popularity, sewer inspection systems equipped with two antipodal cameras are commercial available and also in surveillance applications multiple non-overlapping cameras are used. In many of these situations the relative position of these cameras is of interest.

General methods estimating these rig parameters assume that the cameras have overlapping views such that points lying in these views can be used to register the positions of the cameras with each other [1,2]. This paper suggests an approach for rig parameters estimation from non-overlapping views using sequences of time-synchronous poses of each camera. Such poses can be obtained from SAM algorithms on synchronously captured image sequences. The presented approach works in three stages:

Internal camera calibration: First, the internal calibration of each camera on the rig is computed using standard techniques [4]. The internal camera calibration consists of the focal length, principal point, skew and lens distortion parameters.

Pose estimation: Second, the external pose of each camera in the rig is computed for each frame in arbitrary coordinate systems using SAM techniques [5,1]. Note that without further knowledge the geometry can only be reconstructed up to scale and hence the coordinate systems of the reconstructions of the cameras are related by a similarity transform.

F.A. Hamprecht, C. Schnörr, and B. Jähne (Eds.): DAGM 2007, LNCS 4713, pp. 82–91, 2007.

Rig calibration: The scale of each coordinate system and the internal positions and orientations of the rigidly coupled cameras are estimated using constraints between poses resulting from the previous stage. Nonlinear optimization techniques can be used for refinement.

The paper is organized as follows: After reviewing previous work, the theoretic foundation of the algorithm is explained. Degenerate cases are identified and solutions for these cases are suggested. Finally experiments with synthetic and real data are presented.

2   Previous Work

Sequence reconstruction algorithms profit from rigidly coupled cameras. Frahm e.a. proposed a method for stabilizing 3D scene reconstruction by utilizing images of a moving rig [3]. Broader views of the scene could be reconstructed by using a multi-camera system. In order to perform such a task one has to determine the relative transformations between the cameras of the rig in addition to the intrinsic parameters of each camera (i.e. focal length and principal point). There are many approaches registering the poses of a set of cameras with each other. Most of these approaches, such as metric calibration of a stereo-rig [2], rely on an overlapping field of view. An approach to align non-overlapping image sequences has been made by Caspi and Irani [6] for the case of multi-camera systems sharing the same projection center, but not for general multi camera system. The task at hand is closely related to the field of hand-eye-estimation such as [7] which faces a similar problem: The (fixed) relation between poses measured in different coordinate frames, e.g. between a sensor mounted onto a robot's hand and the hand itself must be estimated. In a similar manner a multi-camera system with cameras fixed in a rig can be interpreted as a hand-eye system where a motion sensor is lacking but pose information can be retrieved from multiple image sequences.

3   Theoretical Background

In the following, superscripts are used to identify a specific time and subscripts are used to identify a specific camera in the rig. For example C_i^κ denotes the center of projection of camera i at time κ.

3.1   Rigid Transformations

The change between two Cartesian reference frames is described by a *similarity transformation*. Each similarity transformation is of the form

$$T = \begin{pmatrix} \lambda R & C \\ 0^T & 1 \end{pmatrix},\tag{1}$$

where $\lambda \in \mathbb{R}$ accounts for the different scales of coordinate systems, $R \in \mathbb{R}^{3\times3}$ is an orthogonal rotation matrix describing the relative orientation and $C \in \mathbb{R}^3$

is the translation between the two reference frames. When the scale λ is equal to 1, T is also called *Euclidean transformation*. Using projective space, the change of reference frame of a projective point vector can be achieved by simple matrix vector multiplication $X^{target} = TX^{source}$. The concatenation of two subsequent changes of reference frames T_1 and T_2 can be computed by a simple matrix multiplication

$$T = T_2 T_1. \tag{2}$$

3.2 Reference Frames and Transformations

The reconstructions from each individual camera are usually given in separate reference frames. The different reference frames are defined next.

Camera Reference Frames: We assume that each reconstruction is described in the coordinate system whose origin and orientation matches the position and orientation of the first camera and whose scale is given such that the baseline between the first two cameras equals 1 as our SAM algorithm delivers. The pose of each camera i at each time κ is described in the reference frame of the reconstruction by its orientation R_i^{κ} and position C_i^{κ}. Obviously the initial pose of each camera is then given by $R_i^0 = I$ and $C_i = (0\ 0\ 0)^T$. These reference frames are denoted as *camera* coordinate system. Each physical camera in the rig has an associated camera reference frame.

Local Reference Frames: Obviously the choice of the first camera for the definition of the camera reference frame is somewhat arbitrary. Any other time $\kappa \neq 0$ could be chosen for the definition of position and orientation of reference frame resulting in the *local* coordinate system. The Euclidean transformation T_i^{κ} relating the camera reference frame with the i-th local reference frame is given by

$$T_i^{\kappa} = \begin{pmatrix} R_i^{\kappa} & C_i'^{\kappa} \\ 0^T & 1 \end{pmatrix}. \tag{3}$$

A local reference frame can be defined for each frame from each sequence resulting in an overall of $m = KN$ reference frames. Here N denotes the number of cameras and K denotes the number of frames in each sequence.

Global Reference Frame: Working with multiple reference frames easily becomes confusing and error-prone. Hence without the loss of generality a dedicated *master camera* is chosen and the associated reference frame is chosen as the *global* coordinate system. The master camera is identified with the subscript index $i = 0$. All other cameras are denoted as *slave* cameras.

3.3 Relations Between Reference Frames

The transformation between the global reference frame and each local reference frame of the slave camera i at time κ can be computed in two alternate

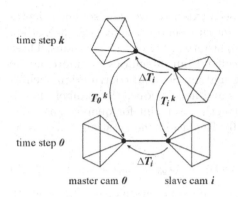

time step k

ΔT_i

$T_0{}^k$ $T_i{}^k$

time step 0

ΔT_i

master cam 0 slave cam i

Fig. 1. Relations between cameras in the rig

ways. Either by first transforming to the local reference frame of the master camera at time κ and afterward using the unknown similarity transforming ΔT_i to get to the local reference frame of the slave camera i at time κ

$$T_0^\kappa \Delta T_i, \qquad (4)$$

or alternatively, by first changing into the camera reference frame ΔT_i and afterward using the Euclidean transform T_i^κ to get to the destination

$$\Delta T_i T_i^\kappa. \qquad (5)$$

This relation is illustrated in figure 1.

4   Estimation of the Rig Parameters from Poses

Equations (4) and (5) must result in the same transformation and hence

$$T_0^\kappa \Delta T_i = \Delta T_i T_i^\kappa \qquad (6)$$

must hold for each time $\kappa = 1, \ldots, K$ and each slave camera $i = 1, \ldots, N$. Equation (6) can be decomposed into one constraint regarding only orientations

$$R_0^\kappa \Delta R_i = \Delta R_i R_i^\kappa \qquad (7)$$

and one constraint linking both orientations and positions

$$R_0^\kappa \Delta C_i + C_0^\kappa = \Delta \lambda_i \Delta R_i C_i^\kappa + \Delta C_i. \qquad (8)$$

Note that the scale $\Delta \lambda_i$ has no influence on (7) because it appears on both sides. Except from the scale factor, this result equals the well-known relation between the different coordinate frames in the hand-eye calibration problem [7], where the master camera defines the sensor frame and the slave camera defines the hand frame.

4.1   General Motion

When the motion of the rig is general, i.e. when it rotates and translates, a two step approach is feasible. First the orientation is recovered using (7) and afterward it is utilized for the recovery of position and scale using equation (8).

Recovery of Orientation: There has been extensive work on solving orientation equations such as (7). Early solutions [8] represent rotations by 3×3-rotation matrices, resp. 9-vectors, resulting in straight forward linear formulations. These approaches tend to be error-prone and suffer from difficulties in enforcing the orthogonality constraint on the resulting matrix. Seminal contribution such as [9] represent rotations by unit quaternions and hence reduce the number of variables from 9 to 4. Further on, the unit length constraint for quaternions is far simpler to enforce than orthogonality [10]. Replacing the rotation matrices by quaternions q in (7) we obtain

$$q_0^\kappa \cdot \Delta q_i = \Delta q_i \cdot q_i^\kappa, \quad \text{or equivalently} \quad (T_{q_0^\kappa} - T_{q_i^\kappa}^*)\Delta q_i = 0, \qquad (9)$$

where T_q, T_q^* define left and right multiplication with quaternion $q = (w, x, y, z)^T$ i.e., (see [11])

$$T_q = \begin{pmatrix} w & -x & -y & -z \\ x & w & -z & y \\ y & z & w & -x \\ z & -y & x & w \end{pmatrix}, \quad T_q^* = \begin{pmatrix} w & -x & -y & -z \\ x & w & z & -y \\ y & -z & w & x \\ z & y & -x & w \end{pmatrix}. \qquad (10)$$

Hence we derive the following linear system of equations with unknowns $\Delta q_i = (\Delta w_i, \Delta x_i, \Delta y_i, \Delta z_i)^T$, fulfilling $|\Delta q_i| = 1$,

$$\underbrace{\begin{pmatrix} w_0^\kappa - w_i^\kappa & -x_0^\kappa + x_i^\kappa & -y_0^\kappa + y_i^\kappa & -z_0^\kappa + z_i^\kappa \\ x_0^\kappa - x_i^\kappa & w_0^\kappa - w_i^\kappa & -z_0^\kappa - z_i^\kappa & y_0^\kappa + y_i^\kappa \\ y_0^\kappa - y_i^\kappa & z_0^\kappa + z_i^\kappa & w_0^\kappa - w_i^\kappa & -x_0^\kappa - x_i^\kappa \\ z_0^\kappa - z_i^\kappa & -y_0^\kappa - y_i^\kappa & x_0^\kappa + x_i^\kappa & w_0^\kappa - w_i^\kappa \end{pmatrix}}_{A_i^\kappa} \begin{pmatrix} \Delta w_i \\ \Delta x_i \\ \Delta y_i \\ \Delta z_i \end{pmatrix} = \begin{pmatrix} 0 \\ 0 \\ 0 \\ 0 \end{pmatrix}, \qquad (11)$$

at each time step $\kappa = 1, \ldots, K$. Apparently one pair of corresponding poses for each camera suffices for the estimation of the internal rotation parameters when the rig motion includes sufficient orientation change. When the rig is purely translating, equation (11) degenerates and can no longer be solved. A detailed investigation of the degenerate case of purely translating motion is presented in section 4.2. Computation of the rotation matrices from unit quaternions can be found in [11]. The quaternion constraint can be explicitly modelled by using the Lagrangian multiplier as described in [7].

Recovery of Position and Scale: Once an estimate for the internal rotation ΔR_i of slave camera i has been found, the internal position ΔC_i and scale $\Delta \lambda_i$ can be found by solving the linear system (8), obtaining the linear system

$$\underbrace{\begin{pmatrix} I - R_0^\kappa & \Delta R_i C_i^\kappa \end{pmatrix}}_{B_i^\kappa} \begin{pmatrix} \Delta C_i \\ \Delta \lambda_i \end{pmatrix} = C_o^\kappa. \qquad (12)$$

The system (12) consists of 3 equations per pose correspondence and 4 unknowns and hence at least 2 corresponding pose pairs for each slave camera are necessary for a unique solution.

4.2   Pure Translation

When the rig motion is purely translational, the relative orientations q_0^κ and q_i^κ in (11) are both given by the quaternion representing zero rotation $(1, 0, 0, 0)^T$ and the matrix A_i^κ becomes zero. Even when the rotation of the rig is very small, A_i^κ is close to zero and the system (11) becomes ill-conditioned[1]. Fortunately this situation can easily be detected simply by looking at the orientations R_i^κ. The estimation of the C_i^κ is not possible in this case, however internal orientation and scale can still be estimated. Assuming that the local rotations R_i^κ are each equal to I and considering only the directions $c_i^\kappa = \frac{C_i^\kappa}{\|C_i^\kappa\|}$, equation (8) becomes

$$\Delta R_i c_i^\kappa = c_0^\kappa, \tag{13}$$

which can be solved linearly in closed form using the quaternion representation [10]. Because a rotation does not change the length of a vector, the scale can be estimated without knowledge about ΔR_i. Mean and variance of the scale are computed using poses from different times κ:

$$\Delta \lambda_i^\kappa = \frac{|C_0^\kappa|}{|\Delta R_i C_i^\kappa|} = \frac{|C_0^\kappa|}{|C_i^\kappa|}, \quad \Delta \lambda_i = \sum_n^N \frac{\Delta \lambda_i^n}{N}, \quad \sigma_{\lambda_i}^2 = \sum_n^N \frac{(\Delta \lambda_i^n - \Delta \lambda_i)^2}{N}. \tag{14}$$

4.3   Nonlinear Refinement

It is obvious that errors in the estimation of the internal rotation will inflict the estimation of the internal translation and scale. Once an estimate for the rig parameters has been found via the LLS approach as described in section 4.1, nonlinear refinement can be used to simultaneously estimate internal orientation, position and scale. The error functional

$$f(\Delta q_i, \Delta C_i, \Delta \lambda_i) = \sum_{\kappa=1}^{K} |A_i^\kappa \Delta q_i|^2 + |B_i^\kappa \left(\begin{matrix} \Delta C_i \\ \Delta \lambda_i \end{matrix} \right) - C_0^\kappa|^2 \tag{15}$$

is minimized using a Levenberg-Marquardt method.

4.4   MAP Refinement

Experiments on real image data revealed that the error functional in (15) is very sensitive to noise. However the situation improved when the scale was held fixed at an approximate value during estimation. To circumvent this problem, the error functional from (15) is augmented by a maximum a posteriori (MAP) term for the scale resulting in

$$f(\Delta q_i, \Delta C_i, \Delta \lambda_i) = \sum_{\kappa=1}^{K} |A_i^\kappa \Delta q_i|^2 + |B_i^\kappa \left(\begin{matrix} \Delta C_i \\ \Delta \lambda_i \end{matrix} \right) - C_0^\kappa|^2 + \frac{(\Delta \lambda_i - \lambda_i)^2}{\sigma_{\lambda_i}^2},$$

with the prior guess of the scale λ_i and uncertainty $\sigma_{\lambda_i}^2$ computed using (14).

---

[1] This is also visible in (12) where B_i^κ grows ill-conditioned when the rotation R_0^κ observed by the master camera is close to I.

5 Experiments

Experiments on synthetic pose data precede experiments on synthetic image data and finally experiments on real image sequences are presented.

5.1 Synthetic Pose Data

Synthetic pose data corrupted with normal distributed error is used for the tests. It is generated as follows: First N random rig parameters ΔR_i, ΔC_i, $\Delta \lambda_i$ and K random master poses R_0^κ, C_0^κ are generated. Afterwards the associated slave poses are computed by applying the rig parameter to the master pose and rotating the resulting ground truth slave pose by ε degrees around a randomly chosen axis to simulate errors resulting from the pose estimation process.

Linear Model Comparison: To compare both linear algorithms (i.e. the purely translational model and the general motion model) the errors are computed under a variety of different conditions, namely different orientations and different input error accuracies. Figure 2 compares the errors of both models and illustrates the equal error boundary for both algorithms.

Sensitivity to Input Pose Errors: To analyze the dependency of the estimation results on noise of the input data, tests on a large number of randomly generated input poses are performed. Figure 3 shows the average resulting orientation error of the estimated internal orientations and translations dependent on the input error ε for the linear general motion approach and for the nonlinear optimization. Four input pose pairs were used for each test. The calibration error grows approximately linearly with the input pose error ε.

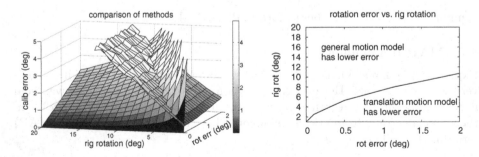

Fig. 2. Comparison of the two linear models. (a): Errors of both models on dependency of rotation and input orientation accuracy. (b): Equal error boundary for general motion model and rotation only model. In conditions above the equal error boundary, the general motion model yields more accurate results than the purely translational model.

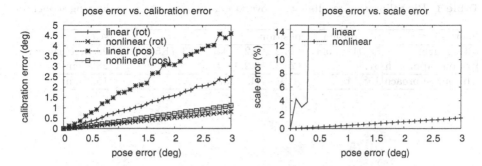

Fig. 3. Sensitivity of the algorithm to errors in the input poses. The resulting rotation and translation orientation error (a), and scale error (b) are shown vs. input pose orientation error for linear solution and the nonlinear refinement.

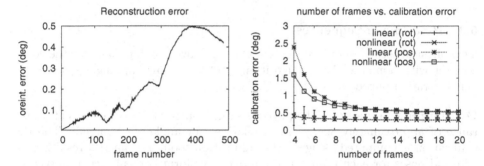

Fig. 4. (a) Orientation error of SAM algorithm on synthetic image sequence. See text for details. (b) Calibration error (orientation and translation) vs. number of randomly selected input poses on synthetically rendered images. The average error over 1000 tries is plotted.

5.2 Synthetic Image Sequences

A synthetic rig consisting of two cameras moves in a synthetic scene resulting in two sequences of synthetically generated images consisting of 500 frames each. The SAM results are transformed in a global coordinate system such that the rig constraints strictly hold on the first two frames. Note that the pose estimates from the SAM algorithm have a rotation error of up to 0.4 degree (figure 4(a)). $\Delta R_i^\kappa = R_i^\kappa (R_0^\kappa)^T$ is estimated from the two orientations for each frame and the error with the respect to ground truth is plotted for each frame in figure 4(a).

The dependency of the calibration error on the number of input poses (i.e. frames) is shown in figure 4(b) for the linear estimation methods with general motion model and for the nonlinear estimation. The input poses again derive from the SAM results on the synthetic image sequences. It can be seen that the estimation results do not improve significantly for $K \geq 10$.

Table 1. Rig calibration results for (a) overlapping and (b) non-overlapping sequence

method	orientation	position	scale
(a) Bouget	$56.94° \pm 0.54°$	$(25.2 \pm 0.2, -3.9 \pm 0.3, 11.5 \pm 0.06)$	$28\text{cm} \pm 0.66\text{cm}$
(a) our approach	$57.56°$	$(25.8, -3.2, 11.4)$	28.37cm
(b) our approach	$158.14°$	$(0.9, -7.4, -13.3)$	15.29cm

Fig. 5. Photo of real rig (a) and 3D model of the rig calibration estimate (b)

5.3 Real Image Sequences

Two physical setups were investigated: One with overlapping views for the comparison with a marker based algorithm, and a non-overlapping sequence for demonstration purposes.

Overlapping Sequence: The physical setup consists of two cameras at a distance of approximately 30cm with a relative yaw angle of about 60°. The rig calibration is computed using (i) the calibration toolbox from [12] resulting in external poses for each frame. The relative transform is computed robustly as the average over 24 frames. Additionally the rig calibration is estimated (ii) using the suggested MAP refinement algorithm. To enhance stability a RANSAC algorithm is used in combination with our approach. The orientation difference between the two results (i) and (ii) was 0.62°, the direction difference of the two resulting translation vectors was 1.52°, and the translation length error was about 1.33 percent (see table 1(a)). The rig calibration result is in the same order of magnitude as the result from the marker based approach.

Non-overlapping Sequence: For the non-overlapping sequence the cameras were rotated approx. about 160° with respect to each other and set up at with a distance of about 15cm. Figure 5 shows a photo of the rig and a 3D model with the reconstructed rig parameters. The rig internal translation is roughly along the optical axis such that the cameras look in opposite directions. The rig was rotated around its center and translated slightly parallel to the image planes such that the sequences do not overlap. The estimated internal rig rotation was 158.14° around axis $(0.4, 0.74, 0.51)^T$, and the internal translation direction was estimated to be $(0.06, -0.48, -0.87)^T$ with length 15.29cm (see table 1(b)). The resulting calibration meets the expectation by qualitative evaluation. Future work will include tests on non-overlapping sequences with ground truth data available.

6 Conclusions

A novel approach for the estimation of rig parameters using non-overlapping sequences was introduced. Two nonlinear refinement algorithms for the rig parameters have been proposed and tested on synthetic poses and on synthetic and real image sequences. It has been shown that the achievable accuracy resides in the same order of magnitude as marker based approaches achieve. In addition, the calibration can also be achieved in a non-overlapping setup where no marker calibration is possible. Of course the accuracy is dependent on the results of the SAM algorithm.

Future Work. Future work could investigate the benefit of direct integration of the calibration process into the SAM algorithm. Also other methods circumventing the dependency of the calibration on SAM results should be found and investigated. Because we do not depend on visual image information, poses received from sensor data can also be utilized for camera alignment.

References

1. Hartley, R., Zisserman, A.: Multiple View Geometry in Computer Vision. Cambridge University Press, Cambridge (2000)
2. Zisserman, A., et al.: Metric Calibration of a Stereo Rig. In: Proc. WRVS (1995)
3. Frahm, J.M., et al.: Pose Estimation for Multi-Camera Systems. In: Rasmussen, C.E., Bülthoff, H.H., Schölkopf, B., Giese, M.A. (eds.) Pattern Recognition. LNCS, vol. 3175, Springer, Heidelberg (2004)
4. Tsai, R.Y.: A Versatile Camera Calibration Technique for High-Accuracy 3D Machine Vision Metrology Using Off-the-Shelf TV Cameras and Lenses. IEEE Jour. RA 3(4), 323–344 (1987)
5. Pollefeys, M., et al.: Visual Modeling with a Hand-Held Camera. IJCV 59(3), 207–232 (2004)
6. Caspi, Y., Irani, M.: Alignment of Non-Overlapping Sequences. In: Proc. ICCV (2001)
7. Horaud, R.P., Dornaika, F.: Hand-Eye Calibration. IJRR 14(3), 195–210 (1995)
8. Shiu, Y.C., Ahmad, S.: Calibration of Wrist Mounted Robotic Sensors by Solving Homogeneous Transform Equations of the Form $AX = XB$. IEEE Jour. RA 5(1), 16–29 (1989)
9. Chou, J.C.K., Kamel, M.: Finding the Position and Orientation of a Sensor in a Robot Manipulator Using Quaternions. IJRR 10(3), 240–254 (1991)
10. Horn, B.K.P.: Closed-Form Solution of Absolute Orientation Using Unit Quaternions. J. Opt. Soc. Am. A 4(4), 629 (1987)
11. Foerstner, W., Wrobel, B.: Mathematical Concepts in Photogrammetry. In: McGlone, J.C. (ed.) Manual of Photogrammetry, 5th edn. ASPRS, pp. 47–49 (2004)
12. Bouguet, J.Y.: Camera Calibration Toolbox for Matlab, http://www.vision.caltech.edu/bouguetj/calib_doc/index.html

Fluid Flow Estimation Through Integration of Physical Flow Configurations

Christoph S. Garbe*

IWR, University of Heidelberg
`Christoph.Garbe@iwr.uni-heidelberg.de`

Abstract. The measurement of fluid flows is an emerging field for optical flow computation. In a number of such applications, a tracer is visualized with modern digital cameras. Due to the projective nature of the imaging process, the tracer is integrated across a velocity profile. In this contribution, a novel technique is presented that explicitly models brightness changes due to this integration. Only through this modeling is an accurate estimation of the flow velocities feasible. Apart from an accurate measurement of the fluid flow, also the underlying velocity profile can be reconstructed. Applications from shear flow, microfluidics and a biological applications are presented.

1 Introduction

Recently, modern techniques of motion estimation have made their arrival in the field of fluid dynamic measurements. Here, the main emphasis has been on regularizing the flow field, either by div-curl regularization [1] or by modeling the flow field based on physical constraints [2,3].

Apart from regularizing the flow field, brightness changes play an important role in a number of fluid dynamic applications. Often, due to transport phenomena the density of tracers change. The same holds true for temperature fields in the case of thermographic visualizations. An accurate modeling of these intensity changes based on the transport phenomena is fundamental to achieving accurate flow estimates. Moreover, apart from the flow field, additional information can be extracted from estimating parameters of brightness change models. These can be the air-water net heat flux from infrared image sequences of the air-water interface or chemical reactions from satellite remote sensing. These are important parameters in their own right.

For flow visualization, scalar quantities such as tracer particles or dyes are added to the flow. Also, heat can be used to visualize interfacial fluid flow. These scalars are visualized with digital or thermographic cameras, respectively. Due to the projective nature of the imaging process, the scalar concentration is integrated along the line of sight of the imaging optics. Depending on the flow configuration and the imaging set-up, frequently an integration across velocity

---

* The author acknowledges financial support by the DFG within the priority programs 1114 and 1147.

F.A. Hamprecht, C. Schnörr, and B. Jähne (Eds.): DAGM 2007, LNCS 4713, pp. 92–101, 2007.
© Springer-Verlag Berlin Heidelberg 2007

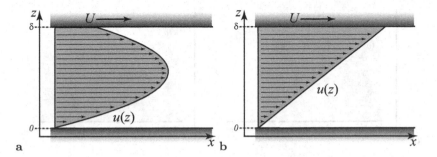

Fig. 1. Flow between parallel plates. The bottom plate is stationary, the upper one moving to the right at the velocity U. In **a** an additional pressure gradient $dp/dx < 0$ is driving the fluid, in **b** Plane Couette flow is shown ($dp/dx = 0$).

profiles has to be performed. In the case of parabolic flow profiles this process is also known as Taylor dispersion [4]. The visualized structures appear to diffuse anisotropically due to the integration. Very often, this unwanted effect cannot be circumvented experimentally. In this contribution, general motion models will be presented that explicitly model the projective process across flow profiles of different orders. This makes it feasible to accurately estimate the velocity and reconstruct the three dimensional flow profile at the same time.

Based on the novel motion models, the model parameters are estimated in a local extended structure tensor framework. If physically based regularization is of interest to the application, the presented framework can readily be incorporated into variational frameworks. However, this is not the topic of this contribution. The novel framework will be applied to shear flow configurations, microfluidics and biological applications.

2   Flow Profiles

2.1   Plane Couette Flow

The equation of motion for a flow of uniform density ρ is given by the Navier-Stokes equation for an incompressible fluid [5]:

$$\frac{d\boldsymbol{u}}{dt} = \boldsymbol{g} - \frac{1}{\rho}\nabla p + \frac{\mu}{\rho}\nabla^2 \boldsymbol{u} = -\frac{1}{\rho}\nabla p_d + \nu\nabla^2 \boldsymbol{u}, \tag{1}$$

where μ is the viscosity and $\nu = \mu/\rho$ is the kinematic viscosity. $\boldsymbol{g}$ is the acceleration of gravity and ∇p is a pressure gradient incident on the fluid. $\boldsymbol{u}$ is the fluid velocity we are interested in. The dynamic pressure is given by $p_d = p - p_s$ and $\boldsymbol{g} = 1/\rho \cdot \nabla p_s$ results from the hydrostatic pressure for a fluid at rest.

Such a flow is generally driven by a combination of an externally imposed pressure gradient and the motion of the upper plate at uniform velocity U, as

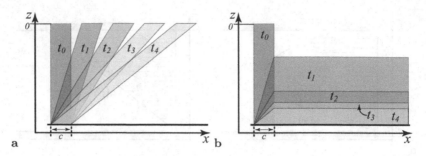

Fig. 2. Sketch of a marker in plane Couette Flow during time steps $t_1 - t_4$ in **a**. The marker is written at time t_0. It is sheared due to the flow. Shown in **b** is the depth integration of the marker, as visualized with the camera.

shown in Figure 1. The two plates are separated by the distance δ. Applying the appropriate boundary conditions [5] this results in the equation

$$u(z) = \frac{z \cdot U}{\delta} - \frac{z}{2\mu} \frac{dp}{dx} (\delta - z).$$ (2)

In the case of plane Couette flow, illustrated in Figure 1b, the flow is driven by the motion of the upper plate alone, without any externally imposed pressure gradient. For this case, Equations (2) reduces to

$$u(z) = \frac{z \cdot U}{\delta}$$ (3)

Plane Couette flow is a very good approximation for a number of shear driven flows. It can be used to describe the velocity structure at the wind driven sheared interface between atmosphere and ocean, particularly in the event of a surfactant covered interface. This is due to the fact that surfactants suppress waves and can be thought of as a rigid interface.

For a number of scientific and industrial applications, it is of interest to accurately measure the flow and velocity profile of the plane Couette flow. This is a straightforward task when the flow is accessible from the side (along the y-axis in Figure 1). In this case the velocity can be measured at a range between the two plates and the gradient with respect to z computed.

Very often, it is not possible to measure the fluid flow in this fashion, since the flow is not accessible from the side. This can either be due to the minute separation of the plates in microfluidic applications or because a very small boundary layer is modulated by relatively high waves at the air-water interface.

The velocity profile in plane Couette flow is given by Equation (3). This leads to the time dependence $x = \frac{z}{\delta} U \cdot t = \frac{z}{\mu} \tau \cdot t$ of the position of a marker attached to the flow at $t = t_0 = 0$. Here the viscous shear τ is given by $\tau = \mu / \delta U$.

It shall be assumed that the fluid elements are marked at time $t_0 = 0$ with an appropriate technique. For microfluidic applications, such a technique relies on the activation of caged dyes with a XeF Excimer laser. At the air-water interface,

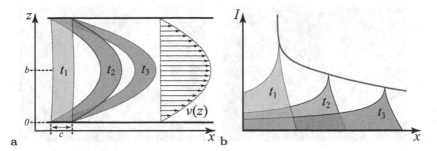

Fig. 3. A sketch of the intensity profile of the dye for a Poiseuille flow at three times t_1-t_3 is shown in **a** together with the velocity profile $v(z)$. The projection of these profiles onto one plate as seen by the camera is shown in **b**.

water parcels are heated up with ca CO_2 laser and visualize with an infrared camera. Without taking the Lambert-Beer law into consideration and thus no attenuation with depth, the marker highlights a homogeneous three dimensional structure inside the viscous boundary layer. A sketch of such a structure is presented in Figure 2a.

Once the structure is written at time t_0, it is sheared due to the velocity profile as indicated in the same figure in successive time steps $t_1 - t_4$. In the imaging process the dimension of depth z is lost through integration. The projection of intensities I onto the surface at $z = \delta$ is given by

$$I(x,t) = \int_{\frac{\delta \cdot (x-c)}{U \cdot t}}^{\frac{\delta \cdot x}{U \cdot t}} 1 \, dz = \frac{x \cdot \delta}{t \cdot U} - \frac{(x-c) \cdot \delta}{t \cdot U} = \frac{c \cdot \delta}{t \cdot U} = \frac{\mu \cdot c}{t \cdot \tau} \tag{4}$$

Here c denotes the width of the area marked, as can be seen in Figure 2.

Differentiating Equation (4) with respect to time leads to

$$\frac{dI}{dt} = \frac{d}{dt}\left(\frac{c \cdot \delta}{t \cdot U}\right) = -\frac{1}{t}I. \tag{5}$$

Estimating the velocity of the intensity structures subject to a plane Couette type shear flow with a linear velocity gradient can thus be computed by solving the differential equation $dI/dt = -(t)^{-1}I$ which can be written in an extension of the well known brightness change constraint equation (BCCE) [6] as

$$\frac{dI}{dt} = u_1 \frac{\partial I}{\partial x} + u_2 \frac{\partial I}{\partial y} + \frac{\partial I}{\partial t} = -\frac{1}{t}I. \tag{6}$$

Rewriting this equation in vector notation leads to

$$\frac{dI}{dt} = d^\top \cdot p = \left[\frac{1}{t}I \ \frac{\partial I}{\partial x} \ \frac{\partial I}{\partial y} \ \frac{\partial I}{\partial t}\right] \cdot \left[1 \ u_1 \ u_2 \ 1\right]^\top = 0 \ . \tag{7}$$

This equation can be thought of as the motion equation of density structures visualized through integration across a plane Couette type flow.

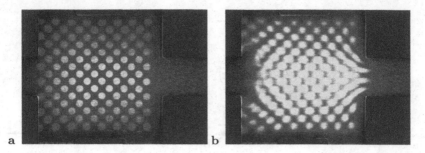

Fig. 4. In **a** and **b** two frames of a microfluidic image sequence are shown. The implication of Taylor dispersion can be clearly observed. Structures seem to diffuse in the direction of fluid flow [7].

2.2   Plane Poiseuille Flow

In Poiseuille flow, the configuration is similar to that of Couette flow. Once more, a fluid is bounded by two infinite plates separated by a distance $\delta = 2 \cdot b$. However, for Poiseuille flow both plates are stationary ($U_\delta = U_0 = U = 0$) and the flow is driven only by a pressure difference dp/dx. In this configuration, Equation (2) reduces to

$$u(z) = -\frac{z}{2\mu}\frac{dp}{dx}(\delta - z) = -\frac{z}{\mu}\frac{dp}{dx}\left(b - \frac{z}{2}\right) = \frac{a}{2}z^2 - a \cdot b \cdot z \quad \text{with} \quad a = \frac{1}{\mu}\frac{dp}{dx}. \quad (8)$$

This type of flow and the associated quantities are visualized in the sketch of Figure 3 **a**.

Similar to plane Couette flow as presented in Section 2.1, plane Poiseuille flow has a broad range of applications, especially in microfluidics. In these types of applications it is important to measure the velocity of fluid parcels in between parallel plates. However, due to the boundary conditions of the microfluidic devices, it is not possible to visualize the cross section of the flow. A marker such as a caged dye is introduced into the fluid and a pattern is written to the fluid at time $t = 0$. In later times, this structure is sheared by the parabolic velocity profile developed by the Poiseuille flow. The 2D cut of this process is shown for three time steps t_1-t_3 in Figure 3a. Through this projection, it appears as though the structure written to the fluid is smeared in the direction of the fluid flow over time. This process which might appear similarly to anisotropic diffusion, is also known as Taylor dispersion [8]. An image of this type of process can be seen in Figure 4.

The marker is visualized through one of the plates, leading to an integration of the dye with respect to depth z. This results in

$$I = \int_{b\pm\sqrt{b^2 + \frac{2x}{at}}}^{b\pm\sqrt{b^2 + \frac{2(x+c)}{at}}} 1 dz = \sqrt{b^2 + \frac{2 \cdot (c+x)}{a \cdot t}} - \sqrt{b^2 + \frac{2 \cdot x}{a \cdot t}}. \quad (9)$$

The projected intensity structure is given by Equation (9). This structure can be developed in a Taylor series around $t = 0$. This results in

$$I = \sqrt{\frac{2}{t}} \left(\sqrt{\frac{c+x}{a}} - \sqrt{\frac{x}{a}} \right) + \frac{b^2 \sqrt{t}}{2\sqrt{2}} \left(\sqrt{\frac{a}{c+x}} - \sqrt{\frac{a}{x}} \right) + \mathcal{O}\left(t^{3/2} \right). \qquad (10)$$

Differentiating the first term of the expansion in time leads to

$$\frac{dI}{dt} = \frac{d}{dt} \left(\sqrt{\frac{2}{t}} \left(\sqrt{\frac{c+x}{a}} - \sqrt{\frac{x}{a}} \right) \right) = -\frac{1}{2t} I. \qquad (11)$$

Estimating the velocity of the intensity structures subject to Taylor dispersion can thus be computed by solving the differential

$$\frac{dI}{dt} = u_1 \frac{\partial I}{\partial x} + u_2 \frac{\partial I}{\partial y} + \frac{\partial I}{\partial t} = -\frac{1}{2t} I. \qquad (12)$$

This linear differential equation can be rewritten in vector notation which leads to

$$\frac{dI}{dt} = d^\top \cdot p = \left[\frac{1}{2t} I \; \frac{\partial I}{\partial x} \; \frac{\partial I}{\partial y} \; \frac{\partial I}{\partial t} \right] \cdot \left[1 \; u_1 \; u_2 \; 1 \right]^\top = 0. \qquad (13)$$

2.3 n-th Order Velocity Profiles

For a number of fluid flow configuration, the velocity profile can be approximated to leading order by

$$u(z) = A \cdot z^n, \qquad (14)$$

where A is a term independent of z and t. The integration across the profile results in

$$I = \int_{\sqrt[n]{\frac{x-c}{A \cdot t}}}^{\sqrt[n]{\frac{x}{A \cdot t}}} 1 \, dz = \sqrt[n]{\frac{x}{A \cdot t}} - \sqrt[n]{\frac{x-c}{A \cdot t}}. \qquad (15)$$

Differentiating this expression with respect to time directly leads to the following differential equation

$$\frac{dI}{dt} = u_1 \frac{\partial I}{\partial x} + u_2 \frac{\partial I}{\partial y} + \frac{\partial I}{\partial t} = -\frac{1}{n \cdot t} I, \qquad (16)$$

which can be written in vector notation giving

$$\frac{dI}{dt} = d^\top \cdot p = \left[\frac{1}{nt} I \; \frac{\partial I}{\partial x} \; \frac{\partial I}{\partial y} \; \frac{\partial I}{\partial t} \right] \cdot \left[1 \; u_1 \; u_2 \; 1 \right]^\top = 0. \qquad (17)$$

It is quite easy to see that this is a generalization of the previous cases of plane Couette flow ($n = 1$), compared to Equation (6) and (7) and of plane Poiseuille flow ($n = 2$), compared to Equations (12) and (13).

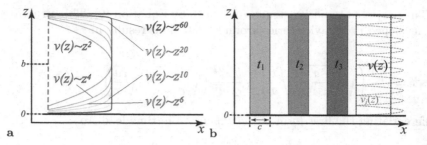

Fig. 5. In **a** a sketch of velocity profiles $v(z) \sim z^n$ with $n \in \{2, 4, 6, 10, 20, 60\}$. The higher the order n the better the approximation of a constant profile as shown in **b**. In the xylem of plants, the flow can be approximated by a number of small hollow tubes with a Poiseuille flow in between, as shown in **b**.

The both relevant flow configuration between parallel plates discussed so far have been plane Couette flow and plane Poiseuille flow. It might seem superfluous to expand the model to n-th order. However, there are flows for which higher order flow profiles are relevant. In Figure 5a the velocity profiles for a range of higher order models is sketched. It becomes apparent, that the central part of the profile becomes increasingly flat. Choosing ever higher order up to $\lim_{n \to \infty}$, we end up with a constant velocity profile with sharp edges. Water carrying tissue in plants can be approximated by an array of Poiseuille flows as sketched in Figure 5b. For an increasing number of such small "'pipes"', this flow can be approximated by this $\lim_{n \to \infty}$ flow.

It is interesting to note that the motion Equations (16) and (17) reduce to

$$\frac{dI}{dt} = u_1 \frac{\partial I}{\partial x} + u_2 \frac{\partial I}{\partial y} + \frac{\partial I}{\partial t} = -\frac{1}{n \cdot t} I, \quad \text{and} \quad n \overset{\lim}{\to} \infty \quad \frac{dI}{dt} = 0, \tag{18}$$

which is the standard BCCE [6]. This means that in the case of a constant velocity profile with depth, integration over depth does not matter and the standard BCCE can be used for estimating velocities of projected quantities. Intuitively this does make sense and is quite an expected behavior.

3   Parameter Estimation

The technique of simultaneously estimating optical flow and change of image intensity is well known in literature [9,10,11,12]. Details of the technique employed in the context of this manuscript are an extension of the structure tensor approach [13] and have been explained previously [14]. Accuracy improvements were introduced in [15] and [16].

Basically, the relevant constraint equations (7), (13) and (17) provide one constraint in two unknowns leading to an ill-posed problem. This can be solved

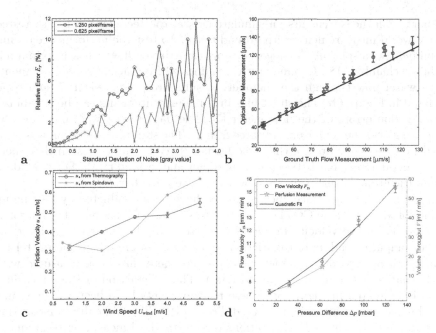

Fig. 6. a Relative error for Gaussian test sequences with two different velocities ($u_1 =$ 0.625 pixel/frame and $u_2 = 1.25$ pixel/frame) and varying noise levels. **b** Comparison of measured values (red circles) compared to ground truth measurement (solid blue line). Error bars: deviations in three successive frames. **c** Measurements conducted in a small wind wave facility. **d** Perfusion measurements of the center vein of a ricinus leaf.

from additional constraints. A commonly made assumption is that of a locally smooth motion field. Therefore, the aforementioned constraint equations can be pooled over a local neighborhood, leading to an overdetermined system of equations. This system can be solved for the parameter v using a weighted total least squares approach [17].

4 Applications

In order to test the presented motion models, test measurements were performed. First, the basic applicability was tested on synthetic sequences. The injection of a tracer into Couette and Poiseuille flow was modeled and the integration was performed. The distribution of the tracer in the projection plane was modeled to be a 2D Gaussian. This test pattern was corrupted with normally distributed noise of varying standard deviation. Also different flow velocities were simulated. The results of these measurements are shown in Figure 6a for the case of Poiseuille flow. It should also be noted that the velocity computed is that of the center layer in between the two plates. From this center plate velocity, the full flow profile can be reconstructed.

Apart from measurements on simulated data, the technique was also tested on real world measurements with ground truth. To test the performance on microfluidic flow, a spatially homogeneous pressure driven flow was set up in a microfluidic chamber [18]. Ground truth was derived from accurate measurements of the water flow through the chamber. Results are presented in [7] and recapitulated in Figure 6b. The slight bias in some measurements can be attributed to calibration errors of the flow meter [7]. The data points were measured by integrating over the center part of three frames. The standard deviation was computed over the same area of the three frames. It can clearly be seen that there exists a good agreement between measurement and ground truth. For most data points, the ground truth value is well within the error bar.

At the air-water interface, measurements have been conducted by heating up patches of water with an CO_2 laser leading to similar patterns as in the microfluidic case. From the velocity profile of Couette flow, the shear at the interface can be computed leading to the friction velocity u_*, an important parameter for parameterizing air-water interactions. This parameter has been measured with an alternative instrument for ground truth. The comparison of these measurements is presented in Figure 6c. These measurements have been the first time that this parameter could be measured directly [19]. The difficulty of measuring this parameter is reflected in deviations to the standard measuring technique.

Similar to the microfluidic application, ground truth measurements have been performed in a botanical applications [20]. The leaf of a ricinus plant was perfused and thus the pressure driven water flow through it was measured. A CO_2 laser was used for writing patterns on the leaf and these patterns were visualized with an infrared camera. The velocity of these structures were measured and compared to the perfusion measurements. The results showing excellent agreement are presented in Figure 6d for different flow velocities [20].

5   Conclusion

In this contribution, motion models were presented incorporating brightness changes due to the integration of a tracer across velocity profiles. These models connect the motion of an object in the scene with gray value changes in the acquired image sequences. This brightness change is very similar in appearance to anisotropic diffusion. Expressions for first- and second-order flow profile have been developed as well as general n-th order profiles. Applications of these models were presented, including shear flow at the air-water interface, Poiseuille flow in pressure driven microfluidic applications and an n-th order model in an botanical application. The validity of the presented motion models was tested on simulations as well as on ground truth image sequences. The parameters of these motion models were estimated in a local structure tensor approach. Only through this approach is the accurate estimation of fluid flow possible. This made the presented applications feasible for the first time. This framework can be readily extended to incorporate physically based regularization to increase accuracy of the results further.

References

1. Corpetti, T., Etienne, M., Perez, P.: Dense estimation of fluid flows. IEEE PAMI 24(3) (March 2002)
2. Ruhnau, P., Kohlberger, T., Nobach, H., Schnörr, C.: Variational optical flow estimation for particle image velocimetry. Exp. in Fluids 38, 21–32 (2005)
3. Ruhnau, P., Schnörr, C.: Optical stokes flow: An imaging based control approach. Exp. in Fluids 42, 61–78 (2007)
4. Taylor, J.A., Yeung, E.S.: Imaging of hydrodynamic and electrokinetic flow profiles in capillaries. Anal. Chem. 65(20), 2928–2932 (1993)
5. Kundu, P.K.: Fluid Mechanics. Academic Press, London (1990)
6. Haußecker, H., Spies, H.: Motion. In: Jähne, B., Haußecker, H., Geißler, P. (eds.) Handbook of Computer Vision and Applications, vol. 2, Academic Press, London (1999)
7. Garbe, C.S., Roetmann, K., Beushausen, V., Jähne, B.: An optical flow mtv based technique for measuring microfluidic flow in the presence of diffusion and taylor dispersion. Exp. in Fluids (accepted, 2007)
8. Taylor, G.: Conditions under which dispersion of a solute in a stream of solvent can be used to measure molecular diffusion. Proc. Royal Soc. London Ser. A 225, 473–477 (1954)
9. Negahdaripour, S., Yu, C.H.: A generalized brightness chane model for computing optical flow. In: ICCV, Berlin, pp. 2–7 (1993)
10. Zhang, D., Herbert, M.: Harmonic maps and their applications in surface matching. In: CVPR'99, June 1999, Fort Collins, Colorado (1999)
11. Haußecker, H., Garbe, C., Spies, H., Jähne, B.: A total least squares framework for low-level analysis of dynamic scenes and processes. In: DAGM, Bonn, Germany, pp. 240–249. Springer, Heidelberg (1999)
12. Haußecker, H., Fleet, D.J.: Computing optical flow with physical models of brightness variation. IEEE PAMI 23(6), 661–673 (2001)
13. Bigün, J., Granlund, G.H., Wiklund, J.: Multidimensional orientation estimation with application to texture analysis and optical flow. IEEE PAMI 13(8), 775–790 (1991)
14. Garbe, C.S., Spies, H., Jähne, B.: Estimation of surface flow and net heat flux from infrared image sequences. J. of Math. Im. and Vis. 19(3), 159–174 (2003)
15. Garbe, C.S., Jähne, B.: Reliable estimates of the sea surface heat flux from image sequences. In: Radig, B., Florczyk, S. (eds.) Pattern Recognition. LNCS, vol. 2191, pp. 194–201. Springer, Heidelberg (2001)
16. Garbe, C.S., Spies, H., Jähne, B.: Mixed ols-tls for the estimation of dynamic processes with a linear source term. In: Van Gool, L. (ed.) Pattern Recognition. LNCS, vol. 2449, pp. 463–471. Springer, Heidelberg (2002)
17. Van Huffel, S., Vandewalle, J.: The Total Least Squares Problem: Computational Aspects and Analysis. In: SIAM, Philadelphia (1991)
18. Roetmann, K., Schmunk, W., Garbe, C.S., Beushausen, V.: Micro-flow analysis by molecular tagging velocimetry and planar raman-scattering. Exp. in Fluids (accepted, 2007)
19. Garbe, C.S., Degreif, K., Jähne, B.: Estimating the viscous shear stress at the water surface from active thermography. In: Garbe, C.S., Handler, R.A., Jähne, B. (eds.) Transport at the Air Sea Interface, pp. 223–239 (2007)
20. Garbe, C.S., Pieruschka, R., Schurr, U.: Thermographic measurements of xylem flow in plant leaves. New Phytologist (in preparation) (2007)

Rigid Motion Constraints for Tracking Planar Objects

Olaf Kähler and Joachim Denzler

Chair for Computer Vision, Friedrich-Schiller University Jena
{kaehler,denzler}@informatik.uni-jena.de
http://www4.informatik.uni-jena.de

Abstract. Typical tracking algorithms exploit temporal coherence, in the sense of expecting only small object motions. Even without exact knowledge of the scene, additional spatial coherence can be exploited by expecting only a rigid 3d motion. Feature tracking will benefit from knowing about this rigidity of the scene, especially if individual features cannot be tracked by themselves due to occlusions or illumination changes. We present and compare different approaches of dealing with the spatial coherence in the context of tracking planar scenes. We also show the benefits in scenes with occlusions and changes in illumination, even without models of these distortions.

1 Introduction

Tracking features is one of the preliminaries for many further processing steps, like e.g. 3d reconstruction. Efficient tracking algorithms exploit the temporal coherence of feature locations in successive frames [1,2]. The basic idea is that small camera or object motions between a pair of views will only lead to small motions of the tracked features in the images.

If a static scene is observed with a moving camera, the motion of features is further constrained by the rigidity of the scene. This is also valid for rigidly moving objects as parts of more general, dynamic scenes. In typical tracking algorithms, this *spatial* coherence is not taken into account. In cases of occlusions, unsuitable viewing angles or illumination changes in parts of the scene, knowledge about the coherent motion can predict and constrain the location of features and hence drastically improve tracking robustness, even without models of illumination or occlusion.

Planar structures, as they are abundant in man-made environments, are particularly attractive for spatial coherence constraints. The points on each plane itself have a highly coherent motion, which can be modeled with the well-known homography transformations. But also for several, rigidly moving planes, motion constraints have been developed [3,4].

Our major contribution is to incorporate the spatial coherence resulting from a rigid scene motion into the tracking process for planar scenes. To achieve this, we use a parameterization of the plane induced homographies with inherent rigidity constraints, by expressing them in terms of plane parameters, which are

F.A. Hamprecht, C. Schnörr, and B. Jähne (Eds.): DAGM 2007, LNCS 4713, pp. 102–111, 2007.

constant over time, and camera parameters, which are constant for all planes observed in one image.

We compare this approach to two different possibilities of dealing with the spatial coherence. As one alternative, the rigid motion is ignored and the planes are tracked by independently estimating one homography per plane and view. The second alternative is a constrained homography estimation [4], where the same over-parameterization is used, but additionally the rigidity of motion is explicitly formulated and enforced as a constraint on the parameters. Our new formulation will also give insights, when and why such constraints can be applied.

The proposed approach can be seen as an intensity-based bundle adjustment problem [5]. It is also highly related to model based tracking approaches [6,7], where an explicit 3d model of the static scene or object is known, while the camera or object poses are estimated. Similarly a completely known camera calibration can be used to estimate the scene geometry from image intensities [8]. In our system, both the scene geometry and camera poses are included in the estimation process, while the intrinsic camera parameters are assumed to be known. In addition to the more robust tracking process, also 3d information is gathered this way.

2   Tracking Planes

Before introducing any constraints arising from rigid motions, we will outline the basic tracking process used in our work. The theoretical foundations of tracking planar scenes are shortly revised and formulated as a non-linear optimization problem. Also several practical issues of such a tracking system are accounted for, providing the basis for reliable tracking of planar features.

2.1   Intensity-Based Tracking

The task of tracking is to locate an object observed in a reference image I_0 in another image I_t taken at time t. It is assumed that the appearance of the object is identical in the two intensity images. The positions of the points $\mathbf{x}$ on the object have been affected by a motion, which is modeled by the function $\mathbf{f}$:

$$I_0(\mathbf{x}) = I_t(\mathbf{f}(\mathbf{p}, \mathbf{x}))\tag{1}$$

where $\mathbf{p}$ are the parameters of the motion between two particular images. The problem is to determine these parameters $\mathbf{p}$, given the two images, a region of interest in the first image (i.e. a set of points $\mathbf{x}$), and a motion model.

From equation (1), an error function $\epsilon(\mathbf{p})$ can be formulated. It has proved beneficial to use a compositional approach [2]. The overall motion is therefore decomposed into a previously estimated motion with parameters $\mathbf{p}'$ and a part to be estimated further on with the unknown parameters $\mathbf{p}$:

$$\epsilon(\mathbf{p}) = \sum_{\mathbf{x}} \left(I_t(\mathbf{f}(\mathbf{p}', \mathbf{f}(\mathbf{p}, \mathbf{x}))) - I_0(\mathbf{x})\right)^2 = \mathbf{d}^T(\mathbf{p})\mathbf{d}(\mathbf{p})\tag{2}$$

Here $\mathbf{d}(\mathbf{p})$ are the residuals for all sample points $\mathbf{x}$ stacked into one vector.

With standard methods from non-linear optimization, this error function ϵ can be iteratively minimized by optimizing the motion parameters $\mathbf{p}$. As a general optimization scheme, the Newton Iteration is used, resulting in:

$$\mathbf{p}_{i+1} = -\left(\frac{\partial^2}{\partial \mathbf{p}_i^2}\epsilon(\mathbf{p}_i)\right)^{-1}\frac{\partial}{\partial \mathbf{p}_i}\epsilon(\mathbf{p}_i) \tag{3}$$

For least squares problems, it is common to reduce the computational effort of evaluating derivatives of $\epsilon(\mathbf{p})$ by assuming that second order derivatives of $\mathbf{d}(\mathbf{p})$ are negligible. This leads to the Levenberg-Algorithm used in our work:

$$\frac{\partial^2}{\partial \mathbf{p}^2}\epsilon(\mathbf{p}) \approx \left(\frac{\partial}{\partial \mathbf{p}}\mathbf{d}(\mathbf{p})\right)\left(\frac{\partial}{\partial \mathbf{p}}\mathbf{d}(\mathbf{p})\right)^T + \lambda \mathrm{Id}$$

In the more specific task of tracking, a further approximation was introduced [1] to avoid recomputing the gradients online in each step of the iteration:

$$\frac{\partial}{\partial \mathbf{x}}I_t(\mathbf{f}(\mathbf{p}',\mathbf{x})) \approx \frac{\partial}{\partial \mathbf{x}}I_0(\mathbf{x})$$

2.2   Tracking of Planar Objects

The motion model $\mathbf{f}$ for the tracking process yet has to be specified. It is well known that points residing in one common 3d plane π are transferred between two images by a common projective 2d-2d transformation, a homography. Such a homography is characterized by 8 independent parameters, stored as $\mathbf{p}^{(\pi)}$, resulting in the following motion model for planar surfaces:

$$\mathbf{f}(\mathbf{p}^{(\pi)},\mathbf{x}) = \frac{1}{p_{31}x + p_{32}y + p_{33}}\begin{pmatrix} p_{11}x + p_{12}y + p_{13} \\ p_{21}x + p_{22}y + p_{23} \end{pmatrix}$$

Due to the temporal coherence, the location of the plane in the previous frame can be assumed as a good prediction of the location in the next frame, and is hence used as a starting point for the iteration.

Several refinements can be employed to achieve a more stable tracking process. One of the most common is to use a resolution hierarchy and apply a coarse to fine optimization of the motion parameters. This way, larger displacements of the tracked object can be handled [9]. Also different motion models like an affine motion are frequently assumed to approximate the full projective transformation [1]. We use such simplifying motion models to initialize the estimation of the more general models, i.e. in the optimization problem of equation (2), at first only the parameters p_{13} and p_{23} of a pure translation are estimated until convergence, then the six parameters of an affine transformation and finally the full set of eight parameters, each utilizing the previous steps as an initialization. Finally note that some of the partial derivatives of the motion model are quadratic in the pixel coordinates $\mathbf{x}$, others are linear and some are constant. A preconditioning of the problem, like a coordinate normalization of the $\mathbf{x}$ to the interval $[0...1]$, hence dramatically improves the numerical stability of the algorithm [10].

3   Rigid Motion Constraints

As depicted in figure 1, the system presented so far can readily be used to estimate independent homographies for several independent planes. With the planes rigidly aligned to each other in a common 3d world coordinate system, the spatial coherence provides additional constraints on the homographies, however. We will first prove this by a counting argument on the number of parameters and degrees of freedom. Then we will present one possible constraint in greater detail and show applicability for tracking multiple planes under rigid motion.

3.1   Motivation of Static Scene Constraints

Each individual homography is determined by 8 independent parameters. To formulate a multiplane tracking problem with independent homographies, a total of $8p(v - 1)$ parameters is therefore needed for p planes and v views. This also includes one reference view for each plane.

If a global, rigid motion is assumed, the actual number of degrees of freedom is much less. Each camera or scene motion can then be expressed as an Euclidian transformation with 6 dof. The projection with intrinsic parameters adds 5 dof, such that there is a total of $11v$ dof for v views of the scene. Further each plane in 3d space has 3 dof. The global position, orientation and scaling of the scene are not relevant for the tracking problem, hence removing 7 dof. Altogether the number of degrees of freedom is hence $11v + 3p - 7$, or even less in case of constant or known camera intrinsics.

This indicates that the $8p(v - 1)$ parameters of independent homographies are overdetermined and constraints can be applied to enforce the globally rigid motion of the scene. With unknown intrinsic parameters, it is easy to count that such constraints are possible for 2 views of at least 4 planes [3], or for 4 views of at least 2 planes [11], but also for 3 views of at least 3 planes. With unknown but constant intrinsic parameters, further constraints can be expected for 2 views of at least 3 planes, or even for a single plane observed in at least 5 views. While it is simple to show the existence of such constraints, only the two first mentioned have been formulated explicitly.

Note that extending these constraints to more views or more planes is not always trivial, as the scaling of the homography matrices, the ninth parameter of the 3×3 transformation matrix, cannot be recovered from image data alone. A comprehensive summary and ideas on such extensions were presented in [4].

3.2   Constrained Tracking

In the following, we will shortly review the constraint for 2 views of at least 4 planes [3]. The advantage of this constraint is that it can be directly used to incorporate spatial coherence into a system tracking multiple planes between two frames. The other known constraint developed in [11] is based on the slightly more complex planar homologies and requires the estimation of at least 4 frames to be performed at once.

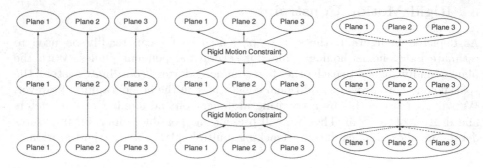

Fig. 1. The three approaches of tracking with the knowledge of rigid motions from left to right: Independent estimation of the planes, independent estimation with a rigid motion constraint at each step and combined estimation of all planes in a bundle

Let π_i be the 3d plane defined by $\mathbf{n}_i^T \mathbf{X} = d_i$, with the plane normal $\mathbf{n}_i$ and the distance d_i to the origin. Let R and $\mathbf{t}$ be the relative rotation and translation between two images, and K_1 and K_2 the projections into the images. The homography H_i transferring points on π_i between the two images is then:

$$
\begin{aligned}
H_i &= K_2 R K_1^{-1} + \tfrac{1}{d_i} K_2 \mathbf{t} \, \mathbf{n}_i^T K_1^{-1} \\
&= \quad H_\infty \quad + \quad \mathbf{q} \quad \mathbf{v}_i^T
\end{aligned}
\tag{4}
$$

Let the 9-vector h_i be composed of the entries of the homography matrix H_i. If n of these vectors are stacked in one big $9 \times n$ matrix $\mathcal{H}$, this can be written as:

$$
\begin{aligned}
\mathcal{H} = \left(h_1 \Big| ... \Big| h_n \right) &= \left(h_\infty \Big| ... \Big| h_\infty \right) + \begin{pmatrix} \mathbf{q}\,0\,0 \\ 0\,\mathbf{q}\,0 \\ 0\,0\,\mathbf{q} \end{pmatrix} \left(\mathbf{v}_1 \, ... \, \mathbf{v}_n \right) \\
&= \underbrace{\begin{pmatrix} \mathbf{q}\,0\,0 \\ 0\,\mathbf{q}\,0\ h_\infty \\ 0\,0\,\mathbf{q} \end{pmatrix}}_{9 \times 4} \underbrace{\begin{pmatrix} \mathbf{v}_1 \, ... \, \mathbf{v}_n \\ 1 \, ... \, 1 \end{pmatrix}}_{4 \times n}
\end{aligned}
\tag{5}
$$

Obviously, $\mathcal{H}$ has at most rank 4. It follows that for 2 views of at least 4 planes, the homographies induced under a rigid motion reside in a 4d subspace of all possible homographies in dynamic scenes.

It is particularly easy to incorporate this constraint into a tracking problem with multiple planes $\pi_1, ..., \pi_I$ and parameters $\mathbf{p}^{(C)} = \{ \mathbf{p}^{(\pi_1)}, ..., \mathbf{p}^{(\pi_I)} \}$. The planes are no longer tracked independently now, but as a whole. The objective function from equation (2) is therefore extended by a sum over all planes:

$$
\epsilon(\mathbf{p}^{(C)}) = \sum_i \sum_{\mathbf{x} \in \pi_i} \left(I_t(\mathbf{f}(\mathbf{p}'^{(\pi_i)}, \mathbf{f}(\mathbf{p}^{(\pi_i)}, \mathbf{x}))) - I_0(\mathbf{x}) \right)^2
\tag{6}
$$

Note the parameters $\mathbf{p}^{(C)}$ computed in the nonlinear optimization process will be a stacked version of all the $\mathbf{p}^{(\pi_i)}$ computed for the individual planes π_i in the independent homography tracker from 2.2. This is because the parameters of the j-th homography only depend on observations of points on the j-th plane. The derivative $\frac{\partial}{\partial \mathbf{p}^{(\pi_j)}} \epsilon(\mathbf{p}^{(C)})$ in equation (3) will be non-zero only for terms $i = j$, and a block-diagonal structure will result for the Hessian matrix $\frac{\partial^2}{\partial \mathbf{p}^{(\pi_j)2}} \epsilon(\mathbf{p}^{(C)})$.

The main difference is, after computing new parameters $\mathbf{p}^{(C)}$ and composing them with the previous estimation, the constraint from equation (5) is applied, as shown schematically in figure 1. This way, the spatial coherence resulting from a rigid motion is enforced for the homographies at each iteration step.

4   Minimal Parameterization

As an alternative to using an over-parameterization and enforcing constraints afterwards, we propose to use a minimal set of parameters from the beginning, and estimate them as a bundle, as sketched in figure 1. We will first outline the idea of such an approach, then present the resulting optimization problem, and finally give some ideas for an implementation.

4.1   Tracking as Bundle-Adjustment

The objective function used in the following is essentially the same as in equation (6), except that another sum is taken over all the frames of the image sequence. As the main difference, the motion function $\mathbf{f}$ is no longer parameterized using 8 independent entries. Instead we use decomposition (4) to define the homography matrices in terms of plane parameters and camera motions relative to a reference view. Accordingly, instead of solving for the $8p(v-1)$ independent homography parameters, we try to find optimal view poses and plane parameters.

Note that the parameters optimized for one plane are now influenced by its observations in multiple views, as well as the parameters for one camera pose are influenced by all planes observed in that view. Due to this, the tracking problem actually becomes an intensity-based bundle adjustment problem [5]. The spatial coherence is enforced, as the plane parameters are identical for all the views and the camera parameters of one view are identical for all planes.

4.2   Parameterization of Homographies

The decomposition of homographies given in (4) still allows different parameterizations of camera poses and planes. In the following we will shortly present and motivate the one chosen in this work.

First note, this decomposition arbitrarily fixes the world coordinate system to the camera of the first view. Without loss of generality, we take this as the common reference view for all planar patches in the tracking problem. This simplifies the problem, but can be overcome easily, as was shown e.g. in [7].

A plane π_i has 3 degrees of freedom, but we use 4 parameters and define it by the equation $\mathbf{n}_i^T \mathbf{X} = d_i$. The vector $\mathbf{n}_i$ is normalized to length 1 at each step of the iteration. Although dividing by d_i might avoid this normalization, a singularity is then introduced for planes passing the origin of the world coordinate system, and an ill-conditioned system for planes nearby such a configuration.

For the camera translation $\mathbf{t}$, a simple 3-vector is used. The camera orientation is represented by a quaternion, again having 4 parameters for 3 degrees of freedom. With a compositional approach and enforcing the normalization constraint directly in the optimization, only the 3 independent parameters contribute to the iterative update steps [12].

With the overall set of parameters $\mathbf{p}^{(B)}$, the motion model $\mathbf{f}_i$ for the i-th plane then is:

$$\mathbf{f}_i(\mathbf{p}^{(B)}, \mathbf{x}) = \mathrm{Proj}\left(K_2 \left(\mathbf{T}(\frac{1}{\mathbf{q}\mathbf{q}^*}\mathbf{q})\mathbf{T}(\mathbf{q}') + \frac{1}{d_i}\mathbf{t}\mathbf{n}_i^T \right) K_1^{-1}\mathbf{x} \right) \tag{7}$$

Here, $\mathrm{Proj}(\mathbf{x})$ computes the projection of $\mathbf{x}$ to inhomogeneous coordinates, $\mathbf{T}(\mathbf{q})$ creates the rotation matrix equivalent to rotation with quaternion $\mathbf{q}$, and $\mathbf{q}'$ results from the previous iterations of the compositional optimization process.

In our setting, the free parameters are $\mathbf{q}$, $\mathbf{t}$, $\mathbf{n}_i$ and d_i, while we assume the intrinsic parameters K_1 and K_2 to be known. For the non-linear optimization, one has to compute derivatives of ϵ and hence $\mathbf{f}_i$ with respect to the unknowns, which are not shown here for lack of space.

4.3   Implementation Issues

As typical for bundle-adjustment problems, many sparse matrices appear in the derivatives and allow for an efficient implementation [5]. We will not go into the details at this point, as an efficient implementation is not the main scope of this work.

To further increase the computational speed of processing an image sequence, a sliding window can be applied. The idea is to take into account only the latest v images and compute only the latest v camera poses, instead of all parameters for the whole sequence. Also the idea of using a resolution hierarchy is transferred easily to this formulation of the tracking problem.

A critical point about bundle-adjustment and non-linear optimization in general is the initialization of the iteration. In our current implementation, new planes are initialized such that they are facing straight to the camera with the plane normal parallel to the optical axis, and the distance from the optical center is arbitrarily set to 1. For each new view, the camera pose is initialized with the pose estimated for the previous frame. Convergence to a stable, local optimum has not been a problem in our experiments.

5   Experiments

We have performed several experiments to evaluate the different methods, and especially to show the benefits of using the spatial coherence in the tracking process. We will first describe the used setup, before presenting the results.

Fig. 2. The red, green, blue and yellow polygons mark planar patches tracked through an image sequence. Despite the severe occlusion in the middle image, the locations of the regions are correctly estimated. This is based solely on the knowledge of observing a rigid scene, no occlusion models are applied.

Fig. 3. The colored polygons mark tracked, planar regions. Although the appearance of the CD-cover in the middle of the scene drastically changes due to specular reflections, the knowledge of observing a static scene allows successful tracking.

5.1 Basic Setup

For the experiments, image sequences of a static scene of books and boxes were recorded with a handheld camera. Planar regions were manually marked in the first image to initialize the tracking. As only the camera was moving, these tracked features were underlying a global, rigid motion.

During tracking, a resolution hierarchy with 3 levels was used. For the bundled tracking, a sliding window over the last 10 frames was applied. Otherwise the parameters were identical for all compared methods.

As mentioned in section 4.3, the implementation is not yet optimized for speed. With planes densely covering about 70% of the 640×480 images, the tracker with independent homographies currently reaches about 7.5 fps, the constraint based tracker about 1.5 fps and the tracker with a minimal parameterization about 0.1 fps on a Intel Pentium 4 with 3.4 GHz and 1GB RAM. With further optimizations, realtime or close to realtime performance seems possible.

5.2 Experimental Evaluation

The tracking accuracy can hardly be expected to improve by imposing static scene constraints. In fact, as the homographies now have to fulfill more conditions than with an independent estimation, the ability to fit the observations even

Table 1. Average tracking durations in percent of the sequence duration. Each row is for one sequence, each column for one of the presented tracking approaches.

sequence	independent	constrained	minimal
box1	71.87	71.87	100.00
box2	29.79	31.58	100.00
box_occlude	53.33	57.66	100.00
books1	69.61	54.34	100.00
books2	72.80	73.60	100.00

decreases slightly. The main benefit however is the improved robustness in cases, where a single plane cannot be estimated from the image data. We hence compare the average tracking duration as a measure for the robustness.

In table 1, the average tracking durations are given for the test sequences. In the setups box1 and box2, planes are temporarily seen with a very small viewing angle. The sequence box_occlude additionally features an occlusion, where one of the planes is covered to approx. 50% by an object in front (see figure 2). Finally, the sequences books1 and books2 show surfaces with specular reflections (see figure 3 for an excerpt of books2).

In all of the cases, tracking the planes independently does not succeed. The constrained homography estimation does slightly improve the tracking robustness. With the tracker using a minimal parameterization, the regions are successfully tracked despite all distortions. Note that no models of illumination or occlusions are required, but instead the knowledge suffices that all image motion is due to just one, rigid scene motion.

The performance of the constraint based tracker most likely is poor, because only a rigid motion between two frames is enforced. This is close to the minimal configuration of where the method can be applied at all, and hence imposes only a weak constraint on the homography estimation. An extension to multiple frames is possible [4], but currently not used. For the tracker with minimal parameterization, a sliding window of 10 frames was applied, hence enforcing a rigid motion between several frames and imposing a much stronger constraint.

6   Conclusions

For tracking problems, the temporal coherence has frequently been used as a helpful cue when tracking features through an image sequence. The basic idea is that features only underlie a small motion, if the camera motion between successive frames is small. We additionally proposed the idea of spatial coherence as a second important cue for tracking. As an example, the rigid 3d motion of a planar scene can be exploited for tracking the features, even if they are partially occluded or their appearance drastically changes.

To evaluate this concept, we have presented three different tracking approaches. The first was ignoring the spatial coherence by tracking features independently of each other. The second was basically still tracking features independently, but then enforcing the constraint of one common, rigid 3d motion upon the feature locations. Finally we proposed a third approach, using a minimal parameterization to directly realize the spatial coherence in terms of a constant 3d geometry of the tracked object or scene.

We used the scenario of tracking piecewise planar objects or scenes, as constraints enforcing a rigid motion for such scenes are readily available [3,11]. These constraints are very inflexible however, e.g. requiring at least 4 planes to be visible in the scene. Also we did not investigate the extensions to multiple views presented in [4]. Instead we developed a formulation as an intensity-based bundle-adjustment problem [5], which we believe to be a lot more flexible.

In the experiments we showed that spatial coherence in itself, without any models of illumination or occlusion, does significantly improve the tracking robustness. Especially in situations, where individual planes cannot be tracked, the knowledge about the location of other planes can be exploited to estimate the positions of occluded features.

References

1. Hager, G.D., Belhumeur, P.N.: Efficient region tracking with parametric models of geometry and illumination. IEEE Transactions on Pattern Analysis and Machine Intelligence 20, 1025–1039 (1998)
2. Baker, S., Matthews, I.: Lucas-Kanade 20 years on: A unifying framework. International Journal of Computer Vision 56, 221–255 (2004)
3. Shashua, A., Avidan, S.: The rank 4 constraint in multiple (>=3) view geometry. In: Proc. 4th European Conference on Computer Vision, Cambridge, UK, vol. II, pp. 196–206. Springer, Heidelberg (1996)
4. Zelnik-Manor, L., Irani, M.: Multiview constraints on homographies. IEEE Transactions on Pattern Analysis and Machine Intelligence 24, 214–223 (2002)
5. Triggs, B., McLauchlan, P.F., Hartley, R.I., Fitzgibbon, A.W.: Bundle adjustment – a modern synthesis. In: Vision Algorithms: Theory and Practice, pp. 298–372. Springer, Heidelberg (2000)
6. Cobzas, D., Sturm, P.: 3d ssd tracking with estimated 3d planes. In: Proc. 2nd Canadian Conf. on Computer and Robot Vision, Victoria, Canada, pp. 129–134 (2005)
7. Ladikos, A., Benhimane, S., Navab, N.: A real-time tracking system combining template-based and feature-based approaches. In: Proc. Intl. Conf. on Computer Vision Theory and Applications, Barcelona, Spain, vol. 2, pp. 325–332 (2007)
8. Habbecke, M., Kobbelt, L.: Iterative multi-view plane fitting. In: Proc. Vision, Modeling, and Visualization Conference 2006, Aachen, Germany, pp. 73–80 (2006)
9. Bergen, J.R., Anandan, P., Hanna, K.J., Hingorani, R.: Hierarchical model-based motion estimation. In: Proc. 2nd European Conference on Computer Vision, pp. 237–252. Springer, Heidelberg (1992)
10. Hartley, R., Zisserman, A.: Multiple View Geometry in Computer Vision, 2nd edn., Camebridge University Press, Camebridge (2003)
11. Zelnik-Manor, L., Irani, M.: Multi-view subspace constraints on homographies. In: Proc. 7th International Conference on Computer Vision, Kerkyra, Corfu, Greece, vol. 2, pp. 710–715. IEEE Computer Society, Los Alamitos (1999)
12. Wheeler, M.D., Ikeuchi, K.: Iterative estimation of rotation and translation using the quaternions. Technical Report CMU-CS-95-215, Computer Science Department, Carnegie Mellon University (1995)

Detectability of Moving Objects Using Correspondences over Two and Three Frames

Jens Klappstein, Fridtjof Stein, and Uwe Franke

DaimlerChrysler AG
71059 Sindelfingen, Germany

Abstract. The detection of moving objects is crucial for robot navigation and driver assistance systems. In this paper the detectability of moving objects is studied. To this end, image correspondences over two and three frames are considered whereas the images are acquired by a moving monocular camera. The detection is based on the constraints linked to static 3D points. These constraints (epipolar, positive depth, positive height, and trifocal constraint) are discussed briefly, and an algorithm incorporating all of them is proposed. The individual constraints differ in their action depending on the motion of the object. Thus, the detectability of a moving object is influenced by its motion. Three types of motions are investigated: parallel, lateral, and circular motion. The study of the detection limits is applied to real imagery.

1 Introduction

Robots and autonomous vehicles require the knowledge about objects moving in the scene in order to avoid collisions with them. Beside radar and lidar sensors also cameras can be utilized to observe the 3D scene in front of the vehicle. In this paper up to three images taken by a moving monocular camera are evaluated. Since we do not know a priori where moving objects are in the scene we cannot check for them directly. However, given the optical flow (image correspondences) and the ego-motion we are able to triangulate the viewing rays yielding reconstructed 3D points. If the 3D point is actually a static point the reconstruction will be fine, but if the actual 3D point is moving the reconstruction will fail (in general). What does this mean?

A reconstructed 3D point has to fulfill certain constraints in order to be a valid static 3D point. If it violates any of them the 3D point is not static, hence it must move. Thus, the detection of moving objects is based on the constraints a static point fulfills.

Although many constraints exist, there are some kinds of motion which (nearly) fulfill all constraints and thus are not detectable. This paper investigates these detection limits, and is organized as follows: At first (section 2) the available constraints are discussed. In section 3 an error metric is developed combining all constraints. Based on this metric the detection limits are investigated in section 4. Experimental results are given in section 5.

F.A. Hamprecht, C. Schnörr, and B. Jähne (Eds.): DAGM 2007, LNCS 4713, pp. 112–121, 2007.

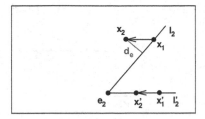

Fig. 1. Epipolar constraint. The image of the second view is shown. The camera moves along its optical axis. An object moves lateral w.r.t. the camera inducing an horizontal optical flow shown by the correspondences $x_1 \leftrightarrow x_2$ and $x_1' \leftrightarrow x_2'$. The subscripts 1 and 2 denote entities in the first and the second view, respectively. x_2 does not lie on the epipolar line l_2 inducing the epipolar error d_e. x_1' moves along its epipolar line l_2' and thus fulfills the epipolar constraint. e_2 is the epipole.

Please note that the ego-motion, i.e. the motion of the camera from frame to frame, must be known in order to perform the detection. Furthermore, the location of the camera with respect to the road (ground plane) is required. The information is considered as given here. Specifically, it is assumed that the fundamental matrix, the road homography between the first two views, and the trifocal tensor are given.

The reader is referred to [1,3,7] which address the estimation of the ego-motion. Beside these two-view methods one can estimate the ego-motion over all three views [9].

2   Constraints for Static 3D Points

In this section we discuss briefly the constraints a static 3D point fulfills. On the basis of traffic scenarios we will see how each constraint acts on different kinds of motion. Thereby we differentiate between parallel motion (preceding and overtaking objects), and lateral motion (crossing objects).

The first three constraints, discussed in detail in [5], apply for correspondences over two frames. The fourth constraint is applicable if correspondences over three views are available. Each individual constraint raises the quality of detection.

- **Epipolar Constraint**
  The epipolar constraint expresses that the viewing rays of a static 3D point (the lines joining the projection centers and the 3D point) must meet. A moving 3D point in general induces skew viewing rays violating the constraint. Figure 1 illustrates it.
- **Positive Depth Constraint**
  The fact that all points seen by the camera must lie in front of it is known as the positive depth constraint. It is also called cheirality constraint. If viewing rays intersect behind the camera, as in figure 2a, the actual 3D point must be moving.

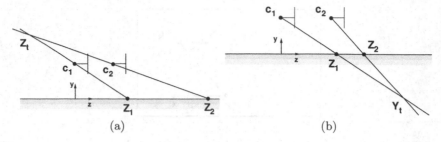

(a)   (b)

Fig. 2. Side view: Positive depth (a) and positive height (b) constraint. The camera is moving from c_1 to c_2. A 3D point on the road is moving from Z_1 to Z_2. In (a) the traveled distance of the point is greater than the distance of the camera (overtaking object). The triangulated 3D point Z_t lies behind the camera, violating the positive depth constraint. In (b) the traveled distance of the point is smaller (preceding object). The triangulated 3D point Y_t lies underneath the road, violating the positive height constraint.

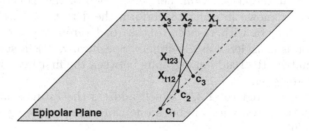

Fig. 3. Trifocal Constraint. The camera observes a lateral moving 3D point (X_1 to X_3) while moving itself from c_1 to c_3. The triangulated point of the first two views is X_{t12}. The triangulation of the last two views yields X_{t23} which does not coincide with X_{t12} violating the trifocal constraint.

- **Positive Height Constraint**
  All 3D points must lie above the road. If viewing rays intersect underneath the road, as in figure 2b, the actual 3D point must be moving.
- **Trifocal Constraint**
  A triangulated 3D point utilizing the first two views must triangulate to the same 3D point when the third view comes into consideration. This constraint is also called trilinear constraint. In figure 3 it is violated.

3   Error Metric Combining All Constraints

With the constraints described above, the objective is to measure quantitatively to which extent these constraints are violated. The resulting measurement function, called error metric, shall be correlated to the likelihood that the point is moving, i.e. higher values indicate a higher probability.

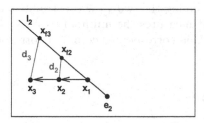

Fig. 4. Combined error metric. The image of the second view is shown. The camera moves along its optical axis observing a lateral moving point $x_1 \leftrightarrow x_2 \leftrightarrow x_3$. The closest point to x_2 fulfilling the two-view constraints is x_{f2}. The error arising from two-views is the distance d_2. Transferring the points x_1 and x_{f2} into the third view yields x_{f3}. If the observed 3D point was actually static its image x_3 would coincide with x_{f3}. However, the 3D point is moving which causes the trifocal error d_3. The overall error is $d = d_2 + d_3$. Note, that in general x_1 and x_{f3} do not lie on the epipolar line l_2.

The error metric is developed in two steps. First, the two-view constraints are evaluated taking view one and two into account. Afterwards, the trifocal constraint is evaluated using the third view, too.

3.1 Two-View Constraints

An error metric combining the two-view constraints has been introduced in [5]. It measures the distance of a given image point in the first view to the closest point fulfilling all constraints (epipolar, positive depth, and positive height constraint). For the ease of computational complexity image points in the second view are considered noise free. We use this metric here but swap the roles of the views, i.e. we compute the error (distance) in the second view. This is illustrated in figure 4.

We first consider the correspondence $x_1 \leftrightarrow x_2$ in the views one and two. The closest point to x_2 fulfilling the two-view constraints is x_{f2}. It lies on the epipolar line $l_2 = Fx_1$ with F the fundamental matrix. Note that the vector from x_{f2} to x_2 is not necessarily perpendicular to l_2. The distance d_2 between x_{f2} and x_2 is the error arising from the first two views. For the computation of d_2 see [5].

3.2 Three-View Constraint

We now add the third view and consider the correspondence $x_1 \leftrightarrow x_2 \leftrightarrow x_3$. As the point x_{f2} is defined such that it fulfills the two-view constraints the reconstructed 3D point arising from the triangulation of the points x_1 and x_{f2} constitute a valid 3D point. This 3D point is projected into the third view yielding x_{f3}. The measured image point x_3 will coincide with x_{f3} if the observed 3D point is actually static. Otherwise there is a distance d_3 (figure 4) between them which we call trifocal error. x_{f3} is computed via the point-point-point transfer using the trifocal tensor [2]. This approach avoids the explicit triangulation of the 3D point.

The overall error combining the two-view constraints and the three-view constraint is $d = d_2 + d_3$. It measures the minimal required displacement in pixels necessary to change a given correspondence into a correspondence belonging to a valid static 3D point.

4 Detection Limit

In this section we deal with the key question: Utilizing the different constraints, which kinds of motion are detectable and to which extent? In order to detect a moving object reliably the error metric developed in section 3 must be greater than a certain threshold T, whereas the threshold should reflect the noise in the correspondences (optical flow). A reasonable choice is $T = 3\sigma$ with σ the standard deviation of the correspondences.

In the following we consider the three most frequent kinds of motion in traffic: parallel, lateral and circular motion. We model the motion of the camera and the object as shown in figure 5. It is not necessary to investigate camera rotations about its projection center, since they do not influence the detection limit. One can always compensate these rotations by a virtual inverse rotation.

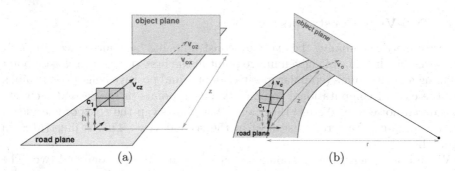

Fig. 5. Motion model utilized for the investigation of the detection limit. The cameras projection center in the first view is c_1. The moving object is modeled as a plane. (a) Linear motion: The (object)plane moves parallel (w.r.t. the camera) with speed v_{oz} and lateral with speed v_{ox}. The distance of the camera to the object is z, to the road it is h. The camera moves along its optical axis with speed v_{cz}. (b) Circular motion: Both, camera and object, move along a circle with radius r. The tangential speed of the camera is v_c, that of the object is v_o.

4.1 Linear Motion

The detection limits for the linear motions (parallel and lateral motion) are illustrated by means of three examples:

1. Overtaking object: The object moves parallel to the camera but faster.
   $v_{cz} = 30\text{km/h}, v_{oz} = 40\text{km/h}, v_{ox} = 0\text{km/h}$

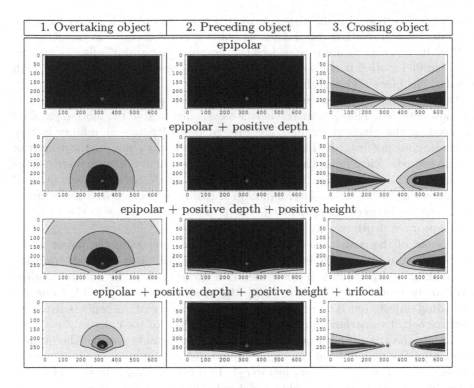

Fig. 6. Detection limits for different kinds of linear motion and constraints. The images show the first view (compare to fig. 5). They are truncated at row 290, since below there is no object but the road. Inside the black regions the motion is not detected. The contour lines $2T$ and $4T$ are also shown. The red point marks the epipole, the red cross is the point of collision. Further explanation is given in the text.

2. Preceding object: The object moves parallel to the camera but slower.
   $v_{cz} = 30\text{km/h}$, $v_{oz} = 20\text{km/h}$, $v_{ox} = 0\text{km/h}$
3. Crossing object: The object moves lateral to the camera.
   $v_{cz} = 30\text{km/h}$, $v_{oz} = 0\text{km/h}$, $v_{ox} = -5\text{km/h}$

The subscripts stand for: c = camera, o = object, z = longitudinal direction, x = lateral direction. Anti-parallel motion ($v_{cz} > 0\text{km/h}$, $v_{oz} < 0\text{km/h}$, $v_{ox} = 0\text{km/h}$) is not of interest here, since it is completely not detectable [4]. In the examples other important parameters are: focal length $f = 1000\text{px}$, principal point $(x_0, y_0) = (320, 240)$, height of camera above the road $h = 1\text{m}$, distance to object $z = 20\text{m}$, time between consecutive frames $\Delta t = 40\text{ms}$.

The detection limits of the linear motions are shown in figure 6. Each image shows the first view. Inside the black regions the error metric is lower than $T = 0.5\text{px}$ (assuming a std. dev. in the correspondences of $\sigma = 0.167\text{px}$). Parts of the object seen in these regions are not detected as moving. There is one important point in the image: the point of collision. This is the point where the camera will collide with the object, provided that the object is slower than the camera. We will see that this dangerous point is not detectable in many cases.

The first row of figure 6 considers the epipolar constraint only. As can be seen parallel motion is not detected at all. Lateral motion is detected to a high extent. The black region is shaped like a bow tie.

In the second row the positive depth constraint is added. Overtaking objects are now detected. The error metric in this case is identical to the motion parallax induced by the plane at infinity. The optical flow of points at infinity is zero (camera does not rotate). Thus, the motion parallax is equal to the length of the measured optical flow. The contour lines (lines where the error metric takes on a constant value) are circular around the epipole. Preceding objects are still not detected. In the case of lateral motion the bow tie is cracked. The motion is also detected between the epipole and the point of collision due to the violation of the positive depth constraint.

The use of the positive height constraint (third row) gains the power of detection for the image part below the horizon. In the cases of parallel motion (overtaking and preceding objects) the error metric below the horizon is identical to the motion parallax induced by the road plane. It is possible to detect preceding objects but it is a challenging task. Lateral motion benefits from the positive height constraint only on the right-hand side of the epipole.

Adding the trifocal constraint yields the best achievable results. The parallel motion profits mainly from the larger driven distance of the camera, since the camera moves from c_1 to c_3 (not just to c_2). This just increases the signal to noise ratio. Similar results would be obtained if only the first and the third view would be evaluated. This does not hold for the lateral motion. The trifocal constraint allows a detection also to the left of the epipole.

The reason for that is given in figure 3. There the camera moves from c_1 to c_3 observing a point moving from X_1 to X_3. A situation is chosen such that the trajectories of the camera and the point are co-planar. They move within the epipolar plane. Considering the first two views the two-view constraints are fulfilled. The viewing rays meet perfectly in the point X_{t12}. This point lies in front of the cameras and above the road. Consequently, this kind of motion is not detected over two views alone. Considering the third view reveals the motion, since the triangulated point X_{t23} of the second and third view is different from X_{t12}.

We have seen that in case of the linear motion the strength of the trifocal constraint is not very high. The trifocal constraint shows its strength if the cameras translational direction changes over time as it is the case in the circular motion.

4.2   Circular Motion

The circular motion is modeled as shown in figure 5b. To demonstrate the detection limit for this case we consider an example similar to the "preceding object" example: $v_c = 30$km/h, $v_o = 20$km/h, $z = 20$m, and $r = 100$m.

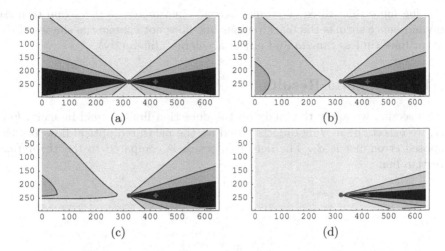

Fig. 7. Detection limit in the case of circular motion. The images show the first view (compare to fig. 5b). They are truncated at row 274, since below there is no object but the road. Inside the black regions the motion is not detected. The contour lines $2T$ and $4T$ are also shown. The red point marks the epipole, the red cross is the point of collision. (a) Epipolar constraint. (b) + positive depth constraint. (c) + positive height constraint. (d) + trifocal constraint.

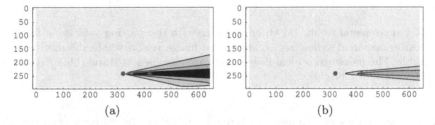

Fig. 8. Detection limit in the case of circular motion with tripled time period Δt compared to figure 7. (a) Epipolar + positive depth + positive height constraint. (b) + trifocal constraint.

Figure 7 shows the detection limit. Although the object is slower than the camera, which was a problem for the parallel motion case, the circular motion is detected to a high extent (fig. 7a). With the positive depth constraint taken into account the entire region to the left of the epipole is detected. It seems that the trifocal constraint (fig. 7d) just shrinks the black region, meaning that it only improves the signal to noise ratio. This is, however, not true. If we triple the time period $\Delta t = 120$ms the black region vanishes (figure 8b). Consequently, the entire object is detected as moving and so is the point of collision. The power of the two-view constraints is insufficient to detect that point.

Taking more than three views into account just increases the signal to noise ratio and hence shrinks the black regions but does not change the shapes of the contour lines (unless camera and object accelerate differently).

5   Experimental Results

In this section we apply the study on the detection limit to real imagery. Further, we detect the moving objects based on the measured optical flow and the proposed error metric d_2. The detection result is compared to the theoretical detection limit.

(a)   (b)

Fig. 9. Experimental result. (a) Original image with two moving vehicles in front. (b) The semi-transparent yellow region shows the image region where the motion is not detectable. The measured optical flow vectors are classified as static (blue / dark) and moving (magenta / bright).

Figure 9a shows two vehicles driving in front of the camera (ego-vehicle). They are faster than the camera and move parallel to it. First, the detection limit is computed. To this end, the distance to the objects and the speed of them are required. The on-board radar sensor provides this information: $z = 16.5$m and $v_{oz} = 62.9$km/h. The speed of the camera, retrieved by odometry, is $v_{cz} = 53.5$km/h. With this information together with the camera calibration the non-detectable region computes to that shown in figure 9b. Thereby the two-view constraints are considered.

The actual detection of the vehicles is carried out by the evaluation of the two-view error metric d_2 utilizing the measured optical flow. Radar data are ignored. The required ego-motion as well as the road homography are estimated using [6]. Flow vectors with $d_2 > T = 1.7$px are classified as moving. The result is shown in figure 9b. One can see that the theoretical detection limit matches well to the practical one.

The vehicle on the right side is completely detected whereas only the lower part of the vehicle in the middle of the image is detected.

6   Conclusion

We have presented the detection limits of independently moving objects utilizing all available constraints existing for static 3D points. We have seen that:

– Objects which are faster than the camera are detected to a higher extent than those which are slower. That is a pity because slower objects are the dangerous ones. We will not collide with a faster object.
– In the event of linear motion the dangerous point of collision is not detected at all, what an irony of fate!
– The trifocal constraint emphasizes its potential if the motion of the camera is circular (non-linear). Then the point of collision is detectable (in principle).

References

1. Armangué, X., Araújo, H., Salvi, J.: Differential Epipolar Constraint in Mobile Robot Egomotion Estimation. In: IEEE International Conference on Pattern Recognition (ICPR), Québec, Canada, pp. 599–602 (2002)
2. Hartley, R., Zisserman, A.: Multiple View Geometry in computer vision, 2nd edn. Cambridge Press (2003)
3. Ke, Q., Kanade, T.: Transforming Camera Geometry to A Virtual Downward-Looking Camera: Robust Ego-Motion Estimation and Ground-Layer Detection. In: IEEE International Conference on Computer Vision and Pattern Recognition (CVPR), Madison, USA, pp. I-390- I-397 (2003)
4. Klappstein, J., Stein, F., Franke, U.: Flussbasierte Eigenbewegungsschätzung und Detektion von fremdbewegten Objekten. In: Workshop Fahrerassistenzsysteme (FAS), Löwenstein, Germany, pp. 78–88 (2006)
5. Klappstein, J., Stein, F., Franke, U.: Monocular Motion Detection Using Spatial Constraints in a Unified Manner. In: IEEE Intelligent Vehicles Symposium (IV), Tokyo, Japan, pp. 261–266 (2006)
6. Klappstein, J., Stein, F., Franke, U.: Applying Kalman Filtering to Road Homography Estimation. In: Workshop on Planning, Perception and Navigation for Intelligent Vehicles in conjunction with IEEE International Conference on Robotics and Automation (ICRA), Rome, Italy (2007)
7. Nistér, D.: An efficient solution to the five-point relative pose problem. In: IEEE Transactions on Pattern Analysis and Machine Intelligence (PAMI), June 2004, pp. 756–770 (2004)
8. Torr, P.H.S., Zisserman, A., Murray, D.W.: Motion Clustering using the Trilinear Constraint over Three Views. In: Mohr, R., Wu, C. (eds.) Europe-China Workshop on Geometrical Modelling and Invariants for Computer Vision, pp. 118–125. Xidan University Press/Springer–Verlag (1995)
9. Trautwein, S., Mühlich, M., Feiden, D., Mester, R.: Estimating Consistent Motion From Three Views: An Alternative To Trifocal Analysis. In: International Conference on the Analysis of Images and Patterns (CAIP), Ljubljana, Slovenia, pp. 311–320 (1999)

An Analysis-by-Synthesis Camera Tracking Approach Based on Free-Form Surfaces

Kevin Koeser, Bogumil Bartczak, and Reinhard Koch

Institut für Informatik, Christian-Albrechts-Universität Kiel
D-24098 Kiel, Germany
{koeser,bartczak,rk}@mip.informatik.uni-kiel.de

Abstract. We propose a model-based camera pose estimation approach, which makes use of GPU-assisted analysis-by-synthesis methods on a very wide field of view (e.g. fish-eye) camera. After an initial registration, the synthesis part of the tracking is performed on graphics hardware, which simulates internal and external parameters of the camera, this way minimizing lens and perspective differences between a model view and a real camera image. We show how such a model is automatically created from a scene and analyze the sensitivity of the tracking to the model accuracy, in particular the case when we represent free-form surfaces by planar patches. We also examine accuracy and show on synthetic and on real data that the system does not suffer from drift accumulation. The wide field of view of the camera and the subdivision of our reference model into many textured free-form surfaces make the system robust against moving persons and other occlusions within the environment and provide a camera pose estimate in a fixed and known coordinate system.

1 Introduction and Previous Work

Camera tracking is nowadays used in many applications, e.g. robotics, visual navigation or augmented reality [16,8]. It can suffer from poor localization of visual features, ill-posed estimation (aperture problem, too small field of view), drifting references and occluded or moving scene content. To overcome these issues we propose a fish-eye camera as a visual pose sensor, which captures the surrounding scene in an offline phase and can then be used in an online phase for real-time tracking. Fish-eye cameras have the advantage that they have a very wide field of view compared to a standard perspective camera. Therefore they always "see" large parts of the static scene even if objects or persons move and occlude parts of the background and when the camera rotates. Furthermore, pose estimation is better conditioned than for perspective cameras [9,17,18]. In our approach, the scene in which the camera moves does not need to be set up with expensive calibrated markers as in [3] and can therefore be any location which provides textured surfaces for tracking, e.g. outdoor in front of a building.

During the last years several online camera tracking systems have been proposed: Commercially available systems (e.g. [3]) need special calibrated markers, fast structure-from-motion [1] is prone to drift on long sequences due to a missing

F.A. Hamprecht, C. Schnörr, and B. Jähne (Eds.): DAGM 2007, LNCS 4713, pp. 122–131, 2007.

absolute reference. Object tracking approaches usually cannot cope with clutter and occlusion as moving objects or persons within the scene [11]. Other systems tend to jitter, because they apply fast 2D feature extraction methods to every single image [5,2], which can suffer from few features or poor feature localization and have to be regularized by temporal pose filtering. Our system overcomes these limitations. The key idea is that feature tracking is improved by compensating the features' appearances with respect to 3D viewpoint and lens effects, which can efficiently be done on graphics hardware with sub-pixel accuracy. The approach is separated into an offline and an online phase. During the offline phase, a very wide field of view camera (e.g. fish-eye with 180°) is moved within a scene and a structure-from-motion-approach [1] is applied to reconstruct the environment as a textured triangle mesh. Since no time-constraints are imposed during offline-processing, an optimal batch tracking with bundle adjustment and multi-camera depth estimation is possible, yielding high quality models. Next, robust 2D features (e.g. MSER [7]) are extracted from reference images, their 3D coordinates are computed and the features are stored in a database according to [4]. The textured triangle mesh and the robust features database serve as an offline reference model.

In the online phase, robust features are extracted from the first image and matched to the robust features of the offline database similar to [4]. Using these correspondences an approximate camera pose is estimated for initialization of the system. Our contribution here focuses on the subsequent tracking part of the online system: From the approximate pose, we synthesize a fish-eye image of our offline model using the same (intrinsic and extrinsic) camera parameters as the real fish-eye camera has (see section 2). We need to minimize the difference between rendered and real camera image to obtain the correct camera pose. However, since we want to cope with outliers and moving scene content, we do not use a direct gradient based approach to estimate the pose parameters as in [11] but search for local 2D offsets of individual free-form surfaces using the KLT [6]. From the exact locations of the surfaces in the camera image we can compute the final camera pose as described in section 3. Section 4 is dedicated to the evaluation of the system on real and synthetic data followed by a conclusion.

2   Spherical Camera

We propose to use a wide field-of-view camera, e.g. with a fish-eye lens, which has a nearly linear and isotropic relation between distance in pixels to the principal point and the angle between the ray and the optical axis[17]. Fleck [10] calls this the equidistant projection. A comparison between spherical and perspective cameras regarding tracking can be found in [9], who showed that pose estimation is more accurate with a wider field of view and that the lower angular resolution of the fish-eye lens is more than compensated by its wide field of view. Furthermore, such a camera covers a larger solid angle and therefore features can be seen for a longer period of time in image sequences. Let $P()$ be the function that computes a 2D image point x_i from a 3D scene point X_i, which takes care of all internal and external camera parameters of our real camera (CCD size, lens distortion, camera pose p, ...): $P(p, k, X_i) = x_i$

P is actually composed of extrinsic camera parameters, i.e. the pose p (position and orientation), and intrinsic camera parameters k, which describe the mapping of 3D points *in the camera coordinate system* to image coordinates. The internal parameters do not change, since they depend only on the lens and the hardware, we are going to estimate the pose. We describe the internal camera parameters with the function $K_k()$, where $K_k()$ maps projection rays in the camera coordinate system to 2D points in the image depending on a vector of internal parameters k. Therefore when we measure an image point x_i in any camera we can use K_k^{-1} to compute the ray that maps a 2D image point onto the unit sphere within the camera coordinate system. We define the mapping from world coordinates to normalized camera coordinates by $\hat{P}$: $\hat{P}(p, X_i) = K_k^{-1}(x_i) = \hat{x}_i$ where $\hat{P}$ is only a function of the pose and the 3D point. k can be determined by calibration [13]. If the effects of $K_k()$ are removed from the image measurement, we compute on rays in the camera coordinate system, which is easily applicable for all camera models with a single center of projection.

In a similar way we can synthesize fish-eye images using the graphics hardware: Given a camera position, we render 6 perspective views in all 6 directions (cube-mapping of environment). Afterwards we stitch these images together to form a fish-eye image (displacement mapping). This exploits again that for each pixel in the fish-eye image, we know the ray and therefore the coordinates where a perspective camera observes this ray. This can be efficiently implemented using OpenGL/CG and runs directly on the graphics hardware. Furthermore we combine the zBuffer values to produce a spherical depth map in a similar way.

3   Camera Tracking

We will first review the offline model generation process and the general system aspects, then we will study the online correspondence search and pose estimation.

3.1   Offline Model Generation

During the offline phase a video of the scene is captured systematically by scanning the possible range of viewpoints that will be used during online processing. In this way we *learn* a 3D reference model for later use. The intrinsics of the fish-eye camera are known [13], therefore coordinates in the image can be identified with rays in the camera coordinate system. First we perform a feature based reconstruction of the camera path similar to [1] using correspondences from the KLT tracker [6]. Next we generate depth maps by applying a cylindrical rectification method in 3D (again a way of abstracting from the underlying camera distortion) to the fish-eye images to use a standard stereo algorithm. The results are fused to robustify the depth maps (for example see figure 1). From these depth maps, free-form surface models can be built which are represented by textured triangle meshes. If a very fine resolution is chosen, the real surfaces

Fig. 1. Left: 3D view of cube-mapped environment (perspective views) Middle:Fish-eye image with center, 45°, 90°, 135° and 180° field of view circles, Right: Example of Reconstructed Fish-eye Depth Map

are approximated quite well at the cost of a huge number of triangles. If on the other hand a very coarse resolution is chosen, the free-form surfaces are actually approximated by only few planar patches (triangles), which can be rendered more efficiently. Those regions which have been tracked well over long time in the offline phase are obviously visible from several viewpoints and serve as a hint for the online phase where to register the triangle mesh with the camera image.

The textured triangle mesh is a reconstructive model of the scene: It represents the scene well in the sense that we can render a virtual view of the scene from any given viewpoint. However, when the camera is switched on during the online phase, no prior information is given about the viewpoint and we have to initially register the camera with respect to the scene, i.e. we also need a discriminative model. We solve this by creating a database of robust features (e.g. MSER[7]) as described in [4], which allows efficient recognition of scene parts.

3.2 Online Pose Estimation

Once we have set up the model we start the online phase, where the system registers against the database [4] and begins the tracking. The registration is robust and needs no approximate pose. However, the subsequent tracking approach is much faster and also more accurate, therefore the database is only used when the system is lost.

Correspondences between Image and Model. Given an approximate pose, the model is rendered and the true pose is computed from the displacement vectors between regions of the rendered image and the real camera image. By using a fish-eye lens we have all the advantages in visibility and geometrical stability, however the appearance of the model is quite different between distant camera poses. Therefore we need the rendering to undistort these effects by warping the model image into the new viewpoint and allowing to establish correspondences using standard techniques like KLT. After the free-form surfaces are rendered, we check geometrically which ones are projected into the virtual image and search for textured regions with a minimum size (e.g. 7x7 pixels) inside each free-form surface projection. We save its center point x_i and create its corresponding 3D

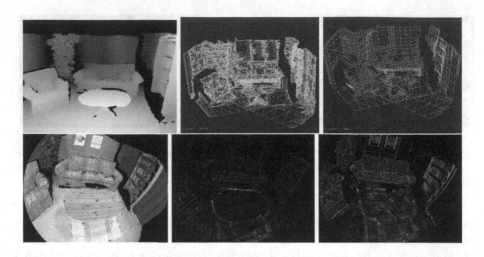

Fig. 2. From Left to Right, Top Row: Perspective Depth Map and Two Reduced Triangle Meshes (87724, 6882 triangles), Bottom Row: Ground Truth Fish-eye Image (left) and Photometric Difference for a sample view from meshes above

point X_i by back-projecting the viewing ray onto the model (using the depth from the renderer). This delivers a 3D model feature.

We start individual gradient-based minimizations [6] of the intensity differences at these locations x_i between the patches in synthesized and real image. This is more robust than a gradient-based global optimization of the pose across the whole image (as in [11]), since several scene parts may be occluded by persons or other unmodeled objects and it is hard to decide within one iteration step, which pixels should be used and which not. For a whole free-form surface we can test the projection error to see whether it is an outlier. Furthermore, the difference minimization is always carried out between a synthesized image and the actual camera image. This way, the offline model serves as a global reference and we will not accumulate drift as it would be the case when one tracks from camera image to camera image. The rendering can be seen as a fish-eye compensation of the patch for tracking. For simplicity, we use the standard KLT tracker, since our prediction (the rendered image) is usually very close. However, if illumination changes occur it is easy to use a more light insensitive version.

Robust Pose Estimation. The resulting 2D-3D correspondences are then processed in a robust non-linear pose estimator (M-Estimator with Huber error function $h()$ to limit the influence of mismatches), which starts at the predicted pose and minimizes the ray error for all 2D-3D correspondences. More precisely, the position x_i and the covariance matrix $C_{x_i x_i}$ from the KLT tracker in the original image are transformed to position $\hat{x}_i$ and a covariance $\hat{C}_i$ which is obtained through an unscented transform[15]. Now the Mahalanobis distance between $\hat{x}_i$

and the ray of the 3D point is minimized, where the transformed covariance $\hat{C}_i$ of the tracked point defines the Mahalanobis error metric.

$$\sum_i h\left((\hat{x}_i - \hat{P}(p, X_i))^T \hat{C}_i^{-1}(\hat{x}_i - \hat{P}(p, X_i))\right) \to min$$

We are looking for the pose p which minimizes the sum of these distances for all points. Once the pose is computed it is possible to render another fish-eye image from that pose and performing the KLT step again, this way iterating towards an even better pose. If and how many iterations are needed depends on the quality of the pose prediction and therefore mainly on the speed and smoothness of camera movement and the speed of computation. Within the camera movement, the rotation is the most critical part, because fast rotations change the fish-eye image more drastically than fast translations (when assuming a certain distance from the scene). In [14] it was found that the critical point is mainly the ability of the KLT tracker to establish the correspondence between rendered and real image at all and that no significant improvement could be observed when rendering more than two times.

4   Experiments

In this contribution the focus is on the analysis-by-synthesis part of the tracking, therefore we assume an approximate initialization in the following evaluation is given. We will compare the approach based on a synthetic scene for ground truth and a real outdoor scene.

4.1   Ground Truth Experiments

As synthetic ground truth we used a model of a real living room scene with real textures as reconstructed by the offline modeling part (see figure 2). The model is fused from four perspective depth maps of the scene, consists of 1.2 million triangles (the bounding box is about 5m x 4m x 2m) and we generated a sequence of 350 fish-eye images (140° field of view, camera translation about 1.5m, rotation in all directions, where the vertical axis rotations dominate by up to 80°) with ground truth pose information.

Sensitivity to Model Accuracy. The accuracy of the pose estimation depends on the goodness of the model used for tracking. Therefore, we compared rendering speed and average pose estimation accuracy (figure 3) at varying resolutions of the triangle mesh for tracking (figure 2). The number of triangles is reduced from 1.200.000 down to 1.600 by a combination of depth map resolution reduction and quad tessellation similar to what has been proposed in [12].

The main result of this evaluation is not surprising: With increasing number of triangles rendering performance goes down; if the GPU resource limit is reached, real-time tracking becomes infeasible. The pose estimation error decreases about logarithmically with increasing number of triangles. In the extreme case of only a

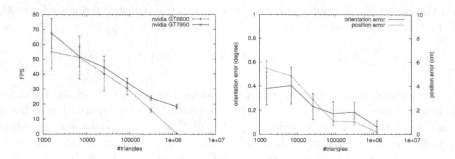

Fig. 3. Model detail in number of triangles. Left: Pure Rendering Frame-rate, Right: Average Orientation and Position Error on Living Room Sequence.

few triangles the scene is actually represented by planar patches, which showed to be only usable as long as the underlying scene is planar. Otherwise the rendering does not fulfill the undistortion goal: the rendered and the camera image look significantly different and cannot be matched by the KLT tracker. Only those points are found which actually do lie on planes and are approximated well.

Comparison of different algorithms. The system has been compared against a) incremental structure-from-motion using the same camera (140° FOV) but no model and b) model-based tracking with a 40° FOV perspective camera with the same number of pixels and same number of surfaces (of which the perspective camera sees not all at once). Pose error is given as position (translational) error in cm and orientation error in $degree$ (axis-angle representation of the rotation between the ground truth camera and the estimated camera). The sequence is run forward and backward, generating a total of 700 frames with image 1 and 700 at identical pose. The results in figure 4 show that the model-based fish-eye tracking outperforms both other approaches. The error is constantly low over the complete sequence (average errors: position: 0.3 cm, orientation: 0.1°).

The structure-from-motion algorithm a) has no prior model and generates the model *on the fly*. Therefore, the average pose error is higher than with the model. Scale was fixed such that the tracking can be compared with the model-based approaches. Drift does not accumulate very much since all features are visible in most images, however we see an error increase as the camera moves away from the initial position. We deliberately left out the bundle adjustment, which would clearly help, but which is not feasible in real-time applications. Average position error is about 2 cm, average orientation error 0.3°.

The perspective model-based tracking b) on the other hand has difficulties in distinguishing between camera rotation and camera translation, which can be seen from the high correlation between orientation and translation error in figure 4. Furthermore it does only see about 100 of the about 500 free-form surfaces in the model at a given time because of its limited field of view. The errors are much higher with average position error 4 cm and orientation error 0.8°.

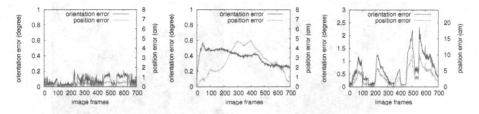

Fig. 4. Algorithm comparison on ground truth living room sequence (350 images forward+backward). Left: Fish-eye Model Tracking, Center: Fish-eye Structure-From-Motion, Right: Perspective Model Tracking (40° FOV) with triple error range.

Real outdoor fish-eye sequence. To prove the applicability of our method we evaluate a real sequence (see also figure 1), which consists of 1400 images of 1200 × 1600pixels, that were taken with a fish-eye lens covering a viewing angle of 185°. The camera was moved handheld and translated approximately 6m sidewards while panning up to 90°. The filmed buildings were up to 20m away and 12m in height. The camera path was reconstructed with the structure from motion approach using the full fish-eye images as explained earlier. The resulting depth map was used to create a mesh yielding a 3D model of the scene which consists of 90303 triangles (compare figure 5, left).

Without ground-truth data, the verification of the estimated camera path is difficult. One way to check for consistent model and camera path reconstruction is to augment the model into a sequence. The right image of figure 5 shows an augmentation of the model rendered with the estimated camera parameters. In order to provide an augmentation which is distinguishable from the background image, the texture of the model was replaced by its gradient magnitude. While evaluating the model tracking, the difference images between the original image and the rendered model view were monitored. This qualitative evaluation showed that the observable tracking error was in the range of one pixel.

In order to analyze potential accumulation of errors in pose estimation for long sequences, 360 consecutive images of the real sequence were processed forward and backwards several times, starting at the middle of the sequence. The central image position is reached eight times and compared to the first pose, which should always be the same. Figure 5 shows the extent of this path which is approximately 2 meters to the left and to the right of the middle camera (green). Looping through this sequence resulted in 2160 images for tracking. Given the pose for the first (central) image, the camera poses for this "oscillating" sequence are estimated using SfM tracking and model based tracking with 400 features for both. Model based tracking uses only one rendering iteration.

Table 1 (top two rows) compares the error development at the middle image over consecutive passes of a looped sequence using tracking on fish-eye images, but without a model. Although the error is not constantly growing with each pass an error increase is visible. On the other hand the tracking error observed

Fig. 5. Left: Perspective view on reference model and extent of camera movement used for drift measurement. The camera is going forward/backward from one end of this path to the other. It passes the green middle camera, where the pose estimation is compared to previous and following passes (see table 1). Right: augmentation of model view and real image using estimated parameters. The texture used for the augmentation is the gradient magnitude of original texture, strong gradient edges colored in red.

Table 1. Pose error evaluation for a looped image sequence, which passed the image under inspection eight times. The SfM rows show the position and orientation error using a structure from motion based tracking and how pose estimation has drifted when passing this image. The model rows prove the avoidance of error accumulation when tracking is supported by a model.

	pass 1	pass 2	pass 3	pass 4	pass 5	pass 6	pass 7	pass 8
ΔT SfM	2.57 cm	1.92 cm	1.92 cm	2.79 cm	2.41 cm	1.06 cm	3.53 cm	3.22 cm
$\Delta\phi$ SfM	0.098°	0.085°	0.085°	0.11°	0.11°	0.02°	0.13°	0.14°
ΔT Model	0.73 cm	0.82 cm	0.69 cm	0.73 cm	0.84 cm	0.68 cm	0.73 cm	0.81 cm
$\Delta\phi$ Model	0.047°	0.047°	0.046°	0.047°	0.048°	0.046°	0.047°	0.047°

using the model (last two rows) is confined and does not increase over consecutive passes. This confirms that the system does not drift. Furthermore the pose error is smaller at all times when compared with the SfM tracking.

5   Conclusion

We have discussed a camera tracking system, which first builds a textured model from the environment and afterwards uses the model in an analysis-by-synthesis approach for tracking. The graphics hardware is exploited to render a distortion-compensated and perspectively warped model image with an approximate pose. Since this compensates the effects of the wide-angle lens, now full advantage can be taken of the fish-eye properties, which proved to be superior to perspective cameras in tracking. It was shown that there is no drift accumulation over time and therefore the system is well-suited to work on infinitely long image sequences. The accuracy of the model approximation should fit well the free-form surfaces, since planar approximations of curved surfaces degrade the accuracy. On current

GPUs a model complexity of about 100.000 triangles is feasible. We showed the applicability of the approach by using a model of a real outdoor building and a semi-artificial living room sequence.

References

1. Pollefeys, M., Van Gool, L., Vergauwen, M., Verbiest, F., Cornelis, K., Tops, J., Koch, R.: Visual modeling with a hand-held camera. IJCV 59(3), 207–232 (2004)
2. Lepetit, V., Lagger, P., Fua, P.: Randomized Trees for Real-Time Keypoint Recognition. In: CVPR 2005, San Diego, CA (June 2005)
3. Thomas, G.A., Jin, J., Niblett, T., Urquhart, C.: A Versatile Camera Position Measurement System for Virtual Reality TV Production. In: Proceedings of International Broadcasting Convention, Amsterdam, pp. 284–289 (1997)
4. Koeser, K., Haertel, V., Koch, R.: Robust Feature Representation for Efficient Camera Registration. In: Franke, K., Müller, K.-R., Nickolay, B., Schäfer, R. (eds.) Pattern Recognition. LNCS, vol. 4174, pp. 739–749. Springer, Heidelberg (2006)
5. Skrypnyk, I., Lowe, D.G.: Scene Modelling, Recognition and Tracking with Invariant Image Features. In: ISMAR 2004, Arlington, pp. 110–119 (2004)
6. Tomasi, C., Kanade, T.: Detection and Tracking of Point Features, Carnegie Mellon University, Technical Report, CMU-CS-91-132 (April 1991)
7. Matas, J., Chum, O., Urban, M., Pajdla, T.: Robust Wide baseline Stereo from Maximally Stable Extremal Regions. In: Proceedings of BMVC02 (2002)
8. Davison, A.J.: Real-Time Simultaneous Localisation and Mapping with a Single Camera. In: Proceedings International Conference Computer Vision, Nice (2003)
9. Streckel, B., Koch, R.: Lens Model Selection for Visual Tracking. In: Kropatsch, W.G., Sablatnig, R., Hanbury, A. (eds.) Pattern Recognition. LNCS, vol. 3663, pp. 41–48. Springer, Heidelberg (2005)
10. Fleck, M.: Perspective Projection: The Wrong Imaging Model. TR 95-01, Computer Science, University of Iowa (1995)
11. Koch, R.: Dynamic 3D Scene Analysis through Synthesis Feedback Control. IEEE Transactions PAMI 15(6), 556–568 (1993)
12. Evers-Senne, J., Koch, R.: Image Based Rendering from Handheld Cameras using Quad Primitives. In: Evers-Senne, J., Koch, R. (eds.) VMV 2003, November 2003, Munich, Germany (2003)
13. Scaramuzza, D., Martinelli, A., Siegwart, R.: A Toolbox for Easy Calibrating Omnidirectional Cameras. In: Proceedings of IROS 2006, October 2006, Beijing, China (2006)
14. Koeser, K., Bartczak, B., Koch, R.: Drift-free Pose Estimation with Hemispherical Cameras. In: Proceedings of CVMP 2006, November 2006, London (2006)
15. Julier, S., Uhlmann, J.: A new extension of the Kalman filter to nonlinear systems. In: Int. Symp. Aerospace/Defense Sensing, Simul. and Controls, Orlando (1997)
16. Bleser, G., Wuest, H., Stricker, D.: Online Camera Pose Estimation in Partially Known and Dynamic Scenes. In: ISMAR 2006, Los Alamitos, California, pp. 56–65 (2006)
17. Neumann, J., Fermuller, C., Aloimonos, Y.: Eyes from eyes: New cameras for structure from motion. In: IEEE Workshop on Omnidirectional Vision, pp. 19–26 (2002)
18. Micusik, B., Pajdla, T.: Structure From Motion with Wide Circular Field of View Cameras. IEEE Transactions on PAMI 28(7), 1135–1149 (2006)

An Adaptive Confidence Measure for Optical Flows Based on Linear Subspace Projections

Claudia Kondermann, Daniel Kondermann, Bernd Jähne,
and Christoph Garbe*

Interdisciplinary Center for Scientific Computing
University of Heidelberg, Germany
claudia.kondermann@iwr.uni-heidelberg.de

Abstract. Confidence measures are important for the validation of optical flow fields by estimating the correctness of each displacement vector. There are several frequently used confidence measures, which have been found of at best intermediate quality. Hence, we propose a new confidence measure based on linear subspace projections. The results are compared to the best previously proposed confidence measures with respect to an optimal confidence. Using the proposed measure we are able to improve previous results by up to 31%.

1 Introduction

Optical flow calculation is a crucial step for a wide variety of applications ranging from scientific data analysis and medical imaging to autonomous vehicle control and video compression. Methods for optical flow computation can be distinguished into local and global approaches. Most local approaches are either based on the idea of Lucas and Kanade [7], Bigün [11] or on the method of Anandan [2], where an energy term is minimized for each pixel individually under utilization of a small neighborhood. Global techniques usually follow the concept of Horn and Schunck [8], which implements prior knowledge on the flow field by spatio-temporally relating neighboring flow estimates by means of global energy functionals. One of the most accurate methods recently has been proposed by Bruhn et al. [9] and combines the advantages of both approaches.

Confidence measures are indispensable to assess and improve the quality of optical flow fields. In 1994, in their landmark paper Barron and Fleet [3] stated that "confidence measures are rarely addressed in literature" even though "they are crucial to the successful use of all [optical flow] techniques". Using the information provided by confidence measures, the accuracy of the estimated flow field can be improved by integrating the confidence measure into the calculation method or by postprocessing, e.g. removing and reconstructing incorrect flow vectors. We have to distinguish between confidence and situation measures. Despite different concepts, both types of measures have been used as confidence

---

* The authors thank the German Research Foundation (DFG) for funding this work within the priority program "Mathematical methods for time series analysis and digital image processing" (SPP1114).

F.A. Hamprecht, C. Schnörr, and B. Jähne (Eds.): DAGM 2007, LNCS 4713, pp. 132–141, 2007.
© Springer-Verlag Berlin Heidelberg 2007

measures in literature. Situation measures assess the mere possibility of an accurate flow computation and yield a low value for example in cases of occlusions, transparent structures, severe noise, aperture problems and homogeneous regions. However, the actual displacement vector is not necessarily considered and can be assessed as unreliable despite its correctness. In contrast, confidence measures evaluate the correctness of a given flow vector independent of the situation in the sequence. A comparison of known situation and confidence measures can be found in [1]. So far, for variational methods only one general type of explicit confidence measures has been proposed in [10]. The idea is to use the inverse of the global energy functional in order to detect violations of the flow computation model. For the well-known structure tensor method proposed by [11] the only confidence measures that have been proposed actually belong to the class of situation measures, as they do not take into account the displacement vector at all when assessing its correctness, e.g. the gradient of the image or other measures described in [4,13,12]. Furthermore, the quality of these measures is unsatisfactory as we have pointed out in [1]. We have also proposed several variational data terms such as the brightness constancy equation and various regularizers [6,5] as confidence measures for the structure tensor method. In fact, these measures turned out more reliable than situation measures, but still did not obtain accurate results. This is mainly due to the problem that each measure assumes a specific flow computation model, which cannot be valid in any situation. Therefore, we propose a new confidence measure for the structure tensor method that is adaptable to the current flow computation problem by means of unsupervised learning. In fact, the measure can be used for all optical flow fields that have been computed with no or minor smoothness assumptions. Even ground truth data which is generally unavailable is not necessary as the model can be learned either from a set of ground truth flow fields or from a previously computed flow field. The linear subspace projection method has been applied for the estimation of optical flows before, directly by Black et al. in [17] and by means of Markov Random Fields by Roth and Black in [16]. In contrast to these approaches, where only spatial information is used, we extend the subspace method to include temporal information of the flow field and derive a new confidence measure. The concept of our confidence measure is based on the idea of learning typical displacement vector constellations within a local neighborhood. The resulting model consists of a set of basis flows, a linear subspace of the flow field, that is sufficient to reconstruct 99% of the information contained in the flow field. Displacement vectors that cannot be reconstructed by this model are considered unreliable. Hence, the reconstruction error is chosen as confidence measure. It performs better than previously proposed confidence measures and obtains a substantial gain of quality in several cases.

2   Definitions

Let a given image sequence $\mathcal{I}$ be defined on a time interval $[0, T]$ as

$$\mathcal{I} : \Omega \times [0, T] \to \mathbb{R}, \ \Omega \subseteq \mathbb{R}^2 \tag{1}$$

The notion "optical flow" refers to the displacement field u of corresponding pixels in subsequent frames of an image sequence

$$u : \Omega \times [0, T] \to \mathbb{R}^2 \tag{2}$$

Then a confidence measure is a mapping c from the image sequence and a two-dimensional displacement vector to the interval $[0..1]$:

$$c : \mathcal{I} \times u \to [0..1] \tag{3}$$

There is an infinite number of possible displacement vector constellations. Hence, none of the previously proposed models is able to represent all of them. Using given ground truth flow fields or computed flow fields we try to derive as much information as possible from the samples in order to incorporate this information into the learned flow model. Since much of the information contained in a flow field is only obvious in the temporal domain, the inclusion of temporal information is indispensable. However, it is rarely used in literature.

3   Linear Subspace Projections

In order to learn the linear subspace model any unsupervised learning method can be used. We apply principal component analysis (PCA) and use a set of given displacement fields for the training. They consist of a horizontal and a vertical flow component. To compute the principal components a spatially and temporally distributed neighborhood containing both components is read into a single vector using a lexicographic order. The matrix containing a large number of such sample vectors will be called M. The idea of PCA is to find a low-dimensional subspace which preserves as much information (variance) of the dataset as possible and in which the different dimensions of the data are decorrelated. The covariance of the matrix M represents the correlation of the dataset along each two dimensions. Hence, the goal is to find a new basis system, where the covariance of each two dimensions is zero, that means the covariance matrix of M is diagonal. As the covariance matrix of M is symmetric and positive definite it can be diagonalized. We can obtain such a basis system by finding an orthogonal matrix S and applying the similarity transformation

$$D = S^T \, Cov(M) \, S \tag{4}$$

e.g. using Givens rotations. The matrix S then contains the eigenvectors of the covariance matrix of M, which form the new basis system. In order to reduce the dimensionality of the data to a meaningful subspace, the axes representing the least information (the smallest variance) of the dataset can be removed. These are the eigenvectors with the smallest eigenvalues. We can select the number of eigenvectors containing the fraction δ of the information of the original dataset by choosing k of the n eigenvectors v_i sorted by decreasing eigenvalue such that

$$\frac{\sum_{i=1}^{k} v_i}{\sum_{i=1}^{n} v_i} \geq \delta \tag{5}$$

With the eigenvectors (*"eigenflows"*) we can now approximately reconstruct any displacement vector neighborhood $\mathcal{N}_x$ centered on position x by a linear combination of the k selected eigenflows using the reconstruction function r

$$r(\mathcal{N}_x, k) = \sum_{i=1}^{k} \alpha_i v_i + m \, , \; m = \frac{1}{n} \sum_{i=1}^{n} s_i \tag{6}$$

where s_i are the data samples in the columns of M. In order to obtain the coefficient vector α containing the eigenflow coefficients α_i, it is sufficient to project the sample neighborhood $\mathcal{N}_x$ into the linear subspace spanned by the eigenflows using the transformation

$$\alpha = S^T(\mathcal{N}_x - m) \tag{7}$$

Figure 1 shows examples for eigenflows derived from computed flow fields. Using temporal information the resulting eigenflows can represent complex temporal phenomena such as a direction change, a moving motion discontinuity or a moving divergence.

The linear combinations of the previously derived eigenflow vectors represent typical flow field neighborhood constellations. Depending on the training data the information contained in the learned model varies. If ground truth flow fields are used many sample sequences are necessary to include most of the possible flow constellations. However, as only very few sequences with ground truth exist the resulting eigenflows only represent an incomplete number of constellations. In contrast, it is possible to compute the flow for a given sequence and use exactly this computed flow as input for the unsupervised learning algorithm. In this way the resulting model will be well adapted to the current flow problem. However, if the flow computation method does not allow certain displacement vector constellations the trained linear subspace will not be sufficient to represent these constellations either, as all training samples are derived from the computed flow field. This is for example the case if the flow computation model demands a smooth flow field, which leads to the problem that the sample flows do not contain any flow edges. In both cases, if we learn from insufficient ground truth flows or from incorrect, computed flow fields, the problem that correct flow constellations cannot be reconstructed from the eigenflows persists. We will compare both methods.

4   A Confidence Measure from Eigenflows

To evaluate the confidence of a given flow vector we have to consider its validity within its spatio-temporal context, that is within its neighborhood $\mathcal{N}_x$ of flow vectors. Given a number of k model parameters, e.g. eigenflows, a confidence measure can be derived based on the assumption that displacement vectors are the more reliable within their neighborhood the better they can be reconstructed from the eigenflows, which represent typical flow constellations. Hence, the reconstruction error of the flow vector will serve as confidence measure:

$$c(x, u) = \varphi(u, r(\mathcal{N}_x, k)) \tag{8}$$

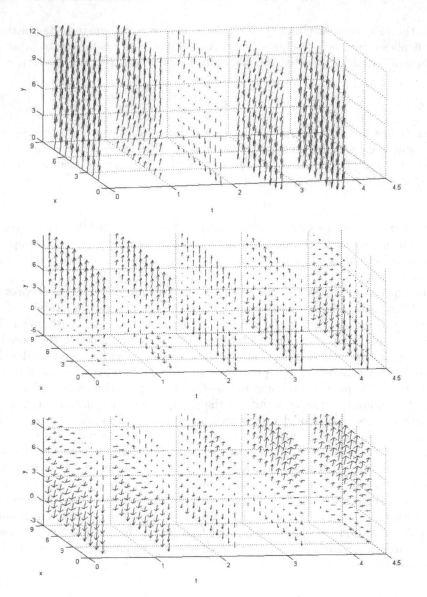

Fig. 1. Examples for eigenflows calculated from computed flow fields using spatial and temporal information; the inclusion of temporal information allows the representation of complex temporal phenomena such as a flow direction change (top), a moving motion discontinuity (center) and a moving divergence (bottom)

The size of the neighborhood $\mathcal{N}_x$ of course has to be the same as for the eigenflows. The function φ represents the error measure evaluating the similarity between the calculated flow vector u and the reconstructed vector $r(\mathcal{N}_x, k)$.

The correctness of computed flow fields is usually evaluated in terms of the angular error. Thus, we will use this error measure to define the function φ. Let the displacement vectors $\boldsymbol{u} = (u_1, u_2)$ be represented as 3-dimensional vectors of unity length $\overline{u} = \frac{1}{\sqrt{u_1^2+u_2^2+1}}(u_1, u_2, 1)$. Then we can derive the function φ based on the angular error α:

$$\varphi(\boldsymbol{u}, \boldsymbol{v}) = 1 - \alpha(\boldsymbol{u}, \boldsymbol{v}) \, , \, \alpha(\boldsymbol{u}, \boldsymbol{v}) = \frac{arccos(\overline{u} \cdot \overline{v})}{\pi} \tag{9}$$

The new confidence measure will be called pcaReconstruction measure.

Our proposed method may fail on rare occasions of untypical flows encountered in the imaged data. These are singular events which in case of underrepresentation in the training data may not be adequately incorporated into our basic PCA framework. A range of more refined algorithms have been developed in the field of statistical learning. Some of these might solve this problem, such as multiclass PCA [18] or partial least squares regression.

5   Evaluation of Confidence Measures

For the comparison of the proposed confidence measures to the best previously proposed confidence measures, we use the technique presented in [1]. It is based on the gradual sparsification (successive removal of least reliable flow vectors to reduce the computation error) of the flow fields. The following problems, which make a fair comparison very difficult, have been stated and solved in [1].

1. The confidence measures are bounded by the interval [0,1], but they all follow different scales, which do not necessarily span all possible values. Therefore a comparison of absolute confidence values is impossible.
2. The confidence values are often highly non-linear.

The basic idea for the comparison of a given to the optimal confidence map is to compare the sparsification order of both confidence measures. In this way non-linearities and different scales do not influence the result. Thus, ground truth for a given confidence measure is necessary. It is defined using the angular error of the computed flow vector $\boldsymbol{u}(\boldsymbol{x})$ and the ground truth flow vector $\boldsymbol{g}(\boldsymbol{x})$

$$c_{opt}(\boldsymbol{x}) = \varphi(\boldsymbol{u}(\boldsymbol{x}), \boldsymbol{g}(\boldsymbol{x})) \tag{10}$$

In [1] we have proposed the confidence measure quality value (CMQV) for the evaluation of a given confidence measure. Let Q be the set of all pixels q in the image sequence. The intuition is to "punish" any deviation from the optimal sparsification *order*. This punishment $P(q)$ at pixel q is weighted by the "damage" $D(q)$ this error in the sparsification order causes. $D(q)$ is defined as the difference in the error that could have been removed in this situation and the error that has been removed by eliminating the current flow vector. Finally the quality value of the confidence measure is calculated as the average over all punishment values weighted by the damage values for all pixels in the image sequence.

$$CMQV(Q) := \frac{\sum_{q \in Q} P(q)D(q)}{|Q|} \tag{11}$$

6   Results

The test of the proposed confidence measure is carried out as described in [1]. We use four test sequences to compare our results to previously known confidence measures based on the CMQV values defined in 11: the Marble and Yosemite sequences as well as the Street and the Office sequences [14] shown in Figure 2.

Fig. 2. A sample frame of each Marble, Yosemite, Street and Office sequence

Table 1. CMQV values scaled by a factor of 100 for the pcaReconstruction measure on all four test sequences for eigenflows based on ground truth flow fields (top) and on computed flow fields (bottom); parameters: number n and spatio-temporal size (x,y,t) of eigenflows in the format (n, x=y, t)

	Marble	Yosemite	Street	Office
ground truth	2.01 (2, 11, 5)	1.81 (6, 3, 1)	1.64 (4, 9, 3)	2.35 (14, 3, 3)
computed	1.98 (5, 19, 5)	1.72 (5, 3, 1)	1.60 (4, 9, 5)	2.38 (5, 3, 3)

Table 2. Comparison of new confidence measure (pcaReconst) to 9 best known confidence measures; the CMQV values are scaled by a factor of 100

Marble	Yosemite	Street	Office
anisoFlowReg (1.85)	**pcaReconst (1.72)**	isoFlowReg (1.44)	**pcaReconst (2.38)**
isoImReg (1.86)	structCt (2.49)	anisoFlowReg (1.47)	spaceTimeReg (3.45)
isoFlowReg (1.86)	isoImReg (2.96)	**pcaReconst (1.60)**	timeReg (3.49)
tvReg (1.88)	crossCorr (3.02)	tvReg (1.61)	anisoImReg (3.50)
homReg (1.88)	anisoImReg (3.06)	anisoImReg (1.64)	isoImReg (3.50)
anisoImReg (1.93)	structEv3 (3.06)	isoImReg (1.78)	tvReg (3.50)
pcaReconst (1.98)	ssd (3.06)	homReg (1.78)	anisoFlowReg (3.51)
timeReg (2.02)	anisoFlowReg (3.08)	spaceTimeReg (1.93)	homReg (3.56)
spaceTimeReg (2.23)	isoFlowReg (3.09)	structEv3 (1.96)	isoFlowReg (3.60)
laplaceConst (2.55)	homReg (3.20)	hessConst (2.13)	structCt (3.94)

We use the CMQV values as basis for the comparison of the proposed confidence measure and the best known measures from literature. A flow field calculated by the structure tensor method with the same parameters as in [1] (7x7x7

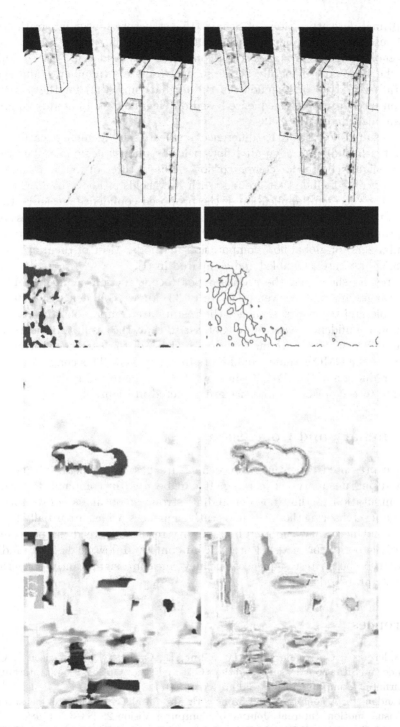

Fig. 3. Comparison to optimal confidence, left: optimal confidence map, right: pcaReconstruction confidence map

flow optimal derivative filters of Scharr [15], structure tensor integration scale $\sigma=4$) is used for the confidence measure test. As explained above, for the computation of eigenflows ground truth or computed flow fields can be used. Table 1 shows the best experimentally determined parameters (number n and spatio-temporal size (x,y,t) of eigenflows in the format (n,x=y,t)) for the pcaReconstruction measure for each sequence based on eigenflows computed from ground truth and calculated flow fields.

The results show that the difference between the eigenflows learned from ground truth and from computed flow fields is almost negligible. The results are even slightly better for computed flow fields in three of the four sequences. Hence, we can conclude that ground truth flow fields are not absolutely necessary for the successful application of the proposed confidence measure. Table 2 contains the ten best confidence measures for the four sequences. The best previously proposed confidence measures are based on energy terms (similarity terms or regularizers) of global flow computation methods. Most of them are derived from [6,5,4] and are assembled and compared in [1].

The results show that the proposed pcaReconstruction confidence measure always ranges among the seven best (out of 33) known confidence measures. For the Marble and the Street sequence the results are comparable to those of the best known confidence measure. In contrast to that, the results on the Yosemite and the Office sequence are far superior to those of the best known confidence measure as the CMQV values could be reduced by 31%. This corresponds to an average reduction of the CMQV value by 11.8 %. The resulting confidence maps compared to the optimal confidence are depicted in Figure 3.

7   Summary and Conclusion

We have presented a new confidence measure based on linear subspace projections using unsupervised learning. It can be used in combination with any flow computation method not demanding strong smoothness constraints, e.g. the structure tensor method. Ground truth sequences, which are usually unavailable, are not necessary to obtain high quality results - instead the performance is slightly superior for models learned from computed flow fields. Tests indicate that for the chosen test sequences the new measure significantly outperforms previously proposed measures.

References

1. Kondermann, C., Kondermann, D., Jähne, B., Garbe, C.: Comparison of Confidence and Situation Measures and their Optimality for Optical Flows. International Journal of Computer Vision (Submitted) (2007)
2. Anandan, P.: A computational framework and an algorithm for the measurement of visual motion. Internat. Journal of Computer Vision 2, 283–319 (1989)
3. Barron, J., Fleet, D., Beauchemin, S.: Performance of Optical Flow Techniques. International Journal of Computer Vision 12(1), 43–77 (1994)

4. Haußecker, H., Spies, H.: Motion. In: Handbook of Computer Vision and Applications. ch. 13, vol. 2, Academic Press, London (1999)
5. Papenberg, N., Bruhn, A., Brox, T., Didas, S., Weickert, J.: Highly Accurate Optic Flow Computation with Theoretically Justified Warping. International Journal of Computer Vision 67(2), 141–158 (2006)
6. Weickert, J., Schnörr, C.: A Theoretical Framework for Convex Regularizers in PDE-Based Computation of Image Motion. International Journal of Computer Vision 45(3), 245–264 (2001)
7. Lucas, B., Kanade, T.: An Iterative Image Registration Technique with an Application to Stereo Vision (DARPA). In: Proceedings of the 1981 DARPA Image Understanding Workshop, pp. 121–130 (1981)
8. Horn, B., Schunk, B.: Determining Optical Flow. Artificial Intelligence 17, 185–204 (1981)
9. Bruhn, A., Weickert, J., Schnörr, C.: Lucas/Kanade meets Horn/Schunck: Combining Local and Global Optic Flow Methods. International Journal of Computer Vision 61(3), 211–231 (2005)
10. Bruhn, A., Weickert, J.: A Confidence Measure for Variational Optic flow Methods. Springer Netherlands, pp. 283–298 (2006)
11. Bigün, J., Granlund, G.H., Wiklund, J.: Multidimensional orientation estimation with applications to texture analysis and optical flow. IEEE journal of pattern analysis and machine intelligence (PAMI) 13(8), 775–790 (1991)
12. Barth, E.: The minors of the structure tensor. In: Proceedings of the DAGM (2000)
13. Mota, C., Stuke, I., Barth, E.: Analytical Solutions For Multiple Motions. In: Proceedings of the International Conference on Image Processing ICIP (2001)
14. McCane, B., Novins, K., Crannitch, D., Galvin, B.: On Benchmarking Optical Flow. Computer Vision and Image Understanding 84(1), 126–143 (2001), http://www.cs.otago.ac.nz/research/vision/Research/OpticalFlow/opticalflow.html
15. Scharr, H.: Optimal filters for extended optical flow. In: Jähne, B., Mester, R., Barth, E., Scharr, H. (eds.) IWCM 2004. LNCS, vol. 3417, Springer, Heidelberg (2007)
16. Roth, S., Black, M.: On the spatial statistics of optical flow. In: Tenth IEEE International Conference on Computer Vision, vol. 1, pp. 42–49. IEEE, Los Alamitos (2005)
17. Black, M., Yacoob, Y., Jepson, A., Fleet, D.: Learning Parameterized Models of Image Motion. In: Proceedings of the Conference on Computer Vision and Pattern Recognition (CVPR) (1997)
18. Nieuwenhuis, C., Yan, M.: Knowledge Based Image Enhancement Using Neural Networks. In: Proceedings of the 18th International Conference on Pattern Recognition, pp. 814–817 (2006)

Bayesian Model Selection for Optical Flow Estimation

Kai Krajsek and Rudolf Mester

J.W. Goethe University, Frankfurt, Germany
Visual Sensorics and Information Processing Lab
{krajsek,mester}@vsi.cs.uni-frankfurt.de
http://www.vsi.cs.uni-frankfurt.de

Abstract. Global optical flow techniques minimize a mixture of two terms: a *data term* relating the observable signal with the optical flow, and a *regularization term* imposing prior knowledge/assumptions on the solution. A large number of different data terms have been developed since the first global optical flow estimator proposed by Horn and Schunk [1]. Recently [2], these data terms have been classified with respect to their properties. Thus, for image sequences where certain properties about image as well as motion characteristics are known in advance, the appropriate data term can be chosen from this classification. In this contribution, we deal with the situation where the optimal data term is *not* known in advance. We apply the Bayesian evidence framework for automatically choosing the optimal relative weight between two data terms as well as the regularization term based only on the given input signal.

1 Introduction

Motion estimation in image sequences is of crucial importance in computer vision, it has a wide range of applications spanning from robot navigation over medical image analysis to video compression. The motion of a single object, i.e. its displacement vector from frame to frame, which can be inferred from brightness changes in the image sequence is denoted as the *optical flow* vector. The set of all optical flow vectors is called the optical flow field. In order to infer the optical flow field from observable entities, e.g. the gray values in an image sequence, a functional relationship between the optical flow field and the observable image signal has to be established. A large number of different types of these *observation equations* has been proposed [2], their properties have been analyzed and classified. It is not very surprising that the simple brightness constancy assumption gives most accurate results when the model assumption - all brightness changes are due to motion - is fulfilled. But if the model assumption is only slightly violated, the accuracy breaks down, leading to highly erroneous results. One way to deal with brightness changes that are not caused by motions is to model the brightness change and optical flow simultaneously [3]. Another way is to relate the optical flow with the signal by observation equations that

F.A. Hamprecht, C. Schnörr, and B. Jähne (Eds.): DAGM 2007, LNCS 4713, pp. 142–151, 2007.

are less sensitive to brightness changes that are not caused by motion [2]. Since they actually disregard parts of the available information, these more robust observation equations have the drawback that they give less accurate results than the simple brightness constancy assumption in case if the model assumption is fulfilled. Furthermore, the most accurate of these illumination-insensitive observation equations induce an orientation dependency such that they are only valid for certain classes of motion [2]. In order to find the best compromise between the different models, it has been proposed to use a combination of different observation equations. But how to find the optimal weight between the different models? The present contribution aims at answering this question which was open so far. It extends the Bayesian evidence framework for choosing the optimal regularization parameter in global optical flow methods presented in [4,5]. Whereas in [4,5] only the optimal weight between data term and regularization term is estimated, the proposed method chooses also the optimal weights between two different model assumptions: the brightness constancy assumption and the generalized constancy assumption that includes the proposed observation equation proposed in [2] as well as the brightness constancy assumption and a new observation equation designed for multiplicative brightness chances.

2   Global Optical Flow Estimation

In the following we describe the image sequence intensity values as a continuous function $s(\boldsymbol{x})$, $\boldsymbol{x} = (x, y, t)$ defined on the continuous Euclidian space denoted as the *space-time volume* $\mathcal{A}$. In order to estimate the optical flow field from the image sequence, a functional relationship, the observation equation, between the signal $s(\boldsymbol{x})$ and the optical flow field $\boldsymbol{u}(\boldsymbol{x})$, has to be established. A simple relation can be derived by the assumption that all intensity variations are due to motion such that the brightness of the signal keeps constant through its evolution in space-time

$$s(x(t), y(t), t) = c \ . \tag{1}$$

This implies the total time derivative to be zero leading to the *brightness constancy constraint equation* (BCCE)

$$g_x u_x + g_y u_y + g_t = 0 \quad \Leftrightarrow \quad \boldsymbol{g}^T \boldsymbol{u}_h = 0 \ , \tag{2}$$

where we have defined $\boldsymbol{g} = (\partial_x s, \partial_y s, \partial_t s)^T$ and $\boldsymbol{u}_h = (u_x, u_y, 1)$. Since it is fundamentally impossible to solve for $\boldsymbol{u}_h$ by a single linear equation (*aperture problem*), additional constraints have to be found and employed. The assumption of spatial [6] or spatiotemporal [7,8] constancy of the flow field $\boldsymbol{u}$ in a local neighborhood V allows the accumulation of all BCCEs in V for a weighted least squares or total least squares optical flow estimation, but this provides the desired disambiguation of optical flow only if the spatial gradients of the image signal vary inside of the regarded neighborhood V. Simoncelli [9] provides a further regularization of the problem by introducing a prior *probability density function* (pdf) which penalizes large optical flow vectors. Whereas local methods minimize a loss function (a *residual*) over a local area $V \subset \mathcal{A}$, global methods [1,10,11,12] estimate the optical flow field by minimizing an error functional (or error function if u is considered on a discrete grid) over the whole space-time. The necessary additional constraint is incorporated by a *regularization term* $\rho(u)$ (ρ denotes an operator acting on the optical flow u) imposing supplementary information on the solution, e.g. the optical flow field should be smooth except for motion boundaries [10]. This means that going from local to global methods is to jump from the simple constant flow assumption directly to expressing smoothness by functionals on derivatives of the resulting flow function. We emphasize here that imposing slightly more complicated local flow models, such as affine, polynomial, etc is still a valid and viable alternative. The *regularization parameter* λ in global approaches specifies the influence of the regularization term $\rho(u)$ relative to the *data term* $\psi \left(g^T u_h \right)$, ($\psi$=real symmetric positive function that is monotonically increasing). There is a certain tradition of estimating the optical flow field by minimizing

$$J(u) = \int_{\mathcal{A}} \left(\psi \left(g^T u_h \right) + \lambda \rho(u) \right) dx \tag{3}$$

with respect to the optical flow field $u(x)$. In principle, the argument of the data term function $\psi(.)$ could be the residual of any valid observation equation. If the brightness constancy assumption does not hold, e.g. due to global brightness changes, (2) does not properly describe the relation between the optical flow and the observable signal any more. One way to deal with this situation is to introduce more complex equations modeling the brightness change and optical flow simultaneously [3]. The drawback is the increase of model parameters that has to be estimated from the input signal. In cases where one is not interested in the brightness model parameters but only in the optical flow it is often more efficient to relate the optical flow with features that are less sensitive to violations of the brightness constancy assumption [2]. A simple and rather popular strategy is to consider the constancy of the spatial gradient of the signal

$$\nabla s(x(t)), y(t), t) = c \ . \tag{4}$$

As in the case of the BCCE, the total time derivative is zero leading to the following equations, denoted as the generalized BCCE (GBCCE) in the following

$$g_{xx}u_x + g_{xy}u_y + g_{xt} = 0 \quad \Leftrightarrow \quad g_x^T u_h = 0 \tag{5}$$

$$g_{yx}u_x + g_{yy}u_y + g_{yt} = 0 \quad \Leftrightarrow \quad g_y^T u_h = 0 \ , \tag{6}$$

where we have defined $g_x = \left(\partial_x^2 s, \partial_x \partial_y s, \partial_x \partial_t s \right)^T$ and $g_y = \left(\partial_y \partial_x s, \partial_y^2 s, \partial_y \partial_t s \right)^T$ respectively. The optical flow is then, as for the case of the brightness constancy assumption, estimated by minimizing the energy functional where we exchange the data term in (3) by $\psi_1 \left(g_x^T u_h \right) + \psi_1 \left(g_y^T u_h \right)$. The gain in robustness with respect to illumination changes has to be payed with the introduction of directional information in the constancy assumption, i.e. the orientation of the spatial gradients. This means that spatial features are required not to change their orientation through the image sequence, e.g. objects should not to perform a rotation. One way to cope with this limitation is to introduce observation equations based on rotationally invariant features as proposed in [2]. The drawback of this strategy is the apparently poorer performance when compared with the generalized BCCE on an image sequence with violation of the brightness constancy assumption. In [2] a linear combination of different data terms has been proposed. An open question is the choice of the relative weight between both data term and also the choice of the regularization term in this context. This contribution fills this gap by presenting a method for estimating the optimal weights based only on the information delivered by the input signal. In the following we propose alternative illumination change robust feature, the derivative of the logarithm of the signal. Let us assume that the observed signal factorizes into a signal that fulfills the brightness constancy assumption and a term that describes the brightness changes that are not caused by motion. If we consider as a feature the spatial gradient of the logarithm of the signal $\nabla \log f = \nabla \log \gamma + \nabla \log \chi$, the feature separates in the sum of a term that depends on the signal which variations describe the motion and another term that describe all other brightness changes. Taking the total derivative with respect to the time yields the two equations

$$\frac{d\nabla \log f}{dt} = \frac{d\nabla \log \gamma}{dt} + \frac{d\nabla \log \chi}{dt} . \tag{7}$$

If we now assume that χ changes only very slowly in spatial direction, its spatial derivative becomes approximately zero and since per definition $\frac{d\nabla \log \gamma}{dt} = 0$, equations (7) lead to the two linear observation equations

$$h_{xx}u_x + h_{xy}u_y + h_{xt} = 0 \quad \Leftrightarrow \quad \boldsymbol{h}_x^T \boldsymbol{u}_h = 0 \tag{8}$$
$$h_{yx}u_x + h_{yy}u_y + h_{yt} = 0 \quad \Leftrightarrow \quad \boldsymbol{h}_y^T \boldsymbol{u}_h = 0 , \tag{9}$$

where we have defined $h_i = \partial_i \log f$.

In the next section, the variational formulations of the energy functions are reformulated into their statistical equivalent formulation and then the Bayesian evidence framework is presented for estimating the optical flow and model weights simultaneously.

3   Bayesian Motion Estimation

In a Bayesian formulation (see e.g. [9]), the optical flow is estimated via a pdf which connects the observable signal or its gradient with the entity of interest, the optical flow. In order to design such a pdf, we assume a regular grid in space-time considering only signal values and optical flow vectors on the knots of the grid. Since N knots in space-time are isomorphic to the Euclidian space $\mathbb{R}^N$, the signal and the optical flow field can be expressed by a set of vectors. The gradients $\boldsymbol{w}$ of the optical flow components $\boldsymbol{u}$ as well as the gradients $\boldsymbol{g}$ of the signal components

s can be written in a compact matrix vector equation $w = Hu \in \mathbb{R}^{6N}$, $g = Ps \in \mathbb{R}^{3N}$. In the Bayesian framework, not only the measured gradients $g = (g(x_1), g(x_2), ..., g(x_N))$, but also the estimated parameters u are considered as random variables with corresponding pdfs $p(u)$ and $p(g)$, respectively. Prior knowledge about u is incorporated into the estimation framework via the *prior* pdf $p(u)$. The *maximum a posteriori* (MAP) estimator infers the optical flow field by maximizing the *posterior* pdf $p(u|g)$. Using Bayes' law, the posterior pdf can be expressed by the *likelihood function* $p(g|u)$, the prior pdf $p(u)$ and the gradient pdf $p(g)$

$$\hat{u} = \arg\max_{u} \left\{ \frac{p(g|u)p(u)}{p(g)} \right\} \tag{10}$$

$$= \arg\min_{u} \left\{ -\ln(p(g|u)) - \ln(p(u)) \right\}. \tag{11}$$

The term in the bracket on the right side of equ.(11) is denoted as the *objective function* $\mathcal{L}$. For Gibbs fields with the partition functions $Z_L(\alpha)$, $Z_p(\beta)$, the energies $J_L(g|u, \alpha)$ and $J_p(u, \beta)$ and the corresponding hyper-parameters α, β, the objective function becomes

$$\mathcal{L} = J_L(g|u, \alpha) + J_p(u, \beta) + \ln\left(Z_L(\alpha)Z_p(\beta)\right). \tag{12}$$

Note that we parameterize the likelihood energy by multiple hyper-parameters α that weigh different observation models and the prior by one prior hyper-parameter. In the following we describe the likelihood and prior energy for the case of the optical flow estimation. Subsequently, the Bayesian evidence framework for estimating the hyper-parameters is presented.

4 Likelihood Functions and Prior Distributions for Motion Estimation

The likelihood function relates the observable input signal s with the optical flow field u. If errors in the spatial gradients can be neglected compared to errors in the temporal gradients, the residuum ε_j of the BCCE's can be assumed to be independent of the optical flow field $g_{sj}^T u + g_{tj} = \varepsilon_j$ [13]. Modeling each random variable ε_j as identical independent distributed, the joint pdf is simply the product $p(\varepsilon_t) = \prod_{j=1}^{N} p(\varepsilon_{tj})$ of the individual pdfs whereas each pdf is modeled by an exponential distribution. The equations (5), (6), (8) and (9) of the gradient brightness constancy assumption can be reformulated in the same way leading to the corresponding distributions $p(\varepsilon_{xt}) = \prod_{j=1}^{N} p(\varepsilon_{xtj})$ and $p(\varepsilon_{yt}) = \prod_{j=1}^{N} p(\varepsilon_{ytj})$, respectively. Due to the linear relationship between the residuum and the temporal gradients g_{tj}, we obtain the following likelihood functions

$$p(g_{kt}|u, g_{ks}, \alpha_k) = \frac{1}{Z_L(\alpha_k)} \exp\left\{ -\alpha_k \sum_{j=1}^{N} \psi_1\left(g_{kj}^T u_{hj}\right) \right\}, \tag{13}$$

where we have introduced $g_1 = g$, $g_2 = g_x$ and $g_3 = g_y$ for notational convenient reasons.If we now assume the different error variables ε_j, ε_{xj} and ε_{yj} to be statistically independent, we can combine all likelihood functions yielding

$$p(\{g_{jt}\}|u, \{g_{js}\}, \{\alpha_j\}) = \prod_{j=1}^{3} p(g_{jt}|u, g_{sj}, \alpha_j) \tag{14}$$

Note that the statistical independence between components of the same gradient is in fact fulfilled, if the temporal gradients are approximated by 1D derivative filter masks. In that case, the error variables of the GBCCE are linear combinations of error variables of the neighborhood of ε_j that do not intersect. In the following, we assume the two hyper-parameters belonging to the GBCCE model are equal reducing the total number of hyper-parameters to α_1 for the BCCE model and α_2 for the GBCCE model.

The prior pdf encodes our prior information/assumption of the optical flow field. The prior pdf corresponding to the smoothness assumption reads

$$p(u) = \frac{1}{Z_p(\beta)} e^{-\beta \sum_{j=1}^{N} \psi_2(|w_j|^2)} , \tag{15}$$

where ψ_2 is again a positive symmetric function.

5   Bayesian Model Selection

In order to determine the likelihood hyper-parameters $\alpha = (\alpha_1, \alpha_2, ..., \alpha_L)$ as well as the prior hyper-parameter β, we extend the evidence approach presented in [4,5] from one likelihood hyper-parameter to at least theoretical arbitrary number of likelihood parameters. The reason which allows us for doing so is mainly based on the assumed statistical independence of the likelihood function at different positions in space-time. Note that this is only approximatively true since they are actually correlated due to the overlapping derivative filter masks. We firstly review the main idea of the Bayesian evidence framework before presenting the extensions in more detail. The evidence framework is based on the MAP estimation, i.e. maximizing $p(\alpha, \beta|g)$ of the hyper-parameters using the evidence $p(g|\alpha, \beta)$ which is in fact the likelihood function of the hyper-parameters (α, β). Multiplying the evidence with the hyper-parameter prior $p(\alpha, \beta)$ yields the joint pdf $p(g, \alpha, \beta)$ of the gradient field and hyper-parameters that is proportional to the desired posterior pdf $p(g|\alpha, \beta)$, i.e. we can obtain the MAP estimate by maximizing also the joint pdf. In the following we assume a constant hyper-parameter prior such that it is sufficient to consider the evidence for estimating the hyper-parameters. The evidence can be obtained from the joint pdf $p(u, g|\alpha, \beta)$ of the gradient field g and the optical flow field u by marginalizing over the optical flow field. The hyper-parameters are then estimated by minimizing the negative logarithm of posterior with respect to α and β for the present realization of the gradient field g. In [4] the evidence for the likelihood parameter and the prior hyper-parameters has been derived. In [5] the approach has been extended to two prior hyper-parameters. Following the derivation in [4], we obtain the approximated evidence for multiple likelihood hyper-parameters

$$\tilde{p}(g|\alpha, \beta, \hat{u}) = \frac{(2\pi)^N}{\tilde{Z}_L(\alpha)\tilde{Z}_p(\beta) \det \mathbf{Q}^{\frac{1}{2}}} \exp\left(-\hat{J}\right) . \tag{16}$$

where $\hat{u}$ denotes the optical flow field that maximizes the posterior pdf $p(u|g, \alpha, \beta)$ and $\hat{J}$ the energy of the joint pdf $p(g, u|\alpha, \beta)$ taken at $\hat{u}$. The matrix $\mathbf{Q}$ denotes the Hessian of the joint pdf energy $J(u, g)$ taken at the maximum of the posterior pdf $p(u|g, \alpha, \beta)$. The partition function are analytically tractable

$$\tilde{Z}_L(\alpha) \propto \prod_j \alpha_j^{-N/2}, \quad \tilde{Z}_p(\beta) \propto \beta^{-N} \tag{17}$$

due to the Gaussian approximation of prior and likelihood. Note that since we are only interested in the functional dependency on the hyper-parameters, we can get rid of the proportional factors in (17) by maximizing the negative logarithm of the evidence. Since the computation of the determinant $\det \mathbf{Q}$ is not feasible for usual image sequence sizes, a further approximation has to be performed. For computing $\det \mathbf{Q}$, we neglect interactions between different pixels, i.e. $\mathbf{Q}$ becomes block diagonal which is in fact the zero order zone determinant expansion [14] of the matrix $\mathbf{Q}$. Then the determinant of $\mathbf{Q}(\hat{u}, \alpha, \beta)$ factorizes into the product of determinants of $\mathbf{Q}_j(\hat{u}, \alpha, \beta) = \mathbf{A}_j + \mathbf{B}_j$. The approximated objective function for the hyper-parameters then becomes

$$\mathcal{L}(\hat{u}, \alpha, \beta) \propto \hat{J} + \frac{1}{2}\sum_{j=1}^N \ln\left(\det \hat{\mathbf{Q}}_j\right) + \frac{N}{2}\sum_{n=1}^L \log(\alpha_n) + N\log(\beta) . \tag{18}$$

and the hyper-parameters are estimated by minimizing $\mathcal{L}$. Since $\hat{u}$ itself depends on the hyper-parameters α, β we have to apply an iterative scheme for estimating the optical flow field and the hyper-parameters simultaneously, i.e. we estimate the optical flow for fixed hyper-parameters and estimate then the hyper-parameters using the previously estimated optical flow. This procedure is repeated until convergence.

6   Experiments

In this section, the performance of our Bayesian Model selection (BMS) algorithm is presented where we combine either the BCCE (with the likelihood hyper-parameter α_1) with the generalized BCCE (GBCCE) with the spatial gradient of the signal (with the likelihood hyper-parameter α_2) or the spatial gradient of the logarithm of the signal (with the likelihood hyper-parameter α_3). We applied the energy function $\psi_i(x^2) = \xi_i^2\sqrt{1 + x^2/\xi_i^2}$ for all prior and likelihood terms where ξ_i is a free parameter that is to be determined by training data. For the experiment we used three image sequences, together with their

Table 1. Results (expressed by the average angular error (AAE)) of the Bayesian model selection (BMS) experiment with the three image sequences: 'Diverging Tree', 'Yosemite' and 'Office' and the linear combination of two out of three models have been applied. The image sequences fulfill either the brightness constancy assumption, obey a linear decrease of the global brightness with three different gradients $\kappa = 0.05, 0.1, 0.15$ or an exponential brightness decay with three different decay constants $\zeta = 0.025, 0.05, 0.075$.

Diverging Tree	$\kappa = 0$	$\kappa = 0.05$	$\kappa = 0.1$	$\kappa = 0.15$	$\zeta = 0.025$	$\zeta = 0.05$	$\zeta = 0.075$
$\alpha_1 = 1; \alpha_2 = 0$	1.11	19.89	38.69	59.51	13.12	22.23	29.39
$\alpha_1 = 0; \alpha_2 = 1$	1.56	2.93	5.39	11.59	2.66	3.57	4,43
BMS(α_1, α_2)	**1.28**	**3.46**	**6.62**	**15.72**	**3.23**	**4.29**	**5.57**
$\alpha_1 = 0; \alpha_3 = 1$	1.49	1.62	1.82	7.17	1.55	1.83	1.99
BMS(α_1, α_3)	**1.27**	**1.55**	**1.72**	**7.54**	**1.52**	**1.68**	**1.77**
Yosemite							
$\alpha_1 = 1; \alpha_2 = 0$	1.84	14.09	31.38	47.25	9.02	17.21	24.73
$\alpha_1 = 0; \alpha_2 = 1$	2.07	2.38	3.07	4.38	3.21	3.65	4.15
BMS(α_1, α_2)	**1.72**	**2.24**	**3.04**	**4.66**	**2.17**	**2.56**	**3.02**
$\alpha_1 = 0; \alpha_2 = 1$	3.12	3.12	3.12	3.12	3.12	3.12	3.12
BMS(α_1, α_3)	**2.19**	**2.66**	**2.67**	**2.67**	**2.65**	**2.66**	**2.66**
Office							
$\alpha_1 = 1; \alpha_2 = 0$	3.28	20.2	31.63	48.54	18.37	26.51	31.77
$\alpha_1 = 0; \alpha_2 = 1$	3.77	4.33	5.32	6.87	4.22	4.81	5.41
BMS(α_1, α_2)	**3.21**	**4.43**	**6.17**	**9.37**	**4.29**	**5.23**	**6.36**
$\alpha_1 = 0; \alpha_2 = 1$	3.68	3.70	3.72	3.79	3.69	3.70	3.71
BMS(α_1, α_3)	**3.66**	**3.65**	**3.65**	**3.72**	**3.65**	**3.64**	**3.64**

true optical flow [1]: 'Yosemite' (without clouds), 'Diverging Tree' and 'Office'. The derivatives occurring in the BCCE were designed according to [15] and are of size $9 \times 9 \times 9$. The optical flow u and the hyper-parameters α_1, α_2/α_3 and β were simultaneously estimated by minimizing the objective function (18).

For performance evaluation, the *average angular error* (AAE) [16] was computed. We optimized all free parameters, i.e. the pre-smoothing of the image sequences, the parameter ξ_i of the energy functions and the prior hyper-parameter (for cases where the hyper-parameters are not estimated) according to the known ground truth of the 'Diverging Tree' sequence. The algorithm is then applied to the 'Yosemite' and 'Office' sequence with this fixed parameters. We apply the algorithm to the original image sequences and to the image sequences that obey either a global linear brightness change with three different gradients $\kappa = 0.05, 0.1, 0.15$ or an exponential brightness decay with the decay constants $\zeta = 0.025, 0.05, 0.075$. Figure 1 (upper left and upper middle) shows two consecutive frames of the 'Office' image sequence with a linear decrease of brightness with $\kappa = 0.1$. The experimental results are depicted in table 1. Note

---

[1] The 'Diverging Tree' sequence has been taken from Barron's web-site, the 'Yosemite' sequence from *"http://www.cs.brown.edu/people/black/images.html"* and the 'Office' sequence from *"http://www.cs.otago.ac.nz/research/vision/"* .

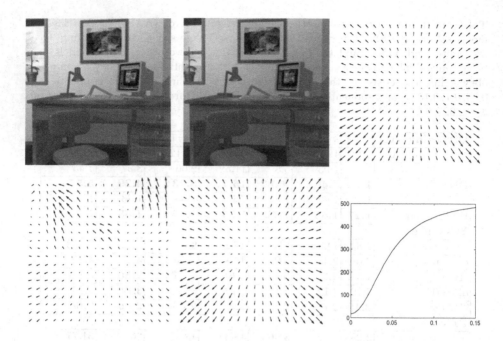

Fig. 1. Upper figures (from left to right): first frame of the 'Office' sequence; second frame of the 'Office sequence' with $\kappa = 0.1$; estimated flow field using $\alpha_1 = 1$ and $\alpha_2 = 0$ for $\kappa = 0$; Lower figures(from left to right):estimated flow field using $\alpha_1 = 1$ and $\alpha_2 = 0$ for $\kappa = 0.1$; estimated flow field using BMS for $\kappa = 0.1$; ratio of both likelihood hyper-parameters α_2/α_1 vs. κ for the BMS algorithm.

that the overall brightness change from one frame to another is rather weak but leads to rather strong erroneous results for the BCCE model ($\alpha_1 = 1$, $\alpha_2 = 0$). The BMS approach gives the most accurate results when applied to the 'test image sequences' 'Yosemite' and 'Office' when compared to fixed models, i.e. only one data term is applied, whose parameters have been tuned to the 'Diverging Tree' sequence . When the brightness constancy assumption is violated the BSE method increases the weight of the second likelihood hyper-parameter α_2 (see figure 1 lower right) in a wide rage depending on the strength of the brightness change leading also to accurate results. Note that in some cases the GBBCE model gives more accurate results than the BMS approach for the sequences with overall brightness changes. But if the optimal model is not known in advance the proposed method estimates automatically the optimal weights between the two models - resulting in most accurate results if the BCCE model is fulfilled and also in most cases in accurate results if the BCCE model assumption is violated.

7   Summary and Conclusion

In this contribution, we presented a Bayesian model selection technique for automatically determining the optimal weights between two data terms in global optical flow methods. We demonstrated the proposed approach with three models: the brightness constancy assumption and gradient brightness constancy assumption of the signal and its logarithm. Further work will examine the expansion of the proposed method to a larger number of models to be selected or weighted. Further research will also focus on the application of the method to the regularization term, i.e. a linear combination of different regularization terms is applied and the optimal weights should optimally be chosen by the Bayesian evidence framework.

References

1. Horn, B., Schunck, B.: Determining optical flow. Artificial Intelligence 17, 185–204 (1981)
2. Weickert, J., Bruhn, A., Brox, T., Papenberg, N.: A survey on variational optic flow methods for small displacements. In: Scherzer, O. (ed.) Mathematical models for registration and applications to medical imaging, pp. 103–136 (2006)
3. Haussecker, H., Fleet, D.: Computing optical flow with physical models of brightness variation. In: Proc. Computer Vision and Pattern Recognition (2000)
4. Krajsek, K., Mester, R.: Marginalized maximum a posteriori hyper-parameter estimation for global optical flow techniques. In: Bayesian Inference and Maximum Entropy Methods In Science and Engineering, Paris, France (2006)
5. Krajsek, K., Mester, R.: A maximum likelihood estimator for choosing the regularization parameters in global optical flow methods. In: IEEE International Conference on Image Processing, Atlanta, USA (2006)
6. Lucas, B., Kanade, T.: An iterative image registration technique with an application to stereo vision. In: Proc. Seventh International Joint Conference on Artificial Intelligence, Vancouver, Canada, August 1981, pp. 674–679 (1981)
7. Bigün, J., Granlund, G.H.: Optimal orientation detection of linear symmetry. In: Proc. ICCV, pp. 433–438. IEEE, Los Alamitos (1987)
8. Jähne, B.: Digital Image Processing, 4th edn. Springer, Heidelberg (1998)
9. Simoncelli, E., Adelson, E.H., Heeger, D.J.: Probability distribution of optical flow. In: Proc. IEEE Conference on Computer Vision and Pattern Recognition, Hawaii, pp. 310–315. IEEE Computer Society Press, Los Alamitos (1991)
10. Weickert, J., Schnörr, C.: A theoretical framework for convex regularizers in pde-based computation of image motion. Int. J. Comput. Vision 45, 245–264 (2001)
11. Black, M.J., Anandan, P.: A framework for the robust estimation of optical flow. In: Proc. Fourth International Conf. on Computer Vision (ICCV93), Berlin, Germany, pp. 231–236 (1993)
12. Alvarez, L., Weickert, J., Sánchez, J.: Reliable estimation of dense optical flow fields with large displacements. Int. J. Comput. Vision 39 (2000)
13. Simoncelli, E.P.: Design of multi-dimensional derivative filters. In: Intern. Conf. on Image Processing, Austin TX (1994)
14. Lee, D.J., Ipsen, I.C.F.: Zone determinant expansions for nuclear lattice simulations. Phys. Rev. C 68, 64003 (2003)
15. Scharr, H.: Optimal Operators in Digital Image Processing. PhD thesis, Interdisciplinary Center for Scientific Computing, Univ. of Heidelberg (2000)
16. Barron, J.L., Fleet, D.J., Beauchemin, S.S.: Performance of optical flow techniques. Int. Journal of Computer Vision 12, 43–77 (1994)

Illumination-Robust Variational Optical Flow
with Photometric Invariants

Yana Mileva, Andrés Bruhn, and Joachim Weickert

Mathematical Image Analysis Group
Faculty of Mathematics and Computer Science, Building E1.1
Saarland University, 66041 Saarbrücken, Germany
{mileva,bruhn,weickert}@mia.uni-saarland.de

Abstract. Since years variational methods belong to the most accurate techniques for computing the optical flow in image sequences. However, if based on the grey value constancy assumption only, such techniques are not robust enough to cope with typical illumination changes in real-world data. In our paper we tackle this problem in two ways: First we discuss different photometric invariants for the design of illumination-robust variational optical flow methods. These invariants are based on colour information and include such concepts as spherical/conical transforms, normalisation strategies and the differentiation of logarithms. Secondly, we embed them into a suitable multichannel generalisation of the highly accurate variational optical flow technique of Brox *et al.* This in turn allows us to access the true potential of such invariants for estimating the optical flow. Experiments with synthetic and real-world data demonstrate the success of combining accuracy and robustness: Even under strongly varying illumination, reliable and precise results are obtained.

1 Introduction

The recovery of the displacement vector field (optical flow) between two consecutive frames of an image sequence is a classical problem in computer vision. In this context, variational methods play an important role, since they allow to incorporate various model assumptions in a transparent way and they yield dense flow fields. Numerous modifications have been introduced since the first variational approaches of Horn and Schunck [8] and Nagel [12]: More recent techniques such as [3,11,4] combine discontinuity-preserving regularisers that respect motion boundaries, robust data terms that improve the performance with respect to outliers and noise, and hierarchical optimisation strategies that handle large displacements. This has led to highly accurate methods. Moreover, efficient numerical schemes allow for a real-time computation of the results [5].

However, there is one topic that has hardly been addressed in the literature on variational optical flow methods, but which is of fundamental importance for their applicability in practice: the robustness of the estimation under realistic illumination changes. Such illumination changes include for instance shadow/shading, specular reflections and globally varying illumination [7,18]. They can provide severe perturbations for important applications such as robot navigation or driver assistance systems.

F.A. Hamprecht, C. Schnörr, and B. Jähne (Eds.): DAGM 2007, LNCS 4713, pp. 152–162, 2007.

So far, most of the illumination-robust optical flow techniques in the literature are local methods: They are easy to implement, but they give non-dense flow fields and do not belong to the currently best performing techniques in terms of error measures. In particular, estimation techniques for colour image sequences are very popular [14,6,18]. Usually, such methods make use of photometric invariants that are derived from the HSI colour space [6,18], from normalised RGB channels [6], or from the $r\phi\theta$ representation that is obtained via the spherical coordinate transform (SCT) [18]. These expressions are in general invariant under illumination changes of multiplicative and/or additive type. Alternatively, in the context of grey value image sequences, different methods have been proposed that tackle the illumination problem by an explicit modelling of the underlying physical process [13,7]. In this case, the optical flow field and the parameters of the illumination model have to be estimated simultaneously. A last class of methods, that are also applicable to grey value image sequences, makes use of image derivatives [17]. However, one should note that derivatives are only invariant under additive illumination changes. Thus, they may not be optimal with respect to realistically varying illumination that always contains a multiplicative part [18].

In face of these strategies and the increasing accuracy of variational methods in the last few years, it becomes evident why recently more efforts have been made to embed such concepts into a suitable variational framework: Prominent examples are the techniques of Brox et al. [4] and Papenberg et al. [15] that are based on higher order image derivatives, as well as the method of Kim et al. [9] that models the illumination changes in an explicitly way. However, with respect to variational techniques that make use of photometric invariants, only one approach is known to us: Barron and Klette [2] incorporate a single invariant expression as part of a multichannel framework into the classical method of Horn and Schunck [8]. Since photometric invariants combine most of the advantages of derivative and model based approaches – they allow for the modelling of multiplicative and additive illumination changes without requiring the estimation of any additional model parameters – it is surprising that there has been no further research done in this direction.

Thus, the goal of the present paper is twofold: First, it shall provide an overview of the most important concepts to design photometric invariants for colour sequences. Secondly, by embedding these invariants into the highly accurate optical flow technique of Brox et al. [4], it shall investigate the true potential of recent variational optical flow methods under realistic illumination conditions.

Our paper is organised as follows. In Section 2 we give a short review on the dichromatic reflection model and discuss the basic properties of photometric invariants. This discussion allows us to propose five different invariants in Section 3. How these invariants can be incorporated into a suitable variational framework is then demonstrated in Section 4. Finally, we investigate the performance of the new method in Section 5. The summary in Section 6 concludes this paper.

2 The Dichromatic Reflection Model

In order to understand the basic concept behind photometric invariants, it makes sense to start by giving a short review of the *dichromatic reflection model* [16,18]. This model describes the observed RGB colour $\mathbf{c}(\mathbf{x}) = (R(\mathbf{x}), G(\mathbf{x}), B(\mathbf{x}))^{\top}$ at a certain location

$\mathbf{x} = (x, y)^\top$ as sum of an interface reflection component $\mathbf{c}_i(\mathbf{x})$ and a body reflection component $\mathbf{c}_b(\mathbf{x})$:

$$\mathbf{c}(\mathbf{x}) = \mathbf{c}_i(\mathbf{x}) + \mathbf{c}_b(\mathbf{x}). \tag{1}$$

While the interface reflection component is caused by specularities or highlights, the body reflection is directly related to the (Lambertian) reflection of the matte body. Physical characteristics of the camera are not modelled explicitly by this equation.

Under *spectrally uniform illumination*, these two terms can be decomposed further. They can be factorized into the overall intensity e, the geometrical reflection factor $m(\mathbf{x})$ and the reflectance colour $\widehat{\mathbf{c}}(\mathbf{x})$. Thus, equation (1) becomes

$$\mathbf{c}(\mathbf{x}) = e\left(m_i(\mathbf{x})\,\widehat{\mathbf{c}}_i(\mathbf{x}) + m_b(\mathbf{x})\,\widehat{\mathbf{c}}_b(\mathbf{x})\right), \tag{2}$$

which actually describes a linear combination of the two reflectance colours $\widehat{\mathbf{c}}_i$ and $\widehat{\mathbf{c}}_b$ with the corresponding geometric reflection factors m_i and m_b as weights. At this point one should note that the interface reflectance colour $\widehat{\mathbf{c}}_i$ cannot be arbitrary: Since we have assumed a spectrally uniform illumination, it is restricted to pure achromatic colours, i.e. grey values of any type. This in turn means that all three channels of $\widehat{\mathbf{c}}_i$ have equal contributions, i.e. $\widehat{R}_i(\mathbf{x}) = \widehat{G}_i(\mathbf{x}) = \widehat{B}_i(\mathbf{x}) =: w_i(\mathbf{x})$.

If we furthermore assume a *neutral interface reflection (NIR)* [10], the value $w_i(\mathbf{x})$ of all three interface channels becomes independent of the location. By defining the vector $\mathbf{1} = (1, 1, 1)^\top$ we can thus rewrite the dichromatic reflection model as

$$\mathbf{c}(\mathbf{x}) = e\left(m_i(\mathbf{x})\,w_i\,\mathbf{1} + m_b(\mathbf{x})\,\widehat{\mathbf{c}}_b(\mathbf{x})\right). \tag{3}$$

One should note that this equation is equivalent to the formulation considered in [18]. However, for a better understanding, we have made all the simplifications explicit.

Now we are in the position to give a concrete definition of photometric invariants: Photometric invariants are those expressions that are constructed from the observed colour $\mathbf{c}$ and that are at least independent of one of the three photometric variables e, m_b or m_i. In general, three different classes of photometric invariants can be distinguished: (i) Invariants with respect to *global multiplicative illumination changes* – these expressions are only independent of the light source intensity e. (ii) Invariants with respect to *shadow* and *shading* – these expressions are independent of the light source intensity e and the geometric body reflection factor m_b, at least for matte surfaces (i.e. $m_i = 0$). (iii) Invariants with respect to *highlights* and *specular reflections* – these expressions are independent of all three photometric variables e, m_b and m_i.

3   Photometric Invariants

After we have discussed the dichromatic reflection model, let us now investigate the main design principles behind photometric invariants. To this end, we consider the colour $\mathbf{c}(\mathbf{x})$ at a certain point $\mathbf{x}$ in terms of its three components $R(\mathbf{x})$, $G(\mathbf{x})$ and $B(\mathbf{x})$, respectively. Then, three main strategies for designing invariants are proposed in the literature: normalisation techniques, the differentiation of logarithmised channels, and the transformation to other colour spaces in terms of spherical/conical coordinates. Let us now discuss all three concepts in detail.

3.1 Normalisation Techniques

The first concept that we consider for designing photometric invariants is the transformation of the RGB colour space by means of normalisation [6]. In general, this transformation can be formulated as

$$(R, G, B)^\top \mapsto \left(\frac{R}{N}, \frac{G}{N}, \frac{B}{N}\right)^\top, \tag{4}$$

where N is a normalisation factor that depends on R, G and B. Such a proceeding yields a so-called *chromaticity space*. Two popular representatives for chromaticity spaces are the *arithmetic* and the *geometric chromaticity space* that are based on the normalisation by the arithmetic mean $N = (R + G + B)/3$ or the geometric mean $N = \sqrt[3]{RGB}$, respectively. However, with respect to the degree of invariance their behaviour is identical: By plugging the dichromatic reflection model (3) into equation (4), one can see that in both cases the photometric variables e and m_b cancel out (if $m_i = 0$). Thus, both the arithmetic and the geometric normalisation strategy yield expressions that are invariant under *shadow* and *shading*.

3.2 Log-Derivatives Strategies

A second class of strategies for creating photometric invariants is the computation of derivatives of the logarithmised colour channels. In the case of first order differential operators this yields the mapping

$$(R, G, B)^\top \mapsto \left((\ln R)_x, (\ln R)_y, (\ln G)_x, (\ln G)_y, (\ln B)_x, (\ln B)_y\right)^\top, \tag{5}$$

where subscripts denote partial derivatives, i.e. $G_x = \partial G/\partial x$. However, in contrast to the previous strategy this concept is not invariant with respect to shadow and shading: Only the overall intensity e is eliminated for $m_i = 0$, since the geometric reflection factor m_b depends on the location $\mathbf{x}$ and thus does not vanish. Therefore log-derivatives are only invariant under changes of the *image intensity*.

Nevertheless, this strategy may be an interesting upgrade possibility for techniques that are originally based on image derivatives such as the ones in [17,4,15]. By logarithmising the colour channels before the computation, such methods are able to handle global multiplicative illumination changes instead of global additive ones. Moreover, if the spatial variations of the geometric reflection factor m_b are rather small, such a strategy also provides a reasonable degree of invariance with respect to *shadow* and *shading*.

3.3 Spherical and Conical Transforms

The last concept for designing invariants that we discuss in this section is the consideration of other colour spaces that are obtained via spherical or conical transforms. Such colour spaces are e.g. the HSV and the $r\phi\theta$ colour space [6,18]. Let us start our discussion with the HSV colour space. This colour space represents each colour in terms of hue, saturation and value. While the hue describes the pure colour and the saturation stands for the achromatic/grey component, the value corresponds to the actual brightness. If we define $M = \max(R, G, B)$ and $m = \min(R, G, B)$, the corresponding transformation is given by:

$$
(R, G, B)^\top \mapsto
\begin{cases}
H = \begin{cases}
\frac{G-B}{M-m} \times 60°, & R \geq G, B, \\
(2 + \frac{B-R}{M-m}) \times 60°, & G \geq R, B, \\
(4 + \frac{R-G}{M-m}) \times 60°, & B \geq R, G,
\end{cases} & \pmod{360°}, \\
S = \frac{M-m}{M} \\
V = M.
\end{cases}
\tag{6}
$$

Evidently, the hue is invariant under both *shadow* and *shading* as well as *highlights* and *specularities*. However, since it involves the ratio of colour channel differences, it also discards the most information of all invariants. The other two channels are less robust: While the saturation allows to cope at least with *shadow* and *shading*, the value channel is not invariant at all.

In contrast to the HSV colour space that describes the RGB colours in terms of a cone, the $r\phi\theta$ colour space is obtained via a spherical transformation of the RGB coordinates. This transformation is given by

$$
(R, G, B)^\top \mapsto
\begin{cases}
r = \sqrt{R^2 + G^2 + B^2} \\
\theta = \arctan\left(\frac{G}{R}\right) \\
\phi = \arcsin\left(\frac{\sqrt{R^2+G^2}}{\sqrt{R^2+G^2+B^2}}\right)
\end{cases}.
\tag{7}
$$

Here, r denotes the magnitude of the colour vector and θ and ϕ are the two angles that describe longitude and latitude, respectively. As one can easily verify, both angles θ and ϕ are invariant with respect to *shadow* and *shading*. However, the colour magnitude r is no photometric invariant.

4   Variational Optical Flow Computation

Since we are interested in incorporating the previously discussed photometric invariants into a variational framework, let us briefly recall the basic idea behind variational methods. To this end, let us consider an image sequence $f(\mathbf{x}, t)$, where $\mathbf{x} = (x, y)^\top$ denotes the location within a rectangular image domain Ω and $t \geq 0$ denotes time. Then, variational optical flow methods compute the dense displacement field $\mathbf{u} = (u, v)^\top$ between two consecutive frames $f(\mathbf{x}, t)$ and $f(\mathbf{x}, t+1)$ as minimiser of an energy functional with the general structure

$$
E(\mathbf{u}) = E_D(\mathbf{u}) + \alpha\, E_S(\mathbf{u}),
\tag{8}
$$

where $E_D(\mathbf{u})$ and $E_S(\mathbf{u})$ denote the data and the smoothness term, respectively, and $\alpha > 0$ is a scalar weight that steers the degree of smoothness. While the data term penalises deviations from constancy assumptions – e.g. the constancy of the grey value of objects – the smoothness term regularises the often non-unique local solution of the data term by assuming (piecewise) smoothness of the result.

4.1   A Multichannel Approach for Photometric Invariants

Having explained the main idea behind variational methods, let us now derive a suitable model for computing the optical flow. Such a model must not only permit the integration of our photometric invariants into the data term, it should also allow the estimation of highly accurate optical flow fields. In order to satisfy both demands, we propose to compute the optical flow as minimiser of an energy functional $E(\mathbf{u})$ with data term

$$E_D(\mathbf{u}) = \int_\Omega \psi_D \Big(\sum_{i=1}^N \gamma_i \, |f_i(\mathbf{x}+\mathbf{u}, t+1) - f_i(\mathbf{x}, t)|^2 \Big) \, dx \, dy \tag{9}$$

and smoothness term

$$E_S(\mathbf{u}) = \int_\Omega \psi_S \left(|\nabla u|^2 + |\nabla v|^2 \right) dx \, dy . \tag{10}$$

Here, $\nabla u = (u_x, u_y)^\top$ and $\nabla v = (v_x, v_y)^\top$ denotes the spatial gradient of the flow component u and v, respectively.

This energy functional can be considered as a 2-D multichannel extension of the high accuracy technique of Brox *et al.* [4]. However, instead of assuming constancy on the grey value and its spatial derivatives, our method is based on the assumption that for corresponding objects in both frames the N different photometric invariants given by the channels f_i remain constant. Thus, for instance, we consider in the case of the spherical coordinate transform constancy assumptions on both channels of the image sequence $\mathbf{f} = (f_1, f_2) = (\phi, \theta)$ which can be obtained from the original colour image sequence $\mathbf{f} = (R, G, B)$ using equation (7) . In this context, the scalars $\gamma_i > 0$ serve as weights that steer the importance of the different channels. In order to allow for a correct estimation of large displacements, all photometric constancy assumptions are employed in their original nonlinear form. Moreover, both the data and the smoothness term are penalised in a non-quadratic way - to render the approach more robust to outliers and noise in the case of the data term and to preserve motion boundaries by modelling a piecewise smooth flow field in the case of the smoothness term. For both purposes the regularised version of the L_1-norm is used. It is given by $\psi(s^2) = \sqrt{s^2 + \epsilon^2}$, where ϵ is a small regularisation parameter. In our case ϵ is set to 10^{-3}.

4.2   Minimisation

In order to minimise the previously proposed energy functional, one has to solve its Euler-Lagrange equations. These equations are given by the following coupled pair of nonlinear partial differential equations (PDEs):

$$0 = \psi_D'(...) \Big(\sum_{i=1}^N \gamma_i \, (f_i(\mathbf{x}+\mathbf{u}, t+1) - f_i(\mathbf{x}, t)) \frac{\partial}{\partial x} f_i(\mathbf{x}+\mathbf{u}, t+1) \Big)$$
$$+ \alpha \, \mathrm{div} \left(\psi_S' \left(|\nabla u|^2 + |\nabla v|^2 \right) \nabla u \right) , \tag{11}$$

$$0 = \psi_D'(...) \Big(\sum_{i=1}^N \gamma_i \, (f_i(\mathbf{x}+\mathbf{u}, t+1) - f_i(\mathbf{x}, t)) \frac{\partial}{\partial y} f_i(\mathbf{x}+\mathbf{u}, t+1) \Big)$$
$$+ \alpha \, \mathrm{div} \left(\psi_S' \left(|\nabla u|^2 + |\nabla v|^2 \right) \nabla v \right) , \tag{12}$$

where $\psi'_D(...)$ is an abbreviation for

$$\psi'_D(...) = \psi'_D\left(\sum_{i=1}^{N} \gamma_i \,|f_i(\mathbf{x}+\mathbf{u},t+1)-f_i(\mathbf{x},t)|^2\right).$$

After discretising these equations by means of finite difference approximations, the resulting nonlinear system of equations is solved via two nested fixed point iterations and a coarse-to-fine warping strategy as proposed in [4]. Alternatively, also a real-time capable multigrid scheme could be used [5].

5   Experiments

In our first experiment, we investigate the usefulness of different photometric constancy assumptions with respect to spatially varying multiplicative and additive illumination changes (using a Gaussian model). To this end, we consider frame 10 and 11 of the *Street* sequence available at http://of-eval.sourceforge.net and

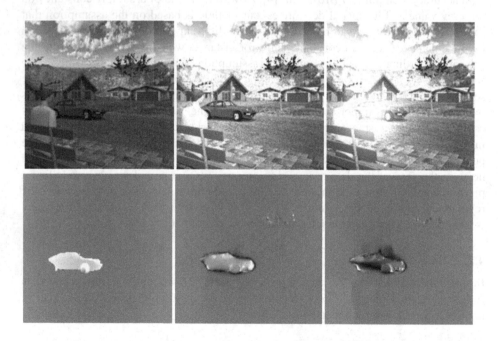

Fig. 1. Robustness of the $\phi\theta$ constancy assumption under varying illumination. *Top Row: (a)* Frame 11 of the *Street* sequence (200×200). *(b)* Frame 11 with spatially varying multiplicative illumination. *(c)* Frame 11 with spatially varying multiplicative and additive illumination. *Bottom Row: (d)* Ground truth (magnitude plot). *(e)* Computed result for (a) and (b). *(f)* Computed result for (c). Colour images and flow fields are available at http://www.mia.uni-saarland.de/bruhn/dagm07/flowfields/index.html.

Table 1. Comparison of the different illumination invariants for the *Street* sequence in its original form (orig.), with locally varying multiplicative illumination (mult.) and with locally varying multiplicative and additive illumination (mult.+add.). All weights γ_i have been set to one. The remaining parameters have been optimised with respect to the average angular error (AAE). #Ch = number of channels.

Concept		#Ch	AAE orig.	AAE mult.	AAE mult. + add.
Standard	RGB	3	2.65°	43.44°	43.44°
Colour Space	HSL (Hue)	1	4.28°	4.28°	4.28°
	spherical (ϕ, θ)	2	**2.07°**	**2.07°**	**3.37°**
Normalisation	RGB (arithm. mean)	3	2.22°	2.22°	3.71°
	RGB (geom. mean)	3	2.26°	2.26°	5.64°
Log-Derivatives	$\nabla \ln(RGB)$	6	2.89°	3.04°	4.35°
Brox et al. (2-D)	RGB + ∇ RGB	9	2.64°	3.89°	3.92°

create two strongly degraded variants of frame 11 with heavily varying illumination (cf. Figure 1). The different photometric constancy assumptions and the corresponding results in terms of the average angular error [1] are listed in Table 1. As one can see, the standard RGB constancy assumption fails completely under varying illumination. Thereby, the error of 43.44° refers to a zero displacement field which means in turn that the underlying method could not make any use of the provided information. In contrast, all techniques based on photometric invariants perform favourably. In particular the constancy assumption on the $\phi\theta$ channels gives excellent results: With average angular errors up to 2.07°, it does not only outperform the hue channel, that offers a higher degree of invariance at the expense of discarding too much information, it also provides better results for the sequence *with* spatially varying multiplicative illumination changes than the 2-D RGB Brox *et al.* for the sequence *without*. Compared to the best result in the literature that is known to the authors – the result of 4.85° by Weickert and Schnörr [19] – this improvement is even more drastical. Thus it is not surprising that the corresponding flow fields of the $\phi\theta$-channels in Figure 1 show a precise estimation of the optical flow: The shape of the car is well preserved and the camera motion is also estimated accurately.

   In our second experiment, we analyse the performance of the different photometric invariants with respect to typical illumination changes in real-world data. To this end, we consider the left frames 205 and 207 of the *DIPLODOC Road* stereo sequence available at http://tev.itc.it/DATABASES/road.html. As one can see from the computed results in Figure 2, the method based on the standard RGB constancy assumptions has again severe problems. Instead of compensating for the varying illumination between both frames, it interprets this change as a global motion in upward direction (street). Since the ego-motion of the camera system induces a divergent flow field, this estimation is completely wrong. However, once again our techniques based on photometric constancy assumptions give very good results. The $\phi\theta$-channels and the normalised RGB values (using the geometric mean) even allow to detect the pedestrian at the lower left border of the image – in spite of the severely changed illumination

Fig. 2. Results under real illumination conditions *Top Row:* (a) Left frame 205 of the *Road* stereo sequence of the DIPLODOC project (size 320 × 240). (b) Left frame 207. (c) Flow with RGB constancy assumption (magnitude plot). *Middle Row:* (d) Hue constancy assumption. (e) $\phi\theta$ constancy assumption. (f) Normalised RGB constancy assumption (arithm.). *Bottom Row:* (g) Normalised RGB constancy assumption (geom.). (h) Log-derivative constancy assumption. (i) 2-D Brox *et al.* (2-D). Colour images and flow fields are available at http://www.mia.uni-saarland.de/bruhn/dagm07/flowfields/index.html.

conditions. This confirms our findings from the first experiment: If suitable photometric invariants are embedded within an accurate variational framework, they may render the underlying method highly robust with respect to realistic changes of the illumination. However, as the first experiment has also shown, one has to be careful not to discard too much information, since otherwise the quality of the estimation decreases.

6   Summary and Conclusions

Photometric invariants and variational methods are two successful concepts in image analysis that have emerged without many interactions so far. In our paper we have demonstrated the benefits of combining them in order to solve a challenging computer vision problem: dense and highly accurate motion estimation under realistic changes of the illumination conditions. We have thereby shown that the performance of variational optical flow methods can be significantly improved, if traditional constancy assumptions are replaced by photometric invariants.

It is our hope that this research serves as another step that helps to bridge the gap between mathematically well-founded theories and more robust real-life applications.

Acknowledgements

Yana Mileva gratefully acknowledges funding by the German Academic Exchange Service (DAAD).

References

1. Barron, J.L., Fleet, D.J., Beauchemin, S.S.: Performance of optical flow techniques. International Journal of Computer Vision 12(1), 43–77 (1994)
2. Barron, J.L., Klette, R.: Quantitative colour optical flow. In: Proc. 16th International Conference on Pattern Recognition, Quebec City, Canada, August 2002, vol. 4, pp. 251–255. IEEE Computer Society Press, Los Alamitos (2002)
3. Black, M.J., Anandan, P.: The robust estimation of multiple motions: parametric and piecewise smooth flow fields. Computer Vision and Image Understanding 63(1), 75–104 (1996)
4. Brox, T., Bruhn, A., Papenberg, N., Weickert, J.: High accuracy optic flow estimation based on a theory for warping. In: Pajdla, T., Matas, J(G.) (eds.) ECCV 2004. LNCS, vol. 3024, pp. 25–36. Springer, Heidelberg (2004)
5. Bruhn, A., Weickert, J., Kohlberger, T., Schnörr, C.: A multigrid platform for real-time motion computation with discontinuity-preserving variational methods. International Journal of Computer Vision 70(3), 257–277 (2006)
6. Golland, P., Bruckstein, A.M.: Motion from color. Computer Vision and Image Understanding 68(3), 346–362 (1997)
7. Haußecker, H., Fleet, D.: Estimating optical flow with physical models of brightness variation. IEEE Transactions on Pattern Analysis and Machine Intelligence 23(6), 661–673 (2001)
8. Horn, B., Schunck, B.: Determining optical flow. Artificial Intelligence 17, 185–203 (1981)
9. Kim, Y.-H., Martínez, A.M., Kak, A.C.: Robust motion estimation under varying illumination. Image and Vision Computing 23(1), 365–375 (2005)
10. Lee, H.C., Breneman, E.J., Schulte, C.P.: Modeling light reflection for computer vision. IEEE Transactions on Pattern Analysis and Machine Intelligence 12, 402–409 (1990)
11. Mémin, E., Pérez, P.: Hierarchical estimation and segmentation of dense motion fields. International Journal of Computer Vision 46(2), 129–155 (2002)
12. Nagel, H.-H.: Constraints for the estimation of displacement vector fields from image sequences. In: Proc. Eighth International Joint Conference on Artificial Intelligence, Karlsruhe, West Germany, August 1983, vol. 2, pp. 945–951 (1983)
13. Negahdaripour, S.: Revised definition of optical flow: integration of radiometric and geometric clues for dynamic scene analysis. IEEE Transactions on Pattern Analysis and Machine Intelligence 20(9), 961–979 (1998)
14. Ohta, N.: Optical flow detection by color images. In: Proc. Tenth International Conference on Pattern Recognition, Singapore, September 1989, pp. 801–805 (1989)
15. Papenberg, N., Bruhn, A., Brox, T., Didas, S., Weickert, J.: Highly accurate optic flow computation with theoretically justified warping. International Journal of Computer Vision 67(2), 141–158 (2006)

16. Shafer, S.A.: Using color to seperate reflection components. Color Research and Applications 10(4), 210–218 (1985)
17. Uras, S., Girosi, F., Verri, A., Torre, V.: A computational approach to motion perception. Biological Cybernetics 60, 79–87 (1988)
18. van de Weijer, J., Gevers, T.: Robust optical flow from photometric invariants. In: Proc. 2004 IEEE International Conference on Image Processing, Singapore, October 2004, vol. 3, pp. 1835–1838 (2004)
19. Weickert, J., Schnörr, C.: Variational optic flow computation with a spatio-temporal smoothness constraint. Journal of Mathematical Imaging and Vision 14(3), 245–255 (2001)

Online Smoothing for Markerless Motion Capture[*]

Bodo Rosenhahn[1], Thomas Brox[2], Daniel Cremers[2], and Hans-Peter Seidel[1]

[1] Max Planck Center Saarbrücken, Germany
rosenhahn@mpi-inf.mpg.de
[2] CVPR Group, University of Bonn, Germany

Abstract. Tracking 3D objects from 2D image data often leads to jittery tracking results. In general, unsmooth motion is a sign of tracking errors, which, in the worst case, can cause the tracker to loose the tracked object. A straightforward remedy is to demand temporal consistency and to smooth the result. This is often done in form of a post-processing. In this paper, we present an approach for online smoothing in the scope of 3D human motion tracking. To this end, we extend an energy functional by a term that penalizes deviations from smoothness. It is shown experimentally that such online smoothing on pose parameters and joint angles leads to improved results and can even succeed in cases, where tracking without temporal consistency assumptions fails completely.

1 Introduction

Tracking 3D objects from 2D images is a well known task in computer vision with various approaches such as edge based techniques [8], particle filters [7], or region-based methods [14,1], just to name a few. Due to ambiguities in the image data, many tracking algorithms produce jittery results. On the other hand, smoothing assumptions of the observed motion can be made due to the inertness of the masses of involved objects. This means, that it is physically unlikely that an object continuously moved by a robot arm or human hand is rapidly changing the direction or even jittering, unless there are physiological diseases. Many tracking procedures do not take this property into account. Hence, the outcome tends to wobble around the true center of the tracked object. To receive a more appealing outcome, the results are often smoothed in a second post-processing step. However, jittery results often indicate errors or ambiguities during tracking. Thus, introducing temporal consistency already during the estimation, can help to eliminate errors at the root of the problem.

In case of human motion capturing and animation, several approaches exist in the literature to smooth motions of joints during synthesis. Bruderlin et al. [3] use a multi target motion interpolation with dynamic time warping in a signal based approach or Sul et al. [16] and Ude et al. [17] propose an extended Kalman filter. While these works have only addressed the smoothing of joint angles, the smoothing of 3D rigid body motions has been addressed in other works: Chaudhry et al. [6] smooth Euler angles and translation vectors. Shoemake [15] proposes quaternions for rotation animation (and interpolation) combined with translation vectors. Park et al. [12] use a rational

---

[*] This work has been supported by the Max-Planck Center for Visual Computing and Communication.

F.A. Hamprecht, C. Schnörr, and B. Jähne (Eds.): DAGM 2007, LNCS 4713, pp. 163–172, 2007.
© Springer-Verlag Berlin Heidelberg 2007

interpolating scheme for rotations by representing the group with Cayley parameters and using Euclidean methods in this parameter space. Belta et al. [4] propose a Lie-group and Lie-algebra representation in terms of an exponential mapping and twists to interpolate rigid body motions.

All these works concentrate on the synthesis, smoothing, and interpolation of given motion patterns, whereas in this work we smooth estimated motions online during a tracking procedure: we use a previously developed markerless motion capture system, which performs image segmentation and pose tracking of articulated 3D free-form sur-face models. In complex scenes (e.g. outdoor environments), we frequently observed the effect of motion jitter as a precursor to tracking failure. Therefore, in this work, we supplement a penalizer to the existing error functional in order to reduce large jit-ter effects. Whereas the penalizer term for joint angles (as scalar functions) is pretty straightforward, the challenging aspect is to formalize penalizers for rigid body mo-tions. To achieve this, we use exponentials of twists to represent rigid body motions (RBMs) and a *logarithm* to determine from a given RBM the generating twist, simi-lar to the motion representation in [11,12]. The gradient of the penalizer leads to linear equations, which can easily be integrated in the numerical optimization scheme as addi-tional constraints. In several experiments in the field of markerless motion capture, we demonstrate the improvements obtained with the integrated smoothness assumptions. As we cannot give a complete overview on the vast variety of existing motion capture systems, we refer to the surveys [9,10].

2   Foundations

In this section, we introduce mathematical foundations needed for the motion penalizer, in particular the twist representation of a rigid body motion and the conversion from the twist to the group action as well as vice-versa. Both conversions are needed later in Section 4 for the smoothing of rigid body motions.

2.1   Rigid Body Motion and Its Exponential Form

Instead of using concatenated Euler angles and translation vectors, we use the twist representation of rigid body motions, which reads in exponential form [11]:

$$M = \exp(\theta\hat{\xi}) = \exp\begin{pmatrix} \hat{\omega} & v \\ 0_{3\times1} & 0 \end{pmatrix} \tag{1}$$

where $\theta\hat{\xi}$ is the matrix representation of a twist $\xi \in se(3) = \{(v,\hat{\omega}) | v \in \mathbb{R}^3, \hat{\omega} \in so(3)\}$, with $so(3) = \{A \in \mathbb{R}^{3\times3} | A = -A^T\}$. The Lie algebra $so(3)$ is the tangential space of all 3D rotations. Its elements are (scaled) rotation axes, which can either be represented as a 3D vector or a skew symmetric matrix:

$$\theta\omega = \theta\begin{pmatrix} \omega_1 \\ \omega_2 \\ \omega_3 \end{pmatrix}, \text{ with } \|\omega\|_2 = 1 \quad \theta\hat{\omega} = \theta\begin{pmatrix} 0 & -\omega_3 & \omega_2 \\ \omega_3 & 0 & -\omega_1 \\ -\omega_2 & \omega_1 & 0 \end{pmatrix}. \tag{2}$$

A twist ξ contains six parameters and can be scaled to $\theta\xi$ for a unit vector ω. The pa-rameter $\theta \in \mathbb{R}$ corresponds to the motion velocity (i.e., the rotation velocity and pitch).

For varying θ, the motion can be identified as screw motion around an axis in space. The six twist components can either be represented as a 6D vector or as a 4×4 matrix:

$$\theta\xi = \theta(\omega_1, \omega_2, \omega_3, v_1, v_2, v_3)^T, \|\omega\|_2 = 1, \qquad \theta\hat{\xi} = \theta \begin{pmatrix} 0 & -\omega_3 & \omega_2 & v_1 \\ \omega_3 & 0 & -\omega_1 & v_2 \\ -\omega_2 & \omega_1 & 0 & v_3 \\ 0 & 0 & 0 & 0 \end{pmatrix}. \tag{3}$$

se(3) to SE(3). To reconstruct a group action $M \in SE(3)$ from a given twist, the exponential function $M = \exp(\theta\hat{\xi}) = \sum_{k=0}^{\infty} \frac{(\theta\hat{\xi})^k}{k!}$ must be computed. This can be done efficiently via

$$\exp(\theta\hat{\xi}) = \begin{pmatrix} \exp(\theta\hat{\omega}) & (I - \exp(\theta\hat{\omega}))(\omega \times v) + \omega\omega^T v\theta \\ 0 & 1 \end{pmatrix} \tag{4}$$

and by applying the Rodriguez formula

$$\exp(\theta\hat{\omega}) = I + \hat{\omega}\sin(\theta) + \hat{\omega}^2(1 - \cos(\theta)). \tag{5}$$

This means, the computation can be achieved by simple matrix operations and sine and cosine evaluations of real numbers. This property was exploited in [2] to compute the pose and kinematic chain configuration in an orthographic camera setup.

SE(3) to se(3). In [11], a constructive way is given to compute the twist which generates a given rigid body motion. Let $R \in SO(3)$ be a rotation matrix and $t \in \mathbb{R}^3$ a translation vector for the rigid body motion

$$M = \begin{pmatrix} R & t \\ 0 & 1 \end{pmatrix}. \tag{6}$$

For the case $R = I$, the twist is given by

$$\theta\xi = \theta(0, 0, 0, \frac{t}{\|t\|}), \quad \theta = \|t\|. \tag{7}$$

In all other cases, the motion velocity θ and the rotation axis ω are given by

$$\theta = \cos^{-1}\left(\frac{trace(R) - 1}{2}\right), \quad \omega = \frac{1}{2\sin(\theta)} \begin{pmatrix} r_{32} - r_{23} \\ r_{13} - r_{31} \\ r_{21} - r_{12} \end{pmatrix}.$$

To obtain v, the matrix

$$A = (I - \exp(\theta\hat{\omega}))\hat{\omega} + \omega\omega^T\theta \tag{8}$$

obtained from the Rodriguez formula (see Equation (4)) needs to be inverted and multiplied with the translation vector t,

$$v = A^{-1}t. \tag{9}$$

This follows from the fact that the two matrices which comprise A have mutually orthogonal null spaces when $\theta \neq 0$. Hence, $Av = 0 \Leftrightarrow v = 0$. We call the transformation from $SE(3)$ to $se(3)$ the logarithm, $\log(M)$.

2.2 Kinematic Chains

Our models of articulated objects, e.g. humans, are represented in terms of free-form surfaces with embedded kinematic chains. A kinematic chain is modeled as the consecutive evaluation of exponential functions, and twists ξ_i are used to model (known) joint locations [11]. The transformation of a mesh point of the surface model is given as the consecutive application of the local rigid body motions involved in the motion of a certain limb:

$$X_i' = \exp(\theta\hat{\xi})(\exp(\theta_1\hat{\xi}_1)\ldots\exp(\theta_n\hat{\xi}_n))X_i. \tag{10}$$

For abbreviation, we note a pose configuration by the $(6+n)$-D vector $\chi = (\xi, \theta_1, \ldots, \theta_n) = (\xi, \Theta)$ consisting of the 6 degrees of freedom for the rigid body motion ξ and the nD vector Θ comprising the joint angles. In the MoCap-setup, the vector χ is unknown and has to be determined from the image data.

2.3 Pose Estimation from Point Correspondences

Assuming an extracted image contour and the silhouette of the projected surface mesh, closest point correspondences between both contours can be used to define a set of corresponding 3D rays and 3D points. Then a 3D point-line based pose estimation algorithm for kinematic chains is applied to minimize the spatial distance between both contours: for point based pose estimation each line is modeled as a 3D Plücker line $L_i = (n_i, m_i)$, with a unit direction n_i and moment m_i [11]. For pose estimation the reconstructed Plücker lines are combined with the screw representation for rigid motions. Incidence of the transformed 3D point X_i with the 3D ray $L_i = (n_i, m_i)$ can be expressed as

$$(\exp(\theta\hat{\xi})X_i)_{3\times1} \times n_i - m_i = 0. \tag{11}$$

Since $\exp(\theta\hat{\xi})X_i$ is a 4D vector, the homogeneous component (which is 1) is neglected to evaluate the cross product with n_i. This nonlinear equation system can be linearized in the unknown twist parameters by using the first two elements of the sum representation of the exponential function:

$$\exp(\theta\hat{\xi}) = \sum_{i=0}^{\infty} \frac{(\theta\hat{\xi})^i}{i} \approx (I + \theta\hat{\xi}). \tag{12}$$

This approximation is used in (11) and leads to the linear equation system

$$((I + \theta\hat{\xi})X_i)_{3\times1} \times n_i - m_i = 0. \tag{13}$$

Gathering a sufficient amount of point correspondences and appending the single equation systems, leads to an overdetermined linear system of equations in the unknown pose parameters $\theta\hat{\xi}$. The least squares solution is used for reconstruction of the rigid body motion using Equation (4) and (5). Then the model points are transformed and a new linear system is built and solved until convergence. The final pose is given as the consecutive evaluation of all rigid body motions during iteration.

Since joints are expressed as special screws with no pitch of the form $\theta_j \hat{\xi}_j$ with known $\hat{\xi}_j$ (the location of the rotation axes is part of the model) and unknown joint angle θ_j. The constraint equation of an ith point on a jth joint has the form

$$(\exp(\theta \hat{\xi}) \exp(\theta_1 \hat{\xi}_1) \ldots \exp(\theta_j \hat{\xi}_j) X_i)_{3 \times 1} \times n_i - m_i = 0 \tag{14}$$

which is linearized in the same way as the rigid body motion itself. It leads to three linear equations with the six unknown twist parameters and j unknown joint angles.

3 Markerless Motion Capture

The motion capturing model we use in this work can be described by an energy functional, which is sought to be minimized [13]. It comprises a level set based segmentation, similar to the Chan-Vese model [5], and a shape term that states the pose estimation task:

$$E(\Phi, p_1, p_2, \chi) = \underbrace{- \int_\Omega (H(\Phi) \log p_1 + (1 - H(\Phi)) \log p_2 + v|\nabla H(\Phi)|) \, dx}_{\text{segmentation}}$$

$$\underbrace{+ \lambda \int_\Omega (\Phi - \Phi_0(\chi))^2 dx}_{\text{shape error}} \tag{15}$$

The function $\Phi \in \Omega \mapsto \mathbb{R}$ serves as an implicit contour representation. It splits the image domain Ω into two regions Ω_1 and Ω_2 with $\Phi(x) > 0$ if $x \in \Omega_1$ and $\Phi(x) < 0$ if $x \in \Omega_2$. Those two regions are accessible via the step function $H(s)$, i.e., $H(\Phi(x)) = 1$ if $x \in \Omega_1$ and $H(\Phi(x)) = 0$ otherwise. Probability densities p_1 and p_2 measure the fit of an intensity value $I(x)$ to the corresponding region. They are modeled by local Gaussian distributions [14]. The length term weighted by $v > 0$ ensures the smoothness of the extracted contour.

By means of the contour Φ, the contour extraction and pose estimation problems are coupled. In particular, the projected surface model Φ_0 acts as a shape prior to support the segmentation [14]. The influence of the shape prior on the segmentation is steered by the parameter $\lambda = 0.05$.

Due to the nonlinearity of the optimization problem, an iterative minimization scheme is chosen: first the pose parameters χ are kept constant, while the functional is minimized with respect to the partitioning. Then the contour is kept constant, while the pose parameters are determined to fit the surface mesh to the silhouettes (Section 2.3).

4 Penalizing Motion Jitter

To avoid motion jitter, the idea is to extend the energy functional in (15) by an additional error term that penalizes deviations of the estimated pose from a smooth prediction generated from the poses of previous frames.

Such a prediction $\underline{\chi} = (\underline{\xi}, \underline{\Theta})$ (as global pose) can be computed by means of the joint angle derivatives,

$$\underline{\Theta} = \Theta_t^s + \partial \Theta_t^s = \Theta_t^s + (\Theta_t^s - \Theta_{t-1}^s), \tag{16}$$

and the twist that represents the predicted position,

$$\underline{\hat{\xi}} = \log\left(\exp(\hat{\xi}_t)\exp(\hat{\xi}_{t-1})^{-1}\exp(\hat{\xi}_t)\right), \tag{17}$$

see Section 2.1. The deviation of the estimate $\chi = (\xi, \Theta)$ from the prediction can now be measured by

$$E_{Smooth} = |\log\left(\exp(\underline{\hat{\xi}})\exp(\hat{\xi})^{-1}\right)|^2 + |\underline{\Theta} - \Theta|^2. \tag{18}$$

Notice that the deviation of the rigid body motion is modeled by the minimal geodesics between the current and predicted pose.

This error value is motivated from the exponential form of rigid body motions: since we linearize the pose, see (13), we have to do exactly the same here. The derivative of the joint angles is simply given by $\underline{\Theta} - \Theta$. To compute the motion derivative we can apply the logarithm from Section 2.1 to get a linearized geodesic [11]. This follows from the fact that the spatial velocity corresponding to a rigid motion generated by a screw action is precisely the velocity generated by the screw itself. To see this, we first set

$$\exp(\hat{\xi}') := \exp(\underline{\hat{\xi}})\exp(\hat{\xi})^{-1}, \tag{19}$$

with $\xi' = \log(\exp(\underline{\hat{\xi}})\exp(\hat{\xi})^{-1})$. Let $g(0) \in \mathbb{R}^3$ be a point transformed to

$$g(\theta) = \exp(\hat{\xi}'\theta)g(0). \tag{20}$$

The spatial velocity of the point is given by [11]

$$\hat{V} = \dot{g}(\theta)g^{-1}(\theta). \tag{21}$$

Since,

$$\frac{d}{dt}(\exp(\hat{\xi}'\theta)) = \hat{\xi}'\dot{\theta}\exp(\hat{\xi}'\theta), \tag{22}$$

we have

$$\hat{V} = \dot{g}(\theta)g^{-1}(\theta) \tag{23}$$

$$= \hat{\xi}'\dot{\theta}\exp(\hat{\xi}'\theta)g(0)g^{-1}(\theta) \tag{24}$$

$$= \hat{\xi}'\dot{\theta}g(\theta)g^{-1}(\theta) = \hat{\xi}'\dot{\theta}. \tag{25}$$

After setting $\dot{\theta} = 1$ $(\theta = t)$, the linearized penalizer term acts as additional linear equation to the pose constraints which further regularize the equations,

$$\frac{\partial E_{Smooth}}{\partial \chi} = (\log(\exp(\underline{\hat{\xi}})\exp(\hat{\xi})^{-1}), \underline{\Theta} - \Theta)^{\top} = 0. \tag{26}$$

Equation (26) yields an additional constraint for each parameter that draws the solution towards the prediction. Note that we do not perform an offline smoothing in a second processing step. Instead, the motion jitter is penalized online in the estimation procedure, which does not only improve the smoothness of the result, but also stabilizes the tracking.

5   Experiments

The experiments are subdivided into indoor and outdoor experiments. The indoor experiments allow for a controlled environment. The outdoor experiments demonstrate the applicability of our method to quite a tough task: markerless motion capture of highly dynamic sporting activities with non-controlled background, changing lighting conditions and full body models.

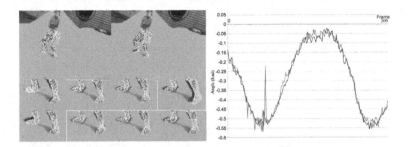

Fig. 1. Left: Example frames of a knee bending sequence. Right: Quantization of outcome: Red: without penalizer, blue: with penalizer. The Penalizer function is suited to penalize rapid movement changes during tracking, not the smaller ones.

5.1   Indoor Experiments

For indoor experiments we use a parameterized mesh model of legs, represented as free-form surface patches.

Figure 1 shows in the left several consecutive example frames of a knee-bending scene in the lab environment. The smaller images in the first row show 4 example feet positions without a smoothness assumption and the last row shows feet positions with such an assumption. The motion jitter in these four consecutive frames is suppressed. The effect is quantified in the right of Figure 1. Here we have overlaid knee angles. The red values indicate the result of the system without the jitter penalizer and the blue one is the outcome with the incorporated penalizer. As can be seen, the penalizer decreases rapid motion changes, but maintains the smaller ones. The red peak around frame 50 is due to a corrupted frame, similar to the one in Figure 3

5.2   Outdoor Experiments

In our outdoor experiments we use two full body models of a male and female person with 26 degrees of freedom. Different sequences were captured in a four-camera setup (60 fps) with Basler gray-scale cameras. Here we report on a running trial and a coupled cartwheel flick-flack sequence, due to their high dynamics and complexity.

Figure 2 summarizes results of the running trial: all images have been disturbed by 15% uncorrelated noise and random rectangles of random color and size. Tracking is successful in both cases, with the smoothness assumption and without it. However,

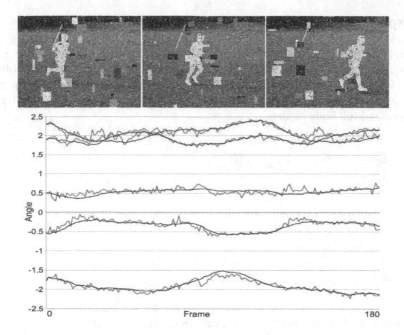

Fig. 2. Running trial of a male person. Top: The images have been disturbed with uncorrelated noise of 15% and random rectangles of random color and size. Bottom: Comparison of (some) joint angles: Red: Without jitter penalizer, black: with jitter penalizer. The curves reveal, that with the jitter penalizer the motion is much smoother.

Fig. 3. Tracking in an outdoor environment: corrupted frames can cause larger errors, which are avoided by adding the penalizer function

the diagram reveals that the curves with a smoothness constraint are much smoother. A comparison with a hand-labeled marker-based tracking system revealed an average error of 5.8 degrees between our result and the marker-based result. More importantly,

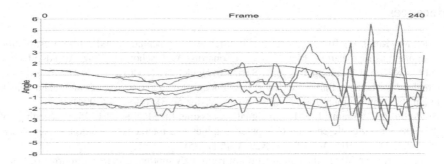

Fig. 4. Red: Tracking fails, Blue: Tracking is successful

Fig. 5. Example frames of the (successful tracked) Cartwheel-Flick-Flack sequence in a virtual environment. The small images show one of the four used cameras.

the variance between our method and the marker-based method has been reduced from 12 degrees to 5 degrees by using the jitter penalizer.

Another impact of our approach is shown in Figure 3: when grabbing images of a combined cartwheel and flick-flack, some frames were stored completely wrong, resulting in leg crossings and self intersections. Due to the smoothness term, the rapid leg movement is reduced and self-intersection avoided. Because of such noise effects, the tracking fails in the latter part of the sequence, see Figure 4, whereas it is successful with the integrated smoothness constraint. This shows that the smoothness assumption can make the difference between a successful tracking and an unsuccessful one. Figure 5 shows key frames of the successfully tracked sequence.

6 Summary

In this work, we have presented an extension of a previously developed markerless motion capture system by integration of a smoothness constraint, which suppresses 3D motion jitter during tracking. In various experiments we have shown that the outcome is smoother and more realistic. There is no need for a second processing step to post-smooth the data. We have further shown that the additional penalizer can be decisive for successful tracking. It also acts as a regularizer that prevents singular systems of equations. In natural scenes, such as human motion tracking or 3D rigid object tracking, the results are generally improved, since an assumption of smooth motion is reasonably due to the involved inertness of masses.

References

1. Bray, M., Kohli, P., Torr, P.: Posecut: Simultaneous segmentation and 3d pose estimation of humand using dynamic graph-cuts. In: Leonardis, A., Bischof, H., Pinz, A. (eds.) ECCV 2006. LNCS, vol. 3952, pp. 642–655. Springer, Heidelberg (2006)
2. Bregler, C., Malik, J., Pullen, K.: Twist based acquisition and tracking of animal and human kinematics. International Journal of Computer Vision 56(3), 179–194 (2004)
3. Bruderlin, A., Williams, L.: Motion signal processing. In: SIGGRAPH '95: Proceedings of the 22nd annual conference on Computer graphics and interactive techniques, New York, NY, USA, pp. 97–104. ACM Press, New York (1995)
4. Belta, C., Kumar, V.: On the computation of rigid body motion. Electronic Journal of Computational Kinematics 1(1) (2002)
5. Chan, T., Vese, L.: Active contours without edges. IEEE Transactions on Image Processing 10(2), 266–277 (2001)
6. Chaudhry, F.S., Handscomb, D.C.: Smooth motion of a rigid body in 2d and 3d. In: IV '97: Proceedings of the IEEE Conference on Information Visualisation, Washington, DC, USA, p. 205. IEEE Computer Society Press, Los Alamitos (1997)
7. Deutscher, J., Reid, I.: Articulated body motion capture by stochastic search. Int. J. of Computer Vision 61(2), 185–205 (2005)
8. Drummond, T.W., Cipolla, R.: Real-time tracking of complex structures for visual servoing. In: Triggs, B., Zisserman, A., Szeliski, R. (eds.) Vision Algorithms: Theory and Practice. LNCS, vol. 1883, pp. 69–84. Springer, Heidelberg (2000)
9. Moeslund, T.B., Hilton, A., Krüger, V.: A survey of advances in vision-based human motion capture and analysis. Computer Vision and Image Understanding 104(2), 90–126 (2006)
10. Moeslund, T.B., Granum, E.: A survey of computer vision based human motion capture. Computer Vision and Image Understanding 81(3), 231–268 (2001)
11. Murray, R.M., Li, Z., Sastry, S.S.: Mathematical Introduction to Robotic Manipulation. CRC Press, Baton Rouge (1994)
12. Park, F., Ravani, B.: Bezier curves on riemannian manifolds and lie groups with kinematics applications. Journal of Mechanical Design 117(1), 36–40 (1995)
13. Rosenhahn, B., Brox, T., Kersting, U., Smith, A., Gurney, J., Klette, R.: A system for markerless motion capture. Künstliche Intelligenz (1), 45–51 (2006)
14. Rosenhahn, B., Brox, T., Weickert, J.: Three-dimensional shape knowledge for joint image segmentation and pose tracking. International Journal of Computer Vision 73(3), 243–262 (2007)
15. Shoemake, K.: Animating rotation with quaternion curves. In: SIGGRAPH '85: Proceedings of the 12th annual conference on Computer graphics and interactive techniques, New York, NY, USA, pp. 245–254. ACM Press, New York (1985)
16. Sul, C., Jung, S., Wohn, K.: Synthesis of human motion using kalman filter. In: Magnenat-Thalmann, N., Thalmann, D. (eds.) CAPTECH 1998. LNCS (LNAI), vol. 1537, pp. 100–112. Springer, Heidelberg (1998)
17. Ude, A., Atkeson, C.G.: Online tracking and mimicking of human movements by a humanoid robot. Journal of Advanced Robotics 17(2), 165–178 (2003)

Occlusion Modeling by Tracking Multiple Objects*

Christian Schmaltz[1], Bodo Rosenhahn[2], Thomas Brox[3], Joachim Weickert[1],
Daniel Cremers[3], Lennart Wietzke[4], and Gerald Sommer[4]

[1] Mathematical Image Analysis Group, Faculty of Mathematics and Computer Science,
Building E1.1, Saarland University, 66041 Saarbrücken, Germany
{schmaltz,weickert}@mia.uni-saarland.de
[2] Max-Planck Institute for Informatics, 66123 Saarbrücken, Germany
rosenhahn@mpi-sb.mpg.de
[3] Department of Computer Science,University of Bonn, 53117 Bonn, Germany
{brox,dcremers}@cs.uni-bonn.de
[4] Institute of Computer Science, Christian-Albrecht-University, 24098 Kiel, Germany
{lw,gs}@ks.informatik.uni-kiel.de

Abstract. This article introduces a technique for region-based pose tracking of multiple objects. Our algorithm uses surface models of the objects to be tracked and at least one calibrated camera view, but does not require color, texture, or other additional properties of the objects. By optimizing a joint energy defined on the pose parameters of all objects, the proposed algorithm can explicitly handle occlusions between different objects. Tracking results in simulated as well as real world scenes demonstrate the effects of occlusion and how they are handled by the proposed method.

1 Introduction

This article deals with 2-D–3-D pose tracking of multiple objects, which is the task to pursue the 3-D positions and orientations of known 3-D object models from a 2-D image data stream [7]. Pose tracking has a wide range of applications, e.g. self localization and object grasping in robotics, or camera calibration. Although the initial work of Lowe [10] was published more than a quarter of a century ago, pose tracking is still a challenging problem, especially in scenes with cluttered backgrounds, partial occlusions, noise, or changing illumination.

A problem similar to pose tracking is pose estimation. The difference is that there is usually no initial pose given in pose estimation, but only a single pose must be estimated. In this article, we will concentrate on pose tracking and not on pose estimation. Thus, the problem to find the necessary approximate model pose for the first frame will not be discussed.

A lot of different approaches for pose tracking have been considered [6]. A common idea is to use feature matching. The features used range from points [1] over lines [3] to more complex features such as vertices, t-junctions, cusps, three-tangent junctions, limb

---

* We acknowledge funding by the German Research Foundation under the projects We 2602/5-1 and SO 320/4-2, and the Max-Planck Center for Visual Computing and Communication.

F.A. Hamprecht, C. Schnörr, and B. Jähne (Eds.): DAGM 2007, LNCS 4713, pp. 173–183, 2007.

and edge injections, and curvature L-junctions [9]. Drummond and Cipolla used edge-detection to achieve real-time tracking of articulated object with their iterative algorithm [5]. In [2], Agarwal and Triggs describe learning-based methods that use regression for human pose tracking. Another learning based approach was proposed by Taycher et al. in [16], in which an undirected conditional random field is used. Moreover, methods based on neural networks [17] have been introduced. Another possible approach to pose tracking is to match a surface model of the tracked object to the object region seen in the images. In doing so, the computation of this region yields a typical segmentation problem. It has been suggested to optimize a coupled formulation of both problems and to solve simultaneously for both the contour and the pose parameters via level sets [4]. In [13], it was proposed to estimate the 3-D pose parameters by minimizing an energy function directly defined on the images, i.e. without using segmentation as an intermediate step. In the present paper, we build upon this framework.

Most works on 3D tracking concentrate on a single object that used to be fully visible in the image. Usually, the techniques run into severe problems when objects occlude each other. In the present work, we deal with such scenes that contain multiple, partially occluding objects, and show that the corresponding problems can be avoided, if the occlusions are explicitly modeled in the tracking framework. Some related works on multiple object tracking are those in [8], where particle filters and a Gibbs sampler are employed for 2-D tracking of a changing number of objects. The same problem is solved in [15] with a Rao-Blackwellized sequential Monte Carlo method. As both works state only a 2-D tracking in the image domain, they are very restricted in handling mutual occlusions.

Our paper is organized as follows: In the following section, we will briefly review the basics of pose estimation from 2-D–3-D point correspondences. After that, an approach for pose tracking of single objects is described in Section 3, followed by an explanation how the algorithm can be extended to yield improved results by tracking several objects. Experimental results are presented in Section 5. Section 6 concludes with a summary.

2   Pose Estimation from 2-D–3-D Point Correspondences

This section introduces basic concepts and notation and briefly describes the point-based pose estimation algorithm in [12]. The main idea is to use 2-D–3-D point correspondences (x_i, q_i), i.e. 3-D points x_i on the object model, which are visible as 2-D points q_i in an image, to find the rigid motion of the object. Section 3 shows how such point correspondences are obtained with our method.

2.1   Rigid Motion and Twists

A rigid body motion in 3-D, i.e. an isomorphism that preserves orientation and distances, can be represented as $m(x) := Rx + t$, where $t \in \mathbb{R}^3$ is a translation vector and $R \in SO(3)$ is a rotation matrix with $SO(3) := \{R \in \mathbb{R}^{3 \times 3} : \det(R) = 1\}$. By means of homogeneous coordinates, we can write m as a 4×4 matrix M:

$$m((x_1, x_2, x_3)^T) = M(x_1, x_2, x_3, 1)^T = \begin{pmatrix} R_{3 \times 3} & t_{3 \times 1} \\ 0_{1 \times 3} & 1 \end{pmatrix} x. \tag{1}$$

Rigid motions are of interest to us, since a rigid body can only perform a rigid motion. The set of all rigid motions is called the *Lie group SE*(3). To every Lie group there is an associated Lie algebra, whose underlying vector space is the tangent space of the Lie group evaluated at the origin. The Lie algebras associated with $SO(3)$ and $SE(3)$ are $so(3) := \{A \in \mathbb{R}^{3\times3}|A^T = -A\}$, and $se(3) := \{(v, \omega)|v \in \mathbb{R}^3, \omega \in so(3)\}$, respectively. Since elements of $se(3)$ can be converted to $SE(3)$ and vice versa, we can represent rigid motions as elements of $se(3)$. Such elements are called *twists*. This is advantageous since a twist has only six parameters while an element of $SE(3)$ has twelve. Both have six degrees of freedom, though.

Since elements of $so(3)$ and $se(3)$ can be written both as vectors $\omega = (\omega_1, \omega_2, \omega_3)$, $\xi = (\omega_1, \omega_2, \omega_3, v_1, v_2, v_3)$ and as matrices,

$$\hat{\omega} = \begin{pmatrix} 0 & -\omega_3 & \omega_2 \\ \omega_3 & 0 & -\omega_1 \\ -\omega_2 & \omega_1 & 0 \end{pmatrix} \in so(3), \qquad \hat{\xi} = \begin{pmatrix} \hat{\omega} & v \\ 0_{3\times1} & 0 \end{pmatrix} \in se(3), \qquad (2)$$

we distinguish these two ways of representing elements by a hat sign. Thus, the matrix $\hat{\xi}$ and the vector ξ are always two different representations of the same element. A twist $\xi \in se(3)$ can be converted to an element of the Lie group $M \in SE(3)$ by the exponential function $\exp(\hat{\xi}) = M$. This exponential can be computed efficiently with the Rodriguez formula. For further details we refer to [11].

2.2   From 2-D–3-D Point Correspondences to a Linear Least Squares Problem

Let (q, x) be a 2-D–3-D point correspondence, i.e. let $x \in \mathbb{R}^4$ be a point in homogeneous coordinates on the 3-D silhouette of the object model and $q \in \mathbb{R}^2$ its position in the image. Furthermore, let $L = (n, m)$ be the Plücker line [14] through q and the corresponding camera origin. The distance of any point a to the line L given in Plücker form can be computed by using the cross product: $\|a \times n - m\|$, i.e., $a \in L$ if and only if $\|a \times n - m\| = 0$.

Our goal is to find a twist ξ such that the transformed points $\exp(\hat{\xi})x_i$ are close to the corresponding lines L_i. Linearizing the exponential function $\exp(\hat{\xi}) = \sum_{k=0}^{\infty} \frac{\hat{\xi}^k}{k!} \approx I + \hat{\xi}$ (where I is the identity matrix), we like to minimize with respect to ξ:

$$\sum_i \left\| \left(\exp\left(\hat{\xi}\right) x_i\right)_{3\times1} \times n_i - m_i \right\|^2 \approx \sum_i \left\| \left(\left(I + \hat{\xi}\right) x_i\right)_{3\times1} \times n_i - m_i \right\|^2 \rightarrow \min, \qquad (3)$$

where the function $\cdot_{3\times1} : \mathbb{R}^4 \mapsto \mathbb{R}^3$ removes the last entry, which is 1.

Evaluation yields three linear equations of rank two for each correspondence (q_i, x_i). Thus, three correspondences are sufficient to obtain a unique solution of the six parameters of the twist. Usually, there are far more point correspondences and one obtains a least squares problem, which can be solved efficiently with the Householder algorithm. Since the twist ξ only corresponds to the pose change it is usually rather small, which justifies the linearization. In order to also allow for larger motions, we iterate this minimization process. This comes down to a variant of the Gauss-Newton method.

3   Region-Based Model Fitting

A lot of existing contour-based pose estimation algorithms expect an explicit contour to establish correspondences between contour points and points on the model surface. This involves a matching of the projected surface and the contour. Here we avoid explicit computations of contours and contour matching. Instead, we stick to [13] and seek to adapt the pose parameters in such a way that the projections of the surface optimally split all images into the object and the background region. For simplicity, we will first review this setting for a single rigid object. The extension to multiple objects, which is the main focus of this paper, will be explained later in Section 4.

3.1   Energy Model

Like in a segmentation task, we seek an optimal partitioning of the image domain Ω. This can be expressed as minimization of the energy function

$$E(\xi) = -\int_\Omega \left(P(\xi,q)\log p_1 + (1-P(\xi,q))\log p_2\right)dq\,, \qquad (4)$$

where the function $P : \mathbb{R}^6 \times \Omega \ni (\xi,q) \mapsto \{0,1\}$ is 1 if and only if the surface of the 3-D model with pose ξ projects to the point q in the image plane. P splits the image domain into two parts, in each of which different feature distributions are expected. These distributions are modeled by *probability density functions (pdf)* p_1 and p_2. Such pdfs also occur in variational segmentation methods [4], where a functional similar to this function is sought to be minimized. However, while in variational segmentation algorithms the partitioning is represented by a contour, i.e. a function, (4) implies only six optimization variables. Moreover, there is no need for a regularization of the object boundary, which can reduce the accuracy of tracking [13]. In order to model the image features by pdfs, we first have to decide which features should be modeled. For the experiments presented later, we have used the color in CIELAB color space.

Since the two pdfs p_1 and p_2 are unknown, we must assume an underlying model to estimate them. We track objects with uniform appearance by means of a non-parametric Parzen density and object with a varying appearance with a local Gaussian distribution [4]. Since there is not enough data available to accurately estimate a multi-dimensional pdf, we consider the separate feature channels to be independent. Thus, the total probability density function is the product of the single channel densities. As soon as the estimated pose changes, and thus the induced partitioning, p_1 and p_2 are recomputed.

3.2   Minimization

Since $E(\xi)$ in (4) is a multi-dimensional function on an open domain, we know from basic calculus that $\nabla E(\xi)$ must vanish at a minimum of $E(\xi)$. However, this nonlinear equation system is far too complex to be solved directly. Hence, we make use of a gradient descent that should result in the desired pose that minimizes $E(\xi)$ locally. In order to compute the gradient of $E(\xi)$, we assume that the function P is differentiable. Then we get:

$$\nabla E(\xi) = -\int_\Omega \left(\nabla P(\xi,q)(\log p_1 - \log p_2)\right)dq\,. \qquad (5)$$

Thus, the energy function (4) is minimized by moving each point on the contour of the projected model to the direction indicated by the gradient ∇P. This movement is transfered to corresponding 3-D points on the surface model by using the framework from Section 2. In this way, we estimate the rigid body motion necessary to change the 2-D silhouette in such a way that different features are separated more clearly.

More precisely, we create 2-D–3-D point correspondences (q_i, x_i) by projecting silhouette points x_i, using the current pose ξ, to the image plane where they yield q_i. Each image point q_i obtained in this way which seems to belong to the object region – i.e. those points for which $p_1(q_i)$ is greater than $p_2(q_i)$ – will be moved in outward normal direction to a new point q_i'. Points where $p_1(q_i) < p_2(q_i)$ holds will be shifted into the opposite direction to q_i', respectively. In order to compute the normal direction ∇P, we use Sobel operators. Experimental results indicate that the length $l := \|q_1 - q_2\|$ of the shift vector should be set to a constant depending on the sequence, since the results from experiments with varying l were inferior to those obtained with a constant l.

The 2-D–3-D point correspondences (q_i', x_i) obtained in this way are used in the point based pose tracking algorithm explained above to get a new pose. This forms one optimization step. This step is iterated until the pose changes induced by the force vectors will start to mutually cancel each other. We stop iterating when the average pose change after up to three iterations is smaller than a given threshold. Before changing frames in an image sequence, we predict the object's pose in the new frame by linearly extrapolating the results from the two previous frames. This prediction is very simple and fast, but leads to improved results in case of fast moving objects.

4   Extension to Multiple Objects

The tracking algorithm presented in the last section works fine if there is only a single object in the scene. In this section, we discuss possible problems that can occur as soon as there is more than one object to be tracked and how the tracking framework can be extended in order to deal with such scenes.

4.1   Uncoupled Tracking of Multiple Objects

The basic idea when tracking n objects simultaneously is as follows: Instead of minimizing the energy function (4), which depends on only one pose, the goal is to minimize an energy function depending on the poses of all objects $\xi_1, \ldots, \xi_n$, i.e.

$$E(\xi_1, \ldots, \xi_n) = -\sum_{i=1}^{n} \int_{\Omega} \left(P_i(\xi_i, q) \log p_{i,1} + (1 - P(\xi_i, q)) \log p_{i,2}\right) dq. \tag{6}$$

This function can be minimized in basically the same way as in the single object case: After projecting every object to the image plane, 2-D–3-D point correspondences are gathered along the 2-D silhouette of each object. These correspondences are adapted depending on the pdfs for the inside and outside regions and used to estimate a new pose. Once the movement of one object is below the requested threshold, the iterations on this object can be stopped.

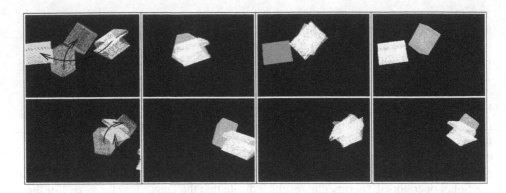

Fig. 1. Leftmost: Here, the 3-D movement which the objects perform is illustrated in the two available views; The puncher moves from the white to the yellow pose while the tea box moves from the cyan to the green pose. The arrows indicate the directions in which the two objects move. **Left:** Tracking result for frame 9 with uncoupled tracking. This is the first frame in which the estimated pose of the puncher is imprecise due to the occlusions. **Right:** Tracking result for frame 17 with uncoupled tracking. As explained in Section 4.1, the estimated pose of the puncher is close to the yellow tea box and is thus incorrect. **Rightmost:** Tracking result for frame 17 with the proposed coupled algorithm. It can be seen that the estimated pose is far better when using the proposed algorithm. **Top:** View 1, **Bottom:** View 2.

One problem that can occur, though, is that one object might occlude a large portion of another object. Although the algorithm can deal with occlusions up to a certain extend, it must fail if too much of the object to be tracked is occluded in the image(s).

To understand the problem, consider Figure 1. In this simulation with 20 frames, the projected model of a tea box (yellow) moves from left to right while the projected model of a puncher (green) moves from right to left. Both objects also rotate slowly. The projections of the models overlap in frames 5 to 16 (first view) and from frame 7 until the end of the sequence (second view). Since the models actually penetrate each other, the projection of the puncher is in front of the projected tea box in some places while it is the other way round in other places.

Since the objects are obviously clearly separated from each other as well as from the background, and since two views are available, this scene should be very easy to track. As can be seen in this figure, the green puncher is not tracked correctly with the current algorithm. This happens because most of the puncher is occluded from the yellow tea box for some frames, i.e. large parts of the puncher region contain yellow pixels. Consequently, the information of the puncher being mainly yellow is included into the pdfs. The algorithm tries to follow the motion of this "mostly yellow" puncher, in fact following the occluding yellow tea box.

4.2   Coupling the Tracking

To solve the problem described in the last section, we change the energy function (6) in such a way that each image point is considered as inside the object region for at most one point. To achieve this, we define $O_i(\xi_i, q)$ as the set of all 3-D points on the object model of the ith object in the pose ξ_i that are projected to the image point q. Furthermore, for the normal Euclidean metric d, let $d_i(\xi_i, q) := d(O_i(\xi_i, q), C)$ be the minimal distance from the camera origin C to a 3-D point in the set $O_i(\xi_i, q)$, i.e.

$$d_i(\xi_i, q) := \min_{x \in O_i(\xi_i, q)} \{d(x, C)\} . \tag{7}$$

Finally, define

$$v_i(\xi_1, \ldots, \xi_n, q) = \begin{cases} 1 \text{ if } d_i(\xi_i, q) = \min_{j \in \{1, \ldots, n\}} \{d_j(\xi_j, q)\} , \\ 0 \text{ else} \end{cases} \tag{8}$$

Then, the integral to be minimized is:

$$E(\xi_1, \ldots, \xi_n) = -\sum_{i=1}^{n} \int_{\Omega} \quad [v_i(\xi_1, \ldots, \xi_n, q) P_i(\xi_i, q) \log p_{i,1}$$
$$+ (1 - v_i(\xi_1, \ldots, \xi_n, q)) P(\xi_i, q)) \log p_{i,2}] dq . \tag{9}$$

In other words, the function $P_i(\xi_i, q)$ is multiplied by a visibility indicator function $v_i(\xi_1, \ldots, \xi_n, q)$, which is 1 if there is no point closer to the camera origin on a different object that is also projected to q, and 0 else. Note that this is a more complex setting than simply stating that one object is in front of another, because the objects can also partially occlude each other.

Algorithmically, this means that those parts of the projected objects which are occluded by another object are discarded in the calculation of the object interior. This results in different pdfs, a different silhouette and thus different 2-D–3-D point correspondences.

Additionally, instead of using all points on the new silhouette for pose estimation, only those points which are on the 2-D silhouette before and after omitting the occluded model parts are used. This is advantageous because, although such points are on the visible silhouette of the projected model, the corresponding 3-D points are not on the 2-D model silhouette as seen from the camera.

The reason why those points are not used might get clearer when looking at the idea behind the pose tracking algorithm: Every contour point "votes" for the direction in the image in which the projected model should move to get closer to the contour of the actual object seen in the image. Thus, the point would benefit from moving the projected model into that direction. However, the points that will be omitted would not benefit: Such a point is either below the other object (if it is moved in outward normal direction) or in the object interior (if it is moved in inward normal direction) after any amount of movement. In both cases, it is not a silhouette point any more, and cannot be used for object tracking anymore.

In contrast to the uncoupled case, every object must be tracked until every object movement is below the requested threshold. This is necessary because every part of the integral depends on all poses, which is not the case for uncoupled tracking.

Although it is possible to choose different parameters for each object (e.g. a different parameter l, a different threshold, other image features etc.), this vastly increases the number of parameters. For the experiments presented here, all parameters are equal for all tracked objects.

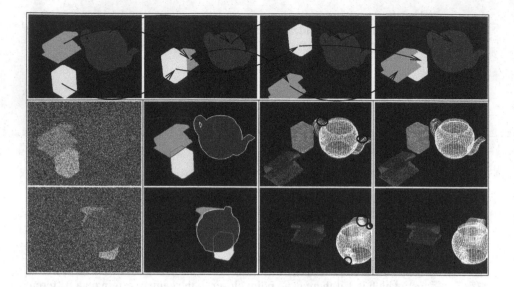

Fig. 2. First row: Four input images (frames 8, 15, 22 and 29) of one of the views. The arrows indicate the movement of the objects. **Leftmost:** Input views for frame 9, including the independent Gaussian noise with a standard deviation of 256. **Left:** Contours of the tracking results of frame 9, shown in images without noise. Note the multiple occlusions. **Right:** Pose results for frame 26 of this sequence. Again, the noise that was added for the pose tracking was removed for the presentation of the results. The black ellipses show areas where it is possible to see that the tracking of the teapot is not optimal due to the noise. **Rightmost:** Pose results obtained without noise in frame 26. **Middle row:** View 1, **Last row:** View 2.

5   Experiments

In this section, we show several tracking results for different objects obtained with the proposed algorithm.

Since the scene shown in Figure 1 is very simple, we present another simulated scene (cf. Figure 2) that was degraded with uncorrelated Gaussian noise with a standard deviation of 256. This time, an additional third object (a teapot projected in dark red) must be tracked. All objects move in a circle with radius 7cm around a certain point with a speed of one full rotation every 25 frames. Since the yellow tea box and the green puncher circle around the same center, the tea box occludes the puncher in some frames while it is the other way round in other frames. The red teapot performs only a slight movement when seen from the first view and a strong movement as seen from the second view, which further complicates the tracking. As can be seen, simple simulated scenes in which the objects are clearly distinguished can be tracked even with a high amount of noise and in the presence of several occlusions.

In Figure 3, tracking results for a real world stereo scene are shown. In this scene, the objects to be tracked are built from Lego Duplo® bricks. The object built with

Fig. 3. From Left to Right: Tracking results for frame 10, 90, 140 and 170 of three Lego Duplo objects. (cropped) **Top:** View 1, **Bottom:** View 2.

Fig. 4. From Left to Right: Input images for frame 110 and tracking results of the three Lego Duplo objects for the frames 50, 80 and 110 (cropped). **Top:** View 1, **Bottom:** View 2. Note that the blue object is nearly completely occluded in the second view of frame 110.

blue, light green, and dark green bricks moves between the two objects build from red, yellow, and ocher bricks. Thus, it both occludes and is occluded. As can be seen, all three objects have been tracked simultaneously with the proposed algorithm.

Figure 4 shows tracking results for another stereo sequence in which three different objects have been tracked. Again, the objects have been made from Lego Duplo bricks. One of the objects is made from blue bricks while the other two are made from red bricks. Although the blue object is nearly completely occluded in the second view, the tracking results with the new algorithm are still good.

6   Summary

We have presented a region based method for coupled pose tracking of multiple objects that can handle an arbitrary number of objects. In particular, the simultaneous 3-D tracking of multiple objects allows to model mutual occlusions of these objects explicitly. We introduced a visibility function for this purpose. This way, even cases where two objects partially occlude each other are handled correctly. We presented tracking results for simulated as well as real world scenes to demonstrate that the proposed algorithm is able to track different objects in different scenes.

References

1. Abidi, M.A., Chandra, T.: Pose estimation for camera calibration and landmark tracking. In: Proc. International Conf. Robotics and Automation, Cincinnati, May 1990, vol. 1, pp. 420–426 (1990)
2. Agarwal, A., Triggs, B.: Recovering 3D human pose from monocular images. IEEE Transactions on Pattern Analysis and Machine Intelligence 28(1) (January 2006)
3. Beveridge, J.: Local Search Algorithms for Geometric Object Recognition: Optimal Correspondence and Pose. PhD thesis, Department of Computer Science, University of Massachusetts, Amherst (May 1993)
4. Brox, T., Rosenhahn, B., Weickert, J.: Three-dimensional shape knowledge for joint image segmentation and pose estimation. In: Kropatsch, W.G., Sablatnig, R., Hanbury, A. (eds.) Pattern Recognition. LNCS, vol. 3663, pp. 109–116. Springer, Heidelberg (2005)
5. Drummond, T., Cipolla, R.: Real-time tracking of multiple articulated structures in multiple views. In: Vernon, D. (ed.) ECCV 2000. LNCS, vol. 1843, pp. 20–36. Springer, Heidelberg (2000)
6. Goddard, J.: Pose And Motion Estimation From Vision Using Dual Quaternion-Based Extended Kalman Filtering. PhD thesis, Imaging, Robotics, and Intelligent Systems Laboratory, University of Tennessee, Knoxville-College of Engineering, Tennessee (1997)
7. Grimson, W., Lozano–Perez, T., Huttenlocher, D.: Object Recognition by Computer: The Role of Geometric Constraints. MIT Press, Baton (1990)
8. Hue, C., Cadre, J.L., Perez, P.: Tracking multiple objects with particle filtering. IEEE Trans. on Aerospace and Electronic Systems 38(3), 791–812 (2002)
9. Kriegman, D., Vijayakumar, B., Ponce, J.: Constraints for recognizing and locating curved 3D objects from monocular image features. In: Sandini, G. (ed.) ECCV 1992. LNCS, vol. 588, pp. 829–833. Springer, Heidelberg (1992)
10. Lowe, D.: Solving for the parameters of object models from image descriptions. In: Proc. ARPA Image Understanding Workshop, College Park, April 1980, pp. 121–127 (1980)
11. Murray, R.M., Li, Z., Sastry, S.S.: A Mathematical Introduction to Robotic Manipulation. CRC Press, Boca Raton (1994)
12. Rosenhahn, B., Sommer, G.: Adaptive pose estimation for different corresponding entities. In: Van Gool, L. (ed.) Pattern Recognition. LNCS, vol. 2449, pp. 265–273. Springer, Heidelberg (2002)
13. Schmaltz, C., Rosenhahn, B., Brox, T., Cremers, D., Weickert, J., Wietzke, L., Sommer, G.: Region-based pose tracking. In: Martí, J., Benedí, J.M., Mendonça, A.M., Serrat, J. (eds.) Pattern Recognition and Image Analysis, Girona, Spain, June 2007. LNCS, vol. 4478, pp. 56–63. Springer, Heidelberg (2007)
14. Shevlin, F.: Analysis of orientation problems using Plucker lines. In: Proc. 14th International Conference on Pattern Recognition, Washington, DC, USA, vol. 1, pp. 685–689. IEEE Computer Society Press, Los Alamitos (1998)
15. Särkkä, S., Vehtari, A., Lampinen, J.: Rao-Blackwellized Monte Carlo data association for multiple target tracking. In: Proc. 7th International Conference on Information Fusion, vol. 1, pp. 583–590 (2004)

16. Taycher, L., Shakhnarovich, G., Demirdjian, D., Darrell, T.: Conditional random people: Tracking humans with CRFs and grid filters. In: Proc. 2006 IEEE Computer Society Conference on Computer Vision and Pattern Recognition, New York, NY, December 2006, pp. 222–229. IEEE Computer Society Press, New York (2006)
17. Winkler, S., Wunsch, P., Hirzinger, G.: A feature map approach to real-time 3-D object pose estimation from single 2-D perspective views. In: Paulus, E., Wahl, F. (eds.) Mustererkennung 1997 (Proc. DAGM), pp. 129–136. Springer, Berlin (1997)

Simultaneous Estimation of Surface Motion, Depth and Slopes Under Changing Illumination

Tobias Schuchert and Hanno Scharr

ICG III, Research Center Jülich, 52425 Jülich, Germany
{T.Schuchert,H.Scharr}@fz-juelich.de

Abstract. In this paper we extend a multi-camera model for simultaneous estimation of 3d position, normals, and 3d motion of surface patches
[17] to be able to handle brightness changes coming from changing illumination. In the target application only surface orientation and 3d motion
are of interest. Thus color related surface properties like bidirectional
reflectance distribution function do not need to be reconstructed. Consequently we characterize only changes of the brightness using a second-
order power series. We test two new models within a total least squares
estimation framework using synthetic data with ground truth available.
Motion estimation results improve severely with respect to the brightness
constancy model when brightness changes are present in the data.

1   Introduction

Our target application is plant leaf growth analysis at a time range of minutes
and spatial resolution of several micrometers. Growth is the divergence of the
motion vector field projected onto the leaf surface, thus we need very accurate
subpixel motion estimates. As temporal resolution is not 30Hz 'real-time' but
minutes, image acquisition at multiple camera positions may be done by a single
camera mounted on a moving stage as long as overall acquisition time for one
'time instance' is only a few seconds. Thus we can use elaborate camera setups
at low cost like e.g. a 5×5 camera grid with grid-spacing even smaller than
physical camera dimensions instead of really using 25 cameras (as e.g. in [13]).

In our experiments we illuminate the scene using 880nm light emitting diodes
resulting in a directed, but not completely homogeneous illumination. We are
restricted to this, as plants react on visible light. While this is no issue for 3d
reconstruction, it is a major problem when measuring motion using a brightness
constancy assumption. When plant leaves grow, they change their position and
surface orientation with respect to the stationary illumination. Even if brightness changes due position change could be suppressed by optimally homogeneous
illumination, brightness changes due to surface orientation change remain significant. These changes depend on the bidirectional reflectance distribution function
(BRDF) of the leaf surface, thus there is no way to suppress this change experimentally without disturbing the plant.

Related Work. Estimating parameters of dynamic scenes like 3d surface position and orientation as well as motion of objects is a problem central to computer

F.A. Hamprecht, C. Schnörr, and B. Jähne (Eds.): DAGM 2007, LNCS 4713, pp. 184–193, 2007.
© Springer-Verlag Berlin Heidelberg 2007

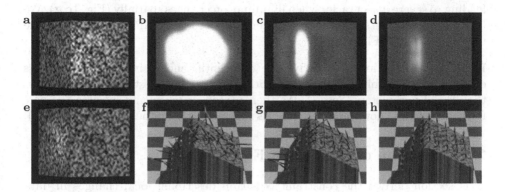

Fig. 1. Motion estimation of cube moving towards camera with spot light moving around cube center. (**a**, **e**): first and last image taken with central camera. (**b–d**): color coded model errors (projected on contrast reduced cube) for models without (**b**), constant temporal (**c**), and spatially varying temporal brightness change (**d**). Below the model errors, scaled motion estimates for the models are depicted, respectively (**f–h**).

vision research. For subpixel motion estimation as needed here, as well as stereo reconstruction optical flow techniques are applied successfully since many years [10,12] and became more and more accurate [1,9,2,15]. More complex models like affine motion [5,6], scene flow [20] and physics-based brightness changes [4,7] have been proposed. Stereo reconstruction extensions to curved surfaces [11] and depth estimation via optical flow and epipolar geometry [18] have been presented recently. Simultaneous motion and stereo analysis are addressed in [19,21,3,17]. The currently richest optical-flow-like model for local scene reconstruction [17] handles translational motion of slanted surfaces. There the basic idea is to interpret the camera position (s_x, s_y) as additional data dimensions. Hence all image sequences (x-y-t data blocks) acquired by a 2d camera grid are interpreted as a 5d-Volume in x-y-s_x-s_y-t-space. The scene model boils down to be an affine optical flow model with 3 dimensions (s_x, s_y, t) behaving like time dimension in an usual affine optical flow model.

Our Contribution. Two extensions of that model [17] need to be addressed in order to be applicable to our application: rotational motion and brightness changes. In the current paper we only deal with brightness changes. Therefore we closely follow [17] in the derivation of the geometrical part of the model, including all approximations, even though we will have to change them for rotational motion in future work. Thus, we will not look at rotating objects under nonmoving illumination in this paper, but all our tests use translating objects and rotating illumination. This means that only synthetic sequences fully fulfill the model presented here. Thus we are restricted to synthetic data for now. Without modeling brightness changes motion estimates are corrupted by illumination changes, cmp. Fig. 1b,f. Being an optical-flow-like model we follow [7] for physics-based brightness changes. The models derived there assume spatially constant brightness change parameters leading to severe inaccuracies when illumination changes spatially (Fig. 1c,g). We therefore also model spatial changes of temporal changes leading to more accurate motion estimates (Fig. 1d,h).

Paper organization. We derive the differential model including brightness changes in Sec. 2 followed by a description of parameter estimation and disentangling of parameters (Sec. 3). We then present experiments showing the performance of the known and new models for various brightness changes (Sec. 4).

2   Derivation of the Model Equation

This section derives the constraint equation describing local changes in data acquired with a camera grid, following [17]. It combines a 3d object/motion model, a camera model and a brightness change model. For completeness we briefly present the full derivation, but focus on the brightness change model.

The dynamic surface patch is modeled by its geometry X, which can be described by its initial world coordinate position (X_0, Y_0, Z_0), velocity (U_x, U_y, U_z) and X- and Y-slopes Z_x and Z_y (i.e. surface normal $(-Z_x, -Z_y, 1)$)

$$X(\Delta X, \Delta Y, t) = \begin{pmatrix} X \\ Y \\ Z \end{pmatrix} = \begin{pmatrix} X_0 + U_x t + \Delta X \\ Y_0 + U_y t + \Delta Y \\ Z_0 + U_z t + Z_x \Delta X + Z_y \Delta Y \end{pmatrix} \quad (1)$$

with time t and local world coordinates $(\Delta X, \Delta Y)$. It is projected into the images by pinhole cameras at world coordinates $(s_x, s_y, 0)$, looking in Z-direction

$$\begin{pmatrix} x \\ y \end{pmatrix} = \frac{f}{Z} \begin{pmatrix} X - s_x \\ Y - s_y \end{pmatrix} \quad (2)$$

A camera grid samples camera position space equidistantly. The cameras convert light intensity L into image intensities I (i.e. gray values). In order to derive a model for dI/dt, the temporal changes visible in the data, we look into the dependencies of L. In this paper, a translating surface patch is illuminated by a spatially smoothly varying, translating and rotating light source (see Sec. 1). Direction n_i of incident irradiance E may vary smoothly with time and space but reflectance direction n_r is kept constant.[1] Visible light intensity i.e. reflected radiance L depends on incident irradiance E and on the patch's bidirectional reflectance distribution function (BRDF) B (cmp. e.g. [8]) according to

$$L(X(\Delta X, \Delta Y, t), t, n_r) = B(X(\Delta X, \Delta Y, t), n_i(t), n_r)E(\Delta X, \Delta Y, t, n_i(t)) \quad (3)$$

and the BRDF depends on the material and hence on the position on the surface patch as well as the directions of incidence n_i and reflectance n_r. We assume that the material does not change with time and therefore

$$B(X(\Delta X, \Delta Y, t), n_i(t), n_r) = B(X(\Delta X, \Delta Y, 0), n_i(t), n_r) \quad (4)$$

---

[1] Reflectance direction n_r obviously also varies with pixel position in the cameras, but for this paper we do not use this extra information.

If the BRDF is smooth enough, which is typically given at sufficient angular distance from specularities, changes due to smoothly changing incidence direction $n_i(t)$ can be modeled using a smooth function $h_B(t)$ with $h_B(0) = 1$

$$B(\boldsymbol{X}(\Delta X, \Delta Y, t), \boldsymbol{n}_i(t), \boldsymbol{n}_r) = B(\boldsymbol{X}(\Delta X, \Delta Y, 0), \boldsymbol{n}_i(0), \boldsymbol{n}_r)h_B(t) \qquad (5)$$

Being spatially inhomogeneous the moving irradiance E changes not only by a time dependent factor, but by a factor also varying smoothly in space

$$E(\Delta X, \Delta Y, t, \boldsymbol{n}_i(t)) = E(\Delta X, \Delta Y, 0, \boldsymbol{n}_i(0))h_E(\Delta X, \Delta Y, t) \qquad (6)$$

Here again $h_E(\Delta X, \Delta Y, t)$ is a smooth function with $h_E(\Delta X, \Delta Y, 0) \equiv 1$. Plugging Eq. 5 and Eq. 6 in Eq. 3 the reflected radiance L becomes

$$L(\boldsymbol{X}(\Delta X, \Delta Y, t), t) = L(\boldsymbol{X}(\Delta X, \Delta Y, 0), 0)h_B(t)h_E(\Delta X, \Delta Y, t) \qquad (7)$$

We assume image intensities I to be proportional to the radiance L, i.e. the characteristic curve of the used camera to be linear, and therefore

$$I(\boldsymbol{X}(\Delta X, \Delta Y, t), t, s_x, s_y) = I(\boldsymbol{X}(\Delta X, \Delta Y, 0), 0, s_x, s_y) \exp(h_I(\Delta X, \Delta Y, t)) \qquad (8)$$

where $h_I(\Delta X, \Delta Y, t) := ln(h_B(t)h_E(\Delta X, \Delta Y, t))$. The sought for temporal derivative of Eq. 8 is thus

$$\begin{aligned}
\tfrac{\mathrm{d}}{\mathrm{d}t}I &= I(\boldsymbol{X}(\Delta X, \Delta Y, 0), 0, s_x, s_y) \exp(h_I(\Delta X, \Delta Y, t))\tfrac{\mathrm{d}}{\mathrm{d}t}h_I(\Delta X, \Delta Y, t) \\
&= I(\boldsymbol{X}(\Delta X, \Delta Y, t), t, s_x, s_y)\tfrac{\mathrm{d}}{\mathrm{d}t}h_I(\Delta X, \Delta Y, t)
\end{aligned} \qquad (9)$$

The most common assumption in optical-flow-like approaches is brightness constancy, boiling down to $h_I(\Delta X, \Delta Y, t) \equiv 0$. Haussecker and Fleet [7] derive models for changing surface orientation and a moving illumination envelope approximating h_I as a second order power series respecting temporal changes only

$$h_I(\Delta X, \Delta Y, t) \approx h_{HF}(t, \boldsymbol{a}) := \sum_{i=1}^{2} a_i t^i \qquad (10)$$

where a_1 and a_2 are treated as local constants in the estimation process. Looking at Fig. 1f and **g** we observe that for highest accuracy this is not sufficient. Therefore we introduce a more accurate approximation of h_I explicitly modeling spatial variations still respecting $h_I(\Delta X, \Delta Y, 0) \equiv 0$

$$h_I(\Delta X, \Delta Y, t) \approx h(\Delta X, \Delta Y, t, \boldsymbol{a}) := \sum_{i=1}^{2} (a_i + a_{i,x}\Delta X + a_{i,y}\Delta Y)t^i \qquad (11)$$

The temporal derivative of h is then

$$f(\Delta X, \Delta Y, t, \boldsymbol{a}) := \frac{\mathrm{d}}{\mathrm{d}t}h(\Delta X, \Delta Y, t, \boldsymbol{a}) = \sum_{i=1}^{2} i\,(a_i + a_{i,x}\Delta X + a_{i,y}\Delta Y)\,t^{i-1} \qquad (12)$$

using the notation $\boldsymbol{a} = (a_1, a_2, a_{1,x}, a_{1,y}, a_{2,x}, a_{2,y})$. Following [17] the brightness change model is finally formulated as total differential $\mathrm{d}I = If\mathrm{d}t$ or

$$I_x\mathrm{d}x + I_y\mathrm{d}y + I_{s_x}\mathrm{d}s_x + I_{s_y}\mathrm{d}s_y + I_t\mathrm{d}t = If\mathrm{d}t \qquad (13)$$

where lower indices at I indicate partial derivatives, e.g. $I_x = \partial I/\partial x$.

2.1   Combination of Patch-, Camera-, and Brightness-Models

We will now briefly summarize how to combine the dynamic surface patch (Eq. 1), camera model (Eq. 2) and the brightness change model (Eq. 13). A more detailed and comprehensive derivation can be found in [17].

Points (X, Y, Z) of a surface element (Eq. 1) are projected onto the camera chip at pixel position (x, y) via Eq. 2

$$\begin{pmatrix} x \\ y \end{pmatrix} = \frac{f}{Z} \begin{pmatrix} X_0 + U_x t + \Delta X - s_x \\ Y_0 + U_y t + \Delta Y - s_y \end{pmatrix} \tag{14}$$

At fixed surface locations with constant ΔX and ΔY differentials dx and dy are

$$\begin{pmatrix} dx \\ dy \end{pmatrix} = \frac{f}{Z} \begin{pmatrix} (U_x - U_z \frac{x}{f})dt - ds_x \\ (U_y - U_z \frac{y}{f})dt - ds_y \end{pmatrix} \tag{15}$$

being nonlinear in U_z as $Z = Z_0 + U_z t + Z_x \Delta X + Z_y \Delta Y$. Using image-based expressions 3d optical flow, disparity, local pixel coordinates, and projected slopes

$$u_x = \frac{f}{Z_0} U_x, \quad u_y = \frac{f}{Z_0} U_y, \quad x = x_0 + \Delta x, \quad \Delta x = \frac{f(1 - Z_x \frac{x}{f})}{Z_0} \Delta X, \quad z_x = \frac{Z_x}{Z_0(1 - Z_x \frac{x}{f})}$$

$$u_z = -\frac{1}{Z_0} U_z, \quad v = -\frac{f}{Z_0}, \quad y = y_0 + \Delta y, \quad \Delta y = \frac{f(1 - Z_y \frac{y}{f})}{Z_0} \Delta Y, \quad z_y = \frac{Z_y}{Z_0(1 - Z_y \frac{y}{f})} \tag{16}$$

omitting $U_z t$ in Z by the assumption $|Z_0| \gg |U_z t|$ and linearizing f/Z by

$$\frac{-f}{Z_0 + Z_x \Delta X + Z_y \Delta Y} \approx v + z_x \Delta x + z_y \Delta y \tag{17}$$

we get an affine-optical-flow-like model [6] when plugging all this into Eq. 13

$$\begin{pmatrix} I_x \\ I_y \end{pmatrix} \left[\begin{pmatrix} v ds_x + (u_x + x_0 u_z) dt \\ v ds_y + (u_y + y_0 u_z) dt \end{pmatrix} + \begin{pmatrix} z_x ds_x + u_z dt & z_y ds_x \\ z_x ds_y & z_y ds_y + u_z dt \end{pmatrix} \begin{pmatrix} \Delta x \\ \Delta y \end{pmatrix} \right]$$
$$+ I_{s_x} ds_x + I_{s_y} ds_y + I_t dt - I f dt = 0 \tag{18}$$

where all nonlinear terms coming from multiplications with $z_x \Delta x$ and $z_y \Delta y$ are suppressed. We decompose Eq. 18 into data vector $\boldsymbol{d}$ and parameter vector $\boldsymbol{p}$:

$$\boldsymbol{d} = (I_x, I_y, I_x \Delta x, I_x \Delta y, I_y \Delta y, I_y \Delta x,$$
$$I_{s_x}, I_{s_y}, I_t, I, I \Delta x, I \Delta y, It, It \Delta x, It \Delta y)^T$$
$$\boldsymbol{p} = (v ds_x + (u_x + x_0 u_z) dt, v ds_y + (u_y + y_0 u_z) dt, \tag{19}$$
$$z_x ds_x + u_z dt, z_y ds_x, z_y ds_y + u_z dt, z_x ds_y,$$
$$ds_x, ds_y, dt, b_1 dt, b_{1,x} dt, b_{1,y} dt, b_2 dt, b_{2,x} dt, b_{2,y} dt)^T$$

where f has been substituted by the novel brightness change model from Eq. 12 and the brightness change parameters are

$$b_1 = -a_1 \qquad b_{1,x} = -a_{1,x} \frac{Z_0}{f(1 - Z_x \frac{x}{f})} \qquad b_{1,y} = -a_{1,y} \frac{Z_0}{f(1 - Z_y \frac{y}{f})}$$
$$b_2 = -a_2 \qquad b_{2,x} = -a_{2,x} \frac{Z_0}{f(1 - Z_x \frac{x}{f})} \qquad b_{2,y} = -a_{2,y} \frac{Z_0}{f(1 - Z_y \frac{y}{f})} \tag{20}$$

For simpler brightness models or when a 1d camera grid is used (i.e. $ds_y = 0$) terms with non-existing parameters are simply omitted. Eq. 18 is a model equation of the form $\boldsymbol{d}^T \boldsymbol{p} = 0$ (cmp. Eq. 19).

3   Parameter Estimation

Also for total least squares parameter estimation we closely follow [17]. For every 5d-pixel a constraint equation of the form $\boldsymbol{d}^T\boldsymbol{p} = 0$ is given. To get an over-determined system of equations, we assume that all equations within a local neighborhood Ω are solved by the same parameter vector, i.e. $\boldsymbol{d}_i^T\boldsymbol{p} = e_i$ for all pixels i in Ω, with errors e_i. The errors are minimized in weighted L_2-norm

$$||e|| = ||\mathbf{D}\boldsymbol{p}|| = \boldsymbol{p}^T\mathbf{D}^T\mathbf{W}\mathbf{D}\boldsymbol{p} =: \boldsymbol{p}^T\mathbf{J}\boldsymbol{p} \stackrel{!}{=} \min \qquad (21)$$

with $\mathbf{D}_{ij} = (\boldsymbol{d}_i)_j$ and a diagonal matrix $\mathbf{W}$ containing the weights. As in [17] Gaussian weights with variance σ^2 are used (see Sec. 4). The matrix $\mathbf{J}$ is called structure tensor. For a 2d camera grid the space of solutions $\tilde{\boldsymbol{p}}$ is spanned by the 3 eigenvectors to the smallest eigenvalues of $\mathbf{J}$. From these eigenvectors the sought for parameters are derived by linear combination of the eigenvectors $\tilde{\boldsymbol{p}}$ such that all but exactly one component of $\{ds_x, ds_y, dt\}$ vanish. From the linear combination with $dt \neq 0$ and $ds_x = ds_y = 0$, we calculate motion and brightness change components. First u_z is derived and then used to calculate u_x and u_y from the first and second component of this linear combination. From the other 2 eigenvector combinations with $dt = 0$ we derive depth and normals. The parameters v, z_x, z_y and u_z occur twice in the model (Eq. 18) and therefore can be estimated independently from different components and/or different linear combinations of the eigenvectors. The estimates for these parameters can be combined according to their error estimates, provided that their covariance matrix (see [14]) is diagonal. This is made sure by suitable coordinate transformations in x-y-space (for u_z) or s_x-s_y-space (for v, z_x, and z_y).

4   Experiments

We show a systematic error analysis using sinusoidal patterns, and a reconstruction of a cube with a high contrast noise texture raytraced with *povray* [16].

4.1   Sinusoidal Pattern

Sinusoidal pattern data is used to evaluate systematic errors and noise dependence of the estimation process. In Fig. 2 two images of such a sequence are shown. The wavelengths are 8 pixel in x- and 80 pixel in y-direction and amplitude changing according to Eq. 11. We generated data sets for different values of brightness change parameters a_1, $a_{1,x}$, a_2, and $a_{2,x}$, but not for $a_{1,y}$ and $a_{2,y}$ as they work like the respective x-parameters. The other parameters are $U_X = U_Y = Z_X = Z_Y = 0$, $Z_0 = 100$, $f = 10$ and $U_Z = 0.1$. As performance measure for a parameter Q we use the mean absolute value either of the relative error if $Q_{ref} \neq 0$ or of the absolute error if $Q_{ref} = 0$

$$Q_{rel} = \frac{1}{N}\sum_i^N \frac{|Q_i - Q_{ref}|}{|Q_{ref}|} \qquad Q_{abs} = \frac{1}{N}\sum_i^N |Q_i - Q_{ref}| \qquad (22)$$

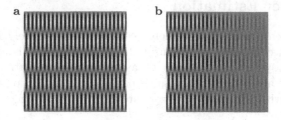

Fig. 2. Sinusoidal pattern data. (**a, b**): first and last image taken at central camera position, $a_1 = a_{1,x} = 0$, $a_2 = -0.2$ and $a_{2,x} = -0.002$ (cmp. Eq. 11).

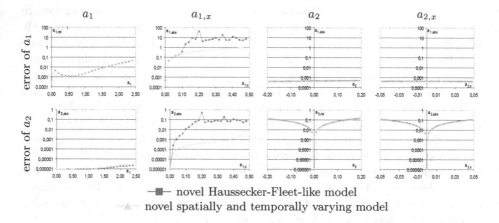

Fig. 3. Mean absolute value of relative or absolute error of brightness change parameters a_1 (top) and a_2 (bottom) versus the brightness change parameters a_1, $a_{1,x}$, a_2, and $a_{2,x}$. Noise free data.

where the sum runs over all pixels not suffering from border effects and the lower indices *rel* stand for 'relative error', *abs* for 'absolute error' and *ref* for 'reference'. Parameter estimation was done according to Sec. 3, with weighting matrix **W** implemented via a 65-tab Gaussian with standard deviation $\sigma = 16$.

The first experiment evaluates systematic error of and cross talk between brightness change parameters. In Fig. 3 errors of a_1 and a_2 versus brightness change parameters a_1, $a_{1,x}$, a_2, and $a_{2,x}$ are shown. We observe that the relative error of a_1 is well below 0.5% if $a_1 < 1$ and then moderately raises. This is due to the fact that temporal derivatives of the data I_t become less and less accurate when exponential behavior of the data becomes more and more prominent. The same explanation holds for the linear error increase of a_2 with increasing a_2. And as local brightness changes due to $a_{1,x}$ come close to changes due to a_1 if $a_1 = a_{1,x}\Delta X$ for the same local patch, we expect and observe severe cross talk between $a_{1,x}$ and a_1, more severe for the model not containing $a_{1,x}$. This is also true for $a_{2,x}$ and a_2, but there the cross talk is the same for both models, thus modeling $a_{2,x}$ is of no advantage here. Further a_1 is almost independent of a_2

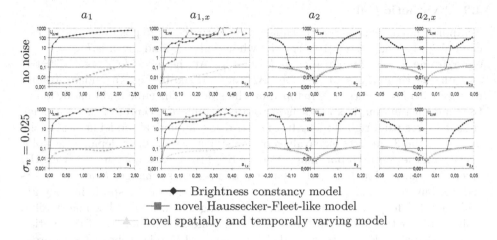

Fig. 4. Mean absolute value of relative error of U_Z versus the brightness change parameters a_1, $a_{1,x}$, a_2, and $a_{2,x}$. Noise free (top row) and noisy data (bottom).

and $a_{2,x}$, as well as a_2 of a_1. But while a_2 does depend on $a_{1,x}$ if $a_{1,x}$ is not modeled, the error of a_2 is about 1 to 2 orders of magnitude smaller if $a_{1,x}$ is modeled. The positive effect on accuracy of the method if $a_{1,x}$ is modeled is even higher for U_Z, as we see next.

In Fig. 4 results for $U_{Z,rel}$ versus brightness change parameters are shown, using noise free data and data with Gaussian noise of standard deviation $\sigma_n = 0.025$ being 2.5% of the amplitude of the signal at $t = 0$. As before all parameters except the one on the ordinate have been kept fix. U_Z is the most relevant motion parameter, because errors in U_Z directly also influence U_X and U_Y (see the first 2 components of the parameter vector p in Eq. 19). Let us first look at the noise free case. As soon as a_1 is significantly larger than 0 the brightness constancy model immediately breaks down, errors get unacceptably high. For the two other models U_Z does not react on small a_1 and only weak for larger values of a_1. When brightness changes due to $a_{1,x}$ are present only the model containing spatial changes remains stable, brightness constancy and Haussecker-Fleet-like models have severe problems. Looking at $U_{Z,rel}$ with changes due to a_2 or $a_{2,x}$ we observe that a_2 and $a_{2,x}$ cause similar errors in U_Z. This is in complete consistency with our earlier observation in Fig. 3. While all models behave the same for small absolute value of a_2 or $a_{2,x}$, the brightness constancy model rapidly breaks down at $|a_2| \approx 0.1$ or $|a_{2,x}| \approx 0.02$. Comparing errors of U_Z for noise free and noisy data sets, we see only a small effect when a_2 or $a_{2,x}$ are close to 0. For larger a_2 or $a_{2,x}$ the plots for noisy and noise free data look almost identical. Also for large a_1 and $a_{1,x}$ errors remain unchanged. But for smaller a_1 and $a_{1,x}$ the influence of noise can be quite high. We observe that errors increase from well below $U_{Z,rel} = 0.01$ up to nearly $U_{Z,rel} = 0.1$.

We conclude that modeling $a_{1,x}$ is worth the effort while $a_{2,x}$ does not really help. Noise may be an issue, thus it has to be kept as low as possible.

4.2 Synthetic Cube

Temporal image sequences with 9 images were created at 25 positions of a 2d 5×5 camera grid using *povray* [16]. For the whole cube ground truth is $U_X = U_Y = 0$mm/frame, $U_Z = 2$mm/frame, and $Z_Y = 0$. At the left side $Z_X \approx 1.73 \hat{=} 60°$ and on the right $Z_X \approx 0.577 \hat{=} 30°$. As one can see in Fig. 1a and **e**, a noise texture with high contrast is mapped on the sides of the cube and in addition to the ambient illumination a spot light rotates around the center of the cube such that it moves from right to left. In Fig. 1**b-d** the numerical model error, i.e. the largest of the 3 smallest eigenvalues of the structure tensor is depicted as color overlay on the central input image. For the brightness constancy model (Fig. 1**b**) error is highest. Modeling spatially constant brightness changes (Fig. 1**c**) errors reduce, but at the edge of the cube and at the border of the spotlight they are still high. With spatially varying temporal changes errors again become smaller, visible only at the edge of the cube. The components U_X and U_Y of the motion vectors shown in Fig. 1**f-h** are scaled by a factor 135 relatively to U_Z in order to visualize estimation errors (U_X and U_Y should be 0). Even with this large accentuation of errors motion vectors estimated with the richest model point in the correct direction almost everywhere. The other models yield much less accurate vector fields.

5 Summary and Outlook

In this paper we extended the brightness constancy model presented in [17] by brightness change parameters. They are derived as a power series approximation of the changes in reflected radiance due to (1) changes of illumination direction and (2) changes in incoming light intensity caused by moving inhomogeneous incident irradiance. While the first effect may be modeled by spatially constant temporal changes, the latter one causes spatially variant temporal changes. The sinusoidal pattern experiments reveal that modeling spatial variations of brightness changes result in increased motion estimation accuracy with respect to $a_{1,x}$, but not with $a_{2,x}$ (cmp. Eq. 11). Motion vector fields of a translating cube illuminated by a moving spotlight have been estimated using brightness constancy assumption and brightness change model with or without spatial changes. The richest model yields significantly better results than the other ones.

In future work we will extend this model to be able to handle rotating objects. Rotation leads to divergence visible in the image data, currently used for the estimation of U_Z, leading to erroneous motion estimates.

References

1. Barron, J.L., Fleet, D.J., Beauchemin, S.S.: Performance of optical flow techniques. IJCV 12(1), 43–77 (1994)
2. Bruhn, A., Weickert, J., Schnörr, C.: Lucas/kanade meets horn/schunck: Combining local and global optic flow methods. IJCV 61(3), 211–231 (2005)
3. Carceroni, R., Kutulakos, K.: Multi-view 3d shape and motion recovery on the spatio-temporal curve manifold. In: ICCV (1), pp. 520–527 (1999)

4. Denney Jr., T.S., Prince, J.L.: Optimal brightness functions for optical flow estimation of deformable motion. IEEE Trans. Im. Proc. 3(2), 178–191 (1994)
5. Farnebäck, G.: Fast and accurate motion est. using orient. tensors and param. motion models. In: ICPR, pp. 135–139 (2000)
6. Fleet, D.J., Black, M.J., Yacoob, Y., Jepson, A.D.: Design and use of linear models for image motion analysis. IJCV 36(3), 171–193 (2000)
7. Haußecker, H., Fleet, D.J.: Computing optical flow with physical models of brightness variation. PAMI 23(6), 661–673 (2001)
8. Haussecker, H.: Interaction of radiation with matter. In: Handbook of Computer Vision and Applications, vol. 1, pp. 37–62. Academic Press, London (1999)
9. Haußecker, H., Spies, H.: Motion. In: Jähne, B., Haußecker, H., Geißler, P. (eds.) Handbook of Computer Vision and Applications, Academic Press, London (1999)
10. Horn, B.K., Schunck, B.G.: Determining optical flow. Art. Int. 17, 185–204 (1981)
11. Li, G., Zucker, S.W.: Differential geometric consistency extends stereo to curved surfaces. In: Leonardis, A., Bischof, H., Pinz, A. (eds.) ECCV 2006. LNCS, vol. 3953, pp. 44–57. Springer, Heidelberg (2006)
12. Lucas, B., Kanade, T.: An iterative image registration technique with an application to stereo vision. In: DARPA Im. Underst. Workshop, pp. 121–130 (1981)
13. Nakamura, Y., Matsuura, T., Satoh, K., Ohta, Y.: Occlusion detectable stereo–occlusion patterns in camera matrix. In: CVPR, pp. 371–378 (1996)
14. Nestares, O., Fleet, D.J., Heeger, D.J.: Likelihood functions and confidence bounds for total-least-squares problems. In: CVPR, pp. 523–530 (2000)
15. Papenberg, N., Bruhn, A., Brox, T., Didas, S., Weickert, J.: Highly accurate optic flow computation with theoretically justified warping. IJCV 67(2), 141–158 (2006)
16. Pov-ray 3.6, http://www.povray.org
17. Scharr, H., Schuchert, T.: Simultaneous motion, depth and slope estimationwith a camera-grid. In: Vision, Modeling and Visualization 2006, pp. 81–88 (2006)
18. Slesareva, N., Bruhn, A., Weickert, J.: Optic flow goes stereo: A variational method for estimating discontinuity-preserving dense disparity maps. In: Kropatsch, W.G., Sablatnig, R., Hanbury, A. (eds.) Pattern Recognition. LNCS, vol. 3663, pp. 33–40. Springer, Heidelberg (2005)
19. Szeliski, R.: A multi-view approach to motion and stereo. In: CVPR (1999)
20. Vedula, S., Baker, S., Rander, P., Collins, R., Kanade, T.: Threedimensional scene flow. In: ICCV 1999, pp. 722–729 (1999)
21. Vedula, S., Baker, S., Seitz, S., Collins, R., Kanade, T.: Shape and motion carving in 6d. In: CVPR 2000, pp. 592–598 (2000)

Recursive Estimation with Implicit Constraints

Richard Steffen[1] and Christian Beder[2]

[1] Department of Photogrammetry
Bonn University, Germany
`rsteffen@uni-bonn.de`
[2] Computer Science Department
Kiel University, Germany
`beder@mip.informatik.uni-kiel.de`

Abstract. Recursive estimation or Kalman filtering usually relies on explicit model functions, that directly and explicitly describe the effect of the parameters on the observations. However, many problems in computer vision, including all those resulting in homogeneous equation systems, are easier described using implicit constraints between the observations and the parameters. By implicit we mean, that the constraints are given by equations, that are not easily solvable for the observation vector.

We present a framework, that allows to incorporate such implicit constraints as measurement equations into a Kalman filter. The algorithm may be used as a black-box, simplifying the process of specifying suitable measurement equations for many problems. As a byproduct, the possibility of specifying model equations non-explicitly, some non-linearities may be avoided and better results can be achieved for certain problems.

1 Introduction

Recursive estimation or Kalman filtering is a classical technique [10] and has been widely used in computer vision [15] and photogrammetry [4]. All those recursive estimation schemes assume a functional model, where the observations are explained by an explicit function in the unknown parameters.

However, many problems encountered in computer vision naturally result in implicit constraints between the observations and the parameters [6,8,13,7]. For instance, all problems resulting in homogeneous equation systems fall into this class. Although it is always possible to reduce the solution of an implicit problem to the solution of an explicit problem [11, p.231ff], to our knowledge no recursive estimation scheme is readily available in this case. The main goal of this paper is to provide a recursive estimation scheme, that can be applied to such problems comprising of implicit constraints in a black-box manner thereby simplifying the task of recursive estimation from the modeling point of view. The scope is not to present a run-time optimized estimation scheme tailored specifically for the task of structure-from-motion, as the proposed method is a framework, which is applicable in a much broader context.

F.A. Hamprecht, C. Schnörr, and B. Jähne (Eds.): DAGM 2007, LNCS 4713, pp. 194–203, 2007.

The Kalman filter consists of two parts, namely a time update and a measurement update. The scope of our work is not the time update but the measurement update, for which we will present a solution based on implicit constraints.

Recently the Kalman filter based on the unscented transformation [9] has obtained a lot of attention, which aims at improving the stochastic properties of the filter. Our work on the other hand aims at simplifying the specification of measurement equations, which are often much easier and straightforward to derive as implicit functions. By allowing more freedom in the task of modeling a certain problem the effects arising from non-linearities in the model equations can possibly be reduced resulting in more stable algorithms.

We will demonstrate the applicability of our approach for the task of on-line structure-from-motion from image sequences, which may be modeled using explicit functions [2] as well as using implicit functions (see section 3.1). The two approaches will be compared in section 3.2.

We are aware that a lot of highly optimized non-linear methods for the task of on-line structure-from-motion from image sequences are available [14,5,3], which exploit the specific structure of the normal equation matrix. However, this is not the scope of our paper as the presented methods are applicable to a variety of problems beyond structure-from-motion, which can be specified using implicit functions. The structure-from-motion problem is only used to demonstrate the applicability of the proposed method, as it is well-known to many researchers and test-sequences are readily available.

In the following section a recursive estimation scheme based on implicit functions will be derived. Section 2.3 summarizes the results and presents an easily applicable algorithm based on the derived equations. Finally we will compare the presented method to [2] in section 3.

2 Recursive Estimation Using Implicit Functions

2.1 Estimation Using Implicit Functions

We will now derive a recursive estimation scheme for the case of implicit constraints, which are functions relating the parameters p and the observations l as

$$g(\tilde{p}, \tilde{l}) = 0 \ . \tag{1}$$

Note, that such implicit functions are often much easier derived than explicit functions of the form $\tilde{l} = f(\tilde{p})$. The best linear unbiased estimate of the parameter vector $\hat{p}$ given observations l together with their covariance matrix C_{ll} may be obtained iteratively by solving the linear normal equation system [4, p.85]

$$A^{\mathsf{T}}(B^{\mathsf{T}}C_{ll}B)^{-1}A\widehat{\Delta p} = A^{\mathsf{T}}(B^{\mathsf{T}}C_{ll}B)^{-1}c_g \tag{2}$$

using the Jacobians at appropriate initial values

$$A = \left.\frac{\partial g(p, l)}{\partial p}\right|_{\hat{l},\hat{p}} \qquad\qquad B = \left.\frac{\partial g(p, l)^{\mathsf{T}}}{\partial l}\right|_{\hat{l},\hat{p}} \tag{3}$$

the contradiction vector

$$c_g = -g(\hat{p}, \hat{l}) - B^T(l - \hat{l}) = -g(\hat{p}, \hat{l}) + B^T v \tag{4}$$

and the residual of the observations

$$v = \hat{l} - l = C_{ll} B (B^T C_{ll} B)^{-1} (c_g - A\widehat{\Delta p}) . \tag{5}$$

In the following we will analyze the effect additional observations have on this estimation scheme.

2.2   Recursive Estimation

The task of recursive estimation is now to incorporate additional observations into the model. Hence, the model equation is augmented by a second implicit constraint block

$$\begin{bmatrix} g_1(\tilde{p}, \tilde{l}_1) \\ g_2(\tilde{p}, \tilde{l}_2) \end{bmatrix} = 0 . \tag{6}$$

Applying the same reasoning as before the solution of this new model equation may be obtained using the new normal equation system with

$$A^T (B^T C_{ll} B)^{-1} A = \begin{bmatrix} A_1^T \\ A_2^T \end{bmatrix} \left(\begin{bmatrix} B_{11}^T & B_{21}^T \\ B_{12}^T & B_{22}^T \end{bmatrix} \begin{bmatrix} C_{11} & C_{12} \\ C_{21} & C_{22} \end{bmatrix} \begin{bmatrix} B_{11} & B_{12} \\ B_{21} & B_{22} \end{bmatrix} \right)^{-1} \begin{bmatrix} A_1 \\ A_2 \end{bmatrix} \tag{7}$$

on the left hand side and

$$A^T (B^T C_{ll} B)^{-1} c_g = \begin{bmatrix} A_1^T \\ A_2^T \end{bmatrix} \left(\begin{bmatrix} B_{11}^T & B_{21}^T \\ B_{12}^T & B_{22}^T \end{bmatrix} \begin{bmatrix} C_{11} & C_{12} \\ C_{21} & C_{22} \end{bmatrix} \begin{bmatrix} B_{11} & B_{12} \\ B_{21} & B_{22} \end{bmatrix} \right)^{-1} \begin{bmatrix} c_{g_1} \\ c_{g_2} \end{bmatrix} \tag{8}$$

on the right hand side with the respective Jacobians in the block matrices.

In the following we will assume that the two observation blocks are stochastically independent, i.e. $C_{12} = C_{21} = 0$, as well as functionally independent, i.e. $B_{12} = B_{21} = 0$. Observe that this is analogous to classical recursive estimation with explicit functions in the Kalman filter. Now we can reformulate the left hand side of the normal equation system

$$A^T (B^T C_{ll} B)^{-1} A = A_1^T (B_1^T C_{11} B_1)^{-1} A_1 + A_2^T (B_2^T C_{22} B_2)^{-1} A_2 \tag{9}$$

as well as the right hand side of the normal equation system

$$A^T (B^T C_{ll} B)^{-1} c_g = A_1^T (B_1^T C_{11} B_1)^{-1} c_{g_1} + A_2^T (B_2^T C_{22} B_2)^{-1} c_{g_2} . \tag{10}$$

Using the substitution $W = B^T C_{ll} B$ the final solution, that incorporates both observations l_1 and l_2, may be obtained iteratively as

$$\widehat{\Delta p} = (A_1^T W_{11}^{-1} A_1 + A_2^T W_{22}^{-1} A_2)^{-1} (A_1^T W_{11}^{-1} c_{g_1} + A_2^T W_{22}^{-1} c_{g_2}) . \tag{11}$$

In the following the dependence on the first set of observation l_1 should be removed.

The goal of recursive estimation is now to derive such a solution $\widehat{\Delta p_2}$ for the combined constraints using the solution of the first constraint block g_1 represented by $\widehat{\Delta p_1}$ and its covariance matrix $Q_{\widehat{p}\widehat{p}11}$ as well as the new constraint block g_2 together with the new observations l_2 and their covariance matrix C_{22}. In order to achieve this goal equation (11) may be re-written as

$$\widehat{\Delta p_2} = \underbrace{(\underbrace{A_1^{\mathsf{T}} W_{11}^{-1} A_1}_{Q_{\widehat{p}\widehat{p}11}^{-1}} + A_2^{\mathsf{T}} W_{22}^{-1} A_2)^{-1}}_{Q_{\widehat{p}\widehat{p}22}}(\underbrace{A_1^{\mathsf{T}} W_{11}^{-1} \bar{c}_{g_1}}_{Q_{\widehat{p}\widehat{p}11}^{-1}\,\widehat{\Delta p_1}} + A_2^{\mathsf{T}} W_{22}^{-1} c_{g_2} + A_1^{\mathsf{T}} W_{11}^{-1} \Delta c_{g_1})$$

(12)

with the contradictions being separated into

$$c_{g_1} = \bar{c}_{g_1} + \Delta c_{g_1} \;. \tag{13}$$

Observe that the contradictions for the first contradiction block g_1 change due to the change of parameters resulting from the new contradiction block g_2, due to the dependence on $\hat{p}$ of equation (4). As a consequence the residuals for the observations of the first contradiction block change as well

$$v_1 = C_{11} B_1 W_{11}^{-1}(\bar{c}_{g_1} + \Delta c_{g_1} - A_1 \widehat{\Delta p_2}) \tag{14}$$

$$= \underbrace{C_{11} B_1 W_{11}^{-1}(\bar{c}_{g_1} - A_1 \widehat{\Delta p_1})}_{\bar{v}_1} + \underbrace{C_{11} B_1 W_{11}^{-1}(\Delta c_{g_1} - A_1(\widehat{\Delta p_2} - \widehat{\Delta p_1}))}_{\Delta v_1}. \tag{15}$$

The expression $Q_{\widehat{p}\widehat{p}22}$ in equation (12) is the inverse of a sum and can be decomposed as follows [11, p.37]

$$Q_{\widehat{p}\widehat{p}22} = Q_{\widehat{p}\widehat{p}11} - Q_{\widehat{p}\widehat{p}11} A_2^{\mathsf{T}} (W_{22} + A_2^{\mathsf{T}} Q_{\widehat{p}\widehat{p}11} A_2)^{-1} A_2 Q_{\widehat{p}\widehat{p}11} \tag{16}$$

$$= Q_{\widehat{p}\widehat{p}11} - F A_2 Q_{\widehat{p}\widehat{p}11} \tag{17}$$

$$= (I - F A_2) Q_{\widehat{p}\widehat{p}11} \tag{18}$$

with F being the well known gain matrix. Note that this update does not involve the inversion of the full normal equation matrix. Substituting this back into equation (12) we obtain

$$\widehat{\Delta p_2} = (I - F A_2) Q_{\widehat{p}\widehat{p}11} Q_{\widehat{p}\widehat{p}11}^{-1} \widehat{\Delta p_1} + (I - F A_2) Q_{\widehat{p}\widehat{p}11} A_2^{\mathsf{T}} W_{22}^{-1} c_{g_2} + \tag{19}$$

$$(I - F A_2) Q_{\widehat{p}\widehat{p}11} A_1^{\mathsf{T}} W_{11}^{-1} \Delta c_{g_1}$$

$$= \widehat{\Delta p_1} - F A_2 \widehat{\Delta p_1} + F c_{g_2} + (I - F A_2) Q_{\widehat{p}\widehat{p}11} A_1^{\mathsf{T}} W_{11}^{-1} \Delta c_{g_1} \tag{20}$$

using the identity [11, p.37]

$$F = (I - F A_2) Q_{\widehat{p}\widehat{p}11} A_2^{\mathsf{T}} W_{22}^{-1} \;. \tag{21}$$

The only remaining part still depending on l_1 is now the change of the contradictions (see equation (4))

$$\Delta c_{g_1} = c_{g_1} - \bar{c}_{g_1} = -g_1(\widehat{p_2}, \widehat{l_1}) + B_1^{\mathsf{T}} v_1 + g_1(\widehat{p_1}, \widehat{l_1}) - B_1^{\mathsf{T}} \bar{v}_1 \;. \tag{22}$$

In order to get rid of this remaining dependence on the previous observations observe, that the whole first contradiction block in the Kalman filter is encoded in the first two moments of the parameter vector only. We therefore replace the first constraint block by a direct observation of the parameters itself, i.e. $l_1 = \widehat{p_1}$ and $C_{11} = Q_{\widehat{p}\widehat{p}_{11}}$, so that

$$g_1(\widehat{p_1}, l_1) = \widehat{p_1} - l_1 = 0 \tag{23}$$

immediately fulfills the constraint and therefore $\bar{c}_{g_1} = 0$, $\bar{v}_1 = 0$ and $\widehat{\Delta p_1} = 0$. Furthermore the Jacobians are given by $A_1 = I$ and $B_1 = -I$.

Now equation (20) simplifies to

$$\widehat{\Delta p_2} = Fc_{g_2} + (I - FA_2)\Delta c_{g_1} \tag{24}$$

with

$$\Delta c_{g_1} = -g_1(\widehat{p_2}, \widehat{l_1}) - v_1 \tag{25}$$

and equation (14) boiling down to

$$v_1 = -\Delta c_{g_1} + \widehat{\Delta p_2} . \tag{26}$$

For the second contradiction block we can compute the residuals

$$v_2 = C_{22}B_2 W_{22}^{-1}(c_{g_2} - A_2\widehat{\Delta p_2}) \tag{27}$$

and the contradictions

$$c_{g_2} = -g_2(\widehat{p_2}, \widehat{l_2}) + B_2^{\mathsf{T}} v_2 . \tag{28}$$

We now have derived all required equations for incorporating an additional implicit constraint into an estimation. In the following section those equations will be summarized and put together into an easily applicable algorithm.

2.3   The Final Algorithm

We will now summarize the recursive estimation algorithm, which can be applied as a black-box if only the Jacobians of the implicit model function are supplied. From a previous estimation or prediction step of the filter, a current state vector p_1 together with its covariance $Q_{p_1 p_1}$ is known. We now gather additional observations l_2 together with their covariance matrix C_{22} in a subsequent measurement step. The following algorithm may then be applied to update the state vector accordingly.

1. set $\widehat{\Delta p_2} = 0$
2. set $\widehat{p_2} = p_1$
3. set $v_1 = 0$
4. set $v_2 = 0$, hence $\widehat{l_2} = l_2$

5. iterate until $\widehat{\Delta p_2}$ is sufficiently small
   (a) compute Jacobians A_2 and B_2 at $\widehat{p_2}$ and $\widehat{l_2}$
   (b) compute the gain matrix F as shown in equation (17)
   (c) compute c_{g_2} according to equation (28)
   (d) compute Δc_{g_1} according to equation (25)
   (e) compute $\widehat{\Delta p_2}$ according to equation (24)
   (f) update $\widehat{p_2}$ with $\widehat{\Delta p_2}$
   (g) compute v_1 according to equation (26)
   (h) compute v_2 according to equation (27)
   (i) update $\widehat{l_2}$ with v_2
6. compute $Q_{\widehat{p}\widehat{p}_{22}}$ according to equation(18)

After the algorithm is converged we finally obtained the updated state vector $\widehat{p_2}$ together with its covariance matrix $Q_{\widehat{p}\widehat{p}_{22}}$. The only problem specific part is the computation of the Jacobians in step 5a, which has to be adapted by the user. This completes the measurement update using the implicit constraint and a subsequent time update may be performed.

3   Results

The algorithm presented in the previous section is applicable to a broad range of problems. In the following we will demonstrate the applicability of the framework for the task of structure-from-motion using a single camera [2]. We will first briefly sketch the involved model equations and then give some results on a test sequence, where we will compare our approach to [2].

3.1   Model Equations

In [2] a popular model for on-line structure from motion using a single camera is presented, which uses the following state vector

$$p = \begin{pmatrix} r^W \\ q^{RW} \\ v^W \\ \omega^R \\ X_1 \\ \vdots \\ X_i \end{pmatrix} \tag{29}$$

comprising of the camera state followed by a set of features parameters. The uncertainty is coded in the covariance matrix Q_{pp}, which is a square matrix of equal dimension. The camera trajectory is represented by its actual position r^W, orientation quaternion q^{RW}, velocity vector v^W and angular velocity vector ω^R. The 3d point coordinates are represented by their Euclidean points X_i.

The time update for the camera position and orientation can easily be compute as

$$\widehat{p} = \begin{pmatrix} r^W_{new} \\ q^{RW}_{new} \end{pmatrix} = \begin{pmatrix} r^W + v^W \Delta t \\ q^{RW} \times q(\omega^R \Delta t) \end{pmatrix} \tag{30}$$

where velocity, angular velocity and Euclidean points do not change. The uncertainty of the predicted state is computed using error propagation and adding some system noise (see [2]). We will use this time update model in both approaches we compare.

In the approach of [2] the measurement model is based on the co-linearity equations, which can be written as homogeneous equations

$$\mathbf{x}_i = \lambda_i \mathsf{P} \mathbf{X}_i \qquad \text{with} \qquad \mathsf{P} = \mathsf{K} R(\mathbf{q}) \left[I_{3 \times 3} \mid -\mathbf{r} \right] . \tag{31}$$

Rewriting this in Euclidean coordinates, we get $\{u_i, v_i\}$ as image coordinate observations

$$u_i = \frac{P_{11} X_i + P_{12} Y_i + P_{13} Z_i + P_{14}}{P_{31} X_i + P_{32} Y_i + P_{33} Z_i + P_{34}} \tag{32}$$

$$v_i = \frac{P_{21} X_i + P_{22} Y_i + P_{23} Z_i + P_{24}}{P_{31} X_i + P_{32} Y_i + P_{33} Z_i + P_{34}} \tag{33}$$

which are explicit functions in the observations as required by the classical Kalman filter. The fraction introduces a degree of non-linearity into the model equations, that could be avoided using implicit functions.

As our approach is able to cope with implicit functions, we re-formulate the co-linearity constraint using the cross-product as follows: Introducing the matrix

$$S(t) = \begin{pmatrix} 0 & -t_3 & t_2 \\ t_3 & 0 & -t_1 \end{pmatrix} \tag{34}$$

the co-linearity equations can be stated as implicit equation

$$S(\mathbf{x}_i) \mathsf{P} \mathbf{X}_i = -S(\mathsf{P} \mathbf{X}_i) \mathbf{x}_i = \mathbf{0} . \tag{35}$$

Obviously, those implicit constraints are equivalent to the explicit constraints. Also observe that they are also non-linear in the camera pose parameters. However, there is no fraction involved, so that the effects introduced by the non-linearity turn out to be reduced, as will be seen in the next section.

3.2   Experimental Evaluation

In order to assess the performance of the presented technique for the non-linear structure-from-motion problem, we used the well-known rotating dinosaur sequence depicted in figure 1, where ground-truth camera calibration and orientation data were available. We extracted point features and tracked them across the sequence.

Because the initialization of a Kalman filter based reconstruction approach is known to influence the result significantly (see [12], [1]), we used the result of a bundle adjustment of the first five frames for initialization of both approaches. New points, that were introduced into the estimation, were initialized at the centroid of the point cloud and given a large initial covariance matrix.

We estimated the camera trajectory and the 3d point cloud using the approach based on explicit functions presented in [2] as well as using our own approach

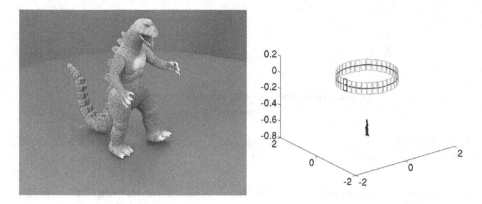

Fig. 1. *Left:* A single frame of the well-known rotating dinosaur sequence. The sequence consists of 36 images rotated in 10° steps around the dinosaur. Ground-truth for the camera calibration, position and rotation is available and will be used to quantify the performance of the presented methods. *Right:* Camera positions and orientations computed using a bundle adjustment of tracked feature points. The frame marked in black is the last in the sequence. Note that the features were tracked, so that no correspondences between the first and the last frame were used to close the loop.

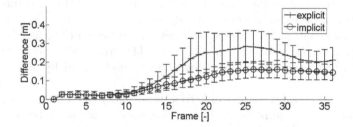

Fig. 2. The mean distances and standard deviations of the estimated projection centers to the ground truth for both methods with simulated noise plotted against the frame number

based on implicit functions as described in the previous section. Both algorithms were initialized using the same values, and the system noise and time update model were identical. Furthermore we iterated the measurement update until convergence for both approaches unlike proposed in [2], where only one iteration is performed.

To evaluate the new algorithm, we added noise to the ground truth observations, estimated the projection centers based on the noisy data with both methods and compared the results with the ground truth projection centers. We ran the experiment 20 times. The results can be observe in figure 2. We see that the proposed approach improves the accuracy of the estimated parameters.

Figure 3 shows the distance of the estimated projection centers to the ground truth projection centers plotted against the frame number of the real data.

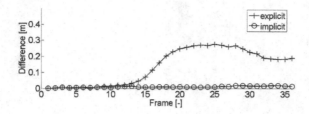

Fig. 3. The distances of the estimated projection centers to the ground truth for both methods plotted against the frame number

Observe, that the recursive estimation scheme based on the implicit function performs slightly better after the 15th frame.

4   Conclusion

We presented a new type of recursive estimation framework in a Kalman filter approach, which enables us to use implicit constraint functions, rather than being restricted to explicit ones. By allowing implicit constraints, not only the task of modeling recursive estimation schemes is eased significantly, but also those could lead to more linear models in the estimation part of a Kalman filter, which improves the robustness of such approaches.

We demonstrated the feasibility of this new algorithm for the task of structure-from-motion from monocular image sequences. The proposed implicit constraints turned out to be more robust than the explicit model used by [2] on our test sequence.

The presented method is applicable to a broad range of computer vision problems, including all those resulting in homogeneous equation systems, so that a lot of estimation task might benefit, which is a topic of further research. Furthermore it might be interesting, how the proposed measurement update might improve the performance of recursive estimation tasks in combination with the unscented transformation in the time update equations.

A MATLAB reference implementation of the presented estimation algorithm is available at **www.ipb.uni-bonn.de/~richard/imEKF/**.

References

1. Beder, C., Steffen, R.: Determining an initial image pair for fixing the scale of a 3d reconstruction from an image sequence. In: Franke, K., Müller, K.-R., Nickolay, B., Schäfer, R. (eds.) Pattern Recognition. LNCS, vol. 4174, pp. 657–666. Springer, Heidelberg (2006)
2. Davison, A.J.: Real-Time Simultaneous Localisation and Mapping with a Single Camera. In: Proceeding of the 9th International Conference on Computer Vision, pp. 674–679 (2003)
3. Engels, C., Stewenius, H., Nister, D.: Bundle Adjustment Rules. Photogrammetric Computer Vision (PCV) (September 2006)

4. Förstner, W., Wrobel, B.: Mathematical Concepts in Photogrammetry. In: Mc-Glome, J.C., Mikhail, E.M., Bethel, J. (eds.) Manual of Photogrammetry, pp. 15–180, ASPRS (2004)
5. Grün, A.: An Optimum Algorithm for On-Line Triangulation. International Society for Photogrammetry and Remote Sensing 24 - III/2, 131–151 (1982)
6. Hartley, R., Zisserman, A.: Multiple View Geometry in Computer Vision. Cambridge University Press, Cambridge (2000)
7. Heuel, S.: Points, Lines and Planes and their Optimal Estimation. In: Radig, B., Florczyk, S. (eds.) Pattern Recognition. LNCS, vol. 2191, pp. 92–99. Springer, Heidelberg (2001)
8. Heuel, S.: Uncertain Projective Geometry - Statistical Reasoning for Polyhedral Object Reconstruction. Springer, Heidelberg (2004)
9. Julier, S., Uhlmann, J.: A new extension of the Kalman filter to nonlinear systems. In: Int. Symp. Aerospace/Defense Sensing, Simul. and Controls, Orlando, FL (1997)
10. Kalman, R.E.: A New Approach to Linear Filtering and Prediction Problems. Journal of Basic Engineering, 35–45 (1960)
11. Koch, K.R.: Parameter Estimation and Hypothesis Testing in Linear Models, 2nd edn. Springer, Heidelberg (1999)
12. Montiel, J., Civera, J., Davison, A.: Unified Inverse Depth Parametrization for Monocular SLAM. In: Proceedings of Robotics: Science and Systems, Philadelphia, USA (2006)
13. Perwass, C., Gebken, C., Sommer, G.: Estimation of geometric entities and operators from uncertain data. In: Kropatsch, W.G., Sablatnig, R., Hanbury, A. (eds.) Pattern Recognition. LNCS, vol. 3663, pp. 459–467. Springer, Heidelberg (2005)
14. Triggs, B., McLauchlan, P., Hartley, R., Fitzgibbon, A.: Bundle Adjustment – A Modern Synthesis. In: Triggs, B., Zisserman, A., Szeliski, R. (eds.) Vision Algorithms: Theory and Practice. LNCS, vol. 1883, pp. 298–375. Springer, Heidelberg (2000)
15. Welch, G., Bishop, G.: An Introduction to the Kalman Filter. Technical Report, University of North Carolina at Chapel Hill (1995)

Optimal Dominant Motion Estimation Using Adaptive Search of Transformation Space

Adrian Ulges[1], Christoph H. Lampert[2], Daniel Keysers[3],
and Thomas M. Breuel[1]

[1] Department of Computer Science, Technical University of Kaiserslautern
{a_ulges,tmb}@informatik.uni-kl.de
[2] Department for Empirical Inference
Max-Planck-Institute for Biological Cybernetics, Tübingen
chl@tuebingen.mpg.de
[3] Image Understanding and Pattern Recognition Group
German Research Center for Artificial Intelligence (DFKI), Kaiserslautern
keysers@iupr.net

Abstract. The extraction of a parametric global motion from a motion field is a task with several applications in video processing. We present two probabilistic formulations of the problem and carry out optimization using the RAST algorithm, a geometric matching method novel to motion estimation in video. RAST uses an exhaustive and adaptive search of transformation space and thus gives – in contrast to local sampling optimization techniques used in the past – a globally optimal solution. Among other applications, our framework can thus be used as a source of ground truth for benchmarking motion estimation algorithms.

Our main contributions are: first, the novel combination of a state-of-the-art MAP criterion for dominant motion estimation with a search procedure that guarantees global optimality. Second, experimental results that illustrate the superior performance of our approach on synthetic flow fields as well as real-world video streams. Third, a significant speedup of the search achieved by extending the model with an additional smoothness prior.

1 Introduction

We address the estimation of the dominant parametric motion from a sequence of video frames. Such dominant motion is usually equated with background motion, and its precise and robust estimation is required for several applications in the context of video analysis, like motion-based segmentation or motion compensation (which again serves as a building block in modern video encoders or in video mosaicing).

Like most practical video processing systems, we estimate a global parametric motion from a field of local motion probes – a problem that is difficult due to measurement noise, inaccuracies of the previous motion estimation step, and deviant foreground motion. In terms of dominant motion estimation, such foreground motion probes are "outliers" that have to be recognized and discarded during the fitting process.

F.A. Hamprecht, C. Schnörr, and B. Jähne (Eds.): DAGM 2007, LNCS 4713, pp. 204–213, 2007.

We view the problem from a parameter estimation perspective and propose two Bayesian formulations, one of them including a smoothness prior. The resulting optimization problems are solved using the RAST algorithm [3]. While other methods are based on a local sampling of search space and do not guarantee optimal solutions, RAST performs an adaptive, but exhaustive branch-and-bound search and finds the global optimum. This fact is proven by experimental results on synthetic motion fields as well as real-world video data.

Our main contributions are: first, the novel combination of a state-of-the-art MAP criterion with a search procedure that guarantees global optimality up to any accuracy desired. Second, experimental results that illustrate the superior performance of our approach on synthetic flow fields as well as real-world video streams. Third, a novel extension to the RAST algorithm with a smoothness prior that leads to a better search strategy with a significant speedup.

2   Related Work

Motion interpretation has often been called a "chicken-egg" problem: motion estimation is inaccurate without knowledge of motion boundaries due to the aperture problem [1], while on the other hand motion segmentation requires local motion estimates.

Methods to solve this problem can be divided into direct and indirect (or "feature-based" [8]) methods. Approaches from the first category jointly estimate motion and group it into coherent regions. Some estimate a parametric motion over image regions – like regression [1], mixture models [9], clustering methods [16] or formulations imposing additional shape priors [4]. Other direct methods are nonparametric and assume piecewise smoothness of the motion field, which leads to formulations related to Markov Random Fields [12,17].

In contrast to this, indirect methods are two-step procedures: first, a motion field is estimated using correlation-based techniques [15], feature tracking [14] or optical flow. The result forms the input to a segmentation step, which must cope with local outliers and inaccuracies due to noise in the measurement process, error-prone motion estimation, and foreground objects in motion. For this, greedy local search procedures have been used in the past, like robust least squares, RANSAC [5], least median of squares or least trimmed squares [10].

Since local errors in the motion estimation step cannot be undone, indirect methods do not reach the robustness of direct ones. Nevertheless, they offer simple and fast alternatives that are more popular in practice, and are applied to several video processing tasks, like in state-of-the-art video codecs or video mosaicing [13]. Our approach belongs to this second category. More precisely, we assume a motion field is given and focus on the motion interpretation step.

3   Statistical Framework

We assume that a motion field $D = \{(x_1, v_1), .., (x_n, v_n)\}$ of 2D positions x_i associated with 2D motion vectors v_i is given. These probes can correspond to a dense optical flow field or to sparse probes obtained from block matching or tracked point features.

The task is now to extract a parametric motion $v_\theta : \mathcal{R}^2 \to \mathcal{R}^2$ that fits D "well", i.e. $v_i \approx v_\theta(x_i)$. Such parameterized motion has proven a simple and often sufficiently accurate approximation to projected 3D scene motion. From the parameterizations proposed in the literature [8,13], we choose the similarity transform consisting of a rotation by an angle α, a scaling s (e.g., due to zooming), and a translation $(d_x, d_y)^T$.

As an optimality criterion, we use a statistical formulation of the problem, i.e. we choose the global motion $\hat{\theta} = (\hat{s}, \hat{\alpha}, \hat{d}_x, \hat{d}_y)$ that maximizes the posterior:

$$\hat{\theta} = \arg\max_\theta P(\theta|D) = \arg\max_\theta P(D|\theta) \cdot P(\theta) \tag{1}$$

3.1   Criterion Q_1: Local Independence

For our first formulation, we assume a uniform prior $P(\theta)$ and independent motion probes drawn from a distribution $p(v_i|\theta)$. If we also neglect competitive foreground motion and use isotropic Gaussian noise to model inaccuracies of motion estimation and of the capturing process, $p(v_i|\theta)$ is a Gaussian distribution with mean $v_\theta(x_i)$ and diagonal covariance $\sigma^2 I$. In practical flow fields, however, *outliers* occur – again, due to inaccuracies of the motion estimation process, but also due to foreground objects moving in a different direction. Since we do not have prior knowledge about the motion of such objects, we assume a uniform distribution $p(v_i|\theta) = c$ of foreground motion. This gives a more realistic scenario including outliers:

$$p(v_i|\theta) \propto \max\left(\mathcal{N}(v_i; v_\theta(x_i), \sigma^2 I), c\right) \tag{2}$$

We insert this term into the overall likelihood and obtain

$$p(D|\theta) = \prod_i p(v_i|\theta). \tag{3}$$

Maximizing this is equivalent to maximizing the following quality function derived from the log-likelihood (for a detailed derivation, see [18]):

$$Q_1(\theta) = \sum_i \max\left(1 - \frac{(v_i - v_\theta(x_i))^2}{\epsilon^2}, 0\right) =: \sum_i q(v_i, \theta). \tag{4}$$

The only free parameter of this ML criterion, ϵ, determines the allowed deviation of a background motion sample from the parametric motion v_θ. Note that Q_1 consists of local contributions $q(v_i, \theta)$ from the single flow samples, which are in the following referred to as the *support* of a local flow probe v_i for a global motion θ. This support is zero exactly if v_i deviates by ϵ or more from the model motion $v_\theta(x_i)$ (i.e. if v_i is regarded as an outlier). Thus, the evaluation of Q_1 provides a segmentation of the motion field into background and foreground.

3.2 Criterion Q_2: Spatial Coherence Prior

The optimality criterion Q_1 introduced in Equation (4) is derived from the likelihood and neglects the spatial coherence with which motion occurs in real-world videos. Like other researchers before, we use this fact by formulating an additional prior related to formulations in Markov Random Fields [1,6,17].

For this, we first introduce a segmentation as a *labeling* of the motion vectors $L : \{x_1, .., x_n\} \to \{0,1\}$ such that $L(x_i) = L_i = 1$ iff v_i belongs to the background (which is the case exactly if $q(v_i, \theta) > 0$). Note that – given such a labeling – we can automatically compute a motion $\theta(L)$ as a least squares solution over the motion probes in the background region $L^{-1}(1)$. This is why – instead of searching for a motion θ – we instead search for an optimal labeling by maximizing the posterior:

$$P(L|D) \propto P(D|L) \cdot P(L) = P(D|\theta(L)) \cdot P(L) \qquad (5)$$

The first term corresponds to the likelihood criterion from Equation (3). For the prior $P(L)$, we define a neighborhood structure over the motion field sites $\{x_i\}$ (for example, 4-connectedness on a regular grid of sites x_i), which again induces *cliques* of neighbor sites (all pairs of sites (x_i, x_j) which are adjacent). Let $\mathcal{C}$ denote the set of all such cliques. Then we define $P(L)$ as:

$$P(L) \propto \prod_{(x_i, x_j) \in \mathcal{C}} e^{-U(i,j)} \qquad (6)$$

with $U(i,j) = L_i L_j \cdot c_1 + (1 - L_i L_j) \cdot c_2$. This leads to the overall posterior

$$P(L|D) \propto \prod_i p(v_i|\theta) \cdot \prod_{(x_i, x_j) \in \mathcal{C}} e^{-U(i,j)} \qquad (7)$$

maximizing which is again equivalent to maximizing a simpler quality criterion (a detailed derivation is again given in [18]):

$$Q_2(\theta) = Q_1(\theta) + \gamma \sum_{(x_i, x_j) \in \mathcal{C}} L_i L_j \qquad (8)$$

where Q_1 is the quality from Equation (4). The free parameter $\gamma > 0$ determines the weight of spatial coherence relative to the goodness-of-fit term Q_1. It depends on c, c_1, and c_2, and is set manually in practice.

3.3 Optimization Using RAST

Both criteria Q_1 and Q_2 can be highly non-convex for motion fields in practice such that techniques based on a sparse sampling of the space of possible motions may get caught in local minima. We present an alternative based on a full search of parameter space. Though more time-consuming, it is made feasible using an *adaptive* search strategy. Our approach is called RAST (*Recognition by Adaptive*

Search of Transformation space) [3][1]. It has been applied in the domain of geometric matching before, but is novel to dominant motion estimation in video. RAST is based on a branch-and-bound strategy: starting with the full parameter space, a parameter subset is iteratively chosen and subdivided into two parts by splitting along one parameter. We obtain subsequently finer subsets until finishing with a sufficiently small region corresponding to our estimate $\hat{\theta}$ (the user can define the accuracy of the solution via this stopping criterion). The search is guided into promising regions of parameter space by managing subsets in a priority queue, i.e. for each subset an *upper bound* $\mathcal{U}$ of the quality is computed and used to reinsert the subset into the priority queue.

The key part of the search is the computation of $\mathcal{U}$. For Q_1, the associated bound is $\mathcal{U}_1 = \sum_i u_i$, i.e. for each motion probe we find out (e.g., using interval arithmetic [2]) if it can contribute to *any* global motion in the subset. For Q_2, $\mathcal{U}_2 = \mathcal{U}_1 + \gamma \cdot \sum_{(i,j) \in \mathcal{C}} u_{ij}$ with $u_{ij} = 0$ if $u_i = u_j = 0$ and $u_{ij} = 1$ otherwise. i.e. after computing $\mathcal{U}_1$, an additional linear sweep through the motion probes is required to increment the bound for each pair of adjacent potential background sites.

4   Experiments

The most important capability of our approach is its optimality: the combination of our statistical framework and the RAST optimization guarantees an optimal solution up to any accuracy desired given a state-of-the-art statistical model – a fact that is proven by quantitative experiments on synthetic motion fields, which provide a controlled framework for evaluation with a well-known known ground truth segmentation and ground truth motion. To validate that our model is adequate in practice, we also present results for real-world video data.

4.1   General Setup

All input motion fields – synthetic or extracted from video – are defined at 16×16 macroblock positions (though our approach is not restricted to this setup). For video streams, motion is estimated using the MPEG-4 video codec XViD[2] [15]. Global motion is parameterized using a similarity transform. The following methods are tested:

1. *Our Framework*: We test our framework for both quality functions Q_1 and Q_2 ($\epsilon = 2.3$, $\gamma = 1$). The 4-dimensional similarity transform space searched by RAST should contain all reasonable motion between adjacent video frames. We choose: $\sigma \in [0.9, 1.1], \alpha \in [-0.1, 0.1], (d_x, d_y) \in [-40, 40]^2$. Search is stopped if the evaluated subset has dimensions smaller than $(0.0002)^2 \times (0.1)^2$. This means, the solution is determined with an accuracy of 0.1 pixels for the translation, 0.0002 *rad* for the rotation, and 0.0002 for the scale.

---

[1] Open source implementation at http://www.iupr.org/~chl/multirast.tar.gz
[2] www.xvid.org

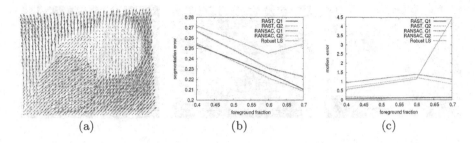

Fig. 1. (a) A synthetic motion field with three blobs each moving in different directions. (b) and (c) Motion estimation results on synthetic blob data. (b) shows the average segmentation error (depending on the fraction of the screen occupied by competitive foreground motion), (b) the squared error of the estimated x translation relative to the ground truth.

2. *Least Squares*: standard least squares regression is equivalent to maximizing a quality function similar to Q_1, but with a pure Gaussian motion vector density instead of a truncated Gaussian one. It is thus expected to perform poorly when competitive foreground motion occurs and serves as a baseline.

3. *Robust Least Squares*: this method alternately computes least squares motion estimates and discards motion samples from D that deviate further than an outlier threshold σ. Our implementation generates a sequence of solutions by decreasing σ according to the schedule $\sigma_{k+1} = 0.95 \cdot \sigma_k$ until $\sigma < 2.3$.

4. *RANSAC*: Random Sample Consensus (RANSAC) [5] is a popular Monte Carlo procedure with excellent robustness to outliers and noise [7,11]. It is based on an iterated random subsampling of D. The probability of failure decreases with the number of iterations, but never reaches 0, such that optimality is not guaranteed. RANSAC is tested for both Q_1 and Q_2.

5. *XViD Dominant Motion Estimation*: this is the dominant motion estimation component that the XViD codec uses for compression purposes. The implementation is comparable to robust least squares, but with a more greedy outlier rejection strategy.

4.2   Synthetic Flow Fields

In a first experiment, we use synthetic flow fields of blob regions moving in front of a moving background with the purpose of simulating the phenomena of noise and spatial coherence in real-world video frames.

Like the example illustrated in Figure 1(a), all motion fields are derived from a dominant motion and three foreground motions. The background motion is randomly drawn from $[-0.05, 0.05] \times [0.95, 1.05] \times [10, 10]^2$. Also, three blobs are initialized with a random motion from $\{0\} \times \{1\} \times [-16, 16]^2$. All blobs are of the same size such that they – when non-overlapping – occupy a certain fraction $f \in \{0.4, 0.6, 0.7\}$ of the field. Also, isotropic Gaussian noise with standard

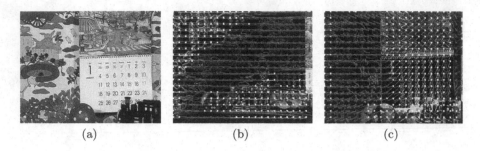

$$\text{(a)} \qquad\qquad\qquad \text{(b)} \qquad\qquad\qquad \text{(c)}$$

Fig. 2. (a) A frame from the mobile sequence. (b) and (c) Motion segmentation (red vectors belong to the background, white ones to the foreground) and difference between motion-compensated frames for XViD (b) and RAST (c). For XViD, a wrong estimate leads to a poor motion compensation on the upper left part of the frame.

deviation $\sigma \in \{1.0, 1.3, 1.6, 2.0, 2.3\}$ is added to each motion vector, obtaining a total of 1000 motion fields.

Numerical results for all test methods except the XViD codec (which we apply to real-world videos only) and least squares (which performed much worse than all other methods) are given in Figures 1(b) and 1(c). In Figure 1(b), the average segmentation error is plotted against the fraction f occupied by the foreground, reaching from 0.4 to 0.7. Note that some intrinsic segmentation error results from outliers due to noise. The rate of such outliers – and thus the segmentation error – constantly drops with f. Our framework gives lower segmentation error rates than all other methods. The robust least squares method tends to break at high foreground fractions. Between RAST and RANSAC (100 iterations), a difference of about 1 % in segmentation error can be observed.

In Figure 1(c), we plot the average error of the estimated motion (more precisely, for the x-translation parameter) for the noise level $\sigma = 2.0$ against the foreground fraction f. Again, our framework shows the best performance. The average mean squared error remains below 0.2 pixels. Also, it can be observed that Q_1 and Q_2 give a similar performance.

4.3   Test Sequences "Mobile" and "Snooker"

To validate its performance on real-world video data, we first apply our framework to MPEG-4 motion vectors derived from the "mobile and calendar" test sequence[3]. The sequence shows a textured background behind three foreground objects, each moving in a different direction approximately perpendicular to the optical axis. We subsampled the sequence in the temporal domain at 1 fps, obtaining 11 frames 22×18 macroblocks each. One frame is shown in Figure 2 together with motion estimates for XViD and RAST. The motion visualization is layed over a motion-compensated difference image. For the RAST result, the difference is low except for foreground regions. For the XViD result, it can be

---

[3] http://www.m4if.org/resources.php

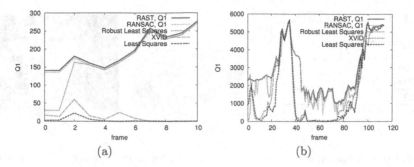

(a)   (b)

Fig. 3. Motion support results for (a) the mobile test sequence (11 frames) and (b) the snooker test sequence (90 frames)

seen that parts of the background (on the upper left) have been classified as foreground and have thus been poorly compensated for.

Figure 3(a) illustrates the motion support Q_1 for several test methods, plotted over the frames of the mobile toot sequence. For RANSAC and RAST, the ML formulation was used.

We also compared the average processing time of RAST for both criteria Q_1 (2.85 sec./frame, 1.6 Ghz Pentium M) and Q_2 (1.07 sec./frame). Interestingly, the spatial prior – though demanding an extra sweep through all motion samples for the evaluation of a subset – leads to a significant speedup (62 %) that can be observed throughout all of our experiments. Obviously, spatial coherence helps to discard bad motion hypotheses early that are scattered over the field, and to guide search into promising regions of transformation space. This insight might be interesting in the geometric matching domain where RAST was developed.

Comparable results can be observed for our second test sequence "snooker" captured from a TV sports broadcast (90 frames), showing a snooker player tracked by a camera with a strong translation. The support Q_1 for the sequence is plotted in Figure 3(b) (for RANSAC, 20 iterations were used). Again, XViD and least squares give relatively poor results. RANSAC and robust least squares perform comparable to our method, but fail occasionally.

For both sequences, the support for our approach serves as an upper bound for the performance of other methods.

4.4   Test Sequence "Foreman"

In this experiment, we test the performance of our approach for motion segmentation on a subsampled version of the MPEG-4 test video sequence "foreman" (80 frames) that comes with a ground truth segmentation mask. The sequence shows strong, chaotic camera motion and a highly non-planar background.

Again, we tested several methods, for RAST and RANSAC (100 iterations) including the spatial prior (Q_2). Segmentation results are compared to the ground truth on block basis (mixed blocks showing more than 5 % of both foreground and background pixels are ignored). The resulting error rates are given in

method	segmentation error rate
RAST	0.24
RANSAC	0.25
Robust LQ	0.26
XViD	0.33
LQ	0.41

(a)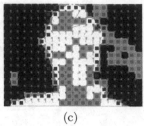

         (a)   (b)   (c)

Fig. 4. (a) Average segmentation error rates for the foreman sequence. (b) A frame from the foreman sequence, and (c) a typical segmentation result evaluated using MPEG-4 ground truth segmentation masks. Blue blocks are ignored, red blocks are misclassified.

Figure 4 (a), a sample segmentation is illustrated in Figure 4 (b) and (c). Our method gives the best results, followed by RANSAC and robust least squares. A high intrinsic error occurs due to two reasons (besides inaccuracies in the motion estimation step): first, the object stands still in some frames and is missed by motion segmentation. Second, the 4D motion model implicitly assumes a planar background surface perpendicular to the optical axis. Since this assumption is heavily violated in the foreman sequence, the optimal motion fit cannot be determined in some frames.

5 Discussion

We have presented a framework for the indirect estimation of a global motion from a given motion field. Our method is based on two alternative probabilistic formulations of the problem: an ML criterion assuming independence of motion samples, and an extension with a spatial coherence prior enforcing piecewise-smooth motion. The optimization of the resulting quality functions is done using RAST, an approach novel to dominant motion estimation in video.

The most important capability of our framework is that our method – in contrast to local search procedures used in the past – guarantees an optimal solution up to any user-defined accuracy. We demonstrate this superior performance on synthetic motion data showing blobs moving in front of a noisy background motion, as well as on several real-world video sequences. Though greedy search procedures may be fast, attractive solutions for online processing, they do not guarantee global optimality. In this context, our framework might provide ground truth for benchmarking global motion estimation in video.

Another novelty we present is the combination of RAST optimization with a spatial prior formulation. In our experiments, we measured a significant speed-up using this extension. Obviously, this approach helps to guide the adaptive search into more promising regions of parameter space – an insight that might be interesting for RAST applications in the area of geometric matching and object recognition.

Acknowledgements

This work was supported in part by the Stiftung Rheinland-Pfalz für Innovation, project InViRe (961-386261/791).

References

1. Black, M.J., Anandan, P.: The Robust Estimation of Multiple Motions: Parametric and Piecewise-Smooth Flow Fields. In: CVIU, vol. 63(1), pp. 75–104 (1996)
2. Breuel, T.M.: On the Use of Interval Arithmetic in Geometric Branch-and-Bound Algorithms. Pattern Recogn. Lett. 24(9-10), 1375–1384 (2003)
3. Breuel, T.M.: Fast Recognition using Adaptive Subdivisions of Transformation Space. In: CVPR 92, pp. 445–451 (1992)
4. Cremers, D., Soatto, S.: Motion Competition: A Variational Approach to Piecewise Parametric Motion Segmentation. Int. J. Comput. Vision 62(3), 249–265 (2005)
5. Fischler, M.A., Bolles, R.C.: Random Sample Consensus: A Paradigm for Model Fitting with Applications to Image Analysis and Automated Cartography. Communications of the ACM 24(6), 381–395 (1981)
6. Geman, D.: Stochastic Model for Boundary Detection. Image Vision Comput. 5(2), 61–65 (1987)
7. Hartley, R., Zisserman, A.: Multiple View Geometry in Computer Vision. Cambridge University Press, New York (2003)
8. Irani, M., Anandan, P.: About Direct Methods. In: ICCV '99: Intern. Workshop on Vision Algorithms, London, UK, pp. 267–277 (2000)
9. Jepson, A., Black, M.J.: Mixture Models for Optical Flow Computation. In: CVPR 93, pp. 760–761 (1993)
10. Kühne, G.: Motion-based Segmentation and Classification of Video Objects. PhD thesis, University of Mannheim (2002)
11. Lepetit, V., Fua, P.: Monocular Model-Based 3D Tracking of Rigid Objects: A Survey. Foundations and Trends in Computer Graphics and Vision 1(1) (2005)
12. Murray, D.W., Buxton, B.F.: Scene Segmentation from Visual Motion using Global Optimization. IEEE Trans. Pattern Anal. Mach. Intell. 9(2), 220–228 (1987)
13. Smolic, A.: Globale Bewegungsbeschreibung und Video Mosaiking unter Verwendung parametrischer 2-D Modelle. PhD thesis, RWTH Aachen (2001)
14. Tomasi, C., Kanade, T.: Detection and Tracking of Point Features. Technical Report CMU-CS-91-132, CMU (1991)
15. Tourapis, A.M.: Enhanced Predictive Zonal Search for Single and Multiple Frame Motion Estimation. In: Proc. SPIE Conf. Visual Communications and Image Processing, Lugano, Switzerland, pp. 1069–1079 (2002)
16. Wang, J.Y.A., Adelson, E.H.: Layered Representation for Motion Analysis. In: CVPR 93, pp. 361–366 (1993)
17. Weiss, Y.: Smoothness in Layers: Motion Segmentation using Nonparametric Mixture Estimation. In: CVPR 97, pp. 520–526 (1997)
18. Ulges, A.: Motion Interpretation using Adaptive Search of Transformation Space. Technical Report, IUPR Research Group, TU Kaiserslautern (2007)

A Duality Based Approach for Realtime TV-L^1 Optical Flow

C. Zach[1], T. Pock[2], and H. Bischof[2]

[1] VRVis Research Center
[2] Institute for Computer Graphics and Vision, TU Graz

Abstract. Variational methods are among the most successful approaches to calculate the optical flow between two image frames. A particularly appealing formulation is based on total variation (TV) regularization and the robust L^1 norm in the data fidelity term. This formulation can preserve discontinuities in the flow field and offers an increased robustness against illumination changes, occlusions and noise. In this work we present a novel approach to solve the TV-L^1 formulation. Our method results in a very efficient numerical scheme, which is based on a dual formulation of the TV energy and employs an efficient point-wise thresholding step. Additionally, our approach can be accelerated by modern graphics processing units. We demonstrate the real-time performance (30 fps) of our approach for video inputs at a resolution of 320×240 pixels.

1 Introduction

The recovery of motion from images is a major task of biological and artificial vision systems. The main objective of optical flow methods is to compute a flow field estimating the motion of pixels in two consecutive image frames. Since optical flow is an highly ill-posed inverse problem, using pure intensity-based constraints generally results in an under-determined system of equations, which is generally known as the *aperture problem*. In order to solve this problem some kind of regularization is needed to obtain physically meaningful displacement fields.

In their seminal work [13], Horn and Schunck studied a variational formulation of the optical flow problem.

$$\min_{\boldsymbol{u}} \left\{ \int_{\Omega} |\nabla u_1|^2 + |\nabla u_2|^2 \, \mathrm{d}\Omega + \lambda \int_{\Omega} \left(I_1(\boldsymbol{x} + \boldsymbol{u}(\boldsymbol{x})) - I_0(\boldsymbol{x}) \right)^2 \mathrm{d}\Omega \right\} . \quad (1)$$

I_0 and I_1 is the image pair, $\boldsymbol{u} = (u_1(\boldsymbol{x}), u_2(\boldsymbol{x}))^T$ is the two-dimensional displacement field and λ is a free parameter. The first term (regularization term) penalizes high variations in $\boldsymbol{u}$ to obtain smooth displacement fields. The second term (data term) is also known as the optical flow constraint. It assumes, that the intensity values of $I_0(\boldsymbol{x})$ do not change during its motion to $I_1(\boldsymbol{x} + \boldsymbol{u}(\boldsymbol{x}))$.

Since the Horn-Schunck model penalizes deviations in a quadratic way, it has two major limitations. It does not allow for discontinuities in the displacement

F.A. Hamprecht, C. Schnörr, and B. Jähne (Eds.): DAGM 2007, LNCS 4713, pp. 214–223, 2007.

field, and it does not handle outliers in the data term robustly. To overcome these limitations, several models including robust error norms and higher order data terms have been proposed. Since discontinuities in the optical flow appear often in conjunction with high image gradients, several authors replace the homogeneous regularization in the Horn-Schunck model with an anisotropic diffusion approach [15,19]. Other proposed modifications substitute the squared penalty functions in the Horn-Schunck model with more robust variants. Blake and Anandan [5] apply estimators from robust statistics and obtain a robust and discontinuity preserving formulation for the optical flow energy. Aubert et al. [3] analyze energy functionals for optical flow incorporating an L^1 data fidelity term and a general class of discontinuity preserving regularization forces. Papenberg et al. [16] employ a differentiable approximation of the TV (resp. L^1) norm and formulate a nested iteration scheme to compute the displacement field.

Most approaches for optical flow computation replace the nonlinear intensity profile $I_1(\boldsymbol{x}+\boldsymbol{u}(\boldsymbol{x}))$ by a first order Taylor approximation to linearize the problem locally. Since such approximation is only valid for small displacements, additional techniques are required to determine the optical flow correctly for large displacements. Scale-space approaches [1] and coarse-to-fine warping (e.g. [2,14,7]) provide solutions to optical flow estimation with large displacements.

In several applications, such as autonomous robot navigation, it is necessary to calculate displacement fields in real-time. Real-time optical flow techniques typically consider only the data fidelity term to generate displacement fields [10,18]. One of the first variational approaches to compute the optical flow in real-time was presented by Bruhn et al. [8,9]. In their work a highly efficient multi-grid approach is employed to obtain real-time or near real-time performance. The aim of their approach is very similar to our objective: obtaining robust and discontinuity preserving solutions for optical flow with highly efficient implementations. Nevertheless, we utilize a completely different solution strategy as described in the next sections.

2   TV-L_1 Optical Flow

In the basic setting two image frames I_0 and $I_1 : (\Omega \subseteq \mathbb{R}^2) \to \mathbb{R}$ are given. The objective is to find the disparity map $\boldsymbol{u} : \Omega \to \mathbb{R}^2$, which minimizes an image-based error criterion together with a regularization force. In this work we focus on the plain intensity difference between pixels as the image similarity score. Hence, the target disparity map $\boldsymbol{u}$ is the minimizer of

$$\int_\Omega \left\{ \lambda \phi \left(I_0(\boldsymbol{x}) - I_1(\boldsymbol{x} + \boldsymbol{u}(\boldsymbol{x}))\right) + \psi(\boldsymbol{u}, \nabla \boldsymbol{u}, \ldots) \right\} d\boldsymbol{x}, \tag{2}$$

where $\phi\left(I_0(\boldsymbol{x}) - I_1(\boldsymbol{x} + \boldsymbol{u}(\boldsymbol{x}))\right)$ is the image data fidelity, and $\psi(\boldsymbol{u}, \nabla \boldsymbol{u}, \ldots)$ depicts the regularization term inducing the shape prior. λ weights between the data fidelity and the regularization force. Selecting $\phi(x) = x^2$ and $\psi(\nabla u) = |\nabla u|^2$ results in the Horn-Schunck model [13].

The choice of $\phi(x) = |x|$ and $\psi(\nabla u)) = |\nabla u|$ yields to the following functional consisting of an L_1 data penalty term and total variation regularization:

$$E = \int_\Omega \left\{ \lambda |I_0(\boldsymbol{x}) - I_1(\boldsymbol{x} + \boldsymbol{u}(\boldsymbol{x}))| + |\nabla u| \right\} d\boldsymbol{x}. \tag{3}$$

Although Eq. 3 seems to be simple, it offers some computational difficulties. The main reason is that both the regularization term and the data term are not continuously differentiable. One approach is to replace $\phi(x) = |x|$ and $\psi(\nabla u)$ with differentiable approximations $\phi_\varepsilon(x^2) = \sqrt{x^2 + \varepsilon^2}$ and $\psi_\varepsilon(\nabla u) = \sqrt{|\nabla u|^2 + \varepsilon^2}$, and to apply a numerical optimization technique on this slightly modified functional (e.g. [12,7]).

In this paper we employ a rather different approach. In [11] Chambolle proposed an efficient and exact numerical scheme to solve the Rudin-Osher-Fatemi energy [17] for total variation based image denoising. In the following, we will describe how to adopt this approach for the optical flow case.

2.1   The 1D Stereo Case

In this section we restrict the disparities to be non-zero only in the horizontal direction, e.g. a normalized stereo image pair is provided. Hence, $\boldsymbol{u}(\boldsymbol{x})$ reduces to a scalar $u(\boldsymbol{x})$, and we use the (sloppy) notation $\boldsymbol{x} + u(\boldsymbol{x})$ for $\boldsymbol{x} + (u(\boldsymbol{x}), 0)^T$. The following derivation is based on [4], but adapted to the stereo/optical flow setting. At first, we linearize image I_1 near $\boldsymbol{x} + u_0$, i.e.

$$I_1(\boldsymbol{x} + u) = I_1(\boldsymbol{x} + u_0) + (u - u_0) I_1^x(\boldsymbol{x} + u_0),$$

where u_0 is a given disparity map and I_1^x is the derivative of the image intensity I_1 wrt. the x-direction. Using the first order Taylor approximation for I_1 means, that the following procedure needs to be embedded into an iterative warping approach to compensate for image nonlinearities. Additionally, a multi-level approach is employed to allow large disparities between the images.

For fixed u_0 and using the linear approximation for I_1, the TV-L_1 functional (Eq. 3) now reads as:

$$E = \int_\Omega \left\{ \lambda |u\, I_1^x + I_1(\boldsymbol{x} + u_0) - u_0\, I_1^x - I_0| + |\nabla u| \right\} d\boldsymbol{x}. \tag{4}$$

In the following, we denote the current residual $I_1(\boldsymbol{x} + u_0) + (u - u_0) I_1^x - I_0$ by $\rho(u, u_0, \boldsymbol{x})$ (or just $\rho(u)$ by omitting the explicit dependency on u_0 and $\boldsymbol{x}$). Moreover, we introduce an auxiliary variable v and propose to minimize the following convex approximation of Eq. 4:

$$E_\theta = \int_\Omega \left\{ |\nabla u| + \frac{1}{2\theta}(u - v)^2 + \lambda |\rho(v)| \right\} d\boldsymbol{x}, \tag{5}$$

where θ is a small constant, such that v is a close approximation of u. This convex minimization problem can be optimized by alternating steps updating either u or v in every iteration:

1. For v being fixed, solve

$$\min_{u} \int_{\Omega} \left\{ |\nabla u| + \frac{1}{2\theta}(u - v)^2 \right\} d\boldsymbol{x}. \tag{6}$$

This is the total variation based image denoising model of Rudin, Osher and Fatemi [17].

2. For u being fixed, solve

$$\min_{v} \int_{\Omega} \left\{ \frac{1}{2\theta}(u - v)^2 + \lambda \, |\rho(v)| \right\} d\boldsymbol{x}. \tag{7}$$

This minimization problem can be solved point-wise, since it does not depend on spatial derivatives of v.

An efficient solution for the first step (Eq. 6) was proposed in [11], which uses a dual formulation of Eq. 6 to derive an efficient and globally convergent scheme. Since this algorithm is an essential part of our method, we reproduce the relevant results from [11]:

Proposition 1. *The solution of Eq. (6) is given by*

$$u = v - \theta \operatorname{div} \boldsymbol{p}\,, \tag{8}$$

where $\boldsymbol{p} = (p^1, p^2)$ *fulfills*

$$\nabla(\theta \operatorname{div} \boldsymbol{p} - v) = |\nabla(\theta \operatorname{div} \boldsymbol{p} - v)| \, \boldsymbol{p}\,, \tag{9}$$

which can be solved by the following iterative fixed-point scheme:

$$\boldsymbol{p}^{k+1} = \frac{\boldsymbol{p}^k + \tau \nabla(\operatorname{div} \boldsymbol{p}^k - v/\theta)}{1 + \tau|\nabla(\operatorname{div} \boldsymbol{p}^k - v/\theta)|}\,, \tag{10}$$

where $\boldsymbol{p}^0 = 0$ *and the time step* $\tau \leq 1/8$.

The next proposition characterizes the minimizer of the second part (Eq. 7):

Proposition 2. *The solution of the minimization task in Eq. 7 is given by the following thresholding step:*

$$v = u + \begin{cases} \lambda\,\theta\,I_1^x & \text{if} \quad \rho(u) < -\lambda\,\theta\,(I_1^x)^2 \\ -\lambda\,\theta\,I_1^x & \text{if} \quad \rho(u) > \lambda\,\theta\,(I_1^x)^2 \\ -\rho(u)/I_1^x & \text{if} \quad |\rho(u)| \leq \lambda\,\theta\,(I_1^x)^2. \end{cases} \tag{11}$$

This means, that the image residual $\rho(v)$ is allowed to vanish, if the required step from u to v is sufficiently small. Otherwise, v makes a bounded step from u, such that the magnitude of the residual decreases.

The proposition above can be shown directly by analyzing the three possible cases, $\rho(v) > 0$ (inducing $v = u - \lambda\,\theta\,I_1^x$), $\rho(v) < 0$ ($v = u + \lambda\,\theta\,I_1^x$) and $\rho(v) = 0$ ($v = u - \rho(u)/I_1^x$).

2.2 Generalization to Higher Dimensions

In this section we extend the method introduced in the previous section to optical flow estimation, i.e. an N-dimensional displacement map u is determined from two given N-D images I_0 and I_1. The first order image residual $\rho(u, u_0, x)$ wrt. a given disparity map u_0 is now $I_1(x + u_0) + \langle \nabla I_1, u - u_0 \rangle - I_0(x)$. Additionally, we write u_d for the d-th component of u ($d \in \{1, \ldots, N\}$).

The generalization of Eq. 5 to more dimensions is the following energy:

$$E_\theta = \int_\Omega \left\{ \sum_d |\nabla u_d| + \sum_d \frac{1}{2\theta}(u_d - v_d)^2 + \lambda |\rho(v)| \right\} \, d\boldsymbol{x}. \qquad (12)$$

Similar to the stereo setting, minimizing this energy can be performed by alternating optimization steps:

1. For every d and fixed v_d, solve

$$\min_{u_d} \int_\Omega \left\{ |\nabla u_d| + \frac{1}{2\theta}(u_d - v_d)^2 \right\} \, d\boldsymbol{x}. \qquad (13)$$

This minimization problem is identical to Eq. 6 and can be solved by the same procedure. Note, that the dual variables are introduced for every dimension, e.g. Eq. 8 now reads as

$$u_d = v_d - \theta \, \mathbf{div} \, p_d. \qquad (14)$$

2. For u being fixed, solve

$$\min_v \sum_d \frac{1}{2\theta}(u_d - v_d)^2 + \lambda \, |\rho(v)|. \qquad (15)$$

The following proposition generalizes the thresholding step from Proposition 2 to higher dimensions:

Proposition 3. *The solution of the minimization task in Eq. 15 is given by the following thresholding step:*

$$v = u + \begin{cases} \lambda \theta \, \nabla I_1 & \text{if } \rho(u) < -\lambda \theta |\nabla I_1|^2 \\ -\lambda \theta \, \nabla I_1 & \text{if } \rho(u) > \lambda \theta |\nabla I_1|^2 \\ -\rho(u) \, \nabla I_1 / |\nabla I_1|^2 & \text{if } |\rho(u)| \le \lambda \theta |\nabla I_1|^2. \end{cases} \qquad (16)$$

This proposition essentially states, that the N-dimensional optimization problem can be reduced to a one-dimensional thresholding step, since v always lies on the line $l^\perp$ going through u with direction ∇I_1 (for every x). This can be seen as follows: The first part in Eq. 15, $\sum_d (u_d - v_d)^2 / 2\theta$, is basically the squared distance of v to u, and the second part, $\lambda |\rho(v)|$, is the unsigned distance to the line l : $\rho(w) = 0$, i.e. $I_1(x + u_0) + \langle \nabla I_1, w - u_0 \rangle - I_0(x) = 0$. If we consider all v_μ with a fixed distance μ to u, then the functional in Eq. 15 is minimized for the v_μ closest to the line l (with minimal normal distance). This is also valid for the true minimizer, hence the optimum for Eq. 15 is on $l^\perp$.

In addition, the one-dimensional thresholding step in gradient direction can be applied (Proposition 2), resulting in the presented scheme.

3 Implementation

This section gives details on the employed numerical procedure and on the GPU-accelerated implementation for the proposed TV-L^1 optical flow approach. Although the discussion in Section 2.2 is valid for any image dimension $N \geq 2$, our GPU-based implementation is specifically tailored for the case $N = 2$.

3.1 Numerical Scheme

The generally non-convex energy functional for optical flow (Eq. 3) becomes a convex minimization problem after linearization of the image intensities (Eq. 4), but this linearization is only valid for small displacements. Hence, the energy minimization procedure is embedded into a coarse-to-fine approach to avoid convergence to unfavorable local minima. We employ image pyramids with a downsampling factor of 2 for this purpose. Beginning with the coarsest level, we solve Eq. 3 at each level of the pyramid and propagate the solution to the next finer level. This solution is further used to compute the coefficients of the linear residual function ρ by sampling I_0 and I_1 using the corresponding pyramid levels. Hence, the warping step for I_1 takes place only once per level. ∇I_1 is approximated by central differences. At the beginning of a new level, v is initialized with u, and all p_d are set to $\mathbf{0}$. At the coarsest level, the displacement field u starts with $\mathbf{0}$.

Avoiding poor local minima is not the only advantage of the coarse-to-fine approach. It turns out, that the filling-in process induced by the regularization occurring in textureless region is substantially accelerated by a hierarchical scheme as well.

The minimization procedure alternates one step of the fixed-point scheme to update all p_d (and therefore u, Eq. 10) with the thresholding step from Proposition 3 to improve v. The implementation of the fixed-point update (Eq. 10) uses backward differences to approximate $\mathbf{div}\,p$ and forward differences for the numerical gradient computation in order to have mutually adjoint operators [11].

3.2 Acceleration by Graphics Processing Units

Numerical methods working on regular grids, e.g. rectangular image domains, can be effectively accelerated by modern graphics processing units (GPUs). We employ the huge computational power and the parallel processing capabilities of GPUs to obtain a fully accelerated implementation of our optical flow approach. The GPU-based procedure is essentially a straightforward Cg implementation of the numerical schemes (Eqs. 10 and 16) with few modifications described as follows.

If we write down the alternating minimization steps explicitly, iteration k performs the following updates on $\boldsymbol{u}$, $\boldsymbol{v}$ and $\boldsymbol{p}_d$:

$$1a. \quad \boldsymbol{v}^{k+1} \leftarrow TH(\boldsymbol{u}^k)$$

$$1b. \quad u_d^{k+1} \leftarrow v_d^{k+1} - \theta \operatorname{div} \boldsymbol{p}_d^k \quad \text{for } d \in \{1, 2\} \tag{17}$$

$$2. \quad \boldsymbol{p}_d^{k+1} \leftarrow \frac{\boldsymbol{p}_d^k + \tau/\theta \nabla u_d^{k+1}}{1 + \tau/\theta |\nabla u_d^{k+1}|} \quad \text{for } d \in \{1, 2\},$$

where $TH(\cdot)$ denotes the thresholding step from Eq. 16. These steps can be immediately implemented on the GPU by appropriate fragment programs using two rendering passes.[1] The first pass implements steps 1a and 1b from Eq. 17. The values $\boldsymbol{v}^{k+1}$ are used only temporarily within the shader program and need not to be saved explicitly. $\boldsymbol{u}^{k+1}$ is written to the target texture. The second shader program corresponds with step 2 from Eq. 17. It turns out, that the utilization of the fragment processors can be improved by updating $\boldsymbol{u}$ and $\boldsymbol{p}_d$ for two pixels simultaneously. The shader programs work on the left and on the right half of the images in parallel, with appropriate handling of border pixels. Our implementation encodes the two components of $\boldsymbol{u}$ using full 32-bit precision, and the overall four components of $\boldsymbol{p}_1$ and $\boldsymbol{p}_2$ are compressed to 16-bit half precision floating point numbers.

We currently use a fixed but tunable number of iterations on each level in our implementation, since determining the maximum update $|\boldsymbol{u}^{k+1} - \boldsymbol{u}^k|$ still requires an expensive reduction operation even on modern GPUs.

4   Results

At first, we provide timing results for our optical flow approach depicted in Table 1. Two hardware setups were used to obtain the timing results: a desktop PC equipped with a NVidia GeForce 7800 GS card, and a high-end laptop supplied with a NVidia GeForce Go 7900 GTX graphics board. The timing results were obtained under the Linux operating system with recent OpenGL graphics drivers and the Cg 1.5 toolkit. The timings in Table 1 are given in frames per second for the depicted fixed number of iterations on each level of the image pyramid. The measured times include the texture uploads to video memory and the final visualization of the obtained displacement field. The timing results indicate, that real-time performance with more than 30 frames per second can be achieved at 256×256 pixels resolution with our approach. Frames from a live video demo application are shown in Figure 1, which continuously reads images from a firewire camera and visualizes the optical flow for adjacent frames. Real-time performance can be achieved with the mobile hardware setup.

---

[1] A single pass variant using only one shader program is possible as well, but the observed performance is inferior in almost all cases.

Table 1. Observed frame rates at different image resolutions and with varying number of iterations on our tested hardware

	GeForce 7800 GS			GeForce Go 7900 GTX		
Image resolution	50 It.	100	200	50 It.	100	200
128×128	56	32.1	17.5	95	57.6	30.9
256×256	18	9.6	5	34.1	17.5	8.9
512×512	5	2.6	1.3	9.3	4.7	2.3

  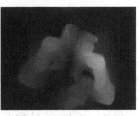

(a) First frame   (b) Second frame   (c) Optical flow field

Fig. 1. Captured frames and generated optical flow field using our live video application. The image resolution is 320×240, and 50 iterations are performed on each level of the image pyramid. The framerate is close to 30 frames per second in this setting. The flow field is visualized using hue to indicate the direction and intensity for the magnitude.

Figure 2 shows common test sequences for optical flow, in particular the *Ettlinger Tor*, the *Rheinhafen* and the *Yosemite* sequences, and their respective flow fields. The results for these datasets indicate, that the reduced 16-bit resolution for the dual variables p_d does not severely affect the quality of the obtained flow fields. Table 2 specifies the obtained average angular error (AAE) of the flow field for the Yosemite dataset wrt. the provided ground truth. If the completely homogeneous sky region is excluded from the AAE calculation, the flow field is essentially converged after 50 iterations. Enabling more iterations yields to slightly inferior results, since the TV-L^1 energy favors piecewise constant flow fields in the limit. If the sky region is included in the evaluation, the AAE error decreases by increasing the number of iterations. In this case the flow field in the sky region converges relatively slowly to the zero displacement.

Table 2. Average angular error for frame 8 and 9 of the Yosemite sequence at different number of iterations

	50 It.	150	250
Without sky	$2.85°$	$2.88°$	$2.89°$
With sky	$5.06°$	$3.7°$	$3.27°$

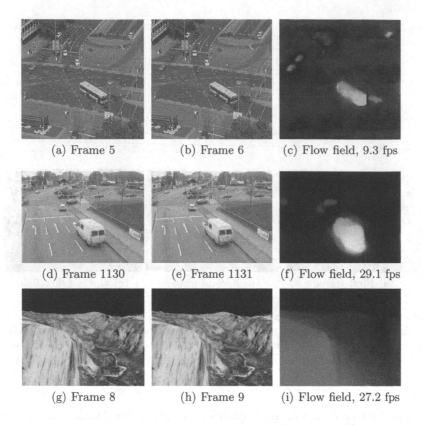

(a) Frame 5   (b) Frame 6   (c) Flow field, 9.3 fps

(d) Frame 1130   (e) Frame 1131   (f) Flow field, 29.1 fps

(g) Frame 8   (h) Frame 9   (i) Flow field, 27.2 fps

Fig. 2. Sample images and obtained flow fields for the *Ettlinger Tor* (512×512 pixels), the *Rheinhafen* (320×240 pixels) and the Yosemite (320×256 pixels) sequences

5   Conclusion

We presented a novel approach for efficient optical flow estimation using a TV-L_1 energy functional. We developed a novel fast numerical scheme which can be efficiently implemented on modern graphics processing units. With this we can show real-time performance using online video streams. The correctness and quality of our implementation is demonstrated on several datasets.

Future work includes the extension of our approach to handle color images as well. Additionally, other image similarity measures, e.g. based on intensity gradients, need to be further explored. The edge preserving nature of total variation can be enhanced, if a suitable weighted TV-norm/active contour model is applied [6]. Future work will address the incorporation of these feature for stereo and optical flow estimation.

Finally, switching from an OpenGL-based implementation to the newer CUDA GPU programming framework is expected to increase the observed performance substantially.

References

1. Alvarez, L., Weickert, J., Sánchez, J.: A scale-space approach to nonlocal optical flow calculations. In: Proceedings of the Second International Conference on Scale-Space Theories in Computer Vision, pp. 235–246 (1999)
2. Anandan, P.: A computational framework and an algorithm for the measurement of visual motion. Int. J. Comput. Vision 2, 283–310 (1989)
3. Aubert, G., Deriche, R., Kornprobst, P.: Computing optical flow via variational techniques. SIAM J. Appl. Math. 60(1), 156–182 (1999)
4. Aujol, J.-F., Gilboa, G., Chan, T., Osher, S.: Structure-texture image decomposition–modeling, algorithms, and parameter selection. Int. J. Comput. Vision 67(1), 111–136 (2006)
5. Black, M.J., Anandan, P.: A framework for the robust estimation of optical flow. In: ICCV93, pp. 231–236 (1993)
6. Bresson, X., Esedoglu, S., Vandergheynst, P., Thiran, J., Osher, S.: Fast Global Minimization of the Active Contour/Snake Model. Journal of Mathematical Imaging and Vision (2007)
7. Brox, T., Bruhn, A., Papenberg, N., Weickert, J.: High accuracy optical flow estimation based on a theory for warping. In: Pajdla, T., Matas, J(G.) (eds.) ECCV 2004. LNCS, vol. 3021, pp. 25–36. Springer, Heidelberg (2004)
8. Bruhn, A., Weickert, J., Feddern, C., Kohlberger, T., Schnörr, C.: Variational optical flow computation in real time. IEEE Transactions on Image Processing 14(5), 608–615 (2005)
9. Bruhn, A., Weickert, J., Kohlberger, T., Schnörr, C.: A multigrid platform for real-time motion computation with discontinuity-preserving variational methods. Int. J. Comput. Vision 70(3), 257–277 (2006)
10. Camus, T.A.: Real-time quantized optical flow. Journal of Real-Time Imaging, Special Issue on Real-Time Motion Analyis 3, 71–86 (1997)
11. Chambolle, A.: An algorithm for total variation minimization and applications. Journal of Mathematical Imaging and Vision 20(1–2), 89–97 (2004)
12. Chan, T.F., Golub, G.H., Mulet, P.: A nonlinear primal-dual method for total variation-based image restoration. In: ICAOS '96, Paris, 1996, vol. 219, pp. 241–252 (1996)
13. Horn, B.K.P., Schunck, B.G.: Determining optical flow. Artificial Intelligence 17, 185–203 (1981)
14. Mémin, E., Pérez, P.: Hierarchical estimation and segmentation of dense motion fields. Int. J. Comput. Vision 46(2), 129–155 (2002)
15. Nagel, H.-H., Enkelmann, W.: An investigation of smoothness constraints for the estimation of displacement vector fields from image sequences. IEEE Transactions on Pattern Analysis and Machine Intelligence (PAMI) 8, 565–593 (1986)
16. Papenberg, N., Bruhn, A., Brox, T., Didas, S., Weickert, J.: Highly accurate optic flow computation with theoretically justified warping. Int'l J. Computer Vision, 141–158 (2006)
17. Rudin, L.I., Osher, S., Fatemi, E.: Nonlinear total variation based noise removal algorithms. Physica D 60, 259–268 (1992)
18. Strzodka, R., Garbe, C.: Real-time motion estimation and visualization on graphics cards. In: IEEE Visualization 2004, pp. 545–552. IEEE Computer Society Press, Los Alamitos (2004)
19. Weickert, J., Brox, T.: Diffusion and regularization of vector- and matrix-valued images. Inverse Problems, Image Analysis and Medical Imaging. Contemporary Mathematics 313, 251–268 (2002)

Semi-supervised Tumor Detection in Magnetic Resonance Spectroscopic Images Using Discriminative Random Fields

L. Görlitz[1,2], B.H. Menze[2], M.-A. Weber[3], B.M. Kelm[2], and F.A. Hamprecht[2]

[1] Corporate Research, Robert Bosch GmbH, Germany
[2] Multidim. Image Processing, Interdisciplinary Center for Scientific Computing (IWR), University of Heidelberg
[3] Department of Radiology, German Cancer Research Center (dkfz), Heidelberg

Abstract. Magnetic resonance spectral images provide information on metabolic processes and can thus be used for in vivo tumor diagnosis. However, each single spectrum has to be checked manually for tumorous changes by an expert, which is only possible for very few spectra in clinical routine. We propose a semi-supervised procedure which requires only very few labeled spectra as input and can hence adapt to patient and acquisition specific variations. The method employs a discriminative random field with highly flexible single-side and parameter-free pair potentials to model spatial correlation of spectra. Classification is performed according to the label set that minimizes the energy of this random field. An iterative procedure alternates a parameter update of the random field using a kernel density estimation with a classification by means of the GraphCut algorithm. The method is compared to a single spectrum approach on simulated and clinical data.

1 Introduction

One major challenge in image processing is to exploit spatial correlation in 2-D images. Certain imaging techniques, however, are not only able to record *one* spatially resolved scalar signal, but provide a full vector of different features per pixel. Spectral images are examples of such multidimensional data sets and are in common use, e.g. in satellite remote sensing or non-invasive diagnostics. If the mapped process can be assumed to exhibit some spatial correlation, combining the information of the spectral and spatial dimension will allow for better decisions than the interpretation of one spectrum alone, especially with noisy spectra. Often these two sources of information are processed in a consecutive manner by first analyzing the spectral image spectrum-by-spectrum, and then using the spatial context in a second *post-hoc* step on the label map resulting from the spectrum-wise processing.

Magnetic resonance (MR) spectroscopy is a non-invasive diagnostic method used to determine the relative abundance of specific metabolites at arbitrary locations *in vivo*. Characteristic changes in the spectral pattern can be linked to

F.A. Hamprecht, C. Schnörr, and B. Jähne (Eds.): DAGM 2007, LNCS 4713, pp. 224–233, 2007.
© Springer-Verlag Berlin Heidelberg 2007

specific changes of the tissue, providing means for the grading and localization of tumors, e.g. in brain, breast and prostate [1]. Magnetic resonance spectroscopic imaging (MRSI) allows to acquire such spectra on two- or three-dimensional grids. Each spectrum is represented by a vector of several hundred spectral channels and shows a low number of relevant resonance lines, e.g. 5-10 for MR spectra of the brain. When searching for tumorous changes of the spectrum, pattern recognition methods can be applied to evaluate the data in a highly automated fashion and to guide the radiologist to the relevant regions of the spectroscopic image [2,3,4,5,6].

Typically, a limited number of spectra are diagnosed manually by a physician, providing patient-specific, diagnostic information on the tumor. In the following we propose an approach for the detection and localization of brain tumors which uses this information in a flexible, semi-supervised classifier for an adaptive processing of the complete spectral image. It allows both to process spectral information and to exploit the spatial correlation of the data in a coherent, highly adaptable framework (section 2). Our approach relies on common chemometric models in the classification of the spectral information and on a spatial model, motivated by Bayesian image processing, for the spatial regularization. Seeking for a time-efficient implementation in the clinical setting, we propose an efficient solver based on the GraphCut algorithm in an iterative strategy. Finally the algorithm is tested on simulated and real data, with results shown in section 3.

2   Spatio-spectral Classification Model

The classification of spatio-spectral data can be separated into two tasks: the inference on the spectral signal alone, a learning problem on highly collinear data, and the formulation of a spatial model on the resulting label map combining information from the single-voxel spectral model with a spatial smoothness assumption on the labels.

2.1   Spectral Model

In the following let $X_i = (X_i^1, \ldots, X_i^p)$ represent a p-dimensional spectrum, and Y_i a binary random variable taking values in $\{0, 1\}$, with $Y_i = 0$ for healthy and $Y_i = 1$ for tumorous tissue.

Given appropriate training data, the information of a spectrum X_i can be mapped to low dimensional scores, e.g. to the probabilities of either showing characteristic tumorous changes of the spectral pattern (with posterior distribution $\pi(Y_i = 1|X_i)$), or to be within the normal range of spectra originating from healthy tissue ($\pi(Y_i = 0|X_i)$). The posterior probability can be estimated with any method, linear (e.g. linear discriminant analysis, partial least squares regression) or nonlinear (e.g. support vector machines, mixture discriminant analysis), parametric or nonparametric, generative or discriminative. A regularization, however, might be indicated, as collinearity between the channels of a spectrum often leads to intrinsic dimensionalities well below the nominal length of the feature vector.

In the current application we have chosen an approach which combines the strong regularization of a chemometric spectral model and the variability of a nonparametric classifier. By assuming a flat prior on the classes ($\pi(Y_i = 0) = \pi(Y_i = 1)$) and by Bayes' rule, it suffices to estimate $\pi(X_i|Y_i = 0)$ and $\pi(X_i|Y_i = 1)$ to predict the most probable assignment of the spectrum X_i. For this, we used a Parzen kernel density estimator with bandwidth chosen according to Silverman's "rule-of-thumb" [7] on a reduced feature subspace defined by the first two principal components of an external training set.

2.2   Spatio-spectral Model

All N spectra $\mathbf{X} = \{X_1, \ldots, X_N\}$ lie, by acquisition, on a regular 2-D or 3-D Cartesian grid. The task is to identify each spectrum X_i with either healthy or tumorous tissue. It is assumed that a tumor is significantly larger than the spatial sampling distance, leading to spatial smoothness of the predicted classes. In order to incorporate this smoothness assumption into the spatio-spectral model, a graph-based method was used. Thus the structure of the spectral image is represented by an undirected graph $G = (S, E)$, with vertices S and edges E, with each site $s \in S$ representing a voxel of spectral acquisition and the set of edges E representing the neighborhood relation and therefore the spatial coupling of the random variables $\{Y_i\}$. In our experiments we chose the set E to be derived from the rectangular 2-D Cartesian acquisition grid, i.e. a 4 neighborhood system, which uses at most pairwise interactions between labels $\mathbf{Y} = \{Y_i\}$ and therefore keeps efficiency in inference and classification.

One of the most widely used methods for modeling spatial interaction are random fields, introduced to image processing by Besag [8], a generative approach to classification. As shown in [9] it is often advantageous to use discriminative models, i.e. a model for $p(\mathbf{Y}|\mathbf{X})$. Therefore a *discriminative* random field (DRF) [10] (a subgroup of conditional random fields [11]) with penalty term given by a parameter-free function was used. The single-site potential is formulated to reflect the information of the spectral model, and is given by

$$\text{ssp}(Y_i|X_i) = -\log \pi(Y_i = 1|X_i) \cdot Y_i - \log \pi(Y_i = 0|X_i) \cdot (1 - Y_i) \qquad (1)$$

and the pair-potential, responsible for the spatial coupling of the labels, is

$$\text{pp}(Y_i, Y_j|\mathbf{X}) = \begin{cases} \nu \cdot \gamma(X_i, X_j) \cdot |Y_i - Y_j| & \text{if } X_i \sim X_j \\ 0 & \text{else} \end{cases} \qquad (2)$$

where $X_i \sim X_j$ means that X_i and X_j originate from connected vertices, $\gamma(X_i, X_j)$ gives the penalty incurred when Y_i and Y_j are classified to different classes, and ν governs the trade-off between the purely voxel based classification and the spatial smoothness of the label map. For each spectral image $\mathbf{X}$ this induces the following probability distribution on $\{0, 1\}^N$, which is an Ising model on $\mathbf{Y}$ given $\mathbf{X}$ [12]:

$$p(\mathbf{Y}|\mathbf{X}) = \frac{1}{Z} \exp\left(-\sum_{i=1}^{N} \text{ssp}(Y_i|X_i) - \sum_{i,j=1}^{N} \text{pp}(Y_i, Y_j|\mathbf{X}) \right) \qquad (3)$$

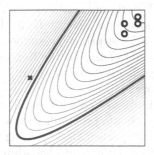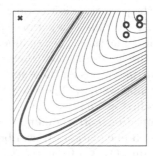

Fig. 1. Point 'x' and its four neighbors 'o' with the posterior distribution in the feature space of the spectral model and decision border indicated; LEFT: label of sample 'x' will flip for low ν, due to different classification of 'o' and weak support for classification; RIGHT: label of 'x' has strong evidence and will not flip, though all neighbors are classified differently

and the sought classification is given as the maximum a posteriori (MAP) estimate of this distribution, which corresponds to using the Bayes estimator for the zero-one loss function. According to $ssp(Y_i|X_i)$, the spectrum X_i is classified to the most probable class. If two neighboring vertices s_i and s_j are assigned to different classes, a penalty $\gamma(X_i, X_j)$ is incurred, which depends on the similarity of the two spectra X_i and X_j. In contrast to the DRF as used in [10], the penalty is given as a function and not inferred from training data, leading to a significant decrease of the number of parameters to be estimated. In the current model we have chosen the square root of the Perona-Malik tensor [13]

$$\gamma(X_i, X_j) = \frac{1}{\sqrt{|X_i - X_j|^2 + 1}} \tag{4}$$

with $|X_i - X_j|$ denoting a distance between the features of X_i and X_j used in the spectral model, i.e. in this case the Cartesian distance of the projection into the subspace spanned by the first two principal components. The function penalizes the assignment of different labels to neighboring spectra, unless they are very dissimilar. An illustrative example is shown in figure 1. The amount of evidence needed for such a classification is governed by the trade-off parameter ν.

A similar model for object extraction by GraphCut has been proposed by Boykov and Funka-Lea [14].

2.3   Semi-supervised Solution

The posterior distributions $\pi(Y_i|X_i)$ are not known in the beginning, as a non-parametric kernel density estimator is used to model both class densities. To optimally adapt to different patients, this estimate is obtained in a semi-supervised, patient dependent manner. In clinical practice, a limited number of spectra in the MRSI is always checked and diagnosed by the physician. The resulting labels, which are optimally adapted to the data, are used for the initialization of the estimate of the posterior distributions $\pi(X|Y = 0)$ and $\pi(X|Y = 1)$. To this end, a kernel density estimate is performed for each class separately, in the reduced two-dimensional feature space spanned by the first principal components of the spectra. As the hand-assigned labels should not change in the iteration process the single-site potentials for these spectra are changed to $\mathrm{ssp}(Y_i|X_i) = \infty \cdot (1 - Y_i)$ for a tumor label and $\mathrm{ssp}(Y_i) = \infty \cdot Y_i$ otherwise.

With this first estimate of the class distributions and with an initial value for ν, the classification, corresponding to the maximum probability state of the distribution given in equation (3), can be efficiently calculated by using Bayes theorem to obtain $\pi(Y_i|X_i)$ from $\pi(X_i|Y_i)$ and the GraphCut algorithm [15,16,17]. The latter is an instance of the well known MinCut/MaxFlow algorithm from graph theory. This results in an updated classification of the spectra which, in the next iteration, is used for an update of the kernel density estimation used to obtain the single-site potentials via Bayes theorem. These two steps are iterated until no spectra changes its classification in subsequent iterations. In our experiments we found that hardly ever more than four iterations were needed until convergence.

This iterative procedure obviously is a version of Dempster's Expectation-Maximization [18] with hard class assignments. It is essential for this approach to start with a good initialization (Fig. 2). Using spectra showing an ambiguous spectral pattern leads to a significantly worse classification result, compared to an initialization with spectra showing a clear pattern for either class.

Fig. 2. Simulated data described in chapter 3; LEFT: true classification, MIDDLE: classification after initialization with spectra showing a clear spectral pattern, RIGHT: classification after initialization with spectra with ambiguous spectral pattern

It is often desirable to show the confidence in the classification. To this end, Gibbs sampling [19] from the posterior distribution $p(\mathbf{Y}|\mathbf{X})$ can be used, a Markov Chain Monte Carlo method [20]. In order to employ a Gibbs sampler, the local characteristics have to be known, which can easily be calculated to be

$$p(Y_i|Y_1,\ldots,Y_{i-1},Y_{i+1},\ldots,Y_N,\mathbf{X}) = \frac{1}{\hat{Z}} \exp\left(\mathrm{ssp}(Y_i|X_i) + \sum_{j:j\sim i} \mathrm{pp}(Y_i,Y_j|\mathbf{X}) \right)$$

(5)

with $\hat{Z}$ denoting the normalization constant.

3   Experiments

The method was tested both on simulated data providing ground truth for a quantitative analysis, and on real data in order to evaluate the practicability in the clinical setting. The artificial data set consisted of 93 simulated MRSI-data sets from three patients (representing three different tumor geometries) with 16% noise on a 64×64-grid (for details see [21]). The first two principal components were calculated in a leave-"one patient"-out fashion, and all spectra of the hold-out patient were projected onto these directions. To imitate the physician, three spectra, having a posterior probability of at least 95%, were randomly selected per class for initializing the kernel density estimation. The hyper-parameter ν of the spatio-spectral coupling was optimized in an additional, internal cross-validation loop. For evaluation the spatio-spectral classification was repeated ten times with different initializations. For comparison, the classification without coupling ($\nu = 0$) was also tested.

The algorithm was also tested on 67 MRSI with a spatial resolution of 16×16 acquired from 14 patients under routine protocol during pre-therapeutic diagnostic and follow up on a 1.5T MR scanner at the German Cancer Research Center (dkfz), Heidelberg. Standard signal processing comprised Fourier transformation of the temporal resonance signal, water peak removal and phasing of the spectrum to its real part. Spectra containing artifacts were singled out using the NoN-score [22], and pair potentials in (2) involving these spectra were set to zero. The spectra were projected onto the first two PCA-directions calculated from an independent, clinically validated set of spectra (for details see [3,4]).

For the initialization of the algorithm on this clinical data set, two tumorous and two healthy spectra were hand-selected and labeled in each MRSI. The trade-off parameter ν depends on the spatial resolution of the MR scanner and the signal-to-noise ratio of the acquired data. As both can be assumed constant and since no ground truth was available, three MRSI slices from different patients were randomly selected, hand-labeled and ν fixed to the value, that gave the smallest cross-validation error. Classification results were compared against the single-voxel results of the external classifier already used in [3].

4   Results

Using the model in eq. (3) on the simulated data with the iterative optimization procedure described in section 2.3 on the simulated data, a mean accuracy of 98.7% was obtained, with an average true positive rate of 97.5% for tumorous tissue (standard deviation $17.0 \cdot 10^{-4}$) and a true negative rate of 98.8% on healthy tissue (standard deviation $6.6 \cdot 10^{-4}$). The single-voxel classification without spatial regularization reached a mean classification accuracy of 98.2%, with a true positive rate of 94.3% for tumor (standard deviation $114 \cdot 10^{-4}$), and 99.1% for normal spectra (standard deviation of $5.4 \cdot 10^{-4}$). The spatial regularization increased the classification accuracy and reduced the variance, leading to better classification results especially on tumorous tissue. Comparing the average over 500 samples from the posterior distribution (3) with the MAP estimate,

Fig. 3. FIRST: ground truth; SECOND: MAP-estimate for posterior distribution; THIRD: single-voxel based classification; FOURTH: average over 500 samples from the posterior distribution in eq. (3)

calculated via GraphCut, shows the ambiguity of the classification only along the tumor border, indicated by the blurred contours of the tumorous region (Fig. 3, fourth image).

The low SNR of the data led to speckle noise and misclassification in the single-voxel processing (Fig. 3), which was the main reason for the worse performance of this approach. Spectra well within the healthy region which were classified as tumorous (Fig. 3, third image) in the single spectrum approach, were classified correctly if the spatially coupled model was used for classification (Fig. 3, second image).

Adapting the algorithm to different patients by using the semi-supervised initialization is of major importance for the good classification results. Using spectra from a different patient in initializing the spectral model often led to disastrous results, to the extent that the tumor is not detected at all or unnecessarily large regions are classified as tumorous (Fig. 4). Using the patient-specific labels assigned by an expert as initialization for the spectral model guarantees an automatic adaption to patient variation and ensures high-quality classification, independent of patient characteristics. From the simulated data, we observe

Fig. 4. LEFT: ground truth; RIGHT: solution of the spatio-spectral model by initializing the density estimate with labeled spectra from a different patient

that the main advantages of the spatio-spectral classification are on the one side its ability to adapt optimally to the patient, by using the semi-supervised initialization, which ensures a highly accurate and reliable classification. On the other hand, it is able to remove isolated misclassifications, depending on the distinctiveness of the spectral pattern. A similar result might be achieved by using morphological operators in a post-hoc processing step, but, in contrast to the proposed approach, all "label islands" will be removed, irrespective of the probability of the voxel belonging to the assigned class. Trading spatial smoothness of the probabilistic result map with the support of a different classification of neighboring spectra by their distance in feature space is one of the main advantages of the presented approach.

On the real data set a high agreement between the results of the spatio-spectral and single voxel approaches could be observed in those voxels which were assigned a high confidence to one of the classes by the single voxel classifier. Voxels with a less stringent assignment were preferably classified according to their neighborhood by the spatio-spectral classifier. A detailed inspection of these cases showed that a main source for these contradicting results was a low quality of the respective spectra, e.g. caused by a low SNR or showing small shifts of the resonance lines. Visual inspection of the spectrum belonging, for example, to voxel (a) in the second image of figure 5 shows that a low data quality was the most likely reason for an assignment to the "intermediate" class by the single-voxel classifier of [3], while the spectral pattern was in fact "healthy", a label predicted also under a slight spatial regularization (Fig. 5, second image). As a

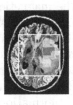

Fig. 5. FIRST, THIRD: Single-voxel classification according to [3], red indicating tumor, green indicating healthy, saturation indicating confidence in respective classification, SECOND: MAP estimate of spatially restricted model (eq. 3) for area indicated by white square in first image; FOURTH: Average over 500 samples from the posterior distribution (eq. (3)) for area indicated by white square in third image

second example, pixel (b) is surrounded by six voxels of tumorous tissue. The spatially regularized classification of the low quality spectrum leads to a distinct "tumor" assignment as opposed to "intermediate" by the single-voxel classifier. Here, the decision for "tumor" is in accordance with the visual inspection of the MR spectrum.

Comparing whole confidence maps of the single-voxel classification (Fig. 5, third image) and the spatio-spectral model (mean over 500 samples from the posterior (3), Fig. 5, fourth image), shows that a consideration of neighborhood information increases the confidence in the assigned labels on low quality data significantly.

Overall, we find that a main advantage of the spatio-spectral classification is its ability to adapt optimally to the individual spectral image, by using the semi-supervised initialization ensuring a highly accurate and reliable classification. Using the patient-specific labels assigned by an expert as initialization for the spectral model guarantees an automatic adaption to patient variation and a high-quality classification, independent of patient characteristics. In addition, the present approach is able to trade local support of a decision with the global support from the labels in its neighborhood. While in a standard post-hoc processing, for example, morphological operators remove all regions below a certain size in the result map, irrespective of the spectral information of the voxels belonging to these areas, the proposed spatio-spectral classification is able to remove isolated misclassifications depending on the distinctiveness of the spectral pattern. On MRSI it is thus able to differentiate between misclassifications resulting from low data quality, often resulting in random class assignments of single spectra, and strongly supported labels of isolated tumor voxels in an otherwise healthy neighborhood.

5   Conclusion

In this paper we have shown that adapting to patient characteristics can be efficiently incorporated into spatially regularized models operating both in spatial and spectral dimension of the magnetic resonance spectroscopic image. By using a DRF with a very versatile single-site potential, obtained from a class-wise kernel density estimate, and a parameter-free penalty function, it is possible to use the few labels generated in standard clinical procedure to segment spectral images with optimal adaption to the patient. An iterative procedure using the GraphCut algorithm was introduced and the necessity of customization to the patient and usage of spatial information was shown.

References

1. Hagberg, G.: From magnetic resonance spectroscopy to classification of tumors. a review of pattern recognition methods. NMR in Biomedicine 11(45), 148–156 (1998)
2. Devos, A., Lukas, L., Suykens, J., Vanhamme, L., Tate, A., Howe, F., Majós, C., Moreno-Torres, A., van der Graaf, M., Arús, C., Van Huffel, S.: Classification of brain tumours using short echo time ^{1}H MR spectra. Journal of Magnetic Resonance 170(1), 164–175 (2004)
3. Menze, B.H., Lichy, M.P., Bachert, P., Kelm, B.M., Schlemmer, H.P., Hamprecht, F.A.: Optimal classification of long echo in vivo magnetic resonance spectra in the detection of recurrent brain tumors. NMR in Biomedicine 19(5), 599–609 (2006)
4. Kelm, B.M., Menze, B.H., Zechmann, C.M., Baudendistel, K.T., Hamprecht, F.A.: Automated estimation of tumor probability in prostate MRSI: Pattern recognition vs. quantification. Magnetic Resonance in Medicine 57, 150–159 (2007)
5. Lukas, L., Devos, A., Suykens, J., Vanhamme, L., Howe, F., Majós, C., Moreno-Torres, A., van der Graaf, M., Tate, A., Arús, C., Van Huffel, S.: Brain tumor classification based on long echo proton MRS signals. Artificial Intelligence in Medicine 31(1), 73–89 (2004)
6. Tate, A., Majós, C., Moreno, A., Howe, F., Griffiths, J., Arús, C.: Automated classification of short echo time in in vivo ^{1}H brain tumor spectra: A multicenter study. Magnetic Resonance in Medicine 49(1), 29–36 (2003)
7. Silverman, B., Silverman, B.: Density Estimation for Statistics and Data Analysis. Chapman and Hall, New York (1986)

8. Besag, J.: Spatial interaction and the statistical analysis of lattice systems. Journal of the Royal Statistical Society 36, 192–236 (1974)
9. Ng, A., Jordan, M.: On discriminative vs. generative classifiers: A comparison of logistic regression and naïve Bayes. In: Proceedings of the 14th Conference on Advances in Neural Information Processing, vol. 14 (2001)
10. Kumar, S., Hebert, M.: Discriminative random fields. International Journal of Computer Vision 68(2), 179–201 (2006)
11. Lafferty, J., McCallum, A., Pereira, F.: Conditional random fields: Probabilistic models for segmenting and labeling sequence data. In: Proc. 18th International Conf. on Machine Learning, pp. 282–289. Morgan Kaufmann, San Francisco, CA (2001)
12. Li, S.Z.: Markov random field modeling in computer vision. Springer, London, UK (1995)
13. Perona, P., Malik, J.: Scale-Space and edge detection using anistropic diffusion. IEEE Transactions on Pattern Analysis and Machine Intelligence 12(7), 629–639 (1990)
14. Boykov, Y., Funka-Lea, G.: Graph Cuts and Efficient N-D Image Segmentation. International Journal of Computer Vision 70(2), 109–131 (2006)
15. Boykov, Y., Veksler, O., Zabih, R.: Fast approximate energy minimization via graph cuts. IEEE Transactions on Pattern Analysis and Machine Intelligence 23(11), 1222–1239 (2001)
16. Kolmogorov, V., Zabih, R.: What energy functions can be minimized via graph cuts. IEEE Transactions on Pattern Analysis and Machine Intelligence 26(2), 147–159 (2004)
17. Boykov, Y., Kolmogorov, V.: An experimental comparison of min-cut/max-flow algorithms for energy minimization in vision. IEEE Transactions on Pattern Analysis and Machine Intelligence 26(9), 1124–1137 (2004)
18. Dempster, A.P., Laird, N.M., Rubin, D.B.: Maximum likehood from incomplete data via the EM-algorithm. Journal of the Royal Statistical Society, Series B 39(1), 1–22 (1977)
19. Geman, S., Geman, D.: Stochastic relaxation, Gibbs distributions, and the Bayesian restoration of images. IEEE Transactions on Pattern Analysis and Machine Intelligence 6(6), 721–741 (1984)
20. Robert, C., Casella, G.: Monte Carlo Statistical Methods, 2nd edn. Springer, Secaucus, NJ, USA (2004)
21. Kelm, B.M., Hamprecht, F.A.: Trading resolution against noise in NMR spectroscopic imaging using conditional random fields. Technical report, IWR, University of Heidelberg (2007)
22. Menze, B.H., Kelm, B.M., Weber, M.A., Bachert, P., Hamprecht, F.A.: Mimicking the human expert: a pattern recognition approach to score the data quality in MRSI. Technical report, Interdisciplinary Center for Scientific Computing, University of Heidelberg (2007)

Regularized Data Fusion Improves Image Segmentation

Tilman Lange and Joachim Buhmann

Institute of Computational Science
ETH Zurich
CH-8092 Zurich, Switzerland
{langet,jbuhmann}@inf.ethz.ch

Abstract. The ability of a segmentation algorithm to uncover an interesting partition of an image critically depends on its capability to utilize and combine all available, relevant information. This paper investigates a method to automatically weigh different data sources, such that a meaningful segmentation is uncovered. Different sources of information naturally arise in image segmentation, e.g. as intensity measurements, local texture information or edge maps. The data fusion is controlled by a regularization mechanism, favoring sparse solutions. Regularization parameters as well as the clustering complexity are determined by the concept of cluster stability yielding maximally reproducible segmentations. Experiments on the Berkeley segmentation database show that our segmentation approach outperforms competing segmentation algorithms and performs comparably to supervised boundary detectors.

1 Introduction

Image segmentation is widely recognized as an important step in low-level computer vision and a prerequisite for subsequent image analysis tasks. It is, for example, employed in medical image analysis or SAR imagery based land-usage classification. The problem of partitioning an image into semantically meaningful regions can be cast as a clustering problem: The n pixels of an image are considered as objects to be clustered; the segmentation into $k \in [n]$ [1] homogeneous regions is often represented by an assignment matrix $\mathbf{W} \in \{0,1\}^{n \times k}$, where $w_{i\nu} = 1$ *iff* object i is assigned to segment ν. Clustering principles rely on a notion of similarity between at least pairs of objects. Different sources of similarity information about objects (pixels) naturally arise in many application scenarios. In image segmentation such information sources (or cues) may, e.g., consist of intensities, edge maps, local texture information, color information etc. These examples underline the need for data fusion combined with feature selection/weighting which endows clustering algorithms with the capability to emphasize *relevant* information.

In this work, we consider a non-negative matrix factorization (NMF) formulation of the pairwise clustering problem and integrate the data fusion approach

---

[1] We use the short-hand $[n] := \{1, \ldots, n\}$.

F.A. Hamprecht, C. Schnörr, and B. Jähne (Eds.): DAGM 2007, LNCS 4713, pp. 234–243, 2007.
© Springer-Verlag Berlin Heidelberg 2007

into it where we build on and substantially extend the previous approach in [5] in the following ways: (i) We use the Frobenius norm instead of the KL divergence for the NMF allowing us to demonstrate the generality of the fusion approach, (ii) a refined version of the stability-based model selection scheme is used and (iii) a large-scale experimental evaluation on the Berkeley Segmentation Database (BSDS) demonstrates that (1) our proposal outperforms other standard segmentation algorithms and (2) is competitive with *supervised* boundary detection procedures on this database [9].

Some work has been devoted to feature selection and weighting in clustering. In [11] a variant of k-means has been studied using Fisher's criterion to assess the importance of features. In [12] and [6], Gaussian mixture model approaches to feature selection were discussed. Kernel Target Alignment [1] based methods try to maximize the (normalized) correlation coefficient between a given labelling and a convex/conic combination of basis kernels.

Algorithms for NMF [7] have recently found a lot of attention, and our proposal is particularly inspired by the recent work in [8] and [3]. The interplay between clustering and NMF has been investigated in [17], [2] and [5].

2   Grouping by Non-negative Matrix Decomposition

We phrase the clustering problem in a *pairwise* setting, where objects are characterized by mutual (dis-) similarity relations. Often, there are multiple ways of measuring the similarity between different objects and each such assessment gives rise to a similarity s_{ij} between objects i and j, where we assume symmetry $s_{ji} = s_{ij}$, and bounded-ness $s_{ij} < \infty$. For n objects, the similarity data can be summarized in an $n \times n$ similarity matrix $\mathbf{S} = (s_{ij}) \in \mathbb{R}^{n \times n}$. The notion of *clustering* refers to the organization of objects into groups (clusters) so that objects in the same cluster are more similar to each other than to those in different groups. This notion can be phrased formally by assuming that the similarities s_{ij} are proportional to the probability of a *joint occurrence* of objects i and j, i.e. $s_{ij} \propto p(i,j)$. This co-occurrence can be explained by a *categorial,* latent class variable with realizations $\nu \in [k]$. Hence, $p(i,j) = \sum_{\nu=1}^{k} p(i,j|\nu)p(\nu)$ reflects the probability that objects i and j belong to the same group. Assuming conditional independence $p(i,j|\nu) = p(i|\nu)p(j|\nu)$, one can simplify the expression to

$$p(i,j) = p(i)p(j|i) = p(i) \sum_{\nu=1}^{k} p(\nu|i)p(j|\nu). \qquad (1)$$

The interesting term is $p(j|i)$, as here the *de-marginalization* in terms of the latent cluster variable comes into play. Clustering can be achieved by finding an NMF based on the similarities $\mathbf{S}$ (as estimate for $\mathbf{P}$).

Standard NMF aims at finding a decomposition of $\mathbf{S} \in \mathbb{R}_+^{m \times n}$, often in two non-negative matrices $\mathbf{W} \in \mathbb{R}_+^{m \times k}$ and $\mathbf{H} \in \mathbb{R}_+^{n \times k}$, where $k \ll \min(m,n)$ such that $\mathbf{S} \approx \mathbf{W}\mathbf{H}^\top$. Two common formulations of the NMF problem rely on the

Frobenius norm and the KL divergence. Finding the best approximation of $\mathbf{S}$ in $\mathbf{WH}^\top$ w.r.t. the Frobenius norm amounts to solving

$$\min_{\mathbf{W}\in\mathbb{R}_+^{m\times k},\mathbf{H}\in\mathbb{R}_+^{n\times k}} \|\mathbf{S} - \mathbf{WH}^\top\|_F^2. \tag{2}$$

The purpose of this section is to show that a variety of clustering criteria can be captured in the $\|\cdot\|_F^2$-based NMF approach to clustering – demonstrating the generality of the fusion method described later. For the clustering problems the standard algorithms can be applied due to the formal equivalences.

Let us assume that the decomposition in eq. (1) exists. Set $\mathbf{H} := (p(i|\nu)) \in [0,1]^{n\times k}$ and $\mathbf{W} := (p(\nu|i)) \in [0,1]^{n\times k}$ and let $\mathbf{D} := \mathrm{diag}(p(1),\ldots,p(n))$. Then, $\mathbf{P} := (p(i,j))$ can be written as $\mathbf{P} = \mathbf{DWH}^\top$. Boundary and normalization constraints are: $\mathbf{W} \geq 0$, $\mathbf{H} \geq 0$, $\mathbf{1}_n^\top\mathbf{H} = \mathbf{1}_k^\top$ and $\mathbf{W1}_k = \mathbf{1}_n$. In the classification case, the entries of $\mathbf{H}$ may be regarded as *class-conditional likelihoods*, while the entries of $\mathbf{W}$ reflect *assignment probabilities*. It makes sense to assume that $\mathbf{D} = \frac{1}{n}\mathbf{I}_n$. This way, one obtains: If $\mathbf{P} = \mathbf{DZ}$, $\mathbf{Z} = \mathbf{WH}^\top$, is symmetric, then $\mathbf{Z}$ is symmetric *iff* $\mathbf{D} = \frac{1}{n}\mathbf{I}_n$. If $\mathbf{D} = \frac{1}{n}\mathbf{I}_n$, $\mathbf{Z}$ is doubly stochastic. Adding double stochasticity, symmetry and normalization constraints to eq. (2) gives a valid pairwise grouping model optimizable by alternating minimization. To ensure consistency of the probability estimates $\mathbf{W}\mathrm{diag}(\mathbf{1}_n^\top\mathbf{W})^{-1} = \mathbf{H}$ has to hold. This yields a symmetric factorization: With $\mathbf{\Delta} = \mathrm{diag}(\mathbf{1}_n^\top\mathbf{W})^{-1/2}$ and $\mathbf{Q} := \mathbf{W}\mathbf{\Delta}$ a *symmetric* decomposition $\mathbf{Z} = \mathbf{QQ}^\top$ is sought. The CP algorithm in [17] optimizes this form. For *hard* clustering, $\mathbf{Q}^\top\mathbf{Q} = \mathbf{I}_k$ holds. Based on this, the following is easy to show:

Lemma 1. *Let* $\mathbf{Q} \in \mathbb{R}_+^{n\times k}$, *such that,* $\mathbf{QQ}^\top$ *is doubly stochastic and* $\mathbf{Q}^\top\mathbf{Q} = \mathbf{I}_k$, *then a unique, binary matrix* $\mathbf{W} \in \{0,1\}^{n\times k}$ *with* $\mathbf{W1}_k = \mathbf{1}_n$ *exists, such that* $\mathbf{Q} = \mathbf{W}(\mathbf{W}^\top\mathbf{W})^{-1/2}$.

For the symmetric factorization, $\mathbf{Q}$ is an optimal solution to the problem

$$\min_{\mathbf{Q}\in\mathbb{R}_+^{n\times k}} \|\mathbf{S} - \mathbf{QQ}^\top\|_F^2 \qquad \text{s.t.} \quad \mathbf{QQ}^\top\mathbf{1}_n = \mathbf{1}_n, \quad \mathbf{Q}^\top\mathbf{Q} = \mathbf{I}_k. \tag{3}$$

According to lemma 1, a feasible solution to (3) uniquely determines a hard clustering solution. One also easily obtains that the mathematical program given in problem (3) is invariant under additive shifts and scalar multiplication applied to the input similarity matrix $\mathbf{S}$. $\mathbf{S}$ can always be shifted to positive semi-definiteness (c.f. [13]); thereby, one can safely assume that $\mathbf{S}$ is an empirical kernel function. As a consequence, one can easily show [13] that problem (3) is equivalent to solving the kernel k-means problem. Hence, kernel k-means can be captured in a constrained NMF problem and, the respective algorithm can be used to solve (3). This result can be extended. The symmetric decomposition problem $\min_{\mathbf{Q}\in\mathbb{R}_+^{n\times k}} \|\mathbf{S} - \mathbf{QQ}^\top\|_F^2$ s.t. $\mathbf{Q}^\top\mathbf{Q} = \mathbf{I}_k$ yields for the Normalized Cut ([16],[2]): An optimal solution to this for $\tilde{\mathbf{S}} = \mathbf{\Delta}^{-1/2}\mathbf{S}\mathbf{\Delta}^{-1/2}$ with $\mathbf{\Delta} = \mathrm{diag}(\mathbf{S1}_n)$ is an optimal solution to the Normalized Cut. Note, that the non-negativity and orthogonality constraints ensure, that $q_{i\nu} > 0$ *iff* i belongs to class ν.

3   Fusion of Information Sources

After having demonstrated how pairwise clustering problems can be formulated as NMF problems, we study fusing multiple similarity measurements. The NMF perspective allows us to propose a generic procedure for combining multiple information sources for several standard grouping methods. In practical applications, the similarity of objects can be assessed in multiple, say, $l \in \mathbb{N}$, different ways: the similarity of proteins can be quantified based on sequence similarity, protein-protein interaction maps, gene expression profiles and so forth. The l different ways to assess protein similarity give rise to l similarity matrices $\mathbf{S}_1, \ldots, \mathbf{S}_l$ with $\mathbf{S}_a = (s_{ij}^{(a)})$. There might be spurious, inconclusive or irrelevant information in some of the matrices and, ideally, this should be discarded. On the other hand, each individual measurement may only convey partial, incomplete information and only the weighted combination may provide the complete picture. Our aim is to introduce a method that can cope with both extremes.

Assume that there is a categorical *source selection random variable* $\chi_{ij} \in [l]$ which is i.i.d. for each pair of objects. Using this random variable, the *observed* similarity $\bar{s}_{ij}$ between objects becomes a random quantity by $\bar{s}_{ij} = s_{ij}^{(\chi)}$. Again, a factorization $\mathbf{Z}$ of $\bar{\mathbf{S}}$ is sought by minimizing the Frobenius norm between data $\bar{\mathbf{S}}$ and approximation $\mathbf{Z}$. The objective function becomes the random variable $\|\bar{\mathbf{S}}(\chi) - \mathbf{Z}\|_F^2$, where $\chi = (\chi_{ij})$ denotes the collection of all source selection variables. Depending on the realization of χ_{ij} one out of the l possibilities for $\bar{s}_{ij}$ is selected. In practice, inference needs to be made about the variables χ and their distribution. To this end, one may average over all choices for $\chi_{ij} \in [l]$ which amounts substituting $\bar{s}_{ij}$ with its expectation $\mathbb{E}_{\chi \sim \alpha}[s_{ij}^{(\chi)}] = \sum_a \alpha_a s_{ij}^{(a)}$. Instead of making inference about χ, one now has to infer α from the data. For fixed α, $\bar{\mathbf{S}}(\alpha) := \sum_a \alpha_a \mathbf{S}_a$ is the *aggregated* similarity matrix and describes an interpretable weighting of information sources. Here, we assume the similarities $\mathbf{S}_a$ to be suitably re-normalized. Hence, the average similarity $\bar{s}_{ij}(\alpha)$ becomes a *mixture* of individual similarities $s_{ij}^{(a)}$, i.e. a mixture of different perspectives on the set of n objects.

Given a factorization $\mathbf{Z}$, we may want to be the least committal to a certain selection (on average) of input similarities. Therefore, adopting the maximum entropy (ME) principle for the estimation of α is a natural choice. The ME principle tells us to pick the distribution maximizing the entropy $H(\alpha)$ while respecting constraints of the form $\mathbb{E}_{\chi \sim \alpha}[c(\chi)] \leq \vartheta$. Here, we choose $c_a := \|\mathbf{S}_a - \mathbf{Z}\|_F^2$, so that the entropy of α should be maximized while maintaining an approximation error of at most ϑ. This gives rise to the mathematical program

$$\max_{\alpha} H(\alpha) \qquad \text{s.t.} \quad \mathbf{c}^\top \alpha \leq \vartheta, \quad \mathbf{1}_l^\top \alpha = 1, \quad \alpha \geq 0. \tag{4}$$

By considering the equivalent formulation

$$\min_{\alpha} \mathbf{c}^\top \alpha - \eta H(\alpha) \qquad \text{s.t.} \quad \mathbf{1}_l^\top \alpha = 1, \quad \alpha \geq 0, \tag{5}$$

one easily gets that the optimal solution to eq. (4) is the Gibbs distribution:

$$\alpha_a \propto \exp(-c_a/\eta). \tag{6}$$

For $\eta \to \infty$ one gets $\alpha_a = 1/l$, while for $\eta \to 0$, only one source is selected; the estimates become the sparser the more the individual c_a differ. The parameter η enables us to explore the space of similarity combinations. We postpone for now the issue of selecting a value for η (c.f. sec. 4).

3.1 Model Optimization

For fixed $\boldsymbol{\alpha}$, all NMF-based clustering methods from sec. 2 can be applied to the (fixed) mixture $\bar{\mathbf{S}}(\alpha)$. Hence, a simple *nested* alternating minimization approach is adopted to find both, $\boldsymbol{\alpha}$ and an approximation $\mathbf{Z}$ to $\bar{\mathbf{S}}(\alpha)$: Fix $\boldsymbol{\alpha}$ to find an optimal factorial approximation $\mathbf{Z}$ of $\bar{\mathbf{S}}(\boldsymbol{\alpha})$ and, then, given the fixed factorization, find the optimal $\boldsymbol{\alpha}$. This strategy leads to a sequence of estimates monotonously decreasing the cost in each iteration. In this optimization, the entropy constraint has a self-stabilizing effect on the estimates of $\boldsymbol{\alpha}$.

4   Model Selection Using Cluster Stability

We have two free parameters, the number of classes k and the parameter η; both are user-supplied or estimated from the data. For a fully unsupervised procedure, the stability concept [4] is used: for both parameters one looks for solutions being highly reproducible. The stability assessment can be regarded as generalization of cross-validation relying on the dissimilarity of solutions generated from multiple *sub-samples*. In a second step, solutions obtained from these sub-samples are extended to the complete data by an appropriate *predictor*. Hence, multiple classifications of the same data are obtained whose similarity can be measured. For two clustering solutions $\mathbf{W}, \mathbf{W}' \in \{0, 1\}^{n \times k}$, we define their disagreement as $d(\mathbf{W}, \mathbf{W}') = \min_{\pi \in \mathfrak{S}_k}(1 - \frac{1}{n} \sum_{i=1}^{n} \sum_{\nu=1}^{k} w_{i\nu} w_{i\pi(\nu)})$ where $\mathfrak{S}_k$ is the set of permutations on $[k]$. The measure quantifies the 0-1 loss after the labels have been permuted so that the two clustering solutions are in best possible agreement. d is a metric on the equivalence classes of partitions modulo permutation. The optimal permutation can be determined in $O(k^3)$.

We refine the stability method of [4]: In the stability analysis, one might observe high instability for a certain pair of values (η, k), but there can be several *locally* stable solutions which are conflicting: E.g. a bi-modal distribution of clustering solutions can happen either due to symmetries in the distribution or because the data admits different interpretations where – depending on the sample – one interpretation dominates. This is amplified by the combination of sources. For such cases, we adopt a local perspective: for every η and k, we look for highly similar clustering solutions and establish a *local* stability score by considering the fraction of solutions belonging to the same *cluster of clustering solutions*. This way one gets a detailed picture of the variability structure. For each pair (η, k), we draw $b \in \mathbb{N}$ sub-samples and compute solutions on the sub-samples which are extended to the full sample by a prediction step. The pairwise similarity between the solutions can be evaluated using d; it can be used in order to look for *clusters of highly similar solutions*. This poses a pairwise clustering problem, which operates on label matrices: Instead of fixing the number of classes for it, we select a threshold $\varepsilon \ll 1$ and require solutions to have an *average* within-cluster disagreement of less than $\varepsilon(1 - \frac{1}{k})$, i.e. for m assignment matrices $\mathbf{W}_j$ in the same cluster of labellings the inequality $\frac{1}{m} \sum_{i=1}^m \sum_{j=1}^m d(\mathbf{W}_i, \mathbf{W}_j) < \varepsilon(1 - \frac{1}{k})$ has to hold. The quantity on the lhs are the per cluster costs whose sum is measured by the pairwise clustering cost function [13]. This strategy is justified since: the expected distance of randomly drawn solutions is upper bounded by $(1 - \frac{1}{k})$ and it is natural to look for homogenous, non-random clusters of clustering solutions. The threshold ε effectively controls the number of clusters by requiring solutions to have an *average* within-cluster disagreement of less than $\varepsilon(1 - \frac{1}{k})$.[2] In practice, Ward's method [15] is used. To get a single solution per solution cluster, representatives need to be selected. We achieve this by simply picking the "median" element in the respective solution cluster, which minimizes the distance to all other solutions in its cluster. For each (k, η), the local stability score of a solution cluster is the *fraction of labellings in that cluster*. Given the scores, each pair (k, η) can be ranked based on the stability measurements.

To generalize a clustering solution to a set of previously unseen objects is important for stability assessments, but also necessary for large scale computations. The predictor is based on linear interpolation: Assume an initial fit using $\mathbb{N} \ni m \ll n$ objects and that we have to predict class memberships for r additional objects, whose similarity to the initially given m objects is summarized in $\tilde{\mathbf{S}} \in \mathbb{R}^{r \times m}$.[3] Let $w_{i\nu}$ be the "posterior" estimated for the i-th object in the data set used for the original fit. The weighted, normalized similarity between a new object o and object i is $\hat{p}_{io} := \tilde{s}_{oi} / \sum_j \tilde{s}_{oj}$. One can think of $\hat{p}_{io}$ as estimate for $p(i|o)$. The posterior $w_{o\nu}$ for a new object o is *approximated* by $\hat{w}_{o\nu} = \sum_{1 \leq i \leq m} w_{i\nu} \hat{p}_{io}$, being an *interpolation* of the $w_{o\nu}$. Classification can be performed by the Maximum A Posteriori (MAP) rule, $\mathrm{argmin}_\nu \hat{w}_{o\nu}$. The procedure requires $O(mrk)$ steps to make predictions for r novel objects.

5 Experimental Evaluation

We apply our proposal to the 100 test images in the Berkeley Image Segmentation Database (BSDS) [9].[4] Generally, it is difficult to objectively assess the quality of image segmentations. This database has the crucial benefit that human beings manually created segmentations which can be used for experimental evaluations. The images in the BSDS have 481×321 pixels, which need to be labelled, and are represented in the LUV space. To the LUV image, a spatial averaging filter was applied. Localized frequency information was collected by computing responses of Gabor filters on 3 scales for 4 orientations for the wavelengths 2, 4 and 8 pixels resulting in 3×4 single-channel images. For each scale, all orientations have been collapsed into a single image. For comparability to other procedures,

---

[2] For the experiments we set $\varepsilon = 1 \cdot 10^{-1}$.

[3] Given the decomposition into $\mathbf{Q}$ and $\mathbf{Q}^\top$ one can recover $\mathbf{W}$ using the lemma 1.

[4] The database can be accessed via
http://www.eecs.berkeley.edu/Research/Projects/CS/vision/bsds/.

we employ the Euclidean scalar products to arrive at similarities; this choice *limits* the possibilities of our proposal and non-linear kernels are expected to improve results.

For the experiments, the NMF formulation in eq. 3 was used. The number of segments was varied in 2–5. Five different values of the regularization parameter η were selected. For every (k, η) pair, $b = 20$ re-samples were drawn. Following the strategy sketched above, we predict class memberships for objects not taken into account during an initial learning phase. To this end, ≈ 5000 image sites on a fixed grid are pre-selected. For model selection, sub-samples consisting of ≈ 2500 sites are generated from these points. The prediction step generalizes solutions to all objects not included in the sub-sample.

Comparison of Aggregated Segmentations with the BSDS: The BSDS contains 100 test images which have been manually segmented by several human beings. As human ground-truth, the BSDS contains *aggregated*, soft edge maps obtained from averaging the human-generated maps. The database was used to bench-mark boundary detection algorithms in [10]. Unfortunately, there is no generally agreed-upon measure for comparing segmentations. Attempts to address this problem, e.g. in [9], suffer from pathologies rendering the assessment question-able. For benchmarking, a matching measure is employed that takes a pair of soft boundary maps as input. Despite all the potential shortcomings of measur-ing the performance of a segmentation algorithm with a measure designed for benchmarking boundary detection algorithms, it may still shed light on some properties of an algorithm.[5] We have, therefore, chosen this method to evaluate the quality of our proposal. The standard benchmarking procedure of the BSDS varies a threshold t on the soft boundary maps, so that several pairs (r_t, p_t) of precision-recall values are obtained. The final score obtained from the matching of two boundary maps is then defined as the maximum attainable F-measure $\max_t f_t$. For comparison of the methods, the results for all stable choices of pa-rameter values (η, k) considered in the local stability assessment and re-samples are aggregated into a single soft boundary map for each image.

The comparison on the benchmark includes the three supervised boundary de-tectors as discussed in [10]: The algorithm *Brightness/Color/Texture Gradients (BCTG)* employs locally measured brightness, color, and texture gradients to detect boundaries. It is the best performing boundary detector in this study and in [10]. The second best algorithm, *Brightness / Texture Gradients (BTG)* relies only on local brightness and texture information and neglects color. The third and simplest pure boundary detection method taken from [10] is the *Color Gra-dient (CG)* method that takes only color information into account. In addition to these boundary detectors, we have additionally applied k-means clustering (KM) and a Gaussian mixture model (GMM) to the naively stacked feature

---

[5] The measure was designed for assessing the performance of boundary detectors. An algorithm producing segmentations is a special type of boundary detector, which is, however, forced to produce closed, connected segment boundaries. This severely constrains the possibly detected boundaries in comparison to those obtained from mere boundary detector in view of the BSDS benchmarking methodology.

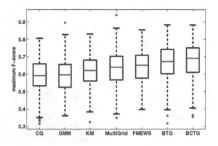

Fig. 1. The figure summarizes the outcome of the comparison of segmentation algorithms using the Berkeley Segmentation Database (BSDS)

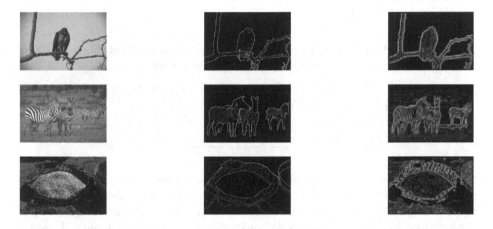

Fig. 2. A sample of aggregated edge maps: Original images are depicted in the left column. The human segmentations in the next column are compared to the output of the algorithms. The third column shows the results for the ME approach. F-scores are 0.85, 0.81 and 0.72 (top-down).

vectors. Furthermore, the ME weighting scheme is called FMEWS. We have also included the multi-grid based segmentation method from [14].

Figure 1 summarizes the results of the study in a box plot, where each plot shows the distribution of F-scores for the respective methods. The scores have been computed with the boundary detection benchmark measure for all 100 test images. In addition to that, the median, lower and upper quartile over the 100 maximal F-scores are given in table 1 for all algorithms. Only best results have been taken into account. The two best performing measures are the supervised boundary detectors from [10], BTG and BCTG. The best unsupervised segmentations are obtained with FMEWS. The strongest competing grouping method is the multi-grid method from [14], which we outperform. k-means (KM) as well as Gaussian mixture models (GMMs) are clearly outperformed by all other clustering methods. Figure 2 shows edge maps and their scores.

Fig. 3. A sample of (in-) stable segmentations along with the input images obtained for varying η and k as produced by FMEWS. The local stability score is $= 1$ in columns 1–3. Unreliable segmentations can often be detected by lack of stability (for the last column local stability is 0.1).

Table 1. (Rounded) Median, lower and upper quartile values (Med, LQ and UQ) of maximal F-scores of the different methods under consideration

	CG	BTG	BCTG	KM	GMM	M-Grid	FMEWS
UQ.	0.66	0.74	0.75	0.68	0.66	0.71	0.71
Med.	0.59	0.67	0.69	0.62	0.60	0.63	0.65
LQ.	0.53	0.60	0.61	0.56	0.53	0.57	0.58

Stable Segmentations: The goal of local stability assessment is to automatically infer meaningful segmentations instead of considering aggregated boundary maps. For stable segmentations, segments often consist of one or more object predominant in a scene. Figure 3 demonstrates this for several images. Thereby, such segmentations provide what supposedly their usage is, e.g., to extract sensible pre-processing information for a subsequent object detection stage. Similarly, highly instable solutions are observed for inaccurate, noisy solutions. Observing instability generally renders the inferred structure questionable as the segmentations exhibit a high variability. We conclude, that the proposed local stability measure gives a reasonable indication about presence or absence of structure.

6   Conclusions

An approach to combining similarity data from multiple sources was introduced and evaluated for image segmentation. Clustering has been phrased as NMF problem, where weights have been introduced. By way of ME inference, a mechanism was devised to control the sparsity of the weights. Cluster stability was refined and employed to determine both, regularization parameter as well as number of clusters. The refined model selection strategy was demonstrated to yield meaningful segmentations in practice. The experiments on the Berkeley Segmentation Database show that our proposal outperforms other segmentation algorithms, and is competitive with *supervised* boundary detectors.

References

1. Christianini, N., Shawe-Taylor, J., Kandola, J., Elisseeff, A.: On kernel target alignment. In: NIPS 14, MIT Press, Cambridge (2002)
2. Ding, C.H.Q., He, X.: On the equivalence of nonnegative matrix factorization and spectral clustering. In: Jonker, W., Petković, M. (eds.) SDM 2005. SIAM, LNCS, vol. 3674, Springer, Heidelberg (2005)
3. Hofmann, T.: Unsupervised learning by probabilistic latent semantic analysis. Mach. Learn. 42(1-2), 177–196 (2001)
4. Lange, T., Braun, M., Roth, V., Buhmann, J.: Stability-based model selection. In: NIPS 15, MIT Press, Cambridge (2003)
5. Lange, T., Buhmann, J.M.: Fusion of similarity data in clustering. In: NIPS 18, MIT Press, Cambridge (2006)
6. Law, M.H.C., Figueiredo, M.A.T., Jain, A.K.: Simultaneous feature selection and clustering using mixture models. IEEE TPAMI 26(9), 1154–1166 (2004)
7. Lee, D., Seung, H.: Learning the parts of objects by non-negative matrix factorization. Nature 401, 788–791 (1999)
8. Lee, D.D., Seung, H.S.: Algorithms for non-negative matrix factorization. In: NIPS 13, MIT Press, Cambridge (2000)
9. Martin, D., Fowlkes, C., Tal, D., Malik, J.: A database of human segmented natural images and its application to evaluating segmentation algorithms and measuring ecological statistics. In: ICCV 2001, vol. 2, pp. 416–423 (2001)
10. Martin, D.R., Fowlkes, C.C., Malik, J.: Learning to detect natural image boundaries using local brightness, color, and texture cues. IEEE TPAMI 26(5), 530–549 (2004)
11. Modha, D.S., Spangler, W.S.: Feature weighting in k-means clustering. Mach. Learn. 52(3), 217–237 (2003)
12. Roth, V., Lange, T.: Feature selection in clustering problems. In: NIPS 16, MIT Press, Cambridge (2004)
13. Roth, V., Laub, J., Kawanabe, M., Buhmann, J.M.: Optimal cluster preserving embedding of nonmetric proximity data. IEEE TPAMI 25(12), 1540–1551 (2003)
14. Sharon, E., Brandt, A., Basri, R.: Fast multiscale image segmentation. In: CVPR 2000, pp. 1070–1077. IEEE Computer Society Press, Los Alamitos (2000)
15. Ward, J.H.: Hierarchical grouping to optimize an objective function. JASA 58, 236–244 (1963)
16. Yu, S.X., Shi, J.: Multiclass spectral clustering. In: ICCV 2003, pp. 313–319. IEEE Computer Society Press, Los Alamitos (2003)
17. Zass, R., Shashua, A.: A unifying approach to hard and probabilistic clustering. In: ICCV 2005, pp. 294–301. IEEE Computer Society Press, Los Alamitos (2005)

Perception-Based Image Segmentation Using the Bounded Irregular Pyramid

Rebeca Marfil, Antonio Bandera, and Francisco Sandoval

Grupo ISIS, Dpto. Tecnología Electrónica
ETSI Telecomunicación, Universidad de Málaga
Campus de Teatinos 29071-Málaga (Spain)

Abstract. This paper presents a bottom-up approach for fast segmentation of natural images. This approach has two main stages: firstly, it detects the homogeneous regions of the input image using a colour-based distance and then, it merges these regions using a more complex distance. Basically, this distance complements a contrast measure defined between regions with internal region descriptors and with attributes of the shared boundary. These two stages are performed over the same hierarchical framework: the Bounded Irregular Pyramid (BIP). The performance of the proposed algorithm has been quantitatively evaluated with respect to ground-truth segmentation data.

1 Introduction

Image segmentation is typically defined as the low-level process of grouping pixels into clusters which present homogeneous photometric properties. However, if the goal of the segmentation process is to divide the input image in a manner similar to human beings, then this definition is not valid. Natural images are generally composed of physically disjoint objects whose associated groups of image pixels may not be visually uniform. This makes extremely difficult to formulate what should be recovered as a region from an image or to separate complex objects from a natural scene [4].

In order to reduce the complexity of segmenting real objects from their background, the particular application could be taken into account. In these cases, the higher-level information is known a priori and it can be used to group the image pixels into logical regions that resemble the real objects. To maintain the generality of use, several authors have proposed generic segmentation methods which are based neither on a priori knowledge of the image content nor on any object model [1,3]. These approaches typically combine a pre-segmentation stage with a subsequent perceptual grouping stage. Basically, the pre-segmentation stage conducts the low-level definition of segmentation as a process of grouping pixels into homogeneous clusters and the perceptual grouping stage performs a domain-independent grouping which is mainly based on properties like the proximity, similarity, closure or continuity. Although the final obtained regions do not always correspond to the natural image objects, they provides a mid-level segmentation which is more coherent with the human-based image decomposition.

F.A. Hamprecht, C. Schnörr, and B. Jähne (Eds.): DAGM 2007, LNCS 4713, pp. 244–253, 2007.

Thus, it must be considered as a precursor to the detection of the real salient objects in the image.

This paper presents a segmentation approach which is also divided into these two successive stages. The pre-segmentation stage groups the image pixels into a set of regions whose spatial distribution is physically representative of the image content. The size of this set of regions is commonly very much less than the original number of pixels. Thus, these regions constitute an efficient image representation that replaces the pixel-based image representation. Besides, these regions preserve the image geometric structure as each significant feature contain at least one region. Our approach accomplishes this pre-segmentation stage by means of an irregular pyramid: the Bounded Irregular Pyramid (BIP). The BIP combines the 2x2/4 regular structure with an irregular simple graph. The regular decimation is applied in the homogeneous parts of the image, while the heterogeneous parts are decimated using a classical irregular process [6,7]. The perceptual grouping stage groups the set of homogeneous regions into a smaller set of regions taking into account not only the internal visual coherence of the obtained regions but also the external relationships among them. For managing this process, a hierarchical segmentation operator (HSO) can be applied [1]. The hierarchical structure is well-adapted to the parallel manipulation of regions, permitting to simultaneously group several regions. Thus, the perceptual organization of the image can be represented by a tree of regions, ordered by inclusion [1]. The roots of the tree is a set of regions which represent the entire scene and the leaves are the finest details. To achieve this perceptual grouping, the proposed approach generates a set of new pyramid levels over the previously built BIP. However, while the nodes of the pre-segmentation pyramid are merged taking into account a colour criterion, the similarity among nodes of these new levels is defined using a more complex distance which takes into account information about their common boundaries and internal features like their colour or size.

The proposed method is related to the previous works of Arbelaez and Cohen [1,2] and Huart and Bertolino [3]. In all those papers, the perceptual grouping is achieved by means of a hierarchical process. Besides, they employ a pre-segmentation stage prior to the perceptual grouping stage: Arbelaez and Cohen propose to employ the extrema mosaic technique [2], and Huart and Bertolino use the localized pyramid [3]. Our approach is very related to this last work. Thus, it uses different decimation techniques in the homogeneous and heterogeneous regions of the input image. The main difference with [3] is that both decimations are performed simultaneously using the BIP, being unnecessary to previously detect the homogeneous areas of the input image. The pre-segmentation stage uses a colour distance to group image pixels into homogeneous regions in a fast manner. The roots of these regions constitute the base level of the perceptual grouping stage. Thus, the perceptual grouping is integrated into the same hierarchical structure. However, the distance employed to achieve this last stage is significantly more complex, complementing the colour contrast between regions with attributes extracted from the local boundary which they shared and internal region features.

The rest of the paper is organized as follows: Section 2 describes the proposed approach. It briefly explains the main aspects of the pre-segmentation stage, which is based on previous works of Marfil et al. [6,8]. This section also describes the perceptual grouping process and the distance employed to group these homogeneous regions. These two stages are achieved using the Bounded Irregular Pyramid (BIP). The experimental results revealing the efficiency of the proposed method are presented in Section 3. The paper concludes along with discussions and future work in Section 4.

2 Perception-Based Segmentation Approach

2.1 Pre-segmentation Stage

Pyramids are hierarchical structures which have been widely used in segmentation tasks [7]. Instead of performing image segmentation based on a single representation of the input image, a pyramid segmentation algorithm describes the contents of the image using multiple representations with decreasing resolution. Pyramid segmentation algorithms exhibit interesting properties when compared to segmentation algorithms based on a single representation. Thus, local operations can adapt the pyramidal hierarchy to the topology of the image, allowing the detection of global features of interest and representing them at low resolution levels [3].

The Bounded Irregular Pyramid (BIP) is a mixture of regular and irregular pyramids whose goal is to combine their advantages. A 2x2/4 regular structure is used in the homogeneous regions of the input image and a simple graph structure in the non-homogeneous ones. The mixture of both structures generates an irregular configuration which is described as a graph hierarchy in which each level $G_l = (N_l, E_l)$ consists of a set of nodes, N_l, linked by a set of intra-level edges E_l. Each graph G_{l+1} is built from G_l by computing the nodes of N_{l+1} from the nodes of N_l and establishing the inter-level edges $E_{l,l+1}$. Therefore, each node n_i of G_{l+1} has associated a set of nodes of G_l, which is called the *reduction window* of n_i. This includes all nodes linked to n_i by an inter-level edge. The node n_i is called *parent* of the nodes in its reduction window, which are called *sons*. Two nodes n_i and n_j of N_l are said to be adjacent or *neighbours* at level l, if their corresponding reduction windows w_i and w_j are neighbours at level $l - 1$. Two reduction windows $w_i \in N_{l-1}$ and $w_j \in N_{l-1}$ are neighbours if there are at least two nodes $n_r \in w_i$ and $n_s \in w_j$ which are connected by an intra-level edge $e_{r,s} \in E_{l-1}$. The set of nodes in N_l which are neighbours of a node $n_i \in N_l$ is called the *neighbourhood* of n_i. An *intra-level path* is a sequence of ordered nodes linked by intra-level edges. Two nodes $n_i \in N_l$ and $n_j \in N_l$ are said to be *connected* if there exists an intra-level path that includes them both. Equivalently, an *inter-level path* is a sequence of ordered nodes linked by inter-level edges. Two nodes $n_i \in N_p$ and $n_j \in N_q$ are said to be *connected* if there exits an inter-level path that includes them both. The *receptive field* r_i of a node $n_i \in N_l$ is the set of nodes at level 0 which are connected to it by an inter-level path.

The successive levels of the hierarchy are built using a regular decimation process and a union-find strategy. Therefore, there are two types of nodes: nodes belonging to the 2x2/4 structure, named regular nodes, and virtual nodes or nodes belonging to the irregular structure. In any case, two nodes $n_i \in N_l$ and $n_j \in N_l$ which are neighbours at level l are linked by an intra-level edge $e_{ij} \in E_l$. This mixture of processes inside the same hierarchical structure presents interesting properties. Thus, the irregular part of the BIP allows to solve the main problems of regular structures: their inability to preserve connectivity or to represent elongated objects [8]. On the other hand, the BIP is computationally efficient because its height is constrained by its regular part [7].

The proposed approach uses a BIP structure to accomplish the segmentation task. In this hierarchy, the first levels perform the pre-segmentation stage using a colour-based distance to group pixels into homogeneous regions. In order to introduce colour information within the BIP, all the nodes of the structure have associated 3 parameters: chromatic phasor $S_{\angle H}(n)$, luminosity $V(n)$ and area $A(n)$, where S, H and V are the saturation, hue and value of the HSV colour space. The chromatic phasor and the luminosity of a node n are equal to the average of the chromatic phasors and luminosity values of the nodes in its reduction window. The area of a node is equal to the sum of the areas of the nodes in its reduction window, i.e. the cardinality of its receptive field.

The employed similarity measurement between two nodes is the HSV colour distance. Thus, two nodes are similar or have a similar colour if the distance between their HSV values is less than a similarity threshold T. This threshold is not fixed for all levels. Its mathematical expression is the following:

$$T(l) = T_{max} * \alpha(l) \tag{1}$$

being

$$\alpha(l) = \begin{cases} 1 - \frac{l}{L_{reg}} * (1 - \alpha) & \text{if } l \leq L_{reg} \\ \alpha & \text{if } l > L_{reg} \end{cases} \tag{2}$$

L_{reg} is the highest level of the regular part of the BIP. This threshold takes into account that usually the receptive field of a vertex in a high level is bigger than the receptive field of a vertex in a low level. Therefore, the linking of two vertices of a high level implies the merging of two larger regions at the base. This threshold makes more difficult this linking process at upper levels.

The graph $G_0 = (N_0, E_0)$ is a 8-connected graph where the nodes are the pixels of the original image. The chromatic phasors and the luminosity values of the nodes in $G_0 = (N_0, E_0)$ are equal to the chromatic phasors and luminosity values of their corresponding image pixels. Then, the process to build the graph $G_{l+1} = (N_{l+1}, E_{l+1})$ from $G_l = (N_l, E_l)$ is the following:

1. *Regular decimation process.* In order to perform this decimation, each regular node has associated two parameters: homogeneity $Hom(i, j, l)$ and parent link $Parent(i, j, l)$. $Hom(i, j, l)$ of a regular node is set to 1 if the four nodes immediately underneath present a similar colour (according to the threshold $T(l)$) and their homogeneity values are equal to 1. Otherwise, it is set to 0.

If the node (i, j, l) is a node of the regular structure with $Hom(i, j, l) = 1$, then the parent link of the four cells immediately underneath (sons) is set to (i, j). It indicates the position of the parent of a regular node in its upper level. A regular node without parent has its parent link set to a NULL value. Parent links represent the inter-level edges of the regular part of the BIP. All the nodes of $G_0 = (N_0, E_0)$ are initialized with $Hom(i, j, 0) = 1$ and $A(i, j, 0) = 1$. Table 1 summarizes this stage in pseudocode, where $d(\cdot, \cdot)$ is the HSV colour distance and `ComputeColour()` determines the colour of the input node using the nodes in its reduction window.

2. *Parent search and intra-level twining.* Once the regular structure is generated, there are some regular orphan nodes (regular nodes without parent). From each of these nodes (i, j, l), a search is made for the most similar regular node with parent in its 8-neighbourhood $\xi_{(i,j,l)}$ (see Table 1). If this neighbour node is found, the node (i, j, l) is linked to the parent of this neighbour node. On the contrary, if for this node a parent is not found, then a search is made for the most similar regular neighbour node without parent to link to it (see Table 1). If this node is found, then both nodes are linked, generating a virtual node at level $l + 1$.

3. *Virtual parent search and virtual node linking.* Each virtual orphan node n_i searches for the most similar virtual node with parent in its neighbourhood ξ_{n_i} (see Table 1). If for n_i a parent is found, then it is linked to it. On the other hand, if a parent is not found, the virtual orphan node n_i looks for the most similar virtual orphan node in its neighbourhood to generate a new virtual node at level $l + 1$ (see Table 1).

4. *Intra-level edge generation in G_{l+1}.* The intra-level edges of G_{l+1} are computed by taking into account the neighbourhood of their reduction windows in G_l.

The hierarchy stops to grow when it is no longer possible to link together any more nodes because they are not similar. In order to perform the pre-segmentation, the orphan nodes are used as roots. The receptive field of each of these nodes is a region of the pre-segmented image. The described method has been tested and compared with other similar pyramid approaches for colour image segmentation [7]. This comparative study concludes that the BIP runs faster than other irregular approaches when benchmarking is performed in a standard sequential computer. Besides, the BIP obtains similar results than the main irregular structures. Fig. 1.b shows the pre-segmentation images associated to the images in Fig. 1.a.

2.2   Perceptual Grouping Stage

After the local similarity pre-segmentation stage, grouping regions aims at simplifying the content of the obtained partition. As it was pointed out by [3], two constraints are respected for an efficient grouping process: first, although all groupings are tested, only the best groupings are locally retained; and second, all the groupings must be spread on the image so that no part of the image is advantaged. For managing this grouping, the BIP structure is used: the roots of

Table 1. Pseudo-code for the regular decimation, parent search and intra-level twinning and virtual parent search and virtual node linking steps of the pre-segmentation stage (see text for details)

```
//Regular decimation process
for i=0:SizeX[1], for j=0:SizeY[1],
  if (Hom(i,j,1) & Hom(i+1,j,1) & Hom(i,j+1,1) & Hom(i+1,j+1,1))
    if (d((i,j,1),(i+1,j,1))<T(1) & d((i,j,1),(i,j+1,1))<T(1) &
    & d((i,j,1),(i+1,j+1,1))< T(1))
      Parent(i,j,1)=(i/2,j/2);Parent(i+1,j,1)=(i/2,j/2);
      Parent(i,j+1,1)=(i/2,j/2);Parent(i+1,j+1,1)=(i/2,j/2);
      Hom(i/2,j/2,1+1)=1; ComputeColour((i/2,j/2,1+1));
    end if

//Parent search and intra-level twining
for i=0:SizeX[1], for j=0:SizeY[1],
  if (Hom(i,j,1) & Parent(i,j,1)==NULL)
    dmin=T(1);sel=NULL;
    for each (m,n,1) ∈ ξ_(i,j,l),
      if (Parent(m,n,1)!=NULL & d((i,j,1),(m,n,1))<dmin)
        dmin=d((i,j,1),(m,n,1));sel=(m,n,1);
    if (sel!=NULL) Parent(i,j,1)=Parent(sel);
    else
      dmin=T(1);
      for each (m,n,1) ∈ ξ_(i,j,l),
        if (Parent(m,n,1)==NULL & d((i,j,1),(m,n,1))<dmin)
          dmin=d((i,j,1),(m,n,1));sel=(m,n,1);
      if (sel!=NULL) CreateVirtualNode((i,j,1),sel);
    end else
  end if

//Virtual parent search and virtual node linking
for i=0:NumberOfVirtualNodes[1],
  if (Parent(n_i)==NULL)
    dmin=T(1);sel=NULL;
    for each (n_m) ∈ ξ_{n_i},
      if (Parent(n_m)!=NULL & d(n_i,n_m)<dmin)
        dmin=d(n_i,n_m);sel=(n_m);
    if (sel!=NULL) Parent(n_i)=Parent(sel);
    else
      dmin=T(1);
      for each (n_m) ∈ ξ_{n_i},
        if (Parent(n_m)==NULL & d(n_i,n_m)<dmin)
          dmin=d(n_i,n_m);sel=(n_m);
      if (sel!=NULL) CreateVirtualNode(n_i,sel); virtualnodes=true;
    end else
  end if
```

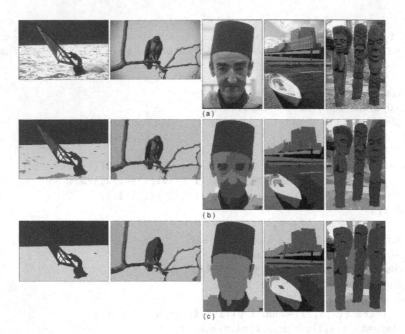

Fig. 1. a) Original images; b) pre-segmentation images; and c) obtained regions after the perceptual grouping

the pre-segmented regions are considered as virtual nodes which constitute the first level of the perceptual grouping multiresolution output. Successive levels can be built using the virtual parent search and virtual node linking scheme previously described in Section 2.1, but, in order to achieve the perceptual grouping process, a specific distance must be defined.

This distance uses the colour information stored in the nodes of the pyramid for measuring the colour contrast between image regions. In order to speed up the process, a global contrast measure is used instead of a local one. It avoids to work at pixel resolution. The contrast measure is complemented with internal regions properties and with attributes of the boundary shared by both regions. To perform correctly, the nodes of the BIP which are associated to the perceptual grouping multiresolution output store statistics about the HSV values of the roots generated by the pre-segmentation stage which are linked to them. Then, the distance between two nodes n_i and n_j is defined as

$$\Upsilon(n_i, n_j) = d(n_i, n_j) \cdot \frac{min(b_i, b_j)}{b_{ij}} \cdot min\{A_i, A_j\} \tag{3}$$

where b_{ij} is the length of the common boundary between n_i and n_j, and $\{b_i, A_i\}$ and $\{b_j, A_j\}$ the total length of the boundaries and area of the nodes n_i and n_j, respectively.

In order to build a new hierarchy level G_{l+1}, the virtual parent search and virtual node linking process described in Section 2.1 is applied. However, a different threshold value T_{perc} is employed. The grouping process is iterated until the number of vertices remains constant between two successive levels. Fig. 1.c shows the set of regions associated to the images in Fig. 1.a. It can be noted that the obtained regions do not always correspond to the set of natural objects presented in the image, but they provide an image segmentation which is more coherent with the human-based image decomposition.

3   Experimental Results

In order to evaluate the performance of the proposed approach, the Berkeley Segmentation Dataset and Benchmark (BSDB) has been employed[1][9]. In this dataset, the ground-truth data is provided by a large database of natural images, manually segmented by human subjects. The methodology for evaluating the performance of segmentation techniques is based on the comparison of machine detected boundaries with respect to human-marked boundaries using the *Precision-Recall framework* [10]. This technique considers two quality measures: precision and recall. The *precision* (P) is defined as the fraction of boundary detections that are true positives rather than false positives. Thus, it quantifies the amount of noise in the output of the boundaries detector approach. On the other hand, the *recall* (R) is defined by the fraction of true positives that are detected rather than missed. Then, it quantifies the amount of ground-truth detected. Measuring these descriptors over a set of images for different thresholds of the approach provides a parametric Precision-Recall curve. The F-measure combines these two quality measures into a single one. It is defined as their harmonic mean:

$$F(P, R) = \frac{2PR}{P + R} \tag{4}$$

Then, the maximal F-measure on the curve is used as a summary statistic for the quality of the detector on the set of images. The current public version of the dataset is divided in a training set of 200 images and a test set of 100 images. In order to ensure the integrity of the evaluation, only the images and segmentations from the training set can be accessed during the optimization phase. Fig. 1 shows the partitions on the higher level of the hierarchy for five different images. The optimal training parameters on the test set have been chosen. It can be noted that the proposed approach is able to group perceptually important regions in spite of the large intensity variability presented on several areas of the input images. The pre-segmentation stage provides an oversegmentation of the image which overcomes the problem of noisy pixels, although bigger details are preserved in the final segmentation results (e.g., the legs of the bird in Fig. 1.c).

The F-measure associated to the individual results ranged from bad to significantly good values. Thus, the F-measure value of all images in Fig. 1 is over 0.75. On the contrary, Fig. 2 shows several images which have associated a low F-measure value. The main problems of the proposed approach are due to its inability to deal with textured regions. Thus, the background, zebras or tigers

---

[1] http://www.cs.berkeley.edu/projects/vision/grouping/segbench/

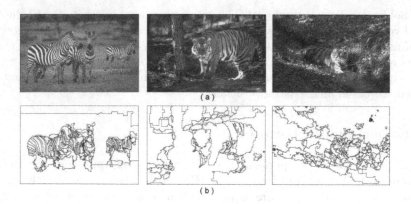

Fig. 2. a) Original images; and b) obtained regions after the perceptual grouping

in Fig. 2 are divided into a set of different regions. In any case, the maximal
F-measure obtained from the whole test set is 0.65. Although this value is less
than the F-measure obtained by Arbelaez [1], it is similar to the value provided by other methods like the gradient paradigm implemented by Martin et
al [10]. This approach optimizes, with respect to the BSDB, the combination of
local discontinuities in feature channels like brightness, color and texture. The
main advantage of the proposed method is that it provides these results at a
relative low computational cost. Thus, the processing times associated to the
pre-segmentation stage are typically less than 200 ms, meanwhile the perceptual grouping stage takes less than 150 ms to process any image on the test set.
Therefore, the processing time of the segmentation approach is less than 350 ms
for any image on the test set.

Finally, the proposed method requires choosing values for a set of parameters.
These parameters are:

- The colour threshold, T_{max}, which determines the maximum distance between two colours that are considered similar at the pre-segmentation
  stage.
- The parameter α determines the colour threshold employed in the highest
  levels of the hierarchy in the pre-segmentation stage.
- The threshold value T_{perc}, which determines the maximum distance between
  two nodes that are considered similar at the perception-based stage.

In order to choose these parameters, several combinations were selected and the
best values were chosen. In our tests, the best choices for the thresholds were
$T_{max}=50$, $\alpha=0.8$ and $T_{perc}=150$.

4   Conclusions and Future Work

This paper presents a new perception-based segmentation approach which is
totally defined in the framework of the Bounded Irregular Pyramid. Thus, the

pre-segmentation and perceptual grouping stages are combined into the same structure, without being necessary to define any threshold to bound these stages. The pre-segmentation is achieved using a colour-based distance and it works faster than similar hierarchical approaches [7]. The roots of the regions defined by the pre-segmentation stage are the first level of the hierarchy associated to the perceptual grouping stage. This second stage employs a distance which is also based on the colour difference between regions, but it includes information of the area and boundary of each region. The processing time of this second stage is also reduced because the obtained pre-segmentation regions constitute an efficient image representation.

Future work will be focused on testing different perception-based grouping parameters [5], studying its repercussion in the efficiency of the method. Besides, it is necessary that the pre-segmentation stage takes into account a texture measure to characterize the image pixels.

Acknowledgments

The authors have been partially supported by the Spanish Ministerio de Educación y Ciencia under project TIN2005-01359.

References

1. Arbeláez, P.: Boundary extraction in natural images using ultrametric contour maps. In: Proc. 5th IEEE Workshop Perceptual Org. in Computer Vision, pp. 182–189. IEEE Computer Society Press, Los Alamitos (2006)
2. Arbeláez, P., Cohen, L.: A metric approach to vector-valued image segmentation. Int. Journal of Computer Vision 69, 119–126 (2006)
3. Huart, J., Bertolino, P.: Similarity-based and perception-based image segmentation. Proc. IEEE Int. Conf. on Image Processing 3(3), 1148–1151 (2005)
4. Lau, H., Levine, M.: Finding a small number of regions in an image using low-level features. Pattern Recognition 35, 2323–2339 (2002)
5. Luo, J., Guo, C.: Perceptual grouping of segmented regions in color images. Pattern Recognition, 2781–2792 (2003)
6. Marfil, R., Rodríguez, J.A., Bandera, A., Sandoval, F.: Bounded irregular pyramid: a new structure for colour image segmentation. Pattern Recognition 37(3), 623–626 (2004)
7. Marfil, R., Molina-Tanco, L., Bandera, A., Rodríguez, J.A., Sandoval, F.: Pyramid segmentation algorithms revisited. Pattern Recognition 39(8), 1430–1451 (2006)
8. Marfil, R., Molina-Tanco, L., Rodríguez, S.F.: Real-time object tracking using bounded irregular pyramids. Pattern Recognition Letters (2007)
9. Martin, D., Fowlkes, C., Tal, D., Malik, J.: A database of human segmented natural images and its application. In: Proc. Int. Conf. Computer Vision, vol. 2, pp. 416–423 (2001)
10. Martin, D., Fowlkes, C., Malik, J.: Learning to detect natural image boundaries using local brightness, color and texture cues. IEEE Trans. on Pattern Anal. Machine Intell. 26(5), 530–549 (2004)

Efficient Image Segmentation Using Pairwise Pixel Similarities

Christopher Rohkohl[1] and Karin Engel[2]

[1] Friedrich-Alexander University Erlangen-Nuremberg
[2] Dept. of Simulation and Graphics, Otto-von-Guericke-University Magdeburg

Abstract. Image segmentation based on pairwise pixel similarities has been a very active field of research in recent years. The drawbacks common to these segmentation methods are the enormous space and processor requirements. The contribution of this paper is a general purpose two-stage preprocessing method that substantially reduces the involved costs. Initially, an oversegmentation into small coherent image patches - or superpixels - is obtained through an iterative process guided by pixel similarities. A suitable pairwise superpixel similarity measure is then defined which may be plugged into an arbitrary segmentation method based on pairwise pixel similarities. To illustrate our ideas we integrated the algorithm into a spectral graph-partitioning method using the Normalized Cut criterion. Our experiments show that the time and memory requirements are reduced drastically ($> 99\%$), while segmentations of adequate quality are obtained.

1 Introduction

The segmentation of images into meaningful regions is an important task of computer vision. One common approach is the definition of a similarity measure $\Phi(i, j)$ between two image pixels i, j based on e.g. color, texture, proximity or contour information. Let N in the following denote the number of image pixels. Usually from Φ a $N \times N$ similarity matrix W is derived with $W_{ij} = \Phi(i, j)$. W may be interpreted as an adjacency matrix for an undirected weighted graph $G = (V, E)$, whose nodes V represent the image pixels which are connected by the affinity-weighted edges in E. In order to receive a partition of the image an arbitrary method may be applied to W. The most popular methods are spectral graph partitioning [1,2], deterministic annealing [3] and stochastic clustering [4]. Unfortunately, for most problems W easily becomes very large and unmanageable. For example, given a relatively small 400×300 image ($N = 120000$) W contains 14.4 billion entries and requires about 53.6 GB of memory at single precision. Thus prevalently the number of connections per pixel is restricted.

We present a two-step preprocessing method which substantially reduces the time and memory requirements such that even much larger problems may be addressed by any pairwise grouping algorithm. The remainder of this paper is organized as follows: In Sect. 2 we discuss related work. We present our algorithm in detail in Sect. 3. The Normalized Cut grouping method into which we

F.A. Hamprecht, C. Schnörr, and B. Jähne (Eds.): DAGM 2007, LNCS 4713, pp. 254–263, 2007.
© Springer-Verlag Berlin Heidelberg 2007

integrated our algorithm is reviewed in Sect. 4. In Sect. 5 we present the results of our method applied to the segmentation of synthetic and natural images.

2   Related Work

A very common procedure to make pairwise grouping methods tractable is the creation of a sparse version of the similarity matrix by zeroing entries, i.e. by removing edges from the graph representation. Shi and Malik [1] proposed the approximation of W by setting a cutoff radius in the image plane such that each pixel is connected to only a few of its neighbors. Alternatives include the zeroing of randomly chosen entries and of, e.g. the smallest matrix entries. This approach was confirmed to be very effective by [5]. However, this requires all matrix elements to be calculated. Fowlkes et al. [5] utilize the Nyström method to approximate the similarity matrix. Initially, a set of randomly chosen sample pixels and their corresponding connections to all other pixels are extracted. This small portion of the similarity matrix is then used to estimate all remaining connections. The major reduction of the computational effort is achieved by calculating the row sums of the approximated similarity matrix without the need to estimate all matrix entries. Hence, this approach is attractive for methods that actually require the row sums of W. Keuchel and Schnörr [6] propose a singular value decomposition (SVD) approximation method for W based on probabilistic sampling. Sharon et al. apply a multiscale method to find an approximate solution to normalized cut measures [7].

Several pairwise segmentation techniques may take advantage of the mentioned approximations but not all can do so [8]. More general approaches [8, 9] generate a suitable oversegmentation of the image in terms of a preprocessing step. Ideally this oversegmentation does not miss any boundaries. It thus can be used to derive a new (much smaller) similarity matrix by means of a pairwise measure for the obtained image patches. This in turn is used to feed the pairwise grouping method. Keuchel et al. [8] created an irregular oversegmentation using the mean shift algorithm. The image patch affinities are described using a region feature, e.g. the mean color. Malik et al. [9] proposed to use a sparsified version of the complete similarity matrix in order to separate the image into patches. However, this procedure still does not reduce the costs, as a convenient approximation scheme for W is still required.

In this paper, we propose a method that provides a suitable oversegmentation and concurrently exploits the availability of a pairwise pixel similarity measure. In our approach an oversegmentation into small coherent image patches is obtained in an iterative manner. The algorithm offers a clean interface and may be easily integrated into existing pairwise grouping methods.

3   Our Approach

The high spatial resolution of modern images makes optimization on the level of pixels intractable [10]. However, image pixels are no natural entities, being rather a consequence of the digital discretization process. For these reasons we define image elements as small coherent image patches which we refer to as superpixels [10].

The interpretation and preferences of superpixels can be compared to a jigsaw puzzle. The superpixels are the pieces that make up the segments which reveal the complete image. With increasing size of the tiles the jigsaw gets easier and can be completed significantly faster. This analogy reveals two important aspects our algorithm is based on:

1. The superpixels must respect the boundaries of the true segmentation.
2. The size of the superpixels limits the resolution of the segmentation. Any true segment smaller than the superpixel size cannot be correctly segmented.

For the creation of superpixels our algorithm solely requires the pairwise pixel similarity function Φ. This allows for the use of clever implementation schemes, e.g. a caching mechanism. In our experiments we stored the information needed for the similarity function (e.g. color) and performed the computation on the fly.

3.1   Oversegmentation into Superpixels

The superpixel segmentation is calculated in a two-step process. An initial tiling of the image plane is achieved which is then adapted to the local image structure. Figure 1 shows an example of the superpixel segmentation. To obtain the initial segmentation into k superpixel segments, Ren et al. apply the Normalized Cut algorithm which produces superpixels of similar size and shape [10]. This fact is exploited by our approach which uses a raw segmentation into hexagonal superpixels. We decided for a regular hexagonal grid (see Fig. 2a) as it offers beneficial properties over other tilings [11]. Choosing a proper value for k may require a training stage [10]. However, this shall not be addressed in the scope of this paper. We choose k given a predefined minimum size of the segments, i.e. the granularity of the superpixels is user–supplied.

Starting from this raw segmentation the segments then adapt iteratively to the local image structure characterized by the pairwise pixel similarities. The

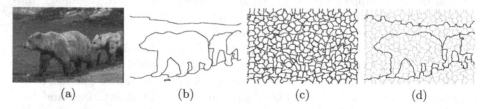

| (a) | (b) | (c) | (d) |

Fig. 1. An example of a superpixel segmentation using color information for $k = 400$ at a sampling rate of $r_{sp} = 0.01$ and $m = 30$ iterations (see text for explanations). (a) the original image from the Berkeley Segmentation Dataset [12]; (b) a reference segmentation; (c) the final superpixel segmentation; (d) a reconstruction of (b) from the superpixel segmentation: each superpixel is assigned to the segment with the maximum overlapping area [10].

(a) 0 iterations   (b) 5 iterations   (c) 15 iterations   (d) 30 iterations   (e) Final result

Fig. 2. Superpixel segmentation process. The background shows the superpixel segmentation of the current iteration. The dark outline constitutes the reconstruction of a reference segmentation [10]. (a) The original image (see Fig. 1) is partitioned into approximately $k = 400$ hexagons. (b) - (d) Given this raw segmentation the segments are iteratively adapted to the local image structure. (e) The final superpixel segmentation after region merging to obtain a maximum of $k = 400$ image patches.

similarity between a pixel i and a segment s can be defined as the average of the similarities between i and all the pixels in s, namely $sim_p(i, s) = \frac{1}{|s|} \sum_{j \in s} \Phi(i, j)$. For a set S of concurrent image patches the most likely segment $s^i \in S$ is the one having maximum similarity to pixel i, i.e.

$$s^i = \arg \max_{s \in S, s \setminus \{i\}} sim_p(i, s) = \arg \max_{s \in S, s \setminus \{i\}} \frac{1}{|s|} \sum_{j \in s} \Phi(i, j) \ . \tag{1}$$

The pixel i is ignored in any segment as it would bias the result. Since the computational effort depends on the size of the segments we introduce a function $R_n(\cdot)$ which returns n randomly selected elements from a set of pixels. Modifying (1) an estimation for the most suitable segment $\hat{s}^i$ for a pixel i is then

$$\hat{s}^i = \arg \max_{s \in S, s \setminus \{i\}} \frac{1}{n} \sum_{j \in R_n(s)} \Phi(i, j) \ . \tag{2}$$

The initial segments adapt to the local image conditions in the following way:

1. For each boundary pixel i of the current segmentation identify the set P of feasible superpixel segments (P will contain the neighboring and the current superpixels. Hence most similarities are ignored.). Select the new superpixel $\hat{s}^i$ from P according to (2).
2. Repeat step 1 until a stopping criterion is fulfilled.
3. Merge the smallest superpixels until a maximum of k superpixel segments is left. The spreading of the pixels is again calculated using (2).

For reasons of simplicity, in our experiments we used color and proximity information to characterize the pairwise pixel similarity, see Sect. 5.2 for details. The number n of random samples used in step 1 is set to a fraction r_{sp} of the size of the current superpixel segment. In the following r_{sp} will be referred to as superpixel sampling rate. A preset number of m iterations was chosen as stopping criterion. (Alternatives may include the supervision of the number of consecutive fails to assign boundary pixels of the current segmentation to a new superpixel, but this shall not be discussed here).

Figures 1 and 2 show the results for an 481×321 image taken from the Berkeley Segmentation Dataset [12] at a sampling rate of 1% for $k = 400$ superpixels and $m = 30$ iterations. To obtain these results in overall ≈ 8 million calls have been made to Φ, which corresponds to 0.04% of all pairwise pixel similarities.

3.2   Definition of a Pairwise Superpixel Similarity

By hypothesis the true segmentation can be computed from the k image patches obtained through the oversegmentation of an image according to Sect. 3.1. To make the superpixels viable for a pairwise grouping method, a pairwise super-pixel similarity measure has to be defined on the basis of the pairwise pixel similarity measure. A straightforward expansion of the measure of similarity $sim_p(i, j)$ between a pixel i and a segment s given in (1), to the similarity of two image segments s_1 and s_2 is obtained using the average similarity of each pixel of s_1 to the segment s_2, namely:

$$sim_s(s_1, s_2) = \frac{1}{|s_1|} \sum_{i \in s_1} sim_p(i, s_2) = \frac{1}{|s_1||s_2|} \sum_{i \in s_1} \sum_{j \in s_2} \Phi(i, j) \ . \tag{3}$$

However, the calculation of all pairwise superpixel similarities requires to compute all pairwise pixel similarities, which is exactly what we wanted to avoid. By means of the function $R_n(\cdot)$ which gives n randomly selected elements for any set of pixels, (3) can be modified. An estimation $\hat{\Phi}(s, t)$ for the similarity between superpixel segments s and t is then given by:

$$\hat{\Phi}(s, t) = \frac{1}{n_1 n_2} \sum_{i \in R_{n_1}(s)} \sum_{j \in R_{n_2}(t)} \Phi(i, j) \ . \tag{4}$$

The numbers n_1, n_2 of random samples can be adapted for each segment using the superpixel sampling rate r_{sp} introduced in the previous section.

By providing a suitable pairwise pixel similarity function Φ along with the parameters for the superpixel segmentation, i.e. k (the number of superpixels), r_{sp} (the superpixel sampling rate) and the number of iteration steps m, the according superpixel similarity measure $\hat{\Phi}$ can be computed. This may be easily plugged into an arbitrary pairwise grouping method, e.g. [1].

4   The Normalized Cut Framework

The Normalized Cut framework introduced by Shi and Malik [1] provides a pairwise grouping method inspired by spectral graph theory. Image segmentation is described in terms of a graph partitioning problem. Recall that W may be interpreted as an adjacency matrix for an undirected weighted graph $G = (V, E)$. Let A, B be a partition of the graph, i.e. $A \cup B = V$, $A \cap B = \emptyset$. The Normalized Cut criterion allows to evaluate the quality of a partition by extracting the global impression of an image:

$$Ncut(A, B) = \frac{cut(A, B)}{assoc(A)} + \frac{cut(A, B)}{assoc(B)}, \tag{5}$$

where $cut(A, B) = \sum_{i \in A, j \in B} W_{ij}$ and $assoc(A) = \sum_{i \in A, j \in V} W_{ij}$. The determination of the best partition is a NP-complete problem. However, fast approximation methods exist. Let D be a diagonal matrix with $D_{ii} = \sum_{j=1}^{N} W_{ij}$. The optimal partition can be computed as follows:

$$y = \arg \min Ncut = \arg \min_y \frac{y^T(D - W)y}{y^T Dy}, \tag{6}$$

with $y \in \{a, b\}^N$ being a binary indicator specifying the group membership for each pixel in either A or B. If y is relaxed to take on real values (6) can be optimized by solving the generalized eigenvalue system $(D - W)y = \lambda Dy$. The eigenvector y with the second smallest corresponding eigenvalue can be used to recursively compute a bipartition of the image. We suppose to check l evenly spaced possible splitting points, such that the resulting partition has the best $Ncut$ value. A complete image segmentation is obtained by further splitting the computed segments, starting e.g. with the largest of the current segments. Any two segments which differ in size for a maximum allowable ratio e are both split. The partition with minimum $Ncut$ value is accepted. The segmentation process can be stopped, e.g. after t partitions, or when a partition exceeds the maximum $Ncut$ value c_{max}.

Our algorithm is plugged into this framework by calculating an approximative similarity matrix $\hat{W}_{st} = \hat{\Phi}(s, t)$ from the superpixel segmentation.

5 Experiments

5.1 Segmentation of a Test Case

In the 25×25 images I_0 displayed in Figs. 3a-3b, the dark and light segments I_0^D and I_0^B were created from the normal distribution $N(\mu = 0, \sigma = 0.1)$ and $N(\mu = 1.2, \sigma = 0.1)$, respectively. The image segmentation $I_0 = I_0^D \cup I_0^B$ was taken as ground truth. The difficulty of the segmentation task was increased by minimizing the difference of the means of the probability distributions of the dark and light segments in I_0. We therefore formally introduce a problem difficulty $p \in [0, 0.75]$. Each image I_p is derived from I_0 according to: $I_p^D = I_0^D + \frac{p}{2}$ and $I_p^B = I_0^B - \frac{p}{2}$. The similarity of two pixels i, j is given by the Gaussian weighted Euclidean distance function $\Phi(i, j) = \exp\left(-|x_i - x_j|/2\sigma^2\right)$, where x_i is the intensity value of pixel i. The quality of the $Ncut$ bipartition provided by the eigenvector with the second smallest eigenvalue is estimated using the Jaccard coefficient [13]: $J(T, S) = n_{11}(n_{11} + n_{10} + n_{01})^{-1} \in [0, 1]$. Here, T is the true solution and S the segmentation to evaluate; n_{11}, n_{01} and n_{10} denote the number of pairs of elements within the same segment in both S and T, only in S and only in T, respectively. For each problem difficulty the parameter σ was optimized by testing several evenly spaced values in the non-approximated segmentation. The number of iterations during the superpixel segmentation was fixed to $m = 30$.

The results of this experiment are presented in Fig. 3. As expected, the number of superpixels used directly influences the quality of the segmentation as well

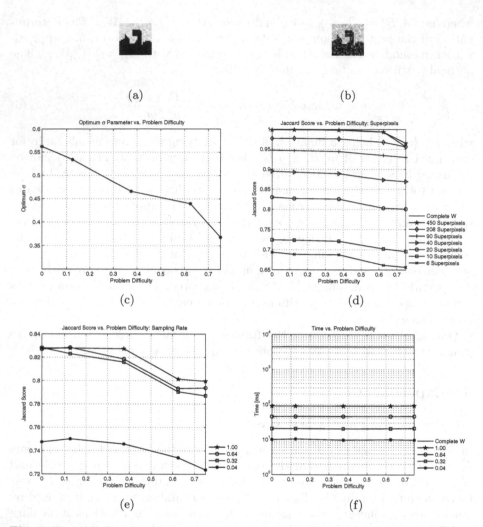

(a)   (b)

(c)   (d)

(e)   (f)

Fig. 3. Top row: Benchmark images of size 25×25 used for evaluating the quality of our approximation scheme. (a) The benchmark image I_0 of difficulty $p = 0$. (b) The benchmark image $I_{0.75}$ of maximum difficulty $p = 0.75$. Second and last row: A study of the segmentation quality depending on the problem difficulty for different configurations of the algorithm in 500 trials. The non-approximated solution to the similarity matrix is denoted "Complete W". (c) The optimum value for σ that maximizes the Jaccard score. (d) Comparison of the segmentation quality for different numbers of superpixel segments at a sampling rate of $r_{sp} = 1$. (e) Estimation of the segmentation quality at different sampling rates given a fixed number $k = 20$ of superpixels. (f) Empirical analysis of the running time for the segmentations of (e).

as the computational effort of our algorithm. Interestingly, for a large number of sampling rates the results are of similar quality and compare to the segmentation quality of the Normalized Cut algorithm. The computation of the segmentation

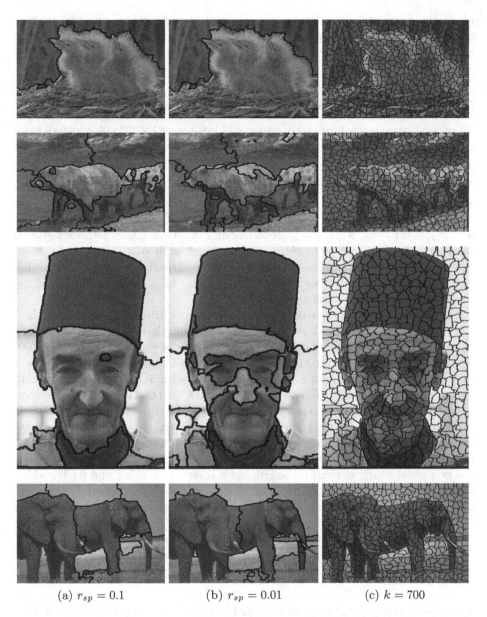

(a) $r_{sp} = 0.1$ (b) $r_{sp} = 0.01$ (c) $k = 700$

Fig. 4. Color image segmentations of our algorithm using color and proximity information. The images are taken from the Berkeley Segmentation Dataset [12] and are of a size of 481×321 pixels. Column (a) shows the segmentation on the basis of $k = 700$ superpixels at a sampling rate of 10%, the average segmentation time was about 4 minutes. In column (b) the images were segmented using the same configuration but a lower sampling rate of 1%. The running time decreased to less than 1 minute. (c) shows the superpixel segmentations obtained during the segmentation of (a) after $m = 30$ iterations. Results on the complete dataset are available at **effpixsegment.oneder.de**.

using the complete similarity matrix W took at average 4.5 seconds. In contrast, $\hat{W}$ could be computed in about 0.045 seconds, using 20 superpixels and a sampling rate of 64%. Approximately 99% savings in calculation time and 97% savings in memory requirements could be achieved at a quality loss of just 15%.

5.2   Segmentation of Natural Images

To present some segmentations of real world images, 481×321 color images from the Berkeley Segmentation Dataset are used [12]. The pairwise pixel similarities are calculated according to: $\Phi(i,j) = \exp\left(-\frac{\|C(i)-C(j)\|_2}{\sigma_{ci}} - \frac{\|X(i)-X(j)\|_2}{\sigma_{sl}}\right)$, where $C(\cdot)$ is the 3-dimensional vector in the nearly perceptual uniform L*a*b* color space and $X(\cdot)$ the spatial location of the image pixels i, j. The parameters are set to 15% of the range of the feature distance function, i.e. $\sigma_{ci} = 0.15 \cdot d_{max}$, and $\sigma_{sl} = 0.15 \cdot D$, where d_{max} denotes the maximum color distance between randomly chosen pairs of pixels and D is the length of the image diagonal. The Normalized Cut implementation was parametrized with: $l = 50$, $e = 0.5$, $c_{max} = 0.5$, $t = 10$ (see Sect. 4). A fixed number of $m = 30$ iterations of the superpixel segmentation was computed.

Figure 4 summarizes some segmentation results (without any postprocessing) for two different configurations of the segmentation algorithm. The first group of segmentations was obtained at a sampling rate of $r_{sp} = 0.1$ and $k = 700$. The whole segmentation process for an image at this configuration took about 4 minutes in unoptimized Java code on a Pentium 4 with 3GHz. The second group was achieved at a sampling rate of $r_{sp} = 0.01$ and $k = 700$. The computation took at average less than one minute. A direct comparison to the non-approximated version is not possible as the complete similarity matrix does not fit into memory. However, to estimate the savings of our approximation scheme the number of all calls to Φ was compared with the number of all pairwise pixel similarities. For the two given configurations we calculated a fraction of 0.75% and 0.03% which resembles to reductions in the order of 99.25% and 99.97% compared to the real solution. The segmentation quality of course highly depends on Φ which in our case utilizes color and proximity information only. The integration of suitable proximity, texture and contour cues [9] would yield better results.

6   Conclusion

We presented a general approach toward making grouping methods based on pairwise pixel similarities applicable to real world problems. The technique is very straightforward and may be plugged into existing systems as a preprocessing step. The pixels are replaced by small coherent image patches - the superpixels. In order to make the superpixels utilizable in a pairwise grouping method, in the second step a new pairwise similarity measure for the superpixels is defined. It relies on the basis of the pairwise pixel similarity function used in the iterative superpixel creation. We demonstrated the integration into the Normalized Cut framework. The speed and memory requirements for segmentation can be reduced drastically without loosing significantly in quality. The savings of our approximation scheme are in the order of $>99\%$ of the original problem size. The reconstructed segmentations are good approximations of the original. Depending on the granularity of the superpixels, some less significant details in the human segmentation may be lost (see Fig. 1). However, we yield comparable results as other approximation and speed–up techniques [8, 7, 10]. Segmentation results and the source code are available at `effpixsegment.oneder.de`.

References

1. Shi, J., Malik, J.: Normalized cuts and image segmentation. In: Proc. IEEE CVPR, vol. 731 (1997)
2. Wang, S., Siskind, J.M.: Image segmentation with ratio cut. IEEE Trans. Pattern Anal. Mach. Intell. 25(6), 675–690 (2003)
3. Hofmann, T., Buhmann, J.M.: Pairwise data clustering by deterministic annealing. IEEE Trans. Pattern Anal. Mach. Intell. 19(1), 1–14 (1997)
4. Gdalyahu, Y., Weinshall, D., Werman, M.: Stochastic image segmentation by typical cuts. In: Proc. IEEE CVPR, vol. 02, p. 2596 (1999)
5. Fowlkes, C., Belongie, S., Chung, F., Malik, J.: Spectral grouping using the Nyström method. IEEE Trans. Pattern Anal. Mach. Intell. 26(2), 214–225 (2004)
6. Keuchel, J., Schnörr, C.: Efficient graph cuts for unsupervised image segmentation using probabilistic sampling and SVD-based approximation. In: 3rd Internat. Workshop on Statist. and Comput. Theories of Vision, France (2003)
7. Sharon, E., Brandt, A., Basri, R.: Fast multiscale image segmentation. In: IEEE CVPR, vol. 1, pp. 70–77 (2000)
8. Keuchel, J., Heiler, M., Schnörr, C.: Hierarchical image segmentation based on semidefinite programming. In: Rasmussen, C.E., Bülthoff, H.H., Schölkopf, B., Giese, M.A. (eds.) Pattern Recognition. LNCS, vol. 3175, pp. 120–128. Springer, Heidelberg (2004)
9. Malik, J., Belongie, S., Leung, T., Shi, J.: Contour and texture analysis for image segmentation. Int. J. Comput. Vision 43(1), 7–27 (2001)
10. Ren, X., Malik, J.: Learning a classification model for segmentation. In: IEEE ICCV, vol. 10 (2003)
11. Brimkov, V.E., Barneva, R.P.: Analytical honeycomb geometry for raster and volume graphics. Comput. J. 48(2), 180–199 (2005)
12. Martin, D., Fowlkes, C., Tal, D., Malik, J.: A database of human segmented natural images and its application to evaluating segmentation algorithms and measuring ecological statistics. In: Proc. IEEE ICCV vol. 2, pp. 416–423 (2001)
13. Halkidi, M., Batistakis, Y., Vazirgiannis, M.: Clustering algorithms and validity measures. In: Proc. 13th Int. Conf. Scient. Stat. Datab. Man., USA, pp. 3–22. IEEE Computer Society, Los Alamitos (2001)

WarpCut – Fast Obstacle Segmentation in Monocular Video

Andreas Wedel[1,2], Thomas Schoenemann[1], Thomas Brox[1], and Daniel Cremers[1]

[1] Computer Vision Group University of Bonn
[2] DaimlerChrysler Research
{wedel,schoenemann,brox,dcremers}@cs.uni-bonn.de

Abstract. Autonomous collision avoidance in vehicles requires an accurate separation of obstacles from the background, particularly near the focus of expansion. In this paper, we present a technique for fast segmentation of stationary obstacles from video recorded by a single camera that is installed in a moving vehicle. The input image is divided into three motion segments consisting of the ground plane, the background, and the obstacle. This constrained scenario allows for good initial estimates of the motion models, which are iteratively refined during segmentation. The horizon is known due to the camera setup. The remaining binary partitioning problem is solved by a graph cut on the motion-compensated difference images.

Obstacle segmentation in realistic scenes with a monocular camera setup has not been feasible up to now. Our experimental evaluation shows that the proposed approach leads to fast and accurate obstacle segmentation and distance estimation without prior knowledge about the size, shape or base point of obstacles.

1 Introduction

Year by year, thousands of people die in car accidents. Many of those accidents could be avoided or alleviated by autonomous collision avoidance systems providing for faster and more adequate reaction of the driver. In this paper we propose a key component for an assistance system, namely a framework for segmenting stationary distant obstacles in the direction of the moving vehicle. See Fig. 1 for an example of a stationary obstacle in the vehicle corridor. Stationary objects pose a particular challenge. Moving objects can easily be detected by optical flow based methods or - in vehicle application - by radar. Accurate segmentation allows for the verification of obstacle hypotheses and enables the driver assistance system to decide whether there is enough space to drive around the obstacle.

Three aspects are of critical importance for such an obstacle segmentation system. Firstly, the segmentations must be generic in the sense that they cannot rely on specific assumptions regarding the color or shape of the obstacles. Secondly, it needs to provide reliable segmentations in particular when objects are still far from the driving vehicle, i.e. where the obstacle is close to the focus of expansion (FOE), thus leaving enough time to induce obstacle avoidance strategies. This is typically a challenge, because at such an early stage the obstacle covers only a small portion of the image and the relative pixel motion is very small [10]. Thirdly, a useful collision avoidance system requires the segmentations results in real-time.

F.A. Hamprecht, C. Schnörr, and B. Jähne (Eds.): DAGM 2007, LNCS 4713, pp. 264–273, 2007.

Fig. 1. Motion segmentation of a stationary obstacle in 36 m distance from monocular video. Notice the two cones, which are difficult to capture by means of their gray value.

In recent time, the graph cut has become very popular for fast computation of globally optimal solutions to binary partitioning problems [2,3,6]. The graph cut method gave rise to numerous interesting applications in computer vision. In [9], a stereo camera and ternary graph cuts are employed to separate a person in front of the camera from the background. In two successive works, the approach was modified to work also with monocular video by relying (predominantly) on the difference image of a moving person [5,13] in front of a static background. For our application, such approaches would not work as the entire scene is moving due to the strong ego-motion of the car. General motion segmentation with graph cuts, without a specific application in mind, has been suggested [1,12]. Mathematically, such unconstrained motion segmentation is a highly ill-posed problem. In addition to the partitioning also the motion fields in the regions have to be estimated. In contrast to segmentation based on difference images as used in [5] and [13], motion segmentation cannot be solved in a globally optimal manner anymore. The iteration of segmentation and motion estimation is likely to end up in unsatisfactory local minima.

It turns out that the obstacle segmentation task considered here actually does provide additional information and constraints. In the following, we will show which additional information is available and how it can be imposed in the graph cuts based segmentation scheme. Experimental results confirm that the integration of additional information will lead to reliable segmentations of obstacles from a driving vehicle.

2   Obstacle Segmentation with Graph Cut

The system is continuously fed with live gray scale video data $I : \Omega \times [0, \infty) \rightarrow \mathbb{R}$ represented as 2-D gray value fields $I_t(x, y)$ at time t and image points $\boldsymbol{x} = (x, y)^{\top}$ in camera coordinates. As soon as another frame becomes available, it is segmented into obstacle and non-obstacle regions, based on the last two frames and the previous segmentation. This is done by computing a binary labeling $L_t(\boldsymbol{x})$ of each pixel $\boldsymbol{x} = (x, y)^{\top}$ in a region of interest (ROI) $\Omega_s \subset \Omega$ of the image I_t at time t, such that

$$L_t(\boldsymbol{x}) = \begin{cases} 1 \text{ if } \boldsymbol{x} \text{ obstacle} \\ 0 \text{ otherwise.} \end{cases} \tag{1}$$

The ROI is the area around the focus of expansion, where potential obstacles in the driving corridor are located. Its size corresponds to the image size of mapped obstacles.

Fig. 2. Motion-compensated difference images. From left to right: original gray value input images and difference images for foreground (E_f) and background (E_b) based on the quadratic difference between the motion-compensated image I_{t-1} and image I_t after the last iteration. The camera translation was 1.9 m. H_f and H_b denote foreground and background motion.

Approximate obstacle distance estimates are given from an obstacle detection system, which will be described in Section 4.

Segmentation by grouping similar gray values is not sensible in our context because the gray value of different obstacles is not fixed and may be similar to the gray value of the street. We therefore base the labeling on motion information. The classical approach to segmentation minimizes an energy on the labeling of the form

$$E(L_t) = E_{Data}(L_t) + \alpha E_{Smooth}(L_t) . \tag{2}$$

2.1   WarpCut

In the following we show how to design the data term in Eq. 2 which is optimally suited for the segmentation of obstacles in the driving corridor of a moving vehicle. While traditionally the data term aims at segmenting the intensities [2] or the motion field [1,12], in this paper we propose to segment the warped image.

We assume that the scene is static and all image motion is caused by the camera installed in the moving vehicle. The camera motion is approximately known from odometric measurements of the vehicle. Due to the given scenario we impose the following assumptions:

1. The street is approximately planar. Hence, the image motion in this area is described by a homography H_s. The homography can be approximated from the known camera motion and the camera parameters.
2. Visible object points on distant obstacles have approximately the same depth. Applying the weak perspective camera model, the motion field in the obstacle region is affine, which can be expressed by another homography H_o.
3. Finally, the background region, i.e., the region above the horizon can be approximated as a plane at infinity, which leads to a third homography H_b.

Consequently, there are three regions, each with a different motion model. The separation of the obstacle region from the other two regions is done by the sought segmentation of the obstacle. The street and background region are separated a-priori by a horizontal line $y = y_{hor}$ that can be derived analytically from the camera parameters which leaves us with a binary partitioning problem.

The key idea of differentiating between obstacles and background is to penalize the difference between the current frame and motion-compensated (*warped*) previous frame. Separate motion predictions are computed for the obstacle and the non-obstacle regions. Notice that for the presented application this is much more sensible than the approaches described in [5,13] as it allows to drop the assumption of a static camera. The motion-compensated images are composed as follows:

$$I_{0,t-1}^{mc}(\boldsymbol{x}) = \begin{cases} I_{t-1}(H_b(\boldsymbol{x})) & y < y_{hor} \\ I_{t-1}(H_s(\boldsymbol{x})) & y \geq y_{hor} \end{cases}, \tag{3}$$

$$I_{1,t-1}^{mc}(\boldsymbol{x}) = I_{t-1}(H_o(\boldsymbol{x})) . \tag{4}$$

Values between grid points are determined by bilinear interpolation. Figure 2 shows the motion-compensated difference images of the introductory example in Figure 1 for $L_t = 1$ and $L_t = 0$, respectively. The data term evaluates the consistency between the warped previous image and the current image. It consists of the sum over the squared differences between both images:

$$E_{Data}(L_t) = \sum_{\boldsymbol{x} \in \Omega_s} (I_t(\boldsymbol{x}) - I_{L_t(\boldsymbol{x}),t-1}^{mc}(\boldsymbol{x}))^2 . \tag{5}$$

2.2 Spatio-temporal Regularity of the Labeling

Additionally to the data consistency term, our energy model incorporates assumptions on the spatial and temporal regularity of the labeling:

$$E_{Smooth} = E_{Spatial} + \beta E_{Temporal} . \tag{6}$$

The spatial regularity is measured by the geodesic length of the segmentation boundary. In particular, the boundary length is locally weighted by the gray value difference along the boundary. With $\mathcal{N}$ being the set of pairs of pixel neighbors (here we use an 8-neighborhood) the spatial regularity constraint reads

$$E_{Spatial}(L_t) = \frac{1}{2} \sum_{(p,q) \in \mathcal{N}} \frac{[L_t(p) \neq L_t(q)]}{\|p - q\|} \left(1 - \frac{|I_t(p) - I_t(q)|}{I_{max}}\right) \tag{7}$$

with I_{max} being the maximum possible gray value. Given two boundary pixels, the energy takes its maximum for equal gray values and decreases linearly.

In addition to spatial regularity, we impose temporal regularity of the labeling setting

$$E_{Temporal}(L_t) = \sum_{\boldsymbol{x} \in I_t} [L_t(\boldsymbol{x}) \neq L_{t-1}(\boldsymbol{x})] . \tag{8}$$

Two aspects are considered here: the spatial smoothness of the labeling and the size of the segments. For relatively small camera movement in stationary scenes one expects the current segmentation to be close to the most recent one. Additionally, we set the parameter β according to the validity of the most recent segmentation. As we explain in the next section, the scale of the foreground region is used to determine the obstacle distance. With known distance, segmentation size, and calibrated camera an obstacle size is deduced. β in our case can be seen as a switch. The parameter is set to zero for unrealistic obstacle size or distance from a given prior (for example in the beginning β is set to zero as no prior segmentation exists). However, β could be continuously changed if other post-processing algorithms are used to evaluate the current segmentation result.

The total energy can be minimized globally via the graph min cut method [6,4].

3   Adaptation of the Motion Fields

The segmentation above was solely based on pre-computed motion fields, derived from the approximate camera motion and assumptions on the planarity of the involved structures. In order to improve the segmentation, we propose to iteratively refine these motion fields. This is related to estimating the camera motion (ego-motion) from the image data [8] but aims at estimating the scene depth for static scenes. Based on the gray value constancy in 5, one can apply an incremental warping technique as originally proposed in [11] and later extended to non-translatory motion. This is detailed for our motion model in the following.

For the homographic motion model H_*, $* \in \{o, b, s\}$, a point x in a given frame is associated with the point

$$H_*(h, x) = \begin{pmatrix} \frac{h_{1,1} \cdot x + h_{1,2} \cdot y + h_{1,3}}{h_{3,1} \cdot x + h_{3,2} \cdot y + 1} \\[2mm] \frac{h_{2,1} \cdot x + h_{2,2} \cdot y + h_{2,3}}{h_{3,1} \cdot x + h_{3,2} \cdot y + 1} \end{pmatrix}$$

in the previous frame, where $h \in \mathbb{R}^8$ is a parameter vector. Given an estimate h^0 of these parameters, one can generate an estimate of the motion-compensated frames for the parameters $h^0 + \Delta h$:

$$I_{*,t-1}^{mc}(h^0 + \Delta h, x) \approx I_{t-1}(H_*(h^0, x)) + \nabla I_{t-1}(H_*(h^0, x)) \left. \frac{dH_*(\cdot, \cdot)}{dh} \right|_{x, h=h^0} \Delta h .$$

This is introduced into our objective function $E_{data}(\cdot)$

$$\sum_{x \in R_*} \left(I_t(x) - I_{*,t-1}^{mc} \left(h^0 + \Delta h, x \right) \right)^2$$

where the region R_* is given by all points associated with the respective model. When setting the derivative w.r.t. Δh to zero, one can solve for the update (with simplified notation):

$$\Delta h = \sum_{x \in R_*} \left(\frac{dH_*}{dh}(x)^\top \nabla I_{t-1}(x)^\top \nabla I_{t-1}(x) \frac{dH_*}{dh}(x) \right)^{-1}$$

$$\cdot \sum_{x \in R_*} \left(I_t(x - I_{*,t-1}^{mc}(h^0, x)) \nabla I_{t-1}(x) \frac{dH_*}{dh}(x) \right) .$$

Such warping schemes are also known as the Gauss-Newton method. In our case, they allow homography estimation without the knowledge of point-correspondences.

In contrast to the segmentation with fixed motion fields, the iteration of graph cuts and motion field adaptation usually does not result in a global optimum anymore. A prior for the homography parameters is given by the car odometer.

4 Initial Obstacle Detection and Depth Estimation

Our segmentation model is based on the restriction of the labeling domain to a region of interest around the focus of expansion. Moreover, the initial motion field in the obstacle region depends on the obstacle's distance to the camera. Although the detection of obstacles is not the focus of this paper, we briefly review a method that has recently been proposed in [14] and which we adopted in order to trigger the segmentation. Alternatively, one could use active sensors, such as radar or lidar, for this purpose.

Assume an image point x_t belonging to a static world point at $(X, Y, Z)^\top$. The camera translates by $(T_X, T_Y, T_Z)^\top$ in camera coordinates from frame I_t to I_{t+1}. Then the world point at $t + 1$ will be projected to

$$
\begin{aligned}
x_{t+1} &= \frac{f}{Z+T_Z} \begin{pmatrix} X + T_X \\ Y + T_Y \end{pmatrix} \\
&= \underbrace{\frac{Z}{Z + T_Z}}_{s} \underbrace{\frac{f}{Z} \begin{pmatrix} X \\ Y \end{pmatrix}}_{x} + \frac{f}{Z+T_Z} \begin{pmatrix} T_X \\ T_Y \end{pmatrix} .
\end{aligned}
$$

Hence, the distance Z of the point can be inferred from the scaling s of x with respect to the focus of expansion. For obstacle detection, we track a number of points over multiple frames using the region tracker in [7]. Distance estimates at locations that are not consistent with the ground plane are considered as potential obstacle points. This way, stationary obstacles within 50 m are detected at interactive frame-rates. For a comparative test we refer to [14]. Given the location and distance of potential obstacle points allows to define the region of interest in which we compute the segmentation. The interest region is chosen large enough to capture obstacles up to a size of 10 m $\times$ 3 m.

In the same manner, one can derive an accurate depth estimate for the obstacle from the scaling of the obstacle region segmented by our approach. Such estimates are then used to verify the depth estimate from region tracking. Notice that the initial region tracking step can be replaced by other sensors such as radar. The segmentation is verified by comparing its distance estimate with the distance predicted by the region based tracker. If the deviation is smaller than 5%, the segmentation is considered trustworthy.

5   Results

We evaluated the method in some real world scenarios. For all the experiments we show in this section, the parameters have been kept fixed. In particular, we set $\alpha = I_{max}$ and $\beta = \frac{5}{I_{max}}$ with $I_{max} = 255$. The camera had a focal length of 8mm, which corresponds to approximately 800 pixels.

Fig. 3. Closeup of segmentation for an obstacle in 17 m distance. The middle image shows the warped foreground with the foreground energy. The right image shows the warped ground plane and according energy. Color warmth denotes higher gray value difference compared to the current image. Notice the correct segmentation across the shadow boundary and the incorrect segmentation of the traffic cone due to occlusion.

Figure 3 demonstrates the accuracy of the segmentation even in areas close to the base point of the obstacle. In these areas the motion model of the street is almost identical to the motion field of the obstacle. As the segmentation is based on differences between those models, the segmentation is much more sensitive to noise here. The correct segmentation even along the bottom of the car reveals the robustness of the overall method even in these critical areas. Another reason for inaccuracies are occlusions of the ground plane by the obstacle. The traffic cone, for instance, is not perfectly segmented due to this fact. Apart from occlusion artifacts, however, the segmentation result is very precise. Moreover, the algorithm runs at interactive frame rates of 5 fps including obstacle detection and segmentation.

Figure 4 shows another result for a scenario with two differently colored obstacles. The color of the gray car actually fits very well to large parts of the background region. Clearly, an intensity based segmentation with graph cuts, as shown in the Figure, is not appropriate here. On the other hand, the motion cues used in the proposed approach can segment the two obstacles very well, though they are still 53 m away. However, with the general motion segmentation approach the obstacles are not segmented from the background and, hence, distance and size estimates are not possible. The motion parallax (motion difference between ground plane and obstacle) decreases non-linearly with increasing distance. Thus, it is quite small in this case. Nevertheless, there is enough difference to outline the shape of the obstacles without implying any prior shape knowledge using our WarpCut algorithm.

The plots in Figure 5 show the size and distance estimates of the approaching obstacle from Figure 7 by means of segmentation. The ideal values are indicated by the straight lines. The estimates by the segmentation are very good. This emphasizes the

Fig. 4. Motion segmentation and distance estimation for different color obstacles in 53 m distance from monocular vision alone. The camera translation was 2.6 m between the frames. The *right plots* show the region of interest with motion segmentation (*top*) and gray value segmentation (*bottom*) for the same frames. Clearly, gray value segmentation is not suitable for the segmentation of different colored obstacles in scenes with arbitrary background.

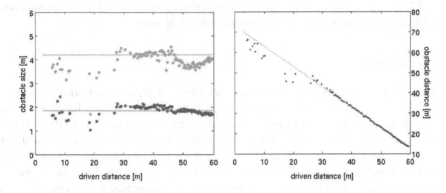

Fig. 5. Distance and obstacle size estimation for the example with one obstacle (ground truth: 4.19 m×1.83 m) in Figure 1

Fig. 6. Detection of a gap between obstacles. Taking the center of mass for the distance measurements results in one detected object. The gap between the two trucks is ignored.

precise segmentation of the obstacle throughout the video sequence, pictured with extracted frames in Figure 7.

Fig. 7. Segmentation and distance estimation from monocular video. The segmentation and distance estimation of the stationary obstacle proves to be precise throughout the video sequence. The early detection and localization of the obstacle leaves time to induce obstacle avoidance strategies.

Figure 6 shows that obstacle *segmentation* is more than just obstacle *detection*. The segmentation allows to detect gaps between obstacles and to measure the size of these gaps in order to decide whether it is possible to drive through this gap. Common radar sensors, for instance, would only consider the center of mass and detect a single object. This example demonstrates the relevance of segmentation for autonomous collision avoidance. Similar scenarios appear in robot navigation.

6   Conclusions

We presented a method for accurate stationary obstacle segmentation from motion in monocular video. In particular, we propose to obtain segmentations based on intensity differences of the current frame and motion-compensated versions of the previous frame. As spatially regularized segmentations are desired in a real-time context, energy minimization via graph cuts on such warped images proved to be very useful. For the motion segmentation to be robust, we exploited a number of assumptions that are reasonable in the context of obstacle segmentation. Experimental results confirmed the validity of these assumptions in several scenes and demonstrated the robust and accurate segmentation of obstacles. Moreover, we showed that from the scaling of the obstacle region in time, one can accurately estimate the obstacle's distance. Also conclusions about obstacle dimensions can be deduced.

References

1. Birchfield, S., Tomasi, C.: Multiway cut for stereo and motion with slanted surfaces. In: International Conference on Computer Vision, pp. 489–495 (1999)
2. Boykov, Y., Jolly, M.P.: Interactive graph cuts for optimal boundary & region segmentation of objects in n-d images. In: International Conference on Computer Vision, vol. 1, pp. 105–112 (2001)
3. Boykov, Y., Kolmogorov, V.: An experimental comparison of min-cut/max-flow algorithms for energy minimization in vision. In: Energy Minimization Methods in Computer Vision and Pattern Recognition, pp. 359–374 (2001)
4. Boykov, Y., Veksler, O., Zabih, R.: Fast approximate energy minimization via graph cuts. IEEE Transactions on Pattern Analysis and Machine Intelligence 23(11), 1222–1239 (2001)
5. Criminisi, A., Cross, G., Blake, A., Kolmogorov, V.: Bilayer segmentation of live video. In: IEEE Computer Society Conference on Computer Vision and Pattern Recognition, Washington, DC, USA, pp. 53–60. IEEE Computer Society Press, Los Alamitos (2006)

6. Greig, D., Porteous, B., Seheult, A.: Exact maximum a posteriori estimation for binary images. Royal Journal on Statistical Society 51(2), 271–279 (1989)
7. Hager, G., Belhumeur, P.: Efficient region tracking with parametric models of geometry and illumination. IEEE Transactions on Pattern Analysis and Machine Intelligence , 1025–1039 (1998)
8. Ke, Q., Kanade, T.: Transforming camera geometry to a virtual downward-looking camera: Robust ego-motion estimation and ground-layer detection. In: IEEE Computer Society Conference on Computer Vision and Pattern Recognition, pp. 390–397. IEEE Computer Society Press, Los Alamitos (2003)
9. Kolmogorov, V., Criminisi, A., Blake, A., Cross, G., Rother, C.: Bi-layer segmentation of binocular stereo video. In: IEEE Computer Society Conference on Computer Vision and Pattern Recognition, pp. 407–417. IEEE Computer Society Press, Los Alamitos (2005)
10. Longuet-Higgins, H., Prazdny, K.: The interpretation of a moving retinal image. Proceedings of the Royal Society of London, Biological Sciences, Series B, vol. 208, pp. 385–397 (1980)
11. Lucas, B.D., Kanade, T.: An iterative image registration technique with an application to stereo vision. In: Proceedings of the 7th International Joint Conference on Artificial Intelligence, Vancouver, pp. 674–679 (1981)
12. Schoenemann, T., Cremers, D.: Near real-time motion segmentation using graph cuts. In: Franke, K., Müller, K.-R., Nickolay, B., Schäfer, R. (eds.) Pattern Recognition. LNCS, vol. 4174, pp. 455–464. Springer, Heidelberg (2006)
13. Sun, J., Zhang, W., Tang, X., Shum, H.-Y.: Background cut. In: Leonardis, A., Bischof, H., Pinz, A. (eds.) ECCV 2006. LNCS, vol. 3952, pp. 628–641. Springer, Heidelberg (2006)
14. Wedel, A., Franke, U., Klappstein, J., Brox, T., Cremers, D.: Realtime depth estimation and obstacle detection from monocular video. In: Franke, K., Müller, K.-R., Nickolay, B., Schäfer, R. (eds.) Pattern Recognition. LNCS, vol. 4174, pp. 475–484. Springer, Heidelberg (2006)

Comparison of Adaptive Spatial Filters with Heuristic and Optimized Region of Interest for EEG Based Brain-Computer-Interfaces

Christian Liefhold[1], Moritz Grosse-Wentrup[1], Klaus Gramann[2,3], and Martin Buss[1]

[1] Institute of Automatic Control Engineering, Technische Universität München, 80333 München, Germany
christian.liefhold@mytum.de, moritz@tum.de, mb@tum.de
[2] Ludwig-Maximilians-Universität München, Department Psychology, 80802 München, Germany
[3] Swartz Center for Computational Neuroscience, Department for Neural Engineering, University of California, San Diego
gramann@psy.uni-muenchen.de

Abstract. Research on EEG based brain-computer-interfaces (BCIs) aims at steering devices by thought. Even for simple applications, BCIs require an extremely effective data processing to work properly because of the low signal-to-noise-ratio (SNR) of EEG signals. Spatial filtering is one successful preprocessing method, which extracts EEG components carrying the most relevant information. Unlike spatial filtering with Common Spatial Patterns (CSP), Adaptive Spatial Filtering (ASF) can be adapted to freely selectable regions of interest (ROI) and with this, artifacts can be actively suppressed. In this context, we compare the performance of ASF with ROIs selected using anatomical a-priori information and ASF with numerically optimized ROIs. Therefore, we introduce a method for data driven spatial filter adaptation and apply the achieved filters for classification of EEG data recorded during imaginary movements of the left and right hand of four subjects. The results show, that in the case of artifact-free datasets, ASFs with numerically optimized ROIs achieve classification rates of up to 97.7 % while ASFs with ROIs defined by anatomical heuristic stay at 93.7 % for the same data. Otherwise, with noisy datasets, the former brake down (66.7 %) while the latter meet 95.7 %.

1 Introduction

Steering wheel chairs, prostheses or technical instruments we use every day only by thoughts is the proximal goal of research in context with brain-computer-interfaces (BCIs). This is mainly beneficial for handicapped people or people suffering from the locked-in-syndrome. In the long term, it could additionally enrich the everyday life for all people.

The technical approach we use for "reading thoughts" consists in recognizing patterns of recorded electroencephalogram data (EEG) from different subjects.

F.A. Hamprecht, C. Schnörr, and B. Jähne (Eds.): DAGM 2007, LNCS 4713, pp. 274–283, 2007.
© Springer-Verlag Berlin Heidelberg 2007

For example, motor imagery leads to a decrease of the variance of the EEG in specific frequency bands over the motor cortex [1]. This event-related desynchronization (ERD) can be used to infer the intention of the user of the BCI [2]. The main problem in this context is the low signal-to-noise-ratio (SNR) of the recorded EEG. This has led to the development of spatial filters, extracting that component of the EEG that carries the most relevant information about the classification task. One of the most successful algorithms for spatial filtering in the context of BCIs is the Common Spatial Patterns (CSP) algorithm ([3], [4]). For two conditions (i.e., imaginary movement of right and left hand), it minimizes the variance of one dataset, while maximizing the variance of the other dataset. This leads to spatial filters that enable very good classification results in combination with linear classification algorithms. However, the CSP algorithm is not robust against artifacts like eye activity or mental states that are not induced by the imagination of the specific movement.

To overcome this disadvantage we use the Adaptive Spatial Filters (ASF) algorithm [5]. In ASF, it is presumed that the imagination of a specific movement causes a change of the EEG in one specific location of the cortex. Since it is well known that imaginary movements of a limb cause an ERD in that part of the motor cortex representing the specific limb [1], this a-priori knowledge can be used to design a spatial filter that attenuates all EEG activity not originating in this region of interest (ROI). With ASFs, we thus only pick out information originating from the desired sources, and eliminate unwanted EEG activity.

To obtain a good adaptation of the spatial filters to the desired EEG sources, it is necessary to estimate their true origins. This estimation can be based on heuristic a-priori knowledge or on source localization by solving data driven optimization problems. The former does not require time-consuming computation while the latter does. Hence, numerical optimization is not the choice for online capable BCIs. In this context, our intention is to analyze the performance of heuristic filter adaptation compared to numerically optimized filter adaptation. We expect that this will help to improve the performance of ASFs and show the achievable limits. More precisely, in [5] experiments with motor imagery of the left and right hand were performed. Two ASFs were trained with a-priori information about the approximate positions of the left and right motor cortex. These positions were heuristically assumed as spherical regions with 5 mm radius and midpoints located on a sphere around the center of the head with radius 6.6 cm, at the points, where radial projections of C3 and C4 cut this sphere. This assumption was based on anatomical knowledge about the human brain, but for sure, it does not exactly hold for all subjects. This raises the following question: *Is there a better way to define the regions of interest (ROI)?* Or more precise: *How far is the location of a numerically optimized ROI from the heuristic one?* By setting up a method to numerically optimize the position of the sources for preprocessed training data, and by comparing the achieved classification results with the results achieved using heuristically adapted spatial filters, we will give the answer to this question.

The structure of the paper is the following. In Section 2, the ASF algorithm is briefly reviewed and the numerical optimization of the ROI is described. In Section 3, we will apply heuristically adapted ASFs as well as numerically optimized ASFs on EEG data of four subjects, and compare the achieved classification results. A discussion of the different results and some prospects on future research will conclude the paper in Section 4.

2   Methods

2.1   Adaptive Spatial Filters

An adaptive spatial filter tries to minimize the signal variance of sources outside a region of interest, while leaving unchanged the signal variance of sources inside the ROI. It can be described by a filter vector $w \in \mathbb{R}^M$, with M the number of EEG electrodes. Applying it on a signal $x(t) \in \mathbb{R}^M$ returns the signal $y(t) \in \mathbb{R}$, caused by sources inside the ROI:

$$y(t) = w^T x(t). \tag{1}$$

The filter vector w can be found by

$$w^* = \underset{w}{\operatorname{argmax}}\{f(w)\} \text{ with } f(w) = \frac{w^T R_{\tilde{x}}(t) w}{w^T R_x(t) w}, \tag{2}$$

where $R_x(t)$ is the covariance matrix of measured EEG data while $R_{\tilde{x}}(t)$ denotes the covariance matrix of model generated EEG data, that shows only activity of sources originating in the ROI. For the latter, a four-shell spherical head model is used to compute the electrical field at a position $r_i \in \mathbb{R}^3$ (i.e., the EEG signal $\tilde{x}_i(t)$ of the i-th EEG electrode, $i = 1 \ldots M$, with M the number of EEG electrodes) caused by an electric dipole at position $r' \in \mathbb{R}^3$ [6]. The basic equation therefore is described by

$$\Phi(r_i, t) = \tilde{x}_i(t) = l(r_i, r')^T p(t). \tag{3}$$

$l(r_i, r') : \mathbb{R}^3 \times \mathbb{R}^3 \mapsto \mathbb{R}^3$ denotes the leadfield equations, describing the projection strength of a dipole at position r' with moment $p(t) \in \mathbb{R}^3$ on a position r_i outside the head with respect to conductive and geometric properties of the head model. Hence, with (3) we can compute the signal $\tilde{x}(t)$ of all EEG electrodes for a given dipole source and adapt a spatial filter to this dipole source by solving (2). This maximizes signal variance, which may seem contradictory to the goal of finding ERDs of an EEG-Signal, i.e., decreases of variance. But these steps are independent. At first we want to attenuate the variance of all EEG sources not within the ROI with an optimal spatial filter found by (2). Then we can proceed with the variance information originating within the ROI to vote for an ERD or not. The process of predefining a ROI can be carried out by applying a-priori information about cortex positions or by data driven, numerical optimization, i.e., source estimation.

2.2   Optimizing the Region of Interest

While in [5] the ROI was chosen heuristically, we will now address the question how the ROI can be optimized numerically. We will utilize source localization for this purpose, i.e., we will try to localize the origin of the ERD changes observed during motor imagery. The aim in source estimation is to find sources which give the best approximation of EEG data generated by a suitable model of EEG conduction, e.g., a dipole placed inside a four-shell head model, to real EEG data taken from an eligible training set. If a good aproximation is obtained, the estimated source locations should be quite close to the true source locations inside the human brain. Therefore, adapting the ASFs to the estimated sources should increase the achievable classification rate.

As we use the signal variance in each ROI as a classification paradigm, we look for a dipole that gives the best approximation of the variance of the measured EEG data. Hence, we perform source estimation using the variance of EEG data. The main steps for estimating the source locations consist in creating a training dataset and in constructing a suitable cost function.

Creation of the Training Dataset. We create a training dataset from EEG data measured during motor imagery of the left and right hand (four subjects, 150 trials of 10 s per condition, see chapter 3.1 or [5] for details of the experimental setup) using the data processing chain depicted in Fig. 1. At first, to reduce artifacts, we perform Independent Component Analysis (ICA) using the extended Infomax algorithm [7] as implemented in [8], and manually reject those components that are obviously induced by eye activity. All remaining components are reprojected onto the observation space. Then, the most reactive frequency band for each subject is determined heuristically. This is done by computing ERD/ERS changes for electrodes C3 and C4 situated over the motor cortex across all trials, and determining that frequency band that shows the highest ERD during motor imagery relative to a baseline during rest. Afterwards, a sixth-order butterworth bandpass (BP) filter is applied to the data, extracting the most reactive subject specific frequency band. Then, we take the same data intervals of motor imagery that are used for later classification as basis for our optimization (6.5 s per each condition and trial). Subsequently, the variance of the chosen interval is computed for each trial condition, imagination of left-hand-movement (IL) and imagination of right-hand-movement (IR), and averaged over all proper trials. At this point, we have two M-dimensional variance vectors for each subject: variance vector of condition IL and variance vector of condition IR. Now, as we want to extract the distinction of these two conditions, we build the difference between them. Only the negative outcomes of this difference will be used, because we are interested in the decrease of the variance (ERD). Positive outcomes are set to zero. Finally, the absolute values of the remaining variances are computed, since only absolute (positive) variances can be modeled. The result forms the data input for the optimization problem, which is described in the next subsection.

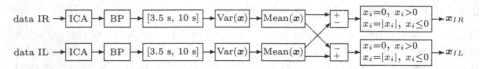

Fig. 1. Data processing chain to compute the training dataset for each subject. See text for more details.

Derivation of the Cost Function. Before we go to the next step of the dipole source estimation, let us assume the following:

- The superposition of many sources originating in each region of interest can be represented by only one single electric dipole.
- For each condition, a dipole can be characterized by a time-invariant dipole position vector r' and a dipole moment vector $p(t)$ with time-invariant orientation, each $\epsilon \, \mathbb{R}^3$.
- The EEG data is of zero mean (due to bandpass filtering) and of stationary variance during each training condition.

Now, we will derive a cost function $J(r', p) : \mathbb{R}^3 \times \mathbb{R}^3 \mapsto \mathbb{R}$. In general, the cost function should express the difference of the reconstructed signal variance and the signal variance of the training set. Our choice is

$$J[r', p(t)] = \| \, \sigma^2_{\boldsymbol{x}(t)} - \sigma^2_{\tilde{\boldsymbol{x}}(t)} \, \|^2_2 \qquad (4)$$

with $\sigma^2_{\boldsymbol{x}(t)}$ the variance of the training set data $x(t)$ and $\sigma^2_{\tilde{\boldsymbol{x}}(t)}$ the variance of the model generated data $\tilde{x}(t)$, each $\epsilon \, \mathbb{R}^M$. Now, let us consider the signal of one single EEG channel $x_i(t) \, \epsilon \, \mathbb{R}$. We can expand the difference of the variances by expressing the variance operators as sample variances (zero-mean assumption) such that

$$\sigma^2_{x_i[n]} - \sigma^2_{\tilde{x}_i[n]} = \frac{1}{2N} \sum_{n=-N}^{N} x_i[n]^2 - \frac{1}{2N} \sum_{n=-N}^{N} \tilde{x}_i[n]^2, \qquad (5)$$

where the variances are computed over $2N$ data samples. According to (3), the model generated signal $\tilde{x}_i(t)$ of the i-th EEG electrode can be written as

$$\tilde{x}_i[n] = l(r_i, r')^T \, p[n] \qquad (6)$$

which is the dot product of the leadfield equations and the dipole moment vector $p[n] \, \epsilon \, \mathbb{R}^{3 \times 1}$. With (6), we can rewrite the model built signal variance to

$$\sigma^2_{\tilde{x}_i[n]} = \frac{1}{2N} \sum_{n=-N}^{N} [l(r_i, r')^T \, p[n]]^2. \qquad (7)$$

Now, we express the dipole moment vector $p[n]$ by an amplitude $s[n] \in \mathbb{R}$ and a normalized moment $\tilde{p} \in \mathbb{R}^{3 \times 1}$, which is independent of n due to our assumptions (time-invariant orientation):

$$p[n] = \frac{p[n]}{\|p[n]\|_2} s[n] = \tilde{p}\, s[n]. \tag{8}$$

We further get

$$\sigma^2_{\tilde{x}_i[n]} = \frac{1}{2N} \sum_{n=-N}^{N} [l(r_i, r')^T \tilde{p}]^2\, s[n]^2. \tag{9}$$

The normalized moment vector $\tilde{p}$ is completely determined by two angles, which are denoted as θ and φ in the following . We can merge together all the nonlinearly influencing variables into a function $g(r, r', \theta, \varphi) : \mathbb{R}^3 \times \mathbb{R}^3 \times \mathbb{R} \times \mathbb{R} \mapsto \mathbb{R}$ and write (9) as

$$\sigma^2_{\tilde{x}_i[n]} = g(r_i, r', \theta, \varphi)^2\, \frac{1}{2N} \sum_{n=-N}^{N} s[n]^2 = g(r_i, r', \theta, \varphi)^2\, \sigma^2_s. \tag{10}$$

The second equation sign holds, as we assumed the signal variance to be stationary for one training condition (σ^2_s denotes the variance of $s[n]$). Now, let's consider all available EEG channels. We can construct a M-dimensional variance vector $\sigma^2_{\tilde{x}[n]}$ by just stacking all M components on top of each other, which results in

$$\sigma^2_{\tilde{x}[n]} = \begin{pmatrix} g(r_1, r', \theta, \varphi)^2\, \sigma^2_s \\ \vdots \\ g(r_i, r', \theta, \varphi)^2\, \sigma^2_s \\ \vdots \\ g(r_M, r', \theta, \varphi)^2\, \sigma^2_s \end{pmatrix} = \mathrm{diag}\{gg^T\}\, \sigma^2_s \tag{11}$$

with $g = g(r', \theta, \varphi) : \mathbb{R}^3 \times \mathbb{R} \times \mathbb{R} \mapsto \mathbb{R}^M$. As the electrode positions $r_1, ..., r_M$ are well known, they are not mentioned as arguments of g. Then, the final cost function yields to

$$J(r', p) = J(r', \theta, \varphi, \sigma^2_s) = \left\| \frac{1}{2N} \mathrm{diag}\{XX^T\} - \mathrm{diag}\{gg^T\}\sigma^2_s \right\|^2_2 \tag{12}$$

with $X \in \mathbb{R}^{M \times 2N}$ the data sample matrix, containing $2N$ data samples of all M EEG channels. Now, an inequality constraint for this cost function is necessary, because we are only interested in sources located inside the brain (i.e., the innermost sphere of the head model). Hence, our optimization problem can be expressed by

$$\min_{r', \theta, \varphi, \sigma^2_s} \{J(r', \theta, \varphi, \sigma^2_s)\} \quad \text{s. t.} \quad \|r'\|_2 \leq R \tag{13}$$

with $R \in \mathbb{R}$ the radius of the innermost head model sphere. If this optimization problem is numerically solved for a given training dataset, we retrieve an optimized dipole position r'_{opt} and optimized moment parameters $\theta_{opt}, \varphi_{opt}, \sigma^2_{s,opt}$.

The optimization problem (13) is solved using sequential quadratic programming as implemented in the Matlab optimization toolbox. To avoid getting stuck in local minima, an equally with 4 cm spaced, three-dimensional grid of start vectors $r'_{0,k}$ ($k = 1 \ldots K$, with $K = 32$ the number of grid points) is processed to find the best global start vector. For each grid point k, optimal moment parameters are computed by minimizing the cost function $J(r' = r'_{0,k}, \theta, \varphi, \sigma_s^2)$. We also perform the optimization under the constraint of radially oriented dipole moments:

$$\min_{r',\theta,\varphi,\sigma_s^2} \{J(r',\theta,\varphi,\sigma_s^2)\} \quad \text{s. t.} \quad \|r'\|_2 \leq R \tag{14}$$

$$\begin{pmatrix} \sin(\theta)\cos(\varphi) \\ \sin(\theta)\sin(\varphi) \\ \cos(\theta) \end{pmatrix} = c\, r'$$

with $c \in \mathbb{R}$. This constraint is due to the fact that the cortical columns in the motor cortex are usually oriented radially to the surface of the cortex [9].

Based on the optimized position of the electric dipole, we create the ROI by placing a spherical dipole grid with radius 5 mm around the midpoint r'_{opt}, while ensuring that no dipole lies outside the innermost sphere of the head model. The moment of each grid dipole is determined by either the optimized moment parameters in the case of unconstrained dipole orientation (13), or by the radial constraint in the case of the radially constrained optimization problem (14).

3   Results

In this chapter, we will briefly describe the setup of the experiment that delivered the EEG data used for the comparison of heuristically and numerically adapted spatial filters. More detailed information can be found in [5]. Afterwards, we will present the classification results achieved with each of the two different adaptation methods.

3.1   Experimental Setup

Four male subjects (S1, S2, S3, S4) took part in the experiment. They were 26, 30, 27 and 24 years old. Wearing an EEG cap with 128 electrodes, the subjects had to perform imaginary movements of the right and left hand, according to the direction of an arrow projected on a screen. The experiment was divided into 300 trials, each of 10 s length. The presentation of the arrow started at 3 s after the beginning of the actual trial and ended with the beginning of the next trial. The pointing direction of the arrow was selected from a list, created by randomizing 150 left directions and 150 right directions. In the first 3 s of each trial, a fixation cross replaced the arrow. The EEG data of each subject was recorded with 500 Hz sampling frequency using a common average reference.

3.2   Experimental Results

Per subject, we performed a heuristic as well as a numerical spatial filter adaptation as described in the methods sections. The resulting ASFs were then applied on two frequency bands of the EEG data. The first frequency band was found during the numerical optimization (see 2.2) while the second frequency band has been fixed between 20 Hz and 30 Hz, as ERD related to motor imagery can also be observed for these frequencies. Then, we computed the variance for each spatially filtered signal within 3.5 s and 10 s of each trial. This delivered a four-dimensional feature vector for each kind of filter and each trial, whereas two dimensions represent the activity in the ROI for the condition IR per spectral band and the other dimensions the activity in the ROI for the condition IL per spectral band. These feature vectors were then classified by using leave-one-out cross validation with Fisher Linear Discriminant Analysis [10].

The results of the classification are listed in Tab. 1. For the subjects S2 and S3, numerical optimization enhanced the classification rate according to our expectation from 81.0 % to 85.7 % and from 93.7 % up to 97.7 %. For the other subjects, a-priori classification still achieved the best classification results. The ROIs of the subjects S2 and S3 (radial constraint), for which numerical optimization improved the classification results, differ from the heuristically set ROIs with 2.38 cm (S2, IL), 1.56 cm (S2, IR), 1.65 cm (S3, IL) and 1.97 cm (S3, IR).

Table 1. Classification results achieved with heuristically and numerically optimized spatial filters for subjects 1-4

Subject	Frequency band 1	heuristic ASF	numerically optimized ASF	
			unconstrained	radial constraint
1	17 − 18 Hz	54.3 %	48.3 %	52.7 %
2	12 − 14 Hz	81.0 %	83.7 %	85.7 %
3	12 − 14 Hz	93.7 %	96.5 %	97.7 %
4	12 − 14 Hz	95.7 %	52.0 %	66.7 %

4   Discussion

Considering only numerically optimized filters, the adaptation using radially constrained dipoles delivered better classification results than adaptation with unconstrained dipole orientations. This may be due to a higher artifact resistance of the constrained optimization problem. This property becomes clearly visible by comparing the variance topographies of subject S3 shown in Fig. 2. Using unconstrained numerical adaptation (Fig. 2, [b]), the model built EEG variance reproduces both, the activity of the motor cortex and the artifacts observed in the region of the occipital lobe. This does not happen with a radially constrained dipole (Fig. 2, [c]).

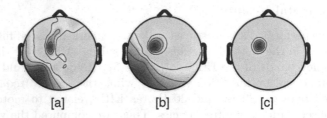

Fig. 2. Variance topographies of subject S3 and condition IR, computed from measured EEG data [a], from unconstrained dipole modeled data [b], and from radial constrained dipole modeled data [c]

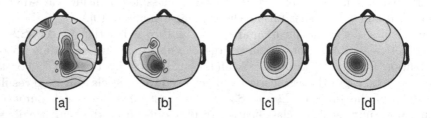

Fig. 3. Variance topographies of subject S4, computed from measured EEG data for IL [a], IR [b] and from model built data variance for IL [c], IR [d]

The collapse of the numerical methods for the data of subject S1 can be explained by the in principle poorly classifiable data set. It shows up many artifacts. Hence, a data driven approach to feature extraction must lead to worse results than one which is strictly independent of training data. The heuristic approach ignores artifacts and extracts the existing classifiable information that corresponds to the assumptions made. The poor classification rate in the case of numerically optimized filter adaptation for subject S4 might be surprising, as the result with a heuristically adapted spatial filter constitutes 95.7 %. But if we take a look at the measured EEG variance of this subject (Fig. 3), the reason becomes evident: There exists a second significant activation region for each condition (IL, IR), which is situated over the parietal cortex. This observation suggests that, contrary to most subjects, subject S4 recruits motor as well as parietal areas for motor imagery. The numerical filter adaptation method introduced in this paper is not able to handle such an occurrence, as we assumed only one activation region for each trial condition. Future work in this context should extend this method, to enable it to adapt to more than one activation region.

In summary, it was shown that numerical optimization of the ROI of an ASF can enhance the quality of the extracted features and thus lead to better classificaton results. This increase in classification accuracy however is not significant and requires an almost artifact-free data set. Furthermore, for those two subjects that showed an improvement in classification accuracy, the centers of the heuristically chosen and numerically optimized ROIs differed on average by 1.89 cm with an average improvement in classification accurcay of 4.35 %. This suggests that mispositioning of the ROI by several centimeters only results in moderate decreases of classification accuracy.

We thus conclude that numerical optimization of the ROI of ASFs is a viable option if artifact-free training data is available, and very high classification accuracies are desired. However, heuristic positioning of the ROI achieves classification accuracies close to those obtainable by numerical optimization of the ROI without the lack of robustness associated with data driven optimization techniques.

References

1. Pfurtscheller, G., Lopes, F.H.: Event-related EEG/MEG synchronization and desynchronization: basic principles. Clinical Neurophysiology 110, 1842–1857 (1999)
2. Pfurtscheller, G., Neuper, C., Flotzinger, D., Pregenzer, M.: EEG-based discrimination between imagination of right and left hand movement. Electroencephalography and Clinical Neurophysiology 103, 642–651 (1997)
3. Ramoser, H., Mueller-Gerking, J., Pfurtscheller, G.: Optimal spatial filtering of single trial EEG during imagined hand movement. IEEE Transactions on Rehabilitation Engineering 8(4), 441–446 (2000)
4. Blanchard, G., Blankertz, G.: BCI competition 2003 - data set IIa: Spatial patterns of self-controlled brain rythm modulations. IEEE Transactions on Biomedical Engineering 51(6), 1062–1066 (2004)
5. Grosse-Wentrup, M., Gramann, K., Buss, M.: Adaptive spatial filters with predefined region of interest for EEG based brain-computer-interfaces. In: Schölkopf, B., Platt, J., Hoffman, T. (eds.) Advances in Neural Information Processing Systems 19, MIT Press, Cambridge, MA (2007)
6. Cuffin, B.N., Cohen, D.: Comparison of the magnetoencephalogram and electroencephalogram. Electroencephalography and Clinical Neurophysiology 47(2), 132–146 (1979)
7. Lee, T.W., Girolami, M., Sejnowski, T.J.: Independent component analysis using an extended infomax algorithm for mixed subgaussian and supergaussian sources. Neural Computation 11, 417–441 (1999)
8. Delorme, A., Makeig, S.: EEGlab: an open source toolbox for analysis of singletrial EEG dynamics including independent component analysis. Journal of Neuroscience Methods 134(1), 9–21 (2004)
9. Nunez, P.L., Shrinivasan, R.: Electric Fields of the Brain. In: The Neurophysics of EEG, 2nd edn., Oxford University Press, Oxford (2006)
10. Duda, R.O., Hart, P.E., Stork, D.G.: Pattern Classification, 2nd edn. Wiley, Chichester (2000)

High Accuracy Feature Detection for Camera Calibration: A Multi-steerable Approach

Matthias Mühlich and Til Aach

Lehrstuhl für Bildverarbeitung, RWTH Aachen University,
52056 Aachen, Germany
{matthias.muehlich,til.aach}@lfb.rwth-aachen.de

Abstract. We describe a technique to detect and localize features on checkerboard calibration charts with high accuracy. Our approach is based on a model representing the sought features by a multiplicative combination of two edge functions, which, to allow for perspective distortions, can be arbitrarily oriented.

First, candidate regions are identified by an eigenvalue analysis of the structure tensor. Within these regions, the sought checkerboard features are then detected by matched filtering. To efficiently account for the double-oriented nature of the sought features, we develop an extended version of steerable filters, viz., multi-steerable filters. The design of our filters is carried out by a Fourier series approximation. Multi-steerable filtering provides both the unknown orientations and the positions of the checkerboard features, the latter with pixel accuracy. In the last step, the feature positions are refined to subpixel accuracy by fitting a paraboloid. Rigorous comparisons show that our approach outperforms existing feature localization algorithms by a factor of about three.

1 Introduction

Accurate camera calibration is a basic prerequisite for many image processing and computer vision algorithms. Jean-Yves Bouguet's camera calibration toolbox (http://www.vision.caltech.edu/bouguetj/calib_doc/) [1,2] has become a de facto standard for this problem, mainly for three reasons: simple usage, high estimation quality and free availability as Matlab and C code. Additionally, its C version is part of the OpenCV library distributed by Intel.

Camera calibration from a set of M input images can be divided into two steps: first extract some feature points, for instance on a checkerboard grid, and then use these points to estimate internal and external camera parameters, see fig. 1. The second step is the actual calibration, where the camera model parameters are estimated. Recent papers focus on this part, e.g., by introducing advanced distortion models [3]. Here, however, we will improve the *first* step of the complete procedure. Evidently, the estimation quality of any calibration scheme can only be as accurate as the quality of the feature points which are used as input for the parameter estimation step.

Any type of camera calibration requires some visual features on a calibration object which can be detected in its images as robustly and accurately as possible.

F.A. Hamprecht, C. Schnörr, and B. Jähne (Eds.): DAGM 2007, LNCS 4713, pp. 284–293, 2007.

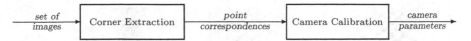

Fig. 1. Camera calibration from images is a two-step procedure: first, a set of point correspondences between world and image coordinates has to be extracted in the input images and then, these points are the input for a non-linear optimization of the sought camera parameters

Common choices for feature points are centers of gravity (of circles or squares), intersections of a line grid, corners, or patterns like the checkerboard pattern. However, centers of gravity are not invariant to perspective distortions, line-based approaches can lead to problems due to varying line thicknesses, and corner-based approaches suffer from biased estimates (see e.g. [4] for a discussion of fitting parametric models to corners). Checkerboard-based approaches, on the contrary, avoid localization bias due to their symmetry and have therefore become the most widely used choice for (2D) calibration patterns recently.

Bouguet's toolbox uses a sub-pixel extension of the famous Harris corner detector [5] which finds prominent regions in the following way: Let $f(x,y)$ denote an image signal and let $\mathbf{g} = \nabla f$ denote its gradient. Then

$$\mathbf{S} = \int_{\Omega} \mathbf{g}\mathbf{g}^{T} \, , \tag{1}$$

where Ω is an area of local integration, defines the so-called *structure tensor* [6]. Its two eigenvalues λ_1 and λ_2 characterize the image region centered at $\mathbf{x} = (x,y)^T$: two small eigenvalues indicate a homogeneous region, one small and one large eigenvalue indicate a linear feature and two large values finally denote features which usually allow exact localization. If the image is known to contain features such as corners or checkerboard crossings, one can safely assume that the corresponding regions can be found by looking for two large eigenvalues. Harris therefore introduced the following measurement for corner strength:

$$M_c = \lambda_1\lambda_2 - \kappa(\lambda_1 + \lambda_2)^2 \, . \tag{2}$$

The tuning parameter κ penalizes regions where the sum but not the product is high, i.e., it penalizes lines or edges. Reasonable values are in the range 0.1 ± 0.05.

Other advanced general feature detectors exist, for instance in the SIFT [7] algorithm, but for camera calibration, their use remains limited. In contrast to applications like motion detection, tracking, panorama stitching, 3D modelling or object recognition, we do not have to consider general objects – there is no need to extract every possible bit of information regardless of form or scale. Instead, we have a pretty good model of what the image of a *known* calibration pattern should look like. Our novel approach to corner detection is therefore based on designing filters specifically for images of the widely used checkerboard calibration patterns.

An existing signal model directly calls for a correlation-based feature detection approach, but what exactly is our signal model? Due to perspective distortions,

Fig. 2. A synthetic checkerboard image (left), the same image with added Gaussian noise (center; SNR = 10 dB), and a region of interest around a crossing (right). It can be seen that checkerboard crossings are characterized by *two* independent edges.

images of checkerboard crossings are black-and-white patterns characterized by *two* independently varying local orientations, see fig. 2, which generate a large family of possible patterns. For any correlation-based approach, this is problematic: Assuming that each angle shall be sampled in 5 degree steps, we would need $72^2/2 = 2592$ checkerboard templates (the 2 in the denominator is due to the symmetry of the checkerboard pattern). The resulting computational load would be absolutely prohibitive.

As a solution, we present a novel feature detection approach which is based on an extension of the concept of steerable filters [8] to *multi-steerability*. Steerable filters have been used in [9] to detect edges and lines. Unfortunately, these linear feature never allow an exact feature localization; only the component orthogonal to the orientation direction can be determined (*aperture problem*, [10]). Therefore, steerable filters have not been used in exact feature localization yet. In this paper, we will show how to extend the steerable filter concept to a multi-steerable detector which allows high precision feature localization.

2 Design of Double-Steerable Filters for Modelling Checkerboard Patterns

Let $f(\mathbf{x})$ denote an image within which we seek a feature which can be modelled as a template $f_0(\mathbf{x})$. Then filtering the image with a filter $h(\mathbf{x}) = f_0(-\mathbf{x})$ yields an output image measuring how strong the feature is present at each location $\mathbf{x}$. This principle is known as *matched filter* [11]. Its application to the detection of a *family* of features is, in general, computationally inefficient, but for one special class of filters, namely rotated versions of some given template, the *steerable filter* approach introduced by Freeman and Adelson in [8] offers a convenient solution: by limiting the class of possible (unrotated) templates to those templates which can be represented in polar coordinates in the form

$$h(r, \phi) = \sum_{p=-P}^{P} a_p(r) \exp(\mathrm{j}p\phi) , \qquad (3)$$

one can represent any rotated version of $h(r, \phi)$ as a linear combination of ν base filters, where the minimum number for ν is given as the number of non-zero

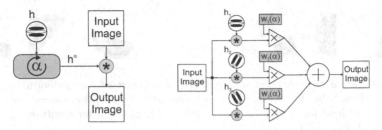

Fig. 3. The steerable filter concept: applying differently rotated filters for arbitrary rotation angles (left) is computationally expensive, while limiting oneself to a class of steerable filters allows a very fast implementation: compute some weights and sum up precomputed filter results

Fourier coefficients in (3). (Note that, in slight abuse of notation, we will always denote an image template as h, regardless whether it is represented in Cartesian or polar coordinates.) Following the notation of Freeman & Adelson and others, let us define a rotation operator: $h^\alpha(r, \phi) = h(r, \phi - \alpha)$. Different variants for designing steerable filters exist, but they all have in common that rotation can be expressed as linear combination of a set of base templates:

$$h^\alpha(r, \phi) = \sum_{a=1}^{\nu} w_a(\alpha)\, h_a(r, \phi)\,. \tag{4}$$

Here, h_a denote the set of base filters. Evidently, the whole dependency on the steering angle is encapsulated in the weight coefficients w_a. The linearity of steerable filters allows to exchange the order of filtering and summation, see fig. 3, thus allowing to precompute a set of filtered images and obtain the correlation between image and template for any given position and angle by a weighted sum of filtered images. Hence, the computational load for correlation-based feature detection is reduced considerably.

In [9], Jacob and Unser applied this *rotated matched filter* approach to the detection of edges and lines in images. Unfortunately, steerable filters are limited to features which are characterized by a *single* steering parameter, viz., the orientation angle of the linear feature. Perspectively distorted checkerboard patterns, however, are characterized by *two* independently varying orientations.

The key idea of our approach now is the following: *can we combine two edges in such a way that they represent a checkerboard and, furthermore, the result is steerable again – but now with two steering angles?* In mathematical form, this can be expressed as

$$h_{\text{check}}^{\alpha,\beta} = h_{\text{edge}}^\alpha \circ h_{\text{edge}}^\beta \tag{5}$$

where $\circ$ is some operator, and we now have to examine whether we can find a mathematical function that fulfills this requirement. Evidently, the sought operator must work for every point in the template individually, i.e.,

$$h_{\text{out}} = h_1 \circ h_2 \quad \Leftrightarrow \quad h_{\text{out}}(\mathbf{x}) = h_1(\mathbf{x}) \circ h_2(\mathbf{x}) \text{ for all } \mathbf{x} \in \Omega \tag{6}$$

Fig. 4. Creation of a checkerboard pattern as product of two individually rotated idealized edges. If black corresponds to -1 and white to 1, this construction principle does not only hold for $\alpha = 0°$ and $\beta = 90°$ (left), but also for *arbitrary* angles like $\alpha = 20°$ and $\beta = 130°$ (right).

where Ω is the size of the templates. The graphical representation in fig. 4 visualizes that the desired steering properties automatically follow if we 'only' find a mathematical representation for four equations:

white ∘ white = white   white ∘ black = black

black ∘ white = black   black ∘ black = white .

A solution is easily found by identifying white with 1, black with -1, and ∘ with (point-by-point) multiplication. Note also that these four equations show that the sought operator *must* be non-linear. Having defined the scaling of black and white, we now multiply two steerable filters:

$$h^\alpha(r,\phi) \cdot h^\beta(r,\phi) = \sum_{a=1}^{\nu} \sum_{b=1}^{\nu} \underbrace{w_a(\alpha) w_b(\beta)}_{w^*_{a,b}(\alpha,\beta)} \underbrace{h_a(r,\phi) \cdot h_b(r,\phi)}_{h^*_{a,b}(r,\phi)} \ . \tag{7}$$

The result can again be represented as a linear combination of base functions $h^*_{a,b}$ which can be computed as point-by-point products of the base functions for the standard steerable filter. In a similar way, the new weight coefficients $w^*_{a,b}$ are found as products of the individual weights; therefore, they now depend on *two* angles, i.e., we have thus introduced a novel *double-steerable* filter. Extension to *multi-steerability* is straightforward.

Generating checkerboard patterns with two arbitrary orientations from (5) now implies replacing idealized edges with *approximated steerable edge functions*. Different approaches for this problem exist: Jacob and Unser [9] used a linear combination of derivatives of the Gaussian function; this has the big advantage of always yielding Cartesian-separable filters. Other authors [12] are interested in *phase-invariant* behavior [13] which means that the filter response should not depend on the signal orthogonal to some orientation; most importantly, lines and edges should lead to the same energy of the filter response. To comply with our needs of multi-steerable edge function approximation, we will propose a novel design concept. This concept is based on the observation that an edge is polar-separable which directly allows a Fourier series expansion. We set

$$h(r,\phi) = q(r)\, h_{\text{ang}}(\phi) \tag{8}$$

with radial function

$$q(r) = \begin{cases} 1 & r \le r_{\max} \\ 0 & \text{else} \end{cases} \tag{9}$$

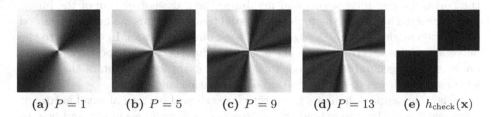

(a) $P = 1$ **(b)** $P = 5$ **(c)** $P = 9$ **(d)** $P = 13$ **(e)** $h_{\text{check}}(\mathbf{x})$

Fig. 5. Checkerboard patterns created by two steerable Fourier expansions of edge-functions for Fourier coefficients $p = 1, 3, \ldots, P$. The higher P is chosen, the better the steerable filter approximates the idealized template shown in (e). A radial weighting can be added if desired.

and idealized angular edge function

$$h_{\text{ang}}^{\text{ideal}}(\phi) = \begin{cases} 1 & 0 \leq \phi < \pi \\ -1 & -\pi \leq \phi < 0 \end{cases} . \tag{10}$$

Note that the radial function $q(r)$ can be designed separately since it does not influence steerability; the disc chosen in (9) is mainly used because of its simplicity. The Fourier approximation of (odd) order P to the angular function $h_{\text{ang}}^{\text{ideal}}(\phi)$ rotated by α then is

$$h_{\text{ang}}^{\alpha}(\phi) = \frac{4}{\pi} \sum_{p=1,3,\ldots}^{P} \frac{1}{p} \sin(p(\phi - \alpha)) . \tag{11}$$

Multiplying with radial function (9) yields the (single-)steerable template (8). This template has $P+1$ non-zero Fourier coefficients; therefore, we need $\nu = P+1$ base filters $h_a(r, \phi)$ which can be chosen exactly in the same way as in Freeman's paper: the approximated edge is rotated to $P+1$ equidistant angles in the interval $[0°, 180°)$. Consequently, the weights $w_a(\alpha)$ can be computed as in Freeman's work. One advantage of this Fourier approach (in comparison to other known steerable filter design concepts) is that increasing the approximation order P allows to increase the approximation quality at the price of higher computational complexity. Fig. 5 shows how the pattern converges to the idealized checkerboard when increasing P.

Having defined the checkerboard pattern as a double-steerable filter, we can now define the *principle of multiply rotated matched filtering*: A multi-oriented feature has M independent orientation angles $\phi_1, \ldots, \phi_M$ and is represented by a template $f_{\text{multi}}^{\phi_1,\ldots,\phi_M}(\mathbf{x})$. A measure of how strong this feature is present in an image $f(\mathbf{x})$ at a fixed position $\mathbf{x}_0$ is $B_{\max}(\mathbf{x}_0)$:

$$B_{\max}(\mathbf{x}_0) = \max_{\phi_1,\ldots,\phi_M} f \circledast f_{\text{check}}^{\phi_1,\ldots,\phi_M}\Big|_{\mathbf{x}=\mathbf{x}_0} = \max_{\phi_1,\ldots,\phi_M} f * h_{\text{check}}^{\phi_1,\ldots,\phi_M}\Big|_{\mathbf{x}=\mathbf{x}_0} \tag{12}$$

where $\circledast$ and $*$ denote correlation and convolution, respectively. In analogy to (single) rotated matched filtering, we define $h_{\text{multi}}^{\phi_1,\ldots,\phi_M}(\mathbf{x}) = f_{\text{multi}}^{\phi_1,\ldots,\phi_M}(-\mathbf{x})$ to be the corresponding filter kernel and maximize the cross-correlation of the image patch centered at $\mathbf{x}_0$ and the multiply rotated template, thus assigning estimated orientation angles $\hat{\phi}_1(\mathbf{x}_0), \ldots, \hat{\phi}_M(\mathbf{x}_0)$ to each image point $\mathbf{x}_0$. In contrast to the detection of linear structures in [9], we are not limited by the aperture problem anymore; this generalized approach also allows *exact* localization of the sought features in addition to the estimation of orientation angles.

So far, this approach allows to detect checkerboard pattern at pixel accuracy. Next, we discuss how to extend the approach to sub-pixel accuracy, and how to increase computational efficiency.

3   Finding Checkerboard Crossings with Sub-pixel Accuracy

Our algorithm consists of three steps: we first determine a list of candidate points, then apply our double-steerable filter (DSF) at these candidate positions to estimate the correlation strengths and, third, fit a paraboloid to each local maximum. The apex of this paraboloid is taken as feature location.

Our double-steerable filter makes correlation-based checkerboard crossing detection feasible, but nevertheless, the angle optimization in it remains the costly part of the procedure. To reduce the computational load, we therefore preprocess with the aim of applying the DSF only where crossings are likely to be found. Over the entire image, we compute the standard structure tensor $\mathbf{S}$, and subsequently only consider those points which are both sufficiently textured and do not represent linear structures, i.e., where the structure tensor exhibits *two* large eigenvalues. This can be tested using trace and determinant only, i.e., without computing eigenvalues:

$$\operatorname{tr}\mathbf{S} > t_1 \quad \text{and} \quad \frac{\det\mathbf{S}}{\operatorname{tr}\mathbf{S}} > t_2 . \tag{13}$$

Usually at most a few percent of all pixels qualify as candidate points, unless low resolution images or images with many checkerboard tiles are used. Only for the image points fulfilling these criteria, we compute the double-orientation structure tensor [14] (occluding model) and solve for two orientations. For every candidate point, these two orientations are then used as initial values for a Levenberg-Marquardt optimization of the two DSF angles α and β.

Having found the best fitting double steerable filter, we find the local maxima of the correlation and fit a paraboloid to the 9 correlation values in a 3×3-neighborhood around each local maximum. Its apex is taken as the final feature location. If not all 8 neighbors of a maximum at pixel resolution were classified as candidates before (unlikely, but it can happen), then some values are missing in the paraboloid fitting step. In such rare cases, the DSF is applied to the missing pixels before carrying out the sub-pixel fitting step.

We do not optimize for angles and crossing position simultaneously because it would require an interpolation step to generate a pseudo-continuous image function. On the other hand, the correlation values around the true sub-pixel maximum could be approximated extremely well with a second-order Taylor expansion, so fitting a paraboloid to the available correlation values at integer positions near maxima is mathematically justified – and also yields very good results.

4 Results

We tested our algorithm on both synthetic and real data. Experiments on synthetic data with known ground truth enable measuring the root mean square (RMS) error of the localization over varying signal-to-noise ratios (SNRs). This also allows a comparison to the corner finder from Bouguet's calibration toolbox.

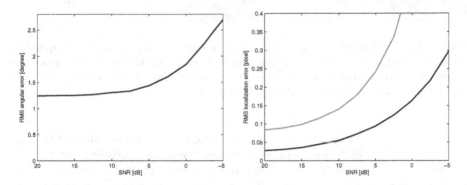

Fig. 6. Left: RMS angular error for our approach over varying SNR. Right: RMS localization error over SNR of our approach (dark) and Bouguet's corner finder (light).

Our experimental setup was as follows: for SNRs from −5 dB to 20 dB in steps of 2.5 dB using additive white Gaussian noise, we calculated 10 noisy realizations for each of three different synthetic input images, resulting in 30 realizations for each noise level. For each realization, we estimated the locations of the crossings in an 8 × 8 tiles checkerboard, i.e., 49 inner crossings. Subsequently, the RMS error was computed. Then the average RMS error of the 30 estimation results was plotted against the noise level. The same was done for Bouguet's corner finder. Here, we even gave Bouguet's corner finder an unfair advantage: it needs an initial value, which we always initialized with the true optimum. The results of both algorithms are shown in fig. 6. The pixel error of our approach is roughly *one third* of Bouguet's approach. For low noise levels, our algorithm achieves a localization accuracy of 0.028 pixels (Bouguet: 0.084). The accuracy of the angle estimates was approximately 1.25° for low and medium noise levels. This result was achieved with approximation order $P = 5$.

Apart from its increased accuracy and robustness, another advantage of our approach is that it needs neither initial values of approximate crossing positions nor assumptions such as small lens distortions. The design of our double-steerable filters makes searching the whole image for crossings feasible. One example,

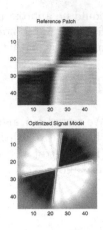

Fig. 7. Left: Estimated crossings in a calibration image taken with an Olympus "CF H-180 AL" endoscope. Right: Image patch and fitted signal model in the marked region of interest. Horizontal orientations are estimated with a slightly increased error because of interlacing artefacts (also visible in image patch).

where the semi-automatic corner finder of Bouguet fails, is the calibration image shown in fig. 7, which was acquired through a wide-angle endoscope; this image exhibits extreme distortions which make (semi-)automatic detection of the crossings difficult. For this 1100×900 pixel image, our approach written in pure Matlab code (i.e., no precompiled C parts) needs approximately one minute on a 3 GHz Dual Pentium computer. This is acceptable for calibration (and definitely less tedious than clicking on all crossings by hand). Note that even the crossings in the strongly distorted regions near the image border were found.

A small bias in the angle estimation can appear if the transition from black to white is not symmetric around the true edge position (overexposure, underexposure, non-linearities). However, due to the symmetry of the checkerboard pattern, it only rotates the estimated edges, but the positions of the crossings, which we are primarily interested in, are *not* affected by this bias.

5   Conclusion and Summary

We have developed a new approach to detect and localize the crossings in checkerboard pattern charts for camera calibration. Its basis is a model characterizing the sought features by multiplicatively combining two edges which are scaled to the range $[-1, 1]$. To allow for perspective distortions, these edges may exhibit arbitrary orientations. The key ingredient of our approach is a multisteerable filter algorithm, which permits efficient matched filtering. The filters are designed using a Fourier series expansion, thus allowing to determine the approximation quality to an ideal edge function by a single parameter. Multisteerable matched filtering then provides not only feature location, but also the orientations, which are determined by Levenberg-Marquard optimization. In our ongoing work, these angles will be used for, e.g.: (i) checking the plausibility of the detected crossings: the estimated orientations must be compatible to the orientations of neighboring crossings, (ii) exploiting additional information for the optimization of the camera parameters, (iii) speeding-up the detection by a sequential detection of crossings: one (or more) already detected crossings plus their orientations directly tell us where to look for the neighboring crossings.

Our technique exhibits two major advantages in comparison to existing approaches. Firstly, fully automatic corner extraction is possible – as we have shown, even in rather noisy conditions – because the whole image can be processed at low computational cost. Secondly, the availability of a signal model ensures much lower feature localization errors. In comparison to the corner finder in Bouguet's camera calibration toolbox, the localization RMSE of our approach is lower by a factor of three.

Matlab demonstration code for double-steerable filters can be downloaded from www.lfb.rwth-aachen.de/en/highlights/multi_steerable_filters.html.

References

1. Zhang, Z.: A flexible new technique for camera calibration. IEEE Trans. Pattern Analysis and Maschine Intelligence 22, 1330–1334 (2000)
2. Bouguet, J.Y.: Visual Methods for Three-Dimensional Modeling. PhD thesis (1999)
3. Kannala, J., Brandt, S.S.: A generic camera model and calibration method for conventional, wide-angle, and fish-eye lenses. IEEE Trans. Pattern Analysis and Machine Intelligence 28, 1335–1340 (2006)
4. Rohr, K.: Recognizing corners by fitting parametric models. International Journal of Computer Vision 9, 213–230 (1992)
5. Harris, C., Stephens, M.: A combined corner and edge detector. In: 4th Alvey Vision Conference, pp. 147–151 (1988)
6. Bigün, J., Granlund, G.H., Wiklund, J.: Multidimensional orientation estimation with applications to texture analysis and optical flow. IEEE Trans. Pattern Analysis and Machine Intelligence 13, 775–790 (1991)
7. Lowe, D.: Distinctive image features from scale-invariant keypoints. International Journal of Computer Vision 60, 91–110 (2004)
8. Freeman, W., Adelson, E.: The design and use of steerable filters. IEEE Trans. Pattern Analysis and Machine Intelligence 13, 891–906 (1991)
9. Jacob, M., Unser, M.: Design of steerable filters for feature detection using Canny-like criteria. IEEE Trans. Pattern Analysis and Machine Intelligence 26, 1007–1019 (2004)
10. Jähne, B.: Digital Image Processing, 6th edn. Springer, Heidelberg (2005)
11. Therrien, C.W.: Decision, Estimation and Classification: Introduction to Pattern Recognition and Related Topics. John Wiley and Sons, Chichester (1989)
12. Simoncelli, E., Farid, H.: Steerable wedge filters. In: Proc. Int. Conf. Computer Vision (1995)
13. Granlund, G., Knutsson, H.: Signal Processing for Computer Vision. Kluwer, Dordrecht (1995)
14. Aach, T., Mota, C., Stuke, I., Mühlich, M., Barth, E.: Analysis of superimposed oriented patterns. IEEE Trans. Image Processing 15, 3690–3700 (2006)

A Subiteration-Based Surface-Thinning Algorithm with a Period of Three

Kálmán Palágyi

Department of Image Processing and Computer Graphics,
University of Szeged, Hungary
palagyi@inf.u-szeged.hu

Abstract. Thinning on binary images is an iterative layer by layer erosion until only the "skeletons" of the objects are left. This paper presents an efficient parallel 3D surface–thinning algorithm. A three–subiteration strategy is proposed: the thinning operation is changed from iteration to iteration with a period of three according to the three deletion directions.

1 Introduction

Skeleton is a region–based shape feature that is extracted from binary image data. A very illustrative definition of the skeleton is given using the prairie–fire analogy: the object boundary is set on fire and the skeleton is formed by the loci where the fire fronts meet and quench each other [4]. In discrete spaces, the thinning process is a frequently used method for producing an approximation to the skeleton in a topology–preserving way [7]. It is based on digital simulation of the fire front propagation: border points of a binary object that satisfy certain topological and geometric constraints are deleted in iteration steps. The entire process is repeated until only the "skeleton" is left.

A simple point is a point whose deletion (or addition) does not alter the topology of the picture [10]. Sequential thinning algorithms delete simple points which are not end–points, since preserving end–points provides important information relative to the shape of the objects. Curve thinning (i.e. a thinning process for extracting medial line) preserves line end–points while surface thinning (i.e. a thinning process for extracting medial surface) does not delete surface end–points.

Parallel thinning algorithms delete a set of simple points simultaneously. A possible approach to preserve topology is to use subiteration–based approach [6]: the thinning operation is changed from iteration to iteration with a period of n ($n \geq 2$); each iteration of a period is then called a subiteration where only border points of certain kind can be deleted. Since there are six kinds of major directions in 3D pictures, 6–subiteration thinning algorithms were generally proposed [3,5,8,9,12,13,18,19]. Note, that 3–, 8–, and 12–subiteration algorithms were also developed [14,15,16].

In this paper, a non–conventional 3–subiteration surface thinning algorithm is proposed. Some experiments are made on synthetic objects and it is demonstrated that the new algorithm is computationally efficient.

F.A. Hamprecht, C. Schnörr, and B. Jähne (Eds.): DAGM 2007, LNCS 4713, pp. 294–303, 2007.

2   Basic Notions

Let p be a point in the 3D digital space $\mathbb{Z}^3$. Let us denote $N_j(p)$ (for $j = 6, 18, 26$) the set of points j–*adjacent* to point p (see Fig. 1a). The sequence of distinct points $\langle x_0, x_1, \ldots, x_n \rangle$ is a j–*path* of length $n \geq 0$ from point x_0 to point x_n in a non–empty set of points X if each point of the sequence is in X and x_i is j–adjacent to x_{i-1} for each $1 \leq i \leq n$. (Note that a single point is a j–path of length 0.) Two points are j–*connected* in the set X if there is a j–path in X between them. A set of points X is j–*connected* in the set of points $Y \supseteq X$ if any two points in X are j–connected in Y.

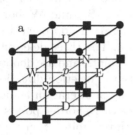 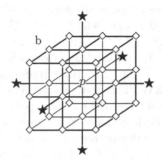

Fig. 1. The frequently used adjacencies in $\mathbb{Z}^3$ (a). The set $N_6(p)$ of the central point $p \in \mathbb{Z}^3$ contains the central point p and the 6 points marked U=$u(p)$, N=$n(p)$, E=$e(p)$, S=$s(p)$, W=$w(p)$, and D=$d(p)$. The set $N_{18}(p)$ contains the set $N_6(p)$ and the 12 points marked "■". The set $N_{26}(p)$ contains the set $N_{18}(p)$ and the 8 points marked "●". The special local neighbourhood of the proposed algorithm (b). The new value of a black point p depends on $N_{26}(p)$ (marked "◇") and six additional points (marked "★").

The *3D binary (m,n) digital picture* P is a quadruple $P = (\mathbb{Z}^3, m, n, B)$ [7]. Each element of $\mathbb{Z}^3$ is called a *point* of P. Each point in $B \subseteq \mathbb{Z}^3$ is called a *black point* and value 1 is assigned to it. Each point in $\mathbb{Z}^3 \backslash B$ is called a *white point* and value 0 is assigned to it. Adjacency m belongs to the black points and adjacency n belongs to the white points. A *black component* (or *object*) is a maximal m–connected set of points in B. A *white component* is a maximal n–connected set of points in $B \subseteq \mathbb{Z}^3$.

We are dealing with $(26, 6)$ pictures. It is assumed that any picture contains finitely many black points.

A black point is called *border point* in $(26, 6)$ pictures if it is 6–adjacent to at least one white point. A border point p is called **U**–*border point* if the point marked by U=$u(p)$ in Fig. 1a is white. We can define **N**–, **E**–, **S**–, **W**–, and **D**–border points in the same way. A black point p is called *interior point* if it is not border point (i.e. $u(p)$, $n(p)$, $e(p)$, $s(p)$, $w(p)$, and $d(p)$ are all black points). A black point is called *simple point* if its deletion does not alter the topology of the picture [7].

We propose a new surface thinning algorithm for extracting medial surfaces from 3D $(26, 6)$ pictures. The deletable points of the algorithm are border points of certain types and not *surface end–points* (i.e. which are not extremities of surfaces). The proposed algorithm uses the following characterization of the surface end–points: a black point is *surface end–point* in a picture if it is border point and it is not 6-adjacent to any interior point. Note, that the same characterization has been used by other authors [1,11].

3   The New Thinning Algorithm

Each conventional 6–subiteration 3D thinning algorithm uses the six deletion directions that can delete certain **U**–, **D**–, **N**–, **E**–, **S**–, and **W**–border points, respectively [3,5,8,9,12,13,18,19]. In our 3–subiteration approach, two kinds of border points can be deleted in each subiteration. The three deletion directions correspond to the three kinds of opposite pairs of points, and are denoted by **UD**, **NS**, and **EW**. The first subiteration assigned to the deletion direction **UD** can delete certain **U**– or **D**–border points; the second subiteration associated with the deletion direction **NS** attempt to delete **N**– or **S**–border points, and some **E**– or **W**–border points can be deleted by the third subiteration corresponding to the deletion direction **EW**. The proposed algorithm is given as follows:

> *Input:*   picture $P = (\mathbb{Z}^3, 26, 6, B)$
> *Output:* picture $P' = (\mathbb{Z}^3, 26, 6, B')$
>
> 3-subiteration_thinning(B, B')
> **begin**
> $B' = B$;
>   **repeat**
> $B' =$ deletion_from_UD(B');   /* *1st subiteration* */
> $B' =$ deletion_from_NS(B');   /* *2nd subiteration* */
> $B' =$ deletion_from_EW(B');   /* *3rd subiteration* */
>   **until** *no points are deleted*;
> **end.**

The new value of a black point depends on the values of $26 + 6 = 32$ additional points. The considered special neighbourhood is presented in Fig. 1b.

Deletable points in a subiteration are given by a set of matching templates. A black point is deletable if at least one template in the corresponding set of templates matches it.

The deletion rule corresponding to the first subiteration is given by the set of templates $T_{\mathbf{UD}}$ (see Fig. 2). Note that Fig. 2 shows only the ten base templates **U1–U5**, **D1–D5**. Additionally, all their rotations around the vertical axis belong to $T_{\mathbf{UD}}$, where the rotation angles are $90°$, $180°$, and $270°$.

It is easy to see that the complete $T_{\mathbf{UD}}$ contains $2 \cdot (1 + 4 + 4 + 2 + 4) = 30$ templates. This set of templates was constructed for deleting some simple points which are neither surface end–points nor extremities of surfaces. The deletable

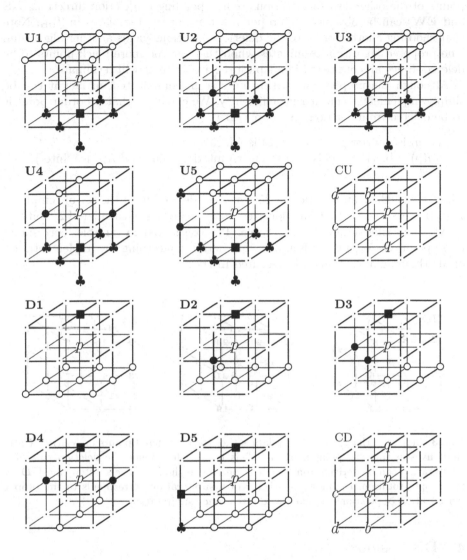

Fig. 2. Base templates **U1–U5**, **D1–D5** and their rotations around the vertical axis form the set of templates T_{UD} assigned to the deletion direction **UD**. Note, that a point p deleted by templates **D1–D5** and their rotated version must be 6–adjacent to at least one interior point.

Notations: each position marked "p", "●", "■", and "♣" matches a black point; each position marked "○" matches a white point; each "." ("don't care") matches either a black or a white point.

Configurations "CU" and "CD", and using different symbols for black template positions help us to prove the topological correctness of the algorithm.

points of the other two subiterations (corresponding to deletion directions **NS** and **EW**) can be obtained by proper rotations of the templates in T_{UD}. Note that choosing another order of the deletion directions yields another algorithm. The proposed algorithm terminates when there are no more black points to be deleted. Since all considered input pictures are finite, it will terminate.

Although the proposed algorithm may seem complicated, in fact it can be simply implemented and it runs efficiently. We can state that a border point is to be deleted from deletion direction **UD** if:

(($d(p)$ is interior point *and* $u(p)$ is white) *or*
($u(p)$ is black *and* p is 6–adjacent to interior point *and* $d(p)$ is white)
) *and* $f(x_0, x_1, \ldots, x_{24}) = 1$,

where f is a Boolean–function of 25 variables derived from the set of templates T_{UD}. It is easy to see, that function f can be given by a pre-calculated 2^{25} bit $\equiv 4$ Mbyte (unit time access) look-up-table. The considered 25 variables correspond to 25 points in $N_{26}(p)$ (see Fig. 3). More details concerning the implementation of 3D thinning algorithms are presented in [17].

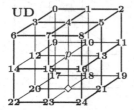 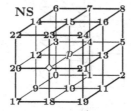 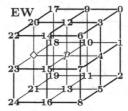

Fig. 3. Indices of the 25 Boolean variables (i.e. the considered points in $N_{26}(p)$). Note, that investigating the point marked "◇" is not needed. Since the deletion rule of a subiteration can be derived from the deletion rule of the reference subiteration **UD** by the proper rotation, the indexing scheme of a subiteration corresponds to the proper permutation of positions assigned to the reference subiteration.

4   Discussion

Thinning algorithms have to take care of the following four aspects:

1. forcing the "skeleton" to retain the topology of the original object (i.e. topology has to be preserved);
2. providing "shape preservation" (i.e. significant features of the original object are to be produced);
3. forcing the "skeleton" to be in its geometrically correct position (i.e. in the "middle" of the object);
4. producing "maximal" thinning (i.e. the desired "width" of the "skeleton" is one point).

The topological correctness (the 1st requirement) of the proposed algorithm is shown in Section 5.

Shape preservation (the 2nd requirement) is a fairly important requirement, too. For example, an object having same shape as letter "b" cannot be thinned to a circular shape. The aim of the thinning is not to produce the topological kernel [2] of an object: the thinning differs from shrinking. That is the reason why end–point criteria are used in thinning. It is easy to see that surface–end points are removed by none of our templates (see Fig. 2).

Geometrical correctness (the 3rd requirement) of the extracted skeleton is mostly achieved by the subiteration (multi–directional) thinning approach. An object is to be shrunk uniformly from each direction.

It is rather difficult to prove that the 4th requirement about maximal thinning is satisfied. Due to the used surface end–point criterion, the produced skeleton may contain 2–point thick surface patches [1,11]. It is easy to overcome this problem (e.g., by applying the final thinning step proposed by Arcelli et al. [1]).

Our algorithm has been tested on objects of different shapes. Here we present five examples (see Figs. 4–5).

Fig. 4. Two synthetic pictures containing a $140 \times 140 \times 50$ horse and a $45 \times 45 \times 45$ cube (top); and their skeletons produced by the proposed surface–thinning algorithm (bottom)

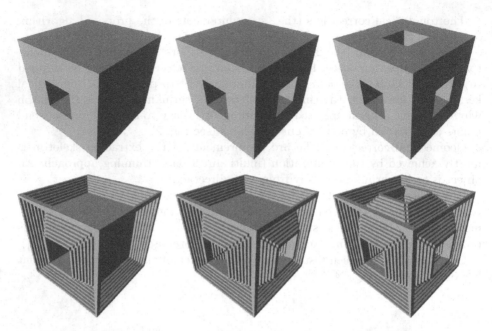

Fig. 5. Three synthetic pictures containing a 45 × 45 × 45 cube with one, two, and three hole(s), respectively (top); and their skeletons produced by the proposed surface–thinning algorithm (bottom)

The computation time of a thinning process depends on the complexity of an iteration step and the required number of iteration steps. The 3–subiteration 3D thinning strategy has been compared with other subiteration–based approaches with periods of 6, 8, or 12. It has been shown that the 3–subiteration approach requires the least number of iterations [16]. If we use unit time access look-up-tables (corresponding the deletion rules of the considered algorithms) and our efficient implemetation method [17] is applied, then 3–subiteration algorithms are the fastest subiteration–based ones. The efficiency of the proposed method is illustrated in Table 1.

Note, that the new algorithm differs greatly from the existing 3–subiteration surface–thinning algorithm [16] in its surface end-point characterization and deletion rule. While in the earlier work a black point p is a surface end-point if $u(p) = d(p) = 0$ or $n(p) = s(p) = 0$ or $e(p) = w(p) = 0$ (see Fig. 1a), in the new algorithm a black point is surface end–point if it is border point and it is not 6-adjacent to any interior point. In addition, the set of matching templates corresponding to a deletion rule of the earlier 3–subiteration surface–thinning algorithm contains only 26 templates [16] in contrast to the 30, used in this work. Consequently, the new and the earlier algorithms produce significantly different medial surfaces.

Table 1. Computation times for the considered five kinds of test pictures. The implemented surface–thinning algorithm was run under Linux on an Intel Pentium 4 CPU 2.80 GHz PC. (Note, that only the thinning itself was considered; reading the input volume and the 4 MB look-up-table, and writing the output image were not taken into account.).

test picture	size	number of object points	running time (sec.)
	$140 \times 140 \times 50$	92 534	0.146
	$45 \times 45 \times 45$	91 125	0.074
	$93 \times 93 \times 93$	804 357	0.377
	$141 \times 141 \times 141$	2 803 221	1.465
	$45 \times 45 \times 45$	81 000	0.033
	$93 \times 93 \times 93$	714 984	0.405
	$141 \times 141 \times 141$	2 491 752	1.493
	$45 \times 45 \times 45$	74 250	0.028
	$93 \times 93 \times 93$	655 402	0.343
	$141 \times 141 \times 141$	2 284 106	1.389
	$45 \times 45 \times 45$	67 500	0.029
	$93 \times 93 \times 93$	595 820	0.393
	$141 \times 141 \times 141$	2 076 460	1.271

5 Verification

The proposed 3–subiteration thinning algorithm is topology preserving for $(26, 6)$ pictures [7]. It is sufficient to prove that reduction operation given by the set of templates T_{UD} is topology preserving. If the first subiteration of the algorithm is topology preserving, then the other two ones are topology preserving as well, since rotation of the deletion templates do not alter their topological properties. Therefore, the proposed algorithm is topology preserving, since it is composed of topology preserving reductions.

We make use of the following result for $(26, 6)$ pictures:

Theorem 1. [10] *Black point p is simple in picture $(\mathbb{Z}^3, 26, 6, B)$ if and only if all of the following conditions hold:*

1. *the set $(B \backslash \{p\}) \cap N_{26}(p)$ contains exactly one 26–component; and*
2. *the set $(\mathbb{Z}^3 \backslash B) \cap N_6(p)$ is not empty and it is 6–connected in the set $(\mathbb{Z}^3 \backslash B) \cap N_{18}(p)$.*

Theorem 1 shows that the simplicity in $(26, 6)$ pictures is a local property; it can be decided in view of the $3 \times 3 \times 3$ neighbourhood of a given point.

We need to consider what is meant by topology preservation when a number of black points are deleted simultaneously. We use the following sufficient conditions for parallel reduction operations:

Theorem 2. [14] *Let F be a parallel reduction operation on $(26, 6)$ pictures. Then F is topology preserving, if for all pictures $P = (\mathbb{Z}^3, 26, 6, B)$, all of the following conditions hold:*

1. *for all points $p \in B$ that are deleted by F and for all sets $Q \subseteq (N_{18}(p) \backslash \{p\})$ $\cap B$ that are deleted by F, p is simple in the picture $(\mathbb{Z}^3, 26, 6, B \backslash Q)$; and*
2. *no black component contained entirely in a $2 \times 2 \times 2$ configuration in $\mathbb{Z}^3$ can be deleted completely by F.*

Unfortunately, there is no room to present the detailed proof concerning the topological correctness. Our proof is based on the following properties of the deletion rule of the first subiteration given by the set of templates T_{UD} (see Fig. 2):

1. Each template in T_{UD} deletes only simple points.
2. The simplicity of a deletable point p does not depend on the points that coincide with a template position marked "♣" and "·".
3. Black points that coincide with template positions marked "■" cannot be deleted by any template in T_{UD}.
4. Let us investigate the configuration "CU" (and its rotations around the vertical axis) and assume that central point p is black and it can be deleted by a template in **U1–U5** (or their rotations). Then the followings hold:
   - If point q is black, then it cannot be deleted by any template in T_{UD}.
   - If point a is black and it can be deleted by a template in T_{UD}, then point b is white.
   - If points a and c are black and they can be deleted by a template in T_{UD}, then point d is white.
5. Let us investigate the configuration "CD" (and its rotations around the vertical axis) and assume that central point p is black and it can be deleted by a template in **D1–D5** (or their rotations). Then the followings hold:
   - If point q is black, then it cannot be deleted by any template in T_{UD}.
   - If point a is black and it can be deleted by a template in T_{UD}, then point b is white.
   - If points a and c are black and they can be deleted by a template in T_{UD}, then point d is white.
6. If a black point p can be deleted by a template in T_{UD}, then p must be 6–adjacent at least one interior point. Hence p cannot be in a small object contained entirely in a $2 \times 2 \times 2$ configuration in $\mathbb{Z}^3$.

Condition 1 of Theorem 2 can be seen with the help of properties 1–5. Condition 2 of Theorem 2 is obvious by property 6. Therefore, the proposed algorithm is topology preserving for $(26, 6)$ pictures.

Acknowledgements

The author is grateful to Stina Svensson (Centre for Image Analysis, Swedish University of Agricultural Sciences, Uppsala, Sweden) for supplying the horse image data (see Fig. 4).

References

1. Arcelli, C., Sanniti di Baja, G., Serino, L.: New removal operators for surface skeletonization. In: Kuba, A., Nyúl, L.G., Palágyi, K. (eds.) DGCI 2006. LNCS, vol. 4245, pp. 555–566. Springer, Heidelberg (2006)
2. Bertrand, G., Aktouf, Z.: A 3D thinning algorithms using subfields. In: Proc. SPIE Conf. on Vision Geometry III, vol. 2356, pp. 113–124 (1994)
3. Bertrand, G.: A parallel thinning algorithm for medial surfaces. Pattern Recognition Letters 16, 979–986 (1995)
4. Blum, H.: A transformation for extracting new descriptors of shape. In: Models for the Perception of Speech and Visual Form, pp. 362–380. MIT Press, Cambridge (1967)
5. Gong, W.X., Bertrand, G.: A simple parallel 3D thinning algorithm. In: Proc. 10th Int. Conf. on Pattern Recognition, pp. 188–190 (1990)
6. Hall, R.W.: Parallel connectivity–preserving thinning algorithms. In: Kong, T.Y., Rosenfeld, A. (eds.) Topological algorithms for digital image processing, pp. 145–179. Elsevier Science, Amsterdam (1996)
7. Kong, T.Y., Rosenfeld, A.: Digital topology: Introduction and survey. Computer Vision, Graphics, and Image Processing 48, 357–393 (1989)
8. Lee, T., Kashyap, R.L., Chu, C.: Building skeleton models via 3–D medial surface/axis thinning algorithms. CVGIP: Graphical Models and Image Processing 56, 462–478 (1994)
9. Lohou, C., Bertrand, G.: A 3D 6-subiteration curve thinning algorithm based on P-simple points. Discrete Applied Mathematics 151, 198–228 (2005)
10. Malandain, G., Bertrand, G.: Fast characterization of 3D simple points. In: Proc. 11th IEEE Internat. Conf. on Pattern Recognition, pp. 232–235 (1992)
11. Manzanera, A., Bernard, T.M., Pretêux, F., Longuet, B.: Medial faces from a concise 3D thinning algorithm. In: Proc. 7th IEEE Internat. Conf. Computer Vision, ICCV'99, pp. 337–343 (1999)
12. Mukherjee, J., Das, P.P., Chatterjee, B.N.: On connectivity issues of ESPTA. Pattern Recognition Letters 11, 643–648 (1990)
13. Palágyi, K., Kuba, A.: A 3D 6–subiteration thinning algorithm for extracting medial lines. Pattern Recognition Letters 19, 613–627 (1998)
14. Palágyi, K., Kuba, A.: Directional 3D thinning using 8 subiterations. In: Bertrand, G., Couprie, M., Perroton, L. (eds.) DGCI 1999. LNCS, vol. 1568, pp. 325–336. Springer, Heidelberg (1999)
15. Palágyi, K., Kuba, A.: A parallel 3D 12–subiteration thinning algorithm. Graphical Models and Image Processing 61, 199–221 (1999)
16. Palágyi, K.: A 3-subiteration 3D thinning algorithm for extracting medial surfaces. Pattern Recognition Letters 23, 663–675 (2002)
17. Palágyi, K.: Efficient implementation of 3D thinning algorithms. In: Proc. 6th Conf. Hungarian Association for Image Processing and Pattern Recognition, pp. 266–274 (2007)
18. Tsao, Y.F., Fu, K.S.: A parallel thinning algorithm for 3–D pictures. Computer Graphics and Image Processing 17, 315–331 (1981)
19. Xie, W., Thompson, R.P., Perucchio, R.: A topology-preserving parallel 3D thinning algorithm for extracting the curve skeleton. Pattern Recognition 36, 1529–1544 (2003)

Holomorphic Filters for Object Detection

Marco Reisert, Olaf Ronneberger, and Hans Burkhardt

University of Freiburg, Computer Science Department,
79110 Freiburg i.Br., Germany
reisert@informatik.uni-freiburg.de

Abstract. It is well known that linear filters are not powerful enough for many low-level image processing tasks. But it is also very difficult to design robust non-linear filters that respond exclusively to features of interest and that are at the same time equivariant with respect to translation and rotation. This paper proposes a new class of rotation-equivariant non-linear filters that is based on the principle of group integration. These filters become efficiently computable by an iterative scheme based on repeated differentiation of products and summations of the intermediate results. Our experiments show that the proposed filter detects pollen porates with only half as many errors than alternative approaches, when high localization accuracy is required.

1 Introduction

In image processing the term 'filter' is mostly related to the special class of image transformations that is characterized by the fact that they are equivariant with respect to the group of translations. If $\mathcal{F}$ is an image transformation, then it is said to be equivariant with respect to a mathematical group $\mathcal{G}$, if $g\mathcal{F}(\mathbf{x}) = \mathcal{F}(g\mathbf{x})$ holds for all images $\mathbf{x}$ and all $g \in \mathcal{G}$. Here the expression $g\mathbf{x}$ denotes the action of the group on the image $\mathbf{x}$. If $\mathcal{F}$ is linear in $\mathbf{x}$ and $\mathcal{G}$ is the group of translations, it is just a convolution of the image with some kernel function known as the impulse response. For nonlinear image transformation this concept is generalized by the so called Volterra filters.

In this work we develop image transformations that are not only equivariant with respect to translations but also with respect to rotations in the image plane. That is, we consider the special Euclidean group of motion $SE(2)$ as the equivariance group. For linear filters the generalization is straight-forward, the only further restriction to an ordinary linear filter is that the impulse response has to be rotationally symmetric. For nonlinear transformation the answer is not quite as simple. We need some kind of generalization of Volterra's principle to $SE(2)$. It will turn out that the concept of group integration gives us such a tool by hand.

Complex calculus provides powerful mathematical concepts for the analysis of 2D rotation. For a fast and cheap computation of our filter we propose a special type of kernel function, which has its origin in complex calculus. Basically,

F.A. Hamprecht, C. Schnörr, and B. Jähne (Eds.): DAGM 2007, LNCS 4713, pp. 304–313, 2007.

it is a Gaussian-windowed holomorphic function. The Gaussian controls the locality and scale of the filter, while the holomorphic part determines the filter characteristics.

The paper is organized as follows: in the following subsection we give references to work that is related to ours. In Section 2 we present the holomorphic filter and show an efficient way of implementation together with a training scheme for the filter parameters. Section 3 presents experiments on microscopical images. The task is to detect so called porates, which are small pores on the surface of pollen grains.

1.1   Related Work

The idea of group integration (GI) to obtain invariants has its origin in classical invariant theory. In pattern recognition it is widely used to obtain invariants that can be used for indexing large image or shape databases for fast retrieval. For an introduction to GI in the field of pattern recognition see [2]. Applications for shape retrieval can be found, e.g., in [9] or [10]. We will use GI to project a nonlinear image transformation onto a rotation- and translation equivariant transformation (see [11]).

Volterra filters are nonlinear transformations that are equivariant with respect to translations. They are widely used in the signal processing community and also find applications in image processing tasks (e.g. [14,6]).

Steerable filters, introduced in [3], are a common tool in early vision and image analysis. For 2D rotations steerable filters get a very simple form in complex notation and are closely related to complex filters [12].

The generalized Hough transform (GHT) [1] is a major tool for the detection of arbitrary shapes. Many modern approaches [5,4] for object detection and recognition are based on this idea that local parts of the object cast votes for the putative center of the object. If the proposed filter algorithm is used in the context of object detection, it may be interpreted as some kind of voting procedure for the object center. This interpretation will later help us to design the scale parameters of the filter.

2   Holomorphic Filters

The image function is represented by a square integrable complex function defined on the complex plane $\mathbb{C}$. It is denoted by $\mathbf{x}$, an element of $L_2(\mathbb{C})$. The 'pixels' of $\mathbf{x}$, i.e. its function values are written in plain face $x(z) = (\mathbf{x})(z)$, where $z = u + \mathbf{i}v$ and (u, v) are the cartesian pixel coordinates. The complex conjugate is denoted by $\bar{z} = u - \mathbf{i}v$. The area measure in the complex plane is denoted by $dz\bar{z}$, which is in ordinary cartesian $dz\bar{z} = du\,dv$. For further introduction in complex analysis see, e.g., [13]. By calligraphic letters, e.g. $\mathcal{A}$, we denote image transformations, i.e. mappings from $L_2(\mathbb{C})$ into itself. The special Euclidean group usually acts on the image function by

$$(g\mathbf{x})(z) := x(e^{-\mathbf{i}\phi}(z - t)), \tag{1}$$

where ϕ is a rotation angle and t a translational shift. We use a small g for denoting the group representation to distinguish it formally from the naturally induced group action on an image transformation $\mathcal{A}$ which is given by

$$(\mathbf{T}_g\mathcal{A})[\mathbf{x}] := g\mathcal{A}[g^{-1}\mathbf{x}].$$

By this definition the fixpoint property $\mathbf{T}_g\mathcal{A} = \mathcal{A}$ is identical to the equivariance of the image transformation $\mathcal{A}[g\mathbf{x}] = g\mathcal{A}[\mathbf{x}]$.

The natural extension of a linear image transformation to a non-linear, homogeneous transformation of nth order is given by

$$(\mathcal{A}[\mathbf{x}])(z_0) = \int_{\mathbb{C}^n} x(z_1)\ldots x(z_n)a(z_0, z_1, \ldots, z_n)dz_1\bar{z}_1 \ldots dz_n\bar{z}_n$$

The function a, the kernel, completely describes the transformation. We propose to use kernels of the following form

$$a(z_0, \ldots, z_n) = h(z_0, \ldots, z_n)e^{-\sum_{k=0}^{n}\lambda_k|z_k|^2}$$

where $\lambda_k \in \mathbb{R}$ and h is anti-holomorphic in z_k for $k < p$ and holomorphic for $k \geq p$, i.e. we can write h as follows

$$h(z_0, z_1, \ldots, z_n) = \sum_{i_0,\ldots,i_n} \alpha_{i_0,\ldots,i_n}\, \bar{z}_0^{i_0} \ldots \bar{z}_{p-1}^{i_{p-1}} z_p^{i_p} \ldots z_n^{i_n}\,,$$

where the sum is $(n+1)$-fold with indices $i_k \geq 0$ that are bounded by some finite cutoff index m. The $\alpha_{i_0,\ldots,i_n} \in \mathbb{C}$ are some expansion coefficients which have to be learned. The natural parameter p will later help us to design the rotation equivariance condition more freely. The choice of the above kernel is driven by the following observation. In [8] Perona introduced the concept of computing optimal steerable approximations of certain image templates. He computed a bank of optimal filters for an elongated edge template. In fact, this bank is very similar to the kernels $z^i e^{-\lambda_0|z_0 - t|^2}$ for $i = 0, \ldots, n$. As edges are one of the most important image features it seems reasonable to choose such functions as the basis for our kernel function. Additionally, this type of kernel can be computed very quickly by the use of complex derivatives as we will see below.

To make the image transformation $\mathcal{A}$ equivariant with respect to the Euclidean motion we use the principle of group integration. We integrate the basis image transformation $\mathcal{A}$ over all possible group actions, i.e.

$$\mathcal{H}[\mathbf{x}] = \int_{SE(2)} (\mathbf{T}_g\mathcal{A})[\mathbf{x}]\, dg = \int_{SE(2)} g\mathcal{A}[g^{-1}\mathbf{x}]\, dg\,.$$

It is easy to show that, if $\mathcal{H}$ converges then it is a $SE(2)$-equivariant transformation. After inserting all the definitions from above we obtain

$$(\mathcal{H}[\mathbf{x}])(z_0) = \sum_{\substack{i_0+\ldots+i_{p-1}=\\ i_p+\ldots+i_n}} \alpha_{i_0,\ldots,i_n}(-1)^{i_0}\, \mathbf{g}_0^{(i_0)} * \left(\prod_{k=1}^{n}(\mathbf{x} * \mathbf{g}_k^{(i_k)})\right)\,, \qquad (2)$$

where $*$ denotes a convolution and $(\mathbf{g}_k^{(i)})(z) = \bar{z}^i e^{-\lambda_k |z|^2}$ for $k < p$ and $(\mathbf{g}_k^{(i)})(z) = z^i e^{-\lambda_k |z|^2}$ for $k \geq p$ (for a detailed derivation see [11]). At first several feature images $\mathbf{x} * \mathbf{g}_k^{(i)}$ are computed. They act like some kind of neighborhood descriptors of each pixel. The larger the Gaussians in $\mathbf{g}_k^{(i)}$ the larger the corresponding neighborhood. According to the constraint $i_0 + \ldots + i_{p-1} = i_p + \ldots + i_n$, all possible point-wise products of such descriptor images are computed. This constraint achieves the rotation equivariance of the filter. Note, that for $p = 0$ the condition is unsatisfiable. Finally, everything is summed up weighted by the parameters $\alpha_{i_0,\ldots,i_n}$.

2.1 Differential Formulation

The convolutions with the functions $\mathbf{g}_k^{(i)}$ are computationally expensive, even if we use a fast Fourier transform or a decomposition into separable filters to speed it up. We will use complex differential calculus to figure out a more efficient way. Actually the function $\mathbf{g}_k^{(i)}$ is proportional to the ith order complex derivative of a Gaussian $\mathbf{g}_k := \mathbf{g}_k^{(0)}$, that is

$$\frac{\partial}{\partial \bar{z}} \left(z^{(i-1)} e^{-\lambda_k |z|^2} \right) = -\lambda_k z^i e^{-\lambda_k |z|^2},$$

where the partial derivative with respect to $\bar{z}$ is defined by $\frac{\partial}{\partial \bar{z}} = \frac{1}{2}(\frac{\partial}{\partial x} + \mathbf{i}\frac{\partial}{\partial y})$. Correspondingly, the z-derivative is defined by $\frac{\partial}{\partial z} = \frac{1}{2}(\frac{\partial}{\partial x} - \mathbf{i}\frac{\partial}{\partial y})$. Inserting this relation into equation (2) and using the fact that convolutions and derivations commute on an unbounded domain gives

$$(\mathcal{H}[\mathbf{x}])(z) = \mathbf{g}_0 * \left(\sum_{i_0=0}^{m} \frac{\partial^{i_0}}{\partial z^{i_0}} \sum_{\substack{i_0 + \ldots + i_{p-1} = \\ i_p + \ldots + i_n}} \beta_{i_0,\ldots,i_n} \prod_{k=1}^{n} (\mathbf{x}_k^{(i_k)})(z) \right),$$

where we used the abbreviation $\mathbf{x}_k^{(i)} = \frac{\partial^i}{\partial z^i}(\mathbf{x} * \mathbf{g}_k)(z)$ for $k < p$ and $\mathbf{x}_k^{(i)} = \frac{\partial^i}{\partial \bar{z}^i}(\mathbf{x} * \mathbf{g}_k)(z)$ for $k \geq p$. The parameters $\beta_{i_0,\ldots,i_n}$ are related to the former by $\beta_{i_0,\ldots,i_n} := (-1)^{i_0} \alpha_{i_0,\ldots,i_n} \prod_{k=0}^{n}(-\lambda_k)^{-i_k}$. For a detailed derivation see [11]. We only have to compute $n + 1$ convolutions with Gaussians, the remaining steps are computations of derivatives which can be performed quickly by the use of finite difference schemes. The computation is sketched in Algorithm 1.

After the initial convolutions with the Gaussians, we have to compute m derivatives. By an iterative scheme the number of outer z-derivatives can be reduced to m. The number of multiplications is at most of order m^n. Of course there is much space for optimization by making use of intermediate results.

To further reduce the number of convolutions we assume that $\lambda_1 = \ldots = \lambda_n$. So, we have to compute the derivatives only for one blurred image $\mathbf{x}_1$. In Figure 1 a workflow graph of a filter with order $n = 2$ and $p = 1$ and $m = 3$ is shown. One can see that we only need to keep the m 'derivative'-images in memory. The rest can be accomplished in place.

Algorithm 1. Filter Algorithm $\mathbf{y} = \mathcal{H}[\mathbf{x}]$

Input: x
Output: y
1: Initialize filter output $\mathbf{y} := 0$
2: Convolve $\mathbf{x}_k := \mathbf{g}_k * \mathbf{x}$ for $k = 1, \dots, n$.
3: Compute derivatives $\mathbf{x}_k^{(i)}$ for $k = 1, \dots, n$ and $i = 1, \dots, m$.
4: **for** $i_0 = m : -1 : 1$ **do**
5:

$$\mathbf{y} := \mathbf{y} + \frac{\partial}{\partial z} \sum_{\substack{\sum i_0 + \dots + i_{p-1} = \\ i_p + \dots + i_n}} \beta_{i_0, \dots, i_n} \prod_{k=1}^{n} \mathbf{x}_k^{(i_k)}$$

6: **end for**
7: Let $\mathbf{y} := \mathbf{y} + \beta_{0, \dots, 0} \mathbf{x}_1$
8: Convolve $\mathbf{y} := \mathbf{g}_0 * \mathbf{y}$

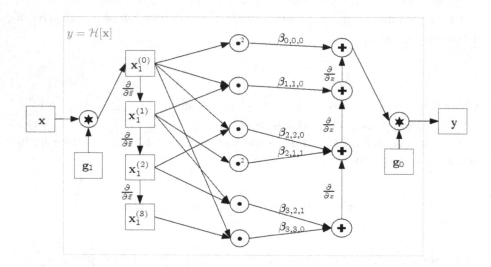

Fig. 1. The workflow of a second order-filter ($n = 2$, $p = 1$). The holomorphic function is expanded up to a degree of $m = 3$. The star '*' in the circle is indicating a convolution of the two incoming images. The dot '·' or the plus '+' indicate the point wise multiplications or addition of the incoming images, and a squared dot a multiplication of the input with itself. The labels at the arrows indicate a multiplication or differentiation, respectively.

2.2 The Training of the Filter Parameters

As the filter is linear in the parameters $\boldsymbol{\beta} = (\beta_{i_0, \dots, i_n})$ a simple linear regression scheme can be applied to adapt the parameters. For a given input image $\mathbf{x}$ and a desired output image $\mathbf{y}$ we have to minimize $J(\boldsymbol{\beta}) = ||\mathcal{H}_\beta[\mathbf{x}] - \mathbf{y}||^2$, which can be accomplished by solving the normal equations (for details see [11]).

3   Experiments

Before starting with the experiments let us clarify some details of the implementation. For speed reasons, we use the FFT to perform the initial and final convolutions (line 2 and line 8 in Algorithm 1). As already pointed out we want to approximate the differentiation (line 3 and 4) by a finite difference scheme. Higher order derivatives are obtained by multiple applications of the first order derivative. This approach is rather crude and inaccurate, because the approximation errors are accumulated by multiple applications of the rough approximation. But it helps to speed up the algorithm and for low orders the effect is not too hazardous. The important issue is that the errors behave 'isotropically', such that the rotation behavior and hence the rotation equivariance is not destroyed. In Figure 2 we try to illustrate the errors which occur when the expansion degree gets too high. We compute the function $\mathbf{g}_0^{(8)}$ in three different ways. First it is computed by the direct use of the formula $z^8 e^{-\lambda_0 |z|^2}$ in an 'accurate' way. Then we iteratively apply a first order finite difference operator Δ_1 or alternatively a second order operator Δ_2 on the plain Gaussian $\mathbf{g}_0^0$. The difference operators are given by

$$\Delta_1 = \begin{pmatrix} 0 & i & 0 \\ 1 & 0 & -1 \\ 0 & -i & 0 \end{pmatrix} \quad \Delta_2 = \begin{pmatrix} 0 & 0 & \frac{-i}{8} & 0 & 0 \\ 0 & 0 & i & 0 & 0 \\ \frac{-1}{8} & 1 & 0 & -1 & \frac{1}{8} \\ 0 & 0 & -i & 0 & 0 \\ 0 & 0 & \frac{i}{8} & 0 & 0 \end{pmatrix}.$$

Figure 2 shows that the approximations obviously produce artifacts around the origin. These artefact's are not compliant with the original rotation behavior anymore. The accurate version in Figure 2 a) has a rotation symmetry of degree 8, the error introduced by the first order scheme has a rotation symmetry of degree 4, i.e. the rotation equivariance of the filter is partially destroyed. One can see that the second order scheme substantially reduces this error, while doubling the computationally load. In the experiments we exclusively used the first-order approximations. We found that, despite the high errors even for low degrees, it makes no difference in practice whether we use Δ_1 or Δ_2 up to degrees of about 8.

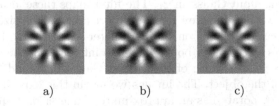

a)   b)   c)

Fig. 2. The real part of the function $\mathbf{g}_0^{(8)}$ in a 32×32 grid is shown. In image a) it is computed explicitly, in b) by a crude approximation with finite difference operator Δ_1 of first order. Image c) shows a approximation with second order finite differences by the use of Δ_2.

All experiments are performed on a *Pentium 4, 2.8GHz* with *MATLAB*. The time consuming parts are implemented in $C++$ using the *MEX*-interface.

3.1   Analyzing Pollen Grains

Analysis techniques for data acquired by microscopy typically demand for a rotation and translation invariant treatment. The microscopical images of particles like cells, pollen grains or spores have usually no predetermined orientation. In this experiment we use the holomorphic filter for the analysis of pollen grains.

Palynology, the study and analysis of pollen, is an interesting topic with very diverse applications like pollen-forecasts or in forensics. An important feature of certain types of pollen grain are the so called porates that are small pores on the surface of the grain. Their relative configuration is crucial for the determination of the species. We want to use the proposed filter to detect such porates. The input images are acquired by transmitted light microscopy, i.e. there may be varying illumination and contrast conditions. Such changes should not have an impact on the detection results. To make the filter invariant against additive change of the gray values the filter must not depend on zero degree $\mathbf{x}_1^{(0)}$ expressions because they carry the information about the local mean of the images. The contrast changes affect the images by a scaling of the gray values. As the local maxima of the filter response will serve as detection hypotheses, a gray scale change will not affect the detection results, because we use a homogeneous filter.

A third order filter ($n = 3$) with degree $m = 5$ is used. We choose $p = 2$, i.e. we search for monomes that fulfill $i_0 + i_1 = i_2 + i_3$. We found 55 monoms fulfilling this selection rule, while not violating the gray value invariance constraint from above. One example is $(i_0, i_1, i_2, i_3) = (4, 1, 3, 2)$. Besides, finding all non-redundant monoms under certain constraints is not a trivial task. The choice of λ_0 and $\lambda_1 = \lambda_2 = \lambda_3$ is motivated by interpreting the filter as some kind of generalized Hough transform [1]. Imagine that the object, in our case the porate, consists of several parts (just for imagination, the parts are actually the pixels of the object). Each part performs some kind of 'voting' for the putative center of the object. The part at position z is described by the derivatives $(\mathbf{x}_1^{(i)})(z)$, which serve as the local descriptors. The size of such hypothetical parts is determined by the width of the input Gaussian $\mathbf{g}_1$. The filter maps these local descriptors of the parts onto a 'voting' function for the object center. The size of the impact of the voting function depends on the parameter λ_0. It has to be chosen, such that also the parts at the outer border have an influence on the decision for the object center. Hence, the width of the output Gaussian should be at least half of the diameter of the object. The images we use in this experiment are of size about 200×200. A porate has an approximate diameter of 40 pixels (compare to Figure 3). So we used an output Gaussian with $\lambda_0 = \frac{1}{20^2}$. The input Gaussian has a size of about $\lambda_1 = \frac{1}{2^2}$.

For the design of filter parameters $\boldsymbol{\beta}$ we used eight betula (birch) pollen, four of them are shown on the left of Figure 3. Each pollen grain possess 3 porates.

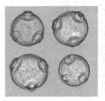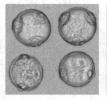

Fig. 3. Example for the porate detection. On the left you see the original input image. On the right the output of the filter. For visualization filter responses below zero are set to zero. The local maxima of the filter output are marked in the left image by red circles.

The target output image is just an indicator image for the porate center. It contains everywhere zeros except at the object center location where the pixel is set to one. The object centers were manually labeled.

3.2   Results

The filter response for the training image is shown on the left of Figure 3. The computation time for this filter is just under $200ms$. The local maxima of the filter response are marked in the original image by red circles. We only show up those local maxima that are above a certain threshold. Obviously, the filter performs very well for the test image and also for an unknown image on the right of Figure 3.

To measure the performance of our system we collected a test set of 150 segmented pollen grains with about 500 porates at all. The pollen in the dataset are sometimes contaminated with dust and dirt particles, which may cause false positive detections. All porate centers were manually labeled. As the porates are not always in the equatorial pose it is sometimes difficult to define an objective ground truth.

We define a detection to be successful if the local maxima of the filter response is at most 10(20) pixels apart from the labeled center (a porate has a diameter of about 40 pixels). All local maxima of the filter responses are collected as detection hypotheses. The filter strength at the putative detection sites are assigned to each hypothesis as a confidence value.

We compared our approach with two different methods. In a first approach we extract SIFT-features at DoG-interest points (following [5]). For compactification of the features we used a PCA. Based on the SIFT(PCASIFT)-features we perform a GHT-like probabilistic voting procedure as done in the ISM model [4]. To achieve rotation invariance we steered the features at the gradient's main orientation and cast votes relative to the orientation as it is done in [7]. For training we used agglomerative clustering to obtain local appearance clusters. The training set is the same as for the holomorphic filter. As the porate dataset does not require a scale invariant treatment the Hough voting map is only two dimensional, just the location of the object. Local maxima of the smoothed voting map serve as detection hypotheses, the absolute values of the maxima as a

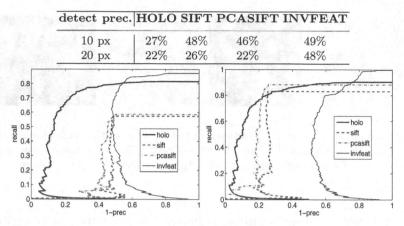

detect prec.	HOLO	SIFT	PCASIFT	INVFEAT
10 px	27%	48%	46%	49%
20 px	22%	26%	22%	48%

Fig. 4. Equal error rates and 1-Precision/Recall graphs for the porate test set. Left graph: with high detection accuracy of 10 pixels. Right graph: with low detection accuracy of 20 pixels.

confidence value. We also tried to use a three dimensional voting map of object position times orientation, but we found that it mostly performed worse, because we got a lot of spurious local maxima and the final localization of the objects was very poor. Secondly, we used an approach (INVFEAT) which extracts a set of rotation invariant features for each pixel and classifies them whether they are an object center or not. As features we use multiple complex derivatives, that is $f_{k,j} = \frac{d^{k+j}x_1}{dz^k d\bar{z}^j}$, up to an order of 8 resulting in $8 \cdot 9/2 = 36$ features per pixel. Rotation invariance is obtained by just taking the absolute value of the feature images $|f_{k,j}|$ as it was done in [12]. To keep the running times comparable to our approach we used a linear classifier for classification and the same training procedure as for our approach.

In Figure 4 we give equal error rates and 1-Precision/Recall graphs for the considered dataset. We made two runs with 10 and 20 pixels detection accuracy. In comparison to our approach (HOLO) the localizations of SIFT and PCASIFT detections are much more imprecise. This might be explained by the imprecise localization of the keypoints which are the basis for the subsequent voting. Our approach does not have such problems because all pixels are taken under consideration. For a low detection precision of 20 pixels, PCASIFT can slightly outperform HOLO in a certain threshold area. Only INVFEAT is able to finally detect nearly all porates by the cost of very high false positive rates.

4   Conclusion

We propose a rotation and translation equivariant image transformation. The output of the holomorphic filter is polynomial in terms of the individual filter responses of a special kind of steerable filter. Thereby the monoms are chosen such that the rotation equivariance is fulfilled.

The filter is applied for rotation invariant detection of objects in microscopical images. Compared to a GHT-based approach relying on SIFT features our approach is competitive for microscopical data. The holomorphic filter provides a much more precise localization of the object, because it does not rely on an intermediate representation by uncertain localized keypoints. Another drawback of the keypoint-based approach is that in fuzzy regions of low contrast no keypoints are detected and hence a detection becomes impossible. The holomorphic filter does not have such problems because all pixels are taken into account. Of course, for more complex vision problems the non-parametric GHT-based approaches will outperform the holomorphic filter, because the model complexity of the filter is very limited. But otherwise, due to the small number of parameters, the filter is able to show better generalization ability for certain data.

References

1. Ballard, D.H.: Generalizing the hough transform to detect arbitrary shapes. Pattern Recognition, 13–12 (1981)
2. Burkhardt, H., Siggelkow, S.: Invariant features in pattern recognition - fundamentals and applications. In: Nonlinear Model-Based Image/Video Processing and Analysis, John Wiley and Sons, Chichester (2001)
3. Freeman, W.T., Adelson, E.H.: The design and use of steerable filters. IEEE Trans. Pattern Anal. Machine Intell., 13(9) (1991)
4. Leibe, B., Leonardis, A., Schiele, B.: Combined object categorization and segmentation with an implicit shape model. In: Proceedings of the ECCV'04 Workshop on Statistical Learning in Computer Vision, Prague (2004)
5. Lowe, D.G.: Distinct image features from scale-invariant keypoints. International Journal of Computer Vision 60, 91–110 (2004)
6. Mathews, V.J., Sicuranza, G.: Polynomial Signal Processing. J. Wiley, New York (2000)
7. Mikolajczyk, K., Leibe, B., Schiele, B.: Multiple object class detection with a generative model. In: Proceedings of the CVPR, vol. 1, pp. 26–36 (2006)
8. Perona, P.: Deformable kernels for early vision. IEEE Trans. Pattern Anal. Machine Intell. 17(5), 488–499 (1995)
9. Reisert, M., Burkhardt, H.: Invariant features for 3d-data based on group integration using directional information and spherical harmonic expansion. In: Proceedings of the ICPR'06 (2006)
10. Reisert, M., Burkhardt, H.: Using irreducible group representations for invariant 3d shape description. In: Proceedings of the 28th DAGM Symposium, Berlin (2006)
11. Reisert, M.: Equivariant holomorphic filters - theory and applications. Technical Report 3, Albert-Ludwig University Freiburg (2007),
    lmb.informatik.uni-freiburg.de/people/reisert
12. Schaffalitzky, F., Zisserman, A.: Multi-view matching for unordered image sets, or 'how do i organize my holiday snaps. In: Heyden, A., Sparr, G., Nielsen, M., Johansen, P. (eds.) ECCV 2002. LNCS, vol. 2350, pp. 414–431. Springer, Heidelberg (2002)
13. Silverman, R.: Introductory complex analysis. Dover Publications (1972)
14. Thurnhofer, S., Mitra, S.: A general framework for quadratic Volterra filters for edge enhancement. IEEE Trans. Image Processing, 950–963 (1996)

Peer Group Vector Median Filter

Bogdan Smolka

Silesian University of Technology, Department of Automatic Control,
Akademicka 16, 44-100 Gliwice, Poland
bogdan.smolka@polsl.pl

Abstract. In this paper, the properties of a novel color image filtering technique capable of impulse noise removal and edge enhancement are analyzed. The new filtering design is a generalization of the well known *Vector Median Filter*. The proposed filtering class is minimizing the cumulated dissimilarity measure of a group of pixels from the filtering window. The described filter is computationally efficient, easy to implement and very effective in suppressing impulsive noise, while preserving image details and strongly enhancing its edges.

1 Introduction

Noise, arising from a variety of sources, is inherent to all electronic image sensors and therefore usually the noisy signal has to be processed by a filtering algorithm that removes the disturbances, while maintaining the original image structures, [1, 2, 3, 4]. Quite often noise corrupting the image is of impulsive nature and mostly it is caused by the sensor malfunctions in the image formation process, aging of the storage material or transmission errors due to natural or man-made sources, [5, 6]. In order to alleviate the problem, much research effort has been directed towards the development of filtering techniques which can cope with image noise, while simultaneously preserving image details and enhancing edges in color images.

In this paper, we analyze a noise filtering design with edge enhancing capabilities, [7]. We show that extending the VMF using the *peer group* concept introduced in [8, 9], it is possible to efficiently remove impulsive noise while sharpening the color image edges.

2 Peer Group Vector Median Filter

Let the color image be defined as a two-dimensional matrix of size $N_1 \times N_2$ consisting of pixels $x_i = (x_{i1}, x_{i2}, x_{i3})$, indexed by i, which gives the pixel position on the image domain. Components x_{ik}, for $i = 1, 2, \ldots, N$, $N = N_1 \cdot N_2$ and $k = 1, 2, 3$ represent the color channel values.

To remove the impulse noise, various filtering approaches based on the ordering of vectors belonging to the filtering window have been proposed, [1]. The most popular ordering scheme called *reduced* or *aggregated ordering* assigns an aggregated dissimilarity measure to each color pixel from the filtering window. The aggregated dissimilarity measure assigned to pixel x_i is defined as

F.A. Hamprecht, C. Schnörr, and B. Jähne (Eds.): DAGM 2007, LNCS 4713, pp. 314–323, 2007.
© Springer-Verlag Berlin Heidelberg 2007

$R_i^n = \sum_{j=1}^n \rho(\boldsymbol{x}_i, \boldsymbol{x}_j)$, $\boldsymbol{x}_i, \boldsymbol{x}_j \in W$, where $\rho(\cdot)$ denotes the chosen dissimilarity measure between color image pixels. The scalar accumulated dissimilarity measures are then sorted and the associated vectors are correspondingly ordered: $R_{(1)}^n \leq \ldots \leq R_{(n)}^n \Rightarrow \boldsymbol{x}_{(1)}^n \leq \ldots \leq \boldsymbol{x}_{(n)}^n$.

In this paper, we will focus on the *vector median* defined using the accumulated sum of distances between vectors, which serves as a dissimilarity measure. The vector median of a set of vectors belonging to a filtering mask W is defined as the vector $\boldsymbol{x}_{(1)}^n$ from W for which the sum of distances to all other vectors belonging to W is minimized, $\boldsymbol{x}_{(1)}^n = \arg\min_{\boldsymbol{x} \in W} \sum_{j=1}^n \|\boldsymbol{x} - \boldsymbol{x}_j\|_\gamma$, where $\|\cdot\|_\gamma$ denotes the L_γ norm (usually L_1 or L_2 is used), with $\|\boldsymbol{x}\|_\gamma = \left(\sum_{k=1}^m |x_k|^\gamma\right)^{1/\gamma}$, and m is the dimension of the vector $\boldsymbol{x}$, [10].

The VMF is the most popular vectorial operator intended for the removal of the spikes injected into the color image by the impulse noise process. This filter is very efficient at reducing the impulses, preserves sharp edges and linear trends, however it does not preserve fine image structures, which are treated as noise and therefore generally the VMF tends to generate or preserve blurry images. This unwanted feature of the VMF is very important, as much of the image information is contained in its edges and sharp edges are pleasing to humans and are desirable in computer vision applications.

The review of the literature devoted to various filters intended to increase the quality of color images leads to the conclusion that simultaneous *noise cancellation* and *edge enhancement* is quite a challenging task. In this paper we analyze a design which can accomplish the two seemingly contradictory aims, [7].

In the new approach the generalized vector median is the vector $\boldsymbol{x}_{(1)}^\alpha$ for which the sum of α smallest distances to other vectors from W is minimized. In other words the output of the PGVMF is the pixel centrally located within a *peer group* of α pixels with minimal aggregated dispersion, expressed as the sum of distances.

If the distance between the vector $\boldsymbol{x}_i$ and $\boldsymbol{x}_j$ is denoted as $\rho_{i,j}$, then we can order the set of distances $\rho_{i,j}$, for $j = 1, \ldots, n$ and obtain the following sequence: $\rho_i^{(1)} \leq \ldots \leq \rho_i^{(\alpha)} \leq \ldots \leq \rho_i^{(n)}$, where $\rho_i^{(k)}$ is the k-th smallest distance from $\boldsymbol{x}_i$ and $\rho_i^{(1)} = \|\boldsymbol{x}_i - \boldsymbol{x}_i\| = 0$. For each pixel in the filtering window the cumulated sum R_i^α is calculated: $R_i^\alpha = \sum_{k=1}^\alpha \rho_i^{(k)}$, and the output of the generalized VMF is the pixel for which the trimmed sum of distances R^α is minimized, [7].

3   Filtering Efficiency

For the evaluation of the efficiency of the proposed filter, a series of experiments has been performed utilizing natural and artificial color images contaminated by impulse noise. For the generation of noisy images the impulsive *uniform* or *random-valued* noise, which changes randomly all the color channels of the percentage p of the image pixels was applied.

For the measurement of the restoration quality, the *Root Mean Squared Error* (RMSE) expressed through the *Peak Signal to Noise Ratio* (PSNR) was used.

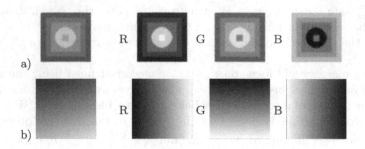

Fig. 1. Synthetic test images with their RGB channels

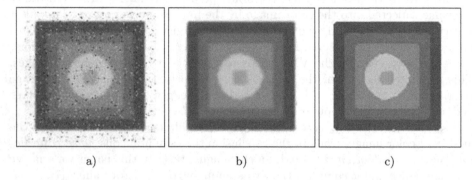

a)   b)   c)

Fig. 2. Edge enhancing and noise attenuating properties of the PGVMF as compared with the VMF: a) blurry test image distorted by impulsive noise of $p = 0.1$, b) VMF output, c) filtering result obtained using the PGVMF with $\alpha = 6$

For the evaluation of the detail preservation capabilities of the proposed filtering design the *Mean Absolute Error* (MAE) has been utilized.

In order to evaluate the edge enhancing and noise cancellation properties of the proposed filter, a synthetic, blurry color test image has been prepared, (see Fig. 1a). This image has been contaminated by 10% impulsive noise as shown in Fig. 2a. Figure 2b depicts the output of the VMF when applied to the noisy test image. As can be noticed the VMF removes the impulse noise and preserves the blurred edges. This behavior is not present when inspecting the output of the PGVMF filter, which is able to enhance image edges while suppressing the impulsive noise, (Fig. 2c).

The edge enhancing abilities of the PGVMF are clearly visible in Fig. 3 which depicts the blue channel intensity plot of the middle row of Fig. 1a. As can be observed, the VMF ($\alpha = 9$) removes the impulses and retains the roof-like edges. The PGVMF besides the cancellation of the spikes introduced by the noise process, strongly enhances the edges, producing steep, step-like image discontinuities as shown in Fig. 4.

The overall good noise reduction abilities of the proposed filter class are presented in Figs. 5a, b, which show the dependence of the PSNR and MAE on the

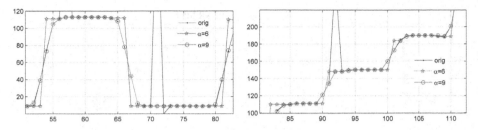

Fig. 3. Plots of the blue channel intensity of the middle row of the enhanced noisy test image depicted in Fig. 2a. Note the steep edges generated by PGVMF, ($\alpha = 6$).

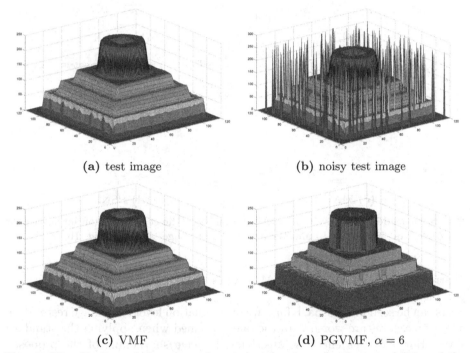

(a) test image

(b) noisy test image

(c) VMF

(d) PGVMF, $\alpha = 6$

Fig. 4. Visualization of the edge enhancing and noise reduction capabilities of the generalized VMF: (a, b) 3D representation of the inverted blue channel of the test images depicted in Figs. 2a, b, (c) result of the VMF, (d) output of the PGVMF with $\alpha = 6$.

noise intensity level and α parameter value of the PGVMF when restoring the *LENA* noisy image.

As can be observed, the PGVMF with $\alpha > 3$ is comparable with the VMF in terms of the objective noise reduction efficiency measures. The edge enhancing effect caused a small decrease of the PSNR and is also reflected by higher MAE values. However, excellent noise reduction properties are visible in the case of uniform noise, for high contamination rates ($p \in [30\%, 70\%]$). In the case

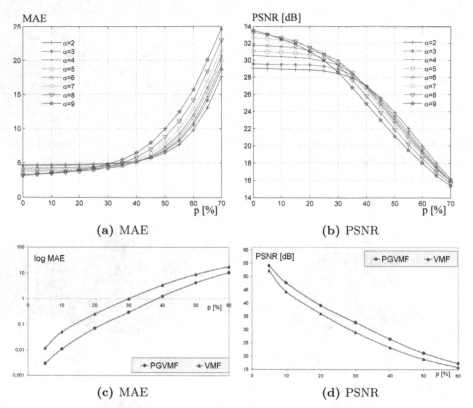

Fig. 5. Dependence of PSNR and MAE measures on the contamination intensities for the *LENA* test image, (a, b) and the artificial test image shown in Fig. 1b, (c, d).

of strong impulse noise the PGVMF excels over VMF independently of the α parameter.

As can be seen in Figs. 5a, b for low contamination levels the image restoration quality measures are worse than the ones obtained when applying the standard VMF. However, this effect is caused by the edge sharpening of the proposed filter. In order to validate this, a series of experiments was performed on a test color image shown in Fig. 1b which has the property that the VMF and also PGVMG do not change any of its pixels. Thus, as the image does not contain any edges, injecting the noise, we are able to examine the real noise reducing capabilities of the PGVMF.

Figures 5c, d show that for the test image without any edges the proposed filtering design is superior to the VMF, which indicates that the PGVMF has overall better noise cancellation properties for the whole range of contamination levels.

The satisfying efficiency of the newly proposed filtering design is confirmed in Tab. 1 which provides the comparison of the quality measures obtained using the PGVMF and various denoising techniques. The results of experiments performed

Table 1. Comparison of the new filtering design with some of the denoising techniques using the *LENA* test image contaminated with impulse noise of intensity $p = 30\%$. Filters used for comparison with the *Peer Group Vector Median Filter* (PGVMF) with $\alpha = 5$: *Vector Median Filter* (VMF) in the RGB and Lab color space, *Directional Distance Filter* (DDF), *Basic Vector Directional Filter* (BVDF), *Fast Modified Vector Median Filter* (FMVMF), *Adaptive Nearest Neighbor Filter*, (ANNF), *Hybrid Directional Filter* (HDF), *Digital Path Approach*, (DPA), *Fast Peer Group Filter* (FPGF) [1, 2, 3, 4, 11, 12].

FILTER	MAE	PSNR	NCD
NONE	23.20	13.85	0.2610
PGVMF$_{\alpha=5}$	**4.39**	**29.54**	**0.0482**
VMF$_{RGB}$	4.79	28.48	0.0527
VMF$_{Lab}$	4.99	27.97	0.0524
DDF	4.81	28.49	0.0521
BVDF	5.91	25.46	0.0569
FMVMF	2.22	29.97	0.0235
ANNF	7.61	26.89	0.0899
HDF	5.19	28.21	0.0656
DPA	4.79	29.65	0.0511
FPGF	2.51	29.26	0.0272

a)   b)   c)   d)

Fig. 6. PGVMF noise reduction efficiency as compared with the VMF: a) part of the test image *PARROTS*, b) noisy image contaminated by impulse noise of $p = 0.4$, c) output of VMF, d) output of PGVMF with $\alpha = 6$

on the *LENA* image contaminated by impulse noise of $p = 30\%$ show that the presented filter yields better or comparable results as the state of the art filters.

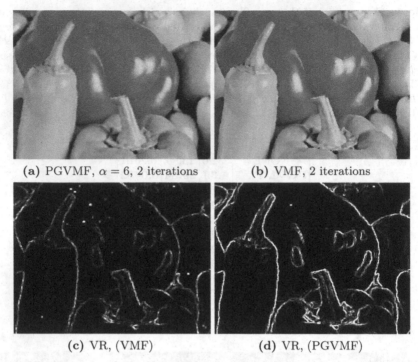

(a) PGVMF, $\alpha = 6$, 2 iterations   (b) VMF, 2 iterations

(c) VR, (VMF)   (d) VR, (PGVMF)

Fig. 7. Performance of the *Vector Range* edge detector applied on the noisy test image, ($p = 0.3$) filtered with VMF and PGVMF: a) VMF and b) PGVMF output, c) VR edge detector output when applied on the noisy test image filtered with VMF, d) result of VR when performed on the noisy test image filtered with PGVMF

The good efficiency of the proposed algorithm in the presence of uniform impulsive noise with high contamination level ($p = 0.4$) is demonstrated in Fig. 6. The visual inspection of the outputs of VMF and PGVMF reveals that the latter not only performs better with regard to noise cancellation ability, but also produces an image with strong, visually pleasing edges. It can be also observed that the VMF heavily softens the image and retains noisy pixels grouped into clusters, (blotches) which is a well known drawback of this filtering technique. This negative effect is not present when evaluating the output of the new filter which is able to better discriminate between the original, undisturbed samples and pixels injected to the image by the impulsive noise process.

The proposed filter intended primarily for noise reduction can also be used for sharpening color images. Figure 7a shows a part of the the test image *PEPPERS* and Fig. 7b depicts its sharpened version obtained using the PGVMF with $\alpha = 6$. As can be observed the sharpness of the image is significantly increased, no false colors are generated and cleaner-looking image is produced.

The edge enhancing properties of the newly designed filter can be exploited in the task of edge detection in color images. Figures 7b and 7c present the output of the *Vector Range* edge detector defined as the distance between the vectors

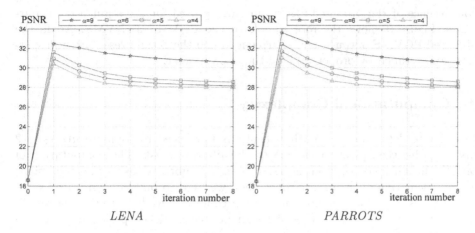

Fig. 8. Dependence of the PSNR measure on the iteration number, for test images contaminated with impulse noise, $(p = 0.1)$

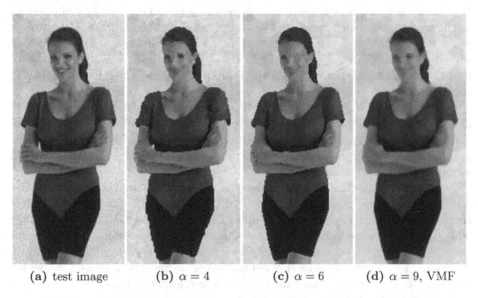

(a) test image (b) $\alpha = 4$ (c) $\alpha = 6$ (d) $\alpha = 9$, VMF

Fig. 9. Root signals of the test image *WOMAN* for the PGVMF and VMF

$x_{(1)}^n$ and $x_{(n)}^n$ from the filtering window W, when performed on the noisy test image filtered with the VMF and PGVMF. As can be seen the quality of the edge maps is increased when the pre-filtering with the described PGVMF filter is performed.

Another advantage of the proposed filter is its quick convergence to the root signal as depicted in Fig. 8. This figure also shows that for low contamination intensities, best filtering results are achieved in the first iteration. The quick convergence of the proposed algorithm can be used for the segmentation purposes. Figure 9 shows the root signals of the PGVMF and VMF. Again the obtained PGVMF outputs have sharp edges and the detail preservation properties can be tuned by proper value of the α parameter.

4   Computational Complexity

In order to determine the VMF output, first we need to compute $n(n-1)/2$ distances between pixels belonging to the filtering mask. The computation of one Euclidean distance requires 2 additions, 3 subtractions, 3 multiplications and a calculation of the square root. Then we need to build n aggregated sums of distances R_i^n, which requires $(n-1)$ additions and we have to find the smallest value of R_i^n, for $x_i \in W$, which can be accomplished performing $(n-1)$ comparisons.

To find the PGVMF output we need the same number of distances as in the case of VMF. In order to find the accumulated sum of α distances, we have to sort $(n-1)$ distances from the pixel under consideration to all other pixels in W. Using the quicksort algorithm, this requires $(n-1)(n-2)/2$ comparisons in the worst case, which increases the complexity of the algorithm. However, to build the accumulated sum of distances R_i^α, we only need $(\alpha-2)$ additions of sorted distances, instead of $(n-1)$ in the VMF method. Finally, we have to find the smallest value of R_i^α, as in the case of VMF, for which we need $(n-1)$ comparisons.

So, the PGVMF differs from the VMF, in the additional sorting of the $(n-1)$ distances for each pixel in W and also in the calculation of aggregated sum of distances, for which we need fewer additions than in the VMF. In this way, the additional computational burden is to some extent compensated by the decreased number of necessary additions.

For the VMF with a 3×3 window, we need 36 distances, which require $36 \cdot 9 = 324$ operations. Then we need to perform $9 \cdot 8 = 72$ additions and 8 comparisons, which gives a total of 404 operations. The PGVMF also requires 324 operations for the calculation of the distances, and additionally in the worst case $(8 \cdot 7/2) \cdot 9 = 252$ comparisons for the sorting operation and $(\alpha - 2) \cdot 9$ additions. Finally, we also need 8 comparisons to find the smallest R_i, which outputs the $x_{(1)}$ vector. Thus, for the 3×3 window, the PGVMF with $\alpha = 6$ requires $324 + 252 + 36 + 8 = 620$ operations. The real, necessary total number of operations is significantly smaller, as on average the quicksort algorithm needs fewer calculations and the computationally demanding sorting, can be terminated after the α smallest distances are found. Moreover, for higher α values in order to find the accumulated distances R_i^α, it is favorable to find the $(n - \alpha)$ highest distances and to subtract them from the sum of all distances associated with a pixel under inspection.

As shown, the computational complexity of the VMF and the proposed filter are comparable, and they can be further decreased applying less demanding vector norms and fast implementations of the vector median algorithm.

5   Conclusions

In this paper, the properties of a novel filtering design has been examined. The proposed filter can be regarded as a generalization of the standard *Vector Median Filter*. Besides its excellent noise reducing capabilities, its unique feature is its ability to enhance color image edges. This effect is really beneficial as in many applications sharp image edges are desired to enable the success of further image processing steps.

The novel filter is easy to implement and its computational complexity is comparable with the VMF. The edge enhancing properties of the new filter make it a valuable tool for the enhancement of noisy and blurred color images.

References

1. Plataniotis, K.N., Venetsanopoulos, A.N.: Color Image Processing and Applications. Springer, Heidelberg (2000)
2. Lukac, R., Smolka, B., Martin, K., Plataniotis, K.N., Venetsanopoulos, A.N.: Vector filtering for color imaging. IEEE Signal Processing Magazine, Special Issue on Color Image Processing 22, 74–86 (2005)
3. Smolka, B., Plataniotis, K.N., Venetsanopoulos, A.N.: Nonlinear techniques for color image processing. In: Barner, K.E., Arce, G.R. (eds.) Nonlinear Signal and Image Processing: Theory, Methods, and Applications, pp. 445–505. CRC Press, Boca Raton, FL, USA (2004)
4. Smolka, B., Venetsanopoulos, A.N.: Noise reduction and edge detection in color images. In: Lukac, R., Plataniotis, K.N. (eds.) Color Image Processing: Methods and Applications, pp. 75–100. CRC Press, Boca Raton (2006)
5. Boncelet, C.G.: Image noise models. In: Bovik, A. (ed.) Handbook of image and video processing, pp. 325–335. Academic Press, London (2000)
6. Zheng, J., Valavanis, K.P., Gauch, J.M.: Noise removal from color images. Journal of Intelligent and Robotic Systems 7, 257–285 (1993)
7. Lukac, R., Smolka, B., Plataniotis, K.N.: Sharpening vector median filters. Signal Processing 87, 2085–2099 (2007)
8. Kenney, C., Deng, Y., Manjunath, B.S., Hewer, G.: Peer group image enhancement. IEEE Transactions on Image Processing 10, 326–334 (2001)
9. Deng, Y., Kenney, S., Moore, M.S., Manjunath, B.S.: Peer group filtering and perceptual color image quantization. In: Proceedings of the IEEE Int. Symp. on Circuits and Systems (ISCAS), Orlando, FL, vol. 4, pp. 21–24 (1999)
10. Astola, J., Haavisto, P., Neuvo, Y.: Vector median filters. Proc. of the IEEE 78, 678–689 (1990)
11. Smolka, B., Chydzinski, A.: Fast detection and impulsive noise removal in color images. Real-Time Imaging 11, 389–402 (2005)
12. Smolka, B., Lukac, R., Chydzinski, A., Plataniotis, K.N., Wojciechowski, K.: Fast adaptive similarity based impulsive noise reduction filter. Real Time Imaging 9, 261–276 (2003)

Image Statistics and Local Spatial Conditions for Nonstationary Blurred Image Reconstruction

Hongwei Zheng and Olaf Hellwich

Computer Vision & Remote Sensing, Berlin University of Technology
Franklinstrasse 28/29, Office FR 3-1, D-10587 Berlin
{hzheng,hellwich}@cs.tu-berlin.de

Abstract. Deblurring is important in many visual systems. This paper presents a novel approach for nonstationary blurred image reconstruction with ringing reduction in a variational Bayesian learning and regularization framework. Our approach makes effective use of the image statistical prior and image local spatial conditions through the whole learning scheme. A nature image statistics based marginal prior distribution is used not only for blur kernel estimation but also for image reconstruction. For an ill-posed blur estimation problem, variational Bayesian ensemble learning can achieve a tractable posterior using an image statistic prior which is translation and scale-invariant. During the deblurring, nonstationary blurry images have stronger ringing effects. We thus propose an iterative reweighted regularization function based on the use of an image statistical prior and image local spatial conditions for perceptual image deblurring.

1   Introduction

In the digital imaging world, images are often degraded due to blur and noise. These degradations heavily influence the implementation, automation, and robustness of many visual systems. The primary goal of blind image deconvolution is to uniquely define the convolved signals only from one observed image without any other information. It gives opportunities not only for valuable contributions in solving ill-posed problems but also for the practical demands in early vision.

According to the image degradation model, $g = h * f + \eta$, where $g \in L^2(\Omega)$ is an observed image function and $\Omega \subset \mathbb{R}^2$ an open bounded domain, the problem is to estimate the original image f with unknown noise η and point spread function (blur kernel) h. The two-dimensional convolution can be expressed as $h * f = Hf = Fh$, where H and F are block-Toeplitz matrices and can be approximated by block-circulant matrices with certain boundary conditions.

Due to the complexity of blurring, we classify blurred images into three main groups, shown in Fig. 1. The first group in Fig. 1(a) is *spatial-invariant* blurring. That is, the blur kernel is uniform and stationary for the entire image and can be approximated by one parametric blur kernel like a Gaussian kernel, motion kernel etc. The second group in Fig. 1(b) can be approximated by *spatial-invariant* blurring. Such a blur kernel is uniform but nonstationary, i.e., the blur kernel

F.A. Hamprecht, C. Schnörr, and B. Jähne (Eds.): DAGM 2007, LNCS 4713, pp. 324–334, 2007.
© Springer-Verlag Berlin Heidelberg 2007

Fig. 1. $a|b|c$ columns. (a) Entirely, uniform and relatively stationary blurred image. (b) uniform and nonstationary blurred image. (c) nonuniform, partially blurred image.

cannot be simply represented by a single parametric model. The estimation of blur kernels can thus be considered as a generalization from parametric to nonparametric approximation. The third group in Fig. 1(c) is partial-blurring. Such images are nonuniform *spatial-variant* blurred and the image deblurring should not influence unblurred regions [1]. In this paper, we focus on the restoration of such nonstationary blurred images.

The Bayesian estimation provides a structured way to include prior knowledge concerning the quantities to be estimated. The Bayesian approach is, in fact, the framework in which the most recent blur kernel estimation methods have been introduced, e.g, simultaneous kernel estimation and image restoration [2], estimating Bayesian hyperparameters [3], factorizing kernels into parametric models [4], [5], and measuring the strength of discontinuities in Gaussian scale space [6], etc. However, these methods are limited in certain parametric models to stationary blurred images.

Based on variational Bayesian approaches [7], [8], Miskin and Mackay [4], [5] have firstly applied this method to deal with blind deconvolution using a prior on raw pixel intensities. Results are shown on synthesized image blur. Using an image statistical prior, Fergus et al. [9] have extended this method for removing camera shaking blur from a single blurred image. The blur kernel is estimated and interpolated in high-accuracy using a multi-scale approach [10]. Although the ringing effect has been observed by Fergus et al., the image deblurring is directly using an extended Richardson-Lucy (RL) method without using an image statistical prior and local spatial conditions for deblurring. Inspired by Fergus's et al., in our approach, we use an image statistical prior not only for kernel estimation but also for weighted space-adaptive image deblurring with ringing reduction.

For image deblurring, ringing effects and amplified noise influence the results due to Gibbs phenomena in the Fourier transformation. One type of ringing effects often happens around edges and discontinuities due to the high frequency loss during blurring. The other type of ringing effects is due to the mismatch between nonstationary real blurred images and stationarity assumptions. Such phenomena have been observed by [2], [9], [11]. Since most original scenes are without ringing, such restoration results are usually undesirable. Therefore, the deblurring approach needs to be designed for both types of ringing reduction.

Furthermore, in Bayesian estimation, a generic prior model needs to represent common descriptive or generative information from an observed image. Such prior distributions can be translation and scale-invariant for representing a global image. Natural image statistics based prior learning has such properties to represent image structure, textures [12], discontinuities and blurred edges [9]. On the other hand, natural images are often inhomogeneous with piecewise uniform regions separated by edges and discontinuities. Therefore, the measure of distributions of local edges, textures as well as the pixel intensity values can be used as local spatial conditions for ringing reduction in image reconstruction.

Different from Fergus's work [9], [4], [5], our approach has several effects. First, through some observations and experiments, we classify natural blurred images into three main groups so that we can design an efficient method. Second, in contrast to previous work [4], [5], [9], [13], natural image statistics is used not only for kernel estimation in a global image but also for piecewise image reconstruction in a newly designed regularization function. Therefore, we obtain an approach, which can use the scale-invariant statistical prior for kernel estimation and integrate local spatial conditions for deblurring with ringing reduction.

2   Variational Bayesian Modeling for Kernel Estimation

During the image blurring period, the changes of image discontinuities and edge gradients are larger and more representative than the changes in the piecewise homogeneous regions. Therefore, we construct a probabilistic model based on marginal distributions of image gradients. We process the gradients of f and g and construct the new convolution equation using the original equation $g = h * f + \eta$. Suppose we have a model which tells how a number sequence $\nabla f = \nabla f(1), ..., \nabla f(t)$ transforms into a sequence $\nabla g = \nabla g(1), ..., \nabla g(t)$, we then have $\nabla g(t) = \nabla f(t) * h + \eta(0, \sigma^2)$ with zero-mean identical and independently distributed (iid) Gaussian noise.

Based on this model, the Bayesian MAP estimation utilizes an input $P(\nabla g)$ to achieve two convergent posteriors $p(h)$ and $p(\nabla f)$, and is formulated in,

$$p(\nabla f, h | \nabla g) = p(\nabla g | \nabla f, h) P(\nabla f, h) / p(\nabla g) \propto p(\nabla g | \nabla f, h) P(\nabla f) P(h) \quad (1)$$

In order to apply this model, the model needs to be given in probabilistic terms, which means stating the joint distribution of all the variables in the model. In principle, any joint distribution can be regarded as a model, but in practice, the joint distribution will have a simple form. Here, in $p(\nabla f, h | \nabla g)$, we can easily obtain a more stable prior distribution, e.g., the log-histogram of image gradients. The prior $P(\nabla f)$ on the restored image gradients is a Gaussian mixture model. The blur kernel prior $P(h)$ is a mixture of K blur kernel parametric models with exponential distributions. Some constraints are used for applying the equation such as non-negativity, and energy preservation during the deblurring.

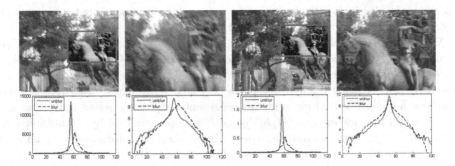

Fig. 2. $\frac{a|b|c|d}{e|f|g|h}$. Comparison of marginal distribution of blurred and unblurred gradients. (a)(b) Blurred image. (c)(d)Unblurred image. (e)(f) Histogram and Log-histogram (y) of gradients $\nabla_x I$. (g)(h) Histogram and Log-histogram (y)of gradients $\nabla_y I$.

2.1 Natural Image Statistics for Global Prior Learning

A generic prior distribution can be incorporated into a probability distribution as a prior model which will bias learning algorithms. For this objective, a translation and scale-invariant prior can be obtained via natural image statistics.

From a combination of psychophysical and computational approaches, Field [14], [15] has presented that real cluttered images obey heavy-tailed distributions in their gradients. The distribution of gradients has most of its mass on small values but gives significant probability to large values in a Student's t-distribution. Later, Olshausen et al. [15] have proposed an approach to understanding such response properties of visual neurons and their relationship to the statistical structure of natural images in terms of efficient coding. In image processing, [10], [16] have shown the non-Gaussian nature of the probability distribution, e.g., high kurtosis, heavy tails; it can be approximated in an exponential function family with exponent less than 1. These heavy-tailed natural image priors have shown in many state-of-the-art methods, e.g., image segmentation [1], [12], denoising [10], [17], removing camera shake [9], etc.

To compute such distributions, one way is to compute the joint statistics of derivative filters at different locations, sizes or orientations [13]. The other way is to observe marginal statistics of more complicated feature detectors [18]. We extend these methods to yielding a translation and scale invariant prior. For example, Fig. 2 illustrates this fact and shows several natural images and their histograms of gradient magnitudes. Similar histograms are observed for vertical derivative filters and for the gradient magnitude ∇I_x and ∇I_y.

2.2 Variational Bayesian Ensemble Learning for Kernel Estimation

Based on the Eq. 1, we can easily find that marginalizing the posterior distribution is difficult. We cannot take a point estimate (e.g., the MAP estimate) because this leads to overfitting. Therefore it is necessary to approximate the posterior density by a more tractable form for which it is possible to achieve any necessary probability mass of the posterior.

Variational ensemble learning [7], [19], [4], [9] is a method for parametric approximations of the posterior distributions. It assumes a Gaussian distribution or another parametric distribution, in which the mean and the variance are allowed to evolve during the learning process. The distributions for each estimated gradient and blur kernel element are represented by their mean and variance. The original full posterior $p(\nabla f, h | \nabla g)$ is then approximated by a tractable distribution $q(\nabla f, h)$ by minimizing the Kullback-Leibler information which acts as a distance measure between the two distributions. It is formulated as,

$$KL\{q(\nabla f, h) \| p(\nabla f, h | \nabla g)\} = \int q(\nabla f, h) \ln \frac{q(\nabla f, h)}{p(\nabla f, h | \nabla g)} d\nabla f dh \qquad (2)$$

$$= \int q(\nabla f, h) \ln \frac{q(\nabla f, h)}{p(\nabla g | \nabla f, h) P(\nabla f, h)} d\nabla f dh + \ln p(\nabla g)$$

The Kullback-Leibler information is greater than or equal to zero, with equality if and only if the two distributions, $p(\nabla f, h | \nabla g)$ and $q(\nabla f, h)$ are equivalent.

Training and learning the approximating ensemble can be done by assuming a fixed parametric form for the ensemble (for instance assuming a product of Gaussian). As a consequence, the parameters of the distributions can be set to minimize the cost function. Therefore, the $q(\nabla f, h) \rightarrow q(\nabla f, h, \sigma^2)$ can be further approximated by adding a noise prior σ^{-2}(inverse variance) in the form of a Gamma distribution. Thus, we have hyper-parameters $x, y : p(\sigma^2 | x, y) = \Gamma(\sigma^{-2} | x, y)$. The variational posterior is $q(\sigma^{-2})$ in a Gamma distribution. If we note that the term $p(\nabla g)$ is constant over all the models, we can define a cost function C_{KL} to obtain the optimum approximating distribution,

$$C_{KL} = KL\{q(\nabla f, h, \sigma^2) \| p(\nabla f, h | \nabla g)\} - \ln p(\nabla g) \qquad (3)$$

$$= \int q(\nabla f) \ln \frac{q(\nabla f)}{p(\nabla f)} d\nabla f + \int q(h) \ln \frac{q(h)}{p(h)} dh + \int q(-\sigma^2) \ln \frac{q(-\sigma^2)}{p(-\sigma^2)} d(-\sigma^2)$$

where the subindex of C_{KL} denotes the variables that are marginalized over in the cost function. In general, they are the unknown variables of the model. Because of the product form of the true posterior density, the cost function C_{KL} can be factorized into a sum of simpler terms. The Kullback-Leibler measure will be sensitive to probability mass in the true posterior distribution rather than the absolute value of the distribution itself.

3   Iterative Reweighted Energy Function for Deblurring

In this section, we first discuss the deblurring error and ringing effects which are closely related to local spatial structures within an image. Then we propose an iterative reweighted energy function using natural image statistical prior weights and image local spatial conditions for deblurring with ringing reduction.

According to $g = h * f + \eta$, using the Tikhonov-Miller regularized solution, the restored image $\hat{F}$ in the frequency domain is,

$$\hat{F}(u,v) = \frac{H^*(u,v)}{|H(u,v)|^2 + \alpha|L(u,v)|^2} G(u,v) = T(u,v)G(u,v) \tag{4}$$

where G, H, F are the DFT of g, h, f, respectively, (u, v) are the spatial frequency variables, $L(u, v)$ represents a regularizing operator with a regularization parameter α. $T(u, v)$ deviates from the inverse of the blur kernel $H^{-1}(u, v)$. The deviation is expressed by the error spectrum $E(u, v; \alpha) = 1 - T(u, v; \alpha)H(u, v)$. The restored image $\hat{F}$ in the frequency domain is given by,

$$\hat{F}(u,v) = T(u,v;\alpha)[H(u,v)F(u,v) + \eta(u,v)] \tag{5}$$
$$= F(u,v) - E(u,v;\alpha)F(u,v) + (1 - E(u,v;\alpha))H^{-1}\eta(u,v) \tag{6}$$

where the restoration error is $\|\hat{F}(u,v) - F(u,v)\|$. On the right side, the second term denotes the error due to the use of filter T, i.e., a regularization error; the third term presents the noise η magnification error. There exists an optimal value α between two types of errors. The noise magnification error has a global degrading effect resulting from the observed noise. Also, the regularization error is a function of F, and its effect will therefore be related strongly to the local spatial structures encountered within the image. Ringing effects can be seen as a structure dependent phenomenon and can be classified as a regularization error.

Therefore, we propose an iterative reweighted regularization function which can use the measure distributions of local edges, textures as well as the pixel intensity values for image deblurring. Similar to Eq. 1, $p(g|f, h)$ follows a Gaussian distribution and $p(f)$ is prior with some constraint conditions,

$$\mathcal{J}(f|g,h) \propto \arg\min\{\frac{1}{2}\sum w_1(g(x) - h(x) * f(x))^2 + \frac{1}{2}\lambda\sum w_2(c_1(x) * f(x))^2\}$$

where $\mathcal{J}(f|h, g) = -\log\{p(g|f, h)p(f)\}$ express that the energy cost $\mathcal{J}$ is equivalent to the negative log-likelihood of the data [19], [2], [1]. λ is a regularization parameter that controls the trade-off between the fidelity to the observation and smoothness of the restored image. The smoothness constraint $c_1(x)$ is an regularization operator and usually is a high-pass filter. The energy function achieves an optimal result by searching for f minimizing the reconstruction error $(g - h * f)^2$ and the weights prior w_2 controlling f to be satisfactorily smooth.

The weights w_1 and w_2 reduce these ringing effects adaptively to achieve better visual evaluation. $w_1 = 1$, if the data at x is reliable, otherwise $w_1 = 0$; the image weight $w_2 = 1/[1 + k\hat{\sigma}_f^2(x)]$, $\hat{\sigma}_f^2(x)$ is the local variance of the observed image $g(x)$ at x in a $P \times Q$ window, k is a contrast parameter. However, it is difficult to directly compute such local variances in a small moving window for a single blurred image and its unknown ideally restored image. In contrast to most existing approaches [2], [9], we use the distributions of statistical edge gradients as the local prior weights, which can bias the results. We use a $w_2' = \exp^{k\hat{\sigma}_f^2(x)}$ from a general exponential function family which has effects similar to w_2 [20].

The heavy-tailed curve of w_2' is directly controlled by using the image statistical prior distribution. The cost function of this equation is minimized in an iterative reweighted optimization approach [21] via conjugate gradient descent.

4   Experiments and Discussion

Experiments on real blurred images are carried out to demonstrate the effectiveness of our algorithm. We perform our experiments on entirely nonstationary blurred images which are collected from videos and photos in real environments.

4.1   Implementation of Blur Kernel Estimation and Deblurring

We firstly present the implementation of blur kernel estimation in the variational Bayesian ensemble learning. Sequentially, we describe the deblurring with ringing reduction in our suggested iterative reweighted energy function.

Weakly-Supervised Variational Bayesian Learning. According to the cost function C_{KL} in Eq. 3, the parameters of the distributions are minimized alternately using the coordinate descent method. The most crucial part is the initial value that we choose the means of the distributions $q(h)$ and $q(\nabla f)$ (a trained prior distribution from another similar type of blurred images). The variance σ^2 is given high value due to the uncertainty of the initial value. The minimization is repeated until the change in C_{KL} becomes negligible. The ensemble learning algorithm is provided online by Miskin and Mackay [4]. Furthermore, multi-scale [10], [9] and multigrid [22] methods have been proven to be very useful in computer vision. These methods can avoid local minima. Following Fergus et al. [9] and Simoncelli [10], we implement our algorithm using multi-scale based coarse-to-fine refinements. At the coarsest level, the blur kernel is initialized at a very coarse level. The initial estimation for ideal image gradients is then adapted to the blur kernel till the edge gradients distribution is well adjusted. At the finest resolution, the blur kernel is fully interpolated.

Iterative Reweighted Energy Function for Deblurring with Ringing Deduction and Denoising.   During the image deconvolution, most of the ringing effects are generated either by the non-accurate blur kernels or by spatial-variant blur around the objects. Our suggested regularization function is designed based on the analysis of ringing effects. The weight distributions in the energy function can be approximated by using image statistical prior distributions which can be computed from other same types of learned blurred images. During image deblurring and image reconstruction, the conjugate gradient descent method minimizes the residual error in an iterative manner. The weight distribution is automatically updated based on the previously iterative restored image results in the spatial domain. Therefore, it needs more computation time.

Fig. 3. $a|b|c$. (a) Blur degraded images. (b) Restored image using the normal RL method with ringing effects. (c) Restored images using the suggested method.

Fig. 4. $a|b|c$ columns. (a) Blur degraded images. (b) Restored image using a similar method in [9]: multi-scale based RL method. (c) Restored images using the suggested method with natural image statistical prior weights and space-adaptive smoothing.

4.2 Deblurring and Reconstruction on Nonstationary Blurred Data

To evaluate this algorithm, the performance of the approach has been investigated by using different types of real images. In these experiments, first, we show that it is easy to get ringing effects in normal deblurring methods. Second, we reconstruct several types of blurred images and compare the results with other methods. Finally, we make a summary of the suggested approach.

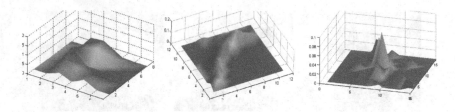

Fig. 5. $a|b|c$. Identified blur kernels with respect to the image of people, street and horse, respectively. (a) for people. (b) for horse. (c) for street.

The first experiment is performed for an indoor image, shown in Fig. 3. Based on the estimated blur kernel in Fig. 5(a), we reconstruct this image using two methods. We can easily find that the classical Richardson-Lucy (RL) method can achieve sharp deblurring results but suffers from stronger ringing effects. Fig. 3(c) is reconstructed using our suggested method with natural image statistical prior weights and space-adaptive smoothing. Compared to the RL method, the reconstructed result in our method is smoother and without ringing effects.

The second experiments present image restoration on blurred images to demonstrate the deblurring and restoration results of the proposed algorithm. The restored images are illustrated in Fig. 4 and their identified blur kernels are shown in Fig. 5, respectively. In this experiment, we compare our deblurring with a multi-scale based RL methods that was used by Fergus et al. [9]. From the results, we note that the multi-scale RL method can achieve sharp restoration results but the noise is also amplified, shown in Fig. 4(b) column. Our method can achieve the sharp deblurring results with more smoothing surfaces due to different reconstruction mechanism, shown in Fig. 4(c). In this experiment, we show three blurred images with different illumination, contrast and environments. The first image is an indoor image of a person, the second image of a copper sculpture has some reflections, and the third one has cluttered movements in the evening. The results show the robustness of image deblurring and reconstruction of the suggested approach for different types of nonstationary real blurred images.

From these experiments, we note that these estimated blur kernels cannot be simply represented by a parametric model. The reason is the random movements and different noise influences (illumination, projective distortion based blur changing, reflections etc.) during the image formation period. In a sense, based on natural image statistics, we can estimate blur kernels in a variational Bayesian learning method and restore and reconstruct the images sequentially in an iterative reweighted energy function. On the other hand, we also note that image noise is smoothed during image deconvolution in our approach.

5   Conclusions and Future Work

In this paper, we have suggested a new approach for weak-supervised image deconvolution with ringing reduction. The integration of variational Bayesian learning and natural image statistics can achieve high-accuracy blur identification. Furthermore, based on the analysis of ringing and noise effects, we have proposed an iterative reweighted energy function for image deblurring and perceptual image reconstruction. In particular, the approach makes effective use of the natural image statistics prior through the learning scheme. By alternating the radius of the natural image statistics, the image statistical prior distribution is not only used for blur kernel estimation in a single blurred image but also used as the local spatial prior weights for image deblurring and reconstruction with ringing reduction in an iterative reweighted energy function. A thorough evaluation has shown that the proposed approach has more flexibilities for identifying and restoring blurred images with ringing reduction in real environments.

References

1. Zheng, H., Hellwich, O.: Introducing dynamic prior knowledge to partially-blurred image restoration. In: Franke, K., Müller, K.-R., Nickolay, B., Schäfer, R. (eds.) Pattern Recognition. LNCS, vol. 4174, pp. 111–121. Springer, Heidelberg (2006)
2. Zheng, H., Hellwich, O.: Double regularized Bayesian estimation for blur identification in video sequences. In: Narayanan, P.J., Nayar, S.K., Shum, H.-Y. (eds.) ACCV 2006. LNCS, vol. 3852, pp. 943–952. Springer, Heidelberg (2006)
3. Molina, R., Katsaggelos, A., Mateos, J.: Bayesian and regularization methods for hyperparameters estimate in image restoration. IEEE Tr. on Sig. 8, 231–246 (1999)
4. Miskin, J., MacKay, D.J.C.: Ensemble Learning for Blind Image Separation and Deconvolution. In: Adv. in Independent Component Analysis, Springer, Heidelberg (2000)
5. Miskin, J.W.: Ensemble Learning for Independent Component Analysis. PhD thesis, Uni. Cambridge (2000)
6. Elder, J.H., Zucker, S.W.: Local scale control for edge detection and blur estimation. IEEE Trans. on PAMI 20, 699–716 (1998)
7. Hinton, G.E., Camp, D.v.: Keeping neural networks simple by minimizing the description length of the weights.s. In: ACM Conf. on Computational Learning Theory, pp. 5–13 (1993)
8. Attias, H.: A variational Bayesian framework for graphical models. In: Leen, T, et al. (eds.) Advances in NIPS, pp. 209–215 (2000)
9. Fergus, R., Singh, B., Hertzmann, A., Roweis, S.T., Freeman, W.: Removing camera shake from a single photograph. In: SIGGRAPH 2006, vol. 25, pp. 787–794 (2006)
10. Simoncelli, E.: Statistical models for images: Compression, restoration and synthesis. In: 31st Asilomar Conf. on Sig., Sys. and Computers (1997)
11. Lagendijk, R., Biemond, J., Boekee, D.: Regularized iterative image restoration with ringing reduction. IEEE Tr. on Ac., Sp., and Sig. Proc. 36, 1874–1888 (1988)
12. Heiler, M., Schnörr, C.: Natural image statistics for natural image segmentation. IJCV 63, 5–19 (2005)
13. Portilla, J., Simoncelli, E.P.: A parametric texture model based on joint statistics of complex wavelet coefficients. IJCV 40, 49–72 (2000)
14. Field, D.J.: Relations between the statistics and natural images and the responses properties of cortical cells. J. Optical Soc. Am. A. 4, 2379–2394 (1987)
15. Olshausen, B.A., Field, D.J.: Emergence of simple-cell receptive field properties by learning a sparse code for natural images. Nature 381, 607–609 (1996)

16. Mallat, S.: A theory for multiresolution signal decomposition: The wavelet representation. IEEE on PAMI 11, 674–693 (1989)
17. Roth, S., Black, M.: Fields of experts: A framework for learning image priors. In: CVPR, San Diego, pp. 860–867 (2005)
18. Zhu, S., Wu, X., Mumford, D.: Minimax entropy principle and its to texture modeling. Neural Computation 9, 1627–1660 (1997)
19. Opper, M., Saad, D.: Advanced Mean Field Methods: Theory and Practice. MIT Press, Cambridge, Massachusetts (2001)
20. Perona, P., Malik, J.: Scale-space and edge detection using anisotropic diffusion. IEEE Trans. PAMI 12, 629–639 (1990)
21. O'leary, D.P.: Robust regression computation using iteratively reweighted least squares. SIAM J. Matrix Anal. Appl. 11, 466–480 (1990)
22. Bruhn, A., Weickert, J., Kohlberger, T., Schnörr, C.: A multigrid platform for real-time motion computation with discontinuity-preserving variational methods. IJCV 70, 257–277 (2006)

The Minimum Volume Ellipsoid Metric

Karim T. Abou-Moustafa and Frank P. Ferrie

The Artificial Perception Laboratory,
Centre for Intelligent Machines, McGill University,
3480 University street, Montreal, QC, Canada H3A 2A7
{karimt,ferrie}@cim.mcgill.ca

Abstract. We propose an unsupervised "local learning" algorithm for learning a metric in the input space. Geometrically, for a given query point, the algorithm finds the minimum volume ellipsoid (MVE) covering its neighborhood which characterizes the correlations and variances of its neighborhood variables. Algebraically, the algorithm maximizes the determinant of the local covariance matrix which amounts to a convex optimization problem. The final matrix parameterizes a Mahalanobis metric yielding the MVE metric (MVEM). The proposed metric was tested in a supervised learning task and showed promising and competitive results when compared with state of the art metrics in the literature.

1 Introduction

The fact that many learning algorithms, supervised, unsupervised, or semi-supervised, depend mainly on a "representative" and a "meaningful" distance metric in the input space, imposes the problem of finding such a metric in the very core problems of machine learning algorithms. The various benefits pointed out in [5,6,9] of having a metric that can better describe similarities in the absence of *a priori* knowledge or side–information [5,9], point to the need for such metrics. This is reflected in the current literature by many new algorithms that tackled the problem directly and indirectly [5,6,7,8,9,11,12], and showed promising results in that regard. The contribution of this paper builds on this research with an algorithm for learning a new distance metric in the input space. The new metric, called the minimum volume ellipsoid metric (MVEM), can be seen as a generalization of existing metrics induced by recent learning algorithms.

Two main objectives and advantages lie behind the MVEM design. First, it is desirable to have a metric that does not depend on *a priori* knowledge, side information as in [5,9], or data labels as in [6,7]. Second, the metric should not depend on the learning paradigm. That is, for any two points $\mathbf{x}, \mathbf{y} \in \mathbb{R}^d$, labeled or unlabeled, from a training set or test set, it is desirable to replace $\|\mathbf{x} - \mathbf{y}\|_2$ by a distance function $D(\mathbf{x}, \mathbf{y})$ which carries more information on the similarity between $\mathbf{x}$ and $\mathbf{y}$.

Our outlook is statistical, with a motivation rooted in robust statistics, and links to maximum likelihood estimation (MLE) with Gaussian distributions. The MVEM is a parameterized version of the general Mahalanobis distance function with a special structure imposed on the symmetric positive definite matrix

F.A. Hamprecht, C. Schnörr, and B. Jähne (Eds.): DAGM 2007, LNCS 4713, pp. 335–344, 2007.

defining the metric. The special structure stems from combined statistical and geometrical properties, with a useful algebraic interpretation that is used later in the proposed algorithm for learning the MVEM. The proposed algorithm, called MiniVenn (or minimum volume ellipsoid of nearest neighbours), depends primarily on the concept of locality in the input space. For a given query point, with its assigned neighborhood (*k-Nearest-Neighbors*, or *ϵ-ball*), similarities between the query point and its neighbors can be found by means of the neighborhood's covariance matrix (i.e. local covariance). In an ideal setting, if the query point is the mean of a normally distributed neighborhood, the covariance matrix defines an ellipsoid which, in principle, should approximately [1] cover (or enclose) the neighborhood [2]. The induced Mahalanobis distance can measure the similarity between the mean and the neighboring points while taking correlations and variances into consideration. With real life data, however, this is hardly the case. Due to the obvious non-normality of the neighboring points with respect to the query point, the curse of dimensionality effect, nonlinearity of the data, and noise, such an ellipsoid poorly covers the desired neighborhood and the induced metric becomes unreliable.

The first motivation for the proposed MVE approach to define a metric stems from the above observation. If the ellipsoid is reshaped to cover the desired neighborhood, as MLE with a Gaussian component does, one can expect that the covariance matrix will better reflect the local structure. Another primary motivation, stems from the statistics literature [14], where the Mahalanobis distance is well known to expose outliers by assigning them very large distance values. Therefore, should the Mahalanobis distance be well parameterized by an accurate estimate of the covariance matrix, one can expect more accurate distances and similarity measures [14].

The paper is organized as follows: First, the motivation for the MVEM is presented in Section 2. Section 3 presents the algorithm for learning the MVEM, followed by a review of related work and similarities with other metric learning algorithms. Experimental results are illustrated in Section 4, and finally, conclusions are drawn in Section 5.

2   Motivation for the MVEM

The Euclidean distance has been and is still extensively used and embedded in many algorithms of the pattern recognition and machine learning literature. There are many reasons, however, that render the Euclidean metric completely inappropriate. First, if the norm is to deal with very high dimensional structured data, the curse of dimensionality and its consequences are inevitable. Second, effects of the random noise in the data and missing values will be reflected in the Euclidean metric. Third, despite an adequately sized training set, it is very likely that the data set is not balanced, resulting in high and low density areas in the

---

[1] Due to the infinite support of the Gaussian.

[2] The axes of the ellipsoid lie along the eigenvectors of the covariance matrix, and the squares of the axes' lengths are its eigenvalues.

input space, causing fragile estimation of densities and intrinsic dimensionality. Moreover, the very definition of the Euclidean metric ignores the effect of scale, variance and correlations of and among the variables. Thus the Euclidean metric may not reflect the true geometry of the underlying manifold structure of points under consideration.

The Mahalanobis distance, on the other hand, is well known in the robust statistics literature as an outlier detector [14]. It exposes outliers by assigning them very large Mahalanobis distances. This, however, depends on an accurate estimate of the covariance matrix that parameterizes this distance. An intuitive approach for obtaining such an estimate is via MLE with Gaussian components. This, however, requires a large number of samples, and converges to a local optimum which might result in an unnecessarily large variance. Our proposed approach is to use a robust estimator for the covariance matrix parameterizing the Mahalanobis distance, where robustness is defined in a statistical sense [17,18]. The MVE [15,16] is such a robust estimator with desirable properties such as intuitive geometric meaning, its formulation as a convex optimization problem which has a global unique solution, and its minimum variance.

2.1   Properties of the Mahalanobis Distance

The Euclidean distance between two points, $\mathbf{x} = (x_1, \ldots, x_d)^T$ and $\mathbf{y} = (y_1, \ldots, y_d)^T$, in the d-dimensional space $\mathbb{R}^d$ is defined as: $D_E(\mathbf{x}, \mathbf{y}) = \sqrt{(\mathbf{x} - \mathbf{y})^T(\mathbf{x} - \mathbf{y})}$. It follows that all non zero points with the same distance from the origin $\mathbf{o}$, satisfy: $x_1^2 + \cdots + x_d^2 = c^2$, $c \in \mathbb{R}^+$, which is the equation of a spheroid. This means that all components of an observation $\mathbf{x}$ contribute equally to the Euclidian distance from $\mathbf{x}$ to the origin or any other reference point. Hence, $D_E(\mathbf{x}, \mathbf{y})$ is meaningful when the data have an equal variance across all its dimensions.

Real life data, however, are usually measurements from various sources at different scales, and are subject to various noise sources. To account for such variability, each component can be assigned a weight that is proportional to the amount of variation across its values, such that components with high variability should receive less weight than those with low variability. Let $\mathbf{u} = (x_1/s_1, \ldots, x_d/s_d)$, and $\mathbf{v} = (y_1/s_1, \ldots, y_d/s_d)$; then, the distance between $\mathbf{u}$ and $\mathbf{v}$ will be: $D_E(\mathbf{u}, \mathbf{v}) = D_\Sigma(\mathbf{x}, \mathbf{y}) = \sqrt{(\mathbf{x} - \mathbf{y})^T \Sigma^{-1}(\mathbf{x} - \mathbf{y})}$ where $\Sigma = diag(s_1^2, \ldots, s_d^2)$, and s_j^2 is the variance of the data across dimension j. Now the distance from $\mathbf{x}$ to the origin equals $D_\Sigma(\mathbf{x}, \mathbf{o}) = \sqrt{\mathbf{x}^T \Sigma^{-1}\mathbf{x}}$, and all points with the same distance to the origin satisfy: $(x_1/s_1)^2 + \cdots + (x_d/s_d)^2 = c^2$, which is the equation of an ellipsoid centered at the origin with its principal axes aligned to the coordinate axes.

By considering correlations between components, this will allow the ellipsoid to rotate its axes and to increase/decrease its size, yielding the well known general form of the distance between two points $\mathbf{x}$ and $\mathbf{y}$, the Mahalanobis distance: $D_\Sigma(\mathbf{x}, \mathbf{y}) = \sqrt{(\mathbf{x} - \mathbf{y})^T \Sigma^{-1}(\mathbf{x} - \mathbf{y})}$, where Σ is a symmetric positive definite matrix, $\Sigma \succ 0$. Consequently, points with the same distance to the origin satisfy: $\mathbf{x}^T \Sigma^{-1}\mathbf{x} = c^2$, which is the general equation of an ellipsoid centered at the origin.

The general Mahalanobis distance enjoys all the properties of distance functions that are defined on a metric space. That is, for any three points $\mathbf{x}$, $\mathbf{y}$, and $\mathbf{z}$ in $\mathbb{R}^d$, the following are satisfied: Symmetry: $D_\Sigma(\mathbf{x}, \mathbf{y}) = D_\Sigma(\mathbf{y}, \mathbf{x})$, Non negativity: $D_\Sigma(\mathbf{x}, \mathbf{y}) > 0$ if $\mathbf{x} \neq \mathbf{y}$, Self reflection: $D_\Sigma(\mathbf{x}, \mathbf{y}) = 0$ if $\mathbf{x} = \mathbf{y}$, and Triangle inequality: $D_\Sigma(\mathbf{x}, \mathbf{y}) \leq D_\Sigma(\mathbf{x}, \mathbf{z}) + D_\Sigma(\mathbf{z}, \mathbf{y})$. Also, it is worth noting that the Euclidean distance can be considered as a special case of the general Mahalanobis form by letting $\Sigma = \mathbf{I}$, where $\mathbf{I}$ is the identity matrix. Alternatively, the general Mahalanobis distance can be seen as a projecting the original $\mathbf{x}$ on the space of $\Sigma^{-1/2}$ and using the Euclidean metric in that space.

2.2 Robust Statistics and the MVE Estimator

Robust statistics [17,18] is the stability theory of statistical procedures. It systematically investigates the effects of deviations from modeling assumptions on known procedures, and if necessary, develops new better procedures [18]. The primary concern of robust statistics is distributional robustness, i.e. the shape of the true underlying distribution deviates slightly from the assumed model (usually the Gaussian law) [17]. Another concern of paramount importance is the design of estimators that can tolerate a large number of outliers before the estimate is affected. Such estimators are known to have a high breakdown point (BP). Finding robust multivariate location and scatter estimators is crucial to make other multivariate techniques such as principal component analysis and discriminant analysis more robust. In addition, distances based on these estimators are more precise than regular ones, and are better suited to expose outliers [14].

The MVE estimator [15,16] is a robust estimator for location (mean) and scatter (covariance matrix) with the highest possible BP value (50%). Geometrically, the estimator finds the minimum volume ellipsoid covering, or enclosing a given set of points. The MVE estimator is a generalization of the least median of squares (LMS) estimator [15,16] for high dimensional data sets, with the extra property of being equivariant to translation, scaling, orthogonal projection and affine transformations. Formulation of the MVE covering a data set is illustrated in the next section.

3   The Minimum Volume Ellipsoid

We consider the problem of finding the minimum volume ellipsoid (MVE) covering a set. Let $\mathcal{X} = \{\mathbf{x}_i \mid 1 \leq i \leq m, \mathbf{x}_i \in \mathbb{R}^d\}$ be a bounded set, where m is the number of vectors, and d is the dimensionality of the input space. The minimum volume ellipsoid that covers $\mathcal{X}$ is known as the $L\ddot{o}wner - John\ Ellipsoid$ of the set $\mathcal{X}$ and is denoted $\mathcal{E}_{lj}$ [2]. The $\mathcal{E}_{lj}$ can be parametrized as follows:

$$\mathcal{E}_{lj} = \{\mathbf{x} \mid \|\Sigma\mathbf{x} - \mathbf{b}\|_2 \leq 1\}, \tag{1}$$

where $\boldsymbol{\Sigma} \in \mathbb{R}^{d \times d}$, $\boldsymbol{\Sigma} \succ 0$, $\mathbf{x}$ and $\mathbf{b} \in \mathbb{R}^d$, and its center is $\boldsymbol{\Sigma}^{-1}\mathbf{b}$. The general ellipsoid can be seen as the inverse image of the Euclidean unit ball under an affine transformation. Using the fact that $\boldsymbol{\Sigma} \succ 0$, it follows that [2]:

$$V(\mathcal{E}_{lj}) \propto \det(\boldsymbol{\Sigma}^{-1}) \propto \frac{1}{\det(\boldsymbol{\Sigma})}, \tag{2}$$

where $V(\mathcal{E}_{lj})$ is the volume of the ellipsoid $\mathcal{E}_{lj}$. Finding the minimum volume ellipsoid covering $\mathcal{X}$ can be formulated as follows:

$$\min_{\Sigma} \ \log\det(\boldsymbol{\Sigma}^{-1}) \quad \textit{or equivalently} \tag{3}$$

$$\max_{\Sigma} \ \log\det(\boldsymbol{\Sigma}) \tag{4}$$

$$\text{subject to } \|\boldsymbol{\Sigma}\mathbf{x}_i - \mathbf{b}\|_2 \leq 1, \quad i = 1, \ldots, m,$$

where the variables of this minimization are $\boldsymbol{\Sigma}$ and $\mathbf{b}$, with an implicit constraint that $\boldsymbol{\Sigma} \succ 0$ which forces the induced distance function to respect all the previously mentioned properties of a metric. The minimization in (3) is a convex optimization problem since the objective and the constraints are convex in the variables $\boldsymbol{\Sigma}$ and $\mathbf{b}$. This is very useful since, theoretically, it allows a global minimum to be found away from local minima. The details of this convex optimization problem are elaborated in [2].

Computing the minimum volume ellipsoid bounding or enclosing a data set can be done in several ways, and the interested reader can see [7,3,13] for a nice review. At the current stage of our research, all our experiments used the CVX MATLAB toolbox for Disciplined Convex Programming [10]. CVX is a general purpose solver that implements an interior point method algorithm that scales efficiently with small to medium size problems.

3.1 The MVE Metric and the MiniVenn Algorithm

The basic idea of the MVEM is that the metric is learned from the perspective of the point itself, should it be a training or a test point, labeled or unlabeled. This should make the metric independent from the learning paradigm since it does not depend on labels as in [6,7], nor on side–information [5,9]. In other words, the metric tries to answer this question, *How does a point perceive the similarity between itself and other neighboring points?* Based on the concept of locality, the metric tries to find the fine differences between a point and its local neighbors, and major differences between the neighborhood and other points in the space.

To find such a metric, we present the Minimum Volume Ellipsoid of Nearest Neighbors (MiniVenn) algorithm, shown in Algorithm 1. Given a query point $\mathbf{x}_q$, the algorithm finds the MVE with $\mathbf{x}_q$ as its center and covering its m nearest neighbors. Recalling the relation in (2), the MiniVenn actually finds a symmetric positive definite matrix with maximum determinant that can parameterize a Mahalanobis distance function from the perspective of $\mathbf{x}_q$. The MiniVenn starts by finding the m nearest neighbors of $\mathbf{x}_q$ using the Euclidean metric; this is

---

Algorithm 1. Minimum Volume Ellipsoid of Nearest Neighbors (MiniVenn):
finds a symmetric positive definite matrix Σ_q with maximum determinant

---

Require: $\mathbf{X}_{n \times d}$, $\mathbf{x}_q$, and m, where $\mathbf{X}$ is the training set with n d-dimensional samples,
$\quad \mathbf{x}_q$ is the query point, and $m \geq d+1$ is a hyper-parameter that controls the size of
$\quad$ the neighborhood.
1: Find the set $\mathcal{X}_q$ that has the m nearest neighbours of $\mathbf{x}_q$ using the Euclidean metric.
2: Find the MVE with center $\mathbf{x}_q$ that covers $\mathcal{X}_q$ using the following convex optimization:

$$\max_{\Sigma} \ \log \det(\Sigma_q)$$

$$\text{subject to } \|\Sigma_q \mathbf{x}_j - \mathbf{b}\|_2 \leq 1, \quad 1 \leq j \leq m, \quad \mathbf{x}_j \in \mathcal{X}_q$$

$$\|\Sigma_q \mathbf{x}_q - \mathbf{b}\|_2 = 0$$

$\quad \{ \textit{The second constraint insures that } \mathbf{x}_q \textit{ will be the center of the MVE, since its}$
$\quad \textit{center is defined as } \Sigma_q^{-1} \mathbf{b}. \}$
3: **return** Σ_q

---

equivalent to considering a spheroid around the query point that covers its m nearest neighbors. Starting from the Euclidean metric is equivalent to setting the initial covariance matrix to the identity matrix which simply reflects our *a priori* assumption that all variables are independent with zero mean and unit variance. This can also be considered as bootstrapping the MVE metric. Next, the convex optimization in (3), reshapes the spheroid into a MVE covering the same set, thereby learning the variances and correlations within and across all variables. The learned Σ_q will be used to measure the Mahalanobis distance from any point $\mathbf{x}$ to $\mathbf{x}_q$. Note that in terms of distances, for any two points $\mathbf{x}, \mathbf{y} \in \mathbb{R}^d$, $D_{\Sigma_\mathbf{x}}(\mathbf{x}, \mathbf{y}) = D_{\Sigma_\mathbf{x}}(\mathbf{y}, \mathbf{x})$ by symmetry. However $D_{\Sigma_\mathbf{x}}(\mathbf{x}, \mathbf{y}) \neq D_{\Sigma_\mathbf{y}}(\mathbf{x}, \mathbf{y})$ since the reference covariance matrix is different.

The advantage of the MVEM stems from its flexibility to be used in any learning paradigm. In an unsupervised setting, and with existence of side–information [5,9], similar samples can be grouped in the same MVE, with the center being their mean. The same applies in the semi–supervised context, when given partially labeled data, which is similar to clustering with side–information. In both cases, m acts as a hyper–parameter that controls clustering affinity.

For supervised learning, two scenarios can take place for learning the metric. In the first, one can learn a full metric $D_\Sigma : \mathbb{R}^d \times \mathbb{R}^d :\mapsto \mathbb{R}$, where MiniVenn will find a MVE for each training point $\mathbf{x}_i$ (i.e. Σ_i). On the one hand, in concept, this makes the MVEM relatively close to the metric found in [5]. On the other hand, as an algorithmic approach, this makes MiniVenn close to the initial step of manifold learning algorithms such as [11,12], albeit without the dimensionality reduction step. The second scenario, on the contrary, learning can be done online using the lazy learning approach [4], where the MVE is computed only on request when a query point $\mathbf{x}_q$ is presented to the training set, and m can be optimized by cross validation. In both scenarios, since there is a training phase to optimize m, the MVEM will generalize well on unseen data sets.

3.2 Links to Other Metric Learning Algorithms

Before proceeding, let us review some basic identities. Let $\mathbf{A} \in \mathbb{R}^{d \times d} \succ 0$ be a symmetric positive definite matrix; then, by eigen decomposition, $\mathbf{A} = V \Lambda V^T$, $\Lambda = diag(\lambda_1, \cdots, \lambda_d)$, where the $\lambda_j s$ are the eigenvalues of $\mathbf{A}$, and the columns of V are its eigenvectors. Then, $\det(\mathbf{A}) = \prod_{j=1}^{d} \lambda_j \succ 0$, and $\det(\mathbf{A}^{-1}) = \prod_{j=1}^{d} 1/\lambda_j \succ 0$. Also, $\|A\|_F^2 = \|V \Lambda V^T\|_F^2 = \|\Lambda\|^2 \succ 0$.

Algorithms found in [5,6,7,8] learn, in general, a parametrized Mahalanobis metric of the form $D_A(\mathbf{x}, \mathbf{y}) = \sqrt{(\mathbf{x} - \mathbf{y}) \mathbf{A}^{-1} (\mathbf{x} - \mathbf{y})}$, and differences between these algorithms are due to the different structures imposed on $\mathbf{A}$. The work in [5,7,8] directly finds an $\mathbf{A}^{-1}$ with minimum $\|\mathbf{A}^{-1}\|_F^2$, i.e. a MVE, accompanied with another term that stems from the problem context, such as minimization of classification error, minimization of distances between similar points, or learning relative relations between points, which ultimately leads to the different flavors of algorithms. Alternatively, the metric in [6] finds directly a matrix $\mathbf{A}^{-1} \succ 0$ that minimizes the Kullback–Leibler divergence between an observed and a desired distribution that will collapse classes to a single point.

The MVEM is relatively close to [5], with no explicit restriction on $\mathbf{A}$ to encode similar samples differently than all other samples, as this is left to the parameter m in the MiniVenn algorithm (1). This can be considered as letting the data speak for itself, but it will be interesting to apply some local constraints similar to those found in [5,9]. Moreover, it does not group similar points together; rather, it is a locally based algorithm. Unlike the proposed methods in [6,7,8], the MVEM does not have any constraints from the problem context; rather, it is the parameter m that is adjusted according to the problem context, and hence the flexibility of the algorithm.

The concept of parameterized Mahalanobis distances also has interesting links with some recent manifold learning algorithms. Charting a manifold [11] and Manifold Parzen Window [12], initially, fix a Gaussian at each training point and then find a local covariance matrix $\mathbf{A}$ based on the neighboring samples. To overcome the poor representation of local covariance matrices, MPW has an embedded dimensionality reduction step by means of spectral decomposition of $\mathbf{A}$, and flattens those components with very small singular values. This acts as a regularized MLE with a Gaussian component, thereby yielding Gaussian pancakes, i.e. a Mahalanobis distance based on a low dimensional projection. In charting a manifold, however, the charting step includes a maximum likelihood estimation, i.e. directly maximizing $\det(\mathbf{A}^{-1})$ (see [2] p. 355), yielding a rotation and an increase of the ellipsoid size, thereby covering a more representative neighborhood. However, neither of the two approaches guarantees a small variance for their estimate.

4   Experimental Results

The experimental setting was designed to validate the MVEM concept and to show its potential. Since the primary objective is to have a metric that can replace the Euclidean metric in any learning paradigm, it is intuitive to evaluate the *"pure"* impact of the new metric without additional aid or complexities from sophisticated learning algorithms. That is, select a simple algorithm that depends solely on the Euclidean metric and replace this metric with the proposed MVEM. The basic and classical k–Nearest Neighbors classifier ($k = 1$) meets such specifications, where optimization of the hyper–parameter m can be based on the training error. Given a training set and a test set, we find the nearest neighbor of each test point using the MVEM.

Table 1. Error rates(%) for EUC, LM, RCA, XING, and MVEM on eleven data sets from the UCI repository using one–out–of–sample criterion

DataSet	classes	size	dim.	EUC	LM	RCA	XING	MVEM
Liver Disorders (bupa)	2	345	6	37.7	38.5	34.5	37.6	35.6
Glass	7	214	9	26.2	34.1	28.5	26.2	23.8
Ionosphere	2	351	34	11.4	16.2	8.3	12.5	8.8
Iris	3	150	4	4.0	2.7	4.0	2.6	2.6
New–Thyroid	3	215	5	5.1	6.9	4.1	5.1	3.2
Diabetes (pima)	2	768	8	32.0	32.4	30.4	32.0	30.4
satImage	6	4435/2000	36	10.6	12.4	22.4	10.6	10.0
Sonar	2	208	60	17.8	24.5	15.9	17.7	15.4
WDBC	2	569	30	9.1	7.9	8.8	9.1	8.4
Wine	3	168	12	4.5	7.3	2.2	10.1	2.8
Yeast	10	1484	6	48.2	46.9	47.2	no convergence	47.5

The MVEM was compared with four other metrics (or metric learning algorithms). Initially, the MVEM was compared to the regular Euclidean metric (EUC), and the Local–Mahalanobis (LM) metric obtained by the local covariance matrix of each test point and its m neighbors from the training set, where m is also optimized based on the training error. Next, the source codes for XING [5] and RCA [9] were downloaded from the authors' web sites in order to compare their performance with the MVEM. XING [5] and RCA [9] algorithms were specifically designed for unsupervised learning with side–information. Unlike the MVEM, these algorithms not only depend on side–information; it is the amount of available side–information that determines their performance. By providing all the true labels for these two algorithms, the uncertainty in the labels is eliminated, and the algorithms should perform at their best.

All five metrics (or algorithms); EUC, LM, RCA [9], XING [5], and MVEM were run on eleven problems from the UCI Machine Learning Repository [1], shown in Table 1, with various sizes, dimensionalities, and difficulties. Except

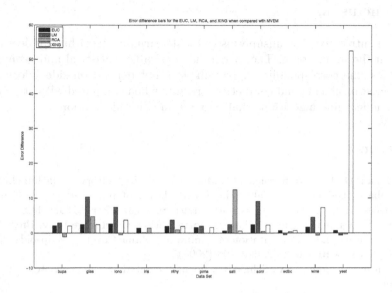

Fig. 1. Error difference bars for EUC, LM, RCA, and XING when compared with MVEM. A positive difference implies that the MVEM is better than the other metric, and negative difference implies the contrary.

for the Sat–Image data set which had explicit training and test sets, the error rates, shown in Table 1, are based on a one–out–of–sample performance using n runs where n is the number of samples in the data set. In order to speed–up the CVX solver, as a preprocessing step, principal component analysis (PCA) was applied to all data sets, except bupa, new–thyroid, pima, and yeast, to keep 99% of their total variance. PCA was obtained from the Sat–Image training set, and from the training set after each split, from all other data sets. The hyper–parameter m (for the case of MVEM and LM) was optimized based on the best training error on the Sat–Image data set, and on the leave–one–out training error after each split for all other data sets.

Discussion: Figure 1 shows error difference bars between all metrics and the MVEM. It can be seen that in overall performance, the MVEM is consistently as good or better than other metrics for most of the cases. In the light of these results, it is worth noting that, in the cases where RCA is slightly better, it is important to recall that RCA was designed for the case when partially labelled data are available, and it achieved this performance when it was provided with the full set of data labels. This is unlike the MVEM which did not use such extra information during its training phase. This makes the MVEM very promising for learning problems where the samples are not labelled, partially labelled, or manually annotated with side–information.

5 Conclusion

We have introduced an unsupervised local–learning algorithm for learning a metric in the input space. The metric has desirable statistical and geometrical properties, the corresponding algorithm does not depend on side–information, and showed promising and competitive results when compared with state of the art metric learning algorithms that depend on side–information.

References

1. Newman, D., Hettich, S., Blake, C., Merz, C.: UCI Repository of Machine Learning Databases University of California, Irvine, Dept. of Information and Computer Sciences (1998), http://www.ics.uci.edu/~mlearn/MLRepository.html
2. Boyd, S., Vandenberghe, L.: Convex Optimization. Cambridge Univ. Press (2004)
3. Sun, P., Freund, R.: Computation of Minimum Volume Covering Ellipsoids. Journal of Operations Research 52, 690–706 (2004)
4. Atkenson, C., Moore, A., Schaal, S.: Local Weighted Learning. AI Review, 11–73 (1997)
5. Xing, E., Ng, A., Jordan, M., Russell, S.: Distance Metric Learning with Application to Clustering with Side-Information. In: NIPS 15, MIT Press, Cambridge (2003)
6. Globerson, A., Roweis, S.: Metric Learning by Collapsing Classes. In: NIPS 18, MIT Press, Cambridge (2006)
7. Weinberger, K., Blitzer, J., Saul, L.: Distance Metric Learning for Large Margin Nearest Neighbor Classification. In: NIPS 18, MIT Press, Cambridge (2006)
8. Schultz, M., Joachims, T.: Learning a Distance Metric from Relative Comparisons. In: NIPS 16, MIT Press, Cambridge (2004)
9. Bar-Hillel, A., Hertz, T., Shental, N., Weinshall, D.: Learning a Mahalanobis Metric from Equivalence Constraints. JMLR 6, 937–965 (2005)
10. Grant, M., Boyd, S., Ye, Y.: Matlab Software for Disciplined Convex Programming (2005), http://www.stanford.edu/~boyd/cvx
11. Brand, M.: Charting a Manifold. In: NIPS 15, MIT Press, Cambridge (2003)
12. Vincent, P., Bengio, Y.: Manifold Parzen Windows. In: NIPS 15, MIT Press, Cambridge (2003)
13. Dolia, A., De–Bie, T., Harris, C., Shawe–Taylor, J., Titterington, D.: The Minimum Volume Covering Ellipsoid Estimation in Kernel–Defined Feature Spaces. In: Fürnkranz, J., Scheffer, T., Spiliopoulou, M. (eds.) ECML 2006. LNCS (LNAI), vol. 4212, Springer, Heidelberg (2006)
14. Rousseeuw, P., Van Driessen, K.: Algorithm for the Minimum Covariance Determinant Estimator. Technometrics 41(3), 212–223 (1999)
15. Rousseeuw, P.: Least Median of Squares Regression. Journal of American Statistical Association 79(388), 871–880 (1984)
16. Rousseeuw, P.: Multivariate Estimation with High Breakdown Point. In: Proceedings of the fourth Pannonian Symposium on Mathematical Statistics, vol. 3, pp. 283–297 (1983)
17. Huber, P.: Robust Statistics. John Wiley Press, Chichester (1981)
18. Hampel, F.: Robust Statistics, ETH–Zurich, Tech. Report No. 94 (2001)

An Attentional Approach for Perceptual Grouping of Spatially Distributed Patterns

Muhammad Zaheer Aziz and Bärbel Mertsching

GET Lab, University of Paderborn, Pohlweg 47-49, 33098 Paderborn, Germany,
<last name>@get.upb.de,
http://getwww.upb.de

Abstract. A natural (human) eye can easily detect large visual patterns or objects emerging from spatially distributed discrete entities. This aspect of pattern analysis has been barely addressed in literature. We propose a biologically inspired approach derived from the concept of visual attention to associate together the distributed pieces of macro level patterns. In contrast to the usual approach practiced by the existing models of visual attention, this paper introduces a short-term excitation on the features and locations related to the current focus of attention in parallel to the spatial inhibition of return. This causes the attention system to fixate on analogous units in the scene that may formulate a meaningful global pattern. It is evident from the results of experiments that the outcome of this process can help in widening the scope of intelligent machine vision.

1 Introduction

A human observer instantly recognizes the patterns formed by arrangement of discrete pieces, such as those given in figure 3, even in the presence of substantial amount of distractors. The individual stars in the European Union flag are of course recognizable patterns by themselves but the macro-level pattern of a circle also has significant meaning for the human vision. This aspect of intelligent viewing helps us in understanding the structures created by spatially distributed items such as shape of a formation of airplanes in an air show, a pattern formed by light bulbs in a signboard, or a design presented by arrangement of windows in an architectural building. Establishing such a relationship is also needed while reading text on large billboards that may be written with horizontal, vertical, or even diagonal arrangement of letters. In psychology this phenomenon is related to the concept of similarity based perceptual grouping [1].

Most of the existing work in this area, such as [2], considers two or already known number of components of distributed patterns in man-made images to formulate a group. We extend the scope to previously unknown number of objects in natural images using a biologically plausible model based upon the phenomenon of visual attention that is utilized by natural vision systems for intelligent viewing. The presented solution will help in picking together the dispersed pieces of the global patterns in a successive sequence so that they could be provided to a higher level recognition process.

F.A. Hamprecht, C. Schnörr, and B. Jähne (Eds.): DAGM 2007, LNCS 4713, pp. 345–354, 2007.

The next section presents the literature related to perceptual grouping and the existing approaches of visual attention modelling. The third section presents the proposed model that includes an explicit influence of behavior in the attention model while introducing the modules for fine grained feature excitation and inhibition in the system. These innovations give rise to a new behavior, we name it as *examine*, which tends to proceed towards the solution of the above mentioned problem. The fourth section explains the details of the *examine* behavior and then the fifth one presents the results of the proposed model in context of integrating parts of distributed patterns followed by a discussion on the achievements from the presented work.

2   Related Work

The concept of grouping texture elements using local conspicuous features called *Textons* [3] has been a significant influence on methods for perceptual grouping. Perception of patterns from random dot distributions known as *Glass Patterns* [4] also has a history of many decades, but these methods have a specific area of application with special restrictions on the input that they can process. The efforts on recognizing dot patterns under gestalt theory are also a step towards determining global structures in the images. One example of such methods is [5], which extracts the perceptual segments of dots grouped together based upon their relative locations and then analyzes the shape of segments. The work in [6] discusses extraction of skeletal shape from 2D dot patterns using self organizing neural networks. The method in [7] uses orientation-tuned receptive field mechanism for determining the local orientation in order to group adjacent tokens consisting of positions and attributes. These methods generally require two restrictions on the input. Firstly the dots should have known size and/or other features and secondly, they should be present in a near neighborhood to each other. Hence, ability to process only a restricted type of artificial data rather than natural images is a major shortcoming.

Another area having relevance to the work discussed in this paper is the illusory contour perception [8] in which completion of imaginary edges is performed between spatially distributed items. Markov random fields have been applied in [9] for completing broken contours in simple images while [10] performs an attentional approach to highlight components of similarly oriented contours in natural images. The work in [11] separates similarly oriented items in images using Gabor responses. The methods mentioned here and other such examples concentrate either on a single feature, mainly orientation, or perform grouping for a specific task using specialized input. On the other hand, the proposed method is an attempt to perform generalized grouping in unrestricted natural scenes as part of the effort to achieve intelligent vision as performed by the biological organisms.

As the proposed solution is based upon artificial visual attention, hence we mention some of the existing models in context of the attention behaviors that they demonstrate. The famous model discussed in [12] and [13] mainly deals with *search* behavior but uses a bottom-up procedure to achieve the target. The recent modification in the model presented in [14] introduces a top-down influence by adjusting weights of feature maps in order to facilitate early pop out of the target. Recent experiments reported by the same group reveal the fine grained nature of the top-down attention, meaning that it is not only the weights of feature maps but the feature values as well that help a target object to pop out first [15]. We have modeled this fact in our approach by explicit excitation on feature values like color, eccentricity, and size etc. The selective tuning model [16] remains in a behavior resembling to *explore* as it does not apply top-down conditions to excite the search target and lets the salient items pop-out during a process involving bottom-up saliency and spatial inhibitions. The models of [17] and [18] are restricted only to exploration while the model given in [19] discusses both *explore* and *search* behavior by integrating bottom-up and top-down biasing in the process of hierarchical selectivity.

The model of [20] considers three behaviors of *explore*, *search*, and *detect changes* while [21] implements *explore* and *search* for dynamic scenes. Work on the early developments in the model proposed here can be seen in [22], [23], and [24] where the main emphasis was on *explore* behavior under the static scenes scenario. Here the model is enhanced to deal with dynamic scenes using memory based mechanism for inhibition of return. Moreover, a new behavior of *examine* is introduced that performs the task of perceptual grouping for spatially distributed patterns by applying excitation on the features of the previously attended object.

3   Proposed Model of Attention

The first major difference of the proposed model of attention from the other models is its region-based nature. Most of the existing models make copies of the input at different scales and apply the attention processes on the pixels of these scaled images whereas a late clustering is implemented to satisfy the needs of object recognition during top-down influence. This leads to fuzzy and dislocated activity clusters and the focus of attention is also unusable by a recognition process. The proposed method first applies a clustering algorithm that produces suitable input for use of the attention process [25] and applies the procedures of visual attention on these pixel clusters. This approach offers many advantages like acceleration in computation, precise localization of activity clusters, and reusability of attention focus into the recognition algorithms.

Figure 1 presents the architectural diagram of the overall model in which a feature extraction function F constructs the feature maps which are combined using the function W that uses weighted averaging to construct a master saliency map. Details of these two functions can be seen in [23] and [24]. The pop-out selection mechanism P picks the highest salient location as the focus of attention which is used by the biasing mechanisms to apply inhibition or excitation according to the active attention behavior handled by module B. The top-down influence affects excitations, inhibitions, and the weights of the feature maps in

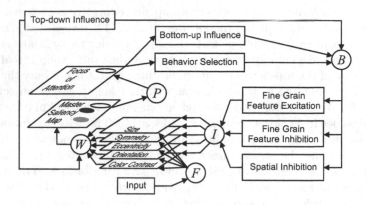

Fig. 1. Architectural diagram of the proposed attention model

order to locate an externally defined target. In this paper we confine our detailed discussion on the fine grain feature excitation and spatial inhibition owing to their active role in the *examine* behavior.

The fine grain feature excitation and inhibition components included here are innovative enhancements in the attention modeling as the existing models apply the top-down or bottom-up influences only by managing weights of the feature maps. The recent experiments on attention such as [15] and [26] suggest that the attention mechanism can excite or inhibit particular values (or a range of values) of features, for example a certain range of hue or some angle of orientation. We include these aspects into our model of attention, which give a feedback to the inhibition/excitation function I. Details of the biasing functions related to the proposed *examine* behavior are discussed in the next section.

4   The *Examine* Behavior

In order to solve the problem of grouping the components of spatially distributed patterns, formed by similar small pieces, we propose a temporary excitation in the feature values resembling the recently attended object coupled with a spatial inhibition on the already attended locations. As we are considering the dynamic input consisting of many frames per second in which the clusters get updated after arrival of each frame, a memory oriented mechanism is introduced for application of biasing effects. This is also an innovation in contrast to the traditional inhibition maps used by the contemporary models. The *examine* behavior works by placing the feature values of the previous pop-out into the feature excitation memory (FEM), denoted by M^e, and its location into the spatial inhibition memory (SIM) denoted by M^s. As the features to be excited remain more or less the same during a cycle of examining, hence the length of M^e is set to only one item. On the other hand the series of locations attended by the system have

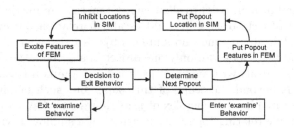

Fig. 2. Execution cycle of *examine* behavior

to be inhibited in order to avoid revisiting of the same objects hence the SIM has a length of m items. We take $m = 13$. Hence

$$M^s = \{M_k^s\}, \, k \in \{1, 2, \ldots, m\} \, .$$

For the latest focus of attention k is set to 1 and it rises with the age of M_k^s in M^s. The overall structure of the examine behavior is sketched in figure 2.

The input for the proposed model is a list of regions $\mathbf{R}$, constructed from the given input frame, containing n regions in which each region is denoted by R_i. Each R_i contains necessary information about the concerned region such as average hue in the region, average saturation, mean intensity, coordinates of the vertices of the bounding rectangle, values of all features from the feature space $\mathbf{F}$, and a list of pointers to the immediate neighbors of R_i in the same list (denoted by η_i). Let $S_f^t(R_i)$ be the saliency of R_i with respect to feature f at time t then the spatial inhibition on R_i is applied as follows:

$$S_f^{t+1}(R_i) = S_f^t(R_i) \cdot \delta \; \forall i \in \mathbf{R} \; \& \; f \in \mathbf{F} \text{ when } D^s(R_i, M_k^s) < r^{inh} \forall k \in \{1, 2, ..m\}$$

where δ is the spatial inhibition factor such that $0 < \delta < 1$, $D^s(R_i, M_k^s)$ is the spatial distance between the considered region R_i and the region in the memory location M_k^s, and r^{inh} is the radius in which inhibition takes effect. Excitation is applied to the regions in $\mathbf{R}$ that are not in M^s and have nearness in features with the last attended region saved in excitation memory M^e. Hence

$$S_f^{t+1}(R_i) = S_f^t(R_i) \cdot \gamma_i \; \forall i \in \mathbf{R} \; \& \; f \in \mathbf{F}, R_i \notin M^s \text{ when } D^f(R_i, M^e) < \theta_f \, ,$$

where $D^f(R_i, M^e)$ gives the difference between R_i and M^e in terms of feature f, θ_f are threshold values and γ_i is the excitation factor such that $\gamma_i > 1$. The value of γ_i is inversely proportional to the distance of R_i from M^e hence it is modeled as

$$\gamma_i = \frac{c \cdot r^{inh}}{D^s(R_i, M^e)} \, ,$$

where c is a scaling factor to keep $\gamma_i \geq 1$ and $D^s(R_i, M^e)$ is the spatial distance between R_i and the previously excited location M^e. To some extent the *examine* behavior has similarity with *search* or *track* behaviors but that would require an inhibition on all objects that differ in features from the target. We do not perform such inhibition in order to allow the system to examine the neighborhood of the attended object so that it could establish relationship even with non-similar surrounding items when no similar objects exist nearby. On the other hand, search and track looks for only one object in a dynamic scene whereas the proposed behavior deals with many objects having common features. Although this discussion is beyond the scope of this paper but such facility can help in learning to integrate pieces of complex objects that do not have common features as well, for example relating together the center of a sunflower with its petals.

5   Results

Experiments were performed using a large set of test images in which high level patterns composed by small objects were present. Figure 3 demonstrates some of these test cases. The model was first executed in exploration mode until it fixated on one of the components of the macro-level pattern and then the behavior was switched to *examine* in order to highlight this pattern in the subsequent saccades. The images of the European Union flag and the night drive scene were among the samples in which a few saccades had to be made before entering the required pattern as visible in figure 4 (a) and (d) where the first focus of attention (marked by 1 in the small rectangle) is outside the main pattern. It is observable in the output given in figure 4 that the model has successfully selected the components of the global pattern in a suitable sequence that follows a scan path reflecting the shape of the respective pattern (figure 5). The circle of stars is picked with fair accuracy, the formation of airplanes is also picked but the scan path needs to be corrected to form a triangle, the letters on the sign board are attended in a suitable sequence that can facilitate reading of the message, and the road side marked by cat eyes is also followed correctly. The arrow formed by the yellow light bulbs and the petals of sunflowers are picked but in an unexpected order while the letter '2' and the rectangle were picked in a correct sequence that highlights their shape. One component at the top left of the digit '2' is missed because the attention moved away from it while following the perceptual group. Due to the attentional nature of the method the sequence of fixations is highly dependant on the visual saliency of the individual items in comparison to their neighborhood that may pull attention of the system before the other items. Hence the scan path may not always draw the concerned shape but this problem can be tackled by normalizing the curve using the points of fixation as guiding information.

The output of the system using the test image given in figure 3 (g) very clearly demonstrates the ability of the method to maintain its focus on the pattern under examination even in presence of distractors that posses higher saliency as compared to the components of the pattern. For example, the rectangles with orange and red colors have higher color saliency than the green ones but the system continues to examine the pattern due to excitation of the examined features. The distracting saliency in the image can be noted by running the system only under exploration behavior. Figure 6 shows output of exploration

Fig. 3. Some images from the data set for experimentation. (a)EU flag (b)air show (c)signboard (d)road at night marked by cat eyes (e)arrow (f)digit 2 formed by oriented rectangles (g)rectangle formed by green boxes (h)circular patterns formed by sunflower petals.

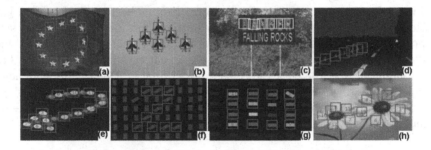

Fig. 4. Locations fixated under *examine* behavior

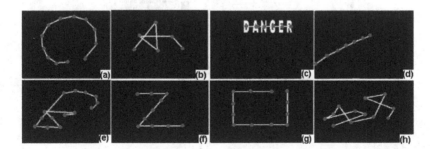

Fig. 5. Scan paths followed by the saccades. Attended regions are also highlighted in (c) to demonstrate the possible utility of the system in reading large graphic texts.

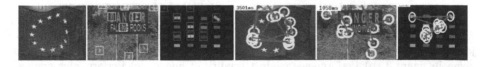

Fig. 6. Output of attention under explore behavior. (Left to right) First three figures show FOA under *explore* behavior using the proposed method and the last three are results using the model of [12].

using the proposed system and the model of [12] using some selected test cases. It is obvious from these results that the fixations under the traditional attention process do not attempt to gather pieces of a high level pattern.

6   Discussion

For a quantitative evaluation of the results from the proposed method we use a scheme adapted from [10]. The test images were presented to human subjects and they were asked to mark the pieces of the most prominent pattern in each. Copies of the same images having low visual quality, obtained by selecting a highly lossy option during JPEG compression, were also used in these experiments. The number of the marked locations were recorded for each case and plotted as a bar graph. Data from the output of the proposed model was collected by counting the locations marked by the system under *examine* behavior. Figure 7(a) shows outcome of this comparison. The proposed system gave identical results as the human subjects on patterns formed by moderately sized components in images with good visual quality. The performance dropped when the pattern components were very small (e.g. in cat eyes image) or do not have clear boundaries (e.g. the petals in the sunflower image). Due the dependency of the model on segmentation, the low image quality of the input causes a significant decline in its performance while the human observers maintain the same efficiency as long as the pattern components remain visible for the eye.

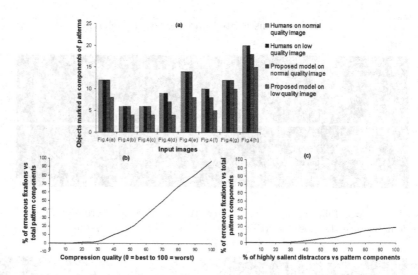

Fig. 7. Performance analysis of the proposed model. (a) Comparison with human subjects in terms of grouping distributed pieces of the most prominent pattern in images given in figure 3 (b) Performance against quality of image. (c) Performance against salient distractors.

The method proposed here depends upon mainly two factors to give good performance. Firstly, it is dependant on the quality of images used as input. Highly compressed images that have noisy shape representations cause decline in performance of the system. Figure 7(b) plots the percentage of fixations placed outside the examined pattern against the quality of image. The actual number of pattern components were obtained by getting the patterns marked by human subjects while different magnitudes of image quality were produced by selecting the parameter of quality during JPEG compression. Low quality of input has minor affect on human observation but significantly degrades performance of the artificial system in the current state of technology. Figure 7(c) shows the effect of presence of highly salient distractors on the performance. It is clear from the results that there is less effect of the presence of distractors that could distract attention in competition to the pattern components. Images of normal quality (without insertion of compression noise) were used in the second experiments.

At this point it is difficult to provide a quantitative comparison of results with the existing methods because such aspect of pattern analysis has not been directly considered in the literature so far and also there are no benchmarks available yet to perform such evaluation. There are many different facets that demand extensive research such as improving the robustness while selecting the component patterns, methods to correlate the components to understand the formed shape, or even an alternate mechanism to perform the same task.

The behavior discussed in this paper is modeled based upon a hypothesis best suited to explain the phenomenon of studying the patterns formed by disjoint components. Psychophysical experiments to prove its existence in the natural vision are yet to be done. Experiments on the model have shown success of the proposed method in advancing towards solution of the said problem that can lead to superior ability of pattern analysis, recognition, and learning in the artificial vision systems.

References

1. Wertheimer, M.: Laws of organization in perceptual forms. In: Ellis, W.D. (ed.) A Source Book of Gestalt Psychology, pp. 71–88 (1938)
2. Ogmen, H., Otto, T., Herzog, M.H.: Perceptual grouping induces non-retinotopic feature attribution in human vision. Vision Research 46, 3234–3242 (2006)
3. Julesz, B.: Textons, the elements of texture perception, and their interactions. Nature, 91–97 (1981)
4. Glass, L.: Moire effect from random dots. Nature 223, 578–580 (1969)
5. Ahuja, N., Tuceryan, M.: Extraction of early perceptual structure in dot patterns: Integrating region, boundary, and component gestalt. Computer Vision, Graphics, and Image Processing 48, 304–356 (1989)
6. Datta, A., Parui, S., Chaudhuri, B.: Skeletal shape extraction from dot patterns by self-organization. In: 13th ICPR, vol. 4, pp. 80–84 (1996)
7. Stevens, K.A., Brookes, A.: Detecting structure by symbolic constructions on tokens. Computer Vision, Graphics, and Image Processing 37, 238–260 (1987)
8. Hund, M., Mertsching, B.: A Computational Approach to Illusory Contour Perception Based on the Tensor Voting Technique. In: Sanfeliu, A., Cortés, M.L. (eds.) CIARP 2005. LNCS, vol. 3773, Springer, Heidelberg (2005)

9. Ackermann, F., Massmann, A., Posch, S., Sagerer, G., Schueter, D.: Perceptual grouping of contour segements using markov random fields. Pattern Recognition and Image Analysis 7, 11–17 (1997)
10. Peters, R.J., Iyer, A., Itti, L., Koch, C.: Components of bottom-up gaze allocation in natural images. Vision Research 45, 2397–2416 (2005)
11. Carreira, M.J., Orwell, J., Turnes, R., Boyce, J.F.: Perceptual grouping from gabor filter responses. In: BMVC 98, Southampton - UK (1998)
12. Itti, L., Koch, U., Niebur, E.: A model of saliency-based visual attention for rapid scene analysis. IEEE Transactions on PAMI 20, 1254–1259 (1998)
13. Itti, L., Koch, C.: A saliency based search mechanism for overt and covert shifts of visual attention. Vision Research, 1489–1506 (2000)
14. Navalpakkam, V., Itti, L.: Modeling the influence of task on attention. Vision Research, 205–231 (2005)
15. Navalpakkam, V., Itti, L.: Top-down attention selection is fine-grained. Journal of Vision 6, 1180–1193 (2006)
16. Rothenstein, A., Tsotsos, J.: Selective tuning: Feature binding through selective attention. In: Kollias, S., Stafylopatis, A., Duch, W., Oja, E. (eds.) ICANN 2006. LNCS, vol. 4132, pp. 548–557. Springer, Heidelberg (2006)
17. Park, S.J., Ban, S.J., Sang, S.W., Shin, J.K., Lee, M.: Implementation of visual attention system using bottom-up saliency map model. In: Kaynak, O., Alpaydın, E., Oja, E., Xu, L. (eds.) ICANN 2003 and ICONIP 2003. LNCS, vol. 2714, pp. 678–685. Springer, Heidelberg (2003)
18. Meur, O.L., Callet, P.L., Barba, D., Thoreau, D.: A coherent computational approach to model bottom-up visual attention. IEEE Transactions on PAMI 28, 802–817 (2006)
19. Sun, Y., Fischer, R.: Object-based visual attention for computer vision. Artificial Intelligence 146, 77–123 (2003)
20. Backer, G., Mertsching, B., Bollmann, M.: Data- and model-driven gaze control for an active-vision system. IEEE Transactions on PAMI 23, 1415–1429 (2001)
21. Frintrop, S., Backer, G., Rome, E.: Goal-directed search with a top-down modulated computational attention system. In: Kropatsch, W.G., Sablatnig, R., Hanbury, A. (eds.) Pattern Recognition. LNCS, vol. 3663, pp. 117–124. Springer, Heidelberg (2005)
22. Aziz, M.Z., Mertsching, B., Shafik, M.S., Stemmer, R.: Evaluation of visual attention models for robots. In: ICVS 06, New York - USA. index–20, IEEE, Los Alamitos (2006)
23. Aziz, M.Z., Mertsching, B.: Color saliency and inhibition in region based visual attention. In: WAPCV 2007, Hyderabad - India, pp. 95–108 (2007)
24. Aziz, M.Z., Mertsching, B.: Pop-out and IOR in static scenes with region based visual attention. In: WCAA-ICVS 2007, Bielefeld - Germany, Bielefeld University eCollections (2007)
25. Aziz, M.Z., Mertsching, B.: Color segmentation for a region-based attention model. In: Farbworkshop 2006, Ilmenau - Germany, pp. 74–83 (2006)
26. Goolsby, B.A., Grabowecky, M., Suzuki, S.: Adaptive modulation of color salience contingent upon global form coding and task relevance. Vision Research, 901–930 (2005)

Classifying Glaucoma with Image-Based Features from Fundus Photographs

Rüdiger Bock[1], Jörg Meier[1], Georg Michelson[2], László G. Nyúl[1],
and Joachim Hornegger[1]

[1] Institute of Pattern Recognition, University of Erlangen-Nuremberg,
Martensstraße 3, 91058 Erlangen
{ruediger.bock,joerg.meier,laszlo.nyul}@informatik.uni-erlangen.de,
joachim.hornegger@informatik.uni-erlangen.de
[2] Department of Ophthalmology, University of Erlangen-Nuremberg,
Schwabachanlage 6, 91054 Erlangen
georg.michelson@augen.imed.uni-erlangen.de

Abstract. Glaucoma is one of the most common causes of blindness
and it is becoming even more important considering the ageing society.
Because healing of died retinal nerve fibers is not possible early detection and prevention is essential. Robust, automated mass-screening will
help to extend the symptom-free life of affected patients. We devised
a novel, automated, appearance based glaucoma classification system
that does not depend on segmentation based measurements. Our purely
data-driven approach is applicable in large-scale screening examinations.
It applies a standard pattern recognition pipeline with a 2-stage classification step. Several types of image-based features were analyzed and are
combined to capture glaucomatous structures. Certain disease independent variations such as illumination inhomogeneities, size differences, and
vessel structures are eliminated in the preprocessing phase. The "vessel-
free" images and intermediate results of the methods are novel representations of the data for the physicians that may provide new insight into
and help to better understand glaucoma. Our system achieves 86 % success rate on a data set containing a mixture of 200 real images of healthy
and glaucomatous eyes. The performance of the system is comparable to
human medical experts in detecting glaucomatous retina fundus images.

1 Introduction

Glaucoma is one of the most common causes of blindness with a mean prevalence
of 4.2 % for ages above 60 years. This disease is characterized by changes in the
eyeground (fundus) in the region of the optic nerve head (ONH): (i) enlarge-
ment of the excavation, (ii) disc hemorrhage, (iii) thinning of the neuroretinal
rim, (iv) asymmetry of the cup between left and right eye, (v) loss of retina nerve
fibers, and (vi) appearance of parapapillary atrophy. It is induced by the progressive loss of retinal nerve fibers in the parapapillary region. Although those
lost fibers cannot be revitalized and there is no possibility for healing glaucoma,
the progression of the disease can be stopped [1].

F.A. Hamprecht, C. Schnörr, and B. Jähne (Eds.): DAGM 2007, LNCS 4713, pp. 355–364, 2007.
© Springer-Verlag Berlin Heidelberg 2007

Nowadays, diagnosis is commonly done by physicians who examine the eye fundus using an ophthalmoscope or digital retina images acquired by devices like the Heidelberg Retina Tomograph (HRT) [2] or the Kowa NonMyd fundus camera.

1.1 State of the Art

In the domain of retina image analysis, automated methods already exist for certain tasks, for instance determination of components of the eyeground (e.g. segmenting the vessels [3] or the ONH [4,5]). These measurements can be used for automated diagnosis of diseases such as diabetic retinopathy [6] or glaucoma. Existing image-based glaucoma detection methods work on HRT images. Swindale et al. [7,8] models a smooth two-dimensional surface that is fitted to the optic nerve head in topography images. Detection of glaucomatous damages can be done via global shape measures of the optic disc (cup and disc area, height variation in HRT images) [9]. This global shape approach is compared with a sector-based analysis by Iester et al. [10]. Zangwill evaluated optic disc parameters and additional parapapillary parameters via Support Vector Machine (SVM) for detecting glaucoma [11]. Greaney states that the detection of glaucoma via separately applied, shape-based methods on different modalities (confocal laser scanning ophthalmoscopy, scanning laser polarimetry, optical coherence tomography) is not better than qualitative assessment of the optic disc by ophthalmologists [12]. All of these shape approaches assume a valid segmentation of the optic disc. However, segmentation based techniques have one major drawback: small errors in segmentation may lead to significant change in the measurements and thus the estimation and diagnosis.

1.2 Our Approach

We build a robust, automated glaucoma detection system using color fundus images in a data-driven way. Therefore, image-based features are provided that are new in the domain of glaucoma detection. This, so called appearance based, approach is well-known from object and face recognition [13,14]. The technique is based on statistical evaluation of the data and does not depend on explicit outlining of the optic disc, as required for global or sector-based shape analysis. Consequently, preprocessing and image-based feature extraction has a major influence on the classification process.

This work shows the influence of different image-based features on the accuracy of glaucoma classification from fundus images. We analyze different types of features (pixel intensity values, textures, spectral features, and parameters of a histogram model) that are intended to capture glaucomatous structures and evaluate the results using three different classifiers (naive Bayes classifier, k-nearest neighbor, and Support Vector Machine). They were used to classify the computed features as is, in combination with an attribute preselection method, and with an iterative attribute selection by AdaBoosting. The combination of features is also considered.

2   Methods

The image processing is structured in a standard 3-stage pipeline: (i) preprocessing, (ii) image-based feature extraction, (iii) classification. In this work, the
preprocessing steps are not changed during the experiments.

2.1   Preprocessing

Our previous studies [15] showed that appearance-based approaches perform
better on images with less disease independent variations. For this reason, a
normalization of the three major variations is applied.

The inhomogeneous illumination caused by deviations in the complex acquisition process are compensated by robust homomorphic surface fitting [6]. Also,
the vessel branches in the images vary much in size, location and shape among
individual cases and introduce a high variance in the data that suppresses variations due to the disease itself. Thus, we roughly segment blood vessels and
spatially inpaint them to gain a "vessel-free" image. These images, as shown in
Fig. 1, provide a novel image representation with irrelevant parts excluded that
support physicians in diagnosing glaucoma.

Fig. 1. Vessel inpainting on color fundus image: Original color fundus image (left),
image with vessel mask overlayed in black (center), "vessel-free" fundus image (right)

The neuroretinal rim is the most important region for detecting glaucoma
[16]. We normalize the images such that the ONH is centered in all images and
appears in the same size. The images are scaled to an uniform size of 128×128
pixels.

2.2   Image-Based Feature Extraction

We propose four feature extraction methods that provide complementary information with different spatial and frequency resolutions. Their influence on
glaucoma classification is evaluated in this paper.

Pixel Intensity Values: The standard appearance based approach takes pixel
intensity values directly as a high dimensional feature vector [13] as input of
a dimension reduction algorithm. We considered principal component analysis
(PCA) as an unsupervised and linear discriminant analysis (LDA) as a supervised method to reduce dimensionality. As evaluated in [15], thirty principal
components capture at least 95 % of data variation.

Textures: The local spatial and spatial-frequency information is characterized by textures. To capture the structural changes caused by glaucoma, we provide a set of Gabor filter banks [17] on preprocessed images. The filter is performed for rotation angles $\theta = 0°, 45°, 90°, 135°$ and frequencies $u_0 = 2^k\sqrt{2}$ for $k = 0, \ldots, 6$. The dimension of each of the computed 28 filter responses ($128 \times 128\,\mathrm{px}$) is reduced by PCA separately. The resulting eigenspaces are then concatenated to a single $(28 \cdot 30)$-dimensional space.

FFT Coefficients: The frequency spectrum contains global frequency information that is translation invariant. We calculate the real and imaginary response as well as the magnitude of the coefficients of the Fast Fourier Transform (FFT). A dimension reduction via PCA is performed on the three responses and combined to a $(3 \cdot 30)$-dimensional space.

Histogram Model: Histograms provide a compact summary of the data distribution in an image. The histogram of an image is relatively invariant to translation and rotation of objects. Comparing histograms of different images is particularly well applicable to the problem of recognizing global intensity changes. The histograms of the preprocessed retina images show three major structural parts corresponding to the background, the papilla rim, and the cup.

The expected variation in the images because of the disease is also represented in the histograms. The increasing cup area and the decreasing rim area cause a shift of the intensity distribution towards higher values. We fit a Gaussian mixture model of three normal distributions to the histogram by a maximum likelihood estimation and the computed distribution parameters, namely the mean, variance and weight, serve as features. The 10 % and 90 % quantiles and the maximum of the histogram are also taken into consideration.

2.3   Classification

Classifiers: The ability of each image-based feature extraction method to separate glaucoma and non-glaucoma cases is quantified by the results of three classifiers. Classifiers achieve good results if their underlying separation model fits well to the distribution of the sample data. As the underlying data distribution is unknown, we tested different classifiers.

Naive Bayes Classifier: This probabilistic classifier directly applies the Bayes rule to determine the probability of a test sample belonging to a class. Three assumptions are made: the feature data is normally distributed, the predictive attributes are conditionally independent given the class, and no hidden or latent attributes influence the prediction process [18].

k-Nearest Neighbor Classifier (k-NN): The k-NN classifier as instance-based classifier, does not assume a specific distribution of the feature data. It adapts well to the sample data, but also tends to overfit. It is also sensitive to noise and to irrelevant features. It is applied with $k = 5$ neighbors.

Support Vector Machine: This linear classifier determines a maximum-margin and soft hyperplane that best separates the considered classes. The data is normalized and transformed via the non-linear radial basis kernel. We use the ν-SVM with penalization parameter $\nu = 0.5$ and cost-parameter $c = 1$ [19].

Classification Enhancement: The feature data distribution might not optimally fit to the classifiers' data model. We analyze the effect of two known methods to improve classification result.

(i) Feature selection removes attributes from the initial set. Features that are highly correlated to a class and have a low correlation to other attributes are kept [20] and the reduced set is used for classification.

(ii) AdaBoosting is a classification scheme to improve classification results. The method iteratively applies one arbitrary classifier. AdaBoosting is able to improve results especially of weak learners on real-world data and is robust to overfitting [21].

Feature Combination: To further improve the classification correctness and robustness, we investigated two ways of combining the four image-based feature types.

(i) Feature Merging concatenates all available feature spaces to a new high dimensional space (970 dim.) that is used for classification.

(ii) 2-stage classification applies the probability score of belonging to the glaucoma class, obtained from each of the four classifiers, as new feature vector input to another classifier.

3 Evaluation

For evaluation, we took images from the Erlangen Glaucoma Registry (EGR) that contains thousands of records of multi-modal fundus images from a long-term screening study. Diagnosis was made by an ophthalmologist based on anamnesis, image data and other measurements. The images were acquired by a Kowa NonMyd α-D digital fundus camera that produced lossless compressed RGB photographs of size 1600×1216 pixels, using a 20° field of view and nasal positioning (papilla-centered).

We evaluated the above described image-based feature extraction methods and classifiers on a test set of 100 preprocessed images (50 healthy and 50 glaucomatous). With this set, the measures were calculated for cross-validation tests and for classification experiments with separated training and test data. The PCA/LDA models, i.e. the eigenimages, as well as the training of the classifiers in the case of separated training and test sets was done with another image set of 100 images (also 50 healthy and 50 glaucomatous cases).

For all experiments we computed the overall classification correctness and the F-measure for healthy (F_h) and glaucomatous eyes (F_g), which is the harmonic mean of sensitivity and precision. To mark promising and robust configurations,

Table 1. Classification performance of the four feature extraction methods. Configurations with "best"-criterion are labeled bold.

Data	Classifier	Structure	Cross-validation			Train-Test		
			Correct (%)	F_h	F_g	Correct (%)	F_h	F_g
PCA on intensities (30 dim.)	Bayes	nothing	73	0.72	0.74	48	0.43	0.52
		AdaBoost	75	0.76	0.74	64	0.65	0.63
		FeatureSel	77	0.75	0.79	63	0.67	0.58
	kNN	nothing	77	0.75	0.79	68	0.75	0.57
		AdaBoost	74	0.75	0.73	70	0.75	0.63
		FeatureSel	82	0.82	0.82	70	0.75	0.62
	SVM	**nothing**	**83**	**0.81**	**0.85**	**81**	**0.83**	**0.78**
		AdaBoost	80	0.78	0.82	79	0.82	0.75
		FeatureSel	85	0.85	0.85	73	0.76	0.69
PCA on textures (840 dim.)	Bayes	nothing	69	0.67	0.70	44	0.44	0.44
		AdaBoost	69	0.70	0.67	70	0.67	0.72
		FeatureSel	76	0.76	0.76	60	0.62	0.57
	kNN	nothing	55	0.21	0.69	64	0.73	0.45
		AdaBoost	64	0.49	0.72	66	0.74	0.51
		FeatureSel	80	0.76	0.83	73	0.77	0.67
	SVM	nothing	67	0.57	0.73	60	0.71	0.35
		AdaBoost	60	0.41	0.70	76	0.77	0.74
		FeatureSel	**80**	**0.78**	**0.82**	**81**	**0.83**	**0.79**
PCA on FFT (90 dim.)	Bayes	nothing	74	0.73	0.75	47	0.40	0.52
		AdaBoost	83	0.83	0.83	59	0.55	0.62
		FeatureSel	78	0.77	0.79	72	0.76	0.66
	kNN	nothing	75	0.71	0.78	66	0.74	0.50
		AdaBoost	74	0.74	0.74	71	0.77	0.60
		FeatureSel	83	0.82	0.84	69	0.74	0.62
	SVM	**nothing**	**76**	**0.74**	**0.77**	**76**	**0.79**	**0.71**
		AdaBoost	77	0.76	0.78	72	0.76	0.67
		FeatureSel	83	0.82	0.84	73	0.77	0.67
Histogram model (10 dim.)	Bayes	nothing	71	0.69	0.73	58	0.60	0.55
		AdaBoost	73	0.71	0.75	65	0.69	0.60
		FeatureSel	71	0.69	0.73	45	0.32	0.54
	kNN	nothing	81	0.80	0.82	54	0.50	0.57
		AdaBoost	72	0.67	0.77	54	0.50	0.57
		FeatureSel	69	0.69	0.68	42	0.39	0.44
	SVM	**nothing**	**73**	**0.72**	**0.74**	**61**	**0.61**	**0.60**
		AdaBoost	80	0.80	0.80	85	0.00	0.92
		FeatureSel	70	0.69	0.71	39	0.30	0.46
LDA on intensities (30 dim.)	Bayes	nothing	78	0.78	0.78	55	0.52	0.58
		AdaBoost	77	0.78	0.76	68	0.71	0.65
		FeatureSel	79	0.78	0.80	67	0.71	0.61
	kNN	nothing	79	0.78	0.80	68	0.75	0.57
		AdaBoost	81	0.80	0.83	74	0.78	0.68
		FeatureSel	84	0.84	0.84	69	0.75	0.60
	SVM	**nothing**	**82**	**0.80**	**0.84**	**76**	**0.80**	**0.71**
		AdaBoost	78	0.78	0.78	68	0.75	0.57
		FeatureSel	80	0.79	0.81	69	0.75	0.60

we defined a "best"-criterion for each feature extraction set. The best configuration within a set has a $F_g \geq 0.60$ and $F_h \geq 0.60$ in the cross-validation test as well as in the separated training and test sets experiments and maximum sum of F-measures $F_g + F_h$.

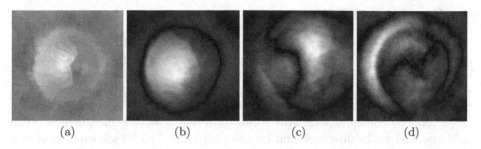

(a)   (b)   (c)   (d)

Fig. 2. (a) "Vessel-free" fundus image, (b)-(c) the first three absolute eigenimages of PCA on intensities. Bright regions indicate high influence on the features.

Table 2. Classification performance of merged features and 2-stage classification

Data	Classifier	Structure	Cross-validation			Train-Test		
			Correct (%)	F_h	F_g	Correct (%)	F_h	F_g
		nothing	71	0.69	0.72	45	0.43	0.47
	Bayes	AdaBoost	79	0.80	0.78	63	0.58	0.67
		FeatureSel	76	0.76	0.76	68	0.71	0.64
Feature Merging		nothing	60	0.33	0.71	63	0.72	0.45
(970 dim.)	kNN	AdaBoost	71	0.69	0.73	66	0.74	0.51
		FeatureSel	81	0.79	0.83	67	0.74	0.56
		nothing	72	0.65	0.77	61	0.72	0.38
	SVM	AdaBoost	61	0.42	0.71	62	0.72	0.71
		FeatureSel	**84**	**0.83**	**0.85**	**80**	**0.82**	**0.77**
	Bayes	nothing	84	0.85	0.86	80	0.82	0.76
		AdaBoost	82	0.82	0.82	80	0.82	0.77
2-stage Classification	kNN	nothing	81	0.80	0.82	80	0.82	0.77
(4 dim.)		AdaBoost	80	0.80	0.80	78	0.81	0.74
	SVM	nothing	85	0.86	0.84	80	0.82	0.77
		AdaBoost	**86**	**0.83**	**0.88**	**80**	**0.82**	**0.77**

In the first step, we tested the four feature extractions with the different classifier types as described in Section 2. Each feature configuration was applied as is, in combination with attribute selection or AdaBoosting. The classification results are given in Table 1. We also computed features based on a LDA model (trained with the separated training set) and classified them according to our scheme. The result is shown in Table 1. The absolute eigenimages generated by PCA on intensities (see Fig. 2) show regions of the fundus with high influence to the features. Those regions might point to relevant glaucomatous areas and help in understanding glaucoma.

In the second step, we evaluated the performance of the feature combinations. Feature merging results are stated in the first block of Table 2. Two stage classification combines the four best classifiers for each feature extraction method. For each feature extraction the class probability for glaucoma was taken as an input to a second classification step. As these features are only 4 dimensional, there was no need for feature selection. The classification result is shown in the second block of Table 2.

4   Results and Discussion

The classification performance using each feature extraction method separately shows that the correctness varies between 55 % and 85 % in cross-validation. Also each feature extraction method itself has varying classification correctness and F-measures for the different classifier configurations. The SVM separates the features most robustly and is always part of configurations labeled with the "best"-criterion. The configurations with "best"-criterion achieve F-measures between 0.72 and 0.81 for healthy case and between 0.74 and 0.85 for glaucomatous case in case of cross-validation. They are always using SVM for classification. Only in case of high dimensional feature space as with PCA on textures (840 dim.) feature selection is necessary to avoid problems with the curse of dimensionality and to achieve similar success rates as PCA on intensities. Although the PCA on pixel values ($F_g = 0.85$) and on texture ($F_g = 0.82$) shows slight better results than PCA on FFT ($F_g = 0.77$) and the histogram model ($F_g = 0.74$), all configurations show a reasonable discriminative power. Comparing the two dimension reduction techniques, LDA shows a smaller variance in the results than PCA. The SVM also classifies the LDA features best.

In case of the feature merging, the highest success rate and F-measures ($F_g = 0.85$, $F_h = 0.83$) are obtained if a feature selection is done before using the SVM in case of cross-validation. In 2-stage classification, the class-probabilities of the "best"-labeled classifier configurations are used as second stage features. This scheme shows success rates with F-measures over 0.80 for all classifier configurations in case of cross-validation. Classification on separate training and test set shows consistent, but slight inferior F-measures. The highest success rate of all experiments (86 %) is gained by SVM with AdaBoosting with $F_h = 0.83$ and $F_g = 0.88$.

As stated in [12], experienced observers achieve an average $F_g = 0.79$ and $F_h = 0.91$ by qualitative assessment of optic nerve head stereophotographs (63 normal and 29 glaucomatous subjects). Regarding classification on separate test and training set, we gain a slightly inferior performance ($F_g = 0.77$) while we get $F_h = 0.82$ for normals.

5   Conclusion

We presented a novel automated glaucoma classification system using digital fundus images. In contrast to the commonly used segmentation based measurements, it is purely data-driven and uses image-based features that are new in the domain of glaucoma recognition. We evaluated several combinations of image-based features and classifier schemes on a set of 200 real fundus images. The 2-stage classification with SVM produced 86 % success rate. The performance of the fully automatic system presented here is comparable to medical experts in detecting glaucomatous eyes and it could be used in mass-screenings. The important features automatically identified by the methods also provide a novel representation of the data for the physicians and may help to better understand glaucoma.

Acknowledgments

The images and diagnoses used in this study were obtained from the Erlangen Glaucoma Registry. The work of R. Bock was supported by the SFB 539 subproject A4, sponsored by the German Research Foundation. The work of J. Meier was supported by a scholarship from the International Max Planck Research School. The work of L.G. Nyúl was supported by a research fellowship from the Alexander von Humboldt-Foundation.

References

1. Sivalingam, E.: Glaucoma: An overview. J. Ophthalmic. Nurs. Tech. 15(1), 15–18 (1996)
2. Malinovsky, V.E.: An overview of the Heidelberg Retina Tomograph. J. Am. Optom. Assoc. 67(8), 457–467 (1996)
3. Staal, J., Abràmoff, M., Niemeijer, M., Viergever, M., van Ginneken, B.: Ridge-based vessel segmentation in color images of the retina. IEEE Trans. Med. Imag. 23(4), 501–509 (2004)
4. Hoover, A., Goldbaum, M.: Locating the optic nerve in a retinal image using the fuzzy convergence of the blood vessels. IEEE Trans. Med. Imag. 22(8), 951–958 (2003)
5. Chrástek, R., Wolf, M., Donath, K., Niemann, H., Paulus, D., Hothorn, T., Lausen, B., Lämmer, R., Mardin, C., Michelson, G.: Automated segmentation of the optic nerve head for diagnosis of glaucoma. Med. Image Anal. 9(4), 297–314 (2005)
6. Narasimha-Iyer, H., Can, A., Roysam, B., Stewart, C.V., Tanenbaum, H.L., Majerovics, A., Singh, H.: Robust detection and classification of longitudinal changes in color retinal fundus images for monitoring diabetic retinopathy. IEEE Trans. Biomed. Eng. 53(6), 1084–1098 (2006)
7. Swindale, N.V., Stjepanovic, G., Chin, A., Mikelberg, F.S.: Automated analysis of normal and glaucomatous optic nerve head topography images. Invest. Ophthalmol. Vis. Sci. 41(7), 1730–1742 (2000)
8. Adler, W., Hothorn, T., Lausen, B.: Simulation based analysis of automated, classification of medical images. Methods Inf. Med. 43(2), 150–155 (2004)
9. Uchida, H., Brigatti, L., Caprioli, J.: Detection of structural damage from glaucoma with confocal laser image analysis. Invest. Ophthalmol. Vis. Sci. 37(12), 2393–2401 (1996)
10. Iester, M., Swindale, N.V., Mikelberg, F.S.: Sector-based analysis of optic nerve head shape parameters and visual field indices in healthy and glaucomatous eyes. J. Glaucoma. 6(6), 370–376 (1997)
11. Zangwill, L.M., Chan, K., Bowd, C., Hao, J., Lee, T.W., Weinreb, R.N., Sejnowski, T.J., Goldbaum, M.H.: Heidelberg retina tomograph measurements of the optic disc and parapapillary retina for detecting glaucoma analyzed by machine learning classifiers. Invest. Ophthalmol. Vis. Sci. 45(9), 3144–3151 (2004)
12. Greaney, M.J., Hoffman, D.C., Garway-Heath, D.F., Nakla, M., Coleman, A.L., Caprioli, J.: Comparison of optic nerve imaging methods to distinguish normal eyes from those with glaucoma. Invest. Ophthalmol. Vis. Sci. 43(1), 140–145 (2002)
13. Hornegger, J., Niemann, H., Risack, R.: Appearance-based object recognition using optimal feature transforms. Pattern Recogn 2(33), 209–224 (2000)

14. Zhao, W., Chellappa, R., Phillips, P.J., Rosenfeld, A.: Face recognition: A literature survey. ACM Comput. Surv. 35(4), 399–458 (2003)
15. Meier, J., Bock, R., Michelson, G., Nyúl, L.G., Hornegger, J.: Effects of preprocessing eye fundus images on appearance based glaucoma classification. In: Procceedings of International Conference on Computer Analysis of Images and Patterns (2007) (accepted for publication)
16. Lester, M., Garway-Heath, D., Lemij, H.: Optic Nerve Head and Retinal Nerve Fibre Analysis. European Glaucoma Society (2005)
17. Jain, A., Farrokhnia, F.: Unsupervised texture segmentation using Gabor filters. In: Proceedings of IEEE International Conference on Systems, Man and Cybernetics, pp. 14–19. IEEE Computer Society Press, Los Alamitos (1990)
18. John, G.H., Langley, P.: Estimating continuous distributions in bayesian classifiers. In: Proceedings of the Eleventh Conference on Uncertainty in Artifical Intelligence, San Mateo, pp. 338–345. Morgan Kaufmann Publishers, San Francisco (1995)
19. Chen, P.H., Lin, C.J., Schölkopf, B.: A tutorial on ν-support vector machines. Applied Stochastic Models in Business and Industry 21(2), 111–136 (2005)
20. Hall, M.A.: Correlation-based Feature Selection for Machine Learning. PhD thesis, University of Waikato, Hamilton, New Zealand (1999)
21. Freund, Y., Schapire, R.E.: Experiments with a new boosting algorithm. In: Procceedings of the Thirteenth International Conference on Machine Learning, pp. 148–156 (1996)

Learning to Recognize Faces Incrementally

O. Deniz, J. Lorenzo, M. Castrillon, J. Mendez, and A. Falcon

Dpto. Informatica y Sistemas. Universidad de Las Palmas de Gran Canaria
Campus de Tafira, Edificio Informatica. 35017 Las Palmas Spain

Abstract. Most face recognition systems are based on some form of batch learning. Online face recognition is not only more practical, it is also much more biologically plausible. Typical batch learners aim at minimizing both training error and (a measure of) hypothesis complexity. We show that the same minimization can be done incrementally as long as some form of "scaffolding" is applied throughout the learning process. Scaffolding means: make the system learn from samples that are neither too easy nor too difficult at each step. We note that such learning behavior is also biologically plausible. Experiments using large sequences of facial images support the theoretical claims. The proposed method compares well with other, numerical calculus-based online learners.

1 Introduction

Face recognition is becoming one of the most researched problems in Computer Vision. The available literature is increasing at a significant rate, and even the number of conferences and special issues entirely devoted to face recognition is growing. Access to inexpensive cameras and computational resources has allowed researchers to explore the problem from many different perspectives, see the survey [5].

Humans are very competent when it comes to recognize faces. A number of face recognition systems have been based, at least partially, on psychophysical or neurophysiological findings related to face recognition in humans. The use of biologically-inspired features for discrimination is a prominent example, with Gabor features topping the list.

Other work has tackled online face recognition. The interest, however, seems to have been mainly practical, rather than based on biological plausibility considerations. In particular, attempts have been made at alleviating the high computational cost of the most common feature selection model used in face recognition, namely Principal Component Analysis (PCA). Incremental PCA [6] aims at updating the PCA basis incrementally and is computationally efficient for large scale problems. Incremental algorithms have been also proposed for classification. Incremental SVM [4], for example, is a computationally efficient version of the successful SVM (Support Vector Machines) classifier, which typically requires solving a quadratic programming (QP) problem in a number of coefficients equal to the number of training samples.

F.A. Hamprecht, C. Schnörr, and B. Jähne (Eds.): DAGM 2007, LNCS 4713, pp. 365–374, 2007.

The ideal situation would be to find a technique that is both sound from a theoretical viewpoint and plausible from a biological viewpoint. This work proposes a novel incremental learning algorithm that is heavily inspired by biological plausibility aspects. The paper is organized as follows. Section 2 describes the notion of *complexity minimization*, and proposes an incremental learning framework for face recognition. Experiments are shown in Section 3. Finally the main conclusions and ideas for future work are outlined.

2   Incremental Learning

As mentioned above, batch supervised learning is behind the vast majority of face recognition systems. A principled way to avoid overfitting in supervised learning is the use of complexity penalization. A well-known complexity penalization technique is Structural Risk Minimization (SRM) [2]. SRM is a procedure that considers hypotheses ranging from simple to complex. For each hypothesis the error in the training set is measured. Basically, the best hypothesis is that which minimizes the sum of its error in the training set and (a measure of) its complexity: $\arg\min_H \; e_{training}(H) + Complexity(H)$.

Hypothesis complexity can be assimilated (although not strictly) to its number of parameters. The more parameters the more the discriminating power, but also the larger its complexity. Hypothesis complexity is commonly measured as a norm in the hypothesis parameter space. This form of complexity penalization has been used in face recognition for some time. In particular, Support Vector Machines [11], which is based on SRM, has been shown to give better results than other techniques for many tasks.

In a complexity penalization framework a search is made for the minimum hypothesis variation with respect to the "zero" hypothesis. The zero hypothesis corresponds to the origin of the functional space, the hypothesis of zero complexity or capacity (i.e. that with no discriminating power). This complexity penalization approach can be made incremental if a search is made for the minimum variation with respect to the current hypothesis, while achieving consistency with a set of new training samples, see Figure 1.

In complexity penalization techniques a search is made for the simplest hypothesis that is consistent with the training samples (x_y, y_i), $y_i = \{\pm 1\}$, $i = 1, .., n$. Hypotheses are generally represented in a functional Reproducing Kernel Hilbert Space (RKHS), a convenient tool from functional analysis [1]. In RKHSs, functions are represented by coefficients or coordinates. The function itself is reproduced as a sum of the coefficients multiplied by symmetric kernel functions centered at the training samples. For classification, the decision function is given by:

$$sig\left(f(x) = \sum_{i=1}^{n} c_i y_i K(x, x_i)\right) \tag{1}$$

The functional to minimize is, [8]:

$$J_n = e_n + \lambda ||f||^2 \tag{2}$$

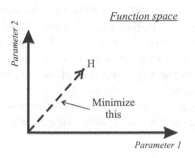 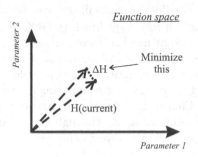

Fig. 1. One-step (batch) complexity minimization (left), incremental complexity minimization (right)

where $e_n = \frac{1}{n}\sum_{i=1}^{n} Err(y_i, f(x_i))$ is the error on the n training samples and $||f||^2$ is the norm of the hypothesis considered. This last term, sometimes called *regularizer*, penalizes the complexity of the hypothesis. For a given kernel and set of training samples, learning algorithms search for a set of non-negative c coefficients that minimize Eq. 2.

Let us divide the learning process in two stages. Let us suppose that we form a hypothesis $f' = f + \cdot f$, where f is the hypothesis obtained from the first $n - m$ samples and $\cdot f$ the hypothesis obtained for the m samples. Let e_{n-m}^f represent the training error in the first $n - m$ samples with hypothesis f, and e_n^f the training error with hypothesis f using all the n samples. Then:

$$
\begin{aligned}
J_n &= e_n^{f'} + \lambda||f'||^2 = e_n^{f'} + \lambda||f + \cdot f||^2 = \\
&= e_n^{f'} + \lambda||f||^2 + \lambda||\cdot f||^2 + 2\lambda < f, \cdot f >= \\
&= e_n^{f'} + e_{n-m}^f - e_{n-m}^f + e_m^{\cdot f} - e_m^{\cdot f} + \lambda||f||^2 + \lambda||\cdot f||^2 + 2\lambda < f, \cdot f >= \\
&= J_{n-m} + J_m + e_n^{f'} - (e_{n-m}^f + e_m^{\cdot f}) + 2\lambda < f, \cdot f >
\end{aligned}
\tag{3}
$$

Note that both f and $\cdot f$ are vectors in a function space. $< \cdot, \cdot >$ is the dot product of that space. Summarizing Equation 3, we have:

$$
J_n = J_{n-m} + J_m + \alpha + 2\lambda\beta
\tag{4}
$$

where:

$$
\alpha = e_n^{f'} - (e_{n-m}^f + e_m^{\cdot f})
\tag{5}
$$

$$
\beta = < f, \cdot f >
\tag{6}
$$

$$
\tag{7}
$$

Our objective is to minimize J_n by minimizing the right hand side of Eq. 4, in an incremental fashion. That is, we want to minimize J_n in steps, first minimizing J_{n-m} and then J_m. The terms α and β would then have to be minimized too. Having minimized J_{n-m} in a previous step, suppose that we minimize J_m. If

m is sufficiently small, e_m^f can be made arbitrarily close to zero. On the other hand, if m is kept fixed, the difference $e_n^{f'} - e_{n-m}^f$ decreases as n grows. Thus, if m is kept fixed α decreases as n grows. Note that $m << n$ does not hold at the beginning of learning, and so it may be necessary to start with a batch learning run in which more than m samples are used in the first step (this, however, was not necessary in the experiments reported below).

Finally, let us turn our attention to the term β. Recall that we are interested in minimizing J_n through the minimization of the right hand side of Eq. 4. Therefore, we have to enforce:

$$|\beta| = |<f, \cdot f>| \approx 0 , \tag{8}$$

Note also that:

$$f(\cdot) = \sum_{i=1}^{n-m} c_i y_i K(\cdot, x_i) \tag{9}$$

and

$$\cdot f(\cdot) = \sum_{j=1}^{m} d_j y_{j+n-m} K(\cdot, x_{j+n-m}) , \tag{10}$$

c_i and d_j being the coefficients obtained in the minimization of J_{n-m} and J_m, respectively. Samples $(x_1, y_1), \dots (x_{n-m}, y_{n-m})$ are used for minimizing J_{n-m}, while $(x_{n-m+1}, y_{n-m+1}), \dots (x_n, y_n)$ are used for minimizing J_m. Then (see [7]):

$$<f, \cdot f> = \sum_{i=1}^{n-m} \sum_{j=1}^{m} c_i y_i d_j y_{j+n-m} K(x_i, x_{j+n-m}) \tag{11}$$

Now let us suppose for simplicity that $m = 1$, then:

$$\cdot f(\cdot) = d_j y_{j+n-1} K(\cdot, x_{j+n-1}) , \tag{12}$$

and

$$<f, \cdot f> = \sum_{i=1}^{n-1} c_i y_i d_j y_{j+n-1} K(x_i, x_{j+n-1}) =$$

$$= d_j y_{j+n-1} \sum_{i=1}^{n-1} c_i y_i K(x_i, x_{j+n-1}) \tag{13}$$

When sample x_{j+n-1} arrives, it would be classified by the (at that moment) current hypothesis using the sign of:

$$f(x_{j+n-1}) = \sum_{i=1}^{n-1} c_i y_i K(x_{j+n-1}, x_i) =$$

$$= \sum_{i=1}^{n-1} c_i y_i K(x_i, x_{j+n-1}) \tag{14}$$

Then, from Eqs. 13 and 14 we see that:

$$< f, \cdot f >= d_j y_{j+n-1} f(x_{j+n-1}) \tag{15}$$

Our original requirement of Eq. 8 is therefore equivalent to:

$$|d_j y_{j+n-1} f(x_{j+n-1})| \approx 0 \tag{16}$$

Note that when the incoming sample is correctly classified by the current hypothesis the product $y_{j+n-1} f(x_{j+n-1})$ of Eq. 16 is larger than zero (in that case the signs are equal). On the contrary, when the incoming sample is incorrectly classified by the current hypothesis the product is negative [1]. This means that Eq. 8 only holds for samples that are neither too "easy" (i.e. a sample correctly classified, with $y_{j+n-1} f(x_{j+n-1}) >> 0$), nor too "difficult" (i.e. a sample incorrectly classified, with $y_{j+n-1} f(x_{j+n-1}) << 0$).

Above, $m = 1$ was used out of simplicity, although in practice m should be at least 2. It can be shown that for $m = 2$ the dot product is made up of two summands, each similar to the right hand side of 15. The interpretation is the same: the dot product will be low when the (two) new samples are neither too easy nor too difficult for the current hypothesis. Note that this theoretical requirement is in line with what occurs in human learning, where learning only progresses if there is scaffolding, see [12]. Consequently, this framework would work if we make the learner process samples that are neither too easy nor too difficult at each step. Such approach would be closely related to what is known as *active learning*.

Another form of achieving scaffolding will be used here. First, note that the left hand side of (16) could be kept low if the coefficient d_j of each new sample is adjusted: the larger the dot product the smaller the adjusted d_j to use. This way, the larger the dot product (which is a measure of similarity of the new sample to the previous ones) the less weight of the of the new sample in the hypothesis.

There is another possibility. Similarities depend on the kernel function $K(x,y)$ (see Eq. 1). In kernel learning this function is commonly considered a similarity measure ([9,10]), which has to be defined a priori. The larger its value, the larger the similarity between samples x and y. A typical kernel function is the RBF kernel:

$$K(x,y) = \exp\left(-\frac{||x-y||^2}{p^2}\right) \tag{17}$$

The larger p the larger the similarity values given by the RBF kernel. Now in this context, what are too-easy and too-difficult samples? The former are samples that are very similar to other (previously seen) samples of its same class, while the latter are samples that are very similar to other (previously seen) samples of the opposite class. Therefore, the value of p is important here: a large p will give large similarity values and thus too-easy and too-difficult samples.

---

[1] The d_j are always non-negative, it is a requirement imposed in the minimization process, see [2].

Scaffolding can be achieved by making the p values dependent on the absolute dot products. That is, the larger the absolute dot product of a new sample the smaller the p to use in the kernel associated to that sample. Such approach requires the dot product of Eq. 15 to be calculated for each new sample. The coefficients d_j and y_{j+n-1} are obtained after the minimization of $\cdot f$, which can be done in constant time (assuming m is kept fixed). The term $f(x_{j+n-1})$ requires evaluating f for each new sample, which has a cost $O(\sum_{i=1}^{n} i) = O(\frac{n(n+1)}{2}) = O(\frac{n^2+n}{2})$, n being the number of samples processed.

Once the dot product is calculated, the new sample will contribute to the hypothesis of Eq. 1 with a kernel p value dependent on the absolute dot product. The larger the absolute dot product the smaller the p used. The exact function used to achieve this will be shown below.

3   Experiments

The incremental learner introduced above was tested in a face recognition problem. The experiments required a large number of images per individual. The EN-CARA2 system was used to collect a number of face image sequences. ENCARA2 is a face detection and normalization system that can detect and track people in real-time, see [3]. ENCARA2 tries to confirm that images actually contain a face and, if so, normalize them so as to be recognized. The final result is a set of frontal face images, normalized and ready to be recognized, see Figure 2.

Fig. 2. Four (partial) face image sequences obtained with the ENCARA2 system

Twenty-five sequences were used, one for each individual. Each sequence had 300 normalized images of 39x43 pixels. Thus, a total of 7500 images were used in the experiments. PCA was initially applied (over the whole set of 40 training images per class, retaining 10 coefficients. Note that, in practice, PCA would be applied to an initial large set of labeled samples. The obtained basis images would then be used from that moment on to transform any incoming image to the new space, exactly as it would have to be done in a batch mode system. It is important to note that this paper is introducing an incremental classifier, not an incremental input space transform.

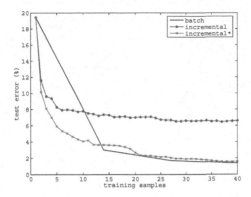

Fig. 3. Error obtained using the batch and incremental learning modes using $p - 800$ (i.e. the p which gave the minimum batch error). The horizontal axis is the number of training samples per class. In order to speed up the experiments, only four n values were calculated for the batch learner. Median of 10 runs.

An SVM classifier with Radial Basis Function (RBF) kernel (Eq. 17) was used. SVM is a binary classifier. $(N(N-1))/2$ binary classifiers were used for N-class classification. In a first experiment the test error rate of the batch learner was obtained for the values of $p = \{100, 200, 400, 800, 1600, 3200, 6400, 12800\}$, using 40 training samples. Error rates for $p = 100$ and $p = 12800$ were 59.4% and 6.4%, respectively. The best batch error (1.13%) was obtained for $p = 800$.

In the figures below, 'Incremental*' is the performance of the incremental learner using the strategy mentioned above. The strategy consists of making the p value associated to the new sample dependent on the corresponding absolute dot product: the larger the absolute dot product, the smaller the assigned p. When the current hypothesis is $f(x)$ and a new sample x_i is received, the p'_i value to use will be given by $p'_i = p_{initial} \cdot K^{-|dotproduct|}$, where $p_{initial}$ is the base p value (i.e. the one used in batch mode) and $K > 1$ is a constant. Note how the dot product is the same as that of Eq. 15. With this equation, the larger the absolute dot product, the smaller the assigned p. The value of K for p'_i equation was obtained using 130 samples -not used for training- per individual as a validation set. Figure 3 shows the results for $p = 800$. Note that in this case $p_{initial} = 800$. 'Incremental' is the performance of the incremental learner using always that $p_{initial}$ value.

More importantly, the 'Incremental*' approach gives lower error than 'incremental'. This difference is statistically significant. A t-test was made with the null hypothesis "means of Incremental and Incremental* errors are equal" vs. "mean of Incremental* is smaller". For $n = 40$ the t-test p-value was $1.2 * 10^{-11}$, a negligible support for the null hypothesis. This confirms the idea that the scaffolding strategy of penalizing too-easy and too-difficult samples has a positive effect. Therefore, the experimental results allow to infer that this incremental

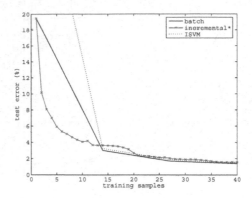

Fig. 4. Learning curves of the three compared learners

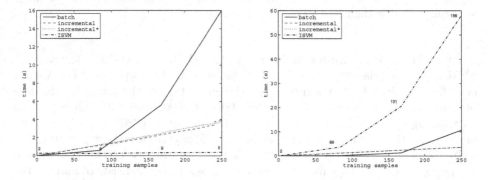

Fig. 5. Computational cost of the compared learners. Measures taken for 2-individual recognition. Left: $p = 800$, right: $p = 100$.

learning framework can work as long as the learner somehow processes samples that are not too-easy or too-difficult.

How well does the proposed learner compare with other incremental learners? In order to answer this we studied the learner proposed by Cauwenberghs and Poggio [4]. This state-of-the-art incremental SVM learner (ISVM in what follows) is based on retaining the *Karush-Kuhn-Tucker* conditions on all previously seen data, while adding a new sample to the hypothesis. According to their authors, ISVM is an *exact* online method. That is, it theoretically gives the same results as the equivalent batch learner. ISVM is an example of a number of incremental learners based on practicality considerations. These learners are generally based on properties of advanced numerical calculus. Figure 4 shows the learning curves of the three compared learners. The ISVM error at $n = 40$ is slightly closer to the batch error (batch=1.29%, incremental*=1.51%, ISVM=1.45%).

Figure 5 compares the computational cost of the three learners. The left figure shows that, for the best batch p value of 800, ISVM is much faster than the other learners. However, the theoretical computational cost of ISVM is $O(s^2)$, s being the number of support vectors. For $p = 800$ the number of support vectors is low (they appear as numbers in the figure). For $p = 100$ (the figure on the right) the number of support vectors is larger, and ISVM rates even worse than the batch learner. Incremental* has a computational cost of $O(\frac{n^2+n}{2})$. $\frac{n^2+n}{2} < n^2$, which suggests that Incremental* may outperform ISVM for particularly complex problems where a large number of support vectors are needed. Incremental* has a storage cost of $O(n)$ (i.e. just the hypothesis itself).

In batch learning, the learner has all of the training samples available from the beginning and thus it can select those that define a good discrimination boundary (i.e. the so-called support vectors). In incremental learning, this is not possible, for only some of the training samples have been given to the learner at a given moment. The natural approach in this case is to gradually span the input space with similarity functions centered in the received training samples. The last processed samples have smaller similarity radii than the first ones. This is what the proposed learner does. The similarity functions are the kernels. The p parameter acts as a radius. The assigned p values decrease with n because the dot products (which represent similarity to the previous samples) increase.

The proposed learner has at least three aspects of a strong biological plausibility. First, it is an online learner. Second, it requires scaffolding to learn. Third, it always classifies each incoming sample with the current hypothesis, being the result of that classification what can make the learner update the hypothesis.

4   Conclusions

A number of existing batch learners used in face recognition, including those based on Support Vector Machines, aim at minimizing both training error and (a measure of) hypothesis complexity. Inspired by biological plausibility considerations, especially those related to the learning process itself, in this work it has been shown that the same complexity minimization can be done incrementally as long as the learning process is aided by some form of "scaffolding", where samples processed by the learner are neither too easy nor too difficult. Within this framework, the feasibility of online learning, both in terms of error difference with respect to batch learning and computational cost at each step, crucially depends on scaffolding. Although there are other ways to achieve scaffolding, a gradually decreasing kernel parameter has been used here. The proposed method has been analyzed in experiments and compared with one state-of-the-art incremental learner. The results show that it compares favorably in terms of biological plausibility and computational and storage cost.

The proposed method seems to be a departure from mainstream approaches in face recognition. We note that this may be only a particular instantiation of a general class of learners that have features generally not found in previous face recognition research, notably a marked biological plausibility of the learning process. Further algorithms may be possible that, like this one, rely on such considerations.

Acknowledgements

This work was funded by research projects *UNI2005/18* and *TIN2004-07087*.

References

1. Aronszajn, N.: Theory of reproducing kernels. Trans. Am. Math. Soc. 68(3), 337–404 (1950)
2. Burges, C.J.C.: A Tutorial on Support Vector Machines for Pattern Recognition. Data Mining and Knowledge Discovery 2(2), 121–167 (1998)
3. Castrillon, M., Deniz, O., Guerra, C., Hernandez, M.: ENCARA2: Real-time detection of multiple faces at different resolutions in video streams. Journal of Visual Communication and Image Representation (2007) (in press)
4. Cauwenberghs, G., Poggio, T.: Incremental and decremental support vector machine learning. In: NIPS, pp. 409–415 (2000)
5. Chellappa, R., Zhao, W. (eds.): Face Processing: Advanced Modeling and Methods. Elsevier, Amsterdam (2005)
6. Hall, P., Marshall, D., Martin, R.: Incremental Eigenanalysis for classification. In: Proceedings of the British Machine Vision Conference, vol. 1, pp. 286–295 (1998)
7. Hofmann, T., Scholkopf, B., Smola, A.J.: A tutorial review of RKHS methods in machine learning (2006), Available at
   http://sml.nicta.com.au/~smola/papers/unpubHofSchSmo05.pdf
8. Poggio, T., Smale, S.: The mathematics of learning: Dealing with data. Amer. Math. Soc. Notice 50(5), 537–544 (2003)
9. Scholkopf, B., Smola, A.: Learning with kernels. MIT Press, Cambridge, MA (2002)
10. Vanschoenwinkel, B., Manderick, B.: Appropriate kernel functions for support vector machine learning with sequences of symbolic data. In: Deterministic and statistical methods in machine learning (First international workshop), Sheffield, UK, September 2004, pp. 256–280 (2004)
11. Vapnik, V.: The Nature of Statistical Learning Theory. Springer, New York (1995)
12. Vygotsky, L.: Mind and society: The development of higher mental processes. Harvard University Press (1978)

Short-Term Tide Prediction

Nils Hasler[1] and Klaus-Peter Hasler[2]

[1] Max-Planck-Institut für Informatik
[2] Bremischer Deichverband am rechten Weserufer

Abstract. Ever since the first fishermen ventured into the sea, tides have been the subject of intense human observation. As a result, computational models and 'tide predicting machines', mechanical computers for predicting tides have been developed over 100 years ago. In this work we propose a statistical model for short term prediction of sea levels at high tide in the tide influenced part of the Weser at Vegesack. The predictions made are based on water level measurements taken at different locations downriver and in the German Bight. The system has been integrated tightly into the decision making process at the Bremen Dike Association on the Right Bank of the Weser.

1 Introduction

The marine industries have always greatly relied on tides. The tide phase governs currents in the coastal regions and many harbours are only accessible when certain water levels are exceeded. So, in order to allow scheduling harbour utilisation and docking and sailing times it is important to predict the times and expected water levels for high and low water.

Another important application of water level forecast can be found in disaster control. Here the authorities attempt to predict storm surges and other abnormal tidal behaviour. This allows them to take actions such as closing flood barrages and flood gates, to warn the population, or even to declare a national state of emergency.

Traditional tide calendars and tide tables provide a good starting point for many naval applications. These calendars are computed assuming that water levels are solely a product of the superposition of influences from different celestial bodies. Water level prediction systems normally focus on forecasting the deviation from the astronomically predicted tide called tide surge. Tide surge is assumed to be primarily a result of the influence of wind on the water. Yet, besides wind speed and direction, water salinity, temperature, and atmospheric pressure have been found to have an influence on tide surge [4]. As we are concerned with very short-term predictions only, we accept that these additional properties can be assumed to be constant and their influence is implicitly contained in the water level measurements we incorporate into the prediction.

In this paper we introduce a statistical approach to very short-term tide prediction. Namely, we focus on the interval 3 to 5 hours before the expected high tide because this is the time frame in which the Bremischer Deichverband am

F.A. Hamprecht, C. Schnörr, and B. Jähne (Eds.): DAGM 2007, LNCS 4713, pp. 375–384, 2007.

rechten Weserufer[1] (BDVR) needs to come to its decisions concerning closing flood barrages and flood gates. While these decisions are frequently made, it may also become necessary to take further action such as alarming the emergency committee.

Our approach employs a statistical model using water level measurements at five different locations downriver and in the German Bight to predict the water level at high tide at Vegesack which is a downriver suburb of Bremen, situated in the tide influenced region of the Weser. Additionally, wind direction and speed are incorporated to improve the prediction. Figure 1 shows the locations of the tide gauges on a map of the German Bight.

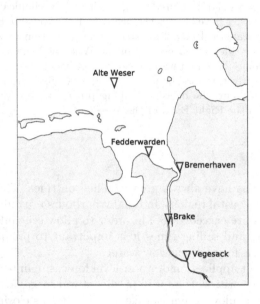

Fig. 1. Tide gauges used for predicting the water level at Vegesack

Water level prediction for the German Bight is also done by the Bundesamt für Seeschifffahrt und Hydrographie[2] (BSH) but their forecasts are focussed on a different timespan. Since they are primarily targeting the marine industries water levels are predicted semi-automatically 6 to 72 hours in advance. Due to this different target time we are able to produce more accurate forecasts although their prediction provides a valuable second opinion on the matter.

The rest of the paper is structured in the following way. Section 2 introduces previous approaches to water level prediction. Section 3 details our approach. Section 4 provides validation of prediction results and a summary is provided in Section 5.

---

[1] Bremen Dike Association on the Right Bank of the Weser.
[2] German Federal Maritime and Hydrographic Agency.

2   Previous Work

Traditionally, only astronomical influences were included into tide forecasts. These were later enhanced by a number of shallow-water constituents to account for different topologies of the sea floor. The parameters are computed using the so-called Harmonic Analysis which is described in more detail below. Despite their simplicity these models are still widely in use since they provide the only means to make long-term predictions. This allows the computation of tide tables and calendars. As these forecasts do not incorporate up-to-date weather information, they are unable to achieve the accuracy of more advanced approaches.

A simple, yet effective statistical system, is used by the BSH. It computes the tide surge as the linear combination of a limited number of carefully chosen parameters. The weights for the linear combination are computed by minimising the prediction error on historical data [4].

Other approaches have included the use of neural networks [5], Kalman filters [8] and chaos theoretical approaches [6].

The most sophisticated systems to date employ three-dimensional simulations of relevant parts of the ocean, incorporating wind, temperature, humidity, and atmospheric pressure data which are provided as input from weather forecast simulations [4].

2.1   Harmonic Analysis

The classical Harmonic Analysis, which was originally developed by Sir William Thomson (the later Lord Kelvin) around 1867, assumes that water levels can be modelled as the superposition of sinusoidal influences of the sun and the moon on the sea [7]. Fitting sines whose frequencies are the linear combination of multiples of the rotation and precession speeds of the celestial bodies relative to the earth to historical tide data leads to a number of constituents as explained by Foreman [1]. Which and how many frequencies to choose depends on the location the predictor is to be generated for and has to be decided manually. In the following v_i represents the ith component's speed and φ_i its phase. A_i is the amplitude of the constituent and $y(t)$ the water level measured at time t. Unfortunately, as a result of increased friction on the ocean floor, the influence of some harmonics lag behind the astronomically predicted phase. Thus, the phases have to be estimated as well as their amplitudes instead of being derived from more accurate astronomical observations.

Commonly, the following equation, derived from the above assumptions, is minimised with respect to the error E to obtain an optimal fit to historical water level measurements $y(t)$.

$$E = \sum_t \left(A_0 + \sum_{i=1}^{N} A_i \cos(v_i t + \varphi_i) - y(t) \right)^2$$

In [7] Thomson and Tait describe a mechanical device that integrates these constituents to predict the water level at a given location. Similar tide predicting machines were in use in various countries until the 1960s.

3   Approach

In a nutshell, we try to predict the water level at high tide at Vegesack on the Weser using a statistical approach that relies on time series of water level measurements taken downriver and in the German Bight up to the time the prediction is made. Additionally, the inclusion of wind speed and direction measurements proved worthwhile.

As the prediction primarily relies on water level measurements it is interesting to investigate what the best encoding of these water levels is. The two considered encodings include using the raw measurement values directly and employing the classical tide surge encoding. Considering the standard deviations of measured tide levels $\mathbf{y}$ and the difference between the astronomically predicted tide levels $\mathbf{p}$ and the measured levels called tide surges or surge water levels $\mathbf{s} = \mathbf{y} - \mathbf{p}$ it may seem advantageous to predict tide surges, since the tide surge is not scattered as widely around its mean as the raw water levels.

$$\text{std}(\mathbf{s_{high}}) = 36.3\,cm < \text{std}(\mathbf{y_{high}}) = 42.7\,cm$$

Yet, experimentation showed that predicting actual water levels produces slightly more accurate results.

Of the four possible encodings only two need to be investigated further. Predicting tide surges from water levels or vice versa is not worth considering because the information about the expected water level is not available to one side of the equation. The achievable accuracies are consequently limited.

Thus only the two remaining variants were compared. While the cross-validation accuracy of the tide surge based prediction reached 24.8 cm, the accuracy achieved by predicting water levels from water levels could be estimated to be 6.6 cm. The better result could probably be achieved because the prediction relies on water levels measured only hours before the predicted event. Since astronomical influences change in the order of days, they can be assumed to be constant during the prediction time span. Their influence is already implicitly included in the water level measurements used in the forecast.

3.1   Wind Direction

In contrast to these results, it was possible to significantly increase the effectiveness of wind measurements, originally available in polar coordinates. Wind levels in this representation are, as Solomantine et al. mention in [6], not sufficiently correlated with the high tide to be of any significant use. The approach the BSH follows is to use the projections of the wind vector onto the coordinate axes as input features. We extended this approach to time dependent projection on different directions.

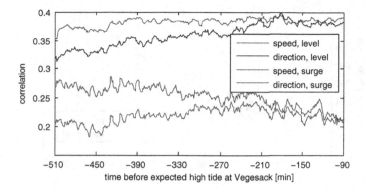

Fig. 2. Correlations between wind speed and direction with water levels and tide surges

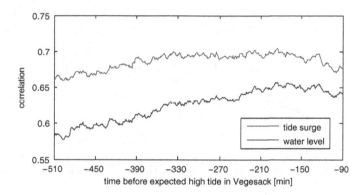

Fig. 3. Correlations between the best projected wind vector with water levels and tide surges

During the time before the astronomically predicted high tide the correlations between wind speed and direction and high tide y_{high} or tide surge s_{high} are given in Figure 2. Since the maximum of these values remains below 0.4, we agree with Solomantine et al. [6] that this is not sufficient to be used directly as a feature.

Fortunately, this problem can be alleviated by assuming that only the component of the wind in a certain direction contributes significantly to the tide surge. While this direction is presumed to be invariant between different tides it is allowed to change during the timespan leading up to the high tide.

To compute the most important wind direction $\omega(t)$ we projected the measured wind vectors on unit vectors sampling the unit circle in steps of $1°$. We then calculated the correlation with the observed water level y_{high} or the tide surge s_{high}. The wind direction with the highest correlation was then chosen for $\omega_y(t)$ and $\omega_s(t)$ respectively. It is interesting to note that the correlation with s_{high} is significantly higher than the correlation with y_{high} (see fig. 3). This finding is not surprising because tide surge is primarily caused by wind. However, in

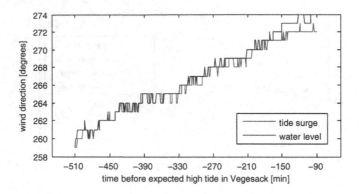

Fig. 4. The best wind direction as a function of time. The wind direction is specified in the nautical system where 0° represents north wind and the angle increases clockwise.

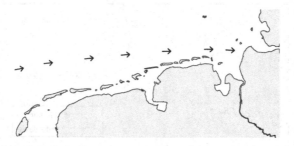

Fig. 5. The best wind direction at the position the tidal wave is situated at at the given time

spite of this convincing edge, the derived wind directions are almost the same, as shown in figure 4. This explains why the difference in prediction accuracy using the two models proved to be minimal.

Interestingly, as can be seen in Figure 3 the wind loses influence on the outcome of the water level at high tide in the last two hours before high tide. To explain this phenomenon consider Figure 5 which plots wind directions and correlations into a map of the Friesian Coast. Wind directions are plotted to the positions the tidal wave is expected to be at at the corresponding time.

Obviously, in order to achieve good results, measurements have to be taken during the same phase in the tide cycle. Unfortunately, the phase cannot be determined exactly as low and high tide not only vary in level but exhibit high variance in time when compared to the expected events as predicted by the harmonic analysis.

So again two different possibilities for anchoring the measurements in time had to be evaluated. On the one hand the tide cycle can be estimated at low or high tide. The first prediction is due approximately 30 minutes after low tide can be detected at the tide gauge Vegesack. Fortunately, since Vegesack is also the place the prediction is made for, the temporal correlation between low water and high water is quite high. Thus, anchoring the measurements at this point in time is a reasonable approach. On the other hand the astronomically predicted cycle can be used for anchoring the prediction. We could not find a great difference in prediction error with either method, so we settled for using the detected time of low tide.

These investigations result in the final formulation of the feature vector used initially for training the model and ultimately for predicting water levels. The vectors are generated by concatenating water level measurements and projected wind speeds taken every minute from three hours before low water at Vegesack until the prediction is made, that is 30–150 minutes after low water at Vegesack or three to five hours before high tide at Vegesack.

3.2   Principal Component Analysis

The third preprocessing step, a principal component analysis (PCA) as described in [2] was used to reduce the dimensionality of the feature vector. By reducing the dimensionality of the data the training time could be reduced tremendously. In comparison with running the optimisation without reducing the dimensionality the observed loss in accuracy could not be found to deteriorate the results. On the contrary, the prediction error could be minimised by choosing the right number of principal components. For the different models that were computed 6 to 56 principal components proved to be optimal.

3.3   Training

Finally, the overdetermined linear system $\mathbf{A}\mathbf{x} = \mathbf{y}$ was solved in a least-squares fashion to determine the coefficients $\mathbf{x}$ of the linear predictor. Here the rows of $\mathbf{A}$ are the feature vectors and the corresponding rows of $\mathbf{y}$ specify the water levels or tide surges that are to be predicted.

By combining the PCA and the linear predictor the prediction model can be reduced to a single scalar product.

$$y_{pred} = \mathbf{x} \cdot \mathbf{f_{PCA}} = \mathbf{x} \cdot (\mathbf{E}\ \mathbf{f}) = (\mathbf{x^T}\ \mathbf{E}) \cdot \mathbf{f}$$

Here y_{pred} is the predicted water level, $\mathbf{f_{PCA}}$ the feature vector as reduced by the PCA, $\mathbf{E}$ the matrix of used eigenvectors, and $\mathbf{f}$ the original feature vector.

4   Validation

The prediction model is computed based on measurements logged by the BDVR in the period from November 1999 to October 2002. Unfortunately, since some measurements are not complete only 1902 of 2117 tide cycles were available for training. For validating the system we used k-fold cross-validation as described by Kohavi [3] employing 10 folds.

Since the system has been installed at the BDVR for several months now and the functionality has reached a stable state, we can also evaluate the accuracy

Table 1. Standard deviations and biases of the predictor by the BSH and our system computed at different times before high tide

	BSH	5h	4h	3h
standard deviation [cm]	30.5	15.5	13.2	8.9
bias [cm]	6.3	4.3	1.7	0.06

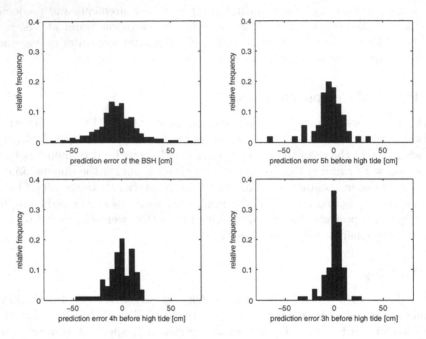

Fig. 6. Error distribution of predictions the BSH made compared to our method computed 5h, 4h, and 3h before high tide

of the live system for the months January and February 2007 and compare our predictions with the forecasts of the BSH. Figure 6 displays the relative frequencies of prediction errors for this period. The cases where tide gauges failed and we were subsequently unable to compute a prediction have been omitted from the evaluation. Table 1 summarises the standard deviations and biases of the predictors in Figure 6. Clearly, the more data is available the more accurate the predictor becomes.

Unfortunately, we were unable to achieve the accuracy on live data that was estimated on the test set specified in Section 3. This is probably a result of the constantly changing depth and consequently changed streaming properties of the Weser. In order to allow larger ships to enter the harbours in Bremen, Brake, and Nordenham the Weser is frequently deepened. As the training data is several years old and the Weser has since been deepened, it is possible that

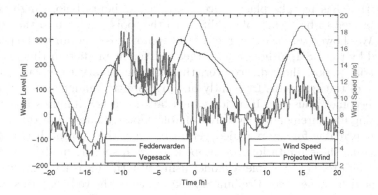

Fig. 7. Water levels and wind speeds around the storm event Kyrill

the model does not represent reality any longer. Apart from this, we would like to stress that as a result of the frequent storms in the winter months predictions are particularly hard to do.

4.1   Kyrill

One disadvantage of statistical prediction systems in general is that they are not particularly good at predicting extreme weather conditions because only very little training data is available for these cases. Unfortunately, these are also the conditions that a prediction system is commonly measured by. So we would now like to present an example of a recent storm that challenged our system. The storm Kyrill that reached hurricane-strength even in the Northern German Planes raged in the night from 18 January to 19 January 2007. At this point our system was already installed and Kyrill provided the first real online test.

The three predictions that were made 5h, 4h, and 3h before expected high tide forecasted 139 cm, 131 cm, and 157 cm above median high tide respectively. The final outcome was 145 cm. While deviation of 12 cm may not seem very accurate, the last prediction by the BSH was 200–250 cm above median high tide. Since the system is statistical in nature, it is hard to tell how it could have foreseen a tide so much lower than was generally expected. Yet, we presume that on the one hand the wind speeds our station picked up were not as high as some of the reported speeds. The highest wind speed we measured corresponds to 8 Bft and the wind direction was only westerly, not corresponding very well to the most significant wind direction. So the overall mean wind speed was registered as only 6 Bft (see fig. 7). This significantly lower wind speed probably caused the system to estimate such a low water level.

5   Summary

We have described a statistical short-term water level prediction system that has been installed at the BDVR. By integrating the system into the decision making process that has to take place twice a day a few hours before high tide, our system proved to be a valuable addition to the tools available to the human in charge. We showed that the accuracy of the approach is superior to the prediction provided by the BSH, although we target a different prediction time span.

The trial period showed, however, that it is necessary to extend the fault-tolerance of the system as frequently one or more tide-gauges fail and the prediction becomes unusable. If a tide gauge fails for a few minutes interpolating the missing measurements proved reasonable. Unfortunately, if a tide gauge becomes unavailable for an extended period of time, this approach is unfeasible. To overcome these limitations we propose to train specific models for different states of failure. For example a model using just the measurements from Vegesack could be generated. Preliminary experiments showed that this approach is practical but the accuracy of the prediction necessarily deteriorates for these models.

References

1. Foreman, M.G.G., Henry, R.F.: Tidal analysis based on high and low water observations. Technical report, Institute of Ocean Sciences, Patricia Bay, Sidney, Canada (1979)
2. Jolliffe, I.T.: Principal Component Analysis. Springer, Heidelberg (2002)
3. Kohavi, R.: A study of cross-validation and bootstrap for accuracy estimation and model selection. In: Proceedings of the International Joint Conference on Artificial Intelligence (IJCAI), pp. 1137–1145 (1995)
4. Müller-Navarra, S.H., Lange, W., Dick, S., Soetje, K.C.: Über die Verfahren der Wasserstands- und Sturmflutvorhersage. promet 29(1–4), 117–124 (2003)
5. Röske, F.: Sea level forecast using neural networks. Deutsche Hydrographische Zeitung 49, 71–99 (1997)
6. Solomatine, D.P., Rojas, C.J., Velickov, S., Wüst, J.C.: Chaos theory in predicting surge water levels in the north sea. In: Proc. 4th Int. Conference on Hydroinformatics, July 2000, Iowa, USA (2000)
7. Thomson, W., Tait, P.G.: Treatise on Natural Philosophy. Oxford University Press, Oxford (1879)
8. Yen, P.-H., Jan, C.-D., Lee, Y.-P., Lee, H.-F.: Application of kalman filter to short-term tide level prediction. Journal of Waterway, Port, Coastal and Ocean Engineering 122(5), 226–231 (1996)

Extraction of 3D Unfoliaged Trees from Image Sequences Via a Generative Statistical Approach

Hai Huang and Helmut Mayer

Institute of Photogrammetry and Cartography, Bundeswehr University Munich
Hai.Huang|Helmut.Mayer@unibw.de
http://www.unibw.de/ipk

Abstract. In this paper we propose a generative statistical approach for the three dimensional (3D) extraction of the branching structure of unfoliaged deciduous trees from urban image sequences. The trees are generatively modeled in 3D by means of L-systems. A statistical approach, namely Markov Chain Monte Carlo – MCMC is employed together with cross correlation for extraction. Thereby we overcome the complexity and uncertainty of extracting and matching branches in several images due to weak contrast, background clutter, and particularly the varying order of branches when projected into different images. First results show the potential of the approach.

1 Introduction

Trees are an essential component of three dimensional (3D) urban information. They add a natural touch and influence the character of an urban scene considerably. Because of their difficult and thus costly acquisition, they are often neglected in 3D urban data sets. This is particularly true if their partially very distinctive shape and texture is to be represented.

Our basic goal is to extract and 3D reconstruct individual unfoliaged deciduous trees from image sequences. Deciduous trees are popular in cities worldwide further away from the equator, as they provide shadow in summer and yet let through most of the light in winter. Thus, they often form the majority of trees in urban areas. From a practical point of view images for data acquisition in cities will often be taken when the trees are unfoliaged as facades etc. are then more readily visible. For us this has the big advantage that one can directly see the branching structure which one can only guess from the foliaged tree.

From a scientific point of view extracting the branching structure in 3D by matching from multiple images is a difficult problem nobody to our knowledge has ever even tried to solve. Extraction and matching of branches is difficult because of bad contrast, clutter by background objects, and because the order of the branches even in neighboring images can vary considerably due to the pronounced 3D structure of trees.

Former work has mostly dealt with tree extraction in aerial images and particularly recently laser scanner data. Much work focuses on forests. The only approach we mention here is [1] as they also use a statistical (Reversible Jump)

F.A. Hamprecht, C. Schnörr, and B. Jähne (Eds.): DAGM 2007, LNCS 4713, pp. 385–394, 2007.

Markov Chain Monte Carlo – (RJ)MCMC [2] approach to model trees, in their case by a spatial point process.

Work for terrestrial urban images is more limited. In [3] foliaged deciduous trees are segmented in color images based on their texture. There is neither a segmentation of individual trees nor any 3D interpretation. Also [4] focuses only on a two dimensional (2D) interpretation, yet for individual trees. The model is based on the particular symmetries of coniferous trees. [5] is mostly concerned with the animation of trees. For their 3D extraction first a volume is generated by intersecting the view cones resulting from the tree silhouettes in multiple images. The voxels of the volume are colored with the average brightness from the rays from the different images. A branching process is started at the ground extending into dark areas assumed to correspond to the trunk or branches. The given results are plausible, but there is much human intervention involved. The most sophisticated approach today is [6]. 3D volumes are generated as in [5]. From the volumes 3D medial axes are constructed. The medial axes are constrained to "botanical fidelity of the branching pattern and the leaf distribution" [6] via an open Lindenmayer-, or in short L-system [7]. Again, a lot of manual interaction is employed to generate results which are good in terms of visualization.

In this paper we show how by means of generative statistical modeling it becomes feasible, to match branches in wide-baseline image sequences taken unconstrained with a standard consumer camera in spite of the problems stated above. We assume, that we can orient images highly precisely by an automatic orientation procedure in the spirit of [8], yet making use of calibration via the five-point-algorithm [9], determining matches by a least-squares procedure highly precisely and bundle-adjusting everything [10]. We note, that our modeling should be useful to find trees in much more explicit laser-scanner data, though the latter is linked to more effort for data acquisition.

In Section 2 the basic idea of generative statistical extraction employing L-systems for the modeling of the 3D characteristics of trees is described. We use statistical sampling in the form of MCMC to generate the parameters of an L-system which comply with the data as described in terms of likelihood.

The generation of 3D hypotheses, their 2D projection and verification are described in Sections 3 and 4. Hypotheses for trunks are generated from vertical lines matched in several images. For the branches suitable prior distributions for the parameters are discussed particularly focusing on issues with the branching angles. The verification of new hypothesis is currently done using the (normalized) cross correlation coefficient (CCC) as (a substitute for) likelihood. After presenting fist results which show the potential of the approach in Section 5, the paper ends up with conclusions.

2   Generative Statistical Extraction Using L-Systems

Branches of trees are difficult to extract from terrestrial urban image sequences due to their weak contrast and background clutter from other objects, e.g., facades or other trees. As we want to construct 3D models of trees, we need to

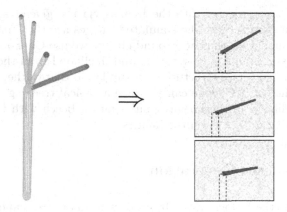

Fig. 1. Left: Stochastical sampling based on an L-system results in a 3D tree hypothesis –
left / right: Projection of a new branch (red) into three empty images with randomly
textured background

match the branches. Because of the complex 3D structure of trees, the ordering
constraint, i.e., a point left of another point on an epipolar line in one image is
also left of the corresponding point on the epipolar line in the other image, often
employed to guide matching, is often not valid even for images taken close to each
other. All this means that the bottom-up extraction of branches and matching
them in 3D does not seem promising and suitable constraints describing the
structure of trees are needed for their 3D reconstruction.

In our case the structure of trees is described in terms of their growing, or
more particularly branching, by an L-system [7]. It is a parallel string rewriting
system representing branching structures in terms of bracketed strings of symbols with associated numerical parameters, called modules. The simulation of
branching starts with an initial string (axiom) and proceeds in a sequence of
steps. By means of productions all modules in the predecessor string are substituted by successor modules. Whether a production is applicable can depend on a
predecessor's context, values of parameters, and like in our case on random factors (also called stochastic L-systems). By means of context-sensitive L-systems
interactions between plant parts can be represented. We do not use this for our
simple first proof-of-concept implementation described in this paper, although it
would certainly be helpful. By recursively using the same productions, L-systems
represent self-similarity, an important biological characteristic of plants.

The modeling with L-systems results in tree-like structures. Yet, L-systems
alone only give means to generate and also visualize trees. For their extraction
from images, they need to be linked to a means for extraction. We decided to
employ a generative statistical approach based on MCMC and L-systems, where
likely candidates of branches are generated by stochastical sampling and are
verified by comparing simulated and real images.

Figure 1 presents the basic idea of our approach. After extracting the trunk
as described below, branches are grown randomly guided by appropriate prior

distributions and are projected into the images via the given highly precisely known orientation parameters. The simulated images are then matched to the given images. As model for the background clutter we use Gaussian noise.

Linking stochastic sampling, L-systems, and likelihood from the images renders it possible to find a tree structure very similar to that of the real tree. I.e., while L-system and MCMC alone can produce a typical tree, e.g., a beech, the link with the likelihood in the images results into a beech with the particular characteristics that can be seen in the images.

3   3D Hypotheses Generation

While we focus on the branches, the basic part of many trees and particularly those we are interested in is the trunk. For it we extract lines, assuming that trunks correspond to thick, mostly vertical lines. The vertical direction is presumed to be known approximately by basically taking images horizontally. It usually can be improved by computing the vertical vanishing point from the vertical edges of trunks or on facades as we focus on urban scenes. Found vertical lines, i.e., hypotheses for trunks, are verified by matching in several images. We use the trifocal tensor [11] derived from our highly precisely known orientation parameters to predict from lines in two images a hypotheses for a line in a third image. We further assume that the position of the tree is determined by the trunk.

The scope of this proof-of-concept paper is limited to the first several levels of branches. We right now assume, that the upper stages of branches with very thin twigs might be grown stochastically to just match the image density, but it is to be seen if and on which level of branching this is a valid assumption.

A new branch is modeled in 3D object-space as a cylinder with known begin and the following parameters (the vertical direction is assumed to be approximately known (cf. above) and the x- and y-axis are taken from the local coordinate system of the first camera after aligning it with the vertical direction):

- Azimuth: angle with x-axis of branch projected into horizontal plane
- Inclination: angle between branch and horizontal plane
- Length
- Diameter

MCMC should basically sample the azimuth with a uniform distribution between $0°$ and $360°$ (cf. blue horizontal dashed line in Fig. 2, right). However, if a limited number of images is taken forming an acute angle together with the trunk as, e.g., the blue area for the three images in Fig. 2, left, accepted branches trend to concentrate in the area of the acute angle. The reason for this is, that in the center of the tree there is usually the vertical trunk, or there are at least only very few thicker vertical branches. All branches with whatever inclination generated in a vertical plane inside the acute angle or close to it will be more likely accepted as they are projected onto the trunk in all given views and are

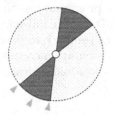 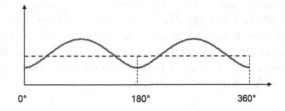

Fig. 2. Left: Area (blue) where for a smaller number of closely-spaced cameras a concentration of hypotheses can occur as hypotheses are not disambiguated from a larger viewing angle – right: Prior distribution (red) for azimuth (with 0° at central camera) helps to reduce the concentration – original uniform distribution as blue dashed line

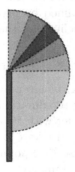

Fig. 3. Prior distribution of inclination – Darker color means higher probability

not disambiguated from another viewing angle. One solution that we have devised for this consists in a modified prior distribution for the azimuth as given as red line in Fig. 2, right.

In combination with the azimuth only a half circle is needed for the inclination (cf. Fig. 3). Moreover, for most types of trees, the majority of branches look upwards. We thus have devised a prior distribution for the inclination shown in Fig. 3 with darker color denoting higher probabilities.

For length and diameter normal distributions are considered. Our first experiments were conducted with a mean of 1 meter for the length for the first level of branches. The diameter is set to a fixed value. For the higher levels of branches we use contraction coefficients.

4   2D Projection and Evaluation

The generated hypotheses are projected into the 2D images, to be evaluated there by comparing the simulated images constructed from the projected hypotheses with the given images. The projection of 3D cylinders entails a larger computational effort. As we do many of these projections in MCMC, we decided for the proof-of-concept prototype, where we did not want to use a graphical processing unit (GPU) due to missing experience with its programming, to use a simple and efficient 2D representation derived from the 3D representation. Another reason for this is that the projection of the branches results into patches of nearly constant brightness anyhow. The chosen 2D representation consists of trapezoids. The color is taken as average of the trunk. A trapezoid is described by the following four parameters:

- Direction: angle with x-axis
- Length
- Width of begin
- Width of end

The parameters of the trapezoid are obtained in the following way: The centers of the begin and the end are obtained by projecting the centers of the circles, i.e., the end points of the axis, delimiting the cylinder on both sides, into the image via

$$\mathbf{x'} = \mathbf{PX}$$

with (homogeneous) 3D points $\mathbf{X}$, image points $\mathbf{x'}$, and the projection matrix $\mathbf{P}$ [11]. To compute reasonable approximations for the widths, we connect the end points of the axis of the cylinder with the camera center and determine one of the normals to this vector. The distance between the projections of the end point of the axis and of the intersection point of the normal with the cylinder surface equals half the width in the image.

The projection of a hypothesis is compared with the corresponding original image i by means of the cross correlation coefficient CCC_i for the intensities computed by HSI color transformation. To compare different hypotheses, the whole images have to be compared with the projections of the complete 3D models. As MCMC sampling consists of a larger number of iterations, the comparison has to be efficient. This is done by an incremental update of only those parts of the 2D projection and the corresponding variances and covariances, which have been changed.

The CCC_i values for the n individual images are combined via multiplication into a global CCC value

$$CCC = \prod_{i=1}^{n} CCC_i \ .$$

Multiplication is used as we interpret the CCC_i values as likelihoods and we assume independence of the images given the 3D model. Additionally, we found empirically that this conservative combination helps to sort out bad hypotheses early. We are aware that the actual size of CCC_i values can be far from correct likelihoods. Yet, our experiments give evidence to assume that they are proportional to correct likelihoods. A function linking raw CCC_i values and likelihoods could be obtained by determining a statistics of CCC_i values for a larger number of known correct and incorrect hypotheses for branches at a certain level. This is subject of further work.

We found empirically that it is not useful to sample all parameters of a branch at the same time. Thus, the MCMC sampling of the parameters is done sequentially. First, only azimuth and inclination are jointly varied over 1000 iterations while the length is kept fixed. The latter is optimized only afterwards with 500 iterations. In future work we plan to relax the sequential sampling via conditional probabilities controlling which parameter to sample next.

5 Results

Fig. 4 and 5 show first results. The input data consists of an image triplet for the former and an image quadruple for the latter, both taken unconstrained with a hand-held 5 Megapixel camera. As output we obtain a VRML (virtual reality modeling language) model describing the trunk and the first two levels of the main branching system of the trees.

Fig. 4. Extraction from an image triplet limited to the the trunk and the first two levels of branches – intermediate stage of processing projected into images (left) and final result (right)

The scenes, taken on different continents under very different lighting conditions demonstrate, that we can basically determine branches on the first two levels. Yet, we note that our proof-of-concept implementation still misses branches

Fig. 5. Extraction from an image quadruple limited to the trunk and the first two levels of branches – images (top) and result (bottom) showing the tree, the cameras as (green) pyramids and points used by the orientation procedure

and reaches only a limited accuracy. We assume that with more experience and particularly by using more levels and RJMCMC, the latter to dynamically generate and delete competing hypotheses via the jumps, we will be able to drop most wrong hypotheses as they will be substituted by better fitting hypotheses.

6   Conclusions

We have proposed a generative statistical approach for the extraction of the branching system of unfoliaged trees. By combining the descriptive power for trees of L-systems with statistical sampling by means of MCMC and simple cross correlation we are able to extract partially occluded branches with possibly weak contrast from image sequences as shown by our first results.

Concerning future work, we first want to generalize the implemented L-system in the direction of open L-systems [7]. We might need to change the parameterization away from the vertically centered azimuth and inclination angles to a more local representation based on branching angles. Yet, we note that generative statistical modeling is not confined to L-systems. We basically just need a means to construct realistic trees that can be efficiently controlled. For this, e.g., also [12] could be a good basis.

Parameters such as contraction rates or branching angles could be learned by extracting a larger number of trees leading to priors probably conditional to the branching level. As already noted above, by correlating against trees and representative samples of the background, a function to upgrade correlation coefficients to likelihoods could also be learned.

An important question will be to decide, how many branches are to be formed on a level and how many levels are appropriate for the tree, i.e., to control the complexity. E.g., for our proof-of-concept implementation, if we had not limited the branching level, a small tree could keep growing, even though new branches are just hallucinated into the background, as there is no obvious way of stopping. This leads to the issue of model selection. The idea is to balance the complexity of a hypothesis, i.e., the size of the tree or more particularly the number of parameters, against its likelihood according to the data. For this, the theory developed for compositional systems [13] might prove helpful, possibly also in conjunction with RJMCMC, to dynamically add and delete hypotheses, the latter, if better solutions evolve.

Acknowledgment

We thank Deutsche Forschungsgemeinschaft for supporting Hai Huang under grant MA 1651/11-1.

References

1. Andersen, H.E., Reutebuch, S., Schreuder, G.: Bayesian Object Recognition for the Analysis of Complex Forest Scenes in Airborne Laser Scanner Data. In: The International Archives of the Photogrammetry, Remote Sensing and Spatial Information Sciences, vol. (34) 3A, pp. 35–41 (2002)
2. Green, P.: Reversible Jump Markov Chain Monte Carlo Computation and Bayesian Model Determination. Biometrika 82, 711–732 (1995)
3. Haering, N., Myles, Z., Vitoria, N.: Locating Deciduous Trees. In: IEEE Workshop on Content Based Access of Image and Video Libraries, pp. 18–25. IEEE Computer Society Press, Los Alamitos (1997)
4. Forsyth, D., Malik, J., Fleck, M., Greenspan, H., Leung, T., Belongie, S., Carson, C., Bregler, C.: Finding Pictures of Objects in Large Collections of Images. In: Object Representation in Computer Vision II, Berlin, Germany, pp. 335–360. Springer, Heidelberg (1996)
5. Sakaguchi, T., Ohya, J.: Modeling and Animation of Botanical Trees for Interactive Environments. In: Symposium on Virtual Reality Software and Technology, pp. 139–146 (1999)

6. Shlyakhter, I., Rozenoer, M., Dorsey, J., Teller, S.: Reconstructing 3D Tree Models from Instrumented Photographs. IEEE Computer Graphics and Applications 21(3), 53–61 (2001)
7. Měch, P.P.: Visual Models of Plants Interacting with Their Environment. In: SIG-GRAPH '96, pp. 397–410 (1996)
8. Pollefeys, M., Van Gool, L., Vergauwen, M., Verbiest, F., Cornelis, K., Tops, J.: Visual Modeling with a Hand-Held Camera. International Journal of Computer Vision 59(3), 207–232 (2004)
9. Nistér, D.: An Efficient Solution to the Five-Point Relative Pose Problem. IEEE Transactions on Pattern Analysis and Machine Intelligence 26(6), 756–770 (2004)
10. Mayer, H.: Robust Least-Squares Adjustment Based Orientation and Auto-Calibration of Wide-Baseline Image Sequences. In: ISPRS Workshop in conjunction with ICCV 2005 "Towards Benchmarking Automated Calibration, Orientation and Surface Reconstruction from Images" (BenCos), Beijing, China, pp. 1–6 (2005)
11. Hartley, R., Zisserman, A.: Multiple View Geometry in Computer Vision, 2nd edn. Cambridge University Press, Cambridge, UK (2003)
12. Lintermann, B., Deussen, O.: Interactive Modeling of Plants. IEEE Computer Graphics and Applications 19(1), 2–11 (1999)
13. Geman, S., Potter, D., Chi, Z.: Composition Systems. Quarterly of Applied Mathematics LX, 707–736 (2002)

Greedy-Based Design of Sparse Two-Stage SVMs for Fast Classification

Rezaul Karim, Martin Bergtholdt, Jörg Kappes, and Christoph Schnörr

University of Mannheim
Dept. Math & CS – CVGPR Group
karim@rumms.uni-mannheim.de

Abstract. Cascades of classifiers constitute an important architecture for fast object detection. While boosting of simple (weak) classifiers provides an established framework, the design of similar architectures with more powerful (strong) classifiers has become the subject of current research. In this paper, we focus on greedy strategies recently proposed in the literature that allow to learn sparse Support Vector Machines (SVMs) without the need to train full SVMs beforehand. We show (i) that asymmetric data sets that are typical for object detection scenarios can be successfully handled, and (ii) that the complementary training of two sparse SVMs leads to sequential two-stage classifiers that slightly outperform a full SVM, but only need about 10% kernel evaluations for classifying a pattern.

1   Introduction

Cascades of classifiers constitute an important architecture for fast object detection. A well-known and promiment example is the work of Viola and Jones [4] on face detection based on a cascade of boosted weak classifiers that only require simple image convolutions for feature extraction and thresholding. This framework is not directly applicable to kernel classifiers like support vector machines (SVMs), for instance, because boosting based on such strong classifiers as components is less effective. In many applications, however, the flexibility of kernel machines is a decisive advantage, as they can be applied to arbitrary features and pattern representations including histograms, sets, graphs, etc. This raises the question of how to design structured architectures for efficient classification using kernel machines as components.

Accordingly, this problem has spurred research recently. Related work can be roughly, but not disjointly, classified

- into approaches [6,5,8,11,1] to the design of *Reduced Support Vector Machines (RSVMs)* that require less computational costs than the standard SVM for classifying a pattern, and
- into approaches [10,5,7,9] that exploit SVMs (either reduced or not) as components of a structured architecture for classification.

Regarding the former class of approaches, RSVMs require only a *fraction of kernel evaluations* for classifying a pattern, either by computing a sparse subset

F.A. Hamprecht, C. Schnörr, and B. Jähne (Eds.): DAGM 2007, LNCS 4713, pp. 395–404, 2007.

of the support vectors of the full SVM [6,1], or by computing a novel small set of vectors in order to replace the support vectors altogether [5,11]. Additionally, wavelet approximations of these latter vectors have been investigated in [8] in order to *efficiently evaluate the arguments* (i.e. dot products between pattern vectors) to which the kernel function is applied.

The latter class of approaches, on the other hand, is focusing on *structured SVM-based classification* for face detection. Heisele et al. [10] studied a hierarchy of linear SVMs including a single nonlinear SVM as top node. Thresholds were tuned for optimizing classification performance and speed, followed by feature selection. Romdhani et al. [5] proposed a single chain of SVMs that is optimized also by threshold tuning, and by approximating a fully nonlinear SVM that has to be computed beforehand, whereas a decision tree with linear SVMs is suggested in [9]. Finally, Sahbi and Geman [7] recently presented a tree-structured hierarchy of SVMs that again is optimized by the reduced set technique used in [5] and threshold selection, and is operating on an application specific partitioning of the space of patterns (faces) according to different poses.

Contribution. In this paper, we assess two different direct greedy strategies [6,1] for designing reduced SVMs (RSVMs) in connection with the sequential combination of *two nonlinear RSVMs*. Such two-stage classifiers form the core of any recursively designed larger structured architecture. Figure 1 illustrates the basic idea underlying the design of RSVMs.

The rationale behind our choice is as follows: Firstly, we focus on *direct* RSVM computation rather than on approximations of fully nonlinear SVMs, in order to avoid the need to train the latter beforehand. Secondly, we refrain from the computation of novel representatives of support vectors as done in [5,11] because this relies on complex optimization problems that are sensitive to initialization, step sizes, etc. Corresponding problems can easily interfere with our main objective, the assessment of structured architectures to classification using RSVMs. Finally, in order to meet error rate specifications, we prefer training with asymmetric costs over threshold tuning because the latter is known to result in classifiers that are not ROC-optimal [3].

Organization. The two greedy strategies [6,1] for designing RSVMs are described in sections 2 and 3. We slightly modified the latter approach by including a bias term (threshold) into the RSVM decision function that is also determined during training. In section 4, we report the results of numerical experiments addressing the following aspects: Validation of the implementation using standard benchmark data, performance evaluation for fixed classifier complexities, coping with asymmetric data and training costs, complementary design of two-stage RSVM classifier.

Notation. False/true and negative/positive error rates are abbreviated with FNR, FPR, TNR and TPR, respectively, and expressed as percentage %. $k(x, y)$ denotes an admissible kernel function (e.g. Gaussian), K_m a $m \times m$ kernel matrix, and $k_m(x)$ the vector $k_m(x) = (k(x_1, x), \ldots, k(x_m, x))^\top$.

Fig. 1. Illustration of RSVMs. From left to right: **(i)** Level-lines of two Gaussian distributions and the decision line of the Bayesian classifier. The Bayes error is $L^* \approx 16.465\%$. **(ii)** The Bayesian classifier and a sample of 200 patterns. **(iii)** The decision surface of the standard SVM trained with all sample patterns, and with optimized parameters. The number of support vectors is 93. The error rate is $L_{full} \approx 17.005\%$. **(iv)** A RSVM with 4 support vectors indicated by circles. The error rate $L_{red} \approx 17.71\%$ is only slightly worse than that of the standard SVM, whereas the kernel evaluations have been reduced by a factor of about 23.

2   RSVM-1: Design by Feature Subset Search

The approach of Franc and Hlavac [6] to the design of RSVMs with fixed classifier complexity involves two phases that we describe next:

(i) Search for an optimal subset of samples $\mathcal{X}_m \subset \mathcal{X}_n = \{x_1, \ldots, x_n\}$, $m \ll n$.
(ii) Compute a classifier with computational costs proportional to the evaluation of $k_m(x)$.

Let $\phi(\cdot)$ denote the feature mapping induced by $k(x, y)$, that is $k(x, y) = \phi(x) \cdot \phi(y)$. To simplify notation, we treat $\phi(\cdot)$ as any other vector.

In phase (i), the subset $\mathcal{X}_m$ is iteratively determined as $\mathcal{X}_r = \{x_1, \ldots, x_r\} \subset \mathcal{X}_n$ for $r = 2, \ldots, m$, $m < n$, such that for each $r < m$, the next pattern to be included satisfies

$$x_{r+1} = \operatorname*{argmax}_{x \in \mathcal{X} \setminus \mathcal{X}_r} d_r(x) ,$$

where $d_r(x)$ is the distance of $\phi(x)$ to the subspace spanned by $\phi(x_1), \ldots, \phi(x_r)$. It is straightforward to check that this distance between $\phi(x)$ and its orthogonal projection $P_r\phi(x)$ is given by

$$
\begin{aligned}
d_r^2(x) &= \|\phi(x) - P_r\phi(x)\|^2 \\
&= k(x, x) - 2k_r(x)^\top \beta_x + \beta_x^\top K_r \beta_x , \qquad \beta_x = K_r^{-1}k_r(x) .
\end{aligned}
$$

After termination of the greedy search $\mathcal{X}_m$ is given, and based on the Cholesky factorization $K_m = U^\top U$, all feature vectors $\phi(x_i)$, $x_i \in \mathcal{X}_n$, are approximated by their projections

$$\left(P_m\phi(x_i)\right) \cdot \left(P_m\phi(x_j)\right) = \beta_i^\top K_m \beta_j = \beta_i^\top U^\top U \beta_j =: \gamma_i^\top \gamma_j .$$

As a result, each training pattern $x_i \in \mathcal{X}_n$ is represented by a vector $\gamma_i \in \mathbb{R}^m$. In phase (ii) of the approach, we compute a standard SVM with $\mathcal{X}$ replaced by $\Gamma := (\gamma_1, \dots, \gamma_n)$:

$$\min_{w,b} \left\{ \frac{1}{2} \|w\|^2 + C_+ \sum_{y_i > 0} \xi_i + C_- \sum_{y_i < 0} \xi_i \right\}, \quad \text{s.t.} \quad D_y(\Gamma^\top w + be) \geq e - \xi, \ \xi \geq 0 .$$

Here, D_y denotes the diagonal matrix with the class variables $y_i \in \{+1, -1\}$. In order to classify a novel pattern x, we compute its representative $\gamma_x = U\beta_x = UK_m^{-1}k_m(x)$ and evaluate the decision function

$$f_m(x) = w^\top \gamma_x + b , \quad w = \Gamma D_y \alpha = \sum_{i=1}^{n_s} \alpha_i y_i \gamma_i .$$

Re-inserting the definitions of γ_x and γ_i, these two steps amount to compute

$$f_m(x) = \sum_{i=1}^{n_s} \alpha_i y_i \beta_i^\top k_m(x) + b ,$$

with n_s denoting the number of support vectors. Note that the computational complexity is dominated by the *fixed* number of m kernel evaluations $k_m(x)$.

3   RSVM-2: Direct Greedy-Based Design

We outline a slight modification of the approach [1]. The modification concerns asymmetric training costs and the inclusion of a bias b into the decision function

$$f_m(x) = w^\top \phi(x) + b = \beta^\top k_m(x) + b , \quad w = \sum_{i=1}^{m} \beta_i \phi(x_i) .$$

Similar to the previous section, the basic idea is to perform a greedy search of an optimal subset $\phi(x_1), \dots, \phi(x_m)$ in feature space, and to train directly a RSVM by minimizing the primal objective function

$$E(\beta, b) = \frac{1}{2} \beta^\top K_m \beta + \frac{C_+}{2} \sum_{y_i > 0} \max \left\{ 0, 1 - \left(\beta^\top k_m(x) + b \right) \right\}^2$$

$$+ \frac{C_-}{2} \sum_{y_i < 0} \max \left\{ 0, 1 + \left(\beta^\top k_m(x) + b \right) \right\}^2$$

with the following Newton-like iteration: Let k be the iteration counter, (β^k, b^k) the current iterate, and I_+ and I_- denote the indices of training patterns whose regularization term does not vanish: $1 - y_i \left(\beta^k \cdot k_m(x) + b^k \right) > 0$. Then we compute

$$(\beta^{k+1/2}, b^{k+1/2}) = (\beta^k, b^k) - \left[H_E(\beta^k, b^k) \right]^{-1} \nabla E(\beta^k, b^k)$$

followed by the line search

$$(\beta^{k+1}, b^{k+1}) = \underset{t \in [0,1]}{\arg\min} \, E\Big((1-t)(\beta^k, b^k) + t(\beta^{k+1/2}, b^{k+1/2})\Big).$$

The gradient and the Hessian are given by

$$\nabla E(\beta, b) = \begin{pmatrix} K_m \beta + C_+ K_{I_+,m}^{\mathsf{T}}(f_{I_+} - y_{I_+}) + C_- K_{I_-,m}^{\mathsf{T}}(f_{I_-} - y_{I_-}) \\ C_+ e_{I_+}^{\mathsf{T}}(f_{I_+} - y_{I_+}) + C_- e_{I_-}^{\mathsf{T}}(f_{I_-} - y_{I_-}) \end{pmatrix},$$

$$H_E(\beta, b) = \begin{pmatrix} K_m + C_+ K_{I_+,m}^{\mathsf{T}} K_{I_+,m} + C_- K_{I_-,m}^{\mathsf{T}} K_{I_-,m} & C_+ K_{I_+,m}^{\mathsf{T}} e_{I_+} + C_- K_{I_-,m}^{\mathsf{T}} e_{I_-} \\ C_+ e_{I_+}^{\mathsf{T}} K_{I_+,m} + C_- e_{I_-}^{\mathsf{T}} K_{I_-,m} & C_+ |I_+| + C_- |I_-| \end{pmatrix},$$

where $|I_+|, |I_-|$ denote the respective number of indices, e_{I_+}, e_{I_-} are one-vectors of the corresponding dimensions, and f_{I_+}, f_{I_-} and $K_{I_+,m}, K_{I_-,m}$ are vectors and matrices, respectively, formed by selecting decisions function values $f_m(x_i)$ and the rows of K_m as indexed by I_+, I_-.

During the greedy search procedure, this parameter fitting is done for increasing dimensions $r = 2, \ldots, m$. For fixed r and minimizing parameters (β, b), $\beta \in \mathbb{R}^r$, the criterion for selecting the next pattern x_{r+1} is the largest change of the energy determined by optimizing the two variables $\min_{\beta_{r+1}, b} E(\beta_{r+1}, b)$ with $\beta = (\beta_1, \ldots, \beta_r)$ kept fixed.

4   Numerical Performance Evaluation

This section summarizes our experimental evaluation of RSVM-1 and RSVM-2 under various aspects. With the exception of the real data experiment reported in subsection 4.5, all experiments were conducted with computer-generate data in order to determine the test error rates accurately.

4.1   Validation of the Implementation

The approach described in section 3 reproduced the performance measures reported in [1] for the benchmark data sets [2]. For example, Figure 2 shows the average error rate (%) as a function of the number of support vectors.

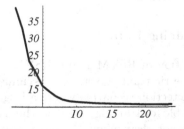

Fig. 2. Average error rate (%) of the RSVM-2 for the Banana data set [2] as a function of the number m of support vectors

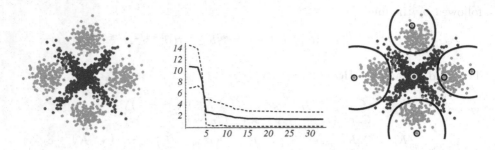

Fig. 3. Left: Training set for a 2-class problem. The standard SVM returns FNR/FPR(%)=0.45/2.12 and 68 support vectors. **Center:** Error rate (thick line) and FNR/FPR (thin lines) for the RSVM-2 that significantly outperforms RSVM-1 (cf. Table 1). **Right:** The first 6 SVs and the corresponding decision line of the RSVM-2 (FNR/FPR(%)=0.51/4.93). On the average, RSVM-2 shows an acceptable performance at about 10% computational costs of a standard SVM.

Table 1. Performance of the reduced SVMs for various fixed classifier complexities. RSVM-2 considerably outperforms RSVM-1. The standard SVM returns FNR/FPR(%)=0.45/2.12 and 68 support vectors.

# SVs	4	10	15	20	30
RSVM-1: FNR/FPR (%)	47.86/56.13	40.74/18.01	14.44/13.93	2.14/8.48	0.39/2.50
RSVM-2: FNR/FPR (%)	13.98/7.40	0.45/4.21	0.25/3.10	0.22/2.88	0.21/2.72

4.2   Performance for Fixed Classifier Complexity

In compare the different greedy strategies underlying RSVM-1 and RSVM-2, respectively, we fixed the classifier complexities to $m \in \{4, 10, 15, 20, 30\}$ and evaluated the FNR and FPR of both reduced machines. The details are given in Figure 3 and Table 1.

It turned out that RSVM-2 is consistently superior to RSVM-1 and shows an performance comparable to the full SVM while needing only 10% of the number of support vectors on the average.

4.3   Asymmetric Training Data

We performed an evaluation of RSVM-1 and RSVM-2 similar to the previous section, but with asymmetric training sets and asymmetric training costs. This situation is typical for detection scenarios where a large number of background patterns are easily available for training, whereas the number of object patterns is limited. A priori, it is not clear whether greedy search breaks down in such situations. Figure 4 and Table 2 provide the quantitative details.

While the RSVM-2 perform as well as in the symmetric case (previous subsection), the performance of the RSVM-1 becomes even worse. Likewise, the

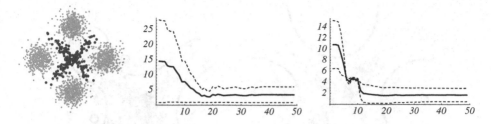

Fig. 4. Left: An *asymmetric* training set (fore-/background samples = 1/10). The standard SVM returns FNR/FPR(%)=3.79/0.86 and 92 support vectors for symmetric training costs, and FNR/FPR(%)=1.08/2.16 and 153 support vectors for an asymmetric choice of the training costs. **Center:** Error rate (thick line) and FNR/FPR (thin lines) for the RSVM-2 trained with symmetric costs, that significantly ourperforms RSVM-1 also in such asymmetric scenarios (cf. Table 2). The greedy optimization, however, mainly focuses on the larger background sample set (lower dashed line), yielding a suboptimal overall performance **Right:** Asymmetric training costs enables to steer the greedy search and to optimize the overall performance (note that the ordinate-scale differs from the figure in the middle). For 15 support vectors, that is about 10% classification costs of the full SVM, the RSVM-2 returns FNR/FPR(%)=0.2/3.5.

Table 2. Performance of the reduced SVMs for various fixed classifier complexities and *asymmetric* training costs. RSVM-2 considerably outperforms RSVM-1. The standard SVM returns FNR/FPR(%)=1.08/2.16 and 153 support vectors.

# SVs	4	10	15	20	30
RSVM-1: FNR/FPR (%)	54.59/32.15	51.74/12.40	43.00/10.79	1.87/6.34	0.87/2.85
RSVM-2: FNR/FPR (%)	14.92/6.44	4.25/4.82	0.2/3.5	0.21/3.03	0.41/2.98

relationship of approximation quality and computational complexity of the RSVM-2 relativ to the fully nonlinear SVM did not change noticeably.

4.4   Two-Stages Sparse SVM Classification

The objective of this section is to show that in principle two sparse SVMs can be combined sequentially without loss of classification performance, but at considerably reduced computational classification costs. Being inferior to RSVM-2, we did not consider RSVM-1 in this context, and we simply denote RSVM-2 by RSVM in this section. We use subscripts 1 and 2 for the RSVM at stage 1 and 2, respectively.

Figure 5, left and right, show two RSVMs designed as stage-1 and stage-2 classifiers. The RSVM at stage 1 was asymmetrically designed so as to yield a very low FNR. For the stage-2 RSVM, only those background patterns were used for training that were accepted as false positives at stage 1. This is reasonable

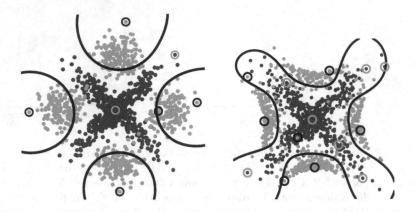

Fig. 5. Sequential classification by two RSVM-2. Both stages were trained by direct greedy optimization. **Left:** Asymmetrically trained stage-1 RSVM with minimal FNR (fraction of missed objects). **Right:** Stage-2 RSVM asymmetrically trained on positive examples and false positives accepted by the stage-1 RSVM. The overall performance is FNR/FPR(%) = 0.52/0.45 (see text for more details).

because in practice typically a large number of background patterns are available. The performance data of the two classifiers are:

$$\text{FNR}_1/\text{FPR}_1(\%) = 0.0035/15.83 \qquad (\#\text{SV} = 7)$$
$$\text{FNR}_2/\text{FPR}_2(\%) = 0.51/2.84 \qquad (\#\text{SV} = 14)$$

Then the overall performance is

$$\text{FNR} = \text{FNR}_2\text{TPR}_1 + \text{FNR}_1 \approx 0.51\% , \qquad \text{FPR} = \text{FPR}_2\text{FPR}_1 \approx 0.45\% ,$$

which compares favourably with the full SVM (see the caption of Figure 3).

The average computational costs per pattern are largely dominated by the first-stage classifier which typically requires 10% computation time relative to the full SVM. Assuming that the second RSVM has twice the number of support vectors, that is 20%, and that an object occurs at 0.1% of all image locations, than the two-stage classifier requires on the average about

$$0.2\,(0.001\,\text{TPR}_1 + 0.999\,\text{FPR}_1) + 0.1 \approx 13\%$$

of the computation time of the full SVM.

Evaluation of benchmark data. We also applied the two-stages classifier combining a very sparse RSVM at stage 1, followed by the RSVM designed as reported in section 4.1, using the bechmark data[2], and averaged the results over the corresponding 100 training-test pairs of data sets. The effective number of support vectors is the sum of #SVs of the first machine plus #SVs of the second machine multiplied by the acceptance rate of the first machine.

Table 3 shows that in comparison to [1] the classification cost can be further reduced without a significance loss of performance.

Table 3. Benchmark evaluation of the two-stages sparse SVM. The effective number of SVs minimizes the classification costs and yields comparable classification performance.

Dataset	Our Cascade		Keerthi *et al* [1]		SVM[1]	
	Effictive #SVs	Error	#SVs	Error	#SVs	Error
Breast	4.67(0.66)	26.80(4.92)	12.1(5.6)	29.22(2.11)	185.8(16.44)	28.18(3.00)
Diabetis	6.48(0.54)	26.32(2.28)	13.8(5.6)	23.47(1.36)	426.3(26.91)	23.73(1.24)
German	4.41(0.63)	27.80(2.45)	14.0(7.3)	24.90(1.50)	630.4(22.48)	24.47(1.97)
Ringnorm	9.79(0.19)	2.04(0.28)	12.9(2.0)	1.97(0.57)	334.9(108.54)	1.68(0.24)
Thyroid	5.45(0.41)	5.61(2.41)	10.6(2.3)	5.47(0.78)	57.80(39.61)	4.93(2.18)
Waveform	9.16(0.40)	12.75(1.33)	14.4(3.3)	10.66(0.99)	246.9(57.80)	10.04(0.67)

4.5 Real Data

Although specific applications are not within the scope of this paper, we report the performance of the RSVM-2 for an experiment with real data, to assure that the findings reported above generalize to other data sets.

For a real-world challenge, we considered head detection on a set of 1042 images containing humans in various poses at approximately the same scale. We divided the data-set into 603 training images and 439 test images, such that there are no two images of individuals under similar conditions in the test set, and all are mutually distinct to the training set. As a result, we may expect realistic general performance measures. From these images, small patches of size 32x32 were extracted at the head location (provided by the user), and the popular SIFT-features [12] were computed from the patches. We used 4x4 location and 8 orientation bins resulting in 128-dimensional feature vectors. Contrary to the original formulation, we did no local orientation or scale normalization.

For the background, we computed 9934 features at locations not containing any heads, which we divided into 4967 training and 4967 test features. Note the asymmetry in the data, with a ratio of background/foreground of $\approx 8/1$ for training and $\approx 11/1$ for testing.

Training a fully nonlinear SVM with asymmetric costs resulted in 1720 support vectors and error rates FNR/FPR (%) = 14.35/1.39. The RSVM-2 showed a comparable performance, FNR/FPR (%) = 10.02/4.11, for only 47 support vectors, however, that is with classification costs reduced by a factor of about 36!

5 Conclusions

We compared two greedy strategies recently proposed for the direct design of reduced nonlinear SVMs. One of these strategies, suggested in [1], performed uniformly well irrespective of the nature of the data set, and also in asymmetric situations that are typical for object detection scenarios.

It should be pointed out that the factor of decreasing computational costs reported in this paper has to be *multiplied* by the acceleration factors reported in [8], that are obtained by an independent technique as discussed in section 1.

We showed that the complementary design of two reduced SVMs results in sequential two-stage classifiers that may even outperform fully nonlinear SVMs. Such classifiers may form the core of larger structured classifiers using RSVMs as components. This will be investigated in our future work.

Acknowledgement. This work has been supported by the European Marie Curie Research Training Network VISIONTRAIN (contract number MRTN-CT-2004-005439).

References

1. Keerthi, S.S., Chapelle, O., DeCoste, D.: Building support vector machines with reduced classifier complexity. J. Mach. Learning Res. 7, 1493–1515 (2006)
2. Rätsch, G.: Benchmark data sets,
   http://ida.first.fraunhofer.de/projects/bench/benchmarks.htm
3. Bach, F.R., Heckerman, D., Horvitz, E.: Considering cost asymmetry in learning classifiers. J. Mach. Learning Res. 7, 1713–1741 (2006)
4. Viola, P., Jones, M.J.: Robust real-time face detection. Int. J. Comp. Vision 57(2), 137–154 (2004)
5. Romdhani, S., Torr, P., Schölkopf, B., Blake, A.: Efficient face detection by a cascaded support-vector machine expansion. Proc. Royal Soc. A 460, 3283–3297 (2004)
6. Franc, V., Hlaváč, V.: Greedy algorithm for a training set reduction in the kernel methods. In: Petkov, N., Westenberg, M.A. (eds.) CAIP 2003. LNCS, vol. 2756, pp. 426–433. Springer, Heidelberg (2003)
7. Sahbi, H., Geman, D.: A hierarchy of support vector machines for pattern detection. J. Mach. Learning Res. 7, 2087–2123 (2006)
8. Rätsch, M., Romdhani, S., Teschke, G., Vetter, T.: Over-complete wavelet approximation of a support vector machine for efficient classification. In: Kropatsch, W.G., Sablatnig, R., Hanbury, A. (eds.) Pattern Recognition. LNCS, vol. 3663, pp. 351–360. Springer, Heidelberg (2005)
9. Zapién, K., Fehr, J., Burkhardt, H.: Fast support vector machine classification using linear SVMs. In: 18th International Conference on Pattern Recognition (ICPR 2006), vol. 3, pp. 366–369. IEEE, Los Alamitos (2006)
10. Heisele, B., Serre, T., Prentice, S., Poggio, T.: Hierarchical classification and feature reduction for fast face detection with support vector machines. Pattern Recognition 36(9), 2007–2017 (2003)
11. Wu, M., Schölkopf, B., Bakir, G.: A direct method for building sparse kernel learning algorithms. J. Mach. Learning Res. 7, 603–624 (2006)
12. Lowe, D.G.: Distinctive image features from scale-invariant keypoints. Int. J. Comp. Vision 60(2), 91–110 (2004)

How to Find Interesting Locations in Video: A Spatiotemporal Interest Point Detector Learned from Human Eye Movements

Wolf Kienzle[1], Bernhard Schölkopf[1], Felix A. Wichmann[2,3], and Matthias O. Franz[1]

[1] Max-Planck Institut für biologische Kybernetik, Abteilung Empirische Inferenz, Spemannstr. 38, 72076 Tübingen
[2] Technische Universität Berlin, Fakultät IV, FB Modellierung Kognitiver Prozesse, Sekr. FR 6-4, Franklinstr. 28/29, 10587 Berlin
[3] Bernstein Center for Computational Neuroscience, Philippstr. 13 Haus 6, 10115 Berlin

Abstract. Interest point detection in still images is a well-studied topic in computer vision. In the spatiotemporal domain, however, it is still unclear which features indicate useful interest points. In this paper we approach the problem by *learning* a detector from examples: we record eye movements of human subjects watching video sequences and train a neural network to predict which locations are likely to become eye movement targets. We show that our detector outperforms current spatiotemporal interest point architectures on a standard classification dataset.

1 Introduction

Interest point detection is a well-studied subject in the case of still images [14], but the field of spatiotemporal detectors for video is fairly new. Currently, there exist essentially two methods. The earlier one is a spatiotemporal version of the *Harris* corner detector [4] proposed by *Laptev* [9]. This detector has been shown to work well in action classification [15]. However, spatiotemporal corners are a relatively rare event, resulting in overly sparse features and poor performance for many real-world applications [1,11]. To remedy this, the *periodic* detector was introduced by *Dollár* [1]. It responds to simpler spatiotemporal patterns, namely intensity changes in a certain frequency range. The authors show that a simple recognition framework based on this detector outperforms the Harris-based approach of [15].

As both of these approaches are relatively new, they are still far from being as well-understood and empirically justified as their spatial counterparts. Clearly, spatiotemporal corners and temporal flicker of a single frequency are only a subset of all potentially interesting events in a video. Here, we present a new approach to spatiotemporal interest point detection. Instead of *designing* new interesting spatiotemporal features, we *learn* them from an already working and very effective interest point detector: the human visual system. Our basic idea

F.A. Hamprecht, C. Schnörr, and B. Jähne (Eds.): DAGM 2007, LNCS 4713, pp. 405–414, 2007.

is to record eye movement data from people watching video clips and train a small neural network model to predict where people look. Used as an interest point detector, the neural network is shown to outperform existing methods on the same dataset which has been used as a benchmark for both the Harris and the Periodic detector.

The connection between eye movements and interest operators has been made before by several authors. In [13], a biologically inspired attention model was used for object recognition in images. The idea of designing an interest point detector directly from eye movement data was recently proposed in [7,8]. They found that humans attend to center-surround patterns, similar to what is already being used in some engineered detectors, e.g., [10]. However, their approach only considers still images, and they do not report how their system performs on typical computer vision tasks.

2 Eye Movements

The human visual system has its highest resolution at the center of gaze, or *fovea*, which covers about one degree of visual angle. In fact, a disproportionately large amount of cortical processing power is devoted to this small area. Towards the periphery, both resolution and processing power decrease quickly [17]. As a consequence, a visual scene does not enter the visual system as a whole, but is *sampled* by the eyes moving from one location to another. During eye movements, the center of gaze is either held fixed over a constant image area during *fixations*, follows moving objects during *smooth pursuit*, or changes rapidly during *saccades* in which visual input is mostly turned off (*saccadic suppression*) [2]. The choice of which image regions become saccade targets is not random, however. In part, it can be explained by typical patterns in the local image structure occurring at fixated image locations [12,8]. Thus, the human eye movement mechanism bears a resemblance to interest point detectors in that it uses local image statistics to decide where to sample visual input for subsequent processing.

The aim of this work is to build an interest point detector that imitates this effect. To this end, we recorded eye movement data from 22 human subjects. Each subject viewed 100 short clips from the movie *Manhattan (1979)*, presented on a 19" monitor at 60cm distance at 24 frames per second with a resolution of 640×480 pixels. Each clip was 167 frames long (about seven seconds), and the clips were sampled uniformly from the entire film (96 min) such that no cuts occurred during a clip. Each subject viewed all 100 clips in random order and with blanks of random duration in between. No color transform was applied, since the movie is black and white. Eye movements were recorded using an *Eyelink II* tracker, which, after careful calibration, yielded measurements of typically 0.3 degrees accuracy. Figure 1 shows three frames from an example clip together with the recorded fixations from all 22 subjects.

In a post-processing step we discarded all fixations that occurred before frame 38 or after frame 148 to ensure a sufficient number of video frames both before and after each fixation. Also, a set of background (negative) examples was

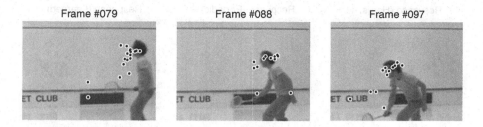

Fig. 1. Recorded eye movements on a sample video from our dataset (Section 2). Fixations from all 22 users are shown as circles (there are no markers for subjects which did not fixate, but moved their eyes during the respective frame).

generated using the same fixation positions, but with the video data taken from *wrong*, i.e., randomly chosen clips. This way of generating background examples is common practice in eye movement analysis and prevents artifacts caused by the non-uniform sampling prior due to the limitations of the viewing field and head motion in the eye tracking setup [12]. Finally, we split the set of all fixations and background points into a training set (18691 samples), and a test set (9345 samples). The training set was used for designing the *learned* detector (Section 3.3), the test set was used to compare the three interest point algorithms in terms of how well they predict human fixations (Section 4.1).

3   Spatiotemporal Interest Point Detectors

3.1   The Spatiotemporal Harris Detector

The spatiotemporal *Harris* detector is due to *Laptev* [9] and extends the widely-used Harris corner detector [4] to the time axis. Analogously to the spatial case, the spatiotemporal Harris detector is based on the 3×3 second-moment matrix M, which describes the local gradient distribution, spatially at scale σ and temporally at scale τ. Interest points are computed as the local maxima of the quantity

$$S_H = \det M - k(\text{trace } M)^3, \tag{1}$$

where $k = 0.005$ is an empirical constant [9], corresponding to the well-known magic number 0.04 in the original spatial detector [4]. Here, we refer to S_H as the *saliency function* of the detector, according to the biological term *saliency* [5] which is used to describe the *interestingness* of locations in an image. Note that the output of the detector is a discrete set of locations, while S_H is defined on the entire video clip. In practice, a second set of scales σ_i, τ_i is used for the integration of the moment matrix over a spatiotemporal window [9], usually taken to be a multiple of σ, τ. Throughout this paper we used the implementation from [1], with the default setting of $\sigma_i = 2\sigma$, $\tau_i = 2\tau$. Thus, the detector has two free parameters, the spatial scale σ and the temporal scale τ.

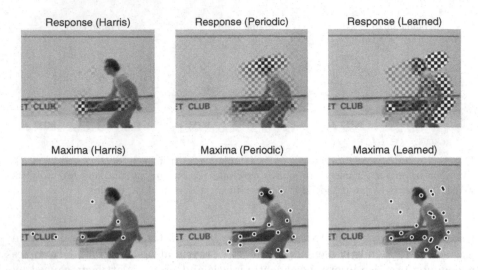

Fig. 2. Qualitative comparison of detector responses S_H (eq. 1), S_P (eq. 2), and S_L (eq. 3). The blended checkerboard texture in the top row illustrates detector responses on frame 88 from Figure 1. The bottom row shows the corresponding regional (2D) maxima. Parameters were set to $\sigma = 2$, $\tau = 3$ for all detectors.

The response of the spatiotemporal Harris detector can be characterized similarly to the 2D case: the saliency function S_H, or *cornerness*, is large if the spatiotemporal gradient varies significantly in all three dimensions. *Laptev* intuitively describes the detected events as split or unification of image structure and as spatial corners changing direction. The applicability of this concept to action classification was shown in [15]. S_H computed on the center frame of our sample sequence in Figure 1 is shown in Figure 2 (left column). The highest values are achieved where the racket passes the black bar in the background.

It should be mentioned that in the conceptual simplicity of the spatiotemporal Harris detector lies also a possible drawback. Clearly, the time axis is not just a third image dimension, such as in volume data [3], but it describes a very different entity. Perhaps not surprisingly, it was found that the 3D-Harris detector can lead to unsatisfactory results, in that it tends to produce too few interest points [1,11]. This has given rise to the development of the *Periodic* detector, which we describe in the following section.

3.2   The Periodic Detector

The so-called *Periodic* detector was proposed by *Dollár* [1] as an alternative to *Laptev*'s method. In *Dollár*'s approach, the image is smoothed spatially and then filtered temporally with a quadrature pair of one-dimensional Gabor filters. The squared outputs of the two Gabor filters are added to get the saliency function

$$S_P = \sum_{i=1}^{2}(I * G(\sigma) * F_i(\tau,\omega))^2 \tag{2}$$

where I denotes the 3D image, $G(\sigma)$ is a 2D spatial Gaussian filter with standard deviation σ, and $F_1(\tau, \omega)$, $F_2(\tau, \omega)$ are 1D temporal Gabor filters with frequency ω and scale τ (with odd and even phase, respectively, as illustrated in Figure 3, right plot). Interest points are again the local maxima of the saliency function over space and time. In the implementation we use [1], the frequency is fixed to $\omega = 0.5/\tau$. In effect, this detector has the same parameters as the Harris detector, namely σ for the spatial scale and τ for the temporal scale.

Intuitively, the saliency S_P is large where image intensity changes temporally at a rate $\omega = 0.5/\tau$. Accordingly, the authors [1] refer to this detector as the *Periodic* detector. Figure 2 shows its output on frame 88 of our example sequence (Figure 1). This suggests that, as intended [1], S_P takes significant values in larger regions than the Harris measure S_H.

3.3   The Learned Detector

The Harris and Periodic detector are based on analytic descriptors of local image structure assumed to be useful for computer vision applications. The interest point detector we propose here is instead based on image features selected by the human visual system.

The architecture of our detector is motivated by that of the Periodic detector (2). It consists of a simple feed-forward neural network model with sigmoid basis functions

$$S_L = b_0 + \sum_{i=1}^{k} \alpha_i \tanh(I * G(\sigma) * W_i + b_i), \tag{3}$$

i.e., the input video I is first convolved with a spatial Gaussian low pass G of width σ, then by k temporal filters W_i. The k filter outputs are fed into tanh nonlinearites (with bias b_i) and then added together using weights α_i and a global bias term b_0. Note that this generalizes the Periodic detector to an arbitrary number of arbitrarily shaped input filters: instead of two quadratic basis functions we now have k sigmoids, and the temporal filters will be fitted to the eye tracking data instead of being fixed Gabor filters. Additionally, each basis function contributes to the output S_L with a different weight and bias.

In the learning step, we fit the saliency function (3) to our recorded eye movement data: we optimize the filters W_i, the weights α_i, and the biases b_i using regularized logistic regression, i.e., by minimizing

$$E = \sum_{i=1}^{m}(y_i s_i - \log(1 + \exp s_i)) + \lambda \sum_{i=1}^{k} \alpha_i^2 \tag{4}$$

Here, the s_i are the values of S_L at the training samples (see Section 2). The corresponding labels y_i are set to 1 if i is a fixation, and 0 if it is a background example. Note that this corresponds to a maximum a posteriori estimate in a logit model, i.e., the learned saliency function S_L has a probabilistic interpretation: it equates to the logarithmic odds ratio of a fixation by a human observer, $S_L = P(Y = 1|I)/P(Y = 0|I)$. To carry out the optimization of (4) we used a

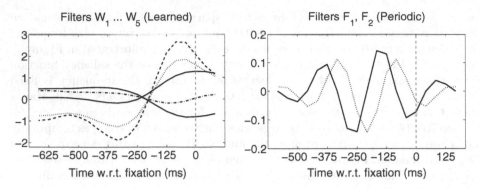

Fig. 3. The 19-tap temporal filters from the Learned (*left*) and the Periodic (*right*) detector. Shown on the horizontal axis is the time relative to the beginning of a predicted fixation (horizontal gray line). Note that both detectors have different offsets in time, corresponding to the values which are optimal in terms of predictivity (cf. Table 1): -7 and -5 frames (w.r.t. the central tap) for the Learned and Periodic detector, respectively .

scaled conjugate gradient method [16]. Prior to training, the training data were denoised to 95% variance by projecting out the least significant PCA components. The network weights were initialized to random values.

During learning, several design parameters have to be set: the regularization parameter λ, the number of filters k, and the spatial scale σ of the Gaussian. The size of the temporal filter W_i was set to 19 frames which corresponds to three times the value of $\tau = 3$ in the Harris and the periodic detector, the standard setting used in [1,11] and also throughout this paper. Additionally, we introduce a temporal offset Δt, which denotes the position of the center of the temporal filters W_i relative to the beginning of a fixation. The rationale behind this is that the time at which a fixation is made does not necessarily coincide with the time at which the video contains the most useful information to predict this. As an example, the typical *saccade latency*, i.e., the time between seeing something interesting and making a saccade is 150–200ms (6–8 frames at 24 fps) [2]. The design parameters were found via 8-fold cross-validation, where the performance was measured in area under the ROC curve (ROC score), the standard measure for predicting eye movements [7]. The search space was a 4D grid with $\log_2 \sigma \in [-1 \ldots 8]$ in steps of 2/3 ranging from single pixels to the full screen, $\Delta t = -29 \ldots 9$ in steps of 2, $k = 1, 2, 5, 10, 20$, and $\log_{10} \lambda = -4, -2, 0, 2$. We found a clear performance peak at $\sigma = 1$, $\Delta t = -7$, $k = 5$ and $\lambda = 0.01$. We will refer to the detector trained with these parameters in the following as the *learned* detector.

The right plot in Figure 2 shows the output S_L on our example sequence from Figure 1. Note that, similarly to the periodic detector, our detector has a large response over extended areas. Interestingly, the largest Harris response (at the racket) leads to a high response, too. The five learned filter kernels W_i

are shown in Figure 3 (left plot). As found during learning, the optimal temporal alignment of the filter kernels is at $\Delta t = -7$, which centers them at about 300ms before the fixation event. Examining the shape of the learned kernels, we find that all kernels have a steep slope 200ms before the fixation event, which means that the detector is tuned to temporal intensity changes occurring at that time. Interestingly, this matches very well with the typical saccade latency of 150-200 ms, i.e., the time between deciding to make and making a saccade (the saccades themselves are typically very short (20-50ms)). Note that we did not put any such assumption into the design of our detector. Therefore, this property must stem from the data, meaning that our detector has in fact *learned* a biologically plausible feature of bottom-up saliency.

4   Experiments

4.1   Eye Movement Prediction

For still images it has been shown that simple local image statistics such as increased RMS contrast attract the human eye [12]. As most spatial interest point detectors strongly respond to local contrast, they do in fact explain some of the variance in human eye movements. For time-varying images, it is known that flicker and motion patterns attract our attention [2]. Since the Harris and Periodic detector respond to such features, we expect a significant correlation with human eye movements in this case as well. To quantify this, we computed ROC scores of the saliency functions R_H (Harris), R_P (Periodic), and R_L (Learned) on our test set (Section 2). ROC scores are the standard measure for eye movement prediction [8]. In still images, the state-of-the-art for purely *bottom-up* (based on image content only) models is around .65 [8]. Note that this seemingly low score makes perfect sense, since eye movements are also controlled by more high-level, *top-down* factors, such as the observers thoughts or intentions [18], which are not considered by bottom-up models by construction.

Here, we compare the three detectors in terms of how well they predict human fixation locations. To reduce the inherent advantage of the *Learned* detector— which was built for this task—we also trained the free parameters of the Harris and the *Periodic* detector: analogously to Section 3.3, we fixed $\tau = 3$ and optimized σ and Δt on the training set via cross-validation. Test ROC scores (averaged over eight random subsets of the test set, $\pm$ standard error) are shown in Table 1, together with the optimal values for σ and Δt found in cross-validation. This shows that our detector outperforms the two others by a large margin, reaching state-of-the-art performance. This is not surprising since we specifically designed the Learned detector for this, while the others were not. Another observation is that the optimal temporal offset Δt is very similar in all three cases, and in agreement with the typical saccadic latency of $6 - 8$ frames (cf. Section 3.3). Also, all detectors have scores significantly above chance level, which means that they are indeed related to the spatiotemporal features that the human eye is attracted to.

Table 1. How human eye movements are prediced by spatio-temporal interest point detectors (Section 4.1)

Detector	ROC score	$\log_2\sigma$	Δt
Learned	.634 ±.007	0.0	-7
Periodic	.554 ±.015	-1.0	-5
Harris	.522 ±.005	3.3	-8

4.2 Action Classification

We have seen that the Learned detector outperforms existing methods in terms of predicting eye movements. This, however, should be regarded only as a proof of concept, since our main interest is to solve actual computer vision problems, not to predict eye movements. To make a fair comparison, we tested our detector within the domain for which the Harris and Periodic detectors were designed. We used the KTH action classification dataset [15], which was also used by the inventors of the Harris and Periodic detector to test their approaches. The dataset contains 598 videos (160×120 pixels, several seconds long) of 25 people performing 6 different actions (walking, jogging, running, boxing, handwaving, handclapping) under varying conditions (indoor, outdoor, different scales). Figure 4 shows one example frame from each class.

In this experiment, we adapt *Dollár*'s method for video classification, as used in [1,11]). The original method is based on the periodic detector. At each interest point, a block of video data (a *cuboid*) is extracted. Then, a codebook is built by applying PCA and K-means clustering. That way, a video is described by the histogram of its cuboids, quantized to the codebook entries. As multiclass classifier on top of this feature map, [1] train RBF (Radial Basis Function) SVMs and [11] use pLSA (probabilistic Latent Semantic Analysis). To test our approach we use *Dollár*'s *Matlab* code with all settings to standard (in particular $\sigma = 2$, $\tau = 3$), but with the *Periodic* detector replaced with our *Learned* detector. The periodic detector uses a threshold of 0.0002 on S_P below which all local maxima are rejected. For our detector, a natural choice for this threshold is zero, since S_L can be interpreted as the log odds of a fixation where $S_L = 0$ corresponds to a fixation probability above .5.

As in [11], we compute a leave-one-out estimate of the test error by training on the data of 24 persons, and testing on the remaining one. This is repeated 25 times. Codebooks are generated using 60,000 random samples of the training cuboids, 100 PCA components and 500 centers in K-means. Classification is done with a hard margin linear SVM. The confusion matrix and the average accuracy (the mean of the diagonal elements of the confusion matrix) are shown in Figure 4. This shows that our method outperforms previous approaches. Note that we intentionally kept most of the settings in *Dollár*'s original method in order to isolate the effect that the new interest point detector has on the performance. We therefore expect that our results improve further if we tune the entire system to suit our detector best.

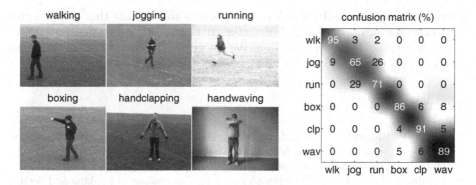

	walking	jogging	running				confusion matrix (%)					

Fig. 4. Action classification results. Top left: The KTH action classification dataset [15]. Top right: The confusion matrix of our classification system, which uses the Learned interest point detector. Bottom left: A comparison against existing algorithms.

Algorithm	Accuracy
our method	82.8
Niebles et al. [11]	81.5
Dollár et al. [1]	81.2
Schüldt et al. [15]	71.7
Ke et al. [6]	63.0

4.3 Real-Time Demo and Matlab Implementation

For many applications it is vital that interest points can be computed very efficiently. Being conceptually similar to the periodic detector, the learned detector works also very efficiently. With five (eq. 3) instead of two (eq. 2) temporal filters, we expect the number of operations to be about 2.5 times higher. A demo application which shows the learned saliency function S_L superimposed onto a webcam feed in real-time (as in Figure 2, top right) can be downloaded at http://www.kyb.mpg.de/~kienzle. The *Matlab* code for detecting interest points, which plugs into *Dollár*'s feature extraction framework [1], is provided at the same location.

5 Discussion

We have presented a new spatiotemporal interest point detector based on a very simple neural network which predicts where a human observer would look in a given video. The detector was trained on real eye movement data and we showed that it predicts the location of human eye movements on independent test clips with state-of-the-art accuracy. We also tested our approach in a computer vision environment. We found that the learned detector, plugged into a simple classification framework, outperforms previous action classification methods on a large real-world dataset. This indicates that a biologically inspired measure of interestingness can be indeed beneficial for computer vision applications. This is a nontrivial result, since existing detectors were specifically designed for computer vision problems, whereas our detector was designed to mimic human eye movements. A possible drawback of our present approach is that the detector is spatiotemporally separable, which makes it blind to time-varying spatial patterns, such as the direction of motion. We are currently working on an improved version which takes this into account.

References

1. Dollar, P., Rabaud, V., Cottrell, G., Belongie, S.J.: Behavior recognition via sparse spatio-temporal features. In: International Workshop on Performance Evaluation of Tracking and Surveillance, pp. 65–72 (2005)
2. Findlay, J.M., Gilchrist, I.D.: Active Vision: The Psychology of Looking and Seeing. Oxford University Press, Oxford (2003)
3. Frantz, S., Rohr, K., Stiehl, H.S.: On the Localization of 3D Anatomical Point Landmarks in Medical Imagery Using Multi-Step Differential Approaches. In: Proc. DAGM, pp. 340–347 (1997)
4. Harris, C., Stephens, M.: A combined corner and edge detector. In: Alvey Vision Conference, pp. 147–151 (1988)
5. Itti, L., Koch, C., Niebur, E.: A model of saliency-based visual attention for rapid scene analysis. IEEE PAMI 20(11), 1254–1259 (1998)
6. Ke, Y., Sukthankar, R., Hebert, M.: Efficient visual event detection using volumetric features. In: Proc. ICCV, pp. 166–173 (2005)
7. Kienzle, W., Wichmann, F.A., Schölkopf, B., Franz, M.O.: Learning an interest operator from eye human movements. In: IEEE CVPR Workshop, p. 24. IEEE Computer Society Press, Los Alamitos (2006)
8. Kienzle, W., Wichmann, F.A., Schölkopf, B., Franz, M.O.: A nonparametric approach to bottom-up visual saliency. In: Proc. NIPS 19 (in press) (2007)
9. Laptev, I.: On space-time interest points. IJCV 64, 107–123 (2005)
10. Lowe, D.G.: Distinctive image features from scale-invariant keypoints. IJCV 60(2), 91–110 (2004)
11. Niebles, J.C., Wang, H., Wang, H., Fei Fei, L.: Unsupervised learning of human action categories using spatial-temporal words. In: Proc. BMVC (2006)
12. Reinagel, P., Zador, A.M.: Natural scene statistics at the center of gaze. Network: Computation in Neural Systems 10(4), 341–350 (1999)
13. Rutishauser, U., Walther, D., Koch, C., Perona, P.: Is bottom-up attention useful for object recognition? In: IEEE Proc. CVPR, pp. 37–44. IEEE Computer Society Press, Los Alamitos (2004)
14. Schmid, C., Mohr, R., Bauckhage, C.: Evaluation of interest point detectors. IJCV 37(2), 151–172 (2000)
15. Schüldt, C., Laptev, I., Caputo, B.: Recognizing human actions: A local SVM approach. In: Proc. ICPR, pp. 32–36 (2004)
16. The Netlab Toolbox, available at http://www.ncrg.aston.ac.uk/netlab/
17. Wandell, B.A.: Foundations of Vision. Sinauer Associates, Inc. (1995)
18. Yarbus, A.: Eye movements and vision. Plenum Press (1967)

A Fast and Reliable Coin Recognition System

Marco Reisert, Olaf Ronneberger, and Hans Burkhardt

University of Freiburg, Computer Science Department,
79110 Freiburg i.Br., Germany
reisert@informatik.uni-freiburg.de

Abstract. This paper presents a reliable coin recognition system that is based on a registration approach. To optimally align two coins we search for a rotation in order to reach a maximal number of colinear gradient vectors. The gradient magnitude is completely neglected. After a quantization of the gradient directions the computation of the induced similarity measure can be done efficiently in the Fourier domain. The classification is realized with a simple nearest neighbor classification scheme followed by several rejection criteria to meet the demand of a low false positive rate.

1 Introduction

The goal of a coin recognition system is to automatically sort and classify high volumes of coins with high accuracy within a small amount of time. In 2003 ARC Seibersdorf research GmbH created the sorting device called *Dagobert* [1]. The recognition unit of Dagobert is able to discriminate between over 600 different coin types based on over 2000 different coin faces. In 2006 ARC Seibersdorf formulated together with the MUSCLE[1] Network of Excellence and the PRIP, Vienna University of Technology the *Coin Image Seibersdorf (CIS) Competition 2006*[2] to foster the development of robust coin recognition algorithms. The present paper proposes the price winning algorithm.

The proposed system roughly follows the ideas in [1]. The similarity of two coin images is computed by the use of registration techniques. In a first step the translational pose of the coin is determined by a segmentation algorithm that makes an estimate of the coin's radius and its center. The comparison of two coins is done by aligning them with respect to their rotational pose, i.e. we have to optimize only one parameter, which makes the registration feasible. Having defined a similarity measure any classification scheme may be used. Because of the highly reliable embossing process for the coins we believe that a registration technique is the first choice to reach good results. The only difficulty is to find robust similarity measures that tolerate the, sometimes severe, abrasion and fouling of the coins, but still give response for the reliable embossment which determines the class membership. Additionally this similarity measure has to be

---

[1] http://www.muscle-noe.org/
[2] http://muscle.prip.tuwien.ac.at/index.php

F.A. Hamprecht, C. Schnörr, and B. Jähne (Eds.): DAGM 2007, LNCS 4713, pp. 415–424, 2007.
© Springer-Verlag Berlin Heidelberg 2007

computable in a fast manner such that the resulting algorithm can cope with large databases.

The article is organized as follows: In the following subsection we give a short overview over related work. In Section 2 we present our algorithm for coin segmentation that is based on the Hough transform. In Section 3 we present the features that are used for alignment and similarity computation followed by some implementation details. The classification scheme is presented in Section 4. Finally we show results on the CIS Benchmark datasets. In Section 6 we give a conclusion and ideas for further improvement.

1.1   Previous Work

Recent approaches for coin recognition can roughly be divided in methods based on rotational invariant features and methods based on registration. In [5,6] invariant features are used to compare coins in a rotational invariant manner. In [5] very high false positive rates are reported. In [1,7] the similarity computation is based on registration techniques. It seems possible that these approaches are able to fulfill the reliability demanded in the benchmark specifications.

2   Coin Segmentation

In [1] a simple segmentation scheme is used which works by thresholding the grayvalues. This approach is based on the assumption that the coins itself are brighter than its background. Having a look at the benchmark database this is mostly but not always the case. So, we have to search for another solution. The Hough transform is known to be a very robust segmentation tool. We use a generalized Hough transform (GHT) [2] to segment the coins. In [3] the same method was used for a fast segmentation of cell-nuclei. We use a three dimensional voting space, namely the two coordinates of the coin's center and its radius r. Let us call the gray-valued image function $I : \mathbb{R}^2 \mapsto \mathbb{R}$ and the voting function $P : \mathbb{R}^3 \mapsto \mathbb{R}$. The idea is to let each pixel cast a vote for possible circle centers at particular radii. To keep the running time low the votes are performed only for those points that are colinear with current gradient vector. Formally we search maxima of the following function

$$P(\mathbf{x}, r) = \int_{\mathbb{R}^2} \left(\delta \left(\mathbf{x} + r \frac{\nabla I(\mathbf{y})}{\|\nabla I(\mathbf{y})\|} \right) + \delta \left(\mathbf{x} - r \frac{\nabla I(\mathbf{y})}{\|\nabla I(\mathbf{y})\|} \right) \right) \|\nabla I(\mathbf{y})\| \, d\mathbf{y},$$

where δ is some indicator function giving contribution whenever its argument is nearby zero, for example a gaussian or a rectangle-function. Each gradient in the image votes for a possible center of the coin, where the hypothetical center has to be along the gradient's direction. Since we do not know whether the coin is darker or brighter than the background we have to vote in positive and negative direction.

Before starting to compute the integral we blur the image with a first-order IIR-Filter to get smooth gradients. The computation of the integral is straightforward. Just run linearly over the image I and compute the gradient $\nabla I(\mathbf{y})$ and its magnitude. Now for every position $\mathbf{y}$ and for discrete radii values r_i accumulate the voting function at positions $\mathbf{y} + r_i \frac{\nabla I(\mathbf{y})}{||\nabla I(\mathbf{y})||}$ and $\mathbf{y} - r_i \frac{\nabla I(\mathbf{y})}{||\nabla I(\mathbf{y})||}$ with weight $||\nabla I(\mathbf{y})||$. The shape of the accumulation depends on the indicator function δ. We just round the estimated coordinates to the nearest integers and accumulate the single pixels. After all accumulations are done the voting function P is smoothed by an IIR-Filter. Hence, the indicator function is just the impulse response of this filter.

Since we know that there is only one coin present in a image, we can use a hierarchical voting scheme to get better estimates for the radius. For a first rough estimate we take 16 different values for the radius covering the whole range of possible coin sizes. After the determination of the first maximum we distribute again 16 radius bins around the first rough estimate. Overall we repeat this procedure four times resulting in an accurate estimate. On an *Intel P4 2.8Ghz* the overall segmentation procedure needs less than one second for one image. In Figure 1 we show three examples of segmented coins.

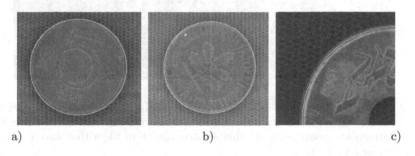

a)   b)   c)

Fig. 1. Coins segmented by our algorithm. Coin a) and b) have very bad contrast conditions, however our algorithm is able to make a good segmentation. In c) a section of a coin is shown where our algorithm makes a small mistake. Due to a strong circle-like structure at the border of the coin the estimated radius is a little bit too small. However, this is a systematical error, and if it happens for every coin from the specific class it shall not confuse the classification algorithm.

3   Feature Extraction and Registration

Having a look at the benchmark database one can guess that the actual gray values of the images are not very discriminative. In [1] a Canny Edge-Detector is used to compute more reliable features. This is, of course, a much better idea than working on the plain gray values, but it has still some disadvantages. At first, the results depend heavily on the choice of the parameters of the edge-detector. These parameters have to be chosen properly depending on the illumination conditions and the quality of the images. And secondly, the orientation of the edges are completely neglected. We want to follow a different approach. We want to use solely the direction of the gradients in the image and totally neglect its magnitude. This has the advantage that we are independent of illumination and contrast changes. One can argue that only considering the direction is a very dirty approach, since we also compute gradient directions in homogeneous, flat regions where theoretically the gradient has to be zero and hence no reliable direction exists. But however, there are several reason to follow this idea. First, if the direction in homogeneous regions can be assumed to be equidistributed with respect to its angle, then the similarity measure can be designed such that this regions give only a constant bias. Further, we do not need any threshold, i.e. we never need to decide whether there is an edge or not. This advantage becomes important considering Figure 2. Due to abrasion coins show typical patterns near structural steps and edges. One can see several slight gradients near the edges. It would be ignorant to neglect this information. An algorithm, which makes only use of edges has problems to also incorporate this information.

Fig. 2. Abrasion effects. Due to abrasion several slight gradients are introduced near the edges. Not only the edges contain structural information that may be considered, also putative flat regions contain valuable structure. Our algorithm also uses this information for recognition.

During segmentation we determined the radius and center of the coin. From now on we assume that the center is shifted to the origin and the radius is normalized to 1. For convenience we represent the image I in polar coordinates $I(r, \varphi)$ with $r \in [0, 1]$ and $\varphi \in [0, 2\pi]$. The basis for our features is the normalized gradient image $\mathbf{g} = (g_r, g_\varphi)^T$ given by

$$g_r(r, \varphi) = \frac{\partial_r I}{\epsilon + \sqrt{(\partial_r I)^2 + (r \partial_\varphi I)^2}}, \quad g_\varphi(r, \varphi) = \frac{r \partial_\varphi I}{\epsilon + \sqrt{(\partial_r I)^2 + (r \partial_\varphi I)^2}},$$

where ϵ is a small positive constant avoiding division by zero. We choose the radial and tangential derivatives because they do not change while rotating the coin. A rotation of the coin just shifts the φ coordinate of $\mathbf{g}$ cyclically. Based on the gradient image we compute the angle image $a \in [0, \pi]$ given by

$$a(r, \varphi) = \text{sign}(g_\varphi(r, \varphi)) \arcsin(g_r(r, \varphi))$$

describing the angle to the tangent of the circle. The sign modification leads to invariance against inverting the contrast. We found that it is not important whether an edge is descending or ascending, because, e.g. by dirt or abrasion of the coin, the contrast conditions are sometimes inverted. So only one half of the circle is represented by this function, the other half is mapped by point reflection to the former. The function a is now used for comparing two coins. Let a and a' be two feature functions from two different coins, we define their correlation function by

$$c(\phi) = \int_0^{2\pi} \int_0^1 \delta(a(r, \varphi) - a'(r, \varphi - \phi)) \, dr d\varphi,$$

where δ is again some indicator function deciding whether two angles are different or equal. It can be imagined as a delta distribution, for example. So $c(\phi)$ counts how often the angles of the gradients of the two coins coincide at a specific relative angle ϕ. The maximum value of c is defined as our similarity measure

$$k(a, a') = \max_{\phi \in [0, 2\pi]} c(\phi) \tag{1}$$

It is well known that the computation of a cross correlation function which is based on the scalar product can be efficiently done in the Fourier domain. But c is not an ordinary scalar product; to get us into the position to apply the Fourier transform we first have to rewrite our correlation function. For any function g there exists the so called convolutional square root $g^{1/2}$, which fulfills the following relation

$$g(x - y) = \int_{\mathbb{R}} g^{1/2}(x - z) g^{1/2}(z - y) \, dz.$$

Using this formula for our indicator function δ we can rewrite the correlation

$$c(\phi) = \int_0^{2\pi} \int_0^1 \int_{\mathbb{R}} \underbrace{\delta^{1/2}(a(r, \varphi) - z)}_{f(r, \phi, z)} \underbrace{\delta^{1/2}(z - a'(r, \varphi - \phi))}_{f'(r, \varphi - \phi, z)} \, dz dr d\varphi.$$

Indeed we introduced an additional integration but now $c(\phi)$ looks like an ordinary correlation of two functions f and f', which can efficiently be computed in the Fourier domain. Let us call $f(r, \phi, z)$ our final feature function and $\tilde{f}(r, k, z) = \int f(r, \varphi, z) e^{-ik\varphi} d\varphi$ its Fourier transform with respect to the angle parameter. The feature with respect the z-parameter can be interpreted as a some kind of indicator function contributing whenever there is a gradient with the specific angle z in the original image.

Using the Fourier features the Fourier representation of $c(\phi)$ looks then

$$\tilde{c}(k) = \int_0^1 \int_{\mathbb{R}} \tilde{f}^*(r, k, z) \tilde{f}'(r, k, z) \, dr dz,$$

where $\cdot^*$ is the complex-conjugate. The last step is just to transform $\tilde{c}(k)$ back into the spatial domain and search for its maxima.

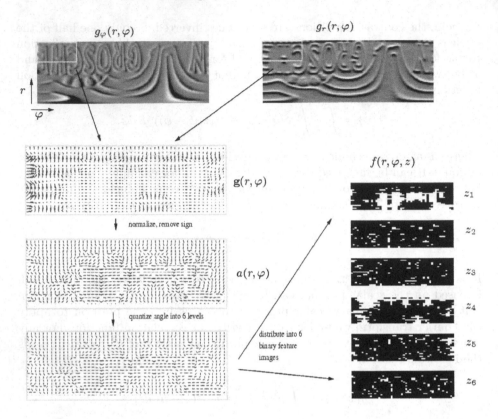

Fig. 3. Sketch of the feature extraction process. After the computation of radial and angular gradients the angle function $a(r, \varphi)$ is computed. For clarity we only visualize the yellow marked upper left corner of the image. In the $a(r, \varphi)$ the arrow-tips are omitted because the sign of the direction does not count anymore. One can see that also regions with relatively low gradient magnitude contain valuable, structured information. In the last step the directions are discretized in six discrete directions. Finally one binary feature image is created for each direction.

3.1   Implementation

Preprocessing and Gradient Computation. Given the segmented image in cartesian coordinates we first applied a blur using the same IIR-filter used for segmentation. To get the polar gradient image we directly sample the gradients from the blurred image with 1024 steps in angular direction and 256 steps in radial direction using bilinear interpolation. We used a stepsize of 1 pixel in the original image for computing the finite differences for the gradient. In radial direction we only sample from 0 to 0.9, i.e. we leave out the outer 10 percent of coin, because it seems that it mostly contains useless information (see also [1]). Then we blur the image again with the IIR-filter and downsample it to the desired size; for the competition we use a size of 256 × 64. Finally we normalize the gradients and compute the angles according to the equations from above.

Discretizing the Angles and Final Feature Computation. The gradient angle parameter z is discretized in M steps, i.e. we have a stepwidth of $\Delta z = \pi/M$. So the final feature image consists of M binary images of size 256×64. The binary image with number i contains entries whenever $\frac{a(r,\varphi)}{\Delta z}$ falls within the interval $[i, i+1]$ with $0 \le i < M$. In Figure 3 we visualize the algorithm. Having a closer look at the angle function $a(r, \varphi)$ one can see that also regions with relatively low gradient magnitude contain valuable information.

To become more robust against small gradient changes we additionally use some kind of 'inverse' bilinear interpolation (also called fuzzy histograms, see [4]) to generate the entries. For each entry the two nearest pixel get a contribution depending linearly on the distance to the pixel's center. We also conduct some smoothing in radial direction to be robust against small shifts in radial direction. Such radial shifts usually come from small errors during the segmentation process.

Finally the Fast Fourier Transform (FFT) of the feature function in φ direction can be precomputed to speed up the comparison later, i.e. we compute the FFT of the rows of the binary feature images on the right of Figure 3.

4   Classification

For classification we use a very simple nearest neighbor scheme. This is mainly due to complexity and memory considerations. For example, considering the feature parameters used for the competition, one feature is of size $256 \cdot 64 \cdot 6 \cdot$ sizeof(float) $= 392$KByte. The training database consists of over two thousand different coin types, so we already need nearly one GigaByte storage. Although, the training set provides a set of different samples per type, we only use one sample for training. But still, a whole scan of those would take about 6 seconds on a *Pentium P4 2.8Ghz* for just one side of the coin, while the benchmark specifications only allowed about 5 seconds to classify one coin, which involves the scan for both sides. To meet this goal we have to restrict to search only in a subset of the two thousand training images. Since we have a good estimate of the radius of the examined coin, the search is only performed in some neighborhood of the estimated radius. We search in a range of $2\Delta = 4mm$ around the estimated radius. Mostly, the search includes around 200 comparison depending on the coin's radius, that is a speed up of a factor of 10 in comparison to an exhaustive search. After the algorithm has determined the nearest neighbors within this range it is checked whether the predicted labels for the front and backside of the coin are consistent. If they do not, the coin is immediately rejected and classified as unknown. Otherwise we compute a prediction confidence C which is based on the similarity scores, thickness, radius and angle pose differences. First we normalize the similarity scores. Imagine that two images are compared that have totally random gradient orientation, then their similarity is expected to be $k = 256 \cdot 64/6 \approx 2730$. Hence, we normalize the similarity score by $k' = k - 2730$. We further compute the thickness differences Δt_1 and Δt_2 for the front and backside of the coin to its matched partners from the training database. And we

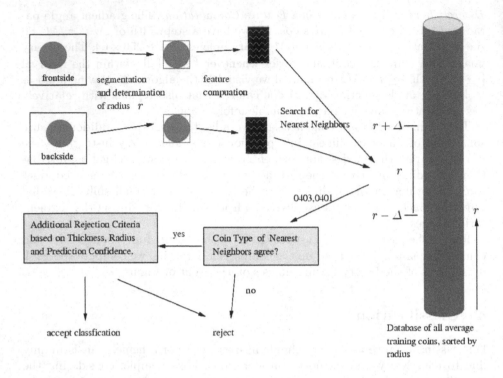

Fig. 4. Complete workflow of the classification system. After segmentation of the coins the features $\tilde{f}(k, r, z)$ according to section 3 are computed. Then, nearest neighbors are searched with respect to the similarity measure (1). The search is only performed within a neighborhood of the estimated radius, not on the whole database. If the nearest neighbors of both coin sides agree the coin is a possible candidate for acceptance, otherwise it is immediately rejected. Finally additional rejection criteria are checked and some classes get a special treatment.

do the same for the radius. Due to the construction of the coin acquisition system front and backside of the coin should have a fixed rotational pose relation. We found that the relation is slightly unreliable, but we also included it with a small weight in our confidence score,

$$C = k_1' k_2' \exp\left(-\frac{(\Delta r_1 + \Delta r_2)}{0.17\ mm} - \frac{(\Delta t_1 + \Delta t_2)}{0.07\ mm} - \frac{(\Delta\phi)}{10°}\right).$$

If this confidence is below 10^{-5} the coin is rejected. Additionally, we will make a reject if the thickness difference is above $0.25mm$ or the $\Delta\phi$ is above $70°$. Besides, all this additional reject criteria do not have too much influence on the overall performance, the most powerful rejection criteria is definitely the consistency of the votes for the front and backside of the coin. In Figure 4 we give a rough overview over the complete classification system.

5   Experiments

We conducted some experiments to get good settings for the parameters. We found that for the angular/radial resolution 256×64 is a good trade-off betwees accuracy and speed of the classification. In general one can say that the higher the resolution the better the results, while the ratio $256/64 = 4$ seems to be optimal and should be kept fix. As already mentioned we use 6 discritization steps for the z-resolution.

Table 1. Experimental results for all three tranches (left) and the competetion results (right). RC is the number of classes which got at least one correct classification. (T/F)(P/N) means True/False Positives/Negatives. TP+TN gives the total number of correct classification. FN+TN is the total number of rejects, i.e. the number of coins classified as unknown. FP gives the number of unknown coins, which are classified to some known class and the number of known coins classified to a wrong known class. The assessment score is calculated by score = RC*25 + TP+TN - 100*(FP).

Tranche	1A (no rej.)	1A	1B	1C	FR	MA
RC	322	320	309	398	**339**	278
TP+TN (%)	97.64	97.27	97.20	94.31	**97.24**	67.31
FN+TN (%)	5.20	5.64	5.94	9.42	**5.18**	32.50
FP (%)	0.06	0.02	0.02	0.03	**0.0**	2.21
Ass. Score	17211	17527	17245	19081	**18199**	-8419

In Table 1 we show the obtained results on the CIS benchmark dataset. The system shows very good performance, classification rate are mostly above 97% and the false positive rate is very low. In the first column results for tranche 1A with no additional reject criteria are shown. Obviously the additional criteria improve the system; less false positives and only marginal shrinkage of the classication rate can be observed, and hence also a higher assessment score is obtained. Further we show results for tranches 1B and 1C with the additional reject criteria. On all tranches, together 30000 coins, we have in total 7 coins which are wrongly classified to be known, while they are labeled as unknown. Six of these coins are very similar to known coin classes or are wrongly labeled. The results for the final competition results are also reported (details in [9]). Our results (FR) are compared to an approach based on invariant features (MA) [8].

6   Conclusions

We presented a coin recognition system which is based on gradient directions only. The results show that the directional information is enough to build a reliable classification system while the system is very robust to illumination and contrast changes. We have shown that the demand of a very low false positive rate is possible to reach. There might be several improvements of the system. Further fitting of the parameters like resolution, oversampling multiplier or smoothing width may improve the accuracy of the system. More sophisticated reject criteria and confidence values could also help to avoid false positives. Unfortunately the test set sizes of ten thousand coins are still to small to validate false positive rates of 0.01 percent.

References

1. Nölle, M., Penz, H., Rubik, M., Mayer, K., Holländer, I., Granec, R.: Dagobert - A new Coin Recognition and Sorting System. In: Proceedings of the 7th Internation Conference on Digital Image Computing - Techniques and Applications (DICTA'03), Sydney, Australia (2003)
2. Ballard, D.H.: Generalizing the hough transform to detect arbitrary shapes. Pattern Recognition, 13–2 (1981)
3. Schulz, J., Schmidt, T., Ronneberger, O., Burkhardt, H.: Fast Scalar and Vectorial Grayscale based Invariant Features for 3D Cell Nuclei Localization and Classification. In: Franke, K., Müller, K.-R., Nickolay, B., Schäfer, R. (eds.) Pattern Recognition. LNCS, vol. 4174, Springer, Heidelberg (2006)
4. Siggelkow, S., Burkhardt, H.: Improvement of Histogram-Based Image Retrieval and Classification. In: Proceedings of the International Conference on Pattern Recognition, vol. 3, pp. 367–370 (2002)
5. Haber, Ramoser, Mayer, Penz, Rubik: Classification of coins using an eigenspace approach. Pattern Recognition Letters 26(1), 61–75 (2005)
6. Fukumi, M., Omatu, S., Takeda, F., Kosaka, T.: Rotation-invariant neural pattern recognition system with application to coin recognition. IEEE Transactions in Neural Networks 3(2), 272–279 (1992)
7. Adameck, M., Hossfeld, M., Eich, M.: Three color selective stereo gradient method for fast topographic recognition of metallic surfaces. In: Proceedings of Electronic Imaging, Science and Technology, Machine Vision Application in Industrial Inspection XI, vol. SPIE 5011, pp. 128–139 (2003)
8. van der Maaten, L., Boon, P.: COIN-O-MATIC: A fast system for reliable coin classification. In: MUSCLE CIS Coin Recognition Competition Workshop (2006), http://muscle.prip.tuwien.ac.at
9. Nölle, M., Rubik, M., Hanbury, A.: Results of the MUSCLE CIS Coin Competition 2006. In: MUSCLE CIS Coin Recognition Competition Workshop (2006), http://muscle.prip.tuwien.ac.at

3D Invariants with High Robustness to Local Deformations for Automated Pollen Recognition

Olaf Ronneberger, Qing Wang, and Hans Burkhardt

Albert-Ludwigs-Universität Freiburg, Institut für Informatik, Lehrstuhl für Mustererkennung und Bildverarbeitung, Georges-Köhler-Allee Geb. 052, 79110 Freiburg, Deutschland
{ronneber,qwang,burkhardt}@informatik.uni-freiburg.de

Abstract. We present a new technique for the extraction of features from 3D volumetric data sets based on group integration. The features are invariant to translation, rotation and global radial deformations. They are robust to local arbitrary deformations and nonlinear gray value changes, but are still sensitive to fine structures. On a data set of 389 confocally scanned pollen from 26 species we get a precision/recall of 99.2% with a simple 1NN classifier. On volumetric transmitted light data sets of about 180,000 airborne particles, containing about 22,700 pollen grains from 33 species, recorded with a low-cost optic in a fully automated online pollen monitor the mean precision for allergenic pollen is 98.5% (recall: 86.5%) and for the other pollen 97.5% (recall: 83.4%).

1   Introduction

Nearly all worldwide pollen forecasts are still based on manual counting of pollen in air samples under the microscope. Within the BMBF-founded project "OMNIBUSS" a first demonstrator of a fully automated online pollen monitor was developed, that integrates the collection, preparation and microscopic analysis of air samples. Due to commercial interests, no details of the developed pattern recognition algorithms were published within the last three years. This is the first time that we show how this machine works behind the scenes.

Challenges in pollen recognition. Due to the great intra class variability and only very subtle inter-class differences, automated pollen recognition is a very challenging but still largely unsolved problem. As most pollen grains are nearly spherical and the subtle differences are mainly found near the surface, a pollen expert needs the full 3D information (usually by "focussing through" the transparent pollen grain). An additional difficulty is that pollen grains are often agglomerated and that the air samples contain lots of other airborne particles. For a reliable measurement of high allergenic pollen (e.g. Artemisia. A few such pollen grains per m^3 of air can already cause allergic reactions) the avoidance of false positives is one of the most important requirements for a fully automated system.

State of the art. Almost all published articles concerning pollen recognition deal with very low numbers of pollen grains from only a few species and use

F.A. Hamprecht, C. Schnörr, and B. Jähne (Eds.): DAGM 2007, LNCS 4713, pp. 425–435, 2007.
© Springer-Verlag Berlin Heidelberg 2007

manually prepared pure pollen samples, e.g. [1]. Only [4] used a data set from real air samples containing a reasonable number of pollen grains (3686) from 27 species. But even on a reduced data set containing only 8 species and dust particles, the recall was only 64,9% with a precision of 30%.

Main Contribution. In this paper we describe the extension of the Haar-integration framework [9,6,7,8] (further denoted as "HI framework") to global and local deformations. This is achieved by creating synthetic channels containing the segmentation borders and employing special parameterized kernel functions. Due to the sparsity of non-zero-values in the synthetic channels the resulting integral features are highly localized in the real space, while the framework automatically guarantees the desired invariance properties.

For efficient computation of these integrals we make use of the sparsity of the data in the synthetic channels and use a Fourier or spherical harmonics ("SH") series expansion (for the desired rotation invariance) to compute multiple features at the same time.

 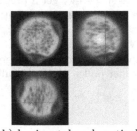 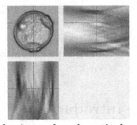

a) volume rendering of confocal data set   b) horizontal and vertical cuts of confocal data set   c) horizontal and vertical cuts of transmitted light data set

Fig. 1. 3D recordings of Betula pollen grains. In transmitted light microscopy the recording properties in z-direction (the direction of the optical axis) are significantly different from those in the xy-direction, because the effects of diffraction, refraction and absorption depend on the direction of the transmitted light. Furthermore there is a significant loss of information in z-direction due to the low-pass property of the optical transfer function.

2   Material and Methods

Data Sets. To demonstrate the generality of the proposed invariants and compare them to earlier results, we use two different pollen data sets in this article. Both contain 3D volumetric recordings of pollen grains.

The *"confocal data set"* contains 389 pollen grains from 26 German pollen taxa, recorded with a confocal laser scanning microscope (fig 1a,b). For further details on this data set refer to [6].

The *"pollen monitor data set"* contains about 180,000 airborne particles including about 22,700 pollen grains from air samples that were collected, prepared and recorded with transmitted light microscopy from the online pollen monitor from March to September 2006 in Freiburg and Zürich (fig. 1c). All 180,000 particles were manually labeled by pollen experts.

Segmentation. To find the 3D surface of the pollen grains in the *confocal data set*, we use the graph cut algorithm described in [2]. The original data were first scaled down. The edge costs to source and sink were modeled by a Gaussian distribution relative to the mean and minimum gray value. We added voxel-to-voxel edges to the 124 neighborhood, where the weight was a Gaussian of the gray differences. The resulting binary mask was then smoothly scaled up to the original size.

The first step in processing the *pollen monitor data set* is the detection of circular objects with voxel-wise vector based gray-scale invariants, similar to those in [8]. For each detected circular object the precise border in the sharpest layer is searched: As parts of the object border are often missing or not clear, we use snakes to find a smooth and complete border. To avoid the common problem of snakes being attracted to undesired edges (if plain gradient magnitude is used as force field), we take the steps depicted in fig 2.

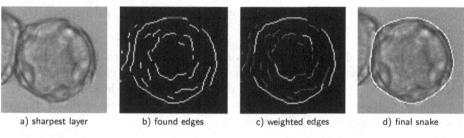

a) sharpest layer   b) found edges   c) weighted edges   d) final snake

1. Applying modified Canny edge detection.
As pollen grains have a nearly round shape, the edges that are approximately perpendicular to the radial direction are more relevant. We replace the gradient with its radial component in the original Canny edge detection algorithm.

2. Model-based weighting of the edges.
The curvatures and relative locations of the edges are analyzed and each edge is given a different weight. Some edges are even eliminated. As a result, a much clearer weighted edge image is obtained.

3. Employing snakes to find the final border.
The initial contour is chosen to be the circle found in the detection step. The external force field is the so-called "gradient vector flow" [10] computed from the weighted edge image

Fig. 2. Segmentation of transmitted light microscopic images

2.1   Construction of Invariants

For the construction of invariants we use the combination of a normalization and Haar-integration [9,6,7,8](see eq. (1)) over a transformation group containing rotations and deformations (Haar-integration has nothing to do with Haar wavelets). In contrast to the very general approach in [6], we now use the object center and the outer border found in the segmentation step to extract more distinctive features describing certain regions of the object.

$$T[f](X) := \int_G f(gX)dg$$

$\quad$ G : transformation group
$\quad$ g : one element of the transformation group
$\quad$ dg : Haar measure $\qquad$ (1)
$\quad$ f : nonlinear kernel function
$\quad$ X : n-dim, multi-channel data set

Invariance to translations. Invariance to translations is achieved by moving the center of mass of the segmentation mask to the origin. The final features are quite insensitive to errors in this normalization step, because they are computed "far" away from this center and only the direction to it is used.

Invariance to rotation. Invariance to rotation around the object center is achieved by integration over the rotation group. In the *confocal data set* we can model a 3D rotation of a real-world object by a 3D rotation of the recorded volumetric data set (see fig. 1b). In contrast to this, the transmitted light microscopic image stacks from the *pollen monitor data set* show very different characteristics in xy- and z-direction, (see fig. 1c). A rotation around the x- or y-axis of the real-world object results in so different gray value distributions, that it is more reasonable to model only the rotation around the z-axis, resulting in a planar rotation invariance.

Invariance to global Deformations and Robustness to local Deformations. The deformation model consists of two parts. The global deformations are modeled by a simple shift in radial direction $\mathbf{e}_r$, which depends only on the angular coordinates (see figure 3a). For full 3D-rotations described in spherical coordinates $\mathbf{x} = (x_r, x_\varphi, x_\vartheta)$ this model is

$$\mathbf{x}' = \mathbf{x} + \boldsymbol{\gamma}(\mathbf{x}) \qquad \text{with} \quad \boldsymbol{\gamma}(\mathbf{x}) = \gamma(x_\varphi, x_\vartheta) \cdot \mathbf{e}_r(x_\varphi, x_\vartheta) \ . \tag{2}$$

For rotations around the z-axis described in cylindrical coordinates $\mathbf{x} = (x_r, x_\varphi, x_z)$ we get

$$\mathbf{x}' = \mathbf{x} + \boldsymbol{\gamma}(\mathbf{x}) \qquad \text{with} \quad \boldsymbol{\gamma}(\mathbf{x}) = \gamma(x_\varphi) \cdot \mathbf{e}_r(x_\varphi) \ . \tag{3}$$

Please note, that this deformation is well defined only for $r > -\gamma(\varphi)$, which is no problem in the present application, because the features are computed "far" away from the center.

$\quad$ The smaller local deformations are described by an arbitrary displacement field $\mathbf{D}(\mathbf{x})$ such that

$$\mathbf{x}' = \mathbf{x} + \mathbf{D}(\mathbf{x}) \tag{4}$$

(see fig. 3b). For the later partial Haar-integration [3] over all possible realizations of this displacement field, it is sufficient to know only the probability for the occurrence of a certain relative displacement $\mathbf{r}$ within this field as

$$p\big(\mathbf{D}(\mathbf{x} + \mathbf{d}) - \mathbf{D}(\mathbf{x}) = \mathbf{r}\big) = p_d\,(\mathbf{r}; \|\mathbf{d}\|) \qquad \forall \mathbf{x}, \mathbf{d} \in \mathbb{R}^3 \ , \tag{5}$$

a) Global deformation model (radial)   b) Local deformation model (arbitrary)

Fig. 3. Possible realizations of the deformation models

where we select $p_d\left(\mathbf{r}; \|\mathbf{d}\|\right)$ to be a rotationally symmetric Gaussian distribution with a standard deviation $\sigma = \|\mathbf{d}\| \cdot \sigma_d$.

While we achieve full invariance to radial deformations by full Haar-integration we can only reach robustness to local deformations by partial Haar-integration. But this non-invariance in the second case is exactly the desired behavior. In combination with appropriate kernel functions this results in a continuous mapping of objects (with weak or strong local deformations) into the feature space.

The kernel functions. Instead of selecting a certain fixed number of kernel functions, we introduce parameterized kernel functions here. Embedded into the HI framework, each new combination of kernel parameters results in a new invariant feature. For multiple kernel parameters, we now have a multidimensional invariant feature array describing the object.

Robustness to gray value transformations. To become robust to gray value transformations the information is split into gradient direction (which is very robust even under nonlinear gray value transformations) and gradient magnitude. This was already successfully applied to the HI framework in [8] and to confocal pollen data sets in [5].

Synthetic channels with segmentation results. To feed the segmentation information into the HI framework we simply render the surface (confocal data set) or the contour of the sharpest layer (transmitted light data set) as delta-peaks into a new channel S and extend the kernel-function with two additional points that sense the gray value in this channel. The only condition for this technique is that the computation of the synthetic channel and the action of transformation group can be exchanged without the result being changed (i.e., we must get the same result if we first extract the surface and then rotate and deform the volume and vice versa).

Resulting kernel function. To achieve the requested properties we construct 4-point kernels, where 2 points of the kernel $\mathbf{a}_1$ and $\mathbf{a}_2$ sense the segmentation channel and the other 2 points $\mathbf{b}_1 = \mathbf{a}_1 + \mathbf{q}_1$ and $\mathbf{b}_2 = \mathbf{a}_2 + \mathbf{q}_2$ sense the gradient ∇X of the gray values relative to the information in the segmentation channel,

$$
\begin{aligned}
k_1[\mathbf{p}](S, X) = {}& S(\mathbf{a}_1) \cdot \|\nabla X\|(\mathbf{b}_1) \cdot \delta\left(c_1 - \frac{\mathbf{a}_1}{\|\mathbf{a}_1\|} \cdot \frac{\nabla X}{\|\nabla X\|}(\mathbf{b}_1)\right) \\
& \cdot S(\mathbf{a}_2) \cdot \|\nabla X\|(\mathbf{b}_2) \cdot \delta\left(c_2 - \frac{\mathbf{a}_2}{\|\mathbf{a}_2\|} \cdot \frac{\nabla X}{\|\nabla X\|}(\mathbf{b}_2)\right)
\end{aligned}
\tag{6}
$$

while the delta-functions restrict the kernel to "see" only gradients with the given "direction" c_1 and c_2. Not all combinations of $\mathbf{a}_1$, $\mathbf{a}_2$, $\mathbf{q}_1$, $\mathbf{q}_2$, c_1 and c_2 make sense, because the Haar integration returns identical features for all kernels that are equivalent under the given transformation group. Furthermore for certain combinations, only trivial features will be returned. To ensure, that only non-trivial and non-identical features are created, we introduce the low-dimensional parameterization $\mathbf{p}$. Examples of this kernel function are depicted in figure 4.

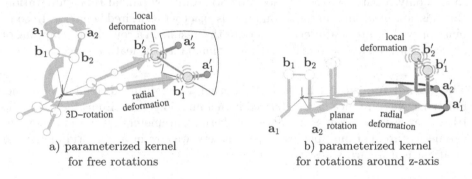

a) parameterized kernel
for free rotations

b) parameterized kernel
for rotations around z-axis

Fig. 4. Action of the transformation group on the selected 4-point kernel functions

As mentioned above, the resulting "structural" features are fully invariant to the global radial deformations. To also extract the shape information, we select the parameterized kernel

$$
k_2[\mathbf{a}_1, \mathbf{a}_2](S) = \|\boldsymbol{\gamma}(\mathbf{a}_1)\| S(\mathbf{a}_1) \cdot \|\boldsymbol{\gamma}(\mathbf{a}_2)\| S(\mathbf{a}_2) ,
\tag{7}
$$

that operates on the synthetic channel. When we use the simple scheme of creating the synthetic channels described above, the resulting features are equivalent to the magnitude of the Fourier coefficients of the contour in the 2D case and spherical harmonic ("SH") coefficients for the surface in the 3D case.

2.2   Fast Simultaneous Computation of the invariants

With the group of radial deformations G_γ, the group of arbitrary deformations G_D and the group of rotations G_R the final Haar integral becomes:

$$
T = \int\limits_{G_R} \int\limits_{G_\gamma} \int\limits_{G_D} f\left(g_R g_\gamma g_D S,\ g_R g_\gamma g_D X\right) p(\mathbf{D})\, dg_D\, dg_\gamma\, dg_R ,
\tag{8}
$$

where $p(\mathbf{D})$ is the probability for the occurrence of the local displacement field $\mathbf{D}$. The transformation of the data set is described by $(gX)(\mathbf{x}) =: X(\mathbf{x}')$, where

$$x' = \underbrace{\mathbf{Rx}}_{\text{rotation}} + \underbrace{\boldsymbol{\gamma}(\mathbf{Rx})}_{\text{global deformation}} + \underbrace{\mathbf{D}(\mathbf{Rx}+\boldsymbol{\gamma}(\mathbf{Rx}))}_{\text{local deformation}} . \tag{9}$$

To ensure a strong coupling of $\mathbf{a}'_1$ and $\mathbf{b}'_1$ (and $\mathbf{a}'_2, \mathbf{b}'_2$ accordingly) we only use kernels, where these two points will be treated equally by the global transformation, i.e., the kernel must fulfill the condition $\boldsymbol{\gamma}(\mathbf{Ra}_i) = \boldsymbol{\gamma}(\mathbf{Rb}_i), \forall \mathbf{R}$ (illustrated by thick connections in fig 4). The transformed kernel points are

$$\mathbf{a}'_i(\mathbf{R}, \boldsymbol{\gamma}, \mathbf{D}) = \mathbf{Ra}_i + \boldsymbol{\gamma}(\mathbf{Ra}_i) + \mathbf{D}(\mathbf{Ra}_i + \boldsymbol{\gamma}(\mathbf{Ra}_i))$$
$$\mathbf{b}'_i(\mathbf{R}, \boldsymbol{\gamma}, \mathbf{D}) = \mathbf{Rb}_i + \boldsymbol{\gamma}(\mathbf{Ra}_i) + \mathbf{D}(\mathbf{Rb}_i + \boldsymbol{\gamma}(\mathbf{Ra}_i)) . \tag{10}$$

Now inserting the kernel into the Haar integral gives:

$$T = \int\limits_{G_\mathbf{R}} \int\limits_{G_\gamma} \int\limits_{G_\mathbf{D}} S(\mathbf{a}'_1) \cdot \|\boldsymbol{\nabla}_{\mathbf{x}'} X\|(\mathbf{b}'_1) \cdot \delta\left(c_1 - \frac{\mathbf{a}_1}{\|\mathbf{a}_1\|} \cdot \frac{\boldsymbol{\nabla}_{\mathbf{x}'} X}{\|\boldsymbol{\nabla}_{\mathbf{x}'} X\|}(\mathbf{b}'_1)\right)$$
$$\cdot S(\mathbf{a}'_2) \cdot \|\boldsymbol{\nabla}_{\mathbf{x}'} X\|(\mathbf{b}'_2) \cdot \delta\left(c_2 - \frac{\mathbf{a}_2}{\|\mathbf{a}_2\|} \cdot \frac{\boldsymbol{\nabla}_{\mathbf{x}'} X}{\|\boldsymbol{\nabla}_{\mathbf{x}'} X\|}(\mathbf{b}'_2)\right)$$
$$\cdot p(\mathbf{D}) \cdot d\mathbf{D}(\mathbf{Ra}_1 + \boldsymbol{\gamma}(\mathbf{Ra}_1)) \cdot d\mathbf{D}(\mathbf{Rb}_1 + \boldsymbol{\gamma}(\mathbf{Ra}_1)) \tag{11}$$
$$\cdot d\mathbf{D}(\mathbf{Ra}_2 + \boldsymbol{\gamma}(\mathbf{Ra}_2)) \cdot d\mathbf{D}(\mathbf{Rb}_2 + \boldsymbol{\gamma}(\mathbf{Ra}_2))$$
$$\cdot d\boldsymbol{\gamma}(\mathbf{Ra}_1) \cdot d\boldsymbol{\gamma}(\mathbf{Ra}_2)$$
$$\cdot d\mathbf{R} ,$$

where $\boldsymbol{\nabla}_{\mathbf{x}'}$ denotes the del operator in the transformed coordinate system. The uncommon notation like $d\boldsymbol{\gamma}(\mathbf{Ra}_1)$ is necessary, because each displacement field is described here with an infinite number of parameters (one displacement for each location in the 3D space). During the integration the outer integral continuously "selects" the integration parameter for the inner integral.

If the synthetic channel is created from a single surface or contour and if we can assume a star-shaped object (which is granted for all considered pollen types) we will find for every given $\mathbf{R}$ only one nonzero response of S during the integration over all deformations $\boldsymbol{\gamma}(\mathbf{Ra}_i)$. By defining this coordinate as $\mathbf{s}(\mathbf{Ra}_i)$ we see that the integral only returns nonzero values for

$$\mathbf{s}(\mathbf{Ra}_i) = \mathbf{a}'_i$$
$$\Rightarrow \boldsymbol{\gamma}(\mathbf{Ra}_i) = \mathbf{s}(\mathbf{Ra}_i) - \mathbf{Ra}_i - \mathbf{D}(\mathbf{Ra}_i + \boldsymbol{\gamma}(\mathbf{Ra}_i)) , \tag{12}$$

which allows to eliminate the direct dependency of $\mathbf{b}'_i$ on $\boldsymbol{\gamma}(\mathbf{Ra}_i)$:

$$\mathbf{b}'_i = \mathbf{s}(\mathbf{Ra}_i) + \mathbf{Rb}_i - \mathbf{Ra}_i + \mathbf{D}(\mathbf{Rb}_i + \boldsymbol{\gamma}(\mathbf{Ra}_i)) - \mathbf{D}(\mathbf{Ra}_i + \boldsymbol{\gamma}(\mathbf{Ra}_i)) . \tag{13}$$

With the additional precondition that the probability for the occurrence of a certain relative displacement $\mathbf{r}$ only depends on the distance of the two considered points (5) we can fully eliminate the dependency of the global transformation $\boldsymbol{\gamma}(\mathbf{Ra}_i)$ and replace the four integrals over the local displacement field

$p(\mathbf{D}) \cdot d\mathbf{D}(\mathbf{Ra}_1 + \boldsymbol{\gamma}(\mathbf{Ra}_1)) \cdots$ by the integration over all relative displacements $\mathbf{r}_i$ weighted with their probability $p_d(\mathbf{r}_1; \|\mathbf{d}_1\|) \cdot p_d(\mathbf{r}_2; \|\mathbf{d}_2\|) \, d\mathbf{r}_1 d\mathbf{r}_2$. The resulting $\mathbf{b}_i'$ is

$$\mathbf{b}_i'(\mathbf{R}, \mathbf{r}_i) = \mathbf{s}(\mathbf{Ra}_i) + \mathbf{Rb}_i - \mathbf{Ra}_i + \mathbf{r}_i . \tag{14}$$

and

$$\|\mathbf{d}_i\| = \|\mathbf{Rb}_i + \boldsymbol{\gamma}(\mathbf{Ra}_i) - \mathbf{Ra}_i - \boldsymbol{\gamma}(\mathbf{Ra}_i)\| = \|\mathbf{b}_i - \mathbf{a}_i\|$$

By the substitution of $\mathbf{q}_i := \mathbf{b}_i - \mathbf{a}_i$ the full Haar integral can be written as

$$T = \int\limits_{G_\mathbf{R}} \int\limits_{\mathbb{R}^3} \|\boldsymbol{\nabla}_{\mathbf{x}'} X\|(\mathbf{b}_1') \, \delta\left(c_1 - \frac{\mathbf{a}_1}{\|\mathbf{a}_1\|} \cdot \frac{\boldsymbol{\nabla}_{\mathbf{x}'} X}{\|\boldsymbol{\nabla} X\|}(\mathbf{b}_1')\right) p_d(\mathbf{r}_1; \|\mathbf{q}_1\|) \, d\mathbf{r}_1$$

$$\int\limits_{\mathbb{R}^3} \|\boldsymbol{\nabla}_{\mathbf{x}'} X\|(\mathbf{b}_2') \, \delta\left(c_2 - \frac{\mathbf{a}_2}{\|\mathbf{a}_2\|} \cdot \frac{\boldsymbol{\nabla}_{\mathbf{x}'} X}{\|\boldsymbol{\nabla} X\|}(\mathbf{b}_2')\right) p_d(\mathbf{r}_2; \|\mathbf{q}_2\|) \, d\mathbf{r}_2 \; d\mathbf{R} . \tag{15}$$

After integration over the local deformations, this results in two scalar functions defined on a sphere (or a cylinder), that are "scanned" by a simple two-point-kernel, which allows to use the framework introduced in [7] for fast but still fully rotation invariant approximation of the solution. For 3D rotations this framework uses a spherical-harmonics series expansion, and for planar rotations around the z-axis it is simplified to a Fourier series expansion.

Parameterization. For the experiments described in this paper we only used kernels with $\|\mathbf{q}_1\| = \|\mathbf{q}_2\|$ and $c_1 = c_2$. For the application on the *confocal data set* (allowing full 3D rotations) this results in 3 parameters for the kernel: The distance q to the segmentation surface, the relative direction of the gradient c and the desired angular resolution n. For the application on the *pollen monitor data set* (rotational invariance only around the z-axis), q is split into a radial distance q_r to the segmentation border and the z-distance to the central plane q_z.

For the computation, each voxel of the dense 3D data is first projected into the sparse representation in the 4D kernel parameter space, defined by each "arm" of the kernel function (q, c, φ, ϑ for confocal data and q_r, q_z, c, φ for the pollen monitor data). The advantage of this sparseness is that fine detail information from the original images "survive" the smoothing effects of the partial Haar-integration over the local deformation model and the extraction of rotation invariant features.

For the selected kernels with $\|\mathbf{q}_1\| = \|\mathbf{q}_2\|$ and $c_1 = c_2$ a further reduction of the complexity can be achieved, because the final features are only a nonlinear combination of the magnitudes of the computed SH- / Fourier coefficients. As this final recombination does not introduce additional informations we can omit it, and instead use the magnitudes of the SH- / Fourier coefficients directly.

The best sampling of the parameter space of the kernel functions (corresponding to the inner class deformations of the objects), was found by cross validation on the training data set, resulting in $N_{q_r} \times N_{q_z} \times N_c \times n = 31 \times 11 \times 16 \times 16 = 87296$ "structural" features (using kernel function k_1) and 8 "shape" features (using kernel function k_2). For combination into one feature vector the structural features were normalized to unit sum and the shape features were multiplied by 0.01 . For the *confocal data set* this resulted in $N_q \times N_c \times n = 64 \times 7 \times 2 = 896$ "structural" features (using kernel function k_1). The "shape" features were not yet used here. For both data sets, σ_d, describing the allowed local deformations, was set to 0.1 .

3 Experiments

Experimental setup. For the *confocal data set* a simple 1 Nearest Neighbor classifier (using the L1-norm) was used.

The *pollen monitor data set* was split to approximately equal sized sets by using the air samples with an even index as training set and that with odd index as test set. From the training set only the "clean" (not agglomerated, not contaminated) pollen and the "non-pollen" particles from a few samples were used to train the support vector machine (SVM) using the RBF-kernel (radial basis function) and the one-vs-rest multi-class approach. The best parameters were selected using cross-validation on the training data set. After that the resulting SVM was used to classify all particles (about 100,000) in the training set and the false classified "non-pollen" objects were added to the final SVM-training set.

The detection step (before segmentation) only finds circular objects. For the very few non-circular (fortunately also non-allergenic) species like pinus, often only fragments are segmented. These fragments are simply labeled as "non-pollen".

Results. On the *confocal data set* we got a recognition rate of **99.2%** with the simple 1NN classifier using a leave-one-out test, which is a significant improvement to best published 1NN result on the same data set: 94,5% [5]

Table 1. Confusion matrix for pollen monitor samples. The pollen grains that the biologists were not able to recognize ("indeterm.") were left out from the statistics. Due to space limitations only the recall of the results with "no rejection" are given.

	rej.	no p.	Cory.	Alnu.	Betu.	Poac.	Arte.	other	recall (%)	recall (%)
	with rejection									no rejection
indeterm.	(826)	(1518)	(5)	(8)	(23)	(40)	(3)	(461)		
no pollen	1882	77430	1	7	3	1	0	119		
Corylus	14	6	75	0	0	0	0	0	78.9	86.3
Alnus	96	41	0	751	2	0	0	0	84.4	90.8
Betula	86	10	1	4	933	1	0	0	90.1	95.7
Poaceae	84	7	0	0	1	576	0	10	85.0	92.5
Artemisia	6	0	0	0	0	0	24	0	80.0	96.7
other pollen	814	195	1	4	5	3	1	5126	83.4	93.6
precision (%)			96.2	98.0	98.8	99.1	96.0	97.5		
mean precision (allergenic):			**98.5%**							**93.8%**
mean recall (allergenic):			**86.5%**							**93%**

On the *pollen monitor data set*, for allergenic pollen species, we got a mean precision of **98.5%** at a recall of 86.5% or a precision of 93.8% at a recall of 93% depending on the selected rejection scheme. The details are shown in table 1. Due to the limited space only the results of the 5 allergenic pollen taxa are explicitly listed, the remaining 28 pollen taxa were combined into the row "other pollen". Objects were rejected, when the SVM returned no or more than one positive decision values. The results in the small table on the right "no rejection" were obtained by always assigning the class with the highest decision value.

There were several air samples with 100% precision and 100% recall and other with very low recall, mainly caused by extreme climate conditions (e.g. snow flakes, that melted on the air sample and created a big cluster of particles in multiple layers) or malfunction of the pollen monitor (e.g. vibrations during the recording of the image stack, misadjustment of the optics , etc.)

4   Conclusions and Outlook

The integration of deformation models into the feature extraction seems to be a central step for a reliable recognition of biological structures. At least for the presented application on automated pollen recognition this technique produced results that are better than all comparable results published elsewhere (e.g., [1,4]). Furthermore it has proven to also work outside the clean laboratory world in a real routine application. Anyhow, we can expect that pollen recognition still remains a challenging research area. In pollen monitor data sets from more than only one machine, one year and two cities, the variations will be even larger.

References

1. Allen, G.P., Hodgson, R.M., Marsland, S.R., Arnold, G., Flemmer, R.C., Flenley, J., Fountain, D.W.: Automatic recognition of light-microscope pollen images. In: Proc of Image Vision and Computing New Zealand (2006)
2. Boykov, Y., Kolmogorov, V.: An experimental comparison of min-cut/max- flow algorithms for energy minimization in vision. IEEE Transactions on Pattern Analysis and Machine Intelligence 26(9), 1124–1137 (2004)
3. Haasdonk, B., Halawani, A., Burkhardt, H.: Adjustable invariant features by partial Haar-integration. In: Proc. of the 17th ICPR, Cambridge (2004)
4. Ranzato, M., Taylor, P.E., House, J.M., Flagan, R.C., LeCun, Y., Perona, P.: Automatic recognition of biological particles in microscopic images. Pattern Recognition Letters 28(1), 31–39 (2007)
5. Reisert, M., Burkhardt, H.: Invariant features for 3d-data based on group integration using directional information and spherical harmonic expansion. In: Proc. of the ICPR, Hong Kong (2006)
6. Ronneberger, O., Burkhardt, H., Schultz, E.: General-purpose object recognition in 3d volume data sets using gray-scale invariants – classification of airborne pollengrains recorded with a confocal laser scanning microscope. In: Proc. of the ICPR, Quebec (2002)

7. Ronneberger, O., Fehr, J., Burkhardt, H.: Voxel-wise gray scale invariants for simultaneous segmentation and classification. In: Kropatsch, W.G., Sablatnig, R., Hanbury, A. (eds.) Pattern Recognition. LNCS, vol. 3663, Springer, Heidelberg (2005)

8. Schulz, J., Schmidt, T., Ronneberger, O., Burkhardt, H., Pasternak, T., Dovzhenko, A., Palme, K.: Fast scalar and vectorial grayscale based invariant features for 3d cell nuclei localization and classification. In: Franke, K., Müller, K.-R., Nickolay, B., Schäfer, R. (eds.) Pattern Recognition. LNCS, vol. 4174, Springer, Heidelberg (2006)

9. Schulz-Mirbach, H.: Invariant features for gray scale images. In: Sagerer, G., Posch, S., Kummert, F. (eds.) 17. DAGM-Symposium "Mustererkennung", Informatik aktuell, pp. 1–14. Springer, Heidelberg (1995)

10. Xu, C., Prince, J.L.: Snakes, shapes, and gradient vector flow. IEEE Transactions on Image Processing 7(3), 359–369 (1998)

The *kernelHMM*: Learning Kernel Combinations in Structured Output Domains

Volker Roth and Bernd Fischer

ETH Zurich, Institute of Computational Science
Universität-Str. 6, CH-8092 Zurich
{vroth,bernd.fischer}@inf.ethz.ch

Abstract. We present a model for learning convex kernel combinations in classification problems with structured output domains. The main ingredient is a hidden Markov model which forms a layered directed graph. Each individual layer represents a multilabel version of nonlinear kernel discriminant analysis for estimating the emission probabilities. These kernel learning machines are equipped with a mechanism for finding convex combinations of kernel matrices. The resulting *kernelHMM* can handle multiple partial paths through the label hierarchy in a consistent way. Efficient approximation algorithms allow us to train the model to large-scale learning problems. Applied to the problem of document categorization, the method exhibits excellent predictive performance.

1 Introduction and Related Work

Kernel methods have been successfully applied to a variety of classification problems with *structured output domains*. Typical learning tasks of this kind are defined by hierarchical (multi-)labelings where the class membership of an object is characterized by *multiple partial paths* through a labeling tree. However, there is a general problem with using kernels which carries over to hierarchical classification: the lack of interpretability of the decision functions in abstract feature spaces makes it difficult to extract further insights into the nature of a given problem. For standard learning settings (i.e. *flat hierarchies*), it has been proposed to address this problem by using *multiple* kernels together with some combination rules, where each of the kernels measures different aspects of the data. Methods for learning sparse kernel combinations have the potential to extract *relevant* measurements for a given task. Moreover, the use of multiple kernels addresses the problem of *data fusion*.

We present a method for learning kernel combinations which explicitly addresses the problem of *hierarchical multilabel classification* in structured output domains. The main ingredient is a hidden Markov model (HMM). The HMM uses a variant of *nonlinear kernel discriminant analysis* (NKDA) [15,16] as a building block for estimating the emission probabilities. The presented variant of NKDA is capable of learning *sparse combinations* of kernel matrices in multilabel settings. The sparsity is obtained by way of *adaptive ridge regression* (AdR).

F.A. Hamprecht, C. Schnörr, and B. Jähne (Eds.): DAGM 2007, LNCS 4713, pp. 436–445, 2007.
© Springer-Verlag Berlin Heidelberg 2007

The contribution of this work is twofold. On the one hand we present a novel strategy for learning kernel combinations that extends previous approaches to multilabel settings. On the other hand, these multilabel classifiers are arranged as layers in a hierarchical hidden Markov model that is capable of handling structured output domains. Inference in this model consists of reconstructing the most probable path(s) through the label hierarchy. We apply this method to the problem of document classification, where the kernel combination mechanism is not only useful for selecting among different text kernels, but also for automatically selecting the model complexity.

Existing algorithms for combining kernels recast the problem either as a *quadratically constrained quadratic program* (QCQP), [11], as a *semi-infinite linear program* (SILP), [18], or within a *sequential minimization optimization* (SMO) framework, [2]. Methods for selecting kernel parameters have also been introduced in the boosting literature, see e.g. [4] or in the context of Gaussian processes, see e.g. [3]. However, none of these approaches has been extended to handling *hierarchical* multilabels consistently. Hierarchical classification problems, on the other hand, have been addressed by several authors, mostly in the context of document classification, see e.g. [14,1]. Many of these approaches use kernels, and some of them can handle incomplete hierarchical labelings, i.e. *multiple partial paths* through the hierarchy. None of these models, however, has been extended to learning *kernel combinations*.

The *kernelHMM* bridges this gap by introducing a method for learning convex combinations of kernel matrices for structured output domains. It can handle multiple partial paths in arbitrary (layered) graphs. It is conceptually similar to the model in [1], but differs in that its generative model allows us to efficiently combine different kernels. The use of discriminant analysis in HMMs has been proposed previously, see e.g. [10].

2   The kernelHMM

Let us assume that the output domain is comprised with a *layer-wise* structure, which for instance could form a *hierarchical* dependency among the classes. We will, however, not restrict ourselves to strict hierarchical orderings in that we allow arbitrary transitions between consecutive layers, see figure 1. If the original structure of the learning problem is of a more general form, we will include "dummy" nodes to enforce a layer structure.

By identifying each layer l in the graph as the possible values of a discrete random variable $\mathcal{Y}^{(l)}$, we arrive at a hidden Markov model for representing structured output domains. Assuming that we are given observations $\mathcal{X}^{(l)}$ generated by a distribution $p(\mathcal{X}^{(l)}|\mathcal{Y}^{(l)})$ in each of the layers, we can identify the values of the random variables $\mathcal{Y}^{(l)}$ as the emitting nodes in an automaton graph: each node within a certain layer emits vectors in some feature space $\boldsymbol{x}_i^{(l)} \in \mathbb{F}^{(l)}$ according to $p(\mathcal{X}^{(l)}|\mathcal{Y}^{(l)})$. We start with a very simple Gaussian model in which all $M^{(l)}$ nodes in one layer share a common covariance matrix: $p(\mathcal{X}^{(l)} = \boldsymbol{x}^{(l)}|\mathcal{Y}^{(l)} = m) = N(\boldsymbol{x}^{(l)}; \mu_m, \Sigma)$. This model will be successively refined for learning kernel combinations and handling multiple labels.

Sparse kernel combinations. We first observe that the ML parameters of the Gaussian model above can be computed by way of linear discriminant analysis (LDA): it is well known in the literature [7] that the LDA solution effectively computes ML estimates in a Gaussian mixture model with common covariance. LDA computes a projection $\beta = \arg\max \beta^\top S_B \beta$ s.t. $\beta^\top S_W \beta = 1$, where $S_{B,W}$ denote the between and within class scatter matrices. The analogy with the ML estimates comes from the fact that in the subspace spanned by β, squared Euclidean distances to class centroids equal Mahalanobis distances in the original space (up to a constant C):

$$\|\boldsymbol{x}^\top \beta - \boldsymbol{\mu}_m^\top \beta\|^2 = (\boldsymbol{x} - \boldsymbol{\mu}_m)^\top \Sigma^{-1}(\boldsymbol{x} - \boldsymbol{\mu}_m) + C. \tag{1}$$

This result carries over to the M-class case where LDA computes as sequence of projections $\beta_1, \ldots, \beta_{M-1}$. It has been shown in [8] that the LDA vectors can be found by first regressing the response matrix Z (which in each row encodes the class membership of an observation $\boldsymbol{x}_i$ as a binary $(0,1)$-vector) against the data matrix X (which contains the observations as row vectors). This regression step is followed by an eigen decomposition which finally yields the LDA vectors. Since there are only $M-1$ nonzero eigenvalues corresponding to the $M-1$ LDA vectors, one can use a transformed response matrix Z' which has only $M-1$ columns and fulfills a certain orthogonality constraint, see [8].

Reformulating LDA as indicator regression procedure has the advantage that one can easily regularize the fits by adding some penalty function, like $\omega \cdot \beta^\top \beta$ in the case of ridge regression, where ω denotes a predefined regularization constant. A different way of regularization called *adaptive ridge regression* has been proposed in [6], where each input dimension is penalized separately: $\sum_j \omega_j \beta_j^2$. For d variables, the individual penalties ω_j are coupled to fulfill the balancing constraint $\frac{1}{d} \sum_j \frac{1}{\omega_j} = \frac{1}{\lambda}$, where λ is again a predefined regularization constant. It has been shown that this model is equivalent to ℓ_1-penalized (or LASSO) regression which produces sparse fits in the sense that typically many of the input variables disappear from the model. Instead of selecting single features, however, we want to derive a model for selecting kernel matrices. The first step towards such a model for sparse kernel combinations is a slight variation of adaptive ridge regression: instead of d individual penalties we divide the d variables into J blocks containing m variables each (for simplicity in notation we assume that there exists an integer m such that $d = J \times m$). We then let the variables within the blocks share a common penalty. Following [6] it is numerically advantageous to introduce new variables $\gamma_{j,i} = \sqrt{\omega_i/\lambda}\, \beta_{j,i}$, $c_i = \sqrt{\lambda/\omega_i}$. Formally, we have to minimize

$$\sum_{k=1}^{M-1} \|\boldsymbol{y}_k - X D_c \boldsymbol{\gamma}_k\|^2 + \lambda \boldsymbol{\gamma}_k^\top \boldsymbol{\gamma}_k, \tag{2}$$

subject to $\boldsymbol{c}^\top \boldsymbol{c} = d$, $c_i > 0$, where D_c denotes a diagonal matrix of the components of $\boldsymbol{c}$. The target vectors $\boldsymbol{y}_k$, $k = 1, \ldots, M-1$ are the columns of the response matrix Z' (see above), and c denotes the vector of shared (transformed) penalties $\boldsymbol{c} = (c_1, \ldots, c_1, \ldots, c_J, \ldots, c_J)^\top$.

Note that for given weights $\boldsymbol{c}$, eq. (2) defines a standard ridge-regression problem in the transformed data $\tilde{X} = X D_c$. It is well-known in the kernel literature that the solution vectors $\hat{\gamma}_k$ lie in the span of these input data, i.e. $\hat{\gamma}_k = \tilde{X}^\top \boldsymbol{\alpha}_k$, which means that the data enter the model only in form of the Gram matrix (or Mercer kernel) $\tilde{X}\tilde{X}^\top$. Since we have assumed that a weight c_i is shared over a whole block of m features, we can decompose this kernel as a weighted sum of J individual kernels:

$$K := \tilde{X}\tilde{X}^\top = \sum_{j=1}^{J} c_j^2 \tilde{X}_{(j)} \tilde{X}_{(j)}^\top =: \sum_{j=1}^{J} c_j^2 K_j. \tag{3}$$

with $\tilde{X}_{(j)}$ denoting a $(n \times m)$ sub-matrix of $\tilde{X}$ consisting of one block of m input features. With the above expression we have arrived at the desired framework for learning sparse combinations of kernel matrices: the kernel matrices K_j in (3) which have been formally introduced by partitioning an initial feature set into J feature blocks can be substituted by arbitrary kernels fulfilling the positive-semidefiniteness condition of valid dot product matrices. On the technical side, we have to minimize the "kernelized" version of eq. (2)

$$\sum_{k=1}^{M-1} \|\boldsymbol{y}_k - (\sum_{j=1}^{J} c_j^2 K_j)\boldsymbol{\alpha}_k\|^2 + \lambda \boldsymbol{\alpha}_k^\top (\sum_{j=1}^{J} c_j^2 K_j)\boldsymbol{\alpha}_k \tag{4}$$

subject to $\boldsymbol{c}^\top \boldsymbol{c} = \sum_{j=1}^{J} c_j^2 = d, \quad c_i > 0$.

The optimal weights $\boldsymbol{c}$ are found iteratively by a fixed-point algorithm similar to that proposed in [6]

$$(c_j^2)_{\text{new}} = J \frac{\sum_{k=1}^{M-1} c_j^2 \hat{\boldsymbol{\alpha}}_k^\top K_j \hat{\boldsymbol{\alpha}}_k}{\sum_{k=1}^{M-1} \sum_{l=1}^{J} c_l^2 \hat{\boldsymbol{\alpha}}_k^\top K_l \hat{\boldsymbol{\alpha}}_k}. \tag{5}$$

Note that in every layer l we are using the above equation for computing *non-linear kernel discriminant analysis* (NKDA) projections of vectors $\boldsymbol{x}_i^{(l)}$ in some kernel-induced feature space $F^{(l)}$. Given these projections in all layers of our HMM with Gaussian emission probabilities in the associated kernel spaces, we can then compute the likelihood of a sample for which we have access to observations at any layer of the graph. Typically, however, we have observations only at the leaf-nodes, which suggests replicating the observations in every layer. Without a sparsifying mechanism such replications would lead to a severe modeling problem, since now the replicated variables would be conditionally independent given the values of the hidden variables $\mathcal{Y}^{(l)}$. Since in every layer we compute sparse combinations of kernels, however, we typically end up with almost orthogonal feature spaces $F^{(l)}$ which might justify the conditional independence assumption (at least on a qualitative level).

Individual covariances per class. The above model is rather restrictive in that it uses a "pooled" covariance matrix shared by all mixture components in a certain layer. This assumption might be violated in practice, for instance in the presence of "dummy" classes that contain samples from many individual classes, see figure 3 for an example of this kind. The flexibility of Mercer kernels, however, helps to overcome this problem. While a pooled covariance model leads to linear class boundaries, individual covariances produce quadratic discriminant functions. In our regression context, we can easily simulate such quadratic discriminant functions by augmenting the set of kernels by quadratic variants thereof: given an initial kernel function which computes dot products in some feature space, $k(x_1, x_2) = \phi(x_1) \cdot \phi(x_2)$, a quadratic kernel of the form

$$k_{\text{quad}}(x_1, x_2) = (1 + \phi(x_1) \cdot \phi(x_2))^2 = (1 + k(x_1, x_2))^2 \qquad (6)$$

implicitly maps into the space of quadratic polynomials and, thus, allows us to switch from linear decision boundaries to quadratic ones. Note that this increased flexibility of the decision functions is the essential difference between individual covariances and a pooled one.

Multiple labels. The origin of multiple labels might be many-fold. A document might contain one paragraph about *sports* and another one about *politics*. If we have decided to consider the whole document as one entity, such a situation gives rise to use a multi-label (*sports,politics*). A different situation might occur if the document deals explicitly with the influence of politics on sports. In such a situation we can expect that each paragraph will contain keywords from both topics. Using the common "bag-of-words" representation, however, both situations would be similar in the sense that both documents will contain a mixture of keywords which are typical for both *sports* and *politics*, so that we might model the generative process as a mixture of topic-specific word distributions.

Another reason might be a discordant collective of supervisors, giving rise to fractional labels: for instance, 70% of the supervisors voted for category *sports* and 30% for *politics*. On the technical side, however, we might represent such label uncertainty again by assuming a generative process in form of a mixture of topic-specific word distributions.

A conceptually different reason for multilabels, however, might be the decision of a single supervisor that a document belongs to both *sports* and *politics* and that it contains words which are neither typical for each of the single categories, so that the underlying generative process cannot be modeled as a mixture distribution. While such situations might occur theoretically, we believe that in the context of document categorization with "bag-of-words" encoding the generative mixture model over category-specific word distributions is more plausible.

Thus we represent a document by its bag-of-words vectors and model the generative process as a mixture of topic-specific distributions over a label set $\mathbb{L}$ with mixture weights π_m: $p(x) = \sum_{m \in \mathbb{L}} \pi_m p(x | \mathcal{Y} = y_m) = \sum_{m \in \mathbb{L}} \pi_m N(x; \mu_m, \Sigma)$. We fit such a Gaussian model with mean μ_m and covariance Σ in each layer of the HMM. The mixing proportions are estimated uniformly as $\pi_m = 1/|\mathbb{L}|$, if the m-th class is a member of the label set $\mathbb{L}$, and zero otherwise.

In practice, the fractional labels are treated as the outcome of one (supervised) E-step in the EM algorithm, and the optimization reduces to finding the ML parameters in one M-step, given a collection of (possibly) multilabeled documents. This M-step estimate can be carried out by an augmented and weighted discriminant analysis which again can be reformulated as a regression problem, followed by an eigen decomposition, see [7]. On the technical side, we only have to replace the (binary) response matrix Z with its probabilistic counterpart $\tilde{Z}$ that encodes the fractional labels. In [7] this matrix $\tilde{Z}$ is called "blurred response matrix". Thus, we can still use the adaptive ridge penalties for finding sparse combinations of kernel matrices as described in the last section. Concerning the estimates for the transition probabilities associated with the edges in the automaton graph, we simply compute the (weighted) empirical frequencies of (fractional) class membership in the training set.

Predicting the class memberships for new test objects amounts to finding the most likely paths through the automaton graph. In the ideal case, the bag-of-words vector of a document belonging to classes *sports* and *politics* will be identified as a mixture of both categories with mixing weights π_{sports} and $\pi_{politics}$ summing to one. This observation suggests to sort the individual paths according to their likelihood and to select the number of labels assigned to an observation by thresholding this ordered sum, i.e. by finding the smallest integer k such that

$$\sum_k \pi_k^{\text{ordered}} \geq \theta. \tag{7}$$

In practice we learn the optimal threshold θ on a validation set.

Efficient implementation. If we can hold objects of the size of *one* kernel matrix in the main memory, the $M-1$ minimizing vectors $\hat{\alpha}_k$, $k = 1, \ldots, M-1$ in eq. (4) can be found simultaneously in a very efficient way by employing *block conjugate gradient methods*, [5]. If the memory capacity is exceeded, we propose to approximate the multiclass discriminant analysis classifiers by a probabilistic pairwise coupling approach [9] where we only have to keep kernels of two classes in the main memory.

The problem of finding the most likely paths can be solved efficiently via the *Tree-Trellis* variant of Viterbi algorithm [19] with a time complexity that is linear in both the number of nodes and the length of the paths (i.e. the number of layers in the HMM) and which scales like $k \log k$ in the number k of paths.

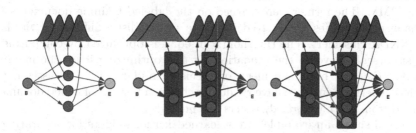

Fig. 1. A flat hierarchy (left), two hierarchical layers (middle), additional "dummy" node to complete partial paths (right). Each layer l contains emitting nodes which correspond to the values of a random variable $\mathcal{Y}_l$. Hierarchical multilabels correspond to multiple paths from the leftmost node ("begin") to rightmost one ("end").

3 Experiments

One of the major applications for hierarchical multilabel models is the classification of documents. For example, a document that belongs to the category *football* is also likely to belong to the category *sports*. Neglecting these dependencies typically leads to a decline of predictive performance.

We tested our approach on the *Reuters Corpus Volume 1* (RCV1) database, [13]. This dataset consists of 4 super-classes (MCAT, GCAT, ECAT, CCAT) which are refined hierarchically. We used the *expanded hierarchy* which contains a 117 node forest of Reuters Topics categories.

The documents are represented by 8 different kernel matrices: a linear kernel $K^{\text{lin-TF}}$ that directly works on a TFIDF-weighted bag-of-words vectors, a RBF kernel $K_{ij}^{\text{rbf}} = \exp(-D_{ij}^2/\sigma_1)$ with D_{ij}^2 denoting the Euclidean distance between the bag-of-words vectors x_i and x_j of documents i and j, a probabilistic text kernel $(K_2^{\text{NU}})_{ij} = \exp(-a\|x_i - x_j\|_1)$ that has been shown to be the best kernel among a family of probabilistic kernels introduced in [12], and a uniform (i.e. non TFIDF-weighted) bag-of-words kernel $K^{\text{lin-u}}$. In order to let the model decide whether or not to choose individual covariances per class, we also included for each of the above kernels their quadratic counterparts $K_{ij}^{*\text{-quad}} = (1 + K_{ij}^*)^2$.

In the training phase we used the dataset $lyrl2004\_vectors\_train.dat^1$, which contains bag-of-words representations for 23149 documents. For estimating the free model parameters, we divided this set into 2/3 training and 1/3 validation examples. One of these free parameters is the regularization constant λ (see eq. 4). In order to make the different kernels comparable we propose the following normalization step which involves another set of parameters: we first train the model only with the linear kernel and select the optimal regularization λ. For each of the other kernels we optimize a scaling parameter δ which rescales a kernel matrix according to $K' = \delta \cdot K$. Some of the kernels have a second parameter (e.g. the width of the RBF kernels) which is optimized together with δ on a grid of values according to best performance on the validation set.

Further parameters of the model are the transition- and emission probabilities in the HMM. The former were learned on the labeled training documents. The emission probabilities are derived from the probabilistic outputs of the layer-wise NKDA classifiers. The threshold θ in eq. 7 is optimized by computing the precision-recall curve on the validation set and optimizing it for the maximum *F1-value* (i.e. the harmonic mean of precision and recall). For assessing the predictive performance, we have randomly chosen a test set of 40000 documents, sampled from the files $lyrl2004\_vectors\_test\_pt0-3.dat$.

Figure 3 shows an example of the learned kernel weights for separating the classes "E3" $\leftrightarrow$ "GWEA" and "C1" $\leftrightarrow$ "Ex" (we used the pairwise coupling approach for computing the discriminant analysis classifiers). These two examples nicely demonstrate the capability of the model to select appropriate class models: while in the first example a pooled covariance matrix has been chosen (the

---

[1] *http://www.ai.mit.edu/projects/jmlr/papers/volume5/lewis04a/lyrl2004_rcv1v2_README.html*

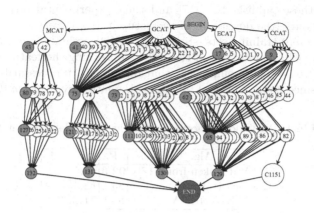

Fig. 2. The HMM for the RCV1 corpus. "Dummy" nodes are marked in green

linear kernels dominate), the problem of separating the first subclass "C1" (node no. 5 in figure 2) in the CCAT hierarchy from the "dummy" class "Ex" (node no. 17 in figure 2) in the ECAT tree seems to require more complex Gaussians with individual covariances. Overall, the linear and the rbf-kernel are the most important ones, followed by the probabilistic text kernel K_2^{NU}.

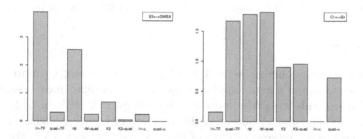

Fig. 3. The learned kernel weights for separating classes "E3" ↔ "GWEA" and "C1" ↔ "Ex". The kernels are (from left to right): linear-TFIDF, quadratic-TFIDF, rbf, rbf-quadratic, K_2^{NU}, $K_2^{NU\text{-}quadratic}$, linear-unweighted, quadratic-unweighted.

In order to quantify the predictive performance, we compare our results with those presented in [17], where only the CCAT subtree was under consideration. Other labels counted only as indicators for not belonging to the CCAT class. We emulated this setting by collapsing all other nodes to a path of "dummy" nodes that "shortcuts" the CCAT subtree. We measured the performance by way of *precision/recall* and *F1* (harmonic mean of the latter) measures based on all labels in all predicted paths through the HMM (with exception of the "shortcut" path summarizing the non-CCAT documents). The *kernelHMM* outperforms the other methods in terms of higher recall and F1 values. Since we compared our

results with those published in [17] and their experimental setup might have
differed from ours (the desription of the setup in [17] is very vague, they might
have used different training sets, stemming, TFIDF weights, etc.), however, this
comparison should be interpreted carefully. Concerning the features used in the
classifier, we would like to emphasize that our approach necessarily differs from
that in [17], since it was our goal to extend the latter by using *multiple* kernels.

Table 1. Prediction performance for the CCAT label hierarchy

Alg.	P	R	F1
H-SVM (taken from [17])	**92.3**	63.4	75.1
H-M^3-$l_{\tilde{H}}$ (taken from [17])	85.4	68.3	75.9
KernelHMM	85.1	**71.8**	**77.9**

On the full hierarchy (i.e. on all four subtrees) we obtain the following preci-
sion/recall/F1 values: P = 0.89, R = 0.75, F1= 0.813. These values coincide with
the results of the best methods presented in [13]. We further tested the influence
of learning kernel combinations by switching off the kernel selection mechanism
(i.e. simply adding all kernels), which yielded a lower F1-value of 0.803. The
availability of such sparse combinations allows the user to get detailed insights
into preferred kernels (mostly linear and rbf) and the appropriate model complexity: in most cases pooled covariance models are sufficient. When separating
dummy nodes from others, however, individual covariances are preferred.

4   Discussion

Structured output domains as well as objects that belong to more than one
category are common in many applications. Several methods have been proposed
for problems of this kind, the most of which employ kernels in order to allow
nonlinear decision rules. A potential shortcoming of kernel models, on the other
hand, is the lacking interpretability of the inferred decision rules. For standard
(i.e. non-hierarchical) models this problem has been addressed by using multiple
kernels together with a strategy to learn weighted combinations.

This work focuses on the combined problem of learning kernel combinations in
hierarchical multilabel scenarios. The key ingredient is a HMM architecture that
uses a multilabel version of nonlinear kernel discriminant analysis as building
blocks. The capability of learning convex combinations of kernel matrices is
based on using adaptive ridge penalties. While the standard adaptive ridge model
presented in [6] selects individual input features, our version leads to a nonlinear
model of discriminant analysis that combines different *kernel matrices*.

From the experiments we conclude that our model exhibits state-of-the-art
predictive performance for the problem of document categorization. Due to the
built-in capability of learning convex kernel combinations, the model can automatically adjust to different learning tasks in the hierarchical levels. The identification of dominant kernels might lead to a better understanding of important

aspects in representing documents. Last but not least, there exist highly efficient approximation algorithms for training the *kernelHMM* model, which make it possible to address large-scale problems like the Reuters RCV1 corpus.

References

1. Altun, Y., Tsochantaridis, I., Hofmann, T.: Hidden markov support vector machines. In: ICML'03, pp. 3–10 (2003)
2. Bach, F.R., Lanckriet, G.R.G., Jordan, M.I.: Multiple Kernel Learning, Conic Duality, and the SMO Algorithm. In: ICML'04 (2004)
3. Peña Centeno, T., Lawrence, N.D.: Optimising kernel parameters and regularisation coefficients for non-linear discriminant analysis. J. Machine Learning Research 7, 455–49 (2006)
4. Crammer, K., Keshet, J., Singer, Y.: Kernel design using boosting. In: NIPS 15, pp. 537–544. MIT Press, Cambridge (2002)
5. Dubrulle, A.A.: Retooling the method of block conjugate gradients. Electron. Trans. Numer. Anal. 12, 216–233 (2001)
6. Grandvalet, Y.: Least absolute shrinkage is equivalent to quadratic penalization. In: ICANN'98, pp. 201–206. Springer, Heidelberg (1998)
7. Hastie, T., Tibshirani, R.: Discriminant analysis by gaussian mixtures. J. Royal Statistical Society B 58, 158–176 (1996)
8. Hastie, T., Tibshirani, R., Buja, A.: Flexible discriminant analysis by optimal scoring. J. American Statistical Association 89, 1255–1270 (1994)
9. Hastie, T., Tibshirani, R.: Classification by pairwise coupling. In: NIPS 10, The MIT Press, Cambridge (1998)
10. Kumar, N., Neti, C., Andreou, A.: Application of discriminant analysis to speech recognition with auditory features. In: 15th Annual Speech Research Symposium, pp. 153–160. Johns Hopkins University, Baltimore (1995)
11. Lanckriet, G.R.G., Deng, M., Cristianini, N., Jordan, M.I., Noble, W.S.: Kernelbased data fusion and its application to protein function prediction in yeast. In: Pacific Symposium on Biocomputing, pp. 300–311 (2004)
12. Lehmann, A., Shawe-Taylor, J.: A probabilistic model for text kernels. In: ICML '06 (2006)
13. Lewis, D., Yang, Y., Rose, T., Li, F.: RCV1: A new benchmark collection for text categorization research. J. Machine Learning Research 5, 361–397 (2004)
14. McCallum, A.: Multi-label text classification with a mixture model trained by EM. In: AAAI'99 Workshop on Text Learning (1999)
15. Mika, S., Rätsch, G., Weston, J., Schölkopf, B., Müller, K.-R.: Fisher discriminant analysis with kernels. In: Proceedings of IEEE Neural Networks for Signal Processing Workshop, vol. 9, pp. 41–48 (1999)
16. Roth, V., Steinhage, V.: Nonlinear discriminant analysis using kernel functions. In: NIPS 12, pp. 568–574. MIT Press, Cambridge (2000)
17. Rousu, J., Saunders, C., Szedmak, S., Shawe-Taylor, J.: Learning hierarchical multi-category text classification models. In: ICML '05, pp. 744–751 (2005)
18. Sonnenburg, S., Rätsch, G., Schäfer, C.: A general and efficient multiple kernel learning algorithm. In: Weiss, Y., Schölkopf, B., Platt, J. (eds.) NIPS 18, pp. 1275–1282. MIT Press, Cambridge (2006)
19. Soong, F.K., Huang, E.-F.: A tree-trellis based fast search for finding the n best sentence hypotheses in continuous speech recognition. In: Proceedings of a workshop on Speech and natural language, pp. 12–19 (1990)

Intrinsic Mean for Semi-metrical Shape Retrieval Via Graph Cuts

Frank R. Schmidt[1], Eno Töppe[1], Daniel Cremers[1], and Yuri Boykov[2]

[1] Department of Computer Science
University of Bonn
Römerstr. 164, 53117 Bonn, Germany
{schmidtf,toeppe,dcremers}@cs.uni-bonn.de
[2] Computer Science Department
University of Western Ontario
London, ON, Canada
yuri@csd.uwo.ca

Abstract. We address the problem of describing the mean object for a set of planar shapes in the case that the considered dissimilarity measures are semi-metrics, i.e. in the case that the triangle inequality is generally not fulfilled. To this end, a matching of two planar shapes is computed by cutting an appropriately defined graph the edge weights of which encode the local similarity of respective contour parts on either shape. The cost of the minimum cut can be interpreted as a semi-metric on the space of planar shapes. Subsequently, we introduce the notion of a mean shape for the case of semi-metrics and show that this allows to perform a shape retrieval which mimics human notions of shape similarity.

1 Introduction

To decide whether two given objects are similar to one another and to cluster subsets of similar objects is an important challenge in Computer Vision. In the last years, this problem has been tackled for shapes by defining *dissimilarity measures* [6]. These measures proved themselves as useful in the context of shape recognition, clustering, classification and statistical modeling [5,9]. In particular, the study of metrics has been very promising to generalize statistical concepts like average objects or standard deviations [9]. But not every useful dissimilarity measure is a metric [3,2]. Indeed, most of them are semi-metrics, i.e. they violate the triangle inequality. But how can the statistical concept of a mean shape be defined, if there is no metric at hand? Since an embedding into an Euclidean space is not possible, we will approach the question of defining a template for a given collection of shapes only by studying the given semi-metric. The semi-metric that we like to study exemplarily is an energy functional that arises in the context of shape matching.

1.1 Dissimilarity Measures for Shapes

In order to abstract from location and rotation, the term *shape* refers to a complete class $\mathcal{C}$ of closed curves $c : \mathbb{S}^1 \to \mathbb{R}^2$ embedded in the plane $\mathbb{R}^2$. This

F.A. Hamprecht, C. Schnörr, and B. Jähne (Eds.): DAGM 2007, LNCS 4713, pp. 446–455, 2007.

class shall be invariant under rigid body transformations, i.e. translations and rotations. The set of all these shapes form a Riemannian manifold [8]. Any continuous transformation from one shape into another can be represented by a path in this curved space and geodesics, i.e. paths of minimal length, define a metric on these spaces [8,5]. Since only such paths are allowed that are placed *inside* the manifold, we are talking of *intrinsic paths*.

From a practical point of view, we often like to compare two different planar shapes. This task of matching two different shapes has been approached by minimizing a given functional [7]. Such a matching functional can be used as dissimilarity measure, just like the intrinsic length presented above.

1.2   Dissimilarity Measures and Statistics

Since the classical mean for a collection of objects is only defined if these objects are elements of a vector space, the generalization of a mean object has been of broad interest. In the case of manifolds, the Karcher mean [4] was introduced as minimum of an energy function and the concept of this metric-oriented mean has been applied to shape spaces [5]. Since distance functions that are robust to outliers will typically violate the triangle inequality [3], we are interested in such semi-metrical distance functions. Semi-metrics have been already considered for segmentation tasks [7,2]. But to the best of our knowledge, there are no statistical approaches for semi-metrics since there is no canonical definition of a mean object. In this paper, we will overcome this limitation by presenting a generalization of the Karcher mean for semi-metrics to which we will refer as *shape template*. These templates will be used to describe the *center of a cluster* and to perform the task of retrieving similar shapes from a given database. Because the definition of a mean *within* a manifold does not use the exterior vector space, such a template provides an *intrinsic mean*.

This paper is organized as follows. In Section 2, we propose an approximation scheme for matching an arbitrary collection of shapes. In Section 3, the result of this synchronistic shape matching will be used to construct a template for a given shape cluster. This cluster template will be used to retrieve similar shapes from a database. In Section 4, we analyze the runtime of the given methods and show some retrieving results for the well known LEMS database. In particular, we experimentally verify that this proposed intrinsic mean gives rise to superior retrieval rates. In Section 5, we will provide a conclusion of our work.

2   Shape Matching

In this section, we will present a method to solve the shape matching task for more than two given shapes. To this end, we first present the shape matching method developed in [10] for *two* different shapes by cutting a specific planar graph. Subsequently, we consider the more general problem of simultaneously matching *multiple* shapes and propose an efficient approximative solution.

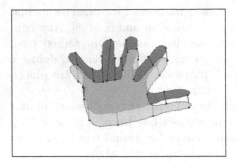 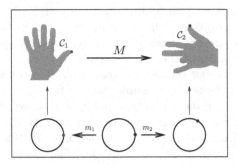

Fig. 1. Matching. *Left hand side:* Matching two shapes amounts to computing a correspondence between pairs of points on both shapes. *Right hand side:* Instead of looking for a mapping $M : \mathcal{C}_1 \to \mathcal{C}_2$, a matching $m = (m_1, m_2) : \mathbb{S}^1 \to \mathbb{S}^1 \times \mathbb{S}^1$ is defined on the parameterization domains.

2.1   Matching of Two Shapes Via Graph Cut

As a shape $\mathcal{C}$ we understand the class of closed curves $c : \mathbb{S}^1 \to \mathbb{R}^2$ that is invariant under rigid body motions. These shapes form the shape space $\mathcal{S}$. Since it is well known that the curvature $\kappa : \mathbb{S}^1 \to \mathbb{R}$ is a unique description of every shape $\mathcal{C}$, the shape space can be described in terms of these curvature functions[1]:

$$\mathcal{S} := \left\{ \kappa : \mathbb{S}^1 \to \mathbb{R} \,\middle|\, \int_{\mathbb{S}^1} \exp\left[i \int_0^t \kappa(\tau)\mathrm{d}\tau \right] \mathrm{d}t = 0 \right\} \qquad (1)$$

By the definition of $\mathcal{S}$, all rigid body motions are eliminated and we can focus on the non-rigid shape transformations. To decide whether two shapes are similar, we want to detect local transformations like stretching and contraction. Therefore, we are looking for a correspondence mapping that maps the points of one shape to the corresponding points on the second shape. Since the points of a shape define an arbitrary subset of the plane $\mathbb{R}^2$, it is much simpler to find the correspondence directly on the parameterization domain $\mathbb{S}^1$ – see also Figure 1. To ensure that a matching covers both parameterization domains exactly once, a matching consists of two orientation preserving bijective mappings $m_1, m_2 : \mathbb{S}^1 \to \mathbb{S}^1$ that simultaneously sample the points of both parameterization domains. The space of all these sampling mappings will be called $\mathrm{Diff}^+(\mathbb{S}^1)$. Given two shapes $\mathcal{C}_1$ and $\mathcal{C}_2$ with their curvature functions κ_1 resp. κ_2, we are interested in a matching $m \in \mathrm{Diff}^+(\mathbb{S}^1) \times \mathrm{Diff}^+(\mathbb{S}^1)$ that minimizes the following functional

$$E_{\kappa_1}^{\kappa_2}(m) = \int_{\mathbb{S}^1} [(\kappa_1 \circ m_1 - \kappa_2 \circ m_2)(s)]^2 \mathrm{dm}(s). \qquad (2)$$

In this functional, the *data term* $(\kappa_1 - \kappa_2)^2$ is therefore integrated along the *matching* $s \mapsto (m_1(s), m_2(s))$. Since $\mathrm{dm}(s) = \|m'(s)\| \, \mathrm{ds}$ holds, the *smoothness*

---

[1] For a detailed study of this manifold, we are referring to [5].

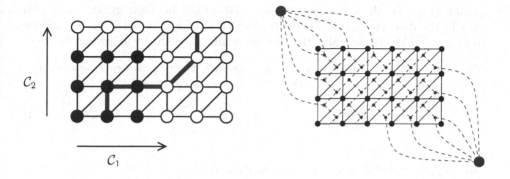

Fig. 2. Left hand side: Sampling two shapes C_1 and C_2 by N points, we receive a squared graph (filled vertices). If we copy the bottom line onto the top and the received construction to the right (blank vertices), every matching can be represented by a path from the matching vertex $(a, 0)$ to the vertex $(a + N, N)$. By identifying $(a, 0)$ with $(a + N, N)$, every matching becomes a shortest cycle. **Right hand side:** Every cycle in G describes a cut on the dual graph G^* (dashed edges). A minimal graph cut in G^* has therefore the same weight as the shortest cycle in G.

term m' is directly coupled to the data term. Using (2), a distance function on the shape space S can be defined as follows.

Definition 1 (Shape Distance). *Given two shapes $C_1, C_2 \in S$ with their curvature functions $\kappa_1 : \mathbb{S}^1 \to \mathbb{R}$ and $\kappa_2 : \mathbb{S}^1 \to \mathbb{R}$ resp., we will call*

$$\mathrm{dist}(C_1, C_2) := \min_{m \in \mathrm{Diff}^+(\mathbb{S}^1)^2} E_{\kappa_1}^{\kappa_2}(m)^{\frac{1}{2}} \qquad (3)$$

the distance of these shapes. Every matching fulfilling this minimum will be called a minimal matching of C_1 and C_2.

It is well known that the calculation of this semi-metrical distance can be done by finding the shortest path in a graph. In Figure 2, the appropriate graph $G = (V, E, w)$ is sketched. The vertices $(x_1, x_2) \in V$ represent a possible match between $c_1(x_1)$ and $c_2(x_2)$ and the data term of this vertex is $(\kappa_1(x_1) - \kappa_2(x_2))^2$. Therefore, the weight w of any edge $(x_1, x_2) \to (y_1, y_2)$ carries the value of the path integral along this edge. If we sample each shape by N points, any path from $(a, 0)$ to $(a + N, N)$ describes a matching. Hence, $\mathrm{dist}(C_1, C_2)$ can be calculated by finding an initial correspondence $(a, 0)$ and afterwards the path of minimal weighted length from $(a, 0)$ to $(a + N, N)$. Given an initial correspondence $(a, 0)$, the classical way to calculate the shortest path length is the Dynamic Time Warping (DTW) method which takes linear time in the size of the given graph. Testing all initial correspondences leads therefore to a runtime of $\mathcal{O}(N^3)$ [3,7].

On the other hand, if we identify any possible initial matching $(a, 0)$ with $(a+N, N)$, the graph becomes a cylinder and the formerly shortest path describes a shortest cycle on this cylindrical graph. Whitney proved in [12] that for any planar graph G, there is a one-to-one relationship between cycles on G and cuts in the dual graph G^*. Therefore, the value of a minimal edge cut will be $\text{dist}(\mathcal{C}_1, \mathcal{C}_2)^2$. Mathematically, this can be summarized in the following theorem.

Theorem 1. *Let $\mathcal{C}_1$ and $\mathcal{C}_2$ be two shapes with their curvature functions $\kappa_1 :$ $\mathbb{S}^1 \to \mathbb{R}$ and $\kappa_2 : \mathbb{S}^1 \to \mathbb{R}$ resp. Then, the following equation holds*

$$\text{dist}(\mathcal{C}_1, \mathcal{C}_2)^2 = \min_{\substack{X^* \subset E^* \\ X^* \ edge \ set \ of \\ a \ graph \ cut \ in \ G^*}} \sum_{e^* \in X^*} w(e) \tag{4}$$

Proof. For a detailed proof, we are referring to [10].   □

To calculate the graph cut, we use the algorithm presented in [1]. In Section 4, we will analyze the runtime of this method in comparison to the shortest path method. We will demonstrate that for similar shapes the graph cut method is favorable over the shortest path method.

2.2 Synchronistic Shape Matching

After introducing the shape matching of two shapes, the question arises how a whole collection of shapes can be set in correspondence. Since any shape carries some artifacts according to the chosen discretization, a matching between two shapes could emphasize these artifacts and hence provide a matching that does not coincide with the human notion of point correspondence. If a synchronistic matching of a whole collection of shapes is to be achieved, the noisy artifacts of one shape shall be inhibited by the other shapes. To provide a synchronistic shape matching is therefore a challenging task and the goal of this subsection.

Analogously to (2), we define a functional for the *synchronistic shape matching*. Given a collection $\mathcal{T} = \{\mathcal{C}_1, \ldots, \mathcal{C}_n\}$ of n shapes, a matching m consists of n different mappings $m_i \in \text{Diff}^+(\mathbb{S}^1)$ that minimize the pairwise curvature differences. Let $\kappa_1, \ldots, \kappa_n$ be the curvature functions of the shapes $\mathcal{C}_1, \ldots, \mathcal{C}_n$ resp. Then, we like to minimize the following functional.

$$E_\mathcal{T}(m) = \int_{\mathbb{S}^1} \sum_{i,j=1}^n [(\kappa_i \circ m_i - \kappa_j \circ m_j)(s)]^2 \mathrm{dm}(s) \tag{5}$$

To calculate any synchronistic shape matching is a computationally challenging task. Analogously to Section 2.1, we can find the matching mapping $m \in \text{Diff}^+(\mathbb{S}^1)^n$ by searching for a closed circle in a n-dimensional grid. If we use a sampling rate of 100 points for every shape, we would need ten billion grid points to match a small collection of five shapes. Since this is too expensive, we are interested in an approximation scheme.

Given a matching mapping $m = (m_1, \ldots, m_n)$, the mapping $(m_i, m_j) \in \text{Diff}^+(\mathbb{S}^1)^2$ describes a matching between the two shapes $\mathcal{C}_i, \mathcal{C}_j \in \mathcal{T}$. Since $m_{i,j} := (m_i, m_j)$ does not necessarily minimize (2), we can reformulate the functional (5) as a compromise between (2) and the property that $m_{i,j}$ and

Fig. 3. Synchronistic Shape Matching. If we compare the first two shapes, we receive a matching that cannot detect the two missing fingers. If we add a third shape (middle), the matching can be improved using (6). The last two images represent the matching according to $\gamma = 10^{-6}$ and $\gamma = 10^{-4}$. Note that the location of the sixth and eighth shape point have been changed.

$m_{j,k}$ describe $m_{i,k}$. As abbreviation, we like to introduce $\tilde{m}_{i,j} := m_{i,j}^2 \circ (m_{i,j}^1)^{-1}$ for a given pairwise matching $m_{i,j} = (m_{i,j}^1, m_{i,j}^2)$. With this notation, $m_{i,j}$ becomes the graph of $\tilde{m}_{i,j}$ and the described compromise can be formulated as the following functional.

$$E_{\mathcal{T}}\left((m_{i,j})_{i,j=1,\ldots,n}\right) = \sum_{i,j=1}^{n} E_{\kappa_i}^{\kappa_j}(m_{i,j})+ \tag{6}$$

$$\gamma \cdot \sum_{i,j,k=1}^{n} \int_{\mathbb{S}^1} \|(\tilde{m}_{i,j} - \tilde{m}_{k,j} \circ \tilde{m}_{i,k})(s)\|^2 \, \mathrm{d}m_{i,j}(s),$$

Note that (6) is a major relaxation of (5). Instead of the n matching functions $m_1, \ldots, m_n$, we are dealing now with the n^2 binary matching functions $m_{i,j} = (m_{i,j}^1, m_{i,j}^2) \in \text{Diff}^+(\mathbb{S}^1)^2$. To solve (6), we start with the matchings $m_{i,j}$ that minimize (2). Then iteratively, every matching $m_{i,j}$ is improved according to (6) using the predefined $m_{i,j}$. Since we assume that all shapes are similar, we use the proposed graph cut method to solve the binary matchings during the whole iteration process. This is done according to the result in Section 4 that for similar shapes the graph cut method outruns the DTW method. In Figure 3, we see how the synchronistic shape matching improves a given matching.

3   Shape Classification Given a Synchronistic Matching

In this section, we will present a way to describe a shape cluster using the synchronistic shape matching of Section 2.2. For this purpose, we present a generalization of the Karcher mean [4] for the space $\mathcal{S}$ in respect to the semi-metric $\text{dist}(\cdot, \cdot)$. Afterwards, we show that this template improves the retrieval result considerably.

3.1   Cluster Template

Given a set $\mathcal{T} = \{\mathcal{C}_1, \ldots, \mathcal{C}_n\}$ of training shapes, we want to tackle the problem of finding the center of this shape cluster. Thus, we are looking for a *template*

C_T that is close to all shapes in T. The next definition describes this task as a minimization problem.

Definition 2 (Template). *Given a collection $T = \{C_1, \ldots, C_n\}$ of shapes with the curvature function $\kappa_1, \ldots, \kappa_n$ resp. Moreover, let $(m_{i,j})_{i,j=1,\ldots,n}$ be a minimum of (6). Then a minimum κ_T of the functional*

$$\kappa \mapsto \sum_{i=1}^{n} \int_{\mathbb{S}^1} [(\kappa \circ m_{1,i}^1 - \kappa_i \circ m_{1,i}^2)(s)]^2 \mathrm{dm}_{1,i}(s). \tag{7}$$

is called a template *of the cluster T.*

Note that we used the synchronistic shape matching for a realignment of all shapes in the training set T. Therefore, the Euler-Lagrange equation of (7) is linear and the template is therefore easy to calculate. While the intrinsic mean constructed above will generally not correspond to a meaningful shape, we shall demonstrate that it form an excellent basis for shape retrieval.

3.2   Cluster-Based Retrieval

In the Section 3.1, we presented a method to find a template C_T for a given cluster T. Now, we want to retrieve from a database those shapes that are similar to the shapes of T. Therefore, we have to decide if an arbitrary shape fits to a given cluster T. We are doing this by calculating the distance of a given shape C to the template C_T. If this distance is small enough, we classify C as an element of T. If different clusters $T_1, \ldots, T_k$ are at hand, we choose the following algorithm:

1. Given a shape $C \in S$, calculate for every $i = 1, \ldots, k$ the distances $d_i = \mathrm{dist}(C, C_{T_i})$.
2. Find $i_0 := \arg\min_i d_i$.
3. If $d_{i_0} < \lambda_{i_0}$, classify C as a shape of cluster T_{i_0}.
4. Otherwise, state that C cannot be classified properly.

The choice of λ_i for a given cluster T_i is important for the appropriate description of the class T_i. In fact, we may choose λ_i differently for different clusters. In Section 4, we will present a representative example to show how well this classification method works.

4   Experimental Results

In this section, we will analyze the proposed methods on real shapes. For this purpose, we use the shapes that are provided by the LEMS laboratory of the Brown University [11] and apply the curvature descriptor introduced in [10]. In detail, we analyze the runtime of the graph cut algorithm in comparison to the classical method using Dynamic Time Warping (DTW). Afterwards, we demonstrate how well shapes can be retrieved with the help of the introduced cluster template.

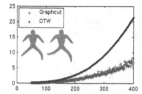 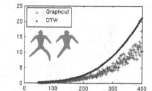 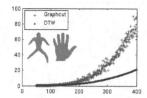

Fig. 4. Runtime comparison. The runtime of the DTW and the proposed graph cut method are plotted against the sampling rate of both shapes. In the first two cases the graph cut matching works faster than the classical DTW approach. The plots indicate that the graph cut method should be favored over DTW if one expects similar shapes. Otherwise, one should benefit of the granted constant DTW runtime.

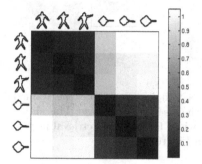 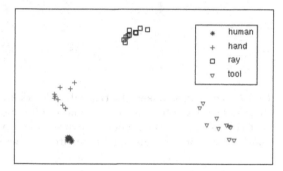

Fig. 5. Clustering. On the left hand side, the pairwise dissimilarity of six given shapes according to $\mathrm{dist}(\cdot, \cdot)$ are color-coded. On the right hand side, 40 shapes are projected into the Euclidean plane based on their pairwise distance. In general, this projection will not preserve pairwise distances since $\mathrm{dist}(\cdot, \cdot)$ is not a metric. But even this approximation indicates that the distance function incorporates the human notion of shape similarity.

4.1   Runtime Comparison

The bottleneck of the classical DTW method is the search for an initial correspondence. If a complete search over all possible initial matchings is done, the runtime is always $\mathcal{O}(N^3)$ for a fixed sampling rate of N points per shape. On the other hand, the runtime of the graph cut method depends very much on the input data. Figure 4 demonstrates the runtime of the graph cut method in respect to the DTW method. The plots indicate that the matching of two shapes is very fast with the graph cut method, if these shapes are similar to one another. One the other hand for distinctively different shapes, the classical DTW method outruns the graph cut method. Therefore, we used the DTW method to cluster the whole database. But for the template calculation of a given cluster, we always used the proposed graph cut method.

Fig. 6. Shape-based Retrieval. Using one of the training shapes (boxed) as a representative for retrieval gives an unsatisfactory retrieval performance: In order to extract all hands from the data base one needs to determine the 15 best hits.

Fig. 7. Template-based Retrieval. We define a template based on the framed shapes. The eleven best hits correspond to all hand shapes in the database. This shows that the distance to the proposed intrinsic mean provides for superior retrieval performance than using an individual template as done in Figure 6.

4.2   Proposed Retrieval Method

The presented retrieval method works in two phases – the learning phase and the retrieval phase. In the learning phase, the shapes that define a shape class were matched via the proposed synchronistic shape matching and thus define a template. During the second phase, the distance between the calculated templates and the unknown shapes from a database are calculated. According to this distance, the unknown shapes can be classified. On the left hand side of Figure 5, we see an example of how well the dissimilarity measure function $\mathrm{dist}(\cdot, \cdot)$ divides the shape database into appropriate clusters. Nonetheless, the question how the number of cluster can be estimated is still unsolved. Therefore, we applied a 4-means run for a subset of the LEMS database that is projected via multidimensional scaling on the right hand side of Figure 5. Since Figure 5 illustrates that the class *ray* and the class *human* are very easy in respect to the given database, we want to analyze the retrieval for the class *hand*. Figure 6 shows the classical retrieval according to one selected shape. We need 15 shapes to find all eleven hand shapes. Since the database consists of only eleven hand shapes, it is remarkable that the first eleven hits according to the template-based (cf. fig. 7) retrieval are in fact these shapes. Note that the learned shapes are not necessarily the best hits. Due to the semi-metric, the template can be closer to some shapes than to others.

5   Conclusion

In this paper, we introduced a generalization of the Karcher mean for semi-metrical spaces. To this end, we approximate the computationally infeasible simultaneous matching of n shapes by a consistent iteration of pairwise matchings. The latter problem can be solved by computing the minimal cut through a graph whose nodes encode the local similarity of respective contour parts on each shape. The presented experiments indicate that for the matching of similar shapes, this graph cut approach provides a speed-up factor up to 4 relatively to the classical method using Dynamic Time Warping (DTW). Just as humans have no problem in finding the correspondence on two similar shapes, the proposed method finds an initial match and the complete correspondence simultaneously and faster than the usual approach via DTW.

In a shape retrieval experiment on the LEMS database, we demonstrated that the proposed intrinsic mean for semi-metrical shape spaces provides for superior retrieval performance than individual shape instances do.

References

1. Boykov, Y., Kolmogorov, V.: An experimental comparison of min-cut/max-flow algorithms for energy minimization in vision. IEEE PAMI 26(9), 1124–1137 (2004)
2. Cremers, D., Soatto, S.: A pseudo-distance for shape priors in level set segmentation. In: Paragios, N. (ed.) IEEE 2nd Int. Workshop on Variational, Geometric and Level Set Methods, Nice, pp. 169–176 (2003)
3. Gdalyahu, Y., Weinshall, D.: Flexible syntactic matching of curves and its application to automatic hierarchical classication of silhouettes. IEEE PAMI 21(12), 1312–1328 (1999)
4. Karcher, H.: Riemann center of mass and mollifier smoothing. Comm. Pure and Applied Math. 30, 509–541 (1977)
5. Klassen, E., Srivastava, A., Mio, W., Joshi, S.H.: Analysis of planar shapes using geodesic paths on shape spaces. IEEE PAMI 26(3), 372–383 (2003)
6. Latecki, L.J., Lakämper, R.: Shape similarity measure based on correspondence of visual parts. IEEE PAMI 22(10), 1185–1190 (2000)
7. Manay, S., Cremers, D., Hong, B.-W., Yezzi, A., Soatto, S.: Integral invariants for shape matching. IEEE PAMI 28(10), 1602–1618 (2006)
8. Michor, P., Mumford, D.: Riemannian geometries on spaces of plane curves. J. of the European Math. Society (2003)
9. Pennec, X.: Intrinsic statistics on Riemannian manifolds: Basic tools for geometric measurements. Journal of Mathematical Imaging and Vision 25(1), 127–154 (2004) (A preliminary appeared as INRIA RR-5093, January 2004)
10. Schmidt, F.R., Töppe, E., Cremers, D., Boykov, Y.: Efficient shape matching via graph cuts. In: Energy Minimization Methods in Computer Vision and Pattern Recognition (to appear)
11. Sharvit, D., Chan, J., Tek, H., Kimia, B.: Symmetry-based indexing of image databases (1998)
12. Whitney, H.: Congruent graphs and the connectivity of graphs. Amer. J. Math. 54, 150–168 (1932)

Pedestrian Recognition from a Moving Catadioptric Camera

Wolfgang Schulz[1], Markus Enzweiler[2], and Tobias Ehlgen[1]

[1] DaimlerChrysler AG, Group Research & Advanced Engineering
[2] Univ. of Mannheim, Dept. of Mathematics and Computer Science, CVGPR Group
{wolfgang.s.schulz,uni-mannheim.enzweiler,
tobias.ehlgen}@daimlerchrysler.com

Abstract. This paper presents a real-time system for vision-based pedestrian recognition from a moving vehicle-mounted catadioptric camera. For efficiency, a rectification of the catadioptric image using a virtual cylindrical camera is employed. We propose a novel hybrid combination of a boosted cascade of wavelet-based classifiers with a subsequent texture-based neural network involving adaptive local features as final cascade stage. Within this framework, both fast object detection and powerful object classification are combined to increase the robustness of the recognition system. Further, we compare the hybrid cascade framework to a state-of-the-art multi-cue pedestrian recognition system utilizing shape and texture cues. Image distortions of the objects of interest due to the virtual cylindrical camera transformation are both explicitly and implicitly addressed by shape transformations and machine learning techniques. In extensive experiments, both systems under consideration are evaluated on a real-world urban traffic dataset. Results show the contributions of the various components in isolation and document superior performance of the proposed hybrid cascade system.

1 Introduction

The real-time detection of pedestrians from a moving camera is a challenging and important problem. Worldwide, more than 476,000 pedestrians are involved in traffic accidents each year where approximately 8% are fatal accidents [20]. In urban traffic environments, difficulties arise from highly cluttered environments and a limited field of view of conventional vison-based systems. Catadioptric camera systems [13] providing a hemispherical field of view are able to monitor a much larger area surrounding the vehicle [6], particularly with regard to blind spots, where pedestrians are at increased risk. Motivated by this situation, we address the recognition of pedestrians from a moving vehicle-mounted catadioptric camera in an urban environment.

2 Previous Work

A large body of research has been done in the field of vision-based pedestrian recognition using conventional cameras [10]. Most techniques determine region

F.A. Hamprecht, C. Schnörr, and B. Jähne (Eds.): DAGM 2007, LNCS 4713, pp. 456–465, 2007.

of interests (ROIs) in a pre-processing step based on object motion [7], stereo [12] or a sliding window approach [5,15,17]. Further processing of ROIs incorporates cues such as shape and texture. Explicit shape-based recognition has been proposed employing both discrete [12] and continuous [4] representations. Texture-based approaches often employ classification techniques involving local texture-based features [16], where both adaptive [23] and non-adaptive [5,14,17] features are available. Recently, a fast variant of the sliding window approach has been proposed [21], consisting of a cascade of several wavelet-based detectors, where fast detectors in the early cascade stages are combined with more complex (but slow) detectors in the final cascade layers. In each cascade stage, features are selected by AdaBoost [8], controlled by user-supplied performance criteria. Up to now, there has been no work done on pedestrian recognition using catadioptric cameras, which requires appropriate rectification of the catadioptric image to gain efficiency. Most systems only incorporate low-level obstacle detection based on motion [9] or disparity [2] bypassing an actual classification step, which is necessary to distinct pedestrians from arbitrary obstacles.

Optical systems can be separated into two kinds, dioptric and catadioptric ones [13]. The former includes vision systems using lenses to enlarge the field of view. The largest field of view possible for this kind of cameras is approximately 180°. By contrast, catadioptric cameras are systems that combine mirrors and lenses to achieve a larger field of view. Catadioptric systems in turn can be separated into single viewpoint systems and non-single viewpoint systems. Single viewpoint catadioptric systems measure only the intensity of light passing through a single point called effective viewpoint. In contrast to non-single viewpoint systems, the image can be transformed to new views because every light ray maps a picture element to a distinct direction.

In this work, we consider the detection and classification of pedestrians from a moving catadioptric camera in an urban environment. We employ a rectification of the catadioptric image using a virtual camera with a cylindrical image plane. This simplifies the appearance of pedestrians and allows to make use of additional constraints, e.g. the ground-plane constraint, for added efficiency. We propose an extension to the boosted wavelet-based cascade framework [21] by using a texture-based neural network involving adaptive local features as final cascade stage. This hybrid cascade architecture combines fast object detection and powerful object classification in a unified framework to increase the robustness of the recognition system. In extensive experiments involving a dataset captured in urban traffic, we compare the novel hybrid cascade framework to a state-of-the-art multi-cue pedestrian recognition system based on [12], where shape-based detection is combined with texture-based classification.

3   Reference Pedestrian Recognition Systems

3.1   Boosted Cascade of Haar-Like Features

Many pedestrian recognition systems employ a combination of a multi-scale sliding window approach and powerful classification techniques, i.e. [5,17]. The cascade framework [21,22] provides an efficient extension to such systems by introducing a cascade of increasingly complex detectors based on simple rectangular features (similar to Haar-wavelets) that can be evaluated very fast. The early cascade layers are designed to quickly determine candidate regions in the image which are then processed by more complex (but slower) detectors in the later cascade stages. In each cascade layer, AdaBoost [8] is used to construct a classifier based on a weighted linear combination of optimal features. Additionally, training samples are re-weighted to focus the training process on misclassified examples. Each cascade layer is trained on a new dataset consisting of the initial pedestrian training samples and a new set of non-pedestrian samples which is generated by collecting false positives of the cascade up to the previous layer on a set of images which do not contain any pedestrians. Subsequent layers are added to the cascade until user-specified performance criteria are met.

3.2   Shape-Texture-Based Pedestrian Recognition

Pedestrian recognition systems combining multiple orthogonal cues, i.e. depth, motion, shape, texture [10,12], have been shown to reach state-of-the-art performance by making maximum use of the available image information. In case of monocular images, two prominent pedestrian attributes are shape and texture. In this work, we consider a monocular version of the *PROTECTOR* system [12] as performance reference by employing the shape-based pedestrian detection module in combination with the texture-based pedestrian classification module.

Shape-based detection [12] is achieved by efficient matching of an exemplar-based shape hierarchy to the image data at hand. The shape hierarchy is constructed off-line in an automatic fashion from a set of pedestrian shape templates covering different scales and poses. On-line matching involves traversing the shape hierarchy with the Chamfer distance [3] between a shape template and an image sub-window as a smooth and robust similarity measure. Image locations, where the similarity between shape and image is above a user-specified threshold, are considered detections.

Detections of the shape matching step are subject to verification by a texture-based pattern classifier. Here, we employ a multi layer feed-forward neural network operating on local adaptive receptive field features (referred to as NNLRF in the remainder) [23], which has shown to strike a good balance between classification performance and computational efficiency [16]. Further, [16] has shown, that adaptive features are key to the performance of the NNLRF classifier which are particularly superior to non-adaptive features, i.e. Haar-like wavelets. The training set for the NNLRF classifier consists of a set of pedestrian samples and non-pedestrian samples which were obtained by collecting false positives of the shape detection module with a relaxed threshold setting.

4   Catadioptric Image Transformation

In this section, we will describe the transformations which are necessary to use the catadioptric image to perform efficient pedestrian detection. Remaining

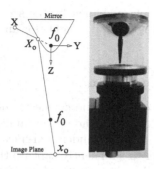
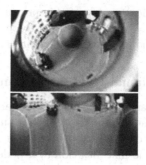

Fig. 1. Left: Diagram and physical catadioptric camera system. Upper right: catadioptric image captured from the camera, lower right: transformed image using a virtual cylindrical camera.

distortions of the pedestrian shape and texture, which are due to the specific camera setup, are handled both explicitly and implicitly, as follows. In case of the shape templates of the shape-texture-based detector (see Section 3.2), we propose to explicitly transform the existing set of templates by generating "virtual" shapes based on known camera geometry. This is motivated by the fact that exact shape contours are usually manually labeled in a laborious and costly process. Further, we want to reuse existing shape templates for comparison purposes instead of obtaining new shape templates. In contrast, distortions in the pedestrian texture are implicitly learned by the pattern classifiers using manually labeled bounding boxes which are much easier to obtain from the rectified images.

4.1 Catadioptric Camera Model

The catadioptric camera used in our system consists of a hyperbolic mirror and a perspective camera. This ensures that all light rays pass through a single point which is one of the two foci of the hyperboloid (f_0 in Fig. 1). The center of projection of the pinhole camera is placed in such a way that it coincides with the second focus f_1.

A two-sheet hyperboloid is given by $\frac{(Z-c)^2}{a^2} - \frac{X^2+Y^2}{b^2} = 1$ where $a > 0$ is the semimajor axis, $b > 0$ the semiminor axis of the hyperboloid and $c = \sqrt{a^2 + b^2}$.

Given an arbitrary point $\mathbf{X} = (X, Y, Z)^T$, the corresponding point $\mathbf{X}_0$ on the hyperbolic mirror is given by the intersection of a line $g = \mathbf{f}_0 + \lambda(\mathbf{X} - \mathbf{f}_0)$ (see Fig. 1), with

$$\lambda_{1,2} = \frac{b^2}{\pm a\|\mathbf{X}\| + cZ} \, , \|\mathbf{X}\| = \sqrt{X^2 + Y^2 + Z^2}. \tag{1}$$

Here, the intersection with the mirror is given by λ_1 (see [19]), thus $\mathbf{X}_0 = \lambda_1\mathbf{X}$, if the origin of the coordinate system is placed in $\mathbf{f}_0$. The point $\mathbf{X}_0$ on the hyperbolic mirror is perspectively projected to $\mathbf{x}_0$, which is the image of $\mathbf{X}_0$.

The optical center of this perspective projection is defined by the second focal point $\mathbf{f}_1 = (0, 0, 2c)^T$ of the hyperboloid. See Fig. 1 (upper right) for an example of catadioptric image acquisition.

4.2   Virtual Cylindrical Camera Transformation

In contrast to conventional planar perspective cameras where pedestrians, standing on the ground, appear in an upright position, the catadioptric camera model maps pedestrian appearance to multiple orientations under non-linear distortions. The instantiation of a pedestrian model to sufficiently capture the whole appearance space would either be very complex or require a large number of training patterns. Further, constraints to restrict the search space, e.g. the ground-plane constraint, where pedestrians are assumed to stand in an upright position on the ground, are complex to incorporate.

Hence, we opted for a transformation of the catadioptric image to obtain a perspective image using a virtual camera model with a cylinder as image plane. The cylindrical camera preserves the aspect ratio of objects with a small horizontal extent and offers a wide field of view. Pedestrians on the ground-plane appear in an upright position which significantly constrains the appearance space and facilitates compact pedestrian models. Further, points at equal distances from the camera map to lines in the cylindrical representation, allowing for a direct application of the ground-plane constraint.

A cylinder is defined in world coordinates $X^2 + Y^2 = 1$, with cylinder height Z, such that the axis of symmetry of the cylinder is orthogonal to the ground-plane. The cylindric surface is subsampled using a discrete grid. Each point on the surface grid, $\mathbf{X}_g = (X_g, Y_g, Z_g)^T$ (represented as $\mathbf{X}_c = (\theta_c, \phi_c, 1)^T$ in cylinder coordinates, with elevation θ_c, azimuth ϕ_c and unit radius), is projected to the catadioptric image plane, yielding $\mathbf{x}_g$, using the transformation described in Section 4.1. The pixel intensity is sampled from the catadioptric image at location $\mathbf{x}_g$ and assigned to $\mathbf{X}_g$. Finally, the cylindric surface is unfolded to a two-dimensional image, with elevation θ corresponding to the image y-axis and azimuth ϕ comprising the image x-axis (see Fig. 1).

Remaining distortions in the objects of interest depend on the properties and the position of the physical camera. For instance, in case of an elevated viewpoint the common assumption that pedestrians have their torso and all extremities in the same distance from the camera (i.e. they are "flat"), is no longer valid. Thus, non-linear distortions are introduced which have to be handled by the pedestrian model underlying the detector. See Fig. 2 (left). The straightforward way to handle these distortions is to use a larger training set which includes distorted examples. While bounding box labels to train texture-based pattern classifiers are relatively easy to obtain, the generation of discrete shape templates, which are used in shape-based approaches, requires much more manual effort.

Hence, we propose a technique to generalize the shape-texture-based detector (see Section 3.2) to arbitrary camera setups, by transforming existing valuable shape templates, guided by camera calibration. Given a set of shape templates, that were obtained using a camera setup C_0, each shape is projected to world

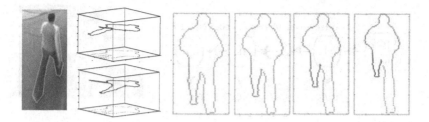

Fig. 2. Left to right: Pedestrian seen from an elevated viewpoint. 3-D shape transformation. A modified shape template, back-projected by the virtual cylindrical camera at distances of 10m, 5m, 2m and 1m from the camera.

coordinates using prior knowledge about the objects of interest, i.e. the ground-plane constraint. In world coordinates, shape templates are modified to simulate object properties such as human gait patterns. At this point, appropriate transformations are applied explicitly to (parts of the) shape contour points while incorporating heuristics about physical properties and constraints. For instance, the legs of pedestrians can be transformed to simulate a full human stride. Orthogonally to an explicit transformation of shape contour points, model-based approaches to create virtual shapes can be incorporated [11]. Finally, the modified shapes are projected back using a second camera setup C_1, yielding the transformed set of shape templates.

Fig. 2 depicts an example of the transformation of shape templates which were acquired using a conventional planar pinhole camera at a height of 1.25m, to be used with our cylindrical camera setup with a camera height of 2.1m. Here, the legs of the pedestrian shape have been modified in z-dimension simulating a human stride and transformed to the cylindrical view to explicitly model non-linear distortions occurring from the elevated view point. Other sources of distortions can be handled by using the same technique.

5   Hybrid Cascade Framework

While the boosted cascade framework using local non-adaptive wavelet-based features (see Section 3.1) has been shown to yield good performance on real-time object detection problems, c.f. [21], it suffers from two significant drawbacks. Firstly, while the local rectangular image features can be computed very fast, their representational capabilities are limited. In an extensive experimental study [16], where several combinations of state-of-the-art features and classifiers have been investigated, it was shown that local features which are able to adapt to the underlying image data outperform non-adaptive local features. Secondly, the feature selection process involving AdaBoost [8] in each cascade layer is a greedy technique, where features and their weights are iteratively determined and linearly combined. Thus, neither the selected features nor the corresponding weights can be regarded as the global optimum for the whole cascade. While

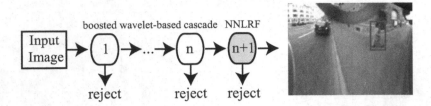

Fig. 3. Hybrid cascade framework overview. A NNLRF classifier is appended to a boosted wavelet-based cascade to combine fast object detection and powerful classification.

extensions to the AdaBoost procedure addressing these drawbacks have been proposed [18], we opt for a hybrid combination of the boosted cascade with a powerful neural network classifier using local receptive fields (NNLRF, see Section 3.2).

In the hybrid cascade framework, as shown in Fig. 3, the NNLRF classifier is appended to the original n-layer wavelet-based cascade as additional layer $n + 1$. Similar to the training process of the cascade framework (see Section 3.1), the NNLRF classifier is trained on the initial pedestrian dataset and a new set of non-pedestrian samples, generated by scanning the boosted cascade over a set of non-pedestrian images and collecting false-positives. Hence, the limitation of the non-adaptive wavelet-based features is eliminated by the richer set of adaptive local receptive field features of the NNLRF. Online detection involves matching the whole $n + 1$-layer cascade in a sliding window fashion to the image data at hand. Here, the early n cascade layers provide fast identification of candidate regions which are subject to classification by the complex (and slow) NNLRF classifier in the final cascade stage. Thus, the proposed hybrid cascade framework unifies fast object detection and powerful object classification in a single framework to increase the robustness of the whole recognition system.

6 Experimental Evaluation

In this section, we evaluate the performance of the proposed hybrid cascade framework and compare it to a shape-texture-based detector (see Section 3.2) on a real-world urban traffic dataset under daytime conditions. Our training set consists of approx. 35 different persons occurring in 1,398 rectified images (see Section 4.2). From these images 2,134 labeled pedestrian examples are available. Other than assuming pedestrians standing in an upright position, we pose no constraints on pose and appearance. Negative training samples are acquired from the same images by collecting false positives of the corresponding detectors for each system under consideration. Here, resulting negative samples contain a bias towards more "difficult" patterns. All training examples were commonly scaled to 9×18 (cascade) and 18×36 (NNLRF), including a border of a few pixels in order not to lose contour information. See Fig. 4. Additionally, an independent

Fig. 4. Positive (left) and negative (right) examples from the dataset

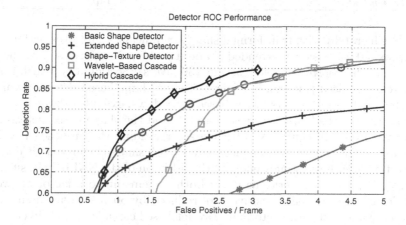

Fig. 5. ROC performance comparison of pedestrian recognition systems under consideration, along with the performance of individual system components

hierarchy of 2,959 pedestrian shapes is available for the shape-texture-based detector. This hierarchy has been adapted to our custom camera setup to include 5,918 shapes by generating virtual shapes, as denoted in Section 4.1. The cascade makes use of a set of pre-defined rectangular features of size up to 3×3 pixels, whereas the NNLRF classifier employs 5×5 pixel local adaptive receptive fields.

All systems are tested on an independent image sequence comprising 689 images and 992 pedestrian labels (created from approx. 15 different real-world persons). No real-world pedestrian appears in both training and test set. Performance evaluation is subject to the following criteria: The detectors are applied to the test set images (540×400), where rectification allows to use the ground-plane constraint to restrict the search space: pedestrians are assumed to stand in upright position on the ground. The system output is compared to manually labeled ground-truth by comparing the 2D locations and size. Any system entity E_s is compared to any ground-truth sample E_g using bounding box coverage, where a correct detection is given by $cov(E_s, E_g) > 0.2$. ROC curves are created by varying the system output thresholds: the threshold of the successive layers for the cascade architecture, NNLRF threshold for both the hybrid cascade and the shape-texture-based detector and a threshold on the Chamfer distance measure in case of the shape-based detector running in isolation. See Fig. 5.

In a first experiment, the effect of extending the shape hierarchy for the shape-based detector with transformed shapes (see Section 4.1) is evaluated without any subsequent texture classification. From Fig. 5 one observes that extending

Table 1. Frame-level processing time comparison

Pedestrian Recognition System	Processing Time (Frames / Second)
Basic / Extended Shape Detector	2.8 fps
Shape-Texture Detector	2.5 fps
Wavelet-Based Cascade	5.1 fps
Hybrid Cascade	4.9 fps

the shape hierarchy with transformed shapes significantly improves performance by approx. 50 % (basic vs. extended shape detector). Not surprisingly, the performance of the boosted wavelet-cascade (30 layers) (Section 3.1), which utilizes richer texture-based features, is superior to the shape-based detector which is restricted to the shape cue (wavelet-based cascade vs. extended shape detector).

Further, both the boosted wavelet-cascade and the shape-based detector are augmented by a subsequent NNLRF classifier yielding the proposed novel hybrid cascade framework (see Section 5) and the shape-texture-based detector (see Section 3.2). Interestingly enough, the addition of the NNLRF classifier significantly improves the performance of both systems up to a factor of two: at equal detection rates, false positives are reduced by 50 % (extended shape detector vs. shape-texture detector and wavelet-based cascade vs. hybrid cascade). Here, the hybrid cascade framework outperforms all other approaches under consideration, in particular the state-of-the-art shape-texture-based pedestrian recognition system (see Section 3.2).

Frame-level processing time has been evaluated using implementations in C/C++ on a 3.2 GHz Pentium IV processor, see Table 1. Compared to a regular wavelet-based cascade system, the proposed hybrid cascade architecture shows a significant increase in detection performance, paid for only with a minor increase in processing time (5.1 fps vs. 4.9 fps). The cascade architecture provides efficient and fast rejection of non-pedestrian areas in the image. In [15], it is shown that support vector machines (SVM) yield even better classification performance compared to the NNLRF, however at a significantly lower processing speed (up to 20 times slower). We therefore regard the NNLRF as state-of-the-art compromise between representational capability and processing speed.

7   Conclusion

We have introduced a framework for real-time pedestrian recognition using a catadioptric camera. A virtual camera transformation has been presented which allows to combine a wide field of view with efficient detection using the ground plane constraint. The wavelet-based cascade framework has been extended to a hybrid formulation unifying fast detection and powerful classification by adding an NNLRF classifier as final cascade stage. The proposed hybrid cascade system achieves superior performance in comparison to a state-of-the-art shape-texture-based detector [12] at real-time processing speeds. Future work could involve additional ROI generation, e.g. using stereo or motion cues as well as the incorporation of other classifiers than the NNLRF, e.g. support vector machines.

References

1. Baker, S., Nayar, S.: Single viewpoint catadioptric cameras. In: Benosman, R., Kang, S.B. (eds.) Panoramic Vision, ch. 4, pp. 39–71 (2001)
2. Bertozzi, M., et al.: Stereo vision-based start-inhibit for heavy goods vehicles. In: IEEE Int. Vehicles Symp., pp. 350–355 (2006)
3. Borgefors, G.: Distance transformations in digital images. Computer Vision, Graphics, and Image Processing 34(3), 344–371 (1986)
4. Cootes, T.F., Edwards, G.J., Taylor, C.J.: Active appearance models. IEEE PAMI 23(6), 681–685 (2001)
5. Dalal, N., Triggs, B.: Histograms of oriented gradients for human detection. In: Proc. CVPR (2005)
6. Ehlgen, T., Pajdla, T.: Monitoring surrounding areas of truck-trailer combinations. In: Proc. of the Int. Conf. on Comp. Vis. Sys. (2007)
7. Elzein, H., Lakshmanan, S., Watta, P.: A motion and shape-based pedestrian detection algorithm. In: IEEE Int. Vehicles Symp., pp. 500–504. IEEE Computer Society Press, Los Alamitos (2003)
8. Freund, Y., Schapire, R.E.: A decision-theoretic generalization of on-line learning and an application to boosting. In: Proc. of the European Conf. on Comp. Learn. Theory, pp. 23–37 (1995)
9. Gandhi, T., Trivedi, M.M.: Motion-based vehicle surround analysis using an omnidirectional camera. In: IEEE Int. Vehicles Symp., pp. 560–565 (2004)
10. Gavrila, D.M.: Sensor-based pedestrian protection. IEEE Int. Sys. 16(6), 77–81 (2001)
11. Gavrila, D.M., Giebel, J.: Virtual sample generation for template-based shape matching. In: Proc. CVPR, pp. 676–681 (2001)
12. Gavrila, D.M., Munder, S.: Multi-cue pedestrian detection and tracking from a moving vehicle. IJCV 73(1), 41–59 (2007)
13. Hecht, E.: Optik, 4th edn. (2002)
14. Leibe, B., Seemann, E., Schiele, B.: Pedestrian detection in crowded scenes. In: Proc. CVPR, vol. 1, pp. 878–885 (2005)
15. Mohan, A., Papageorgiou, C., Poggio, T.: Example-based object detection in images by components. IEEE PAMI 23(4), 349–361 (2001)
16. Munder, S., Gavrila, D.M.: An experimental study on pedestrian classification. IEEE PAMI 28(11), 1863–1868 (2006)
17. Papageorgiou, C., Poggio, T.: A trainable system for object detection. IJCV 38, 15–33 (2000)
18. Sochman, J., Matas, J.: Adaboost with totally corrective updates for fast face detection. In: IEEE Int. Conf. on Autom. Face and Gesture Rec., pp. 445–450 (2004)
19. Svoboda, T., Pajdla, T., Hlavac, V.: Central panoramic cameras: Geometry and design. Technical report, Technical University of Prague (December 1997)
20. United Nations Economic Commission for Europe (UNECE). Road traffic accidents (1997), http://www.unece.org/trans/roadsafe/rs3ras.html
21. Viola, P., Jones, M., Snow, D.: Detecting pedestrians using patterns of motion and appearance. IJCV 63(2), 153–161 (2005)
22. Wender, S., Löhlein, O., Gross, H.M.: Multiple classifier cascade for vehicle occupant monitoring using an omnidirectional camera. Technical report, Fortschritt-Berichte VDI (2004)
23. Wöhler, C., Anlauf, J.: An adaptable time-delay neural-network algorithm for image sequence analysis. IEEE Transactions on Neural Networks 10(6), 1531–1536 (1999)

Efficient Learning of Neural Networks with Evolutionary Algorithms

Nils T. Siebel, Jochen Krause, and Gerald Sommer

Cognitive Systems Group, Institute of Computer Science
Christian-Albrechts-University of Kiel
Olshausenstr. 40, 24098 Kiel, Germany
nils@siebel-research.de, {jk,gs}@ks.informatik.uni-kiel.de

Abstract. In this article we present EANT, a method that creates neural networks (NNs) by evolutionary reinforcement learning. The structure of NNs is developed using mutation operators, starting from a minimal structure. Their parameters are optimised using CMA-ES. EANT can create NNs that are very specialised; they achieve a very good performance while being relatively small. This can be seen in experiments where our method competes with a different one, called NEAT, to create networks that control a robot in a visual servoing scenario.

1 Introduction

As universal function approximators, artificial neural networks (NNs) are capable of modelling complex mappings between the inputs and outputs of a system up to an arbitrary precision [1]. However, with an increase in complexity of a given task the required complexity of the NN also increases. Such a complex NN is difficult to develop due to the high dimensionality of the space in which its parameters live. This so-called "curse of dimensionality" has always been a significant obstacle in machine learning problems [2].

NNs are characterised by their *structure (topology)* and their *parameters* (which includes the weights of connections) [3]. A number of learning methods exist for generating them. Most of these methods, like the popular "backpropagation" algorithm [3, chap. 7], are methods to adjust the parameters of the network to a given problem, but not its structure. When using such methods the structure of the network has to be fit to the problem beforehand and "by hand", i.e. by the designer of the software. Once the structure is fixed, its parameters are learned. These traditional approaches exhibit the following two problems:

1. The common approach to pre-design the network structure can be difficult or even infeasible for complicated tasks. It may also result in overly complex networks if the designer cannot find a small structure that solves the task.
2. Determining the network parameters by local optimisation algorithms like gradient descent-type methods is impracticable for large problems. It is known from mathematical optimisation theory that these algorithms tend to get stuck in local minima. They only work well for very simple (e.g., convex) problems or if an approximate solution is known beforehand.

F.A. Hamprecht, C. Schnörr, and B. Jähne (Eds.): DAGM 2007, LNCS 4713, pp. 466–475, 2007.

We have previously developed a method, called EANT, "Evolutionary Acquisition of Neural Topologies", that automatically learns both the structure and the parameters of a NN to find a solution to a given problem [4,5]. Both learning parts use evolutionary algorithms (EAs) [6], global optimisation methods that are less prone to get stuck in local minima. With these algorithms the NN is learned from scratch by reinforcement learning [7].

In this article we present recent improvements to EANT that further accelerate the generation of networks that perform well. In order to validate our claim we also present for the first time an experimental comparison of EANT and NEAT, a similar method.

The remainder of this article is organised as follows. Section 2 contains an overview over related methods for evolutionary NN learning and describes our approach to the solution. In Section 3 we formulate the visual servoing problem that is used for testing the NN learning methods. Section 4 contains results from experiments with EANT and NEAT; Section 5 concludes the article.

2 Methods for Evolutionary Learning of Neural Networks

In this section we review existing methods on evolutionary neural network (NN) learning and present our own algorithm, EANT. The paradigm is to learn *both the structure (topology) and the parameters of NNs* with evolutionary algorithms (EAs) without being given any information about the nature of the problem. The development of networks is realised through reinforcement learning [7]. This means that candidate solutions which have been generated by the EA are evaluated by testing them on the target application. A scalar value of their "fitness" is fed back to the algorithm to help it judge and determine what to do with this candidate. These learning algorithm do not depend on the availability of input-output pairs of the NN as supervised learning methods do.

2.1 Overview over Existing Methods

Until recently, only small NNs have been evolved by evolutionary means [8]. According to Yao, a main reason is the difficulty of evaluating the exact fitness of a newly found structure: In order to fully evaluate a *structure* one needs to find the optimal (or, some near-optimal) *parameters* for it. However, the search for good parameters for a given structure has a high computational complexity unless the problem is very simple *(ibid.)*.

In order to avoid this problem most recent approaches evolve the structure and parameters of the NNs simultaneously. Examples include EPNet [9], GNARL [10] and NEAT [11]. EPNet uses a modified backpropagation algorithm for parameter optimisation (i.e. a local search method). The mutation operators for searching the space of neural structures are addition and deletion of neural nodes and connections (no crossover is used). A tendency to remove connections/nodes rather than to add new ones is realised in the algorithm. This is done to counteract the "bloat" phenomenon (i.e. ever growing networks with only little fitness improvement; also called "survival of the fattest" [6]). GNARL is similar in that is also uses no crossover during structural mutation. However, it uses an EA for parameter adjustments. Both parametrical and structural mutation use a "temperature" measure to determine whether large or small random modifications should be applied—a concept known from simulated annealing [12]. In order to calculate the current temperature, some knowledge about the "ideal solution" to the problem, e.g. the maximum fitness, is needed.

The author groups of both EPNet and GNARL are of the opinion that using crossover is not useful during the evolutionary development of neural networks [9,10]. The research work underlying NEAT, on the other hand, seems to suggest otherwise. The authors have designed and used a crossover operator that allows to produce valid offspring from two given NNs by first aligning similar or equal subnetworks and then exchanging differing parts. Like GNARL, NEAT uses EAs for both parametrical and structural mutation. However, the probabilities and standard deviations used for random mutation are constant over time. NEAT also incorporates the concept of speciation, i.e. separated sub-populations that aim at cultivating and preserving diversity in the population [6, chap. 9].

2.2 Developing Neural Networks with EANT

EANT, "Evolutionary Acquisition of Neural Topologies", is an evolutionary reinforcement learning system that realises NN learning with EAs both for the structural and the parametrical part [4]. EANT features a unique and compact genetic encoding that uses a linear genome to represent a NN together with its parameters. The linear genome encodes the topology of the NN implicitly by the order of its elements (genes). The following gene types exist: neurons, inputs to the network, bias neurons, forward connections and recurrent connections. Linear genomes can be evaluated, without decoding, similar to the way mathematical expressions in postfix notation are evaluated. For example, a neuron gene is followed by its input genes. In order to evaluate it, one can traverse the linear genome from back to front, pushing inputs onto a stack. When encountering a neuron gene one pops as many genes from the stack as there are inputs to the neuron, using their values as input values. The resulting evaluated neuron is again pushed onto the stack, enabling this subnetwork to be used as an input to other neurons. Connection genes make it possible for neuron outputs to be used as input to more than one neuron. Together with the bias neurons that are implemented as having a constant value of 1.0, the linear genome can encode any NN in a very compact format. The length of the linear genome is equal to the number of synaptic network weights.

The steps of our algorithm, shown in Figure 1, are explained in detail below.

Initialisation: EANT usually starts with minimal initial structures. A minimal network has no hidden layers or recurrent connections, only 1 neuron per output, connected to some or all inputs. EANT gradually develops these simple initial structures further using the structural and parametrical EAs discussed below. On a larger scale new neural structures are added to a current generation of

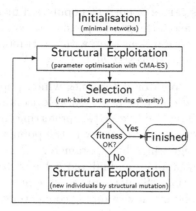

Fig. 1. The EANT algorithm. Please note that CMA-ES has its own optimisation loop which creates in EANT a nested loop.

networks. We call this "structural exploration". On a smaller scale the current structures are optimised by changing their parameters: "structural exploitation".

Structural Exploitation: At this stage the structures in the current EANT population are exploited by optimising their parameters. Parametrical mutation in a previous version of EANT was implemented using evolution strategies (ES) [6]. This means that the strategy parameters in the EA, e.g. the standard deviation for random mutation, were themselves adapted by an EA. This has the advantage that the system needs even less knowledge of the problem than with a different EA, like evolutionary programming. However, using ES for parametrical mutation has the following disadvantages:

1. After a strategy parameter has been adapted it takes many applications of the mutation operator on the corresponding network parameter until the new value of the strategy parameter can be judged. Even then it is unclear when looking at the change in fitness value whether the network performs better/worse because of this adapted strategy parameter or because of other changes that happened during those many generations.
2. The number of strategy parameters adds to the number of total parameters in the system, increasing even further the dimensionality of the space in which ideal parameters are searched.

Disadvantage 1 can be ignored in settings where a very large population size is used. However, it does matter in the context of NN development where large population sizes are prohibitive unless the problem is very simple.

For these reasons newer versions of EANT use CMA-ES ("Covariance Matrix Adaptation Evolution Strategy") [13] in their parameter optimisation. CMA-ES is a variant of ES that avoids random adaptation of the strategy parameters. Instead, the search area that is spanned by the mutation strategy parameters, expressed here by a covariance matrix, is adapted at each step depending on the parameter and fitness values of current population members. CMA-ES uses sophisticated methods to avoid things like premature convergence and is known for fast convergence to good solutions even with multi-modal and non-separable functions in high-dimensional spaces *(ibid.)*.

Selection: The selection operator determines which population members are carried on from one generation to the next. Our selection in the outer, structural exploration loop is rank-based and "greedy", preferring individuals that have a larger fitness. In order to maintain diversity in the population, it also compares individuals by structure, ignoring their parameters. The operator makes sure that not more than 1 copy of an individual and not more than 2 similar individuals are kept in the population. "Similar" in this case means that a structure was derived from an another one by only changing connections, not adding neurons. Again, no network parameters are considered here.

Structural Exploration: In this step new structures are generated and added to the population. This is achieved by applying the following structural mutation operators to the existing structures: Adding a random subnetwork, adding or removing a random connection and adding a random bias. Removal of subnetworks (i.e. neurons together with all their connections) is not done as we found out that this almost never helps in the evolutionary process. The same is valid for a crossover operator, modelled after the one used in NEAT, which is currently not used. New hidden neurons are connected to approx. 50 % of inputs; the exact percentage and selection of inputs are random to enable stochastic search for new structures.

Differences to Other Methods: EANT is closely related to the methods described in the related work section above. One main difference is the clear separation of structural exploration and structural exploitation. By this we try to make sure a new structural element is tested ("exploited") as much as possible before a decision is made to discard it or keep it, or before other structural modifications are applied. Another main difference is the use of CMA-ES in the parameter optimisation. This should yield more optimal parameters more quickly, which is necessary when large networks are to be created. Further differences of EANT to other recent methods, e.g. NEAT, are a small number of user-defined algorithm parameters (the method should be as general as possible) and the explicit way of preserving diversity in the population (unlike speciation).

3   The Visual Servoing Task

In order to study the behaviour of EANT and other algorithms on large problems we simulate the visual servoing setup shown in Figure 2. The robot is equipped with a camera at the end-effector and has to be steered towards an object of unknown pose. This is achieved in the visual feedback control loop depicted in Figure 2. In our system a NN shall be used as the controller, determining where to move the robot on the basis of the object's visual appearance.

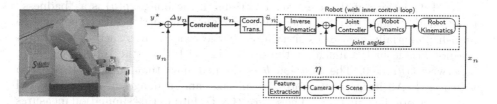

Fig. 2. Robot arm with object and the corresponding visual feedback control loop

The object has 4 identifiable markings, see Figure 2. Its appearance in the image is described by the *image feature vector* $y_n \in \mathbb{R}^8$ that contains the 4 pairs of image coordinates of these markings. The desired pose relative to the object is defined by the object's appearance in that pose by measuring the corresponding *desired image features* $y^\star \in \mathbb{R}^8$ ("teaching by showing"). Object and robot are then moved to a start pose. The object's position is unknown to the controller. The input to the controller is the image error $\Delta y_n := y^\star - y_n$ and additionally the 2 distances in the image of the diagonally opposing markings, resulting in a 10-dimensional input vector. The output of the controller is a relative movement of the robot in the camera coordinate system: $(\Delta x, \Delta y, \Delta z) \in \mathbb{R}^3$.

From a mathematical point of view, visual servoing is the iterative minimisation of an error functional that describes differences of objects' visual appearances, by moving in the search space of robot poses. The traditional solution is equivalent to an iterative Gauss-Newton method to minimise the image error, with a linear model ("Image Jacobian") of the objective function [14,15].

In our case a NN is developed as a controller by reinforcement learning. For the assessment of the fitness (performance) of a network N it is tested by evaluating it in the simulated visual servoing setup. For this purpose 1023 different robot start poses and 29 teach poses (desired poses) have been generated. Each start pose is paired with a teach pose to form a task. These tasks contain all ranges and directions of movements. For each task, N is given the visual input data corresponding to the start and teach poses, and its output is executed by a simulated robot. In order to facilitate easy comparison between different neural networks only one movement is calculated and executed for each of these tasks. The *fitness function* $F(N)$ measures the negative RMS (root mean square) of the remaining image errors after this robot movement, over all tasks. This means that our fitness function $F(N)$ always takes on negative values with $F(N) = 0$ being the optimal solution. $F(N)$ is calculated as follows:

$$F(N) := -\sqrt{\frac{1}{1023} \sum_{i=1}^{1023} \left(\frac{1}{4} \sum_{j=1}^{4} \|(y^\star)_{2j-1,2j} - (y_i)_{2j-1,2j}\|_2^2 + b(y_i) \right)} \quad (1)$$

where y_i denotes the new image features after executing one robot movement starting at start pose i, and $(y)_{2j-1,2j}$ shall denote the vector comprising of the $2j-1$th and $2j$th component of a vector y. The inner sum of (1) thus sums up the squared deviations of the 4 marker positions in the image. $b(y)$ is a "badness" function that adds to the visual deviation an additional positive measure to punish potentially dangerous situations. If the robot moves such that features are not visible in the image or the object is touched by the robot, $b(y) > 0$, otherwise $b(y) = 0$. The function b is defined such that it usually takes on values ≤ 1. All image coordinates are in the camera image on the sensor and have therefore the unit 1 mm. The sensor (CCD chip) in this simulation measures $\frac{8}{3}$ mm $\times$ 2 mm. The average (RMS) image error is -0.85 mm at the start poses, which means that a network N that avoids all robot movements (e.g. a NN with all weights $= 0$) has $F(N) = -0.85$.

4   Experimental Comparison of EANT and NEAT

In order to validate learning methods we use the visual servoing simulation described above, with 1023 start poses and the same definition of the fitness function F, as in equation (1). The 10 inputs and 3 outputs to the neural networks (NNs) are also defined as above. The computationally expensive evaluation of F, requiring 1023 NN evaluations and simulated robot movements makes it a priority to develop networks with as few evaluations $F(N)$ as possible.

4.1   The NEAT System

NEAT by Stanley and Miikkulainen [11] has already been briefly introduced in Section 2.1. It uses one evolutionary optimisation loop in which structures and parameters of NNs are mutated, and networks recombined using a crossover operator. The implementation of NEAT used here is the Java-based NEAT4J which is available as a SourceForge project (http://neat4j.sourceforge.net/). For reference the original NEAT code by Stanley has also been analysed.

The initial population of NEAT4J consists of randomly generated networks without hidden layers that are either fully or sparsely connected (at an option). In each generation the population is split into a number of species so that each two compatible individuals belong to the same species. The split is done using a compatibility measurement that incorporates network size, difference of weights and number of different genes. New species are created if necessary. If a species has a good average fitness, its size will be increased, otherwise the size is decreased. Species become extinct if their size becomes zero or they excess a certain age. The best individual of each species is kept together with their offspring. New members of a species are spawned by crossover and mutation from their parents who are selected among the best individuals in this species. Mutation is done by a stochastic update of weights and structure. Nodes and connections are added with certain probabilities, but never removed. Existing connections can, however, be switched on and off by toggling a flag.

Search for Optimal NEAT4J Parameters: Unfortunately, there is no suggestion how NEAT's 13 evolution and 9 speciation parameters should be set. We have tried many settings and found out that the values from the examples of

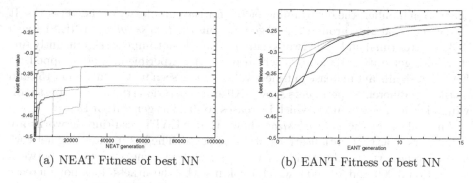

(a) NEAT Fitness of best NN   (b) EANT Fitness of best NN

Fig. 3. Results from 5 runs each of EANT and NEAT

the original NEAT mixed with those of NEAT4J form a suitable starting point. The settings were then adapted to tune the system for our visual servoing task.

NEAT tends to enlarge networks if the *probability of toggling connections* on/off is low and slows down the growing of networks if it is high. We decided to reduce the probability of toggling (PToggleLink 0.0001) so as to enable NEAT4J to sufficiently optimise the network weights before adding a lot of structure. For the same reason we also decreased the *probabilities for structural mutation* (PAddLink=0.0025, PAddNode=0.00125) after some test runs but left the *probabilities for weight changes* high (PMutation=0.25, PWeightReplaced=0.85). NEAT reacts very strongly to *bias neurons* and tends to add many of them. However, this made the evolution process get stuck without improving the fitness in a few test runs. We therefore deactivated biases altogether (which makes sense, considering the visual servoing task). An appropriate *population size* is hard to calculate but concerning the fitness increase over (wall-clock) time a smaller population size usually works better than a bigger. Hence, we tested two sizes of populations, 30 and 150. In most cases the smaller population only performed slightly worse. We did not note a significant change in the test outcome when varying parameters for *speciation*, so we set the number of species to 1.

4.2   The EANT System

The EANT system which was described in detail in section 2.2 was used with the following parameters:

- up to 30 individuals in the structural exploration (global population size)
- each individual spawns 2 children through structural mutation
- 2 parallel optimisations of the same individual by CMA-ES
- stop criteria for CMA-ES: maximum standard deviation in covariance matrix less than 0.00005 or iteration (CMA-ES generation) number over 500.

4.3   Results and Discussion

Figure 3 shows the development of the best individual's fitness value and size. Results from 5 experiments each of EANT and NEAT are shown, plotted against the generation number, the determining factor for the complexity of the networks. It can be seen that after around 25,000 generations the *fitness values* in NEAT reach -0.33 (better runs) and -0.38 (worse runs). They do not improve significantly further until generation 100,000, at which point the experiments were stopped. In EANT, a significant increase in fitness value can be seen up to generation 15 (and further, as different experiments show). After 5 generations the average best individual has a fitness of -0.27, which increases to -0.23 at generation 15.

An analysis of the *network sizes* shows that NEAT's resulting networks are still "sparse", as that initialisation option was used. The best performing network has 17 genes, with only 2 hidden neurons. Only 1 gene was added between generation 3,000 and 100,000, which explains why the fitness does not increase any further. However, without the "sparse" option NEAT generates networks with sizes approx. 80–100 after 3,000 generations; their fitness is around -0.89 to -0.66. EANT's network sizes are larger due to the different initialisation. The mean size at generation 5 is 55 (fitness -0.27), size increasing slower as time goes on, with a mean size of 83 at generation 15 (fitness -0.23).

The fitness values are (modulo $b(\cdot)$) the remaining RMS errors in the image after the robot movement. Both methods quickly develop networks that reduce the image error from the initial -0.85 to as low as -0.23 with 1 robot movement. This is a very good result if one compares to the traditional Image Jacobian approach. Calculating the robot movement using the (undamped) product of the Image Jacobian's pseudoinverse with the negative image error, a standard method [15] yields a fitness of -0.61. The two methods differ in the way networks are generated, and it looks like NEAT performs worse in this scenario. Only when the networks are small and the probability of structural change is low compared to parametrical change can NEAT optimise networks well with its EA. If some options influence NEAT to produce larger networks they have a significantly worse performance compared to EANT networks of the same size. This could mean that NN parameters in NEAT are not optimised as well, or many structural elements exist that do not help the task well, or both.

Overall, EANT created better networks than NEAT and required less parameter tuning to run successfully.

5   Conclusions and Future Work

In this article we have presented EANT, a method to develop both the structure and the parameters of neural networks (NNs) by evolutionary reinforcement learning. EANT differs from other recent methods by implementing a clear separation of structural and parametrical development and the use of CMA-ES during parameter optimisation. In order to validate EANT, it was used with a complete simulation of a visual servoing scenario to learn NNs by reinforcement learning. The same task was given to NEAT [11], a similar method. Results from the experiments show that both evolutionary methods can develop networks that make "useful" robot movements, decreasing the image error and thereby moving towards the goal. The performance of both methods is also significantly better than the traditional visual servoing approach.

A comparison of both methods showed that the NNs created by EANT always have a significantly better performance. NEAT performs good when configured to keep network sizes very small, but then the development of networks comes to a halt, showing almost no improvement over a long runtime. For similar network sizes, EANT's NN perform much better.

For these experiments EANT's parameter optimisation with CMA-ES has been reduced in complexity to make a fair comparison possible; previous experiments used many more CMA-ES generations [5]. Our current work is to study the dependence of EANT on these and other CMA-ES parameters.

References

1. Hornik, K., Stinchcombe, M.B., White, H.: Multilayer feedforward networks are universal approximators. Neural Networks 2, 359–366 (1989)
2. Bellman, R.E.: Adaptive Control Processes. Princeton University Press, Princeton, USA (1961)
3. Rojas, R.: Neural Networks - A Systematic Introduction. Springer, Berlin, Germany (1996)
4. Kassahun, Y., Sommer, G.: Efficient reinforcement learning through evolutionary acquisition of neural topologies. In: Proceedings of the 13th European Symposium on Artificial Neural Networks (ESANN 2005), Bruges, Belgium, pp. 259–266 (2005)
5. Siebel, N.T., Kassahun, Y.: Learning neural networks for visual servoing using evolutionary methods. In: Proceedings of the 6th International Conference on Hybrid Intelligent Systems (HIS'06), Auckland, New Zealand, 6 (4 pages) (2006)
6. Eiben, Á.E., Smith, J.E.: Introduction to Evolutionary Computing. Springer, Berlin, Germany (2003)
7. Sutton, R.S., Barto, A.G.: Reinforcement Learning: An Introduction. MIT Press, Cambridge, USA (1998)
8. Yao, X.: Evolving artificial neural networks. Proceedings of the IEEE 87(9), 1423–1447 (1999)
9. Yao, X., Liu, Y.: A new evolutionary system for evolving artificial neural networks. IEEE Transactions on Neural Networks 8(3), 694–713 (1997)
10. Angeline, P.J., Saunders, G.M., Pollack, J.B.: An evolutionary algorithm that constructs recurrent neural networks. IEEE Transactions on Neural Networks 5, 54–65 (1994)
11. Stanley, K.O., Miikkulainen, R.: Evolving neural networks through augmenting topologies. Evolutionary Computation 10(2), 99–127 (2002)
12. Kirkpatrick, S., Gelatt, C.D., Vecchi, M.P.: Optimization by simulated annealing. Science 220(4598), 671–680 (1983)
13. Hansen, N., Ostermeier, A.: Completely derandomized self-adaptation in evolution strategies. Evolutionary Computation 9(2), 159–195 (2001)
14. Weiss, L.E., Sanderson, A.C., Neuman, C.P.: Dynamic sensor-based control of robots with visual feedback. IEEE Journal of Robotics and Automation 3(5), 404–417 (1987)
15. Hutchinson, S., Hager, G., Corke, P.: A tutorial on visual servo control. Tutorial notes, Yale University, New Haven, USA (1996)

Robust High-Speed Melt Pool Measurements for Laser Welding with Sputter Detection Capability

Nicolaj C. Stache[1], Henrik Zimmer[1], Jens Gedicke[2],
Alexander Olowinsky[2], and Til Aach[1]

[1] Institute of Imaging & Computer Vision,
RWTH Aachen University, 52056 Aachen, Germany
[2] Fraunhofer Institute for Laser Technology, Steinbachstr. 15,
52074 Aachen, Germany

Abstract. Although lasers are widely used for welding in precision engineering industry, it is still a challenge to achieve high accuracy in creating and positioning welding spots at extremely high processing speed.

Towards this end, we propose a system for monitoring the welding process in order to ensure good quality of the welding spots. Our technology enables high speed image acquisition confocally to the laser beam with a direct view onto the melt. This innovative system permits accurate estimation of the melt pool's position and radius, which, however, must be performed at frame rates above 200 fps. We therefore employ fast correlation based approaches for sampling the melt pool's contour and robustly fitting a circle to it. In addition, the approaches enable sputter detection via outlier classification.

To assess the performance of each presented method, extensive experiments are conducted. The proposed paradigms can furthermore be conveniently adapted to a variety of problems dealing with rapid shape estimation in noisy environments.

1 Introduction

Lasers permit to create narrow but deep weldings and they offer contact-free assembling at highest processing speed – among others, these advantages have resulted in an increased use of lasers in the precision engineering industry [1]. However, a profitable use of laser welding, especially in this branch of industry, requires the generation of welding spots at high speed and with high accuracy in size and position. To meet these requirements in industrial environments, it is indispensable to monitor the laser welding process to detect flaws as early as possible. We therefore observe directly the evolution of the pool of melt caused by the laser while the laser pulse is applied. To this end, we employ a confocal laser welding system, which provides a special extension for high speed image acquisition.

The thus acquired image sequences show welding processes of copper and steel performed with a Nd:YAG laser. An additional laser is used for illuminating

F.A. Hamprecht, C. Schnörr, and B. Jähne (Eds.): DAGM 2007, LNCS 4713, pp. 476–485, 2007.

the scene, which allows a direct view onto the generated melt pool without any influence of laser induced plasma. In contrast to plasma monitoring (see Fig. 1a), our direct approach dramatically improves the melt pool estimation (see Fig. 1b) and facilitates further assessment, such as sputter detection, due to the increased amount of relevant details in the images.

The images are captured with a frame rate of 5000 fps using a high-speed CMOS camera, since the welding processes last only 10 ms to 20 ms. However, the throughput of the image processing system, which is predetermined by the cycle time of the welding system (i.e. the time slot between two laser spots), has to be at least 200 fps to prevent the welding machine from stalling. At this rate the parameters, viz. radius and position of the melt pool, have to be estimated in a manner resistant to noise or sputters of the melt.

We therefore present approaches to rapidly estimate these parameters and to detect flaws via robustly fitting a circle to the melt pool's contour and perform basic error classification. For contour estimation, we utilize a novel contour sampling method via correlation of radial profiles with step edge prototypes. To infer the desired parameters from the thus sampled contour, four approaches are applied and compared. The approaches are: a completely newly designed method, adapted types of the Hough Transform, Least Median of Squares regression and RANSAC (RANdom SAmple Consensus).

Recent experiments have shown that the main ideas presented here can be conveniently adapted to various estimation problems such as fast position recognition of bearings in industrial vision and cell recognition for early cancer diagnosis.

The paper is organized as follows: First, our welding and image acquisition system is described. Second, the algorithms for melt pool parameter estimation are introduced. Then, the results of extensive experiments are presented and comparisons of the algorithms are made. The paper concludes with a discussion and an outlook for ongoing work.

2   Welding and Image Acquisition System

Unlike other approaches, which use the radiation of the laser induced plasma for process monitoring with a spatially integrating photo detector (often a photo diode), we employ a special setup which allows the acquisition of 2D images confocally with the laser. This setup is known as *Coaxial Process Control*-system (CPC-system) [4], [5]. Compared to a photo diode system, the CPC-system, when equipped with a high speed camera, provides image data with much more relevant information for the welding process and a strongly increased resolution. To obtain melt pool images without being disturbed by plasma radiation, we extended the basic CPC-system, which is composed of a Nd:YAG laser, a dichroit and a camera, see Fig. 2. As illustrated, the Nd:YAG laser partly shares its optical path with the camera. This is implemented via the dichroit, which reflects the laser wavelength but is transparent for the wavelengths the camera should capture. With only this basic CPC setup, however, the camera would capture the radiation of the laser induced plasma, which prevents a direct view onto the melt.

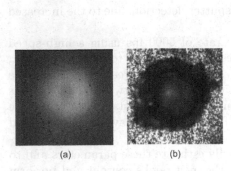

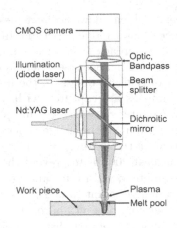

Fig. 1. Frames of a welding sequence: (a) Meltpool without additional illumination (b) with additional illumination – direct view onto the melt pool

Fig. 2. Welding system with extension for image acquisition and additional illumination [5]

To cope with this problem, we extended the setup by using a second beam splitter in front of the camera, which introduces an additional illumination from a diode laser with a wavelength of 830 nm. Additionally, we place an appropriate bandpass filter in front of the camera. The passband of this bandpass is tuned to a small band around 830 nm, where the radiation emitted by the plasma is close to zero. This means, in turn, that the plasma is translucent in this small band and, therefore, we obtain the desired direct view onto the melt pool shown in Fig. 1b).

3   Parameter Estimation

This section describes several techniques for estimating the radii and positions of the melt pools in the image sequences. We concentrate on approaches which use information about the melt pool's contour and fit a circle to estimate radius and position. The advantage of this contour-based method over blob based approaches and derivatives based on matching of entire melt pool frames with sets of prototypes [7], is the higher achievable throughput and the possibility for localizing defects such as sputters in the contour. Conventional approaches, working on entire images, such as the standard Hough Transform [3] are computationally far too expensive. In contrast to the Hough Transform, high throughput can be obtained with the computationally inexpensive fast boundary point analysis in [7] but the robustness of this method to outliers is weak.

To comply with both throughput and robustness constraints, we first estimate contour points, and then robustly fit a circle to these points. Since there are various approaches for robust fitting [6], [3], [8], a rigorous comparison, as mentioned in the introduction, is made.

3.1   Contour Point Estimation

The starting points for the algorithms – except for the Hough Transform, which operates on correlation values – are the points extracted from the melt pool's contour. To estimate these points with low computational effort, we consider n radial profiles of the melt pool images and correlate each profile with a precomputed set of step edges. The positions of the radial profiles for $n = 8$ are highlighted in Fig. 3.

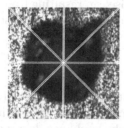

Fig. 3. Melpool with highlighted positions of eight radial profiles

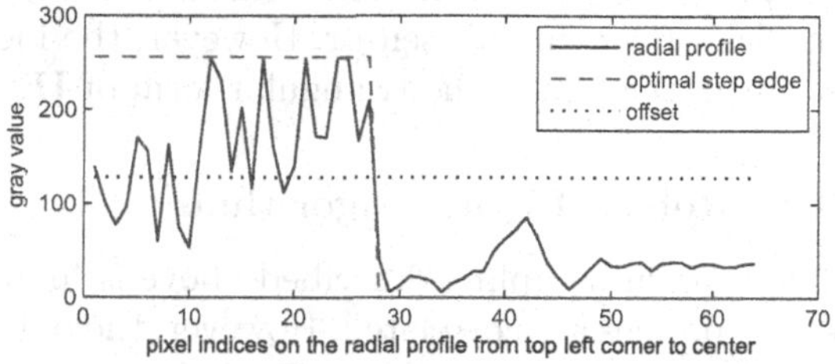

Fig. 4. Radial profile of the top left corner with estimated step edge referring to the sought contour point. Dotted line: Offset which has to be compensated with a gray value shift.

Before the correlations are computed, both the step edges and the profiles have to be freed from their offsets which result in a shift of the gray values. With this operation, the gray values corresponding to the melt pool pixels become negative and the background values become positive. It is important that the symmetry of these values in the radial profile is roughly identical with the symmetry in the precomputed step edges to yield a high accuracy in estimating the edge's position. This leads to a normalization by subtracting the gray value offset. Normalization is followed by correlation computation, which we conveniently implemented as a matrix multiplication. This is similar to linear convolution via multiplication with a Toeplitz matrix and can be described as

$$y = H \cdot x \, , \tag{1}$$

where y denotes the correlation vector, H is the Toeplitz-Matrix, which is composed of the precomputed step edge prototypes and x represents the gray values of the radial profile. An example with idealized x is

$$\underbrace{\begin{pmatrix} 2 \\ 4 \\ 2 \\ 0 \\ -2 \end{pmatrix}}_{y} = \underbrace{\begin{pmatrix} 1 & 1 & 1 & 1 \\ -1 & 1 & 1 & 1 \\ -1 & -1 & 1 & 1 \\ -1 & -1 & -1 & 1 \\ -1 & -1 & -1 & -1 \end{pmatrix}}_{H} \cdot \underbrace{\begin{pmatrix} -1 \\ 1 \\ 1 \\ 1 \end{pmatrix}}_{x} \, . \tag{2}$$

As can be seen, the precomputed step prototypes are stacked in **H**, which, with these ideal models, degenerates to a triangular matrix. Obviously, the second line in **H** fits the best to **x** – consequently, the second entry in **y** exhibits the maximum value. The corresponding contour point can now be determined via the position of the maximum value in **y**.

The challenge in estimating contour points this way is to accurately estimate the gray value offset for normalization because its value varies from frame to frame. We therefore implemented a normalization method by computing the offsets as the mean values of the profiles and the step edges. Thus, these offsets adapt to brightness variations and are insensitive to noise e.g. resulting from bad pixels in the camera's sensor. However, the increased adaptivity and robustness result in the loss of the triangular form of **H**.

3.2   Robust Fitting Algorithms

The contour sampling described above is highly robust to noise because always entire profiles are correlated. However, the obtained contour points are still influenced by sputters or bright reflections in the melt, which should not degrade the melt pool parameter estimation. Therefore, a robust fitting of the circle model with these detected points is vital. We address this challenging task by developing a new approach called "Least Distances (L. Dist.)" and by adapting three widely used paradigms for robust regression to the problem at hand.

Least Distances ("L. Dist."). Compared to the techniques, to be introduced in the following, this approach is closest tailored to the problem stated above, since it uses the highest degree of prior knowledge about the welding process for fitting and rejecting outliers.

Our algorithm is based on the fact that the material to be welded melts continuously. Consequently, the melt pool's radius increases smoothly over successive frames. Thus, undisturbed contour points are distinguished from those disturbed by, e.g., sputter, by evaluating the distance of each contour point to the preceding circle. With this approach we thus make use of the temporal dependencies between the melt pool's parameters of successive frames, due to the physics of welding.

The trusted contour points, chosen by this method and used for circle fitting, are those $m_t = n/2$ points (n = number of contour points, $n \geq 8$), which have the smallest Euclidean distance to the preceding circle. However, to ensure that the trusted points are reasonably distributed, the contour is divided into four quadrants and from each quadrant, at least one point (namely the point with the smallest distance) is selected. This procedure should help to better cope with melt pools which are not perfectly round.

After contour point selection, the circle is fitted via Least Mean Squares to the m_t trusted points.

Hough Transform. The common ground of "L. Dist." (and the following methods) is the attempt of fitting a circle to contour points extracted first. Thus, only the *maxima* of the correlation vectors **y** in (1) are considered, since they represent the points where the contour most likely is to be. However, the strengths of these maxima and the existence of secondary maxima are not considered. These downsides can be addressed by the Hough Transform [3] for finding the circle, whose contour points maximize the correlation in sum over all contour points.

As mentioned before, on our current platform (2.66 GHz, Intel Core2Duo PC), the standard Hough Transform (denoted by "Hough Ext.") can not comply with the stringent real time constraints. Its performance is in the following therefore provided more as a reference. However, the limited number of correlation vectors **y**, the possibility to eventually shrink the Hough accumulator space by invoking additional prior knowledge, and the possibility of further speedup via a lookup table for the pixels to be accumulated, make it an earnest alternative candidate for our application. We thus implemented a trimmed-down and accelerated version, called "Hough Ltd." which inherently makes use of the temporal dependencies described in 3.2 by utilizing the previously estimated circle parameters as initial guess for defining a small sliding search space around these.

RANSAC. The most commonly used approach for robust fitting in industrial vision is RANSAC, introduced by Fishler and Bolles [2]. Unlike "Hough Ltd." or "L. Dist", RANSAC solely uses the given shape model for outlier rejection. For the problem at hand, we implemented RANSAC with the following steps:

1. Select a set of $p = 3$ contour points randomly (three points are required to determine a circle),
2. Construct a circle through these,
3. Count the number of points which lie within an error tolerance of ϵ_{max} to the circle (so-called inliers),
4. If the number of inliers is greater than some threshold n_{min}, do least squares circle fitting for all inliers, else repeat the above process, i.e. start again at 1., until a maximum number m_{max} of trials is reached.

Least Median of Squares. Slightly different to RANSAC, but as well solely based on the shape model, is Least Median of Squares Regression (LMedS), which solves the nonlinear minimization problem

$$\min_{i} \operatorname{med} r_i^2 \,, \tag{3}$$

where r_i^2 denotes the squared residual, i.e. the squared distance of the remaining contour points to the fitted circle. Although (3) looks very similar to Least Mean Squares regression, a closed form solution of this expression is not available. Thus, LMedS has to perform a search in the space of possible estimates generated from data. The procedure we implemented for n given points is composed of the following steps [8]:

1. Draw m random subsamples of $p = 3$ different points,
2. Construct circles through the points of the subsamples,
3. Determine the median of the squared residuals for each circle,
4. Pick the circle yielding the smallest median,
5. Consider the distance of all points to the picked circle and reject points with distances $> t$,
6. Fit a circle via least mean squares with the remaining points.

In contrast to Least Mean Squares, LMedS can resist the effect of 50% of gross outliers in data. Step 5 and 6 help to compensate the poor efficiency of LMedS in the presence of Gaussian noise. According to Rousseeuw in [6], t calculates to

$$t = M \left(3.7065 + \frac{18.5325}{n - p} \right)^2 , \qquad (4)$$

where M denotes the minimal median.

4   Results

This section presents the performances and error rates of the described algorithms compared with a hand selected ground truth. The algorithms were coded in Matlab and executed on a standard PC (Intel Core2Duo, 2.66 GHz, 2 GB RAM). The database for evaluation contains approximately 1020 frames (and the corresponding ground truths) taken from 12 different welding sequences of copper and steel. As mentioned in the introduction, these sequences are recorded with a high-speed camera with 128×128 pixels at 5000 fps. The welding is performed with a Nd:YAG Laser (1064 nm wavelength) and the scene is confocally illuminated with a diode laser (830 nm wavelength). All the presented images exhibit a field of view of 0.8×0.8 mm^2.

To assess the algorithms for both sequences with well-behaved melt pools and sequences with high defect rates (due to sputters and reflections, see Fig. 6) separately, each of these is split into two parts. The first part typically exhibits well-behaved melt pools and the second part exhibits higher defect rates – it can be observed that the defect rate increases with the radius, which in turn increases with the frame number and time, see Fig. 6.

For comparison, the error rates ϵ_1, ϵ_2 and ϵ are computed from the areas in pixels, which are correctly or incorrectly classified by the algorithms compared with ground truths. More specifically, ϵ_1 is the probability of background pixels which are misclassified as melt pool pixels ("false positive rate"), ϵ_2 is the probability of the melt pool pixels being misclassified as background ("false negative rate") and ϵ is the total error rate.

The settings of the algorithms, used for obtaining the following results, are listed in Tab. 1. All settings are carefully chosen to yield reasonable results with the algorithms. In case of LMedS, m is specified to ensure that the probability of drawing at least one completely undisturbed combination is 99% in the presence of 50% disturbed contour points. The results obtained with these settings are depicted in Tab. 2 and Fig. 5.

As can be observed, the two approaches, viz. "L. Dist." and "Hough Ltd.", exploiting temporal dependencies due to the continuity in melt pool changes, perform better than the other approaches and yield moderate error rates. However, among these two, "L. Dist." exhibits higher throughput while "Hough Ltd." is slightly better in total error rate ϵ. The error rates depicted in Tab. 2 might, however, be further improved by optimizing the normalization described in

Table 1. Global settings for the different robust fitting algorithms

Global setting	$n = 16$	number of radial profiles
RANSAC	$p = 3$	initial set of points
	$\epsilon_{max} = 4$ pix.	error tolerance for inliers
	$n_{min} = 4$	minimum number of inliers
	$m_{max} = 80$	maximum number of trials
LMedS	$p = 3$	initial set of points
	$m = 44$	number of initial subsamples
L. Dist.	$m_t = 8$	number of trusted points
Hough Ext.	$s(y, x, r) = 64 \, {}^{+8}_{-8}, \ 64 \, {}^{+8}_{-8}, \ 5 \, {}^{+72}_{0}$	search space in y, x, r direction
Hough Ltd.	$s(y, x, r) = i_y {}^{+2}_{-2}, \ i_x {}^{+2}_{-2}, \ i_r {}^{+5}_{-5}$	search space
	$i_y, \, i_x, \, i_r$	parameters of preceding circle (first initialized with: 64, 64, 15)

Table 2. Results for the different robust fitting algorithms ('Part' refers to the splitting of the sequences into two parts, ϵ_1 = false positive rate in %, ϵ_2 = false negative rate in %, ϵ = total error rate in %, fps = frames per second with a 2.66 GHz Core2Duo, Matlab code).

Algorithm	Part	ϵ_1	ϵ_2	ϵ	fps
RANSAC	1	8.2	1.5	6.1	446.3
	2	12.5	2.2	8.3	442.9
LMedS	1	6.8	0.7	4.9	220.9
	2	10.8	1.1	6.8	221.0
L. Dist.	1	5.0	2.0	4.1	1084.3
	2	8.3	1.8	5.7	1084.2
Hough Ext.	1	5.2	0.7	3.8	39.6
	2	10.3	0.9	6.3	39.6
Hough Ltd.	1	5.0	4.8	4.2	867.5
	2	8.6	0.7	5.5	867.7

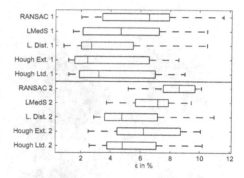

Fig. 5. Boxplot of the total error rate for both sequence parts ("RANSAC 1" e.g. indicates the error rates for part 1 of the sequences, obtained with RANSAC). The lines in the boxes mark the medians, the boxes encompass the two inner quartiles of the quantity of results, whereas the "whiskers" and crosses mark the two remaining outer quartiles.

section 3.1, because the algorithms tend to overestimate the size of the melt pools (ϵ_1 is greater than ϵ_2 – see Tab. 2).

4.1 Edge Model Improvement and Sputter Detection

In case of severe disturbances due to reflections in the melt, the edge model offers the possibility for further improvement. Fig. 6, row a) shows detected contour points with the standard edge model – it can be observed that some contour points are disturbed by reflections in the melt. However, most of these reflections arise in the inner parts and not on the periphery of the melt pools. Consequently, a small (dark) rim of molten material between reflection and background remains. This can be exploited by adapting the precomputed edge prototypes, which is straightforwardly done by inserting stripes of zeros, which cover the inner melt pool region, into the prototypes. As a consequence, the inner parts of the melt pool no longer count for correlation and thus, reflections in these parts no longer disturb the melt pool estimation (see Fig. 6 row b)).

In addition to melt pool estimation, the contour based approach offers the benefit for sputter detection without major effort. A sputter is simply recognized as a contour point lying beyond a threshold distance d_t outside the fitted circle. Fig. 6 (see sputter points) shows an example for melt pool estimation with "L. Dist." and sputter detection ($d_t \geq 4$ pixels like in RANSAC). The accuracy of sputter detection may be increased by detecting more contour points, which of course decreases the detection rate. However, "L. Dist." still yields a throughput of 338 fps with $n = 60$ radial profiles.

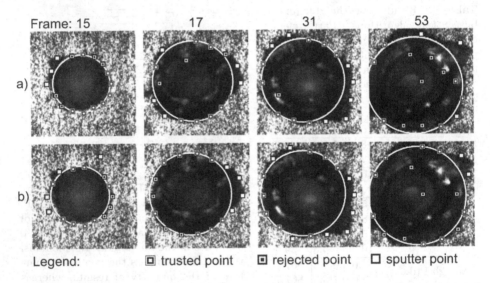

Fig. 6. Melt pool evolution during a welding process of copper. The contour points and circles are obtained with "L. Dist.". Row a): contour points obtained with idealized edge prototypes, row b): contour points and circles obtained with an initial additional stripe of zeros in the edge prototypes.

5   Conclusions

We presented approaches for process monitoring in laser welding via high speed and robust estimation of melt pool parameters. To this end, we employed a special setup with confocal illumination and a bandpass filter in front of the camera to acquire images without influence of plasma radiation. The obtained images thus allow the desired parameter estimation.

All approaches presented in this contribution are based on contour sampling via correlation of step edge prototypes with radial profiles of the images. This sampling is followed by parameter estimation, where two approaches, which use process-pertinent knowledge to achieve the best performance. The main ideas of these algorithms can be easily adapted to other industrial and medical vision tasks as recent experiments have shown.

Our ongoing work is on the extension of the algorithms towards an increased robustness to discontinuities in the background e.g. caused by adjacent melt pools which, in turn, paves the way for monitoring of welding seams.

Acknowledgments

The authors thank Dipl. Ing. Boris Regaard, Fraunhofer ILT who kindly provided the welding sequences used in this paper.

This work is funded by the collaborative research project "INTAKT" in the funding program "InnoNet" from the German Federal Ministry of Economics and Technology (BMWi) with VDI/VDE-IT. The authors gratefully acknowledge this support as well as the active cooperation of all project partners.

References

1. Bollig, A., Mann, S., Beck, R., Kaierle, S.: Einsatz optischer Technologien zur Regelung von Laserstrahlschweißprozessen. Automatisierungstechnik 53, 513–521 (2005)
2. Fischler, M.A., Bolles, R.C.: Random sample consensus: a paradigm for model fitting with applications to image analysis and automated cartography. Commun. ACM 24(6), 381–395 (1981)
3. Hough, P.V.C., Arbor, A.: Method and means for recognizing complex patterns. United States Patent and Trademark Office, 3069654 (1962)
4. Kratzsch, C.: Realisierung eines kamerabasierten Prozessüberwachungssystems am Beispiel des Laserstrahlschweißens. PhD thesis, RWTH Aachen (2003)
5. Regaard, B., Kaierle, S., Schulz, W., Moalem, A.: Advantages of Coaxial External Illumination for Monitoring and Control of Laser Materials Processing. In: ICALEO, pp. 915–919 (2005)
6. Peter, J.R., Annick, M.I.: Robust Regression and Outlier Detection. John Wiley & Sons, New York (1987)
7. Stache, N.C., Zimmer, H., Gedicke, J., Regaard, B., Olowinsky, A., Knepper, A., Aach, T.: Approaches for high-speed melt pool detection in laser welding applications. In: Proc. VMV 2006, pp. 217–224 (2006)
8. Zhang, Z.: Parameter estimation techniques: A tutorial with application to conic fitting. Technical Report RR-2676, INRIA (1997)

Learning Robust Objective Functions with Application to Face Model Fitting

Matthias Wimmer[1], Sylvia Pietzsch[2], Freek Stulp[3], and Bernd Radig[2]

[1] Faculty of Science and Engineering, Waseda University, Tokyo, Japan
[2] Institut für Informatik, Technische Universität München, Germany
[3] Kognitive Neuroinformatik, Universität Bremen, Germany

Abstract. Model-based image interpretation extracts high-level information from images using a priori knowledge about the object of interest. The computational challenge is to determine the model parameters that best match a given image by searching for the global optimum of the involved objective function. Unfortunately, this function is usually designed manually, based on implicit and domain-dependent knowledge, which prevents the fitting task from yielding accurate results.

In this paper, we demonstrate how to improve model fitting by learning objective functions from annotated training images. Our approach automates many critical decisions and the remaining manual steps hardly require domain-dependent knowledge. This yields more robust objective functions that are able to achieve the accurate model fit. Our evaluation uses a publicly available image database and compares the obtained results to a recent state-of-the-art approach.

1 Introduction

Model-based image interpretation systems exploit a priori knowledge about objects, such as shape or texture. The model contains a parameter vector p that represents its configuration, including position, rotation, scaling, and deformation. These parameters are usually mapped to the surface of an image, via a set of feature points, a contour, or a textured region.

Model fitting is the computational challenge of finding the model parameters that describe the content of the image best [1]. This task consists of two components: the fitting algorithm and the objective function. The *objective function* yields a comparable value that determines how accurately a parameterized model fits to an image. In this paper, smaller values denote a better model fit. Depending on context, they are also known as the likelihood, similarity, energy, cost, goodness or quality functions. The *fitting algorithm* searches for the model parameters p that optimize the objective function. Since the described methods are independent of the used fitting algorithm, this paper shall not elaborate on them but we refer to [1] for a recent overview and categorization.

Problem Statement. Fitting algorithms have been the subject of intensive research and evaluation. In contrast, the objective function is usually determined ad hoc and heuristically, using the designer's intuitions about a good measure of

F.A. Hamprecht, C. Schnörr, and B. Jähne (Eds.): DAGM 2007, LNCS 4713, pp. 486–496, 2007.

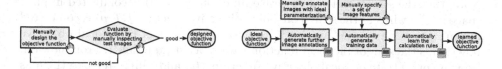

Fig. 1. The traditional procedure for designing objective functions (left), and the proposed method for learning objective functions from annotated training images (right)

fitness. Afterwards, its appropriateness is subjectively determined by inspecting its result, evaluated on example images and example model parameterizations. If the result is not satisfactory the objective function is tuned or redesigned from scratch, see Figure 1 (left). The consequences are that this design approach requires much implicit and domain-dependent knowledge. Its iterative nature also makes it a time-consuming process of unpredictable duration. Furthermore, the best model fit is not objectively determined.

Solution Idea. In contrast, this paper explicitly formulates the properties of *ideal* objective functions and gives a concrete example of such a function based on manual image annotations. Unfortunately, it is impossible to obtain ideal objective functions for real-world scenarios. Therefore, we propose to learn the objective function from comprehensive training data specified by the ideal objective function. This methodology approximates the ideal objective function and therefore achieves high accuracy. It automates most steps and the remaining manual steps require little domain-dependent knowledge, see Figure 1 (right). Furthermore, the *design-inspect* loop is eliminated, which makes the time requirements predictable.

Section 2 describes the design approach and points out its shortcomings. Section 3 specifies properties of ideal objective functions. Section 4 explains the proposed approach in detail. Section 5 experimentally evaluates the obtained results. Section 6 refers to related work and Section 7 summarizes our contributions and suggests further work.

2 Manually Designing Objective Functions

In order to explain the proposed technique, this paper utilizes a two-dimensional, deformable, contour model of a human face according to the Active Shape Model approach [2]. The model parameters $p=(t_x, t_y, s, \theta, b)^T$ describe the translation t_x and t_y, the scaling s, the rotation θ and the deformation b. The function $c_n(p)$ computes the location of the nth contour point with $1 \leq n \leq N$.

Model-based image interpretation requires determining the model that fits best to the image. For this reason, the objective function $f(I, p)$ computes the fitness between the model parameters p and the image I. According to common approaches [2], we split the objective function into N local parts $f_n(I, x)$, one for each contour point $c_n(p)$. These local functions evaluate the image variations around the corresponding contour point and give evidence about its fitness.

Note, that the search on local objective functions $f_n(I, x)$ is conducted in pixel space $x \in \mathbb{R}^2$, whereas the search on global objective function $f(I, p)$ is conducted in parameter space $p \in \mathbb{R}^P$ with $P = dim(p)$. The result of the global objective function is the sum of the local function values, as in Equation 1. From now on, we will concentrate on local objective functions f_n, and simply refer to them as objective functions.

$$f(I, p) = \sum_{n=1}^{N} f_n(I, c_n(p)) \tag{1}$$

Objective functions are usually designed by manually selecting salient features from the image and mathematically composing them. The feature selection and the mathematical composition are both based on the designer's intuition and implicit knowledge of the domain. In [3] for instance, the objective function is computed from edge values of the image. Each contour point is considered to be located well if it overlaps a strong edge of the image. A similar objective function is shown in Equation 2, where $0 \leq E(I, x) \leq 1$ denotes the edge magnitude.

$$f_n^e(I, x) = 1 - E(I, x) \tag{2}$$

As illustrated with the example in Figure 2, the design approach has comprehensive shortcomings and unexpected side-effects. 2a) visualizes one of the contour points of the face model as well as its perpendicular towards the contour. 2b) and 2c) depict the content of the image along this perpendicular as well as the corresponding edge magnitudes $E(I, x)$. 2d) shows the value of the designed objective function f_n^e along the perpendicular. Obviously, this function has many local minima within this one-dimensional space. Furthermore, the global minimum does not correspond to the ideal location that is denoted by the vertical line. Because of this amount of local minima, fitting algorithms have difficulty in finding the global minimum. Even if an algorithm found the global minimum, it would be wrong, because it does not correspond to the ideal location.

3   The Properties of Ideal Objective Functions

This section makes the observations from Figure 2 explicit by formulating two properties P1 and P2. We call an objective function *ideal* once it has both of them. The mathematical formalization of P1 uses the *ideal* model parameters p_I^*, which are defined to be the model parameters with the best fitness to a specific image I. Similarly, $c_n(p_I^*)$ denote the ideal contour points.

P1: Correctness: The global minimum corresponds to the best model fit.

$$\forall x (c_n(p_I^*) \neq x) \quad \Rightarrow \quad f_n(I, c_n(p_I^*)) < f_n(I, x)$$

P2: Uni-modality: The objective function has no local extrema.

$$\exists m \forall x \ (m \neq x) \quad \Rightarrow \quad f_n(I, m) < f_n(I, x) \ \wedge \ \nabla f_n(I, x) \neq 0$$

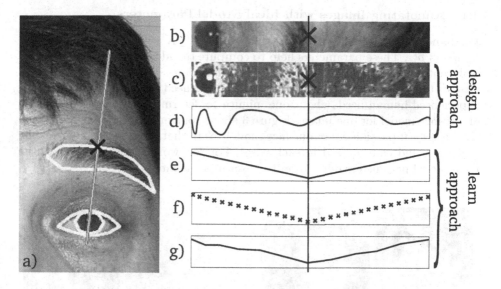

Fig. 2. a) Contour point with perpendicular, b) Image data, c) Edge magnitudes, d) Designed objective function f_n^e, e) Ideal objective function $f_n^\star$, f) Training data, g) Learned objective function f_n^ℓ; Note, b) – g) are taken along that perpendicular visible in a). The vertical line represents the location of the ideal contour point $c_n(p_I^\star)$.

Note that P2 guarantees that any determined minimum represents the global minimum. This facilitates search, because fitting algorithms can not get stuck in local minima. Thereby, the global minimum m does not need to correspond to the best fit. This is only required by the independent property P1.

$$f_n^\star(I, x) = |x - c_n(p_I^\star)| \tag{3}$$

We now introduce a concrete instance of an ideal objective function $f_n^\star(I, x)$, defined in Equation 3. It computes the distance between the ideal contour point $c_n(p_I^\star)$ and a pixel x located on the image surface. A significant feature of $f_n^\star$ is that it uses the ideal parameters $p_I^\star$ to compute its value. This implies that $f_n^\star$ cannot be applied to previously unseen images, because $p_I^\star$ is not known for these images.

4   Learning Robust Objective Functions

This section explains the five steps of our approach that learns objective functions from annotated training images, see Figure 1 (right). The key idea behind the approach is that $f_n^\star$ has the properties P1 and P2, and it generates the training data for learning an objective function $f_n^\ell(I, x)$. Therefore, this learned function will also approximately have these properties. Since it is "approximately ideal" we will refer to it as a *robust* objective function.

4.1 Annotating Images with Ideal Model Parameters

We manually annotate a set of images I_k with $1 \leq k \leq K$ with the ideal model parameters $p^\star_{I_k}$. These parameters help to compute the ideal objective function $f^\star_n$ in Equation 3. This annotation is the only laborious step in the entire procedure of the proposed approach, whereat the time need remains predictable. An experienced human needs about one minute to determine the ideal parameters of our face model for one image. Figure 3 shows four images that are annotated with the ideal parameters of our face model. Note that for synthetic images, $p^\star_I$ is known, and can be used in such cases. For real-world images, however, the ideal model parameters depend on the user's judgment.

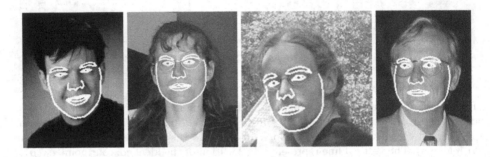

Fig. 3. Four images that are manually annotated with the ideal face model

4.2 Generating Further Image Annotations

According to P1, the ideal objective function returns the minimum $f^\star_n(I, x)=0$ for all image annotations. This data is not sufficient to learn f^ℓ_n, because training data must also contain image annotations, for which $f^\star_n(I, x) \neq 0$. To acquire these annotations, x must be varied. General variations move x to any position within the image, however, it is more practicable to restrict this motion in terms of distance and direction.

Therefore, we generate a number of displacements $x_{k,n,d}$ with $-D \leq d \leq D$ that are located on the perpendicular to the contour line with a maximum distance Δ to the contour point. Taking only these relocations facilitates the later learning step and improves the accuracy of the resulting calculation rules. This procedure is depicted in Figure 4. The center row depicts the manually annotated images, for which $f^\star_n(I, x_{k,n,0})=f^\star_n(I, c_n(p^\star_{I_k}))=0$. The other columns depict the displacements $x_{k,n,d \neq 0}$ with $f^\star_n(I, x_{k,n,d \neq 0})>0$ as defined by P1. At these displacements values of $f^\star_n$ are obtained by applying Equation 3

Due to different image sizes, the size of the visible face varies substantially. Distance measures, such as the return value of the ideal objective function, error measures and Δ, should not be biased by this variation. Therefore, all distances in pixels are converted to the interocular measure, by dividing them by the pixel distance between the pupils.

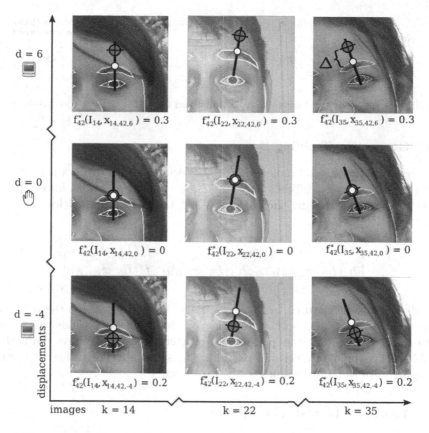

Fig. 4. In each of the K images each of the N contour points is annotated with $2D+1$ displacements. Manual work is only necessary for annotating $d{=}0$, which is depicted in the middle row. The other displacements are computed automatically. Note Δ in the upper right image that indicates the learning radius. The unit of the ideal objective function values and Δ is the interocular measure.

4.3   Specifying Image Features

Our approach learns a mapping from I_k and $\boldsymbol{x}_{k,n,d}$ to $f_n^\star(I_k, \boldsymbol{x}_{k,n,d})$, which is called $f_n^\ell(I, \boldsymbol{x})$. Since f_n^ℓ has no access to $\boldsymbol{p}_I^\star$, it must compute its value from the content of the image. Instead of learning a direct mapping from $\boldsymbol{x}$ and I to $f_n^\star$, we use a feature-extraction method [1]. The idea is to provide a multitude of image features, and let the learning algorithm choose which of them are relevant to the computation rules of the objective function.

In our approach, we use Haar-like image features of different styles and sizes [4], see Figure 5, which greatly cope with noisy images. These features are not only computed at the location of the contour point itself, but also at locations within its vicinity specified by a grid, see Figure 5. This variety of image features enables the objective function to exploit the texture of the image at the model's contour point and in its surrounding area.

Fig. 5. The set of $A=6\cdot3\cdot5\cdot5=450$ features utilized for learning the objective functions

4.4   Generating Training Data

The result of the manual annotation step (Section 4.1) and the automated annotation step (Section 4.2) is a list of $K(2D+1)$ image locations for each of the N contour points. Adding the corresponding target value $f_n^\star$ yields the list in Equation 4.

$$[\qquad\qquad I_k, \quad \boldsymbol{x}_{k,n,d} \qquad\qquad\quad , f_n^\star(I_k, \ \boldsymbol{x}_{k,n,d}) \ ] \qquad\qquad (4)$$

$$[\ \boldsymbol{h}_1(I_k, \ \boldsymbol{x}_{k,n,d}), \ldots, \boldsymbol{h}_A(I_k, \ \boldsymbol{x}_{k,n,d}) \, , f_n^\star(I_k, \ \boldsymbol{x}_{k,n,d}) \ ] \qquad (5)$$

$$\text{with } 1\leq k\leq K, \ 1\leq n\leq N, \ -D\leq d\leq D$$

We denote image features by $\boldsymbol{h}_a(I,\boldsymbol{x})$, with $1\leq a\leq A$. Each of these features returns a scalar value. Applying each feature to Equation 4 yields the training data in Equation 5. This step simplifies matters greatly. We have reduced the problem of mapping images and pixel locations to the target value $f_n^\star(I,\boldsymbol{x})$, to mapping a list of feature values to the target value.

4.5   Learning the Calculation Rules

The local objective function f_n^ℓ maps the values of the features to the value of $f_n^\star$. This mapping is learned from the training data by learning a model tree [5]. Model trees are a generalization of decision trees. Whereas decision trees have nominal values at their leaf nodes, model trees have line segments, allowing them to also map features to a continuous value, such as the value returned by $f_n^\star$. They are learned by recursively partitioning the feature space. A linear function is then fitted to the training data in each partition using linear regression. One of the advantages of model trees is that they tend to use only features that are relevant to predict the target values. Currently, we are providing $A=450$ image features, as illustrated in Figure 5. The model tree selects around 20 of them for learning the calculation rules.

After these five steps, a local objective function is learned for each contour point. It can now be called with an arbitrary pixel $\boldsymbol{x}$ of an arbitrary image I.

5   Experimental Evaluation

This section evaluates learned objective functions in the context of face model fitting. Thereby, we gather 500 images of frontal faces from the Internet.

5.1   Visualization of Global Objective Functions

Figure 6 visualizes how the value of the global objective function depends on varying pairs of parameters from the parameter vector p. The deformation parameter b_1 determines the angle at which the face model is viewed, and b_2 opens and closes the mouth of the model. As proposed by Cootes et al. [3] the deformation parameters vary from -2σ to 2σ of the deviation within the examples used for training the deformable model. It is clearly visible that the learned global objective function is closer to be ideal than the edge-based function. The plateaus with many local minima arise because they are outside of the area on which the objective function was trained. In these areas, the objective function cannot be expected to be ideal.

5.2   Comparison to a State-of-the-Art Approach

In a further experiment, we compare our approach to a state-of-the-art model fitting approach using the BioID database [6]. Figure 7 shows the result of our fitting algorithm using a learned objective function (solid line). We determine the point-to-point distance between the results of the fitted models and the annotated models. Figure 7 visualizes the result of our experiment. The x-axis indicates the point-to-point distance measure between the manually specified

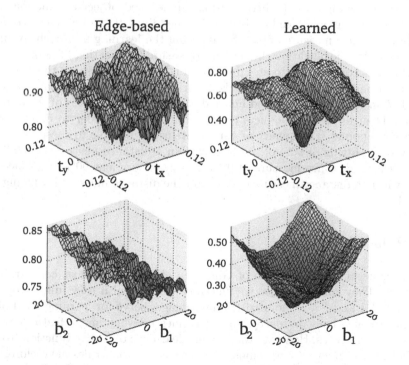

Fig. 6. Comparing the behavior of the edge-based (left column) to the learned (right column) global objective function, by varying pairs of parameters

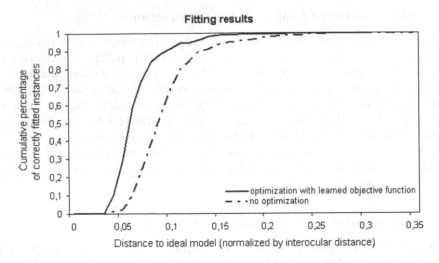

Fig. 7. The initial position of the face model (dashed line) is highly improved by fitting it with a learned objective function (solid line)

models and the results of the fitting step and the y-axis indicates their cumulative percentage. Model fitting using our learned objective function (solid curve) improves global face localization (dashed line). 95% of all faces are fitted within a distance measure of 0.12 by applying the learning approach. Applying only global face localization the distance measure for locating 95% of the faces is 0.16. That corresponds to an up to 30% higher deviation from the annotated model parameters. The set-up of this experiment is directly comparable to the one of [7] in terms of the utilized image database and the format of the obtained results. Their approach conducts template matching in order to determine facial feature points. The quality of our results is comparable to those of [7], who achieved the fitting of 90% of the faces within a distance measure of 0.075 and 96% within a distance measure of 0.15. In our experiment 90% of all faces are fitted within a distance measure of 0.09 and the distance measure for fitting 96% is 0.13.

6   Related Work

The insights and the approach of Ginneken et al. [8] are most comparable to our work. They consider objective functions to be ideal if they fulfill properties similar to P1 and P2. Annotated training images serve for learning local objective functions. Their approach also determines relevant image features from a set of image features. However, they do not learn the objective function from an ideal objective function but manually specify calculation rules. Therefore, their approach aims at obtaining Property P1 but does not consider Property P2.

Furthermore, their approach turns out to be slow, which is a direct result from applying the k-Nearest-Neighbor classifier.

Currently, model fitting is often conducted using Active Appearance Models [2], which do not only contain the contour of the object but also the texture of the surface as it appears in the training images. The objective function is usually taken to be the sum of the square pixel errors between the synthesized texture of the model and the underlying image. Model fitting aims at minimizing this error by conducting a gradient decent approach. Obviously, this approach matches P1 very well. However, this approach does not consider P2 at all. Therefore, model fitting only achieves reasonable results within a small convergence area around the ideal model parameters.

7   Summary and Outlook

In this paper, we formalize the properties of ideal objective functions and give a concrete example of such functions. Since designed objective functions are far from ideal. Therefore, we have developed a novel method that learns objective functions from annotated example images. This approach automates many critical decisions and the remaining manual steps require less domain-dependent knowledge. The resulting objective functions are more accurate, because automated learning algorithms select relevant features from the many features provided and customize each local objective function to local image conditions. Since many images are used for training, the learned objective function generalizes well. Using a publicly available image database, we verify that learned objective functions enable fitting algorithms to robustly determine the best fit.

Ongoing research applies our method to tracking three-dimensional models through image sequences. They exploit knowledge from the current image to bias search in the next image, which makes them perform fast and accurately.

References

1. Hanek, R.: Fitting Parametric Curve Models to Images Using Local Self-adapting Separation Criteria. PhD thesis, Technische Universität München (2004)
2. Cootes, T.F., Taylor, C.J.: Statistical models of appearance for computer vision. Technical report, University of Manchester, Manchester M13 9PT, UK (2004)
3. Cootes, T.F., Taylor, C.J.: Active shape models – smart snakes. In: Proc. of the 3rd British Machine Vision Conference 1992, pp. 266–275. Springer, Heidelberg (1992)
4. Viola, P., Jones, M.: Rapid object detection using a boosted cascade of simple features. In: Computer Vision and Pattern Recognition (CVPR) (2001)
5. Witten, I.H., Frank, E.: Data Mining: Practical machine learning tools and techniques, 2nd edn. Morgan Kaufmann, San Francisco (2005)
6. Jesorsky, O., Kirchberg, K.J., Frischholz, R.: Robust face detection using the hausdorff distance. In: Proc. of the 3rd Int. Conference on Audio- and Video-Based Biometric Person Authentication, Halmstad, Sweden, pp. 90–95. Springer, Heidelberg (2001)

7. Cristinacce, D., Cootes, T.F.: Facial feature detection and tracking with automatic template selection. In: 7th IEEE International Conference on Automatic Face and Gesture Recognition, Southampton, England, pp. 429–434. IEEE Computer Society Press, Los Alamitos (2006)
8. Ginneken, B., Frangi, A., Staal, J., Haar, B., Viergever, R.: Active shape model segmentation with optimal features. Trans. on Medical Imaging 21, 924–933 (2002)

Analyzing the Variability of the 3D Structure of Chromatin Fiber Using Statistical Shape Theory

Siwei Yang[1], Sandra Götze[2], Julio Mateos-Langerak[2], Roel van Driel[2], Roland Eils[1], and Karl Rohr[1]

[1] Biomedical Computer Vision Group, Dept. Theoretical Bioinformatics, DKFZ Heidelberg, and University of Heidelberg, IPMB, Dept. Bioinformatics and Functional Genomics, Im Neuenheimer Feld 267, D-69120 Heidelberg, Germany,
[2] Swammerdam Institute for Life Sciences (SILS), University of Amsterdam, BioCentrum Amsterdam, Kruislaan 318, 1098 SM Amsterdam, The Netherlands
s.yang@dkfz.de

Abstract. The relationship between geometric folding of the chromatin fiber and genome function is a key issue in cell biology. We propose different approaches based on statistical shape theory to investigate the geometric variability of chromatin folding in nuclei of interphase human fibroblasts. Our main purpose is to assess the degree of variability of folding of the chromatin fiber, measured by fluorescent in situ hybridization, using BAC probes in combination with 3D confocal microscopy. We employ point-based registration, the complex Bingham distribution, generalized Procrustes analysis, and the Kendall spherical coordinate system. The approaches have been applied using 337 3D multi-channel microscopy images. We have analyzed the geometric structure formed by gene-rich highly expressed genomic regions and areas that are gene-poor and have a low transcriptional activity. It turned out that the structure formed by these genomic regions exhibit high shape variation, however, most of them can be characterized by a non-uniform shape distribution.

1 Introduction

The common model of the 3D structure of chromatin assumes that the DNA folds around histone octamers, forming arrays of nucleosomes in a 10 nm fiber, which folds into 30 nm diameter chromatin filament. Remarkably, little is known about higher order folding, despite the fact that the 3D organization of the chromatin fiber plays an important role in the control of gene expression [1]. In this work we are interested in the 3D geometric properties of large-scale chromatin fiber of interphase cells. The general motivation consists in relating geometric information to genome function, in order to obtain a better understanding of how the large-scale chromatin structure affects gene regulation in normal and abnormal cells (for recent surveys on this issue we refer to [2] and [3]). The main purpose of our work is to analyze the variability of the 3D geometric structure formed by different genomic regions identified by fluorescent in situ hybridization (FISH) with bacterial artificial chromosome (BAC) probes. We have acquired

F.A. Hamprecht, C. Schnörr, and B. Jähne (Eds.): DAGM 2007, LNCS 4713, pp. 497–506, 2007.
© Springer-Verlag Berlin Heidelberg 2007

337 three-color 3D confocal microscopy images of nuclei of human fibroblasts in which three genomic regions were FISH labelled on the q-arm of chromosome 1. In this way each image contains a cell nucleus with three spots, representing three genomic regions on the same chromosome, that form a triangle, denoted as BAC-triangle (see Fig. 1, top left and bottom). We analyze the gene-rich and highly expressed genomic regions (called ridges [4]) and the gene-sparse genomic regions showing low gene expression (called anti-ridges). To assess the variability of the structures labelled by the BACs we propose different approaches.

Prior to a statistical evaluation we first apply 3D point-based registration to transform the BACs onto the x-y plane. The purpose is to normalize the data and to reduce the dimensionality of the problem from 3D to 2D. Second, we perform statistical shape analysis to evaluate the shape variability of the datasets. Our analysis is based on the following two approaches: The complex Bingham distribution model [5], which involves one parameter that characterizes the degree of variability of the data, and the generalized Procrustes Analysis (GPA) [6], which captures the dominant variation of the data. In addition, we employ Kendall's spherical coordinate system [7] to visualize the shape distribution of the BAC-triangles. According to our knowledge statistical shape analysis has not yet been used to assess the variability of the 3D structure of chromatin fibers.

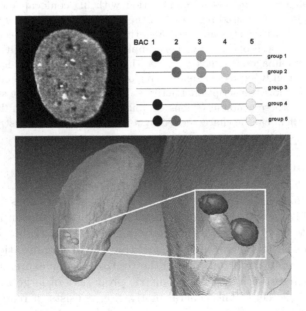

Fig. 1. Top left: One section of a 3D original microscopy image of a cell nucleus; Top right: Relation between BACs and groups of datasets; Bottom: 3D visualization of a cell nucleus and three BACs

2   3D Image Data

Our study is based on 3D microscopy images of human fibroblasts, which were stained by fluorescence in situ hybridization (FISH). The images are multi-channel images and have a resolution of $512 \times 512 \times 100$ voxels. The data was acquired in five different groups according to the scheme sketched in Fig. 1, top right. For subsequent groups there is an overlap of two BACs. For example, within group 1 the BACs 1,2,3 are stained, whereas in group 2 the BACs 2,3,4 are stained. In total, we have acquired 337 datasets that are divided into 10 groups: 5 groups for BACs with low expression level (anti-ridges BACs) and 5 groups for BACs with high expression level (ridge BACs). Each group represents three different BACs (forming BAC-triangles) which were observed in about 30 cells. The labeled BACs appear as fluorescent spots in the images. To localize the spots, we apply threshold-based segmentation and compute the centers of gravity of the BACs.

Besides the real datasets we have generated two sets of simulated data which serve as reference datasets. First, we created 50 triangles with low variability. The vertices of the triangles are isotropic normally distributed $N(\mu, \sigma)$, where $\sigma = 0.05$ and the mean side length of the triangles is 0.82. We denote this dataset by "stable triangles". Also we created a dataset "random triangles" which consists of 50 triangles, whose vertices are uniformly distributed within a unit cube.

3   Methods

3.1   Point-Based Rigid Registration

Prior to applying different techniques from statistical shape theory, we employ 3D point-based rigid registration (translation, rotation) to transform all 3D BAC-triangles onto the x-y plane (reference system). 3D point-based registration can be formulated as follows. Given k source points $\mathbf{p_i}$, and k target points $\mathbf{q_i}$, the task is to find a rigid transformation $\mathbf{R}$ such that $\sum_{i=1}^{k} \|\mathbf{q_i} - \mathbf{p_i} \circ \mathbf{R}\|^2$ is minimized. To register BAC-triangles ($k = 3$) onto the x-y plane, we arbitrarily selected a triangle in this plane as the target structure, and applied the algorithm of Horn [8]. After registration, each vertex of the triangles can be represented by a 2D coordinate or a complex number.

Note, that generally a random 2D triangle is labeled clockwise or counter-clockwise. However, the two labeling orders are equivalent for a 3D triangle, because the counter-clockwise order and the clockwise order can be transformed to each other by a 3D rotation. It means that after 3D point-based registration there is exclusively one kind of labeling order of triangles, i.e. either only clockwise or only counter-clockwise. This is called removing the reflection shape [7].

3.2   Complex Bingham Distribution

After having transformed the BAC-triangles onto the x-y plane, we use the complex Bingham distribution to model the shape distribution. This technique provides an elegant framework for the analysis of 2D shape data [7]. The main advantage is that only one parameter is involved and that this parameter characterizes the degree of shape variability, e.g., it indicates whether the shape distribution of triangles has the tendency to be uniform. Below, we introduce the complex Bingham distribution in the context of our application.

Given a set of n triangles (number of vertices $k = 3$), which have been transformed onto the x-y plane. Each triangle can be represented by a 3D complex vector $\tilde{\mathbf{z}}_i = (\tilde{z}_{i1}, \tilde{z}_{i2}, \tilde{z}_{i3})$, where $\tilde{z}_{ij} \in \mathbb{C}, i = 1, ..., n$, and $j = 1, 2, 3$. A central issue is to examine whether the shape distribution of these triangles is uniform. In this case the shape of the triangles is random. First we have to remove undesirable effects from scaling and translation. To perform this step we need a special transformation (for details we refer to [7]). The transformed triangles are represented by 2D complex vectors $\mathbf{z}_i = (z_{i1}, z_{i2})$. The complex Bingham distribution has the following rotation-invariant probability density function:

$$f(\mathbf{z}) = c(\mathbf{A})^{-1} \exp(\mathbf{z}^* \mathbf{A} \mathbf{z}) \tag{1}$$

where $\mathbf{A}$ is a $(k - 1) \times (k - 1)$ Hermitian matrix, $c(\mathbf{A})$ is the normalizing constant, and $\mathbf{z}^*$ represents the complex conjugate of the transpose of $\mathbf{z}$. In the case of triangles ($k = 3$) $\mathbf{A}$ has two distinct eigenvalues λ_1 and λ_2 where $\lambda_1 > \lambda_2$. In order to investigate the form of the shape distribution, we need to determine λ_1 and λ_2, and examine whether λ_1 and λ_2 are approximately zero. If this is the case, then the triangles tend to have a uniform distribution in shape space. However, in our application the eigenvalues generally cannot be close to zero. The reason is, that for a uniform shape distribution both labeling orders for triangles must be included, however, 3D triangles only have one labeling order. The eigenvalues of $\mathbf{A}$ can be computed based on:

$$c(\mathbf{A}) = 2\pi^2 \sum_{j=1}^{k-1} a_j \exp(\lambda_j), \qquad a_j^{-1} = \prod_{i \neq j}^{k-1} (\lambda_j - \lambda_i) \tag{2}$$

Note, that the Bingham distribution remains unchanged if a constant is added to all eigenvalues. The consequence is that for the λ_i there is no unique solution. Fortunately, this non-uniqueness can be conveniently removed by setting the largest eigenvalue to zero without lost of generality. In our case, we set $\lambda_1 = 0$, which implies that the second eigenvalue λ_2 is negative. Then only one parameter remains, which makes our analysis easier. Hence

$$c(\mathbf{A}) = 2\pi^2 \left(\frac{1}{-\lambda_2} + \frac{\exp(\lambda_2)}{\lambda_2} \right) \tag{3}$$

λ_2 is usually estimated by means of maximum-likelihood estimation (MLE). First let $\mathbf{S} = \sum_{i=1}^{n} \mathbf{z}_i \mathbf{z}_i^*$ be the $(k - 1) \times (k - 1)$ complex sum of squares and products matrix. In the case of triangles ($k = 3$) $\mathbf{S}$ has two positive and distinct eigenvalues, i.e. $l_1 > l_2 > 0$. Note that $l_1 + l_2 = n$. The log-likelihood for the data reads: $L = l_2 \lambda_2 - n \log[c(\mathbf{A})]$ where l_2 is the smaller eigenvalue of the matrix $\mathbf{S}$ defined above.

Test of Uniformity To answer the question whether the data has a random shape, i.e., whether the BAC-triangles have uniform shape distribution, we perform the following statistical test. Generally, the shape space of 2D triangles is a spherical space instead of an Euclidean space. Its southern hemisphere contains all triangles with clockwise labeling, whereas all triangles with counter-clockwise labeling are located on the northern hemisphere. However, the shape space of 3D triangles consist of just one hemisphere [7], since 3D triangles have only one kind of labeling as mentioned above. Thus standard methods of directional statistics, which are particularly designed for statistics of spherical data, are not suited. However, the uniformity on the full sphere implies the uniformity on its both hemispheres. Therefore, one possible solution to overcome this drawback is to map half of the 3D triangles onto the other hemisphere. If the mapped dataset is uniform, then the original one is also uniform. To perform the mapping, for each triangle we randomly assign either its original or its reflected shape as input data. Using this scheme half of the data are located on the northern hemisphere and half of the data are located on the southern hemisphere. Subsequently we apply a statistical test on the spherical data as described by Mardia and Jupp [9]. First we need to establish the sum of squares and products matrix $\hat{\mathbf{S}}$, where the corresponding eigenvalues are $\hat{l}_1$ and $\hat{l}_2$. The test statistic $F = 3(\hat{l}_1 - \hat{l}_2)^2/n$ has a chi-squared distribution, i.e. $F \sim \chi_3^2$. This value can be used to determine whether the data is uniform, which is the case for large values of F at a certain significance level, e.g., for the upper 1% quantile of χ_3^2 we have the value 11.34.

3.3   Generalized Procrustes Analysis (GPA)

Apart from the evaluation based on the complex Bingham distribution we also investigate the dominant shape variation of BAC-triangles. The generalized Procrustes analysis (GPA) uses principal components to characterize the main tendency of structural variability (the term "generalized" indicates, that there are more than two objects involved).

First, it is necessary to compute the full Procrustes estimate of the mean shape [7] for a set of triangles. Afterwards, one can examine how the triangles vary with respect to the mean shape. For this purpose we take advantage of principal components analysis (PCA) of the Procrustes residuals [7]. Let the real vectors $\mathbf{r}_i, i = 1, ..., n$ be the Procrustes residuals, and $\mathbf{M}$ be the sample covariance matrix of $\mathbf{r}_i$, i.e. $\mathbf{M} = \frac{1}{n} \sum_{i=1}^{n} (\mathbf{r}_i - \bar{\mathbf{r}})(\mathbf{r}_i - \bar{\mathbf{r}})^T$ where $\bar{\mathbf{r}} = \frac{1}{n} \sum \mathbf{r}_i$. The orthonormal eigenvectors of $\mathbf{M}$ denoted by γ_i, are the principal components (PCs) of $\mathbf{M}$ with corresponding eigenvalues λ_i. The percentage of variability captured by the ith PC is $100\lambda_i^2 / \sum \lambda_i^2$. The effect of the i−th PC can be visualized by adding $\mathbf{r}$ on the mean shape, where $\mathbf{r} = \bar{\mathbf{r}} + c\lambda_i^{1/2}\gamma_i$ for a range of values of the standardized PC score c, typically $c = \pm 3$.

3.4   Kendall's Spherical Coordinates

To visualize the shape distribution of triangles we use Kendall's spherical coordinate system. Using this coordinate system each triangle is mapped to one point on a sphere. The points on the southern hemisphere represent the reflection shape of those triangles on the northern hemisphere. Furthermore, the two poles of the sphere correspond to an equilateral triangle and its reflection shape, whereas the flat triangles are found in the regions close to the equator. In our case, the reflection shapes of the triangles have been removed after 3D point-based registration. Hence we need to consider only one hemisphere of Kendall's spherical coordinate system. Before constructing this coordinate system it is necessary to compute Kendall's coordinates $(u, v) \in \mathbb{R}^2$ for each triangle (for details we refer to [7]). The Kendall's coordinates can be converted into Kendall's spherical coordinates using the following formula:

$$ x = \frac{1 - r^2}{2(1 + r^2)}, \quad y = \frac{u}{1 + r^2}, \quad z = \frac{v}{1 + r^2} \tag{4} $$

where $r^2 = u^2 + v^2$. Using (4) every triangle can be mapped to a point on the sphere.

Since we need to consider the shape distribution only on one hemisphere, we take advantage of the polar aspect of the Lambert-azimuthal equal-area projection to visualize our data. In this projection the north pole of the sphere is mapped to the center of one circle, whereas the equator is represented by the circle self.

3.5   Multidimensional Scaling (MDS)

To reconstruct the 3D structure of the BACs we apply multidimensional scaling (MDS). As input MDS uses a distance matrix. With this approach it is assumed that the shape variation of the BAC-triangles is relatively low. To establish the distance matrix in our application, we use the mean distances between each two BACs.

4   Experimental Results

For all datasets described in section 2 above we have applied 3D point-based rigid registration. As an example, Figs. 2a,b show the results of the registration for the real datasets AR1 and AR2. Figs. 2c,d visualize the datasets of the stable triangles and the random triangles. The registration removes the reflection shapes in the 2D plane. Therefore the transformed triangles can be evaluated using the complex Bingham distribution. Tab. 1 lists the values of $|\lambda_2|$ for all real datasets. The larger the value of $|\lambda_2|$, the lower is the shape variability of the triangles. For a comparison, we have also calculated the $|\lambda_2|$ value for the stable and random triangles yielding $|\lambda_s| = 162.52$ and $|\lambda_r| = 5.63$, respectively. Apparently, the real data are far from stable shapes. Except AR2 and AR4 all datasets are not random, since their $|\lambda_2|$ values are larger than $|\lambda_r|$. We have also applied the test of uniformity described in section 3.2 using a significance level of 1% yielding $\chi^2_{3;0.01} = 11.34$. The listed values for F in Tab. 1 reveal that all datasets except AR2 and AR4 are not uniformly distributed. This confirms the

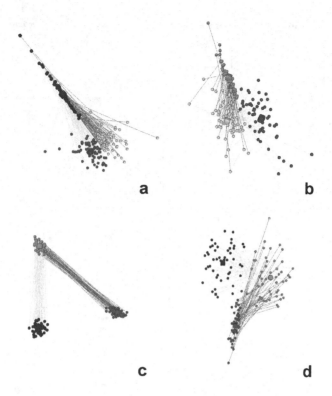

Fig. 2. Results after 3D point-based registration: Datasets AR1 (a), AR2 (b), stable triangles (c) and random triangles (d)

Table 1. Computed absolute values of λ_2 and result of the uniformity test for the real datasets

	Anti-ridge BACs					Ridge BACs				
	AR1	AR2	AR3	AR4	AR5	R1	R2	R3	R4	R5
$|\lambda_2|$	12.28	5.07	8.32	4.52	9.07	10.17	11.35	6.70	10.06	6.69
F	104.2	2.21	49.99	5.56	28.36	52.48	28.81	20.32	41.13	38.26

result using the complex Bingham distribution and the $|\lambda_2|$ values. Moreover, we can draw the same conclusion, if we use the heuristic criterion that the mean length of the triangles should be larger than three times the standard deviation of isotropic normally distributed vertices (which corresponds to a threshold value of $|\lambda_2| = 6.3$).

In Fig. 3 the results of the generalized Procrustes Analysis (GPA) are shown. Figs. 3a,b refer to the real datasets AR1 and AR2, and Figs. 3c,d to the stable and random triangles. The small circles represent the mean shape of the triangles (mean triangle). The vectors (circles attached to line segments) indicate the direction and magnitude of the variation along a certain principal

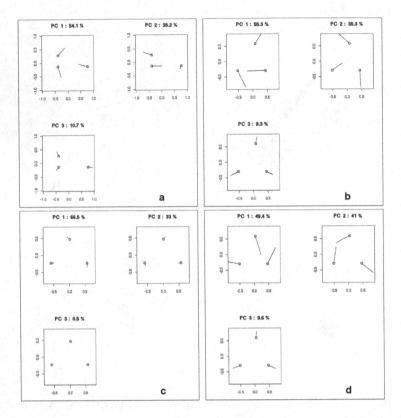

Fig. 3. GPA results including the percentage of variability captured by the i-th PC: Datasets AR1 (a), AR2 (b), stable triangles (c), and random triangles (d)

component (PC) of the Procrustes residual. Generally the first PC captures the most dominant variation. In comparison to the random triangles (Fig. 3d), both real datasets have a larger dominant variation along the first PC compared to the other PCs. However, the other two PCs still have a relatively high variability, in particular, compared to the stable triangles. Note that the magnitude of the vectors for dataset AR1 is smaller than for dataset AR2. Analysing all 10 real datasets it turns out that all BACs-triangles possess high shape variability.

Fig. 4 illustrates the shape distribution of the BAC-triangles using Kendall's spherical coordinate system. The points for dataset AR1 are located primarily in one quarter of the large circle. In contrast, the points for the dataset AR2 are scattered randomly, which is similar to the random dataset. The points of the stable dataset aggregate into a small region as expected. These observations agree with the computed $|\lambda_2|$ values of the complex Bingham distribution.

Finally we show the feasibility of multidimensional scaling (MDS). Fig. 5 displays the polygon through all investigated five anti-ridge and five ridge BACs (based on mean distances between every two BACs as mentioned above). It turns out that the structure of the anti-ridge BACs coils more compactly than that

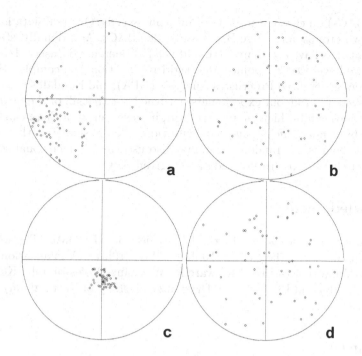

Fig. 4. Kendall's spherical coordinate system using Lambert's azimuthal equal-area projection. The north pole is represented by the center of the large circle. The results correspond to the datasets AR1 (a), AR2 (b), stable triangles (c), and random triangles (d).

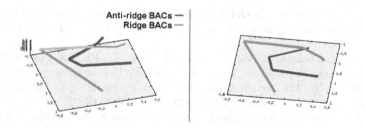

Fig. 5. Result of multidimensional scaling of anti-ridge and ridge BACs displayed from two different perspectives

of ridge BACs, which is what we expect. This is an interesting result, since we applied MDS although knew (based on the analysis above) that two of the ten dataset groups are randomly distributed.

5   Conclusion

We have presented different approaches based on statistical shape theory for analysing and assessing the variability of large-scale structure formed by genomic regions (BACs) on chromatin fibers of interphase cells. Our real data is divided into the two groups: anti-ridge BACs and ridge BACs. Additionally, stable and random datasets have been simulated and used as reference datasets. To evaluate the data we have used 3D point-based rigid registration, the complex Bingham distribution, generalized Procrustes Analysis (GPA), and Kendall's spherical coordinate system. From our experiments it turned out that all of the investigated dataset groups exhibit high shape variation, however, most of them can be characterized by a non-uniform shape distribution. This means that the structure of most of them is not random. We have also used multidimensional scaling to reconstruct the 3D structure based on the given BACs.

Acknowledgment

This work has been supported by the EU project 3DGENOME. The work benefited from the use of the Insight Toolkit (ITK) [10], the Visualization Toolkit (VTK) [11], and the statistical software R. We thank Professor John Kent (University of Leeds) and Professor Ian Dryden (University of Nottingham) for clarifying discussions.

References

1. Sproul, D., Gilbert, N., Bickmore, W.: The role of chromatin structure in regulating the expression of clustered genes. Nature Reviews Genetics 6, 775–781 (2005)
2. Verschure, P.J.: Positioning the genome within the nucleus. Biology of the Cell 96, 560–577 (2004)
3. Cremer, T., Küpper, K., Dietzel, S., Fakan, S.: Higher order chromatin architecture in the cell nucleus: on the way from structure to function. Biology of the Cell 96, 555–567 (2004)
4. Caron, H., van Schaik, B., van der Mee, M., Baas, F., Riggins, G., van Sluis, P., Hermus, M., van Asperen, R., Boon, K., Voute, P., Heisterkamp, S., van Kampen, A., Versteeg, R.: The human transcriptome map: clustering of highly expressed genes in chromosomal domains. Science 291, 1289–1292 (2001)
5. Kent, J.T.: The Complex Bingham Distribution and Shape Analysis. Journal of the Royal Statistical Society, Series B 56, 285–299 (1994)
6. Gower, J.C.: Gerneralized procrustes analysis. Psychometrika 40, 33–50 (1975)
7. Dryden, I., Mardia, K.: Statistical Shape Analysis. John Wiley & Sons, Chichester (1998)
8. Horn, B.: Closed-form solution of absolute orientation using unit quaternions. Journal of the Optical Society of America A 4, 629–642 (1987)
9. Mardia, K.V., Jupp, P.E.: Directional Statistics. John Wiley & Sons, Chichester (2000)
10. Ibanez, L., Schroeder, W., Ng, L., Cates, J.: The ITK Software Guide. Kitware, New York (2005)
11. Schroeder, W., Matin, K., Lorensen, B.: The Visualization Toolkit An Object-Oriented Approach To 3D Graphics, 3rd edn., Kitware, New York (2003)

Image-Matching for Revision Detection in Printed Historical Documents

Joost van Beusekom[1], Faisal Shafait[2], and Thomas M. Breuel[1]

[1] Department of Computer Science, Technical University of Kaiserslautern
D-67663 Kaiserslautern, Germany
joost@iupr.dfki.de, tmb@informatik.uni-kl.de
[2] Image Understanding and Pattern Recognition (IUPR) research group
German Research Center for Artificial Intelligence (DFKI) GmbH
D-67663 Kaiserslautern, Germany
faisal@iupr.dfki.de

Abstract. In the research area of historical documents it is of high interest to reconstruct the process of the emergence of a historical typesetted document. Therefore, the chronological order of the different versions of a typesetted document has to be reconstructed. This is done by manually finding differences in two versions and then deciding on the order between these two versions. In this paper we present an approach to automate the search for differences in both images. This approach uses a globally optimal image matching technique to overlay both images and colors the differences accordingly. We also present a real-world application for this approach on digitized versions of a historical book.

1 Introduction

For historians it is of interest to see how typesetted historical documents have evolved over different versions. At that time, printing a book was mostly a manual process: each letter of each page had to be typesetted manually and printing had also to be done manually. This allowed the typesetter to change characters or even words between the different printings of the book. These modifications allow today's historians to detect the chronological order of the printing of the books.

The process of chronologically sorting the versions starts with a very basic task: finding differences in the two versions. Currently this process has to be done manually: one person reads a version aloud and the other person checks whether the second version contains the same text or not.

This process is costly and time consuming. This first approach to automate the process would be the use of optical character recognition (OCR): however, an OCR-based approach does not work, as current optical character recognition systems do not give reliable results on historical document images. One main problem is the missing support for old fonts. Furthermore, textual noise from the facing book page, presence of many speckles, missing parts of the page and broken characters present frequent and challenging image defects that will further reduce OCR performance. Examples can be found in Figure 1.

F.A. Hamprecht, C. Schnörr, and B. Jähne (Eds.): DAGM 2007, LNCS 4713, pp. 507–516, 2007.
© Springer-Verlag Berlin Heidelberg 2007

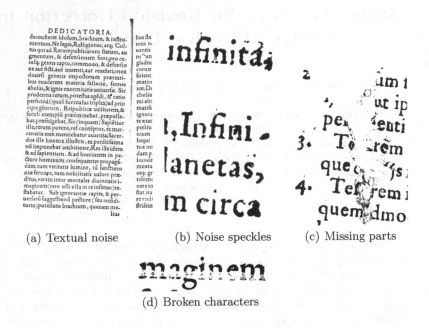

(a) Textual noise   (b) Noise speckles   (c) Missing parts

(d) Broken characters

Fig. 1. Examples for different types of defects in historical document images

Therefore, as a first step to automate this process, we present a method for visualizing differences on a pixel basis in the two documents. The resulting image allows the operator to quickly find relevant differences.

Another strong constraint is that, in our case, only limited influence on the digitization process is possible: some versions are scanned from microfilm, others from paper-based copies. Most images are available in black and white only. This dramatically reduces the available methods for noise removal and quality improvement for degraded document image, as many methods dealing with historical documents work on grey-scale images.

Considering all these problems, we concluded that first of all a global matching between two versions of the same document image has to be established. Therefore, scale, rotation and translation parameters have to be found that allow matching both images. This matching can then be used in later steps to allow comparison of smaller regions or even characters or parts of characters.

Visualizing the differences in historical document images by image matching, as presented in this paper, is closely related to image registration. Many different approaches have been presented for various kinds of tasks: in the field of medical images [MV98] solutions to many practical problems could be found. But also for many other applications, much work has been done. A good overview in this domain can be obtained in [Bro92] and [ZF03].

In the area of document image understanding, different methods for document image registration have been developed: Spitz et al. [Spi97] proposed a method for duplicate finding of document images by a text-based signature.

Other methods use the OCR output for registration. Liang et al. [LDD06] propose a registration method used for mosaicing camera-based document images, where registration is done using PCA-based SIFT descriptors.

As using OCR is no option for historical document images, feature point matching, as done in [LDD06] is a promising way to solve the problem. But as our document images are available only in binarized form, other point of interest as well as other features and a more robust matching method have to be chosen.

In Section 2 our approach is explained. In Section 4 results are presented. Finally Section 5 concludes this paper. Unfortunately, due to the specialized nature of this problem and due to the absence of any ground-truthed dataset for this purpose, no quantitative evaluation could be done. An overview over the system can be found in Figure 2.

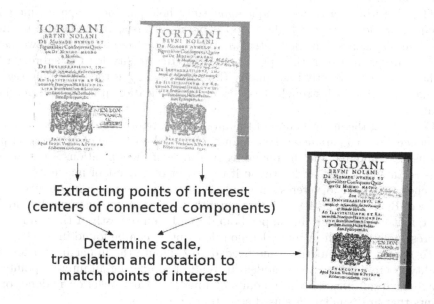

Fig. 2. System overview: first connected components are extracted as points of interest in both images. Then the optimal transformation given by scale, translation and rotation is computed to match the two sets of interest points. In the end, both images are overlaid.

2   Historical Document Image Matching

Given two images I and M. The goal is to find a set of parameters that allows to overlay both images as exact as possible. We define a perfect overlay as the set of parameters that matches the centers of all connected components of image I to the corresponding positions in image M, given that I is obtained by rotating, translating and scaling of M. Thus the quality function to optimize is the number of matching center points of the connected components. The 4 parameters that need to be found are the angle of rotation, the translation in horizontal and vertical direction and the scaling factor.

The method we used to determine the best parameters describing the transformation of the image I onto the image M is called RAST (Recognition by Adaptive Subdivision of Transformation Space) and was first presented by Breuel [Bre92]. This method is capable of finding globally optimal transformation parameters while avoiding to search the whole parameter space. This allows an optimal matching to be found and not, as currently done in many other procedures, only a locally optimal one.

RAST intelligently searches the whole parameter space $\mathcal{R} = [0, 2\pi) \times \mathbb{R}^2 \times \mathbb{R}^*_+$ for the globally optimal parameter set. The pseudo-code, taken from [Bre01], can be found in Figure 3.

The algorithm starts with enqueueing the whole parameter space (line 05). Then the region with the highest upper bound is taken from the queue (line 08). This is then subdivided into two parts (line 10 and 13). The two subregions are enqueued, if the upper bound for the quality for the subregion is higher than the currently best quality (line 19). Finally, if the remaining region is small enough, which strongly depends on the application, it is saved as possible solution.

Computing the upper bound of the quality of a parameter region is the main challenge. Given a parameter region, for each model point the possible target positions are computed and the bounding rectangle of these positions is extracted. This rectangle is used to determine if the point of interest of image M can be matched to a point of interest in image I. If this is the case, the quality is increased. Repeating this for all interest points in M leads to the upper bound for the quality. Computing this upper bound can be quite costly if the number of interest points is high. A more detailed description can be found in [Bre01].

To reduce the computing time needed to compute the upper bound for the quality, a pre-filtering step is added: instead of comparing all interest points of image M to all image interest points of image I, a pre-selection is done: only points that are "similar" are used as potential matches.

2.1   Filtering Using Fourier Descriptors of the Boundary

Using Fourier descriptors to describe boundaries of connected components is a widely used method. Many examples of very different applications of this technique exist, e.g. for shape-based retrieval [ZL01]. As we want to match document images based on connected components positions, one would expect, that a connected component representing an "a" will be matched to another connected component also representing an "a" and not to one representing an "x". Therefore, basing the filtering on features representing the contour of a connected component is a reasonable choice. Another advantage of the Fourier descriptors for the boundary is that they can be made less sensitive to noise by only considering the n first Fourier descriptors.

```
01    Queue active;
02    Region result = nil;
03
04    void match() {
05      enqueue(active, initial_region);
06
07      while(not_empty(queue)) {
08        Region current = dequeue(active) ;
09
10        Region left = expand(split_left(current));
11        if (left != nil) enqueue(active, left);
12
13        Region right = expand(split_right(current));
14        if (right != nil) enqueue(active, right);
15      }
16    }
17
18    Region expand(Region r) {
19      if (quality(r) <= quality(result)) return nil;
20
21      if (region_is_small_enough(r)) {
22        result = r ;
23        return nil ;
24      }
25
26      return r ;
27    }
```

Fig. 3. Pseudo-Code for the RAST algorithm [Brc01]

To obtain the Fourier descriptors of a connected component, the following steps have to be done:

- Step 1: Extraction of the boundary pixels. This is done using Pavlidis algorithm [Pav82]. A sequence of pixel positions is obtained.
- Step 2: "Conversion" of the contour to a sequence of complex values: a pixel position (x, y) is regarded as complex number $x + iy$.
- Step 3: Perform the Fast Fourier Transform (FFT) on the complex number signal. The result is a sequence of complex numbers called "Fourier descriptors".

Depending on the starting position of the pixel sequence describing the contour, the Fourier descriptors change. In order to be invariant to the starting position of the contour (this will happen frequently as images are rotated), the phase information is ignored and only the magnitude of the Fourier descriptor is used.

To define the similarity between two Fourier descriptor sequences, the mean of the differences of the magnitudes of the descriptors is taken.

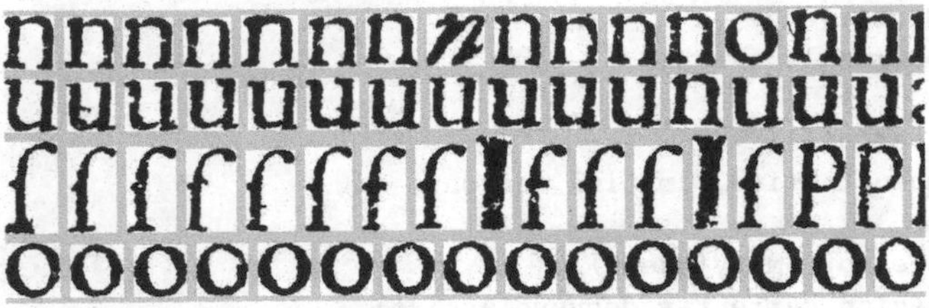

nnnnnnnn⁊nnnnnonnı
uuuuuuuuuuuunuuu⁊
ſſſſſſſſ]ſſſ]ſPPI
ooooooooooooooooo

Fig. 4. Example of similarity based on Fourier descriptors of the boundary. The left-most component in each row is a component from the image, the following are the most similar components from the model.

For each model point only the n most similar image points are taken as possible matches, where $n = 25$ showed to be a reasonable value. The number n should be high enough to ensure that the correct match is also in the list. It should not be too high as it will increase the time needed to estimate the upper bound. An example for some components together with their most similar components can be found in Figure 4.

3   Implementation Details

To reduce the number of connected components a connected component based filtering step has been added, as the most interesting connected components are the one that represent some character. This removes components that are to small or too big compared to the mean component size.

For the similarity measure of the contours only the 64 first Fourier descriptors are used as they contain enough information to give a rough description of the contour. This number may vary depending on the resolution of the document image.

Finally, as the image size of the available images is about 3400 × 4400 pixels, reasonable initial parameter space is defined by −900 to +900 pixels for translation in horizontal direction, −600 to +600 pixels for translation in vertical direction, a scale factor reaching from 0.9 to 1.1 and a rotation angle from −0.2*rad* to 0.2*rad*. A wider initial search space is also possible but increases the memory and time needs for finding the optimal parameter set.

4   Results

We tested our method on 69 pages of the book "De monade numero et figura liber Consequens Quinque De Minimo Magno & Mensura item De innumerabilis immenso & infigurabili; seu De Universo & De Mundis libri octo" written by Bruno Giordano. Two versions of the 69 pages were available. As no ground-truth for the given document images is available and as, to our best knowledge, no publically available dataset with historical document images and ground truth

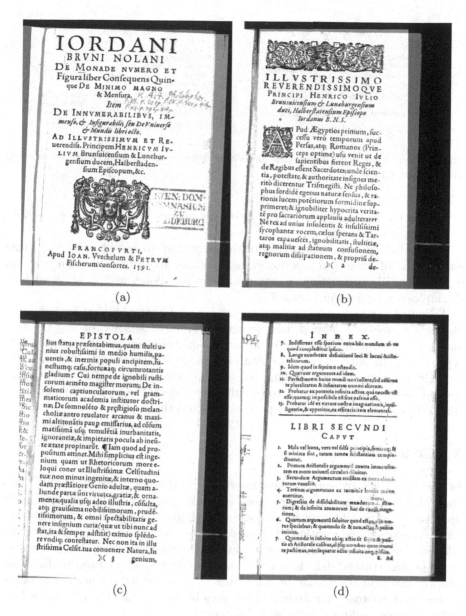

Fig. 5. Examples of correct matches. In Figure (d) one of the two document images was severely degraded. Nevertheless the matching overlaid the two images well.

is available, the only measure for success is visual inspection of the resulting images. This showed that the overlapping worked well in most cases. There are no examples where the matching was totally wrong. In some cases the overall matching was correct, but locally small discrepancies could be noticed. Example images where the matching worked well can be found in Figure 5.

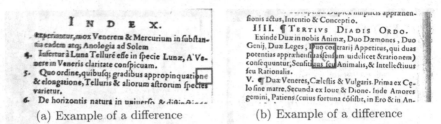

(a) Example of a difference   (b) Example of a difference

Fig. 6. Examples of resulting images containing differences. The differences are marked with a red rectangle.

In Figure 6 two examples of significant differences between the two versions of the book can be seen.

In a few images, there are parts of the page that do not fit as well as other parts. Most of these publicly matchings are due to distortions that can not be described by translation, rotation and scaling alone, as e.g. book curling. Examples can be seen in Figure 7.

A limited evaluation concerning the speed up factor obtained by using the highlighting method showed, that for two untrained persons reading the text aloud an checking for differences, about 5 minutes were needed to process a typical page (a part of the page can be seen in Figure 6 (a)). Checking the overlaid images to find the missing "e" took in mean about 1 minute. Although the number of tested persons is too small to be objective, one can conclude that this technique can speed up this process significantly.

5   Conclusion

In this paper we presented a first approach to automatically highlight differences in different versions of the same historical document. We used an globally optimal image matching technique allowing to find the optimal values for the scale, translation and rotation. Using these parameters, both images are overlaid, allowing the operator to identify quickly the differences between both versions.

As ground-truthed data is not yet available for this specialized problem, no quantitative evaluation could be done. However, we showed the usefulness of the highlighting approach for finding differences by measuring the time needed for a single person to find a word-level difference.

A main problem concerning this method is that it only is capable of matching images deformed by a similarity transform. This explains why curled pages are not matched perfectly (Figure 7). As dewarping curled pages is still an open problem, a local adaption of the obtained parameters on a connected component basis could be a good way to deal with this problem.

Furthermore, the current method is only applicable if the overall page is not changed by a small modification made in the text. This assumption does not hold for modern documents, as often changing a word results in different line

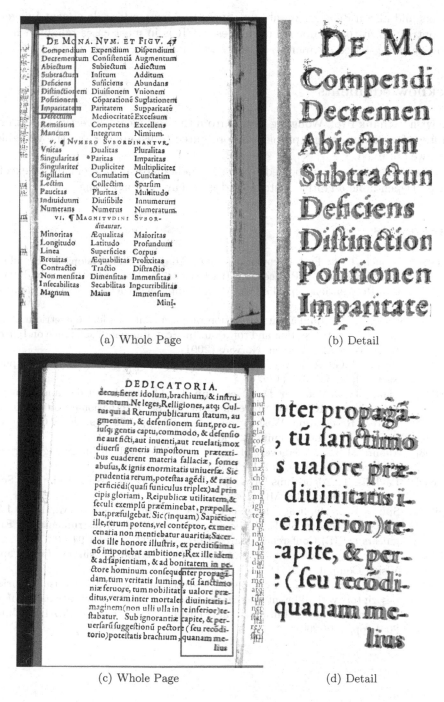

(a) Whole Page

(b) Detail

(c) Whole Page

(d) Detail

Fig. 7. Examples of resulting images that do not fit perfectly in all regions. This is due to non-similarity transforms on one of the images, e.g. book curling.

breaks and also a different number of lines. But for modern document images, in contrast to historical document images, OCR is in most cases reliable which allows a string-based comparing of two versions of a document.

Acknowledgments

We wish to thank Prof. Wolfgang Neuser from the Technical University of Kaiserslautern for the interesting problem he presented to us and also for the valuable data we obtained.

This work has been supported by the Rhineland-Palatinate cluster of excellence "Dependable adaptive systems and mathematical modeling".

References

[Bre92]   Breuel, T.M.: Fast Recognition using Adaptive Subdivisions of Transformation Space. In: Proceedings IEEE Conf. on Computer Vision and Pattern Recognition, pp. 445–451. IEEE Computer Society Press, Los Alamitos (1992)

[Bre01]   Breuel, T.M.: Implicit manipulation of constraint sets for geometric matching under 2d translation and rotation. In: Scandinavian Conference on Image Analysis (SCIA), Bergen, Norway (2001)

[Bro92]   Brown, L.G.: A survey of image registration techniques. ACM Comput. Surv. 24(4), 325–376 (1992)

[LDD06]   Liang, J., DeMenthon, D., Doermann, D.: Camera-based document image mosaicing. In: ICPR '06: Proceedings of the 18th International Conference on Pattern Recognition, Washington, DC, USA, pp. 476–479. IEEE Computer Society Press, Los Alamitos (2006)

[MV98]   Maintz, J.B.A., Viergever, M.A.: A survey of medical image registration. Medical Image Analysis 2(1), 1–36 (1998)

[Pav82]   Pavlidis, T.: Algorithms for Graphics and Image Processing. Computer Science Press, Rockville, MD (1982)

[Spi97]   Spitz, A.L.: Duplicate document detection. In: Vincent, L.M., Hull, J.J. (eds.) Proceedings SPIE, the Society of Photo-Optical Instrumentation Engineers (SPIE) Conference, March 1997, vol. 3027, pp. 88–94 (1997)

[ZF03]   Zitova, B., Flusser, J.: Image registration methods: a survey. Image and Vision Computing 21(11), 977–1000 (2003)

[ZL01]   Zhang, D.S., Lu, G.: A comparative study on shape retrieval using fourier descriptors with different shape signatures. In: Proc. of International Conference on Intelligent Multimedia and Distance Education (ICIMADE), June 2001, pp. 1–9 (2001)

Stochastic Optimization of Multiple Texture Registration Using Mutual Information

Ioan Cleju and Dietmar Saupe

University of Konstanz, Multimedia Signal Processing Group, Fach M697, 78457
Konstanz, Germany

Abstract. We consider the problem of simultaneously registering several images to a 3D model. We propose a global approach based on mutual information that extends previous methods to incorporate the color, and does not require segmentation or feature extraction. We give a stochastic model for joint optimization of multiple image-to-model alignment and we propose a heuristic to solve it. Experiments with synthetic models showed that our algorithm is robust to varying illumination and surface characteristics. Experiments with real data showed that we can achieve very good accuracy even for an object with highly specular surface, in moderate lighting conditions.

1   Introduction

A common framework for creating textured 3D models consists of two steps: firstly the geometry is built, and secondly the texture is mapped from photographs. The texture registration step searches for the projective transformation between the 3D model and the 2D images by solving the camera calibration problem. The parameters that define the projective transformation correspond to the parameters of the camera that acquired the image.

Classical closed-form and iterative numerical solutions for the camera calibration problem use point-feature pair correspondences [4]. Other methods involve more complex features such as silhouettes [6] and lines [2]. If several images are available, it is possible to use 2D-2D pair-features from images to improve the accuracy of the registration [6], [8].

Intensity-based registration techniques rely on global measures such as photo-consistency and mutual information, avoiding feature extraction. Viola and Wells use the mutual information between the normals to the surface and the intensity image to align a 3D model to the image [11]. Several images acquired by a system of cameras with known relative poses were registered to a 3D model using image-model mutual information [7] and photo-consistency [1]. The photo-consistency registration criterion is based on the assumption that any point on a surface with ideal Lambertian reflectance appears with the same color in all images where it is visible. In [5], photo-consistency was used to register two images with unknown relative pose to a 3D model.

We consider the problem of registering several images with unknown relative poses to a 3D model. Our solution extends the intensity-based approaches

F.A. Hamprecht, C. Schnörr, and B. Jähne (Eds.): DAGM 2007, LNCS 4713, pp. 517–526, 2007.

from [7], [1], and [5], considering both image-model and image-image mutual information as registration criteria. The contributions of our work are:

- we extend the mutual information registration method to several uncalibrated cameras;
- we propose a stochastic optimization model for the joint registration of several images to a 3D model;
- we show in experiments the advantages of our approach for complex illumination and surface characteristics;
- we experimentally confirm good accuracy of mutual information for texture registration even for a model with a highly specular surface.

In Section 2 we shortly review the texture registration by maximization of mutual information and we introduce the extension to consider color. In Section 3 we present a model for stochastic joint optimization and we give a heuristic solution. In Section 4 we show and discuss the experimental results, and in Section 5 we draw the conclusions and give some outlines for future work.

2 Texture Registration by Maximization of Mutual Information

Let x be a point on the surface of the 3D model that is visible in the texture image and T the 3D-2D projective transformation. Let $u(x)$ be the normal to the surface in x and $v(T(x))$ the intensity value in the image. The value of $v(T(x))$ is given by the rendering equation and depends on the radiance in the scene, the BRDF of the surface in x and the normal to the surface $u(x)$. The goal of the texture registration is to find the transformation T. Since the BRDF and the radiance are not known, Viola and Wells propose to directly exploit the relation between $u(x)$ and $v(T(x))$ by means of mutual information (MI) [11]. A random variable x on the 3D model that is visible in the image allows defining the random variables 'normal' $u(x)$, 'intensity' $v(T(x))$, and 'normal-intensity' $(u(x), v(T(x)))$. From their entropies we can define the MI between the normals to the surface and the intensity image (equations (1)). The MI between $u(x)$ and $v(T(x))$ is maximized when T aligns the model to the image.

Viola and Wells propose a gradient-based search for the optimal transformation T and a fast method to estimate the gradient of the MI with respect to T. If we consider a random variable y, its entropy $h(y)$ can be estimated from two independent samplings of y. One sampling is used to estimate the probability density function with the Parzen window method [3], which is then evaluated on the second sampling. The complexity of the method is quadratic in the size of the samplings. The MI between $u(x)$ and $v(T(x))$ is estimated from small subsamplings of the data (order of tens of points). When defined in this way, the MI can be differentiated with respect to T.

$$
\begin{aligned}
I(u(x), v(T(x))) &= h(u(x)) + h(v(T(x))) - h(u(x), v(T(x))) \\
\tfrac{d}{dT} I(u(x), v(T(x))) &= \tfrac{d}{dT} h(v(T(x))) - \tfrac{d}{dT} h(u(x), v(T(x)))
\end{aligned}
\tag{1}
$$

Due to the small random subsampling of data, the estimation of the MI gradient is stochastic. Viola and Wells use stochastic gradient descent as the optimization procedure. The subsamplings are changed at each iteration and T is updated in the direction of the gradient. Local maxima of MI can be avoided due to the inherent noise of the gradient.

In [9], a 3D model with reflectance values mapped on its surface was registered to color images using the method of Viola and Wells (the reflectance values were obtained during 3D scanning). The MI has become popular especially in medical image registration.

We extended Viola and Wells' algorithm to register several textures on a 3D model by considering images that contain common patches of the model. If a patch of the surface is visible in two images, we will simply say that the images overlap.

We define image-image MI functions for each overlap. Given two overlapping images i and j with corresponding projective transformations T_i and T_j, let x be a random point on the surface visible in both images. The MI between the colors $v_i(T_i(x))$ and $v_j(T_j(x))$ of the images i and j is then:

$$I(v_i(T_i(x)), v_j(T_j(x))) = h(v_i(T_i(x))) + h(v_j(T_j(x))) - h(v_i(T_i(x)), v_j(T_j(x)))$$
(2)

This extension adds the full color information of the images to the registration objective functions. In our implementation we defined the image-image MI from the chrominance components I and Q of the YIQ color space. The image-image MI is parameterized by the projective transformations associated with both images, and it is maximized when both images are aligned to the model. The gradient estimation follows the same procedure as for the image-model MI.

Compared to other registration criteria, the MI does not need the existence of any 3D-2D feature, including visible outlines in the image, and does not make assumptions on the unknown parameters of the rendering function. It is robust to illumination conditions and even to occlusions [11]. One problem when using the MI objective function is that the value of the global maximum cannot be estimated. In contrast, when registration is done with point correspondences, for instance, the global optimum corresponds to 0 projection error.

2.1   Camera Model

The optimization model does not make assumptions on the projective transformation T, and consequently on the camera model. In our implementation we considered the pinhole camera model [4] with four distortion coefficients (two for radial distortion and two for tangential distortion). The intrinsic parameters field-of-view, optical center, and distortions, were calibrated using Zhang's method [12]. Any of the intrinsic parameters can be further optimized using the mutual information objective functions. We considered the intrinsic parameters fixed and we optimized only the extrinsic parameters. The rotation matrix was parameterized by axis-angle form for its advantages over Euler angles in the iterative optimization [10].

3   A Stochastic Optimization Model for Global Texture Registration

For the joint registration of several images to a 3D model we formulated image-model and image-image MI objective functions. When all images are aligned to the model, all objective functions are maximized. If only the image-model MI functions are considered, each set of camera parameters corresponds to one objective function. In this case the iterative gradient-based optimization updates each set of parameters in the direction of the corresponding gradient. When also image-image MI functions are considered, we estimate several gradients for the parameters of each camera, corresponding to the MI with the model and with other overlapping images. In each iteration we must choose the direction for optimization based on the these gradients. In this section we motivate and discuss the fusion of the gradients for the update direction.

Let n be the number of cameras (images), t_i the approximate parameters for camera i, t_i^* the optimal parameters for camera i and δ_i the error.

$$t_i = t_i^* + \delta_i \quad \text{for} \quad i = 1, \ldots, n \tag{3}$$

Let $g_{i,0}$ be the estimated gradient of the MI between the image i and the model, $g_{i,j}$ be the estimated gradient of the MI between the image i and the (overlapping) image j and $g_{i,j}^*$ the true value of the gradient. Let $\epsilon_{i,j}$ be the error introduced in the estimation of the gradient by the data subsampling. Let overlap$(i, 0)$ state the existence of the overlap between texture i and the model (it is always true), and, for $j \neq 0$, overlap(i, j) the existence of the overlap between the textures i and j, then:

$$g_{i,j} = g_{i,j}^* + \epsilon_{i,j}, \quad \text{for} \quad i = 1, \ldots, n, \quad j = 0, \ldots, n, \quad \text{if overlap}(i, j) = true \tag{4}$$

Let us consider the objective functions corresponding to the image i. Since all of them are maximized for the correct alignment, any linear combination of these functions with positive weights has the global optimum for the same camera parameters. On the other hand, we expect the other local optima to be less related. For example, the image-model MI objective function relies on normals and intensities in comparison to image-image MI objective functions that are based on colors.

Therefore, we think that, in general, a linear combination of the objective functions has a more emphasized global optimum and faded local optima (that are not global) than any of the individual functions. Since the gradient of the summed objective functions is the sum of the gradients, we look for an update direction as a linear combination of individual gradients.

We observe another positive effect of this formulation. The gradients of the objective functions are perturbed by the estimation errors $\epsilon_{i,j}$ as artifacts of sub-sampling. Since the subsamplings are independent, the errors are independent, and their effect is not increased after the linear combination.

The update directions have the form:

$$g_i = \sum_{j=0,\mathrm{overlap}(i,j)}^{n} w_{i,j} g_{i,j} \quad \text{for} \quad i = 1,\ldots,n, \quad j = 0,\ldots,n \qquad (5)$$

The canonical approach is to assign equal weights for each gradient. Following similar intuitive reasoning as above, an even better update direction may be estimated if the weights of the gradients are correlated with the probability that the current estimation lies in the region of attraction of the global optimum of the corresponding objective function. In the following subsection we give a heuristic for this problem.

3.1 Weighted Gradient Fusion

Before defining the weights from equation (5), we introduce some additional variables. The gradient of MI is 'consistent' if its direction does not change considerably for consecutive iterations. For the gradient of MI between items i and j at iteration k, we define the 'instantaneous consistency' $c_k(i,j)$ and the 'consistency' $C_k(i,j)$:

$$
\begin{aligned}
c_k(i,j) &= \tfrac{1}{2}(\cos(g_{k-1,i,j}, g_{k,i,j}) + 1) && \text{for} \quad k \geq 1 \\
C_k(i,j) &= (1-\alpha)C_{k-1}(i,j) + \alpha c_k(i,j) && \text{for} \quad k \geq 1, \quad 0 \leq \alpha \leq 1
\end{aligned}
\qquad (6)
$$

We start with initial values zero for $c_0(i,j)$ and $C_0(i,j)$. $g_{k,i,j}$ is the estimation $g_{i,j}$ at iteration k. $C_k(i,j)$ measures the consistency over a sequence of iterations, where the most recent instantaneous consistencies have a larger weight. A gradient has low consistency if the MI function has poor convexity, if $\epsilon_{i,j}$ is considerable in (4), or if an optimum is already attained. In the implementation α was set to 0.05.

We introduce the 'alignment' variable $A_k(i,j)$ to measure the alignment between the items i and j. The alignment at iteration k is estimated as the maximum value of consistency for that gradient:

$$A_k(i,j) = \max_{l=1,\ldots,k} C_l(i,j) \qquad (7)$$

A large value of $A_k(i,j)$ does not mean that i and j are aligned at iteration k, but rather it indicates that the parameter estimation lies on the region of attraction of a pronounced local optimum. We can estimate that the texture i attained a pronounced local optimum after k iterations if the consistency $C_k(i,0)$ is small but the alignment $A_k(i,0)$ large.

We may now define the weights for equation (5):

$$
\begin{aligned}
w_{i,j} &= C(i,j)A(j,0)(1 - \tfrac{C(j,0)}{A(j,0)}), && \text{for} \quad i = 1,\ldots,n, \quad j = 1,\ldots,n \\
w_{i,0} &= C(i,0), && \text{for} \quad i = 1,\ldots,n
\end{aligned}
\qquad (8)
$$

For simplicity, we omitted the iteration number k in (8). The weights are re-computed in each iteration. From equations (6) and (7) it follows that $w_{i,j}$ are between 0 and 1. The weight $w_{i,j}$ ($j > 0$) is large when the alignment between the texture j and the model is large but the consistency is small (image j and the model are possibly aligned), and when the gradient between i and j is consistent.

4   Implementation Issues and Experimental Validation

We implemented our texture registration method on a point-based framework [13]. We present results for optimization of the extrinsic parameters of the cameras. The probabilities used in the stochastic framework were estimated using 6-dimensional gradients. We used different updating step sizes for rotation and translation. In each iteration, the updating direction was normalized separately for rotation/translation, and we made steps in the updating direction. We are currently working on implementing optimization with adaptive step sizes. For each experiment presented in Fig. 2, the optimization consisted in 2000 iterations.

We compared three registration algorithms. The first algorithm uses only image-model MI (Viola_TR_MI), the second uses equal weights of the gradients in equation (5) (Canonical_TR_MI), and the third algorithm uses adaptive weights computed using equation (8) (Weighted_TR_MI). For a fair comparison, we restricted the computation for the estimation of the gradients (the number of kernel estimations in the Parzen window method) to obtain the same computation effort for all methods. In all experiments we used three texture images, all overlapping. Correspondingly, there are 3 times more MI objective functions for Canonical_TR_MI and Weighted_TR_MI than for Viola_TR_MI. We used subsampling sizes of 100 points for Viola_TR_MI and of 58 for the other two, thus having roughly the same number of kernel estimations in the Parzen window method (the complexity is quadratic in subsampling sizes). Almost all the runtime was spent for gradient estimation. The corresponding speed was roughly 100 iterations per second for each texture, on a Pentium 4 at 3 GHz. From time to time full z-buffer projections have to be done (once for hundreds of iterations). Disregarding cache-memory issues and full z-buffer projections, the running time is independent on the size of the model.

We evaluated the accuracy of the registration using ground truth. For the real case, we estimated the extrinsic camera parameters 5 times, each time with 20-25 point correspondences chosen interactively, and we averaged the parameters. Two types of errors can be defined: parameter error (matrix distance between optimized parameters and ground truth) and projection error. The projection error is the root mean squared distance from the projections of all points of the 3D model on the image plane using optimized parameters to the projections obtained by true parameters [5]. We averaged the errors for the images.

The characteristics of the experiments are summarized in the table. Images of the models are shown in Fig. 1. We randomly perturbed the ground truth (rotation and translation) to simulate initial inexact parameters, and ran the optimization algorithms.

Details	Experiment Index					
	1	2	3	4	5	6
Model Name	Square1	Square2	Square3	Square4	Trilobite	Shakyamuni
Model Type	Synthetic				Real	
No. Points	40 000				726 027	1 693 444
Reflectance	Isotropic		Anisotropic			-
Surface Type	Diffuse and Specular				Diffuse	-
Light	Directional	Directional and Ambient			Directional	Light Tube
Photographs	3 Rendered					3 Real
Resolution	800 × 600				1062 × 864	2048 × 1536
Overlap	Total			Partial		
Ground Truth	Known					Estimated

For experiments 1-4 we used planar square models with normals, colors, diffuse and specular surface reflectance coefficients introduced as a mixture of Gaussians (e.g., the normals were bump mapped) with the same distribution of the variances. The first three models have the surface properties distributed all over the surface. One half of the fourth model has perturbed normals and white color; the other half constant normal and varying color (Fig. 1). For the first three experiments we used images with the whole models, and for the fourth experiment each image covers about 60% of the model, containing the two different halves in different ratios.

In experiment 5 we used the Trilobite model from Arius3D (www.arius3d.com). The model was acquired with a special high resolution scanner capable of sampling the color, and we simulated the photographs by rendering.

The last experiment was performed with the Shakyamuni model from the University of Konstanz (www.inf.uni-konstanz.de/cgip/projects/surfac). The photographs were taken in a room illuminated by one light tube (about 2 meters in length), placed at the ceiling at about 5 meters from the model. We show results for registration of three images taken from front, front-left and front-right. The images were used at full resolution, without any preprocessing. For visual assessment of the registration, we drew two vertical and two horizontal lines on the model (see Fig. 1, bottom left) and we show close views with the model textured with initial and optimized parameters.

We show the results in Fig. 2 plotting the average projection error in pixels over all texture images versus the initial projection error before optimization. We observed a decrease of accuracy when ambient light (experiment 2) and varying reflectance coefficients (experiment 3) were introduced. The accuracy of Canonical_TR_MI and Weighted_TR_MI was similar, considerably higher than Viola_TR_MI.

In the experiment 4, Weighted_TR_MI gave the best accuracy for all runs, performing considerably better than Canonical_TR_MI. For the settings of this experiment, the global optima of some objective functions were pronounced, while other objective functions had many local optima. In particular, the

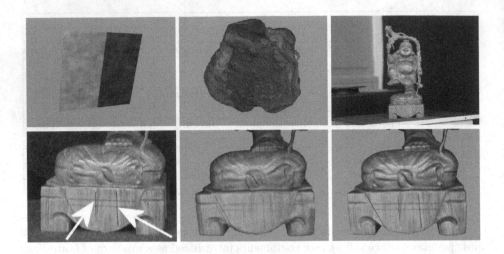

Fig. 1. Models used for evaluation. Top row: Square4 (left), Trilobite (middle), and Shakyamuni (right). Bottom row: part of Shakyamuni photo (left), remark the hand drawn lines; renderings with initial registration (middle) and optimized registration (right) of three photos.

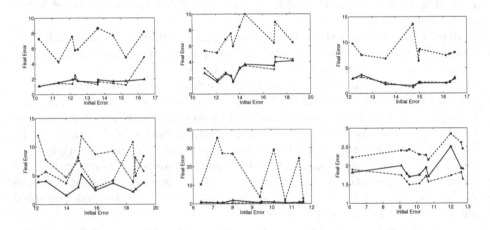

Fig. 2. Comparison between Viola_TR_MI (dashed), Canonical_TR_MI (dashdot), and Weighted_TR_MI (solid) for experiments 1 (upper left) to 6 (bottom right), for several initial parameters. The plots show initial projection error (horizontal axis) versus final projection error (vertical axis) in pixel units. The errors are averaged for all images.

image-model MI was a good objective function for only one of the images. Our heuristic identified and assigned higher weights to the gradients of the functions with pronounced global optima.

For the Trilobite model, in 6 out of 10 runs of Viola_TR_MI the error increased. The other two algorithms achieved the best results out of our experiments: the projection errors of Canonical_TR_MI were under 0.8 pixels, and the largest error of Weighted_TR_MI was 1.8 pixels, while the other 9 errors were under 1.2 pixels. We see two causes for the better accuracy of Canonical_TR_MI and Weighted_TR_MI for the Trilobite model as compared to the synthetic models. Firstly, specular coefficients associated to the surface of the synthetic models allowed modelling of more complex BRDF. Secondly, the distribution of the surface properties on the synthetic models determined MI objective functions with many local maxima.

The most visible features in the images with the Shakyamuni model are the specular highlights, and this may pose serious problems for other registration algorithms. The compared methods gave very good results, with slightly worse performance of Viola_TR_MI. We were even able to register images from an initial average error of about 60 pixels. The visual difference between renderings with estimated ground truth parameters and optimized parameters cannot be perceived.

It is difficult to present direct comparisons to other registration algorithms. Our accuracy is significantly better than the one reported in [5], mean projection error of 5-6 pixels for 512×512 resolution images, and also much faster. Involving only mutual information, the algorithm is conceptually simpler than [8], and does not require the texture image to contain the entire object for the purpose of silhouette extraction as in [8] and [6].

5   Conclusions and Future Work

We motivated and proved experimentally the advantages of joint registration of several images to a 3D model using the mutual information. By considering the image-image mutual information, introduced in this paper, we improved significantly the registration accuracy in all experiments. Our heuristic for the weighted gradient fusion clearly outperformed the canonical approach in only one experiment. We are looking for other heuristics, for instance choosing the update direction using a voting scheme among gradients. Similar methods may be used to adjust the computational effort, e.g., by allocating more run-time to estimate the gradients of the relevant objective functions.

We will study the performance of our algorithm for optimization of the intrinsic camera parameters. After obtaining a good estimation for extrinsic camera parameters with the method described above, a similar refining optimization step should consider all camera parameters. We want to improve the optimization by adaptive step sizes in the gradient descent, using for instance the consistency of the gradient (defined in this paper). This can be combined with a multiresolution approach proposed in other registration methods. Finally, we will complete the texture mapping framework by implementing the texture fusion for 3D point based models.

Acknowledgments

The work was supported by the DFG GK 1042 'Explorative Analysis and Visualization of Large Information Spaces' at the University of Konstanz, Germany. The Trilobite model was provided by Arius3D www.arius3d.com.

References

1. Clarkson, M.J., Rueckert, D., Hill, D.L.G., Hawkes, D.J.: Using photo-consistency to register 2D optical images of the human face to a 3D surface model. IEEE Trans. Pattern Analysis and Machine Intelligence 23(11), 1266–1280 (2001)
2. David, P., DeMenthon, D., Duraiswami, R., Samet, H.: Simultaneous pose and correspondence determination using line features. In: Proc. Computer Vision and Pattern Recognition, pp. 424–431. IEEE Computer Society Press, Los Alamitos (2003)
3. Duda, R., Hart, P.: Pattern Classification and Scene Analysis. John Wiley and Sons, Chichester (1973)
4. Faugeras, O.: Three-Dimensional Computer Vision A Geometric Viewpoint. The MIT Press, Cambridge (1993)
5. Jank, Z., Chetverikov, D.: Photo-consistency based registration of an uncalibrated image pair to a 3D surface model using genetic algorithm. In: Second Int. Symposium on 3D Data Processing, Visualization and Transmission (3DPVT'04), pp. 616–622 (2004)
6. Lensch, H.P.A., Heidrich, W., Seidel, H.-P.: A silhouette-based algorithm for texture registration and stitching. Graphical Models 63(4), 245–262 (2001)
7. Leventon, M., Wells III, W.M., Grimson, W.E.L.: Multiple view 2D-3D mutual information registration. In: Image Understanding Workshop (1997)
8. Neugebauer, P.J., Klein, K.: Texturing 3D models of real world objects from multiple unregistered photographic views. Computer Graphics Forum 3(18), 245–256 (1999)
9. Nishino, K., Sato, Y., Ikeuchi, K.: Appearance compression and synthesis based on 3D model for mixed reality. In: Proc. IEEE Int. Conf. Computer Vision, pp. 38–45. IEEE Computer Society Press, Los Alamitos (1999)
10. Taylor, C.J., Kriegman, D.J.: Minimization on the Lie group SO(3) and related manifolds. Technical report, Center for Systems Science, Dept. of Electrical Engineering Yale University (1994)
11. Viola, P., Wells III, W.M.: Alignment by maximization of mutual information. Int. J. Computer Vision 24(2), 137–154 (1997)
12. Zhang, Z.: Flexible camera calibration by viewing a plane from unknown orientations. In: Proc. Int. Conf. Computer Vision, vol. 1, pp. 666–673 (1999)
13. Zwicker, M., Pfister, H., van Baar, J., Gross, M.H.: Surface splatting. In: Proc. SIGGRAPH, pp. 371–378 (2001)

Curvature Guided Level Set Registration Using Adaptive Finite Elements

Andreas Dedner[1], Marcel Lüthi[2], Thomas Albrecht[2], and Thomas Vetter[2]

[1] Institut für Angewandte Mathematik, Universität Freiburg, Germany
[2] Department of Computer Science, University of Basel, Switzerland

Abstract. We consider the problem of non-rigid, point-to-point registration of two 3D surfaces. To avoid restrictions on the topology, we represent the surfaces as a level set of their signed distance function. Correspondence is established by finding a displacement field that minimizes the sum of squared difference between the function values as well as their mean curvature. We use a variational formulation of the problem, which leads to a non-linear elliptic partial differential equation for the displacement field. The main contribution of this paper is the application of an adaptive finite element discretization for solving this non-linear PDE. Our code uses the software library DUNE, which in combination with pre- and post-processing through ITK leads to a powerful tool for solving this type of problem. This is confirmed by our experiments on various synthetic and medical examples. We show in this work that our numerical scheme yields accurate results using only a moderate number of elements even for complex problems.

1 Introduction

Virtually all methods in pattern recognition and image analysis rely on prior knowledge about the problem to be solved. Often, this prior knowledge is given in the form of statistical information acquired from a set of representative examples. In order to be able to extract meaningful information from several objects of a class, the objects have to be brought into correspondence. That is, to every point in a reference object, one needs to find the corresponding point in all the examples. The problem of establishing correspondence is known as the registration problem.

In this article we consider the problem of dense point-to-point registration of two 3D surfaces. Surface registration is a common problem and has been researched extensively (see [6] for a comprehensive survey). Most common approaches to surface registration are either formulated directly in terms of the given surface triangulation or require the surfaces to be parameterized. The approach we propose in this paper is to represent the surfaces as the zero-level set of the signed distance function to the surface. This formulation yields a problem description that is independent of the topology of the surface. Further, it leads naturally to a variational formulation and allows us to apply the powerful mathematical methods developed in this field (see e.g. [9]).

F.A. Hamprecht, C. Schnörr, and B. Jähne (Eds.): DAGM 2007, LNCS 4713, pp. 527–536, 2007.

While our method is general and can be applied to many surface registration tasks, our particular motivation stems from two problems in medical imaging. The goal is to build a statistical model of the human skull and the femur bone respectively. The human skull is a complex structure and finding a suitable surface parametrization is deemed infeasible. For registration of the femur, the advantage of our representation is that correspondence is established for a neighborhood around the surface, which helps later to fit the inner structures of the bones.

The idea of surface registration using a level-sets representation of the surfaces has been described earlier [18,14]. For the mathematical formulation, our contribution is the inclusion of an additional curvature term in the model that drives the registration in direction tangential to the surface, similar to [12]. The difference to our work is that the curvature is calculated on the parametrization, while we extend the curvature feature to the whole space.

This formulation and its relation to the well known Thirion's Demons algorithm [17] has been detailed in [13]. The main contribution of this paper is a memory-efficient and flexible representation of the data using adaptive finite elements together with its numerical implementation using the DUNE library [2]. The finite element representation gives the flexibility to represent fine details where this is needed (e.g. around the surface) while providing a sparse representation of the function. Further, the numerical method can be easily parallelized.

This paper is structured as follows: In Section 2 we present the mathematical model of our approach. Section 3 describes the finite element discretization and the numerical procedure we employ to solve the registration problem. The feasibility of our approach is illustrated in Section 4 where we show registration results for medical 2D and 3D examples. A more detailed study of the algorithm including variation of parameters and a comparison with a finite difference implementation in ITK [11] is published in [3].

2   Mathematical Model

In this section we present the mathematical model we use for surface registration. In general, registration is an ill-defined problem. The notion of correspondences can greatly vary for different applications. For our application, we define three criteria a good registration has to fulfill: 1) the surfaces should be accurately matched, 2) the curvature at corresponding points should be similar and 3) the deformation should be smooth. In the remainder of this section, we will make these notions precise.

2.1   Level-Set Representation

A common way to model a surface is by representing it as the zero level set of an auxiliary function $I : \mathbb{R}^n \to \mathbb{R}$. This means that the surface Γ is given as:

$$\Gamma := \{x \in \mathbb{R}^n \mid I(x) = 0\}.$$

The main advantage of the level-set representation is the independence of the surface's topology. In practice, the most common choice for representing a given surface $\Gamma \subset \mathbb{R}^n$ through a level set function is to use the signed distance function to Γ:

$$I(x) := d_\Gamma(x) = \begin{cases} \text{dist}(x, \Gamma) & x \in \text{outside}(\Gamma), \\ 0 & x \in \Gamma, \\ -\text{dist}(x, \Gamma) & x \in \text{inside}(\Gamma), \end{cases} \tag{1}$$

where $\text{dist}(x, \Gamma)$ is the Euclidean distance from x to Γ and the inside and outside of Γ have to be assigned in some meaningful way. When calculated on a rectangular domain $\Omega \subset \mathbb{R}^n$, the distance function can be interpreted as an image over Ω. This leads to the problem of intensity based, non-rigid image registration. In fact our formulation of the problem has been derived from Thirion's Demon algorithm, one of the most widely used image-registration algorithms.

2.2   Thirion's Demons

In his landmark paper, Thirion [17] proposed a method for three-dimensional, non-rigid image registration. Originally formulated in a heuristic manner as an optical flow like algorithm, it was later rigorously studied and formalized. In particular, Modersitzki [15] as well as Cachier et al. [16], have presented variational formulations of the Demons Algorithm, on which we base our work.

The Demons algorithm corresponds essentially to the variational problem of minimizing the functional

$$\mathcal{J}[u] = \mathcal{D}[u] + \alpha \mathcal{R}[u],$$

where

$$\mathcal{D}[u] = \frac{1}{2} \int_\Omega \frac{1}{Q_I(x)} (I_0(x + u(x)) - I_1(x))^2 \, dx$$

is a distance measure, and

$$\mathcal{R}[u] = \frac{1}{2} \sum_{l=1}^{3} \int_\Omega |\nabla u_l|^2 \, dx$$

is a regularization term. Here I_0 and I_1 are the images defined on Ω and $u : \Omega \to \mathbb{R}^3$ is the displacement field to be calculated. The parameter $\alpha \in \mathbb{R}$ controls the influence of the regularizer. The weight Q_I is chosen as $Q_I(x) = |\nabla I_0(x)|^2 + (I_0(x) - I_1(x))^2$, motivated by Thirion's original formulation. See [16] for a detailed discussion and interpretation of this term.

The registration problem is thus to find the deformation field u, that solves the following variational problem:

$$\mathcal{J}[u] = \mathcal{D}[u] + \alpha \, \mathcal{R}[u] \to \min. \tag{2}$$

From the calculus of variations, it is known that any solution has to fulfill the Euler-Lagrange equation:

$$\frac{1}{Q_I(x)} (I_0(x + u(x)) - I_1(x)) \nabla I_0(x + u(x)) - \alpha \triangle u(x) = 0, \ \forall x \in \Omega. \tag{3}$$

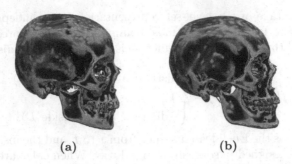

(a)   (b)

Fig. 1. Two skulls colored according to their mean curvature

This is a non-linear elliptic partial differential equation, which can, for example, be solved using the numerical method presented in Section 3.

2.3   Curvature Guided Registration

Thirion's Demons algorithm was designed for the registration of medical images (e.g. CT images), that feature meaningful information on the whole domain. In our approach the only information comes from the surface that represents the zero-level set. Furthermore, on the zero-level set, the value is by definition zero everywhere. We have no information about features that could guide the registration in surface direction. Hence corresponding points are, apart from the influence of the smoothing term $\mathcal{R}$, only sought in the direction normal to the level sets. The resulting correspondences on the zero-level do therefore not necessarily correspond to meaningful features. For a large class of objects, corresponding points in two surfaces have similar curvature. Therefore, we use the mean curvature at a point as an additional feature to be matched. Figure 1 illustrates that for registration of human skulls, the curvature is indeed a reasonable feature to include.

We extend the functional including an additional term which leads to a matching of the curvature

$$\mathcal{C}[u] := \frac{1}{2} \int_\Omega \frac{1}{Q_H(x)} (H_0(x + u(x)) - H_1(x))^2 \, dx.$$

where $H_0(x)$ and $H_1(x)$ are the mean curvatures at point x for I_0 and I_1, respectively. The weight $Q_H(x)$ is chosen analogously to $Q_I(x)$. The registration problem is now to find u that solves the following problem:

$$\mathcal{J}[u] := \mathcal{D}[u] + \beta\mathcal{C}[u] + \alpha\mathcal{R}[u] \to \min. \tag{4}$$

The Euler-Lagrange equation is extended in the obvious way, leading to

$$-\alpha \triangle u = F(u) \tag{5}$$

with

$$F(u) := \frac{I_0(x+u(x))-I_1(x)}{Q_I(x)} \nabla I_0(x + u(x)) + \frac{H_0(x+u(x))-H_1(x)}{Q_H(x)} \nabla H_0(x + u(x)) \, .$$

3   Finite Element Discretization

In this section we describe the steps taken for computing the solution u for given data I_0, I_1, H_0, and H_1 from (5). In [15], Modersitzki showed that the Demons algorithm can be interpreted as a simple fix point iteration scheme for the non-linear elliptic equation (5). The solution u is obtained from an initial solution u^0 by iteratively performing the computation

$$u^{n+1} = u^n + \tau\left(\alpha\triangle u^n + F(u^n)\right).$$

Alternatively, we can interpret this equation as a forward Euler step for the heat equation

$$\partial_t u - \alpha\triangle u = F(u) \tag{6}$$

with step size τ. In this presentation we will focus on deriving methods for computing large time solutions $u = u(t,x)$ of (6). Since we are interested in the large time limit we use as the initial conditions simply $u(0,x) = 0$ in all our calculations. For the simulations shown here we have used Neumann boundary conditions.

Since the elliptic operator in the heat equation leads to a severe time step restriction, coupling the time step τ to the mesh width h via $\tau = O(h^2)$, we use an implicit time discretization for the elliptic part of (6). To avoid problems with the nonlinear term $F(u)$ we want to discretize this term in an explicit fashion. Fixing a time step τ, and using the abbreviation $u^n(x) \approx u(n\tau, x)$ we propose the following semi-implicit scheme:

$$u^{n+1} - \tau\alpha\triangle u^{n+1} = u^n + \tau F(u^n). \tag{7}$$

This approach is similar to Thirion's approach with the exception that the elliptic term is treated implicitly. Similarly higher order implicit/explicit Runge-Kutta schemes for the time discretization can be used [5].

It remains to specify the spatial finite element discretization of the image domain. We use a Discontinuous Galerkin Finite Element approach. This method is very well suited for this type of problem and can be easily used with locally adapted grids and domain decomposition strategies for parallelization on distributed memory computers. Given a tessellation $\mathcal{T}_h = \{T_i\}_{i\in\mathcal{I}}$ of the computational domain Ω into non overlapping elements (see Figures 4 and 2a in the following Section), this scheme follows the same ideas as the standard Galerkin method [7] but employs a discontinuous ansatz space: $V_h^k := \{v_h \ : \ v_i \in P_k(T_i) \text{ for } i \in \mathcal{I}\}$. Here $v_i \equiv v_{h|T_h}$ and $P_k(T_i)$ denotes the space of polynomials on the element T_i of order k. Note that there are no continuity assumptions between elements.

Now, a variational formulation for the implicit and the explicit part

$$L_{\text{impl}} := u - \tau\alpha\triangle u, \quad L_{\text{expl}} := u + \tau F(u) \tag{8}$$

of the semi-implicit scheme (7) is derived: The explicit part is easily discretized on an element T_i by:

$$\int_{T_i} L_{\text{expl},i}\varphi = \int_{T_i} (u_i + \tau F(u_i))\varphi \, dx \tag{9}$$

for all $\varphi \in P_k(T_i)$.

Due to the discontinuous ansatz space, the discretization of the elliptic term is slightly more complicated as in the standard Galerkin approach. We employ the approach known as the *local Discontinuous Galerkin* method, rewriting for given $u_h \in V_h$ the second order equation $L_{\text{impl},h} = u_h - \tau\alpha\triangle u_h$ as a system of first order equations

$$v_h = \nabla u_h, \quad L_{\text{impl},h} = u_h - \alpha\tau\nabla \cdot v_h .$$

$L_{\text{impl},h}$ is now computed from the variation formulation:

$$\int_{T_i} v_i\varphi = \int_{\partial T_i} [u_h]\varphi - \int_{T_i} u_h\nabla\varphi , \tag{10}$$

$$\int_{T_i} L_{\text{impl},i}\varphi = \int_{T_i} u_h\varphi - \int_{\partial T_i} \tau\alpha[v_h]\varphi + \int_{T_i} \tau\alpha v_h\nabla\varphi, \tag{11}$$

for all $\varphi \in P_k(T_i)$; we have used the abbreviation $[v_h]$ to denote the jump of a discrete function $v_h \in V_h$ over element boundaries. For more details see [10,4].

For constructing the tessellation we use the ALUGrid library [1] using hexahedral meshes in 3d and triangular meshes in 2d with non-conforming local adaptivity and the possibility of domain decomposition and dynamic load balancing for parallel computations. The whole numerical scheme is implemented using the generic grid concept from the software library DUNE [2] and the discretization methods from the DUNE-FEM package [8]. Since the DUNE library is implemented in C++ the incorporation of the solution algorithm into the ITK framework [11] presents no major problems so that the pre- and post-processing facilities developed here can be directly used.

4   Results

For the results presented here, the shapes have been aligned prior to registration, to remove large translational and rotational parts. In all the computation we used $\tau = 1, \alpha = 1$, and $\beta = 1$. Using larger values of τ can increase the convergence rate of the numerical scheme and due to the implicit treatment of the elliptic operator does not lead to instability of the scheme; the same holds for smaller values of α but in both cases the smoothness of the displacement field u is decreased in an unsatisfactory manner. For the spatial discretization we have used $k = 0, 1, 2$ i.e., constant, linear, and quadratic polynomials on each element and also higher order time-discretization schemes. Here, we only show results with $k = 1$ together with a first order semi-implicit time discretization scheme.

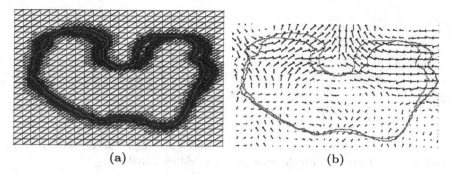

Fig. 2. Registration of two 2D-slices through the femur. Figure 2a shows the outline of the shapes and the discretization of the images, while Figure 2b shows the resulting displacement field.

To increase the rate of convergence and to take advantage of the possibilities offered by local grid adaptation, we start the computation using a coarse grid of less than 100 elements and after performing a number of iterations on this coarse grid, refine the grid elements on which

$$\max\{|I_0(x)|, |I_0(x + u^n(x))|, |I_1(x)|\} < R$$

holds for a given value of R. The indicator R is then decreased and the iteration process is repeated. The full details of the algorithm and a study of the influence of the parameters are published in [3].

4.1   Registration of a Femur

As a first test, we register two 2D slices of a 3D femur bone. Figure 2a shows the two shapes to be registered and the locally adapted tessellation of the image domain. The shape of the slice is well matched and the resulting correspondences are reasonable as demonstrated in Figure 2b where we also show the resulting displacement field.

In Figure 3 we see the registration results for the 3D femora from our database. The image shows that the registered image matches the shape of the target accurately. The discretization used is illustrated in Figure 4a. We see that the resolution is highest around the surface and hence we can represent fine details where this is necessary.

4.2   Registration of a Skull

As a further example, we consider the registration of two skulls. The discretization used is illustrated in Figure 4b.

As previously mentioned, one of the main motivation for the level-set representation was to register surfaces of arbitrary topology. In this example the data is noisy and the topology of the skulls differ due to segmentation artifacts

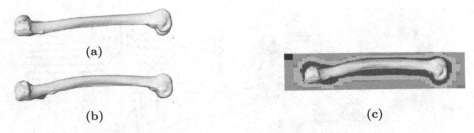

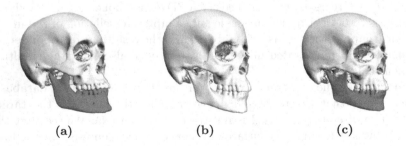

Fig. 3. The reference femur (a) is registered onto a target (b). In (c), the registration result is shown together with the adaption level (blue=2, red=5).

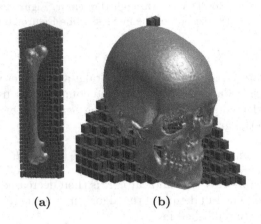

Fig. 4. The discretization for the representation of the skull surfaces and the femur (refinement levels represented by color)

Fig. 5. The labelling of a reference skull (a) is automatically transformed to a target skull (b), (c). Computation time for the skull registration was 4.5 hours on a AMD Opteron 2.4GHz.

and the limited resolution of the original CT-image. Still the shape is accurately matched as can be seen in Figure 5. Although not the main motivation of this work, an immediate application is atlas-based labeling of a target skull. This is illustrated in Figure 5, where the mandible is labeled in a reference skull and the labeling is transformed to an unlabeled target skull using the calculated deformation field u. Moreover, this provides us with a test to validate the quality of the registration result. It can be seen, that the mandible is correctly identified in the target skull.

5   Discussion

Our results demonstrate that even on quite coarse grids and for complex registration problems, the finite element method leads to very good results. Even the challenge posed by the registration of the human skull was met by the algorithm. The advantage of the local grid adaption for this type of problem is evident, since mainly the neighborhood of the surface must be well resolved while outlying regions can be treated with a far lower resolution without reducing the quality of the match. In the calculation for the 3D femura, the resulting finest grid consisted of less than 400.000 hexahedra, compared to more than 10M points used in our ITK implementation. A similar reduction was achieved for the skull example. Also the finite element formulation seems to be very robust, so that additional strategies like using smooth low resolution images do not seem to be required for the convergence of the scheme. The implicit treatment of the elliptic part also enhances the stability of the method so that a wide range of parameters can be used with this scheme.

The consequent focus on the formulation of the problem as a PDE offers a wide range of further approaches for computing the displacement field, e.g., higher order schemes or pre-conditioning strategies like multigrid approaches. These can lead to a further increase in the efficiency of the scheme. The DUNE package used for our implementation is based on a generic interface both for the grid structure and the numerical scheme, thus allowing for a generic implementation of the solution method including local adaptivity and dynamic load balancing. We can therefore easily apply different numerical schemes to the registration problem, such as continuous Galerkin discretizations, fully implicit time stepping schemes or direct methods for the non-linear elliptic equation, and compare these with the method presented here. We will study the possibilities offered by this concept in future work.

Acknowledgment

We would like to thank Dr. Zdzislaw Krol, University Hospital Basel, Dr. Felix Matthews, CARCAS group, and PD Dr. Hansrudi Noser and Dipl. Ing. Thomas Kaup, ADI, AO Foundation, Davos, for providing us with the radiological data. This work was funded by the Swiss National Science Foundation in the scope of the NCCR CO-ME project 5005-66380, the Hasler Foundation in scope of the HOVISSE project and by the Landesstiftung Baden-Württemberg.

References

1. ALUGRID – Adaptive, Load Balanced, and Unstructured Grid Library, http://www.mathematik.uni-freiburg.de/IAM/Research/alugrid/
2. DUNE – Distributed and Unified Numerics Environment, http://dune-project.org/
3. Albrecht, T., Dedner, A., Lüthi, M., Vetter, T.: Curvature sensitive adaptive finite element discretization for surface registration (in preparation)
4. Arnold, D.N., Brezzi, F., Cockburn, B., Marini, L.D.: Unified analysis of discontinuous Galerkin methods for elliptic problems. Siam. J. Numer. Anal. 39(5), 1749–1779 (2002)
5. Ascher, U.M., Ruuth, S.J., Spiteri, R.J.: Implicit-explicit Runge-Kutta methods for time-dependent partial differential equations. Appl. Numer. Math. 25(2-3), 151–167 (1997)
6. Audette, M.A., Ferrie, F.P., Peters, T.M.: An algorithmic overview of surface registration techniques for medical imaging. Medical Image Analysis 4, 201–217 (2000)
7. Braess, D.: Finite elements. Cambridge Univ. Press, Cambridge (1997)
8. Burri, A., Dedner, A., Diehl, D., Klöfkorn, R., Ohlberger, M.: A general object oriented framework for discretizing nonlinear evolution equations. In: Proceedings of the 1st Kazakh-German Advanced Research Workshop on Computational Science and High Performance Computing, Almaty, Kazakhstan (2005)
9. Chefd'Hotel, C., Hermosillo, G., Faugeras, O.: A Variational Approach to Multi-Modal Image Matching. In: IEEE Workshop on Variational and Level Set Methods, pp. 21–28 (2001)
10. Cockburn, B., Karniadakis, G.E., Shu, C.-W.: Discontinuous Galerkin methods. In: Theory, computation and applications. 1st international symposium on DGM. Lect. Notes Comput. Sci. Eng., Newport, RI, USA, May 24–26, 1999, vol. 11, Springer, Berlin (2000)
11. Ibanez, L., Schroeder, W., Ng, L., Cates, J.: The ITK Software Guide, 2nd edn (2005), http://www.itk.org/ItkSoftwareGuide.pdf
12. Litke, N., Droske, M., Rumpf, M., Schröder, P.: An image processing approach to surface matching. In: Symposium on Geometry Processing, pp. 207–216 (2005)
13. Lüthi, M., Albrecht, T., Vetter, T.: A curvature sensitive demons algorithm for surface registration. Technical report, Department of Computer Science, University of Basel (2006)
14. Maurel, P., Keriven, R., Faugeras, O.: Reconciling landmarks and level sets. In: ICPR 2006. 18th International Conference on Pattern Recognition, 2006. vol. 4, pp. 69–72 (2006)
15. Modersitzki, J.: Numerical Methods for Image Registration. Oxford Science Publications (2004)
16. Pennec, X., Cachier, P., Ayache, N.: Understanding the "demon's algorithm": 3D non-rigid registration by gradient descent. In: Taylor, C., Colchester, A. (eds.) Medical Image Computing and Computer-Assisted Intervention – MICCAI'99. LNCS, vol. 1679, pp. 597–605. Springer, Heidelberg (1999)
17. Thirion, J.-P.: Image matching as a diffusion process: an analogy with Maxwell's demons. Medical Image Analysis 2(3), 243–260 (1998)
18. Vemuri, B.C., Ye, J., Chen, Y., Leonard, C.M.: Image registration via level-set motion: applications to atlas-based segmentation. Med Image Anal. 7, 1–20 (2003)

Spline-Based Elastic Image Registration with Matrix-Valued Basis Functions Using Landmark and Intensity Information

Stefan Wörz and Karl Rohr

University of Heidelberg, BIOQUANT, IPMB, and DKFZ Heidelberg,
Dept. Bioinformatics and Functional Genomics, Biomedical Computer Vision Group
Im Neuenheimer Feld 267, 69120 Heidelberg, Germany
{s.woerz,k.rohr}@dkfz.de

Abstract. We introduce a new approach for spline-based elastic image registration using both point landmarks and intensity information. As underlying deformation model we use Gaussian elastic body splines (GEBS), which are analytic solutions of the Navier equation under Gaussian forces and are represented by matrix-valued basis functions. We also incorporate landmark localization uncertainties represented by weight matrices. Our approach is formulated as an energy-minimizing functional that incorporates landmark and intensity information as well as a regularization based on GEBS. Since the approach is based on a physical deformation model, cross-effects in elastic deformations can be handled. We demonstrate the applicability of our scheme based on MR images of the human brain. It turns out that the new scheme is superior to a pure landmark-based as well as a pure intensity-based scheme.

1 Introduction

Image registration plays an increasingly important role in biomedical applications. A main challenge is to cope with the broad range of applications as well as the large spectrum of imaging modalities. In many applications it is not quite clear which type of image information is optimal. Concerning the underlying transformation model generally nonrigid or elastic schemes have to be used (for a survey see, e.g., [1]). Elastic registration approaches are, in general, based on an energy functional or the related partial differential equation. Typically, the solution is computed *numerically* using finite differences or the finite element method, which, however, is generally computationally expensive.

Alternatively, *spline-based* approaches can be used for elastic registration, which can be subdivided into schemes based on a uniform grid of control points, where typically B-splines are used (e.g., [2,3,4,5,6]), and schemes based on a nonuniform grid of control points (e.g., [7,8,9,10,11,12,13,14,15,16,17]). The latter type of schemes generally requires a smaller number of control points (landmarks). Examples of such schemes are based on thin-plate splines (TPS, e.g., [7,10,11,13]), elastic body splines (EBS, e.g., [8]), and Gaussian elastic body

F.A. Hamprecht, C. Schnörr, and B. Jähne (Eds.): DAGM 2007, LNCS 4713, pp. 537–546, 2007.

splines (GEBS, e.g., [15,17]). TPS are based on the bending energy of a thin plate, which represents a relatively coarse deformation model for biological tissues. In comparison, EBS and GEBS are derived from the Navier equation, which describes the deformation of elastic tissues (bodies). GEBS in comparison to EBS have the advantage that more realistic forces are incorporated.

Regarding the used image information, approaches are often based on either landmarks or intensity information. Main advantages of *landmark-based* approaches are computational efficiency, the fact that they can cope with large geometric differences, as well as the relatively easy and intuitive incorporation of user-interaction. In contrast, main advantages of *intensity-based* approaches are that more image information is taken into account and that no segmentation is necessary. In recent years, approaches that combine landmark-based and intensity-based methods have gained increased attention since advantages of both types of methods can be combined (e.g., [18,19,11,20,3,21,22,5,23]). However, so far only relatively few *spline-based* registration approaches exist that integrate both types of information. Typically, the intensity information is only used to determine optimal positions of the control points (e.g., [14,17]) or to establish landmark correspondences (e.g., [4]), i.e. the landmark and intensity information is not directly combined. In addition, often a physical deformation model is not used (e.g., [19,3,4,5,6]) or higher order splines are required (e.g., [22]).

Moreover, in landmark-based registration approaches generally an *interpolation* scheme is applied that forces corresponding landmarks to exactly match each other (e.g., [8,4,15,17]). To include landmark localization uncertainties, *approximation* schemes have been proposed, for example, for TPS [10] and GEBS [16]. Note, however, that in these approaches only landmarks have been used but not intensity information. In [24] both types of information are combined, however, the regularization of the deformation field has been heuristically motivated.

In contrast to previous spline-based registration approaches, the central idea of our approach is to directly combine the landmark and intensity information in a single energy functional as well as to include a regularization based on GEBS, which are analytic solutions of the Navier equation. In addition, we incorporate landmark localization uncertainties. Since GEBS are represented by matrix-valued non-radial basis functions and include a material parameter (Poisson ratio ν) that defines the ratio between transverse contraction and longitudinal dilation of an elastic material, the registration scheme integrates an improved physical deformation model, where the components of the deformation field w.r.t. the different dimensions are coupled, i.e. cross-effects can be handled (which is not the case for, e.g., TPS). Moreover, since GEBS incorporate Gaussian forces we have a free parameter (the standard deviation) to control the locality of the transformation, and, therefore, GEBS are well-suited for the registration of local differences.

2   Spline-Based Registration Using Landmark and Intensity Information

2.1   Interpolating and Approximating GEBS

In the following, we briefly describe the interpolating and approximating GEBS approach. *Interpolating* GEBS are based on the Navier equation of linear elasticity (e.g., [25])

$$\mu \Delta \mathbf{u} + (\lambda + \mu) \nabla (\text{div } \mathbf{u}) + \mathbf{f} = \mathbf{0} \tag{1}$$

with the displacement vector field $\mathbf{u}$ and body forces $\mathbf{f}$. Given Gaussian forces $\mathbf{f}_\sigma(\mathbf{x}) = \mathbf{c} \, f_\sigma(r) = \mathbf{c} \, (\sqrt{2\pi}\sigma)^{-3} \exp(-\frac{r^2}{2\sigma^2})$ with $\mathbf{x} = (x, y, z)^T, r = \sqrt{x^2 + y^2 + z^2}$, and the standard deviation σ, an analytic solution of the Navier equation (1) can be derived [15]. The resulting matrix-valued basis function $\mathbf{G}_\sigma$ (a 3×3 matrix) reads (up to a constant factor)

$$\mathbf{G}_\sigma(\mathbf{x}) = \left(\frac{\alpha r^2 + \sigma^2}{r^3} \text{erf}(\hat{r}) - \beta \frac{e^{-\hat{r}^2}}{r^2} \right) \mathbf{I} + \left(\frac{r^2 - 3\sigma^2}{r^5} \text{erf}(\hat{r}) + 3\beta \frac{e^{-\hat{r}^2}}{r^4} \right) \mathbf{x}\mathbf{x}^T \tag{2}$$

where $\hat{r} = r/(\sqrt{2}\,\sigma)$, $\alpha = 3 - 4\nu$, $\beta = \sigma\sqrt{2/\pi}$, and $\text{erf}(x) = \frac{2}{\sqrt{\pi}} \int_0^x e^{-\xi^2} d\xi$. $\mathbf{I}$ denotes the 3×3 identity matrix and ν is the Poisson ratio $\nu = \lambda/(2\lambda + 2\mu)$, $0 \le \nu < 0.5$ with the Lamé constants $\mu, \lambda > 0$ describing material properties. Using the interpolation condition $\mathbf{q}_i = \mathbf{u}(\mathbf{p}_i)$, the scheme for elastic registration is given by

$$\mathbf{u}(\mathbf{x}) = \mathbf{x} + \sum_{i=1}^{n} \mathbf{G}_\sigma(\mathbf{x} - \mathbf{p}_i) \, \mathbf{c}_i \tag{3}$$

where $\mathbf{p}_i$ and $\mathbf{q}_i$ $(i = 1, \ldots, n)$ denote the positions of the n landmarks of the source and target image, respectively. The coefficients $\mathbf{c}_i$ represent the strength and direction of the Gaussian forces.

Approximating GEBS incorporate the condition $\mathbf{q}_i \approx \mathbf{u}(\mathbf{p}_i)$ and 3×3 covariance matrices $\boldsymbol{\Sigma}_i$ defining anisotropic localization uncertainties of the landmarks $i = 1, \ldots, n$. The energy-minimizing functional consists of an elastic term $J_{Elastic}$ representing the elastic energy according to the Navier equation as well as a data term $J_{Data,L}$ which incorporates the landmark errors. The quadratic Lagrange function is given by [16]

$$L_{Data,L} = \frac{1}{n\lambda_A} \sum_{i=1}^{n} f_\sigma(\mathbf{x} - \mathbf{p}_i) \, (\mathbf{q}_i - \mathbf{u}(\mathbf{x}))^T \, \boldsymbol{\Sigma}_i^{-1} \, (\mathbf{q}_i - \mathbf{u}(\mathbf{x})) \tag{4}$$

where $\lambda_A > 0$ denotes the regularization parameter. The corresponding PDE to the combined functional $J_{Elastic} + J_{Data,L}$ can be stated as

$$\mu \Delta \mathbf{u} + (\lambda + \mu) \nabla (\text{div } \mathbf{u}) + \nabla_{\mathbf{u}} \, L_{Data,L} = \mathbf{0}, \tag{5}$$

and represents an extension of the Navier equation. The solution to (5) can be analytically derived and it is the same as in the case of interpolation.

2.2   Combining Landmark and Intensity Information

The scheme described above has been used for landmark-based elastic registration. Below, we describe a new hybrid approach where both landmark and intensity information is incorporated and GEBS are used as underlying deformation model. To compute the deformation field $\mathbf{u}$ for registering the source image g_1 with the target image g_2, we introduce the functional

$$J_{Hybrid}(\mathbf{u}) = J_{Data,I}\left(g_1, g_2, \mathbf{u}^I\right) + \lambda_I J_I\left(\mathbf{u}, \mathbf{u}^I\right) + \lambda_L J_L\left(\mathbf{u}, \mathbf{u}^L\right) + \lambda_E J_{El.}(\mathbf{u}) \quad (6)$$

which consists of four terms. Besides the searched deformation field $\mathbf{u}$, (6) comprises two deformation fields $\mathbf{u}^I$ and $\mathbf{u}^L$ that are computed based on the intensity and landmark information, respectively (λ_I, λ_L, and λ_E are scalar weights). Concerning the *intensity* information, the first term of (6) represents an intensity similarity measure between the deformed source and target image. As similarity measure we here use the sum-of-squared intensity differences

$$J_{Data,I}\left(g_1, g_2, \mathbf{u}^I\right) = \int \left(g_1\left(\mathbf{x} + \mathbf{u}^I(\mathbf{x})\right) - g_2(\mathbf{x})\right)^2 d\mathbf{x}. \quad (7)$$

The second term J_I couples the intensity-based deformation field $\mathbf{u}^I$ with $\mathbf{u}$ using a weighted Euclidean distance. Since the approach is based on GEBS, we here use Gaussian forces $f_{\sigma_I}(r)$ as weights, which leads to

$$J_I(\mathbf{u}, \mathbf{u}^I) = \int d\mathbf{x} \int d\boldsymbol{\xi}\, f_{\sigma_I}(\mathbf{x} - \boldsymbol{\xi}) \left\|\mathbf{u}^I(\boldsymbol{\xi}) - \mathbf{u}(\mathbf{x})\right\|^2. \quad (8)$$

Regarding the *landmark* information, the deformation field $\mathbf{u}^L$ is computed based on the landmark correspondences using GEBS. To incorporate localization uncertainties, we employ the approximation scheme in [16] (see Sect. 2.1 above). The uncertainties are characterized by weight matrices, i.e. anisotropic landmark errors can be taken into account. The third term of (6) couples $\mathbf{u}^L$ with $\mathbf{u}$ analogously to (8) using Gaussian forces f_{σ_L}.

Finally, the fourth term represents the *regularization* of the deformation field $\mathbf{u}$. In our case, $J_{Elastic}$ represents the elastic energy according to the (force-free) Navier equation. By minimizing J_{Hybrid} in (6), the resulting deformation field $\mathbf{u}$ is, on the one hand, similar to the deformation field obtained from the landmark correspondences, and, on the other hand, the intensities of the deformed source image are similar to those of the target image. In addition, the regularization using GEBS constraints the deformation field to physically plausible deformations in comparison to using other splines such as TPS.

2.3   Minimization of the Functional

An efficient way of minimizing J_{Hybrid} in (6) is to minimize it alternatingly w.r.t. $\mathbf{u}^I$ and $\mathbf{u}$. Note that a minimization w.r.t. $\mathbf{u}^L$ is not required since the landmark correspondences remain unchanged in our approach. For the minimization w.r.t. $\mathbf{u}^I$, the following functional is relevant

$$J_{Data,I}\left(g_1, g_2, \mathbf{u}^I\right) + \lambda_I J_I\left(\mathbf{u}, \mathbf{u}^I\right) \to \min. \quad (9)$$

To simplify this functional, we here omit the weighting based on Gaussian forces f_{σ_I} in J_I. As a consequence, the resulting functional has the advantage that it can be stated independently for *each voxel*, and that for each voxel only sums of squared differences are used. For a certain voxel $\mathbf{x}$ the corresponding Lagrange function of the simplified functional then reads

$$\left(g_1(\mathbf{x} + \mathbf{u}^I(\mathbf{x})) - g_2(\mathbf{x})\right)^2 + \lambda_I \left\|\mathbf{u}^I(\mathbf{x}) - \mathbf{u}(\mathbf{x})\right\|^2, \tag{10}$$

which can be efficiently minimized using the method of Levenberg-Marquardt. The required first order partial derivatives of the source image g_1 are computed using Gaussian derivative filters. For the minimization w.r.t. $\mathbf{u}$, the following functional has to be considered

$$\lambda_I J_I(\mathbf{u}, \mathbf{u}^I) + \lambda_L J_L(\mathbf{u}, \mathbf{u}^L) + \lambda_E J_{Elastic}(\mathbf{u}) \to \min. \tag{11}$$

The corresponding PDE can be derived as (using $\epsilon_I = 2\lambda_I/\lambda_E$ and $\epsilon_L = 2\lambda_L/\lambda_E$)

$$0 = \mu \Delta \mathbf{u} + (\lambda + \mu) \nabla (\operatorname{div} \mathbf{u}) + \epsilon_I \int f_{\sigma_I}(\mathbf{x} - \boldsymbol{\xi}) \left(\mathbf{u}^I(\boldsymbol{\xi}) - \mathbf{u}(\mathbf{x})\right) d\boldsymbol{\xi}$$

$$+ \epsilon_L \int f_{\sigma_L}(\mathbf{x} - \boldsymbol{\xi}) \left(\mathbf{u}^L(\boldsymbol{\xi}) - \mathbf{u}(\mathbf{x})\right) d\boldsymbol{\xi}. \tag{12}$$

Interestingly, (12) can be solved analytically by employing the convolution theorem. An explicit solution using matrix-vector and matrix-matrix convolutions as well as the matrix-valued GEBS basis function $\mathbf{G}_\sigma$ is given by

$$\mathbf{u}(\mathbf{x}) = \mathbf{x} + \boldsymbol{\phi}_I(\mathbf{x}) * \left(\mathbf{u}^I(\mathbf{x}) - \mathbf{x}\right) + \boldsymbol{\phi}_L(\mathbf{x}) * \left(\mathbf{u}^L(\mathbf{x}) - \mathbf{x}\right) \tag{13}$$

where "$*$" denotes the convolution and

$$\boldsymbol{\phi}_I(\mathbf{x}) = \left(\mathbf{G}_{\sigma_I}(\mathbf{x}) + \mathbf{G}_{\sigma_L}(\mathbf{x})\right) * \boldsymbol{\Omega}_I(\mathbf{x}), \quad \hat{\boldsymbol{\Omega}}_I(\boldsymbol{\omega}) = \epsilon_I \hat{f}_{\sigma_I}(\boldsymbol{\omega}) \hat{\boldsymbol{\theta}}(\boldsymbol{\omega})^{-1} \tag{14}$$

$$\boldsymbol{\phi}_L(\mathbf{x}) = \left(\mathbf{G}_{\sigma_I}(\mathbf{x}) + \mathbf{G}_{\sigma_L}(\mathbf{x})\right) * \boldsymbol{\Omega}_L(\mathbf{x}), \quad \hat{\boldsymbol{\Omega}}_L(\boldsymbol{\omega}) = \epsilon_L \hat{f}_{\sigma_L}(\boldsymbol{\omega}) \hat{\boldsymbol{\theta}}(\boldsymbol{\omega})^{-1} \tag{15}$$

$$\boldsymbol{\theta}(\mathbf{x}) = \left(f_{\sigma_I}(\mathbf{x}) + f_{\sigma_L}(\mathbf{x})\right) \mathbf{I} + (\epsilon_I + \epsilon_L) \left(\mathbf{G}_{\sigma_I}(\mathbf{x}) + \mathbf{G}_{\sigma_L}(\mathbf{x})\right) \tag{16}$$

where "$\hat{}$" denotes the Fourier transform and $\hat{\boldsymbol{\theta}}(\boldsymbol{\omega})^{-1}$ is the inverse matrix of $\hat{\boldsymbol{\theta}}(\boldsymbol{\omega})$. Note that the intensity similarity measure $J_{Data,I}$ in (7) is only relevant for the minimization w.r.t. $\mathbf{u}^I$ in (9) but not for the minimization w.r.t. $\mathbf{u}$ in (11). As a consequence, by replacing $J_{Data,I}$ with a different intensity similarity measure such as local correlation or mutual information we only need to change (9) whereas the solution in (13) remains unchanged. Note also that a special case of this hybrid approach is obtained by omitting the landmark information J_L from (6) and in subsequent equations, which results in a pure intensity-based elastic registration scheme.

3   Experimental Results

3.1   MR Images – Ground Truth Deformation

To validate our approach, we considered a simple model of a radial tumor expansion where an analytic solution of the Navier equation is known [26]. We assume

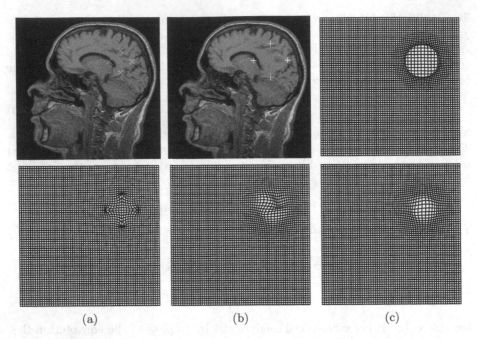

(a)   (b)   (c)

Fig. 1. Registration of 2D MR brain images: Original 2D MR image (top, a), deformed image (b), and ground truth deformation grid (c), as well as the (inverse) deformation grids (bottom) using a pure landmark-based approach (a), a pure intensity-based approach (b), and using the hybrid approach (c).

three different types of tissues: An inner circle with radius R_i representing a tumor, a circular disk between radii R_i and R_o representing normal (elastic) tissue which corresponds to brain tissue, and the region outside of the outer circle with radius R_o representing the rigid skull. We model a tumor expansion by increasing the radius R_i of the inner circle by a value d. To solve the Navier equation, we use cylindrical coordinates and the following boundary conditions: a vanishing displacement at the outer circle (i.e. $u_r(R_o) = 0$) as well as a displacement of $u_r(R_i) \pm d$ at the inner circle, which leads to

$$u_{r,\,expansion}(r) = d\,R_i\,R_o^2\left(R_o^2 - R_i^2\right)^{-1}\left(r^{-1} - r\,R_o^{-2}\right). \tag{17}$$

We have applied this model to real 2D MR images of the human head to obtain physically plausible deformations with ground truth information. For example, Fig. 1 (top) shows the original 2D image (a) as well as the deformed image (b) and the deformation grid (c) using $R_i = 20\,\mathrm{mm}$, $R_o = 55\,\mathrm{mm}$, and $d = 10\,\mathrm{mm}$. Based on this ground truth data, we have registered the deformed image (source) with the original image (target) using four landmarks (see the white markings). Fig. 1 (bottom) shows the (inverse) deformation grids using a pure landmark-based approach (a), a pure intensity-based approach (b), and using the hybrid

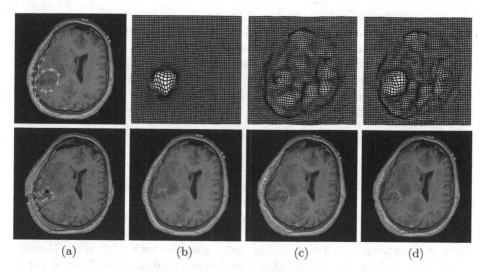

Fig. 2. Registration of 2D MR brain images: Pre- (top, a) and postsurgical image (bottom, a) as well as the (inverse) deformation grids (top) and registered source images (bottom) using a pure landmark-based approach (b), a pure intensity-based approach (c), and using the hybrid approach (d).

approach (c). It can be seen that the *hybrid* approach leads to a significantly better result compared to the other two approaches.

To quantify the registration accuracy, we computed the mean geometric error $\bar{e}_{geom}$ between the ground truth deformation given by (17) and the computed deformations based on the registration results within the outer circle R_o (relevant area of deformation). In addition, we determined the mean intensity error $\bar{e}_{int}$ between the source and target images as well as between the deformed source and target images. For the *hybrid* approach we obtain $\bar{e}_{geom} = 1.17\,\text{mm}$. In contrast, using the *pure intensity-based* approach the error is worse ($\bar{e}_{geom} = 2.03\,\text{mm}$), and using the *pure landmark-based* approach the error is even worse ($\bar{e}_{geom} = 3.15\,\text{mm}$). In addition, using the *hybrid* approach the mean intensity error $\bar{e}_{int}$ improved by 71.9% w.r.t. the unregistered case, whereas the pure *intensity-based* and *landmark-based* approaches yield improvements of only 61.2% and 14.3%, respectively.

3.2   MR Images – Tumor Resection

In this application the task is to register pre- and postsurgical MR images of the human brain. Fig. 2 (a) shows 2D MR images of a patient before (source image, top) and after (target image, bottom) the resection of a tumor. 17 landmarks have been manually placed along the contours of the tumor and the resection area (indicated by crosses). Also shown are the (inverse) deformation grids (top) and registered source images (bottom) using a pure landmark-based approach (b), a pure intensity-based approach (c), and using the hybrid approach (d). It turned out that using only *landmarks* (b) the vicinity of the tumor and resection area are well registered whereas regions without landmarks are not deformed. In contrast, using only *intensity* information (c) yields deformations in different parts of the head, however, the tumor has not been well registered. Applying the *hybrid* approach the registration result is significantly improved in comparison to the previous two approaches since the tumor and resection area are well registered and, in addition, other parts of the head (see Fig. 2d).

4   Conclusion

We have introduced a spline-based registration approach using both landmark and intensity information. Our approach is based on analytic solutions of the Navier equation which are represented by matrix-valued basis functions. In comparison to existing spline-based approaches, our scheme directly combines landmark and intensity information, incorporates a regularization based on Gaussian elastic body splines, as well as takes into account landmark localization uncertainties. We have demonstrated the applicability of the approach based on MR brain images. It turned out that the hybrid approach is superior compared to a pure landmark-based and a pure intensity-based scheme.

Acknowledgment

This work has been funded by the Deutsche Forschungsgemeinschaft (DFG) within the project ELASTIR (RO 2471/2). The original MR images in Fig. 1 have kindly been provided by Philips Research Hamburg and W.P.Th.M. Mali, L. Ramos, and C.W.M. van Veelen (Utrecht University Hospital) via ICS-AD of Philips Medical Systems Best. The original MR images and the tumor outlines in Fig 2 have kindly been provided by OA Dr. med. U. Spetzger and Prof. Dr. J.-M. Gilsbach, Neurosurgical Clinic, University Hospital Aachen of the RWTH. We thank Andrea Steinmetz and Matthias Nohl for implementing the user-interface of the registration program.

References

1. Zitova, B., Flusser, J.: Image Registration Methods: a Survey. Image and Vision Computing 24, 977–1000 (2003)
2. Rueckert, D., Sonoda, L., Hayes, C., Hill, D., Leach, M., Hawkes, D.: Non-rigid Registration Using Free-Form Deformations: Application to Breast MR Images. IEEE Trans. on Medical Imaging 18(8), 712–721 (1999)
3. Kybic, J., Unser, M.: Fast parametric elastic registration. IEEE Trans. on Image Processing 12(11), 1427–1442 (2003)
4. Stewart, C., Lee, Y.L., Tsai, C.L.: An Uncertainty-Driven Hybrid of Intensity-Based and Feature-Based Registration with Application to Retinal and Lung CT Images. In: Barillot, C., Haynor, D.R., Hellier, P. (eds.) MICCAI 2004. LNCS, vol. 3216, pp. 870–877. Springer, Heidelberg (2004)

5. Papademetris, X., Jackowski, A., Schultz, R., Staib, L., Duncan, J.: Integrated Intensity and Point-Feature Nonrigid Registration. In: Barillot, C., Haynor, D.R., Hellier, P. (eds.) MICCAI 2004. LNCS, vol. 3216, pp. 763–770. Springer, Heidelberg (2004)
6. Sorzano, C., Thévenaz, P., Unser, M.: Elastic Registration of Biological Images Using Vector-Spline Regularization. IEEE Trans. on Biomedical Engineering 52(4), 652–663 (2005)
7. Bookstein, F.: Principal Warps: Thin-Plate Splines and the Decomposition of Deformations. IEEE Trans. on Pattern Analysis and Machine Intelligence 11(6), 567–585 (1989)
8. Davis, M., Khotanzad, A., Flaming, D., Harms, S.: A physics-based coordinate transformation for 3D image matching. IEEE Trans. on Medical Imaging 16(3), 317–328 (1997)
9. Joshi, S., Miller, M.: Landmark Matching Via Large Deformation Diffeomorphisms. IEEE Trans. on Image Processing 9(8), 1357–1370 (2000)
10. Rohr, K., Stiehl, H., Sprengel, R., Buzug, T., Weese, J., Kuhn, M.: Landmark-Based Elastic Registration Using Approximating Thin-Plate Splines. IEEE Trans. on Medical Imaging 20(6), 526–534 (2001)
11. Johnson, H., Christensen, G.: Consistent Landmark and Intensity-based Image Registration. IEEE Trans. on Medical Imaging 21(5), 450–461 (2002)
12. Rohde, G., Aldroubi, A., Dawant, B.: The adaptive bases algorithm for intensity based nonrigid image registration. IEEE Trans. on Medical Imaging 22(11), 1470–1479 (2003)
13. Park, H., Bland, P., Brock, K., Meyer, C.: Adaptive registration using local information measures. Medical Image Analysis 8, 465–473 (2004)
14. Rogers, M., Graham, J.: Robust and Accurate Registration of 2-D Electrophoresis Gels Using Point-Matching. IEEE Trans. on Image Processing 16(3), 624–635 (2007)
15. Kohlrausch, J., Rohr, K., Stiehl, H.: A New Class of Elastic Body Splines for Nonrigid Registration of Medical Images. J. of Mathematical Imaging and Vision 23(3), 253–280 (2005)
16. Wörz, S., Rohr, K.: Physics-Based Elastic Image Registration Using Splines and Including Landmark Localization Uncertainties. In: Larsen, R., Nielsen, M., Sporring, J. (eds.) MICCAI 2006. LNCS, vol. 4191, pp. 678–685. Springer, Heidelberg (2006)
17. Pekar, V., Gladilin, E., Rohr, K.: An adaptive irregular grid approach for 3-D deformable image registration. Physics in Medicine and Biology 51, 361–377 (2006)
18. Gee, J., Haynor, D., Reivich, M., Bajcsy, R.: Finite element approach to warping of brain images. In: Loew, M. (ed.) Proc. SPIE Medical Imaging 1994: Medical Imaging, Newport Beach, CA/USA, February 1994. vol. 2167, pp. 327–337. SPIE (1994)
19. Cachier, P., Mangin, J.F., Pennec, X., Rivière, D., Papadopoulos-Orfanos, D., Régis, J., Ayache, N.: Multisubject Non-Rigid Registration of Brain MRI Using Intensity and Geometric Features. In: Niessen, W.J., Viergever, M.A. (eds.) MICCAI 2001. LNCS, vol. 2208, pp. 734–742. Springer, Heidelberg (2001)
20. Hellier, P., Barillot, C.: Coupling dense and landmark-based approaches for non rigid registration. IEEE Trans. on Medical Imaging 22(2), 217–227 (2003)
21. Modersitzki, J., Fischer, B.: Optimal image registration with a guaranteed one-to-one point match. In: Wittenberg, T., Hastreiter, P., Hoppe, U., Handels, H., Horsch, A., Meinzer, H.P. (eds.) Proc. Workshop Bildverarbeitung für die Medizin (BVM'03), Informatik aktuell, Erlangen, Germany. Informatik aktuell, vol. 80, pp. 1–5. Springer, Heidelberg (2003)

22. Cachier, P., Ayache, N.: Isotropic Energies, Filters and Splines for Vector Field Regularization. J. of Mathematical Imaging and Vision 20, 251–265 (2004)
23. Han, J., Hornegger, J., Kuwert, T., Bautz, W., Römer, W.: Feature Constrained Non-rigid Image Registration. In: Hülsemann, F., Kowarschik, M., Rüde, U. (eds.) Frontiers in Simulation, Erlangen, pp. 638–643. SCS Publishing House e.V (2005)
24. Wörz, S., Rohr, K.: Hybrid Spline-Based Elastic Image Registration Using Analytic Solutions of the Navier Equation. In: Proc. Workshop Bildverarbeitung für die Medizin (BVM'07). Munich, Germany, Informatik aktuell, March 2007, pp. 151–155. Springer, Heidelberg (2007)
25. Chou, P., Pagano, N.: Elasticity – Tensor, Dyadic, and Engineering Approaches. Dover Publications, Inc., New York/USA (1992)
26. Chandrasekharaiah, D., Debnath, L.: Continuum Mechanics. Academic Press, San Diego, CA/USA (1994)

Unifying Energy Minimization and Mutual Information Maximization for Robust 2D/3D Registration of X-Ray and CT Images

Guoyan Zheng

MEM Research Center, University of Bern, Stauffacherstrasse 78, CH-3014, Bern,
Switzerland
guoyan.zheng@ieee.org

Abstract. Similarity measure is one of the main factors that affect the accuracy of intensity-based 2D/3D registration of X-ray fluoroscopy to CT images. Information theory has been used to derive similarity measure for image registration leading to the introduction of mutual information, an accurate similarity measure for multi-modal and mono-modal image registration tasks. However, it is known that the standard mutual information measure only takes intensity values into account without considering spatial information and its robustness is questionable. Previous attempt to incorporate spatial information into mutual information either requires computing the entropy of higher dimensional probability distributions, or is not robust to outliers. In this paper, we show how to incorporate spatial information into mutual information without suffering from these problems. Using a variational approximation derived from the Kullback-Leibler bound, spatial information can be effectively incorporated into mutual information via energy minimization. The resulting similarity measure has a least-squares form and can be effectively minimized by a multi-resolution Levenberg-Marquardt optimizer. Experimental results are presented on datasets of two applications: (a) intra-operative patient pose estimation from a few (e.g. 2) calibrated fluoroscopic images, and (b) post-operative cup alignment estimation from single X-ray radiograph with gonadal shielding.

Keywords: similarity measure, mutual information, 2D/3D registration, X-ray, CT, Markov random field, Kullback-Leibler bound.

1 Introduction

2D/3D registration of a limited number of two-dimensional (2D) X-ray images with a three-dimensional (3D) CT volume has shown great potential in various applications including intra-operative patient pose estimation and post-operative prosthesis alignment evaluation. The reported techniques to achieve this registration can be split into two main categories: feature-based methods and intensity-based methods. Feature-based methods require a prerequisite segmentation stage which is error-prone and hard to achieve automatically. The

F.A. Hamprecht, C. Schnörr, and B. Jähne (Eds.): DAGM 2007, LNCS 4713, pp. 547–557, 2007.
© Springer-Verlag Berlin Heidelberg 2007

errors in segmentation can lead to errors in the final registration. In contrast, intensity-based methods directly compare the X-ray image with the associated digitally reconstructed radiograph (DRR), which is obtained by simulating X-ray projection of the CT volume. No segmentation is required.

One of the main factors that affect the accuracy of intensity-based 2D-3D registration is the similarity measure, which is a criterion function that is used in the registration procedure for measuring the quality of image match. An extensive study of six similarity measures applied specifically to 2D-3D registration has been performed by Penney et al. [1]. Using the fiducial markers to get the "gold-standard" registration, the authors ranked these measures based on their accuracy and robustness. They found that pattern intensity [2] was one of the two measures that were able to register accurately and robustly, even when soft tissues and interventional instruments were present in the X-ray images.

In this work, we use maximization of mutual information (MI), an accurate similarity measure for multi-modal and mono-modal image registration tasks [3,4,5]. However, it is known that the standard mutual information measure only takes intensity values into account without considering spatial information and its robustness is questionable [1,7].

Several attempts have been made to adapt the MI-based registration framework to incorporate spatial information of individual images [7][8,9,10,11]. However, the resultant similarity measure either requires to compute the entropy of higher dimensional probability distributions, which is not advisable because of the increase of statistical uncertainties with higher dimensions due to the scarcity of data, or is not robust to outliers.

In this paper, we show how to incorporate spatial information into mutual information without suffering from these problems. Using a variational approximation derived from the Kullback-Leibler bound [12], spatial information can be effectively incorporated into mutual information via energy minimization. The resultant energy function has a least-squares form and can be effectively minimized by a multi-resolution Levenberg-Marquardt optimizer. We point out that several previously introduced similarity measures can be derived from the unified framework.

The paper is organized as follows. In Section 2, we present the derivation of a variational approximation to the MI. In Section 3, we describe in details the realization of the variational approximation via energy minimization. In Section 4, we present the experimental results, followed by conclusions in Section 5.

2   Derivation of a Variational Approximation to the MI

In this work, we assume that the X-ray images are calibrated for their intrinsic parameters and that the X-ray images are corrected for distortion. If multiple X-ray images are used, they are all registered to a common reference frame. Therefore, the goal of a 3D-2D registration is to compute the rigid transformation T that relates the coordinate frame of the CT volume with the reference coordinate frame of the X-ray images. In the following, we focus on the derivation based on the qth X-ray image (where $q = 1, ..., Q$) and its associated DRR.

Let us denote the values of the X-ray image (V) as $v(x)$ and the corresponding values of the DRR (U) created from the CT volume given the current transformation estimation as $u(x; T)$. In this work, we regard the image values $v(x)$ and $u(x; T)$ as random variables with associated probability density functions $p(v(x))$ and $p(u(x; T))$, respectively. The joint probability density function of these two random variables is $p(v(x), u(x; T))$. The conditional probability density function of $v(x)$ given the values of $u(x; T)$ is expressed as $p(v(x)|u(x; T))$.

The mutual information of two random variables is derived from the entropy values of the variables, both separately and jointly, as given by:

$$H(V) = -\int p(v) \log(p(v)) dv; \quad H(V, U) = -\iint p(v, u) \log(p(v, u)) dv du \quad (1)$$

and the conditional entropy of two random variables is:

$$H(V|U) = -\iint p(v, u) \log(p(v|u)) dv du \quad (2)$$

The entropy can be seen as a measure of uncertainty of a random variable. The mutual information between two random variables is defined by:

$$S_{MI}^q(V, U, T) = H(V) + H(U) - H(V, U) = H(V) - H(V|U) \quad (3)$$

After some replacement, we can write Eq. 3 as:

$$S_{MI}^q(V, U, T) = \iint p(v(x), u(x; T)) \log(p(v(x)|u(x; T))) dv du + H(V) \quad (4)$$

The optimal estimation of the rigid transformation can then be obtained by:

$$\hat{T} = \arg \max_T \sum_{q=1}^{Q} S_{MI}^q(V, U, T) \quad (5)$$

Eq. 5 is the standard registration framework using maximization of mutual information. Histogram-based method [4] as well as Parzen window based method [3] have been proposed to compute the mutual information. It is known that the standard mutual information measure only takes intensity values into account without considering spatial information and its robustness is questionable [1,7]. It can be shown using Kullback-Leibler bound [12] that:

$$S_{MI}^q(V, U, T) \geqslant \iint p(v(x), u(x; T)) \log(q(v(x)|u(x; T)) dv du + H(V) \quad (6)$$

where $q(v(x)|u(x; T))$ is an arbitrary variational distribution. We call the right side of Eq. 6 the variational approximation to mutual information (VA-MI) and denote it as $S_{VA-MI}^q(V, U, T)$. The approximation is exact if $q(v(x)|u(x; T)) \equiv p(v(x)|u(x; T))$.

As we are dealing with discrete images, the values $v(x = (i, j))$ and $u((x = (i, j)); T)$ that we observe from the images can be regarded as random samples from $p(v(x), u(x; T))$. Note that $H(V)$ in Eq. 6 does not depend on T. Ignoring this constant term, we can further approximate $S_{VA-MI}^q(v(x), u(x; T))$ by its sample estimate:

$$S_{VA-MI}^q(V, U, T) \approx \frac{1}{I \times J} \sum_{i=1}^{I} \sum_{j=1}^{J} \log(q(v(i, j)|u((i, j); T))) \qquad (7)$$

where $I \times J$ is the size of the X-ray image.

Using Eq. 7, we actually convert the maximization of mutual information to an optimal labeling problem in which the labels are the conditional intensity values. Such a problem can be effectively solved via energy minimization using a maximum a posteriori – Markov random field (MAP-MRF) framework based on the well-known Hammersley-Clifford theorem [13].

3   Realization of the Variational Approximation Via Energy Minimization Using a MAP-MRF Framework

3.1   MAP-MRF Framework for Energy Minimization

To solve the energy minimization problem using a MAP-MRF framework, we thus follow the four steps of the MAP-MRF estimate [13].

1. Construction of a prior probability distribution $p(T)$ for the registration transformation T matching the reference X-ray images to the floating DRRs. In this paper, we do not take advantage of this property. We treat all parameter configurations equally, due to the Euler angle based parameterization of rotation in our approach. But it is possible to use this property to favor certain transformations when different parameterization forms for the rotation component such as quaternions are used.
2. Formulation of an observation model $q(D|T) = q(v(i, j)|u((i, j); T))$ that describes the observed conditional intensity distribution of the difference images D by comparing the reference X-ray images and the floating DRRs given any particular realization of the prior distribution.
3. Combination of the prior and the observation model into the posterior distribution by Bayes theorem

$$p(T|D) \propto q(D|T)) \cdot p(D) \qquad (8)$$

4. Drawing inference based on the posterior distribution.

3.2   Observation Model

To estimate the observed conditional intensity distribution $q(D|T)$, knowing the exact values of $v(i, j)$ and $u((i, j); T)$ is not important. We are more interested in knowing the conditional difference between $v(i, j)$ and $u((i, j); T)$. However, until now we still can not directly compare $v(i, j)$ to $u((i, j); T)$ at each pixel site because there are inherent differences between the X-ray image and the associated DRR. In this paper, we propose to use a local normalization to circumvent this problem. The rationale behind it is that in a local region the intensity differences between different sites are mainly caused by the imaged object, if no external object is present in the field-of-view.

Definition 1: Let $L = \{(i,j) : 1 \leqslant i \leqslant I, 1 \leqslant j \leqslant J\}$ be an $I \times J$ integer lattice; then $D = \{D_{i,j}; (i,j) \in L\}$ denotes a family of random variables, i.e., a random field, defined on L. A rth order neighborhood system for L is defined as $\mathbf{N} = \{N_{i,j}^r; (i,j) \in L\}$, where $N_{i,j}^r$ is the set of sites around (i,j) and is defined as follows:

$$N_{i,j}^r = \{(i',j')|(i',j') \in L, (i',j') \neq (i,j), |(i',j') - (i,j)| \leqslant r\} \qquad (9)$$

where r is a positive integer that determines the size of the neighborhood system.

Definition 2: A clique c is a subset of L, for which every pair of sites is a neighbor. Single pixels are also considered cliques. The set of all cliques related with the pixel site (i,j) is denoted by $C_{i,j}$.

Definition 3: A local region of size r for the pixel site $(i,j) \in L$ is the set of sites defined by:

$$R_{i,j}^r = \{(i',j')|(i',j') \in L, |(i',j') - (i,j)| \leqslant r\} \qquad (10)$$

The local normalization of both the X-ray image and the associated DRR is then performed as follows:

$$\bar{v}(i,j) = \frac{v(i,j) - m_v(R_{i,j}^r)}{\sigma_v(R_{i,j}^r)}; \; and \; \bar{u}((i,j);T) = \frac{u((i,j);T) - m_u(R_{i,j}^r)}{\sigma_u(R_{i,j}^r)} \qquad (11)$$

where $m_v(R_{i,j}^r)$, $\sigma_v(R_{i,j}^r)$ and $m_u(R_{i,j}^r)$, $\sigma_u(R_{i,j}^r)$ are the mean value and the standard deviation calculated from the intensity values of all sites in the local region $R_{i,j}^r$ of the X-ray image and of the associated DRR, respectively.

We can now model the difference image

$$s((i,j);T) = \bar{v}(i,j) - \bar{u}((i,j);T) \qquad (12)$$

as a MRF with respect to the rth order neighborhood system $\mathbf{N}$.

According to the relationship between the probability measure and the energy function of a MRF at a single site [13], we have:

$$\log q(v(i,j)|u(i,j);T) \approx \log p(s((i,j);T); \; and$$
$$\log p(s((i,j);T) = -E(s((i,j);T) = - \sum_{c \in C_{i,j}} W_c(s(i,j);T) \qquad (13)$$

where W_c is called the clique potential. Generally, W_c is a function of the cliques around the site under consideration.

We can further expand the clique potentials in Eq. 13 according to the clique size. In this work, we only consider the cliques of size up to two. Using such an approximation, we unify the mutual information maximization and the energy minimization for deriving a similarity measure. We call any similarity measure derived from the new framework the MRF model based variational approximation to mutual information (MRF-VA-MI) and denote it as $S^q_{MRF-VA-MI}(V,U,T)$. It has the form:

$$-S^q_{VA-MI}(V,U,T) \approx S^q_{MRF-VA-MI}(V,U,T) = \alpha \cdot \sum_{i,j}^{I,J} W_c(s((i,j);T))$$

$$+(1-\alpha) \cdot \sum_{i,j}^{I,J} \frac{1}{card(N^r_{i,j})} \cdot \sum_{(i',j') \in N^r_{i,j}} W_c(s((i,j);T), s((i',j');T)) \tag{14}$$

where $S^q_{VA-MI}(V,U,T)$ is negative because mutual information is maximized, whereas energy must be minimized. The first term of the rightmost side is the potential function for single-pixel cliques and the second term is the potential function for all other pairwise cliques. $card(N^r_{i,j})$ means to compute the number of pixels in neighborhood $N^r_{i,j}$. $\alpha \in [0.0, 1.0]$ is a control parameter.

The selection of the potential function in Eq. 14 is a critical issue in MRF modeling [13]. By choosing different potential functions, we can derive different similarity measures. Here we give two examples of deriving previously published well-known similarity measures based on the present framework.

1. Sum-of-Squared-Difference (SSD): SSD can be derived from Eq. 14 by specifying:

$$\alpha = 1.0$$
$$W_c(s((i,j);T)) = [s((i,j);T)]^2 \tag{15}$$

2. Pattern Intensity: the pattern intensity proposed in [2] has the following form:

$$P_{r,\sigma} = \sum_{i,j} \frac{1}{card(N^r_{i,j})} \sum_{(i',j') \in N^r_{i,j}} \frac{\sigma^2}{\sigma^2 + [s((i',j');T) - s((i,j);T)]^2} \tag{16}$$

where r and σ are two parameters to be experimentally determined. It can be derived from the present framework by specifying $\alpha = 0.0$ and by using following pairwise clique potential function:

$$W_c(s((i,j);T), s((i',j');T)) = -\frac{1}{1 + \frac{[s((i',j');T) - s((i,j);T)]^2}{\sigma^2}} \tag{17}$$

In this work, we simply set $\alpha = 0.5$ and use following potential functions to derive a new similarity measure. We name the newly derived similarity measure as the pairwised MRF model based variational approximation to mutual information (PW-MRF-VA-MI) and denote it as $S^q_{PW-MRF-VA-MI}(V,U,T)$:

$$W_c(s((i,j);T)) = [s((i,j);T)]^2$$
$$W_c(s((i,j);T), s((i',j');T)) = [s((i,j);T) - s((i',j');T)]^2 \tag{18}$$

3.3   Implementation Details

To accelerate the registration process, we exploit a spline-based multi-resolution 3D-2D registration scheme [14]. A cubic-spline data model is used to compute the multi-resolution data pyramids for the CT volume, the X-ray images, the DRRs, as well as for the gradient and the Hessian of the PW-MRF-VA-MI. The registration is then performed from the coarsest resolution to the finest one. At each resolution level, the size of the local region for the normalization is always equal to that of the neighborhood system used in Eq. 14. And to improve the capture range, we use two different sizes of neighborhood systems: r=15 and r=3. The PW-MRF-VA-MI with the bigger neighborhood system is first minimized via a Levenberg-Marquardt non-linear least-squares optimizer. The estimated $\hat{T}$ is then treated as the starting value for optimizing the PW-MRF-VA-MI with the smaller neighborhood system.

4   Experimental Results

We designed and conducted experiments on datasets from two different applications: (a) intra-operative patient pose estimation from a few (e.g. 2) calibrated fluoroscopic images, and (b) post-operative cup alignment evaluation using single X-ray radiograph with gonadal shielding.

4.1   Intra-operative Patient Pose Estimation from a Few Calibrated Fluoroscopic Images

In this experiment, we conducted two studies on X-ray and CT datasets of a plastic phantom and a cadaveric spine segment. The data sizes, the original data resolution, the start and the end resolutions of the X-ray and the CT datasets are summarized in Table 1. The ground truth transformations of both datasets were obtained by performing paired-point matchings on implanted fiducial markers. The phantom was custom-made to simulate a good condition. In contrast, the quality of the X-ray images for the cadaveric spine was poor and there were projections of interventional instruments present.

Using the datasets of both objects downsampled to the start resolution, we first compared the behavior of the PW-MRF-VA-MI to those of a MI-based measure using a histogram-based implementation [4] and of a similarity measure introduced in [14], which is a global normalization based SSD. The results are presented in Fig. 1. It was found that all similarity measures had similar behavior when tested on the phantom dataset but different behavior when tested on the spine segment dataset. The PW-MRF-VA-MI shows a superior behavior compared to others. More specifically, all curves of the PW-MRF-VA-MI have clear minima and are smoother than those of others. It also shows that using bigger neighborhood system, which is equivalent to incorporate wider range of spatial information, leads to smoother energy function whereas using smaller neighborhood system results in higher accuracy.

Table 1. Data specifications

CT Data Specification				
test object	rows × columns × slices	data res. (mm^3)	start res. (mm^3)	end res. (mm^3)
phantom	512 × 512 × 93	0.36 × 0.36 × 2.5	2.88 × 2.88 × 2.5	2.88 × 2.88 × 2.5
spine	512 × 512 × 72	0.36 × 0.36 × 1.25	2.88 × 2.88 × 1.25	2.88 × 2.88 × 1.25
X-ray Data Specification				
test object	width × height × images	data res. (mm^2)	start res. (mm^2)	end res. (mm^2)
phantom	768 × 576 × 2	0.39 × 0.39	3.12 × 3.12	3.12 × 3.12
spine	768 × 576 × 2	0.39 × 0.39	3.12 × 3.12	3.12 × 3.12

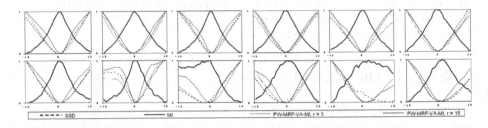

Fig. 1. Probe through the minimum of similarity measures on the phantom data (the first row) and on the spine data (the second row). The ordinate shows the value of similarity measures normalized to the range [0.0, 1.0], which are given as functions of each parameter in the range of $[-15°,15°]$ or [-15mm, 15mm] away from its ground truth (the first three columns represent the translational probe along X, Y and Z axis, respectively; the last three columns represents the rotational probe along each axis).

The second study was performed only on the spine segment dataset to evaluate the performance of the registration scheme using the PW-MRF-VA-MI. In this study, we perturbed the ground truth by randomly varying each parameter in the range of $[-2°, 2°]$ or [-2mm, 2mm] to get 200 positions, and then another 200 positions in the rage of $[-4°, 4°]$ or [-4mm, 4mm], and so on until the range of $[-12°, 12°]$ or [-12mm, 12mm]. We then performed the registration starting from these perturbed positions and counted the success rate. Using a method similar to that reported in [15], we regarded a registration as successful if the mean target registration errors (mTRE) evaluated on the fiducial markers was smaller than 1.5 mm. The capture range was then defined as the the average of the initial mTRE when a 95% success rate is achieved. The study results are presented in Table 2. When the absolute parameter range is $(12°, 12mm)$, the average CPU time tested on a 3.0 GHz Pentium machine was 26.7 seconds. It was found that the capture range of the PW-MRF-VA-MI was much larger than those reported in [10] and in [15], although the attained accuracy was lower than that reported in [15]. This might be explained by the large inter-slice distance (2.5 mm in this work vs. 0.31 mm in [15]) and the region outliers in the X-ray images.

Table 2. Study results using the datasets of cadaveric spine segment

absolute parameter range $(^{\circ}, mm)$	(2, 2)	(4, 4)	(6, 6)	(8, 8)	(10, 10)	(12, 12)
average of the initial mTRE (mm)	2.3	4.6	6.9	9.2	11.5	13.5
success percentage	100	100	100	99	95	85
average of the final mTRE (mm)	0.8	0.8	0.8	0.8	0.8	0.8

4.2 Post-operative Cup Alignment Evaluation from Single X-Ray Radiograph with Gonadal Shielding

2D anteroposterior (AP) pelvic radiographs are the standard imaging method for the evaluation of cup orientation following total hip arthroplasty (THA). While plain pelvic radiographs are easily obtained, their accurate interpretation is complicated by the wide variability in individual pelvic position relative to the X-ray plate. 2D-3D image registration methods [16,17] have been introduced to estimate the rigid transformation between pre-operative CT volume of a patient and post-operative radiograph(s) for an accurate estimation of the post-operative cup alignment relative to an anatomical reference. However, those methods were only evaluated on X-ray radiograph(s) without gonadal shielding, which may pose a challenge for them.

In this experiment, we qualitatively evaluated the present approach to estimate the rigid transformation between a pre-operative CT volume and a post-operative X-ray radiograph on two patients. Fig. 2 shows one example. The input X-ray radiograph is shown in Fig. 2(a). The initial rigid transformation between the radiograph coordinate frame and the CT frame was obtained by an iterative landmark-based registration. Fig. 2(b) shows the initial state of the intensity-based 2D-3D registration. Both the x-ray radiograph and the CT volume data are downsampled to 1/8th of the original sizes. The edges extracted from the DRR are superimposed onto the X-ray radiograph. Fig. 2(c) shows the end of the intensity-based 2D-3D registration. An accurate matching between the X-ray radiograph and the DRR was observed.

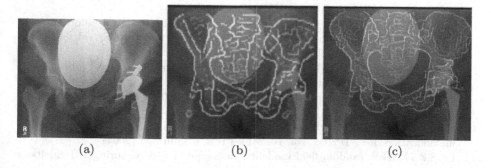

(a)   (b)   (c)

Fig. 2. (a) X-ray radiograph with gonadal shielding; (b) the beginning of the intensity-based 2D-3D registration. and (c) the end of the intensity-based 2D-3D registration.

5   Conclusions

Based on the Kullback-Leibler bound, we present a framework unifying energy minimization and mutual information maximization to derive a similarity measure for 2D/3D registration of X-ray to CT images. The similarity measure derived from the present framework enables us to effectively incorporate spatial information into mutual information. Results from the experiments performed on the datasets of two different applications show that the newly derived similarity measure has a larger capture range than those previously reported and attains satisfactory accuracy even when a large area of the X-ray image(s) is occluded by outliers.

References

1. Penney, G.P., et al.: A comparison of similarity measures for use in 2-D-3-D medical image registration. IEEE Trans Med Imaging 17, 586–595 (1998)
2. Weese, J., et al.: An approach to 2D/3D registration of a vertebra in 2D x-ray fluoroscopies with 3D CT images. In: Troccaz, J., Mösges, R., Grimson, W.E.L. (eds.) CVRMed-MRCAS 1997, CVRMed 1997, and MRCAS 1997. LNCS, vol. 1205, pp. 119–128. Springer, Heidelberg (1997)
3. Wells, W., Viola, P., et al.: Multi-modal volume registration by maximization of mutual information. MedIA 1, 35–51 (1996)
4. Maes, F., Collignon, A., et al.: Multimodality image registration by maximization of mutual information. IEEE Trans Med Imaging 16, 187–1998 (1997)
5. Pluim, J.P., et al.: Mutual information based registration of medical images: a survey. IEEE Trans Med Imaging 22, 986–1004 (2003)
6. Brown, L.M.G., Boult, T.E.: Registration of planar film radiographs with computed tomography. In: MMBIA'96, pp. 42–51 (1996)
7. Pluim, J., et al.: Image registration by maximization of combined mutual information and gradient information. IEEE Trans Med Imaging 19, 809–814 (2000)
8. Rueckert, D., Clarkson, M.J., et al.: Non-rigid registration using higher-order mutual information. SPIE Medical Imaging: image processing 3979, 438–447 (2000)
9. Sabuncu, M.R., Ramadge, P.J.: Spatial information in entropy-based image registration. In: Gee, J.C., Maintz, J.B.A., Vannier, M.W. (eds.) WBIR 2003. LNCS, vol. 2717, pp. 132–141. Springer, Heidelberg (2003)
10. Russakoff, D.B., Tomasi, C., et al.: Image similarity using mutual information of regions. In: Pajdla, T., Matas, J(G.) (eds.) ECCV 2004. LNCS, vol. 3023, pp. 596–607. Springer, Heidelberg (2004)
11. Gan, R., Chung, A.C.S.: Multi-dimensional mutual information based robust image registration using maximum distance-gradient-magnitude. In: Christensen, G.E., Sonka, M. (eds.) IPMI 2005. LNCS, vol. 3565, pp. 210–221. Springer, Heidelberg (2005)
12. Barber, D., Agakov, F.V.: The IM algorithm: a variational approach to information maximization. In: NIPS'03, vol. 16, MIT Press, Cambridge (2004)
13. Li, S.Z.: Markov random field modeling in computer vision. Springer, Heidelberg (1995)
14. Jonić, S., Thévenaz, P., et al.: An optimized spline-based registration of a 3D CT to a set of C-arm images. Int J Biomed Imaging, Article ID 47197, 1–12 (2006)

15. von de Kraats, E.B., Penney, G.P., et al.: Standardized evaluation methodology for 2-D-3-D registration. IEEE Trans Med Imaging 24, 1177–1189 (2005)
16. LaRose, D., et al.: Post-operative measurement of acetabular cup position using X-ray/CT registration. In: Delp, S.L., DiGoia, A.M., Jaramaz, B. (eds.) MICCAI 2000. LNCS, vol. 1935, pp. 1104–1113. Springer, Heidelberg (2000)
17. Jaramaz, B., Eckman, K.: 2D/3D registration for measurement of implant alignment after total hip replacement. In: Larsen, R., Nielsen, M., Sporring, J. (eds.) MICCAI 2006. LNCS, vol. 4191, pp. 653–661. Springer, Heidelberg (2006)

Author Index

Aach, Til   284, 476
Abou-Moustafa, Karim T.   335
Akgul, Yusuf Sinan   62
Albrecht, Thomas   527
Andres, Björn   72
Aziz, Muhammad Zaheer   345

Bajramovic, Ferid   1
Bandera, Antonio   244
Bartczak, Bogumil   11, 122
Beder, Christian   11, 194
Bergtholdt, Martin   395
Bischof, H.   214
Bock, Rüdiger   355
Boykov, Yuri   446
Breuel, Thomas M.   204, 507
Brox, Thomas   163, 173, 264
Bruhn, Andrés   152
Buhmann, Joachim   234
Burkhardt, Hans   304, 415, 425
Buss, Martin   274

Castrillon, M.   365
Cleju, Ioan   517
Cremers, Daniel   163, 173, 264, 446

Dederscheck, David   21
Dedner, Andreas   527
Deniz, O.   365
Denzler, Joachim   1, 102

Ehlgen, Tobias   456
Eils, Roland   497
Engel, Karin   254
Enzweiler, Markus   456
Esquivel, Sandro   82

Falcon, A.   365
Ferrie, Frank P.   335
Fischer, Bernd   436
Franke, Uwe   112
Franz, Matthias O.   405
Friedrich, Holger   21

Gall, Juergen   32
Garbe, Christoph S.   72, 92, 132

Gedicke, Jens   476
Gramann, Klaus   274
Grosse-Wentrup, Moritz   274
Görlitz, L.   224
Götze, Sandra   497

Hamprecht, F.A.   72, 224
Hasler, Klaus-Peter   375
Hasler, Nils   375
Hellwich, Olaf   324
Hornegger, Joachim   355
Huang, Hai   385

Jähne, Bernd   132

Kähler, Olaf   102
Kappes, Jörg   395
Karim, Rezaul   395
Kelm, B.M.   224
Keysers, Daniel   204
Kienzle, Wolf   405
Klappstein, Jens   112
Koch, Reinhard   11, 82, 122
Koeser, Kevin   122
Kondermann, Claudia   132
Kondermann, Daniel   132
Krajsek, Kai   21, 142
Krause, Jochen   466

Lampert, Christoph H.   204
Lange, Tilman   234
Liefhold, Christian   274
Lorenzo, J.   365
Lubeley, Dominik   42
Lüthi, Marcel   527

Marfil, Rebeca   244
Mateos-Langerak, Julio   497
Mayer, Helmut   385
Meier, Jörg   355
Mendez, J.   365
Menze, B.H.   224
Mertsching, Bärbel   345
Mester, Rudolf   21, 142
Michelson, Georg   355

Mileva, Yana   152
Mühlich, Matthias   284

Nordberg, Klas   52
Nyúl, László G.   355

Olowinsky, Alexander   476

Palágyi, Kálmán   294
Pietzsch, Sylvia   486
Pock, T.   214

Radig, Bernd   486
Reisert, Marco   304, 415
Rohkohl, Christopher   254
Rohr, Karl   497, 537
Ronneberger, Olaf   304, 415, 425
Rosenhahn, Bodo   32, 163, 173
Roth, Volker   436

Sandoval, Francisco   244
Saupe, Dietmar   517
Schölkopf, Bernhard   405
Scharr, Hanno   184
Schmaltz, Christian   173
Schmidt, Frank R.   446
Schnörr, Christoph   395
Schoenemann, Thomas   264
Schuchert, Tobias   184
Schulz, Wolfgang   456
Seidel, Hans-Peter   32, 163
Shafait, Faisal   507
Siebel, Nils T.   466

Smolka, Bogdan   314
Sommer, Gerald   173, 466
Stache, Nicolaj C.   476
Steffen, Richard   194
Stein, Fridtjof   112
Stulp, Freek   486

Töppe, Eno   446

Ulges, Adrian   204

van Beusekom, Joost   507
van Driel, Roel   497
Vetter, Thomas   527

Wang, Qing   425
Weber, M.-A.   224
Wedel, Andreas   264
Weickert, Joachim   152, 173
Wichmann, Felix A.   405
Wietzke, Lennart   173
Wimmer, Matthias   486
Woelk, Felix   82
Wörz, Stefan   537

Yang, Siwei   497
Yildiz, Alparslan   62

Zach, C.   214
Zheng, Guoyan   547
Zheng, Hongwei   324
Zimmer, Henrik   476

Lecture Notes in Computer Science

Sublibrary 6: Image Processing, Computer Vision, Pattern Recognition, and Graphics

Vol. 4738: A.C.R. Paiva, R. Prada, R.W. Picard (Eds.), Affective Computing and Intelligent Interaction. XVIII, 781 pages. 2007.

Vol. 4713: F.A. Hamprecht, C. Schnörr, B. Jähne (Eds.), Pattern Recognition. XIII, 560 pages. 2007.

Vol. 4679: A.L. Yuille, S.-C. Zhu, D. Cremers, Y. Wang (Eds.), Energy Minimization Methods in Computer Vision and Pattern Recognition. XII, 494 pages. 2007.

Vol. 4678: J. Blanc-Talon, W. Philips, D. Popescu, P. Scheunders (Eds.), Advanced Concepts for Intelligent Vision Systems. XXIII, 1100 pages. 2007.

Vol. 4673: W.G. Kropatsch, M. Kampel, A. Hanbury (Eds.), Computer Analysis of Images and Patterns. XX, 1006 pages. 2007.

Vol. 4642: S.-W. Lee, S.Z. Li (Eds.), Advances in Biometrics. XX, 1216 pages. 2007.

Vol. 4633: M. Kamel, A. Campilho (Eds.), Image Analysis and Recognition. XII, 1312 pages. 2007.

Vol. 4584: N. Karssemeijer, B. Lelieveldt (Eds.), Information Processing in Medical Imaging. XX, 777 pages. 2007.

Vol. 4569: A. Butz, B. Fisher, A. Krüger, P. Olivier, S. Owada (Eds.), Smart Graphics. IX, 237 pages. 2007.

Vol. 4538: F. Escolano, M. Vento (Eds.), Graph-Based Representations in Pattern Recognition. XII, 416 pages. 2007.

Vol. 4522: B.K. Ersbøll, K.S. Pedersen (Eds.), Image Analysis. XVIII, 989 pages. 2007.

Vol. 4485: F. Sgallari, A. Murli, N. Paragios (Eds.), Scale Space and Variational Methods in Computer Vision. XV, 931 pages. 2007.

Vol. 4478: J. Martí, J.M. Benedí, A.M. Mendonça, J. Serrat (Eds.), Pattern Recognition and Image Analysis, Part II. XXVII, 657 pages. 2007.

Vol. 4477: J. Martí, J.M. Benedí, A.M. Mendonça, J. Serrat (Eds.), Pattern Recognition and Image Analysis, Part I. XXVII, 625 pages. 2007.

Vol. 4472: M. Haindl, J. Kittler, F. Roli (Eds.), Multiple Classifier Systems. XI, 524 pages. 2007.

Vol. 4466: F.B. Sachse, G. Seemann (Eds.), Functional Imaging and Modeling of the Heart. XV, 486 pages. 2007.

Vol. 4418: A. Gagalowicz, W. Philips (Eds.), Computer Vision/Computer Graphics Collaboration Techniques. XV, 620 pages. 2007.

Vol. 4417: A. Kerren, A. Ebert, J. Meyer (Eds.), Human-Centered Visualization Environments. XIX, 403 pages. 2007.

Vol. 4391: Y. Stylianou, M. Faundez-Zanuy, A. Esposito (Eds.), Progress in Nonlinear Speech Processing. XII, 269 pages. 2007.

Vol. 4370: P.P. Lévy, B. Le Grand, F. Poulet, M. Soto, L. Darago, L. Toubiana, J.-F. Vibert (Eds.), Pixelization Paradigm. XV, 279 pages. 2007.

Vol. 4358: R. Vidal, A. Heyden, Y. Ma (Eds.), Dynamical Vision. IX, 329 pages. 2007.

Vol. 4338: P. Kalra, S. Peleg (Eds.), Computer Vision, Graphics and Image Processing. XV, 965 pages. 2006.

Vol. 4319: L.-W. Chang, W.-N. Lie (Eds.), Advances in Image and Video Technology. XXVI, 1347 pages. 2006.

Vol. 4292: G. Bebis, R. Boyle, B. Parvin, D. Koracin, P. Remagnino, A. Nefian, G. Meenakshisundaram, V. Pascucci, J. Zara, J. Molineros, H. Theisel, T. Malzbender (Eds.), Advances in Visual Computing, Part II. XXXII, 906 pages. 2006.

Vol. 4291: G. Bebis, R. Boyle, B. Parvin, D. Koracin, P. Remagnino, A. Nefian, G. Meenakshisundaram, V. Pascucci, J. Zara, J. Molineros, H. Theisel, T. Malzbender (Eds.), Advances in Visual Computing, Part I. XXXI, 916 pages. 2006.

Vol. 4245: A. Kuba, L.G. Nyúl, K. Palágyi (Eds.), Discrete Geometry for Computer Imagery. XIII, 688 pages. 2006.

Vol. 4241: R.R. Beichel, M. Sonka (Eds.), Computer Vision Approaches to Medical Image Analysis. XI, 262 pages. 2006.

Vol. 4225: J.F. Martínez-Trinidad, J.A. Carrasco Ochoa, J. Kittler (Eds.), Progress in Pattern Recognition, Image Analysis and Applications. XIX, 995 pages. 2006.

Vol. 4191: R. Larsen, M. Nielsen, J. Sporring (Eds.), Medical Image Computing and Computer-Assisted Intervention – MICCAI 2006, Part II. XXXVIII, 981 pages. 2006.

Vol. 4190: R. Larsen, M. Nielsen, J. Sporring (Eds.), Medical Image Computing and Computer-Assisted Intervention – MICCAI 2006, Part I. XXXVVIII, 949 pages. 2006.

Vol. 4179: J. Blanc-Talon, W. Philips, D. Popescu, P. Scheunders (Eds.), Advanced Concepts for Intelligent Vision Systems. XXIV, 1224 pages. 2006.

Vol. 4174: K. Franke, K.-R. Müller, B. Nickolay, R. Schäfer (Eds.), Pattern Recognition. XX, 773 pages. 2006.

Vol. 4170: J. Ponce, M. Hebert, C. Schmid, A. Zisserman (Eds.), Toward Category-Level Object Recognition. XI, 618 pages. 2006.

Vol. 4153: N. Zheng, X. Jiang, X. Lan (Eds.), Advances in Machine Vision, Image Processing, and Pattern Analysis. XIII, 506 pages. 2006.

Vol. 4142: A. Campilho, M. Kamel (Eds.), Image Analysis and Recognition, Part II. XXVII, 923 pages. 2006.

Vol. 4141: A. Campilho, M. Kamel (Eds.), Image Analysis and Recognition, Part I. XXVIII, 939 pages. 2006.

Vol. 4122: R. Stiefelhagen, J.S. Garofolo (Eds.), Multimodal Technologies for Perception of Humans. XII, 360 pages. 2007.

Vol. 4109: D.-Y. Yeung, J.T. Kwok, A. Fred, F. Roli, D. de Ridder (Eds.), Structural, Syntactic, and Statistical Pattern Recognition. XXI, 939 pages. 2006.

Vol. 4091: G.-Z. Yang, T. Jiang, D. Shen, L. Gu, J. Yang (Eds.), Medical Imaging and Augmented Reality. XIII, 399 pages. 2006.

Vol. 4073: A. Butz, B. Fisher, A. Krüger, P. Olivier (Eds.), Smart Graphics. XI, 263 pages. 2006.

Vol. 4069: F.J. Perales, R.B. Fisher (Eds.), Articulated Motion and Deformable Objects. XV, 526 pages. 2006.

Vol. 4057: J.P.W. Pluim, B. Likar, F.A. Gerritsen (Eds.), Biomedical Image Registration. XII, 324 pages. 2006.

Vol. 4046: S.M. Astley, M. Brady, C. Rose, R. Zwiggelaar (Eds.), Digital Mammography. XVI, 654 pages. 2006.

Vol. 4040: R. Reulke, U. Eckardt, B. Flach, U. Knauer, K. Polthier (Eds.), Combinatorial Image Analysis. XII, 482 pages. 2006.

Vol. 4035: T. Nishita, Q. Peng, H.-P. Seidel (Eds.), Advances in Computer Graphics. XX, 771 pages. 2006.

Vol. 3979: T.S. Huang, N. Sebe, M.S. Lew, V. Pavlović, M. Kölsch, A. Galata, B. Kisačanin (Eds.), Computer Vision in Human-Computer Interaction. XII, 121 pages. 2006.

Vol. 3954: A. Leonardis, H. Bischof, A. Pinz (Eds.), Computer Vision – ECCV 2006, Part IV. XVII, 613 pages. 2006.

Vol. 3953: A. Leonardis, H. Bischof, A. Pinz (Eds.), Computer Vision – ECCV 2006, Part III. XVII, 649 pages. 2006.

Vol. 3952: A. Leonardis, H. Bischof, A. Pinz (Eds.), Computer Vision – ECCV 2006, Part II. XVII, 661 pages. 2006.

Vol. 3951: A. Leonardis, H. Bischof, A. Pinz (Eds.), Computer Vision – ECCV 2006, Part I. XXXV, 639 pages. 2006.

Vol. 3948: H.I. Christensen, H.-H. Nagel (Eds.), Cognitive Vision Systems. VIII, 367 pages. 2006.

Vol. 3926: W. Liu, J. Lladós (Eds.), Graphics Recognition. XII, 428 pages. 2006.

Vol. 3872: H. Bunke, A.L. Spitz (Eds.), Document Analysis Systems VII. XIII, 630 pages. 2006.

Vol. 3852: P.J. Narayanan, S.K. Nayar, H.-Y. Shum (Eds.), Computer Vision – ACCV 2006, Part II. XXXI, 977 pages. 2006.

Vol. 3851: P.J. Narayanan, S.K. Nayar, H.-Y. Shum (Eds.), Computer Vision – ACCV 2006, Part I. XXXI, 973 pages. 2006.

Vol. 3832: D. Zhang, A.K. Jain (Eds.), Advances in Biometrics. XX, 796 pages. 2005.

Vol. 3736: S. Bres, R. Laurini (Eds.), Visual Information and Information Systems. XI, 291 pages. 2006.

Vol. 3667: W.J. MacLean (Ed.), Spatial Coherence for Visual Motion Analysis. IX, 141 pages. 2006.

Vol. 3417: B. Jähne, R. Mester, E. Barth, H. Scharr (Eds.), Complex Motion. X, 235 pages. 2007.

Vol. 2396: T.M. Caelli, A. Amin, R.P.W. Duin, M.S. Kamel, D. de Ridder (Eds.), Structural, Syntactic, and Statistical Pattern Recognition. XVI, 863 pages. 2002.

Vol. 1679: C. Taylor, A. Colchester (Eds.), Medical Image Computing and Computer-Assisted Intervention – MICCAI'99. XXI, 1240 pages. 1999.